The Powers and Duties of an Arbitrator

The Powers and Duties of an Arbitrator
Liber Amicorum Pierre A. Karrer

Edited by
Patricia Shaughnessy
Sherlin Tung

Published by:
Kluwer Law International B.V.
PO Box 316
2400 AH Alphen aan den Rijn
The Netherlands
Website: www.wolterskluwerlr.com

Sold and distributed in North, Central and South America by:
Wolters Kluwer Legal & Regulatory U.S.
7201 McKinney Circle
Frederick, MD 21704
United States of America
Email: customer.service@wolterskluwer.com

Sold and distributed in all other countries by:
Quadrant
Rockwood House
Haywards Heath
West Sussex
RH16 3DH
United Kingdom
Email: international-customerservice@wolterskluwer.com

Printed on acid-free paper.

ISBN 978-90-411-8413-9

e-Book: ISBN 978-90-411-8414-6
web-PDF: ISBN 978-90-411-8415-3

© 2017 Kluwer Law International BV, The Netherlands

All rights reserved. No part of this publication may be reproduced, stored in a retrieval system, or transmitted in any form or by any means, electronic, mechanical, photocopying, recording, or otherwise, without written permission from the publisher.

Permission to use this content must be obtained from the copyright owner. Please apply to: Permissions Department, Wolters Kluwer Legal & Regulatory U.S., 76 Ninth Avenue, 7th Floor, New York, NY 10011-5201, USA. Website: www.wolterskluwerlr.com

Printed in the United Kingdom.

Editors

Dr Patricia Shaughnessy, Associate Professor, directs the Masters of International Commercial Arbitration Law Program (LLM) at Stockholm University and teaches and researches in related fields. She chairs the "Arbitration and Dispute Resolution Section" of the Stockholm Centre for Commercial Law at Stockholm University. Patricia is the Vice-Chair of the Arbitration Institute of the Stockholm Chamber of Commerce (SCC), having been on its Board since 2006. She sits as an arbitrator and acts as an expert in international cases and, as a consultant, she has led numerous projects related to commercial law and dispute resolution in a number of countries.

Sherlin Tung is currently the Litigation and Arbitration Counsel with Semperit AG Holdings, an international conglomerate specialized in industrial rubber products. Prior to Semperit, Sherlin was a Deputy Counsel with the Secretariat of the ICC International Court of Arbitration where she had the unique opportunity of working in both of its satellite offices (Hong Kong and New York). Sherlin supervised over 300 international arbitration matters with a focus in Asian, Australian, Middle Eastern and North American matters. She began her career in international arbitration in Zurich, Switzerland, where she worked under the direct supervision of Dr. Pierre A. Karrer. She has acted as tribunal secretary in over forty complex international arbitration matters (institutional and ad hoc).

Contributors

Gerald Aksen has many years of experience as counsel and arbitrator in domestic and foreign arbitrations in eighteen different countries. He has acted as arbitrator and mediator with the American Arbitration Association, National Futures Association, International Chamber of Commerce, London Court of International Arbitration, Japan Commercial Arbitration Association, Arbitration Institute of the Stockholm Chamber of Commerce and under UNCITRAL, ARIAS, BERMUDA FORM and other ad hoc rules, as well as with the United States District Court for the Eastern District of New York Early Neutral Evaluation Program. Gerald Aksen has also been an adjunct professor of law at New York University School of Law for thirty years, teaching courses on domestic and international arbitration.

Chiann Bao is the Asia Pacific Counsel for Skadden, Arps, Slate, Meagher & Flom and is based in its Hong Kong office where she focuses on international commercial disputes arising from Asia. Prior to joining Skadden, Ms. Bao served as the secretary-general of the Hong Kong International Arbitration Centre (HKIAC), where she managed hundreds of arbitrations before tribunals in Asia, with a specific focus in China. Ms. Bao worked at an international law firm in New York before joining HKIAC in 2010 where she advised clients in ad hoc and administered arbitrations. She was an adjunct professor at Hong Kong University (2014–2016) and is a frequent lecturer and author on international arbitration.

Louise Barrington FCIArb, C.Arb., is an Independent Arbitrator with over twenty years' experience, based in Hong Kong, Paris and Toronto. She has sat on ICC, HKIAC and ad hoc arbitrations, as sole arbitrator, party-nominated arbitrator and tribunal president, in Europe, Asia and North America. Her experience includes CISG, construction, shareholder agreements, distribution and licensing contracts and insurance. She regularly trains and assesses arbitrators for the Chartered Institute of Arbitrators and is chief editor of "The Danubia Files: Lessons in Award Writing from the Vis Moot." Louise speaks fluent English and French and conversational Spanish.

Contributors

Klaus Peter Berger is Professor of domestic and international business and banking law, comparative and private international law at the University of Cologne and Director of the Institute for Banking Law and the Center for Transnational Law (CENTRAL) at the Cologne law faculty. He has been Honorary Lecturer and Member of the Global Faculty at the Centre for Energy, Petroleum and Mineral Law and Policy, University of Dundee, Scotland, and visiting professor at the University of Virginia School of Law and at Columbia Law School, New York City. He is also a Board Member of the German Institution of Arbitration (DIS)

George A. Bermann is Professor of Law at Columbia Law School (New York City) where he also directs the Center for International Commercial and Investment Arbitration (CICIA). He has served as international arbitrator since 1980. He presides over the Global Board of Advisors of the NY International Arbitration Center and is member of the Standing Committee of the ICC International Chamber of Commerce. He has authored many books and articles and spoken at many conferences on international arbitration, transnational litigation, comparative law, EU Law and related topics. Professor Bermann is also Chief Reporter of the American Law Institute's Restatement of the US Law of International Commercial Arbitration.

David J. Branson has been engaged in the practice of international arbitration for forty years. He was a partner with Charles Brower at White & Case when Pierre Karrer was selected by the ICC to serve as the Chair arbitrator in the case Mr. Branson chose to write about in honor of Pierre.

Nadia Darwazeh is a partner in the International Arbitration Group of Curtis, Mallet-Prevost, Colt & Mosle LLP, based in Paris. She is a Solicitor Advocate and Rechtsanwältin. Nadia has extensive arbitration experience, acting both as counsel and arbitrator. Before joining Curtis, Nadia headed up the EMEA team at the ICC International Court of Arbitration. Prior to the ICC, Nadia practiced for a decade at leading international law firms in Shanghai, Frankfurt and London. Nadia is the first Secretary General of the Jerusalem Arbitration Centre, an ICC joint-venture. Nadia is fluent in French, German and English. She also speaks Dutch and Mandarin Chinese.

Dr. Mariel Dimsey is an international commercial and investment arbitration specialist based in the Hong Kong office of Hogan Lovells. She has over ten years' experience acting as advisor, advocate and arbitrator in numerous international arbitrations covering a wide range of legal systems and industries. She is an Australian Lawyer and received an LLM degree from the University of Cologne and a doctorate in law (Dr. iur.), *summa cum laude*, from the University of Basel, both in investment arbitration. She speaks and publishes regularly on international arbitration and international commercial law topics.

Professor Dr. Siegfried H. Elsing, LL.M. (Yale) is partner in the Düsseldorf office of Orrick, Herrington & Sutcliffe LLP and co-chair of the firm's International Arbitration group. He is admitted as an attorney in both Germany and New York and has more than

Contributors

thirty years of experience as litigation and international arbitration counsel with a particular emphasis on M&A, investment protection, infrastructure, IP and energy related disputes. He also regularly serves as arbitrator in ad hoc as well as institutional arbitral proceedings. Siegfried is Honorary Professor at the University of Dusseldorf and regularly teaches and publishes on arbitration and commercial law subjects.

Emmanuel Gaillard founded and heads Sherman & Sterling's eighty-lawyer International Arbitration practice. He has advised and represented companies, States and State-owned entities in hundreds of international arbitrations. He also acts as arbitrator and expert witness. He is universally regarded as a leading authority and a star practitioner in the fields of commercial and investment treaty arbitration. Emmanuel Gaillard is also a Professor of Law at Sciences Po Law School and a Visiting Professor of Law at Yale Law School. He has written extensively on all aspects of arbitration law, co-authored a leading treatise in the field and authored the first published essay on the legal theory of international arbitration.

Robert Gaitskell, Q.C., practises from Keating Chambers, specialising in technology, engineering and construction disputes, often of an international nature. He was called to the Bar in 1978, appointed Queen's Counsel in 1994 and sat as a Recorder (part-time judge) from 2000-2010. He is both a lawyer and a professional engineer. Robert predominately acts as an arbitrator, adjudicator, dispute board member and mediator. He has conducted over 100 arbitrations throughout the world and regularly lectures on the subject, including for the ICC, SIMC and CIArb. He writes extensively and lectures globally on legal/engineering subjects, including at CERN in Geneva and Xerox PARC in Silicon valley.

Teresa Giovannini is a founding partner of LALIVE specializing in international arbitration (including setting aside proceedings with the Swiss Supreme Court), as well as art law. She has acted – mainly as arbitrator – in more than 170 international arbitrations. Teresa Giovannini is the Swiss Member of the ICC Court of Arbitration and the ICC Commission on Arbitration and ADR since 1 July 2015 and she is part of several panels of arbitrators as well as of arbitration committees. Mrs Giovannini is also a frequent speaker on international arbitration and the author of various publications in the field.

Professor Dr. Daniel Girsberger is a founding member of the Faculty of Law of the University of Lucerne and a tenured professor for Swiss and International Private, Business and Procedural, as well as Comparative Law. Before accepting the Lucerne assignment, he taught at the University of Zurich Law School and as visiting professor at various universities worldwide. He is, moreover, the author of numerous publications focusing primarily on international business law and arbitration. Daniel Girsberger is also of counsel at Wenger & Vieli Ltd., a major Zurich business law firm. In the course of his profession, he has acted as chairman, arbitrator and counsel in various domestic and international arbitration cases.

Contributors

Philipp Habegger is the principal of **Habegger Arbitration** in Zurich, Switzerland. He has acted in more than 170 commercial arbitrations under a variety of arbitration rules and applicable laws. He has been involved in disputes arising out of joint ventures, mergers and acquisitions, international sales, agency and distribution, licensing, franchising, construction and engineering projects, across a wide range of industries. Philipp used to be president of the Arbitration Court of the Swiss Chambers' Arbitration Institution, court member of the ICC International Court of Arbitration, and vice chair of the IBA Arbitration Committee. He teaches international arbitration at the University of Zurich.

Professor Dr. Kaj Hobér is Professor of International Investment and Trade Law at Uppsala University (Sweden). He is Chairman of the Board of the SCC Institute in Stockholm, as well as an associate member of Three Verulam Buildings, Gray's Inn, London.

Günther J. Horvath is partner and leads the International Arbitration Group in the Vienna office of Freshfields Bruckhaus Deringer LLP. His experience comprises around 150 high-profile cases as counsel and arbitrator under the Rules of ICC, VIAC, SCC, Swiss Rules and in ad-hoc arbitrations. His practise specialises in international commercial arbitration with a primary focus on energy, joint venture matters, corporate disputes and industrial engineering. Günther holds law degrees from the University of Graz and New York University. He speaks German, English and some Italian.

Professor Dr. Hans van Houtte is President of the Iran-United States Claims Tribunal and an independent arbitrator. He was a professor of law at the KU Leuven (Belgium) where he taught international public law, international private law, international business law and still teaches arbitration. He sits frequently in commercial and investment arbitrations. He has i.a. been President of the Eritrea-Ethiopia Claims Commission, Judge of the Claims Tribunal for Dormant Accounts and member of the United Nations Claims Commission and the Commission for Real Property Claims in Bosnia.

Benjamin Hughes is an independent arbitrator with Fountain Court Chambers in London and The Arbitration Chambers in Singapore, and Associate Professor of Law at Seoul National University Law School. Prior to launching his practice as an independent arbitrator in 2013, Ben practiced as international arbitration counsel with major US and Korean law firms. Ben has been appointed as arbitrator in over sixty international arbitrations with a total value in despite exceeding USD 1 billion. Chambers & Partners has recognized Ben as one of the *"Most in Demand Arbitrators"* in the Asia-Pacific Region.

Michael Hwang S.C. currently practices as an international arbitrator and mediator based in Singapore. He also serves as the non-resident Chief Justice of the Dubai International Financial Centre Courts. He has two law degrees from Oxford University, to which he gained admission by winning an open scholarship examination. In 2014 he was conferred an Honorary LLD degree by the University of Sydney. His past and present appointments include: (a) Judicial Commissioner of the Supreme Court of

Singapore; (b) Senior Counsel of the Supreme Court of Singapore; (c) Singapore's non-resident Ambassador to Switzerland and Argentina; (d) President of the Law Society of Singapore; (e) Adjunct Professor, National University of Singapore; (f) Commissioner of the United Nations Compensation Commission; and Vice Chair of ICC International Court of Arbitration.

Florence Jaeger, is currently a Visiting Scholar and Ph.D. candidate at Columbia Law School in New York. Florence received her Bachelor's and Master's degrees in Law from the University of Basel.

Professor Doug Jones is a leading independent international commercial and investor/state arbitrator. He is an arbitration member at Arbitration Place, a door tenant at Atkin Chambers in London, and has chambers in Sydney, Australia. The arbitrations in which he has been involved include infrastructure, energy, commodities, intellectual property, commercial and joint venture, and investor-state disputes spanning over thirty jurisdictions. Prior to his full-time arbitration practice, Doug had forty years' experience as an international transactional and disputes projects lawyer. He is an Officer of the Order of Australia, and one of only four Companions of the Chartered Institute of Arbitrators.

Neil Kaplan CBE QC SBS, has been a full-time practicing arbitrator since 1995. He has been involved in several hundred arbitrations as arbitrator. Called to the Bar of England in 1965, Mr. Kaplan has practiced as a barrister, Principal Crown Counsel at the Hong Kong Attorney General's Chambers, and served as a Judge of the Supreme Court of Hong Kong in charge of the Arbitration List. He was Chair of HKIAC for thirteen years and President of the Chartered Institute of Arbitrators in 1999/2000. Since 2017 he has been the President of the Court of the Mauritius Chamber of Commerce and Industry Arbitration and Mediation Centre.

Jennifer Kirby is an internationally recognized arbitration expert, who acts as counsel and sits as arbitrator in a wide variety of arbitration matters. Jennifer served as both Counsel and Deputy Secretary General of the ICC International Court of Arbitration before leaving to join a multinational firm as a partner in their arbitration group. In 2010, Jennifer founded her own boutique arbitration practice, Kirby, in Paris. Jennifer has been recognized by *Chambers Global* as "a true expert in ICC-related disputes" and by *The Who's Who of International Arbitration* as a "very sharp" global player in the field.

Professor Dr. Richard Kreindler is a Partner of the law firm of Cleary Gottlieb Steen & Hamilton LLP and has specialized in international arbitration and litigation matters since 1985. He is a US national, was educated in the US and Germany, is admitted to the Bar in New York and Paris, and is also a professor of law in Germany. He has acted as counsel, arbitrator, expert and mediator in several hundred disputes under the major arbitral rules and regimes, with a focus on post-M&A, construction & infrastructure, energy and intellectual property.

Contributors

Professor Dr. Stefan Kröll is an independent arbitrator in Cologne and an honorary professor at Bucerius Law School in Hamburg. He is one of the directors of the Willem C. Vis Arbitration Moot Court and Germany's national correspondent to UNCITRAL for arbitration. Stefan has acted as arbitrator or emergency arbitrator in over seventy cases with private and state parties and is regularly listed as one of the leading arbitrators in Germany. Stefan has published widely in the field of international commercial arbitration and commercial law.

Lynnette Lee, graduated with an LL.B. from Monash University and was an intern with Michael Hwang Chambers LLC.

Dr. Werner Melis is an independent international arbitrator. He was the former President of the Vienna International Arbitration Centre and is now Honorary President. He was also the former Vice-president of the International Council for Commercial Arbitation and of the London Court of International Arbitration as well as other leading arbitral institutions. He has been an arbitrator in more than 150 international arbitrations world-wide. Dr. Melis has been a member of the Austrian delegation in the negotiations of the UNCITRAL Arbitration Rules, the UNCITRAL Conciliation Rules and the UNCITRAL Model Law on International Commercial Arbitration.

Dr. Michael Moser Michael Moser is an international arbitrator with Twenty Essex Street Chambers, with offices in Hong Kong, Singapore and London. He is Honorary Past Chairman of the Hong Kong International Arbitration Centre, current board member of the Singapore International Arbitration Centre and the Vienna International Arbitration Centre, and past member of the LCIA Court and the SCC Stockholm Chamber of Commerce Arbitration Institute. He has sat as arbitrator in more than 200 cases around the globe.

Alexis Mourre is President of the ICC International Court of Arbitration and past chair of the IBA arbitration committee. He has participated as counsel or arbitrator in more than 230 arbitration proceedings under most international arbitration rules and since 1 May 2015 has established his independent arbitrator practice. He is the author of several books and many articles on international arbitration and private international law. He is fluent in French, English, Spanish and Italian and has good knowledge of Portuguese.

Professor William W. Park is a Professor of Law at Boston University where he teaches courses in tax and financial law. After studies at Yale and Columbia, Park practiced in Paris until returning home to Boston. Park is General Editor of Arbitration International and former President of the London Court of International Arbitration. He served on the Claims Resolution Tribunal for Dormant Swiss Accounts and the International Commission on Holocaust Insurance Claims. The United States appointed Park to the ICSID Panel of Arbitrators. His books include Arbitration of International Business Disputes, International Forum Selection, ICC Arbitration (with Craig &

Paulsson), International Commercial Arbitration (with Reisman, Craig & Paulsson) and Income Tax Treaty Arbitration (with Tillinghast).

Dr. Tom Christopher Pröstler, LL.M. (Sydney) is a registered foreign lawyer with CMS Hong Kong and a visiting lecturer at Humboldt-Universität zu Berlin. His legal practice focuses on representing clients and acting as tribunal secretary in international arbitration proceedings under all major arbitration rules, with a special focus on disputes between western and Asian parties. Dr Pröstler studied law at Humboldt-Universität, Université de Genève and University of Sydney and process management at Ruhr-Universität-Bochum. He obtained his doctorate on a comparative law subject from Humboldt-Universität. Prior to joining CMS Hong Kong, he worked at CMS's Munich office and was a fellow at Humboldt-Universität.

Dr. Axel Reeg is the founding partner of REEG RECHTSANWAELTE, a German niche law firm active in cross-border dispute resolution. Axel holds a Ph.D. in law and is admitted to the Bars in Germany and Spain. He lectures on International Arbitration at the University of Heidelberg. Axel has extensive experience in cross-border dispute resolution, both as an arbitrator, as counsel in international arbitration and before state courts. Axel is, *inter alia*, a member of the Board of Trustees of the Chartered Institute of Arbitrators.

Professor Dr. Klaus Sachs is a partner in the law firm of CMS Hasche Sigle. After attending schools in Paris, Bonn and Brussels, Mr Sachs graduated from Heidelberg University in 1973. He obtained a doctor juris degree in 1975 and was admitted to the bar in 1976. Klaus Sachs has over twenty-five years of experience as party's counsel, co-arbitrator, sole arbitrator and chairman in both ad hoc and institutional arbitration proceedings. He has also acted as chair or co-arbitrator in so far more than fifteen investment treaty arbitrations under the ICSID Rules or the UNCITRAL Arbitration Rules. He is honorary professor for international arbitration law at the Munich University.

Professor Dr. Ulrich G. Schroeter is a Professor of Private Law and Comparative Law at the University of Basel (Switzerland). Prior to starting his position in Basel, he was a Professor at the University of Mannheim (Germany) where he was the Chair for Private Law, International Corporate and Financial Markets Law, European Business Law. Ulrich was educated at the Albert-Ludwigs-University Freiburg (Germany) and the University of Lausanne (Switzerland). He received a *Doctor iuris* from the Freie Universität Berlin. Ulrich works and publishes in the areas of contract law, international trade law, arbitration, treaty law, commercial law, financial markets regulation and European Union law. He regularly speaks at conferences worldwide.

Professor Dr. Ingeborg Schwenzer is the Dean of the Swiss International Law School (SiLS), Professor emerita of Private Law at the University of Basel (Switzerland) and Chair of the CISG Advisory Council. She has also been an adjunct professor at City University of Hong Kong and Griffith University in Brisbane (Australia). She has

Contributors

published numerous books and over 200 articles in the fields of the law of obligations, commercial arbitration as well as family law. She is the editor and main contributor of the world's leading Commentary on the Convention on the International Sale of Goods and its German, Spanish, Portuguese and Turkish counterparts. Ingeborg also regularly acts as arbitrator, counsel and legal expert in international disputes.

Matthew Secomb is a partner in White & Case's International Arbitration Group in Singapore. He specializes in international commercial arbitration, with a focus on energy-related and construction disputes. He has been involved in arbitrations under most of the major arbitral rules, as well as in *ad hoc* arbitrations. In addition to his counsel work, Matthew acts regularly as arbitrator. Before moving to Singapore in 2015, he was based in White & Case's Paris office for nearly ten years. Prior to joining White & Case in 2006, Matthew was counsel to the ICC International Court of Arbitration.

Alexander Shchavelev, LL.M. (UNSW, Sydney) is an associate in the Düsseldorf office of Orrick, Herrington & Sutcliffe LLP and member of the firm's International Arbitration group. His practice focuses on domestic and international arbitration and litigation, with a particular emphasis on M&A, energy and construction related disputes. Another focus are Russia related cross-border transactions and disputes. Alexander also regularly acts as administrative secretary of arbitral tribunals. He holds a PhD in Law from the University of Freiburg and a Master of Laws degree from the University of New South Wales and regularly publishes on arbitration and commercial law subjects.

Jingzhou Tao is the Managing Partner responsible for developing the Asia Practice of Dechert LLP. He has advised many Fortune 500 companies on international mergers and acquisitions, arbitration and corporate matters involving China for more than thirty years. Mr. Tao has represented major American and European and Japanese companies in hundreds of transactions in China involving joint ventures, tax planning, strategic alliances and intellectual property protection. He also has significant experience in international arbitration proceedings both in China and before the major international arbitration institutions.

Marc D. Veit is a Partner at LALIVE and specializes in international arbitration and litigation. He has acted as counsel and arbitrator in a large number of international arbitrations, both ad hoc (including UNCITRAL) and under institutional rules (ICC, Swiss rules, HKIAC, SIAC, SCC, IATA) involving the substantive and/or procedural laws of Switzerland, Germany, Austria, France, England, China, Turkey, Sweden, Singapore, Hong Kong, Georgia, Ukraine, Korea and Albania. He has been ranked for many years by Chambers Global as a leading individual in Arbitration and Litigation in Switzerland, and by Legal 500 as a recommended practitioner in Dispute Resolution in Switzerland.

Contributors

Jeffrey Waincymer has over thirty-two years' experience as a legal practitioner in all aspects of international arbitration, international trade and investment, customers and commercial law. He has acted as arbitrator and expert witness in international arbitration proceedings. Jeffrey has published extensively on international arbitration and litigation and was formerly a Professor of Law at Monash University and Deakin University in Australia.

Professor Janet Walker (JD, DPhil, FCIArb) is a Professor of Law (past associate dean) at Osgoode Hall Law School, a member of the Ontario Bar, and licensed legal consultant of the New York State Bar. She authors Canada's main text on private international law and is general editor of works on comparative procedure and group actions. For more than fifteen years she has served as arbitrator, co-arbitrator and chair under various institutional rules. Janet is based in Toronto at Arbitration Place and in London at Outer Temple Chambers. She has a good working knowledge of Spanish and French.

Jane Willems is an Associate Professor of Law at Tsinghua Law School, Associate Director of the International Arbitration and Dispute Settlement LLM (IADS). She teaches international investment law, private international law and international commercial arbitration. Her Ph.D. thesis focused on Sino-foreign joint ventures contract disputes before international arbitrators. She has participated in numerous international commercial and investment arbitrations and other forms of ADR. She has served as an arbitrator and commercial arbitrations involving the ICC, HKIAC, CIETAC, BAC and UNCITRAL Rules. Jane Willems is a member of the California and the Paris (France) Bar.

Stephan Wilske Dr. iur., Maître en Droit (Aix-Marseille III), LL.M. (The University of Chicago; Casper Platt Award), Rechtsanwalt (Germany) and Attorney-at-Law (New York), admission to various U.S. federal courts, including the U.S. Supreme Court, FCIArb (Chartered Institute of Arbitrators); partner at Gleiss Lutz, Stuttgart; lecturer at the Universities of Heidelberg and Jena. Stephan is a member of the American Law Institute (ALI) and the SIAC Users' Council. He is also an Advisory Committee Member of the Swiss Arbitration Academy, Senior Committee Member of the Contemporary Asia Arbitration Journal and International Correspondent (Germany) of the Revista Română de Arbitraj.

Summary of Contents

Editors	v
Contributors	vii
Foreword	xxxvii
Preface	xxxix

CHAPTER 1
Taming the Twin Dragons of International Arbitration:
Cost and Delay
Gerald Aksen — 1

CHAPTER 2
One Shot Players and Arbitrator Selection: A Fair Shot or a Shot in the Dark?
Chiann Bao — 9

CHAPTER 3
Third-Party Funding and the International Arbitrator
Louise Barrington — 15

CHAPTER 4
The Arbitrator Dr. Martin Regli: Pierre Karrer's *Alter Ego*
Klaus Peter Berger — 25

CHAPTER 5
The Role of National Courts at the Threshold of Arbitration
George A. Bermann — 39

Summary of Contents

CHAPTER 6
Pierre Karrer
David J. Branson — 51

CHAPTER 7
Is Efficiency an Arbitrator's Duty or Simply a Character Trait?
Nadia Darwazeh — 57

CHAPTER 8
The Role of Party-Appointed Arbitrators
Siegfried H. Elsing & Alexander Shchavelev — 65

CHAPTER 9
Concurrent Proceedings in Investment Arbitration
Emmanuel Gaillard — 79

CHAPTER 10
The Role of the Arbitrator in Energy Disputes
Robert Gaitskell Q.C. CEng. — 93

CHAPTER 11
Annulled International Arbitral Awards and Remand: Can/
Should the Same Arbitral Tribunal Take the Case Anew? A Short
Analysis from a Swiss Perspective
Teresa Giovannini — 103

CHAPTER 12
Foreign Mandatory Norms in Swiss Arbitration Proceedings:
An Approach Worth Copying?
Daniel Girsberger — 113

CHAPTER 13
The Arbitrator's Duty of Efficiency: A Call for Increased Utilization
of Arbitral Powers
Philipp Habegger — 123

CHAPTER 14
Latin and International Arbitration
Kaj Hobér — 137

CHAPTER 15
The Angelic Arbitrator Versus The Rogue Arbitrator: What Should
an Arbitrator Strive to Be?
Günther J. Horvath — 143

Chapter 16
Assessment of Future Damages in Arbitration
Hans van Houtte — 153

Chapter 17
The Problem of Undisclosed Assistance to Arbitral Tribunals
Benjamin Hughes — 161

Chapter 18
Standard of Proof for Challenge Against Arbitrators: Giving Them the Benefit of the Doubt
Michael Hwang SC & Lynnette Lee — 169

Chapter 19
The Use of Experts in International Arbitration
Neil Kaplan CBE QC SBS — 187

Chapter 20
How Far Should an Arbitrator Go to Get It Right?
Jennifer Kirby — 193

Chapter 21
Sanctioning of Party Conduct Through Costs: A Reconsideration of Scope, Timing and Content of Costs Awards
Richard Kreindler & Mariel Dimsey — 201

Chapter 22
Promoting Settlements in Arbitration: The Role of the Arbitrator
Stefan Kröll — 209

Chapter 23
The Role of Individuals in International Arbitration
Werner Melis — 225

Chapter 24
The Pre-hearing Checklist Protocol: A Tool for Organizing Efficient Arbitration Hearings
Michael Moser — 229

Chapter 25
About Procedural Soft Law, the IBA Guidelines on Party Representation and the Future of Arbitration
Alexis Mourre — 239

Summary of Contents

CHAPTER 26
Arbitration and Fine Dining: Two Faces of Efficiency
William W. Park   251

CHAPTER 27
Should an International Arbitral Tribunal Engage in Settlement Facilitation?
Axel Reeg   269

CHAPTER 28
Time Limits in International Arbitral Proceedings
Klaus Sachs & Tom Christopher Pröstler   279

CHAPTER 29
Mandatory Private Treaty Application? On the Alleged Duty of Arbitrators to Apply International Conventions
Ulrich G. Schroeter   295

CHAPTER 30
The CISG in International Arbitration
Ingeborg Schwenzer & Florence Jaeger   311

CHAPTER 31
Multi-party, Multi-contract Rules and the Arbitrators' Role in Finding Consent
Matthew Secomb   327

CHAPTER 32
The Emergency Arbitrator
Patricia Shaughnessy   339

CHAPTER 33
Deliberations of Arbitrators
Jingzhou Tao   349

CHAPTER 34
The Importance of Languages in International Arbitration and How They Impact Parties' Due Process Rights
Sherlin Tung   359

CHAPTER 35
Proving Legality Instead of Corruption
Marc D. Veit   373

CHAPTER 36
An Arbitrator, a Gorilla and an Elephant Walk into a Room ...
Jeffrey Waincymer   383

CHAPTER 37
Procedural Order No. 1: From Swiss Watch to Arbitrators' Toolkit
Janet Walker & Doug Jones, AO   393

CHAPTER 38
The Arbitrator's Jurisdiction at Risk: The Case of Hybrid and
Asymmetrical Arbitration Agreements
Jane Willems   403

CHAPTER 39
Work Ethics of the International Arbitrator, or: The Distinction Between
Rendering a Service to the Parties and Being the Parties' Slave
Stephan Wilske   417

Table of Contents

Editors	v
Contributors	vii
Foreword	xxxvii
Preface	xxxix

CHAPTER 1
Taming the Twin Dragons of International Arbitration: Cost and Delay
Gerald Aksen — 1

CHAPTER 2
One Shot Players and Arbitrator Selection: A Fair Shot or a
Shot in the Dark?
Chiann Bao — 9

§2.01	The "One Shot Players" of Asia	10
§2.02	The Responsibility of Appointing an Arbitrator	11
§2.03	The Problem as Faced by the "One Shot Player"	12
§2.04	Where Do We Go from Here?	13

CHAPTER 3
Third-Party Funding and the International Arbitrator
Louise Barrington — 15

§3.01	What Is Third-Party Funding?	15
§3.02	Why All the Fuss?	15
§3.03	Who Are the Funders?	16

Table of Contents

§3.04	Who Uses Third-Party Funding for Arbitration?	17
§3.05	What Concerns May Arise from Third-Party Funder Involvement in an Arbitration Case?	18
§3.06	Should the TPF Be Disclosed to the Opposing Party and the Tribunal?	20
§3.07	Addressing Questions Around Third-Party Funding	22
§3.08	Conclusion	23

CHAPTER 4
The Arbitrator Dr. Martin Regli: Pierre Karrer's *Alter Ego*
Klaus Peter Berger   25

§4.01	Introduction	25
§4.02	Pierre Karrer's Role in the Multimedia Project: The Arbitrator Who Plays Himself	26
§4.03	1001 Q&As: Pierre Karrer's Adaptation of the Idea of Interactive Teaching and Training in Arbitration	27
§4.04	Two Problems and Their Solutions by Dr. Regli and Pierre Karrer	28
	[A] Proactive Procedural Planning	28
	[B] The Pathological Arbitration Clause	32
§4.05	Conclusion	38

CHAPTER 5
The Role of National Courts at the Threshold of Arbitration
George A. Bermann   39

§5.01	Introduction	39
§5.02	On What Grounds Might an Apparent Arbitration Agreement Be Denied Enforcement?	40
§5.03	Approaches to the Threshold Role of National Courts	41
	[A] Comprehensive Judicial Involvement at the Threshold	41
	[B] A "Hands-Off" Role for Courts at the Threshold	42
	[C] Intermediate Positions on the Threshold Judicial Role	43
	[1] Default Rule and Party Autonomy	43
	[2] Heightening the Burden of Proof for Resisting Arbitration	44
	[3] Immediate Court Review of Arbitral Rulings on Jurisdiction	45
	[4] Distinguishing Among Challenges to the Arbitration Agreement	46
§5.04	Conclusion	48

CHAPTER 6
Pierre Karrer
David J. Branson   51

CHAPTER 7
Is Efficiency an Arbitrator's Duty or Simply a Character Trait?
Nadia Darwazeh   57

§7.01	Do Arbitrators Have a Duty of Efficiency in Arbitration?	58
§7.02	What Does it Take for an Arbitrator to Be Efficient?	60
§7.03	What Are the Sanctions if an Arbitrator Breaches the Duty of Efficiency?	62

CHAPTER 8
The Role of Party-Appointed Arbitrators
Siegfried H. Elsing & Alexander Shchavelev   65

§8.01	Introduction	65
§8.02	Some Notes on General Questions	66
	[A] The Right to Choose an Arbitrator	66
	[B] On Independence and Impartiality	68
§8.03	Party-Appointed Arbitrators in UNCITRAL Model Law and Institutional Rules	69
§8.04	Party-Appointed Arbitrator in the Course of Arbitration	70
	[A] Selection and Appointment	70
	[B] Disclosure	71
	[C] Selection of the Chair	72
	[D] Pre-hearing Phase	73
	[E] Hearing Phase	74
	[F] Award Making	75
§8.05	Conclusion	77

CHAPTER 9
Concurrent Proceedings in Investment Arbitration
Emmanuel Gaillard   79

§9.01	The Challenges Arising from Concurrent Proceedings	80
	[A] The Origins of the Problem	80
	[B] Illustrations	83
	[C] Analysis of the Difficulty	85
§9.02	The Potential Solutions	87
	[A] *De lege lata*	87
	[B] *De lege ferenda*	90

Table of Contents

CHAPTER 10
The Role of the Arbitrator in Energy Disputes
Robert Gaitskell Q.C. CEng.   93

§10.01	Introduction	93
§10.02	Types of Energy Disputes	94
§10.03	Outset of the Arbitration	95
§10.04	Conditions Precedent to Arbitration	95
§10.05	Procedural Steps	96
§10.06	Pleadings or Memorials	96
§10.07	Experts and Their Reports	97
§10.08	'Hot-Tubbing' of Experts	97
§10.09	Experts' Meetings and Reports	98
§10.10	The Hearing Bundle	99
§10.11	The Pre-hearing Submissions	99
§10.12	'Chess-Clock' Usage of Time	100
§10.13	Witnesses	100
§10.14	Post-hearing	101
§10.15	The Draft Award	101
§10.16	Conclusion	101

CHAPTER 11
Annulled International Arbitral Awards and Remand: Can/Should the Same Arbitral Tribunal Take the Case Anew? A Short Analysis from a Swiss Perspective
Teresa Giovannini   103

CHAPTER 12
Foreign Mandatory Norms in Swiss Arbitration Proceedings: An Approach Worth Copying?
Daniel Girsberger   113

§12.01	Introduction			113
§12.02	Mandatory Norms in State Court Litigation vis-à-vis Arbitration			114
	[A]	State Court Litigation		114
	[B]	Arbitration		115
		[1]	Swiss FSC	116
		[2]	'Swiss' Arbitral Awards Addressing the Issue	118
§12.03	Is There a Common Denominator?			120
§12.04	Is the Swiss Approach a Recommendable Model?			121

CHAPTER 13
The Arbitrator's Duty of Efficiency: A Call for Increased Utilization
of Arbitral Powers
Philipp Habegger   123

§13.01 Introduction   123
§13.02 Legal Basis for Arbitrator's Duties and Rights Concerning Efficiency   124
§13.03 Party Autonomy Versus Arbitrator's Discretion in Determining
Efficient Procedures   126
    [A] Arbitral Tribunal's Objections to Parties' Procedural
Agreements   126
    [B] Institutional Rules Giving Priority to Party Autonomy
in Matters of Procedure   127
    [C] Institutional Rules Limiting Party Autonomy on Matters of
Procedure   128
§13.04 Mandatory Provisions and Arbitrators' Discretion in Determining
Efficient Procedures   129
§13.05 Arbitrators' Exercise of Power and Discretion: A Shift in
Approach in Case Management   130
    [A] Application of IBA Rules and Other 'Soft Law'   131
    [B] Time to Prepare a Party's Case   131
    [C] Bifurcation of Issues   131
    [D] Document Production   132
    [E] Witness Evidence and Hearings   132
    [F] Written Submissions   133
    [G] Post-hearing Briefs   134
§13.06 Conclusion   135

CHAPTER 14
Latin and International Arbitration
Kaj Hobér   137

§14.01 *Exordium*   137
§14.02 *Legis actio*   138
§14.03 *Ius civile et Ius commercii*   139
§14.04 *Ius Gentium*   140
§14.05 *Conclusio*   141

CHAPTER 15
The Angelic Arbitrator Versus The Rogue Arbitrator: What Should
an Arbitrator Strive to Be?
Günther J. Horvath   143

§15.01 Introduction   143
§15.02 The Angelic Arbitrator: The Ideal   144

Table of Contents

§15.03	The Rogue Arbitrator: The Train Wreck	146
§15.04	The Enlightened Arbitrator: What an Arbitrator Should Strive to Achieve	148
§15.05	Conclusion	151

CHAPTER 16
Assessment of Future Damages in Arbitration
Hans van Houtte — 153

§16.01	Conceptual Framework		154
	[A]	Future *Lucrum Cessans* and *Damnum Emergens*	154
	[B]	Time Span of Future Damages	154
	[C]	Forecasting and Probability	155
	[D]	Different Levels of Certainty	155
§16.02	Procedural Aspects		156
	[A]	"Mind the Gap"	156
	[B]	How to Bridge the Gap?	157
	[C]	The Manageable Excel Sheet	158
	[D]	The Future Shrinks	158
	[E]	Recurrent or Continues Future Damages	158

CHAPTER 17
The Problem of Undisclosed Assistance to Arbitral Tribunals
Benjamin Hughes — 161

§17.01	Introduction		161
§17.02	The Problem		163
	[A]	Confidentiality	163
	[B]	Independence and Impartiality	164
	[C]	Role in the Arbitration	165
	[D]	Remuneration	167
§17.03	The Solution?		168

CHAPTER 18
Standard of Proof for Challenge Against Arbitrators: Giving Them the Benefit of the Doubt
Michael Hwang SC & Lynnette Lee — 169

§18.01	Introduction			169
§18.02	The Standard of Proof for Challenging Arbitrators			171
	[A]	Standard of Proof Spectrum for Challenging Arbitrators		171
		[1]	Academic Commentaries	171
		[2]	Arbitral Rules	173
		[3]	National Arbitration Laws	173
		[4]	Standard of Proof Spectrum	175

§18.03	Applicable Standard of Proof for the 'Justifiable Doubts' Test Under the IBA Guidelines			177
	[A]	The Intentions of the Original Working Group for the Definition of 'Justifiable Doubts'		177
		[1]	The Interpretation of 'Likelihood'	177
		[2]	Best International Practice	177
	[B]	General Standard 2(c): The Explanation of 'Justifiable Doubts'		178
		[1]	The 2004 and 2014 Versions of General Standard 2(c)	179
		[2]	Born's Critique	179
		[3]	Born's Alternative: A Higher Threshold?	179
		[4]	Origins of General Standard 2(c)	180
		[5]	The Litmus Test of Independence	180
		[6]	Application of General Standard 2(c)	181
§18.04	Disclosure Requirements under the IBA Guidelines			182
	[A]	General Standard 3: Disclosure Requirements		182
		[1]	Disclosure Requirements under General Standards 3(a) and 3(c) of the 2004 IBA Guidelines	182
		[2]	Born's Critique: Excessive Disclosure Requirements	183
		[3]	Universal Acceptance of the IBA Guidelines	183
	[B]	Circumstances to Disclose under the IBA Guidelines		184
		[1]	The Orange List 2004 IBA Guidelines	184
		[2]	Born's Critique	184
		[3]	The Concept of Subjective Relevance	184
		[4]	Comparison with ICC Guidance Note on Disclosure Requirements	185
§18.05	Conclusion			186

CHAPTER 19
The Use of Experts in International Arbitration
Neil Kaplan CBE QC SBS   187

§19.01	Tribunal or Party-Appointed Expert?	187
§19.02	No Expert Testimony Without Leave of the Tribunal	189
§19.03	Instructions	190
§19.04	Reports	190
§19.05	Early Opening and Expert Presentation	190
§19.06	Post-Hearing	192

CHAPTER 20
How Far Should an Arbitrator Go to Get it Right?
Jennifer Kirby   193

Table of Contents

CHAPTER 21
Sanctioning of Party Conduct Through Costs: A Reconsideration of
Scope, Timing and Content of Costs Awards
Richard Kreindler & Mariel Dimsey   201

§21.01	Scope of Cost-Relevant Conduct	201
§21.02	Timing of Costs Sanctions	206
§21.03	Form and Content of Costs Sanctions	207
§21.04	Conclusion	208

CHAPTER 22
Promoting Settlements in Arbitration: The Role of the Arbitrator
Stefan Kröll   209

§22.01	Introduction		209
§22.02	Overview of the Different Approaches in Practice		210
§22.03	Connection with Other Developments in International Arbitration Procedure		214
§22.04	The Position Taken by Arbitration Laws and Rules on Settlement Facilitations		215
§22.05	Detailed Evaluation of the Different Measures Suggested		217
	[A]	Information About Preliminary Views on the Issues in Dispute in the Arbitration and the Evidence Needed	217
	[B]	Preliminary Non-binding Findings on Law or Fact on Key Issues in the Arbitration	220
	[C]	Suggested Terms of Settlement as a Basis for Further Negotiation	222
	[D]	Chair Settlement Meetings Attended by Representatives of the Parties at Which Possible Terms of Settlement May Be Negotiated	223
§22.06	Conclusion		223

CHAPTER 23
The Role of Individuals in International Arbitration
Werner Melis   225

CHAPTER 24
The Pre-hearing Checklist Protocol: A Tool for Organizing Efficient
Arbitration Hearings
Michael Moser   229

§24.01	Introduction		229
§24.02	Pre-hearing Planning: Key Points for Consideration		230
	[A]	Dates and Venue	230
	[B]	Attendees	230

		[C]	Hearing Schedule	230
		[D]	Pre-hearing Items	231
		[E]	Order of Play, Witnesses and Sequestration	231
		[F]	Interpretation	231
		[G]	Post-hearing Submissions and the Award	232
§24.03	The Pre-hearing Checklist Protocol			232
§24.04	Conclusion			236

CHAPTER 25
About Procedural Soft Law, the IBA Guidelines on Party Representation and the Future of Arbitration
Alexis Mourre 239

CHAPTER 26
Arbitration and Fine Dining: Two Faces of Efficiency
William W. Park 251

§26.01	The Parties' Legitimate Expectations				251
	[A]	Rival Goals			251
	[B]	Four Aspirations			253
§26.02	Contemplating Alternatives				254
	[A]	Efficiency from Two Perspectives			254
	[B]	Costs and Benefits			255
		[1]	The Last Bad Experience		255
		[2]	Hard Choices		257
			[a]	Contract Drafting	257
			[b]	A Laundry List of Dilemmas	258
			[c]	Institutional Rules	259
§26.03	The Enforcement Stage				260
	[A]	The Law of Arbitration			260
	[B]	The Arbitral Seat: Conflict in Action			260
		[1]	New Theories and Due Process		261
			[a]	Caribbean Niquel	261
			[b]	De Sutter v. Madagascar	262
		[2]	Cost Allocation and Contract Terms		263
§26.04	Good Practices				264
§26.05	Counterpoise and Common Sense				267

CHAPTER 27
Should an International Arbitral Tribunal Engage in Settlement Facilitation?
Axel Reeg 269

§27.01	Is Settlement Facilitation by Arbitrators Viable?: The Common Law and the Civil Law Perspectives	270

Table of Contents

§27.02	Is Settlement Facilitation by International Arbitration Tribunals Desirable?	272
§27.03	Are Hybrid Dispute Resolution Models Truly an Alternative?	273
§27.04	Pre-conditions for Settlement Facilitation by International Arbitration Tribunals	275
§27.05	Summary	277

CHAPTER 28
Time Limits in International Arbitral Proceedings
Klaus Sachs & Tom Christopher Pröstler — 279

§28.01	Establishing Time Limits		280
	[A]	Tribunal Determination	280
	[B]	Parties' Agreement	281
	[C]	Terms of Reference	283
	[D]	Arbitral Institutions and Rules	283
	[E]	Arbitration Laws	285
§28.02	Finding the 'Right' Time Limit		286
	[A]	Overly Long Time Limits	286
	[B]	Overly Short Time Limits	288
	[C]	The 'Right' Time Limits	288
§28.03	Consequences of Breaching Time Limits		288
	[A]	Sanctions Against Parties	288
		[1] Extensions for Non-dilatory Parties	289
		[2] Exclusion of Submissions	289
		[3] Adverse Cost Decisions	289
	[B]	Sanctions Against Arbitrators	290
		[1] Loss of Jurisdiction	290
		[2] Replacement of Arbitrators	291
		[3] Written Report by Arbitrators	291
		[4] Reduction of Tribunals' Fees	291
§28.04	Conclusion		293

CHAPTER 29
Mandatory Private Treaty Application? On the Alleged Duty of Arbitrators to Apply International Conventions
Ulrich G. Schroeter — 295

§29.01	Introduction		295
	[A]	A Duty of Arbitrators to Apply International Conventions?	296
	[B]	Treaty Law and Arbitration Practice: Differences in General Approach	297
§29.02	Duty of Arbitrators to Apply International Conventions Resulting from the Conventions Themselves?		298
	[A]	Wording of International Conventions	298

		[1]	Substantive Law or Conflict-of-Laws Conventions	299
		[2]	Arbitration Conventions	300
	[B]	\multicolumn{2}{l}{Addressees of the Obligation to Apply International Conventions Under Treaty Law}	301
		[1]	International Uniform Private Law Conventions in General	301
		[2]	In Particular: Conventions on the Carriage of Goods	302
		[3]	In particular: European Union Treaties	303
	[C]	\multicolumn{2}{l}{Conclusion and a General Suggestion}	304
§29.03	\multicolumn{3}{l}{The *Lex Arbitri* as Source of an Arbitrator's Duty to Apply International Conventions?}	304
§29.04	\multicolumn{3}{l}{International Conventions as Part of the *Lex Causae*}	306
§29.05	\multicolumn{3}{l}{Duty of State Courts to Apply International Conventions when Reviewing Arbitral Awards?}	307
	[A]	\multicolumn{2}{l}{Perspective of Arbitration Law}	307
	[B]	\multicolumn{2}{l}{Compatibility with Treaty Law}	307
§29.06	\multicolumn{3}{l}{Conclusion}	308

CHAPTER 30
The CISG in International Arbitration
Ingeborg Schwenzer & Florence Jaeger 311

§30.01	\multicolumn{2}{l}{Introduction}	311
§30.02	\multicolumn{2}{l}{CISG as Substantive Law}	313
	[A]	Preliminary Remarks	313
	[B]	Choice of Law by the Parties	314
	[C]	Applicable Law in Absence of a Choice of Law Clause	316
§30.03	\multicolumn{2}{l}{CISG as the Law Applicable to the Arbitration Clause}	317
	[A]	General Remarks Regarding the Applicable Law to the Arbitration Clause	317
	[B]	General Applicability of the CISG to Arbitration Agreements	320
	[C]	Formal Validity	320
	[D]	Substantive Validity	322
	[E]	Interpretation	323
	[F]	Remedies for a Breach of the Arbitration Agreement	324
§30.04	\multicolumn{2}{l}{Conclusions}	324

CHAPTER 31
Multi-party, Multi-contract Rules and the Arbitrators' Role in Finding Consent
Matthew Secomb 327

§31.01 Multi-party/Multi-contract Arbitration: What Business People Care About Versus What Arbitration Rule Drafters Care About 328

Table of Contents

§31.02	How the Parties and Contracts Subject to an Arbitration Are Defined Procedurally	329
	[A] The Bad Old Days Before Multi-party, Multi-contract Provisions	329
	[B] The Brave New World of Multi-contract, Multi-party Provisions	330
	[1] The 'Institution Decides' Approach	331
	[2] The 'Arbitrators Decide' Approach	333
	[3] The Hybrid Approach	334
§31.03	Once the Parties and Contracts Subject to the Arbitration Are Defined, What Happens to Jurisdictional Objections?	334
	[A] Consent's Binary Nature, But with Lots of Combinations and Permutations	334
	[B] Arbitrators' Decisions in Multi-party, Multi-contract Situations	335
§31.04	Why Does This All Matter? Arbitrators' Dual Role for Multi-party, Multi-contract Arbitration	336
§31.05	The Wildcard: National Laws on Consolidation	337
§31.06	Conclusion	338

CHAPTER 32
The Emergency Arbitrator
Patricia Shaughnessy 339

§32.01	Introduction	339
§32.02	Background to Emergency Arbitration	340
§32.03	The Source of the Powers and Duties of an Emergency Arbitrator	341
§32.04	The Developing Practice of Emergency Arbitration	343
§32.05	The Duties and Decision-Making of the Emergency Arbitrator	345
§32.06	Conclusion	347

CHAPTER 33
Deliberations of Arbitrators
Jingzhou Tao 349

§33.01	Introduction	349
§33.02	Issues Relating to Deliberations of Arbitrators	350
	[A] Arbitrators' Duty to Deliberate	350
	[B] Different Types of Deliberations	351
	[C] The Purpose of Deliberations	352
	[D] The Form of Deliberations	352
	[E] The Timing of Deliberations	353
§33.03	The Role of the Chairman in the Process of Deliberations	355
	[A] To Be Responsible for Organizing the Deliberations	355
	[B] To Be Responsible for Managing Potential Clashes Among Arbitrators	356
	[C] To Be Responsible for Drafting the Final Award Afterwards	357
§33.04	Confidentiality of Arbitrators' Deliberations	357

§33.05	Thump-Up Rules in Deliberation Process	358

CHAPTER 34
The Importance of Languages in International Arbitration and How
They Impact Parties' Due Process Rights
Sherlin Tung 359

§34.01	Introduction	359
§34.02	Languages in International Business Transactions	360
	[A] Negotiations Between the Parties	361
	[B] Performance of an Agreement	362
	[C] After the Dispute Arises	363
§34.03	Due Process in International Arbitration	364
§34.04	Languages and Their Impact on Parties' Due Process Rights	368
	[A] Procedural Fairness, Equal Treatment and the Right to Be Heard	369
	[B] CEEG (Shanghai) Solar Science & Technology Co., Ltd. Versus Lumos LLC	371
§34.05	Conclusion	372

CHAPTER 35
Proving Legality Instead of Corruption
Marc D. Veit 373

§35.01	Introduction	373
§35.02	Burden and Standard of Proof	374
§35.03	The Arbitral Tribunal's Right and Duty to Raise Corruption Issues *sua Sponte*	377
§35.04	The Legality Test: The Flipside of the Medal or How Tribunals Can Deal with 'Red Flags' Absent Clear Allegations of Corruption	379

CHAPTER 36
An Arbitrator, a Gorilla and an Elephant Walk into a Room ...
Jeffrey Waincymer 383

§36.01	Introduction	383
§36.02	Conclusion	391

CHAPTER 37
Procedural Order No. 1: From Swiss Watch to Arbitrators' Toolkit
Janet Walker & Doug Jones, AO 393

§37.01	Introduction	393
§37.02	Settling the Procedure Before the Arbitration Begins	393
§37.03	Settling the Procedure at the Commencement of the Arbitration	394
§37.04	Recent Innovations in the Arbitrators' 'Toolkit'	396

Table of Contents

§37.05	Issues Best Left Until Later in the Arbitration		397
	[A]	The Extent of Disclosure and Disputes Concerning Disclosure: The '@#$%&' Redfern Schedule	397
	[B]	The Factual Evidence Actually Needed to Decide the Issues in Dispute	398
	[C]	Expert Evidence: Nature, Extent and Manner of Development	398
	[D]	The Detail of the Evidentiary Hearing	399
	[E]	Written Openings and the 'Education' of the Tribunal	400
§37.06	Conclusion		401

CHAPTER 38
The Arbitrator's Jurisdiction at Risk: The Case of Hybrid and Asymmetrical Arbitration Agreements
Jane Willems   403

§38.01	Introduction		403
§38.02	The Arbitrator's Jurisdiction and Hybrid Arbitration Agreements		404
	[A]	The Arbitrator's Jurisdiction and the Parties' Choice of an Institution to Administer Proceedings under Arbitration Rules Promulgated by Another Arbitration Institution	405
	[B]	The Arbitrator's Jurisdiction and the Parties' Choice of an Institution to Administer the Arbitration under Ad-hoc Arbitration Rules	407
§38.03	The Arbitrator's Jurisdiction and Asymmetrical Arbitration Agreements		410
	[A]	Optional Arbitration Agreements	410
	[B]	The Enforceability of Asymmetrical Clauses Providing for a General Option of Forum	412
	[C]	The Enforceability of Asymmetrical Clauses Providing for an Exception to the General Forum	413

CHAPTER 39
Work Ethics of the International Arbitrator, or: The Distinction Between Rendering a Service to the Parties and Being the Parties' Slave
Stephan Wilske   417

§39.01	The New Focus on the Significance of the "Decision-Makers"		418
§39.02	Often Neglected Work Ethics of Arbitrators: The So-Called Secondary Virtues		419
	[A]	Diligence, Transparency and Predictability	420
	[B]	Time- and Cost-Consciousness	420
	[C]	Honesty	421
§39.03	Enough Is Enough: Neither the Prima Donna nor the Parties' Slave		422
§39.04	Conclusion		424

Foreword

It is an honor for us to join in this celebration of Pierre Karrer's 75th birthday. Pierre has been a friend and a respected colleague whom we have both had the good fortune to know throughout our professional careers. We have had the pleasure of working with Pierre in many capacities: as a committee member colleague working on the IBA Rules of Evidence and other reforms, as co-arbitrator, as an arbitrator hearing our cases, as an officer of various arbitration institutions, and as a fellow aficionado of classical music, among others.

Pierre's is undoubtedly one of the great names in international arbitration. He and his work have influenced practitioners around the world. His contributions to the IBA Rules of Evidence were substantial; his training on both sides of the Atlantic and his global experience enabled him to propose solutions that bridged the common law/civil law divide. As the first Vice Chair of the Arbitration Institute of the Stockholm Chamber of Commerce after it internationalized its Board, he helped devise and implement procedures that offer substantial Board input into every major decision that the Institute needs to make in each case, including in particular the selection of arbitrators.

Pierre is as organized and dedicated an arbitrator as one could hope for – indeed it would be no exaggeration to say that these attributes have become the stuff of legend, sufficient to intimidate anyone ill-advised enough even to think about turning up to a hearing unprepared. He has an extensive box of tools, literally and figuratively, to carry out his trade. In each case, he applies his experience to work with the parties to determine the procedures best suited to that particular arbitration. His presence and demeanor exude efficiency, as do his solutions, but he wears his abilities lightly, so that proceedings before him are always managed with fairness and with a humanity that is readily appreciated. As the hearing progresses, his deft touch is even more keenly felt. Because Pierre is so well prepared in every case, he is able to guide the parties through the case effectively.

The range and quality of articles in this Liber Amicorum, and the diversity and excellence of its contributors, are a testament as much to the esteem and affection in which Pierre is held as to his influence upon, and to his own broad interests in improving, the practice of arbitration. At a time when arbitration is under ever greater

Foreword

scrutiny and subject to ever more searching and sometimes hostile enquiry, his work is an example of how good the process can be when it is in the hands of a master. This volume will be one more substantial contribution resulting from Pierre's career, but more to the point, we hope that he will enjoy it both for its content and as a mark of the appreciation of his professional colleagues and friends for all that he has achieved. We, for our part, offer our warmest congratulations to Pierre and we wish him the happiest of birthdays.

John Beechey[*] and David W. Rivkin[**]

---

[*] **John Beechey CBE** is among the best known arbitrators in the world. He has served as chairman, party-appointed arbitrator, or sole arbitrator on international arbitral tribunals in both 'ad hoc' (including UNCITRAL) and institutional arbitrations under the Rules of, *inter alia*, the European Development Fund (EDF), International Chamber of Commerce (ICC), International Centre for Dispute Resolution/ American Arbitration Association (ICDR/AAA), International Center for the Settlement of Investment Disputes (ICSID), London Court of International Arbitration (LCIA), Permanent Court of Arbitration (PCA), Singapore International Arbitration Centre (SIAC) and the Stockholm Chamber. He is a past President of the International Court of Arbitration of the ICC (2009-2015).

[**] **David W. Rivkin** is Co-Chair of Debevoise & Plimpton's International Dispute Resolution Group and The Immediate Past President of the International Bar Association (IBA). A litigation partner in the firm's New York and London offices, Mr. Rivkin has broad experience in the areas of international litigation and arbitration. Mr. Rivkin is consistently ranked as one of the top international dispute resolution practitioners in the world. He has handled international arbitrations throughout the world and before virtually every major arbitration institution. Mr. Rivkin also represents companies in transnational litigation in the US, including the enforcement of arbitral awards and arbitration agreements.

Preface

Dr. Pierre A. Karrer stands out as an exceptionally accomplished international arbitrator, practitioner and expert. The authors who have contributed to this book – all of whom are also prominent in the field of international arbitration – have come to know and respect Dr. Karrer from sitting with him on tribunals, appearing before him as counsel, and/or working with him on projects such as the IBA Rules on the Taking of Evidence. We the editors had the fortune of getting to know Dr. Karrer through his role as a teacher and mentor. It is within this role that he has enthusiastically helped foster the interest, knowledge, skills and networks of generations of young lawyers. We are therefore pleased and delighted to honor Dr. Karrer's remarkable contributions to developing international arbitration and to enhancing the professionalism and collaboration of the global arbitration community.

When putting together this project, we sought to find a theme that would focus on an important feature of Dr. Karrer's philosophical and practical approach to arbitration After some brainstorming, there was no doubt in our minds that the theme of the book celebrating Dr. Karrer's career should focus on the powers and duties of an arbitrator.

Dr. Karrer exemplifies the characteristics of a "maestro" arbitrator who has built and earned his reputation with talent, skill, creativity, integrity and congeniality. His reputation for his good judgment in an expansive array of cases reflects his wide range of knowledge and interests as well as his openness to new ideas and diverse cultures. Dr. Karrer believes in the importance of the arbitrator conducting the proceedings with attention to detail, careful preparation, a firm hand and an open-mind. He believes in the powers of the arbitrator to ensure a fair and efficient conduct of an arbitration and he takes the duties and responsibilities of the arbitrator seriously. It is well known that "an arbitration is only as good as the arbitrator," and all of the contributors to this book know that when Dr. Karrer is the arbitrator, the arbitration will be expertly conducted.

Attracting prominent contributors to this book was an easy task as Dr. Karrer enjoys professional and collegial friendships across the globe. We tried to bring together a diverse group of his colleagues in this book. Many have enjoyed long careers over many years of interacting with Dr. Karrer, while others more recently had the fortune of getting to know him when they were young practitioners and benefited from his willing helping-hand to bring new talent into the arbitration community. Regrettably, we could not include all of the potential contributors who would naturally be a welcomed part of this book.

We hope that the readers of this book will gain insights into the role of the arbitrator and continue the discussions of the issues addressed in these chapters. Arbitrators continue to develop during their careers and arbitration theory and practice evolves over the years. It is only through the sharing of experience, knowledge and ideas that we can guide the developments and evolution to better achieve the promise of arbitration to promote international trade and relations through resolving disputes in a fair, efficient and reliable manner. Dr. Karrer loves to share his knowledge and experience with students and young practitioners in a variety of settings: at universities, through the Willem C. Vis Arbitration Moot, through his writings, at conferences and seminars, and social events. We are delighted to offer this book to readers to carry-on his tradition of sharing experience and knowledge in the hopes of inspiring discussion and thought, just as Dr. Karrer has inspired us.

We would like to express our appreciation of working with Vincent Verschoor and Eleanor Taylor of Wolters Kluwer, as well as their team. They were immediately on board with the idea of publishing a Liber Amicorum for Dr. Karrer and have offered continuous encouragement and support.

Without the dedication and hard work of the team at Wolters Kluwer and the outstanding contributors, this book would not be the success that it is in honoring Dr. Karrer's career.

Patricia Shaughnessy & Sherlin Tung
April 1, 2017

CHAPTER 1
Taming the Twin Dragons of International Arbitration: Cost and Delay

Gerald Aksen

International Commercial Arbitration has enjoyed solid progress during the last half century. Since the promulgation of the 1958 Convention on the Recognition and Enforcement of Foreign Arbitral Awards, (the NY Convention), there are few contracts in international commercial trade that do not provide for arbitration as the preferred mode of dispute resolution. The process has become so ingrained internationally that there are now over forty institutions around the world that hold themselves out as being neutral administrators of international arbitration and each has a set of rules to follow should a dispute arise. Although the arbitral procedure has become the norm, it is not without its critics. Two of the main complaints against international commercial arbitration are that it has become too expensive and too slow. Some complain that it is therefore beginning to look a lot like court litigation with has always suffered from those same negative factors. This paper looks at the topic and suggests some possible ways to alleviate or avoid these two negative concerns.

In order to understand the reasons for the criticisms of slow and expensive procedures, one must analyze the process itself.

International commercial arbitration was borne out of business necessity. After World War II, international trade and commerce began to flourish and the pace of globalization grew exponentially each year from the late 1950s until the turn of the twenty-first century. More contracts require procedures to resolve disputes since contracts without problems are rare, and the smooth relation among business entities is essential for continued business harmony. Turning to local courts, while certainly a viable possibility, since courts have always been in the business of deciding breaches of contract matters, has never been any vendor's first choice. By definition, an international agreement is between parties from at least two different countries.

There are differences in custom, practice, language, culture and unfamiliar and foreign procedures that hinder the smooth flow of business dealings. The world is blessed with two kinds of lawyers, civil- and common law-trained; that in itself further penetrates the common understanding that two commercial entities need to comprehend before they can navigate successfully the business of selling their products on a worldwide basis. Thus, it was not surprising that contracts began to include a procedure that created more of a commercial and level dispute playing field for the settlement of disputes by those who were experienced in the subject matter of the trade and international business, and had a neutral and unbiased reputation for integrity. To ensure the effectiveness of any resultant award, the N.Y. Convention was promulgated and is now in force in over 150 countries of the world.

There are four distinct constituencies involved in international commercial arbitration – the arbitral institutions, the lawyers, the arbitrators and the parties. They all play an important role in the cost and speed of the process.

The Arbitral Institutions are moving aggressively to address the two problems. First, they are asking arbitrators before they are appointed to indicate their availability to hold hearings in the near term. The International Chamber of Commerce (ICC) International Court of Arbitration of the "ICC" in its procedures requires each nominated arbitrator to indicate the number of pending arbitrations on which they are currently sitting, as well as dates on which they are available to hear cases for the near term. Presumably, a candidate that has a large number of pending cases and a full schedule may not make the confirmation process. Undoubtedly, the ICC believes that if an arbitrator is too busy, it will affect her ability to move cases along quickly. To date, the author is unaware of whether any potential nominees have been denied appointments because they have too large a pending caseload. Indeed, what constitutes a large caseload has yet to be defined. In my practice as a fulltime international arbitrator, I accept from six to eight new cases each year. Invariably, one or two per year at the most settle. In an average year, I am working on approximately eight cases a year (since there are always holdover cases from the previous year). From a time perspective, spending 200 hours on eight cases amounts to 1,600 working hours a year; a full load for anyone my age. At some point in the future, I imagine the ICC Court will inform the arbitral fraternity as to how many cases are too many so that confirmation may be refused.

Further, institutions are also limiting the amount of fees that an arbitrator may charge for her services. The ICC practice, while not limiting fees per se, nonetheless has a kind of cap by tying the fees to the amount in dispute in the case. The London Court of International Arbitration ("LCIA"), for example presently has a limit of Great Britain Pound (GBP) 450 an hour for arbitrator fees. That is considerably less than what counsel receive today for fees in representing clients. Legal fees of GBP 900 per hour are not uncommon. However, arbitrators typically have low overhead as sole practitioners and, if we assume the first figure mentioned above, a busy British arbitrator with 1,600 hours of work can earn about GBP 720,000 per year; which should make for a comfortable life for most neutrals. Even though an arbitrator may have a mix of ICC cases (no hourly rate) and fixed fees of GBP 450, she usually has some ad hoc cases where there may not be any limit on fees so that the average rate of GBP 450 is not a

Chapter 1: Taming the Twin Dragons

farfetched sum to use for guesstimating arbitrators' incomes. In addition, the ICC has now put a procedure in place that alerts its arbitrators to the fact that their fees may be reduced somewhat if they do not render their awards in a reasonably prompt timeframe. Apparently, three months is now considered the outside time within which to complete the award that must be submitted for scrutiny to the ICC Court.

The point is, however, that arbitral institutions are engaging in the process of cracking down on delays and costs by their internal rules and procedures.

Lawyers have a different perspective. Most international arbitrations today are conducted by a limited number of law firms. The complexity of the cases, the use of foreign languages and foreign law and the huge overhead costs of firms have forced them into charging legal fees that are easily in excess of the GBP 450 U.K. cap used by LCIA. In the United States, U.S. Dollars (USD) 1,000 dollars an hour has been reached. The British firms are up to GBP 900 per hour (approximately USD 1,395). The problem is compounded by the fact that many good arbitrators are presently partners in large law firms and they are mandated by peer pressure to charge the same rates as an arbitrator as they receive for being counsel. Unless the partner and her firm are willing to accept a lower amount, then either she cannot serve or she has to negotiate with her firm as to why it should accept a lower hourly rate than the rest of the firm is charging. However, there has been an increased trend for partners to retire early and either join other arbitration chambers or small boutique firms so that they may continue to sit as arbitrators for lesser fees than they would be forced to charge with a large law firm. There are also practical advantages to doing so, since the problem of conflicts looms large when a nominee is a partner with one of the so-called top 100 firms in the international arbitration field. Indeed, a retiring partner at age 60 might have a full career as an international arbitrator for a full twenty years. The average age for experienced arbitrators is from 55 to 75, with a few stalwarts working into the octogenarian years.

The arbitrators are at the bottom of the pecking order. They are not only berated for being too slow and expensive, but often resented by the losing party who sustains the belief that the award was incorrect. Yet, although arbitrators balk at the amount of disclosure required of them – which is ever increasing – and though they dislike any caps on their fees, the number of new entrants into the profession keeps increasing. At a recent speech given by the President of the American Arbitration Association (AAA) this year, she commented that the International Centre for Dispute Resolution ("ICDR"), which is the international division of the AAA, presently lists over 700 arbitrators on its roster of international neutrals and that seemed a sufficient number for the 800 or so cases it receives every year. Her advice to newcomers was not to give up their day jobs until they had a few cases under their belts. Gaining access to the ICDR roster requires more experience than ever before.

Nonetheless, the number of persons retiring every year continues to increase, as well as the number of former general counsel and litigators that believe they can become international arbitrators. While no one has yet marketed herself on a platform of lower arbitrator fees, the possibility looms large.

But it is this constituency than can make a significant contribution to taming the twin dragons.

A dozen examples may prove helpful:

(1) Busy arbitrators should learn to say "No", if they really have a full schedule of cases. An arbitrator with twenty or more pending cases is too busy in my view to accept new work. There is a limit to how many working hours a neutral can work and still distinguish among the cases, lawyers, rules, issues and problem that will arise in a particular case.
(2) It is a good idea to avoid being named by the same law firm over and over again. Whilst there are a limited number of arbitration law firms, there should be enough that you can still have an ample caseload without raising the specter of being "owned" by a particular firm.
(3) One should prepare guidelines (and stick to them) that encourage reasonably prompt times for scheduling and hearing the merits of the case. The case management conference should lay out the full panoply of the schedule and timing, including hearing dates and the initial order should specify that absent exceptional circumstances, the dates are locked in stone. The chair or president should meet early on with her colleagues and stress the importance of giving this case a priority over other business that the co-arbitrators may have.
(4) All international arbitrators should understand that they are independent and neutral and have an obligation to finish the case with a sense of due diligence under the circumstances. Personal inconvenience may have to prevail in many instances. This is especially important if the arbitrator is a law firm partner. She must understand that this case is as important to the parties as the client case is to her back at the office. Co-arbitrators should take no longer than four weeks in selecting the third arbitrator. If agreement is not possible, then the arbitral institution or appointing authority should be promptly asked to select the president.
(5) International arbitration is now a twenty-four hour seven-day business. If the parties send emails on weekends and holidays, the tribunal should try to reply in kind. Some issues affect the lifeblood of a company and the tribunal should accept that responsibility with reasonable flexibility.
(6) The tribunal should expect delays at five pressure points in the case: (i) the pleadings, e.g., statements of case, answers and replies; (ii) document production procedures and ruling on document disputes; (iii) finishing the hearings; (iv) deciding whether post-hearing briefs are necessary or if oral closing arguments will suffice; (v) deliberating and rendering the award. A good tribunal manages all of these with care, fairness and patience while still maintaining a balanced sense of timeliness. In general, taking three years or more is too long; six months or less may be too short; somewhere in between is the right time but it will differ in each case on the complexity and urgency of the facts.
(7) Too often, trial counsel does not fully understand the case that their client has asked them to file. This leads to issues involving requests for amended pleadings and delays the process. If the Request for Arbitration is, however,

Chapter 1: Taming the Twin Dragons

a fairly comprehensive document complete with witness statements and exhibits, it may not be necessary to allow subsequent formal statements of case; perhaps letter amendments to the Request may be sufficient. In many cases where there are no counterclaims in the Answer, replies may not be necessary.

(8) Document production is a necessary evil; but good tribunal management can lessen the impact on delay of the proceeding. A common theme to remember is that the documents should be material and relevant to the case; if not, then prompt denials should help move the case along. It is essential that the tribunal establish a timeframe for parties to request such documents and a timeframe within which it must rule on the admission of said documents or not. Aids such as the well-known Redfern Schedule, can be helpful.

(9) Reaching the hearing with all preliminary procedure behind you is the key goal of the arbitration. Once there, it is essential to provide some semblance of fairness in allocating time to each side. In an international case, the arbitrators, the parties and counsel may be from many different countries and all have a keen desire to finish and return to their homes and offices. Consecutive dates of hearings have become an essential tool in avoiding delay and keeping costs down. This can sometimes mean as many as two or three weeks of hearings in a large complex case. Where parties request staggered hearing dates or bifurcated hearings, the tribunal should think long and hard before granting such requests. It is hard enough to get a minimum of seven people (e.g., three arbitrators, two law firms and two parties), from around the world to agree on a week of available dates. Getting them to agree on several rounds of hearings is, in my view, a frustrating chore. The hearing day should last a minimum of six hours. That means if you sit from 9:30 am to 5:30 pm, you may achieve the six-hour day. There is always a morning break, a lunch break and an afternoon break. Thus, the eight-hour day only provides approximately six hours of actual hearing time. Tribunals that sit from 10:00 am to 4:00 pm usually wind up with some four hours a day of transcript material.

(10) Tribunal deliberations should be held as soon as possible after the hearings have concluded. A good technique is for the president of the tribunal to reserve a day or two at the end of the hearings to share the initial inclinations of her colleagues. If there is general agreement on the outcome, then the post hearings phase may move along smoothly. If however, there is a potential dissent or even the rare situation where there are three different views as to the case outcome, then the tribunal must steel itself for a lengthy and less collegial role in the deliberations. One reason for early deliberations is that it permits the tribunal to put specific questions to the parties on issues that should be addressed in their post-hearing briefs. Sometimes, the answers to the questions may pre-empt potential dissent among the tribunal. In any event, the parties should welcome such questions and it helps them focus their post-hearing submissions. Of

course, if there are no post hearing submissions and the parties concluded with oral arguments, then the tribunal will not have the luxury of asking further questions. However, if the tribunal believes that answers to certain issues are truly crucial to its deliberations, then the tribunal should reopen the proceedings and pose the clarification questions to the parties.

(11) There is no best way to draft the final award. In my experience, the president, after deliberations, prepares a first draft for her colleagues to review, consider and comment upon. The co-arbitrators then have the opportunity to amend, clarify or disagree with certain or many portions of the draft. If the president knows from the deliberations that there will be a dissent, it is helpful if the dissenting arbitrator prepares her draft at the same time so the majority arbitrators will have the benefit of commenting on the dissenter's views in the final award. While many dissenters prefer to await the president's first draft, it does slow down the completion of the process if the tribunal has to await the majority's draft. It is also helpful if the tribunal begins preparation of the draft award even before the post-hearing briefs are submitted. There is usually sufficient material in the pre-hearing submissions and the transcript for a skeleton award to be prepared. Then, when the post-hearing briefs arrive, it is not too difficult to confirm the points in the draft or amend them, as needed. If a final oral argument is needed, despite the post-hearing briefs, then it should be scheduled promptly and, if the lawyers are in different countries, a telephonic oral argument should suffice.

(12) In the end, only the tribunal can decide whether the proceeding is too slow or not. The primary goal is to provide a just award with fairness and equal treatment to all parties. When balancing speed with justice, the latter should always prevail. Sometimes it is difficult to make the right decision. Intervening events such as parallel court proceeding may play a role in the decision. There are international cases that have gone on for years beyond any reasonable timeframe and it is not the fault of the tribunal. Those situations aside, all the tribunal can do is rule on the matter before them. To the extent that they have given the parties the right to present both sides of the picture to them, they will have done their job. In addition, the tribunal has the power to award costs to the prevailing party. This relief, not generally available in U.S. courts, makes it possible for the winning party to retrieve its costs and expenses, including legal fees. Thus, the cost dragon can be slain, at least for one party to the arbitration. And this relief can be substantial. In many large complex cases today the legal fees, which are the single most significant costs of an international arbitration, run into millions of dollars. Typically, the arbitrators' fees are not substantial and the fees of arbitration institution are the lowest costs involved in the case. Of course, the costs must be reasonable. In a recent case, the winning party submitted a bill of costs for USD 3 million and the losing party sought some USD 12 million. The tribunal found the USD 3 million was certainly

Chapter 1: Taming the Twin Dragons

reasonable where the other party's costs were four times higher in the same matter.

It is gospel that the parties and their contracts control the international arbitration process- not the institutions, the arbitrators or the trial counsel. With trepidation, I comment on the responsibility of this constituency in controlling the time and cost of this time honored process.

First, if the parties are to be given the unique responsibility of controlling the international arbitral regime then they must accept that role and act accordingly. Too often a client engages its legendary arbitration lawyer (of whom there are many) and then assumes that the rest of the case should be left in counsel's capable hands. This is a mistake. For example, I have found that if the client attends the case management conference at the beginning of the proceeding, it is easier for the tribunal to achieve a quicker rather than a slower hearing schedule. Clients know that time is money and the longer the case takes the less effective the eventual award may be. With clients in attendance, it is easier to schedule the hearing in six to nine months. Without them, twelve months becomes the agreed norm. There are many times when costs can be cut. For instance, often the party's contract will have provided for a hearing locale that may have been fair and reasonable when the contract was drafted. Years later, however, with an acquiring party now in control, and different executives required to testify, the site may be inefficient. If the tribunal believes that the current seat is inconvenient to all concerned, why not suggest moving the hearing location (not the seat) to a more cost effective place? Sometimes, there may be practical reasons for moving the site. Examples include political instability of the locale due to insurgencies or safety, and legal impediments such as the inability of witnesses to appear in a particular jurisdiction or other similar unanticipated circumstances. Oftentimes, the client itself will prefer the practical solution to the contract provision and will agree to the location change.

Second, choosing the right lawyer for an international arbitration is itself a serious chore for the client. Whilst it may be possible for the client to represent itself, in my experience that is usually a mistake. There is a time-honored rubric stating that a client who represents herself has a fool for a lawyer. This truism may apply even more forcefully to an international arbitration. I do not know how, for instance, a Chinese manufacturer could possibly know how to select an arbitrator for a dispute with a customer in South America where the contract calls for a New York seat with hearings to be conducted in the English language with a New York applicable law clause. Thus, it is essential to engage a law firm that has the credentials to effectively represent that manufacturer in the arbitration. There are numerous web sites that can help the client make that choice.

Indeed, some assert that there is a bewildering choice of leading law firms from which to choose that makes the selection of counsel itself "a chore." *Third*, despite the fact that more international cases go to award than get settled, the client should always stay on top of its case for the possibility of a voluntary business resolution short of the full panoply of arbitration proceedings. Many cases today are ripe for a mediated settlement and institutions encourage that choice. Client relationships are better understood by the client rather than its law firm. Sometimes, keeping that relationship may be more important than a particular dispute may be worth. Only the client can make that decision.

The role of international arbitration continues to evolve. Some recent cases have begged the question as to whether the process can be fair to smaller vendors when it has become so costly. However, with the growth of so-called third-party funders, even this complaint may be remedied. Whilst it is too early to predict the impact of litigation funding on the international commercial arbitration arena, there is at least some good that has arisen from the allegations of expensive arbitration. A new funding source has accepted the challenge of defraying said costs.

Perhaps the business of settling international commercial disputes may always be plagued with the twin demons. So long as language, culture and laws remain different, the difficulty of common understanding will continue to be present. Nonetheless, the cottage industry of international arbitration that has grown exponentially over the past half-century should continue to thrive. The four constituencies have a shared incentive to ensure that the process continues to thrive for another century. All evidence points to the fact that they are aware of the demons and efforts are underway to slay them. In conclusion, in my experience, Swiss arbitrators have time engraved on their psyche. Thus, every Swiss president or co-arbitrator with whom I have ever worked puts strong emphasis on sticking to the schedule and maintaining strict time limits on pre-hearing and hearing procedures. The so-called chess clock procedure for keeping hearings to a rigorous schedule undoubtedly was born in Switzerland. Thus, from birth, Pierre A. Karrer was fine-tuned not to tolerate delay. The world needs more Swiss-like arbitrators.

CHAPTER 2
One Shot Players and Arbitrator Selection: A Fair Shot or a Shot in the Dark?

Chiann Bao

As the "world's most dynamic region" whose integration into the global economy has been deemed the one of the most "striking global developments of the last generation," Asia is spawning homegrown corporations and attracting foreign ones at an historic pace.[1] As a region with many smaller economies, corporations in Asia are inevitably establishing relationships across boundaries. However, save for a few jurisdictions, improvements to the domestic systems of dispute resolution in the region have not kept apace. As a result, corporations are increasingly turning to arbitration as the default dispute resolution mechanism.[2] Drawn predominantly by cross-border friendly characteristics such as global enforcement and avoidance of potentially biased or protectionary national courts, even new players view arbitration not only as an option but rather as their only option.

Once in arbitration, however, these potential new players may find themselves in a system as unfamiliar and unwelcoming as a foreign court. Moreover, as "one shot players" with limited incentive or resources to engage in frequent dispute resolution, these players may find a process in which parties are inherently granted autonomy to make key decisions more daunting than the alternative. Not surprisingly, it is these "new kids on the block" who most often call into question the legitimacy of arbitration and challenge the arbitration community to address these perceived imbalances.

The aim of this chapter is not to equalize resources between these new players and more established participants in the arbitral community. Such a goal, while noble,

---

1. Speech by Christine Lagarde, Managing Director, International Monetary Fund, "Asia's Advancing Role in the Global Economy," Available at: https://www.imf.org/en/News/Articles/2015/09/28/04/53/sp031216, (accessed Sep. 15, 2016).
2. The Queen Mary School of Arbitration's 2015 International Arbitration survey: Improvements and Innovations in International Arbitration ("Queen Mary survey"), Available at: http://www.arbitration.qmul.ac.uk/research/2015/ (accessed Sep. 15, 2016).

is impossible. Rather, this article will draw from anecdotes in Asia in an effort to dissect the issues associated with lack of experience and access to information. It will then focus on the responsibility singularly deemed by scholars, and seen in practice, as the most important decision one might make in the arbitration process: the appointment of the arbitrator and how disparate levels of experience and know-how potentially jeopardize the perceived legitimacy and fairness of the appointment. Resolving these threats to the integrity of the arbitrator appointment process will better ensure that that international arbitration remains the preferred form of dispute resolution in Asia.

§2.01 THE "ONE SHOT PLAYERS" OF ASIA

As a starting point, we consider the origin of the term "one-shotter." The term was first introduced in 1974 by Marc Galanter in his landmark article "Why the 'Haves' Come Out Ahead: Speculations on the Limits of Legal Change" and Catherine Rogers brought the concept into the international arbitration arena in her latest article "The Arrival of the 'Have-Nots' in International Arbitration."[3] As Galanter succinctly put it in his article, it is the "repeat players" who shape the development of law rather than the "one-shotters." According to Galanter, the "one-shotter" is the player that does not have the advantage of "...(1) advance intelligence...(2) expertise and ready access to specialists...(3) opportunities to develop facilitative informal relations with institutional incumbents...[or] (4) interest in his 'bargaining reputation'...."[4] Such issues do not apply only to "one-shotter" companies but can also apply to their counsel. Counsel are themselves either "repeat players" or "one-shotters" who may exacerbate or diffuse these inequalities, depending on the type of client they represent.[5]

Indeed, with the proliferation of "one-shotters" in the Asian dispute resolution scene, the large majority of disputes have "one-shotters" on both sides of the table. During my six years at Hong Kong International Arbitration Centre (HKIAC), for example, only a very small percentage of all parties that engaged in arbitration at the institution came through more than one time.[6] However, this mitigation of the repeat-player advantage was itself somewhat offset by the frequency in which certain counsel with significant arbitration experience appeared on one side of an HKIAC arbitration when the other side was represented by a "one-shot" law firm. Thus, it is often with arbitration counsel—not with the parties themselves—that the risk of "one shotter" disparity arises.

In a region where international commercial arbitration has grown at a frantic pace and where there are so many "one-shotters," one might expect the potential disadvantages faced by "one-shotter" parties (or, more likely, their counsel) to create systemic fairness issues within the Asian commercial arbitration community. Yet, as Rogers has explained, certain characteristics inherent to international commercial

---

3. 9 Law. & Soc'y Rev. 95, 98 (1974) and Nevada Law Journal Vol. 8 (2007).
4. Galanter at 4.
5. *Id.* at 21.
6. The exception to this is the maritime industry where the same claimants would appear frequently on the docket.

arbitration help to mitigate these disadvantages in ways that the national courts may not. First, the institution of international commercial arbitration inherently requires an inclusive approach in order for its practitioners, and, more specifically, for the institutions responsible for administering these disputes, to survive; unlike publicly-funded court systems who have no built-in incentive to accommodate all-comers, the practice of international commercial arbitration is primarily self-funded, and its growth depends on attracting and retaining new players. Second, the variance of national legislation places a check on the arbitral infrastructure, protecting the "one-shotters" from egregious inequalities and providing opportunities for "one-shotters" to create obstacles in the process.[7]

§2.02 THE RESPONSIBILITY OF APPOINTING AN ARBITRATOR

There is perhaps no decision that parties can make more important to both the process and outcome of an arbitration than that of the selection of arbitrator. Indeed, those surveyed in the Queen Mary survey designated selection of arbitrators as one of the top most value characteristics of arbitration, with 76% of respondents preferring party-appointed arbitrators. And, the top four worst characteristics of international arbitration—cost, lack of effective sanctions during the arbitral process, lack of insight into arbitrators' efficiency, and lack of speed—can all be affected by the arbitrator chosen.

It should not be surprising then, that regardless of the sophistication of parties or whether such parties are "one-shotters," parties (and their counsel) nearly always wish to have the power to make such an important decision. The most recent ICC statistics on arbitrator appointments also show that 74% of the appointments made are party appointed.[8] In Asia, similar statistics from HKIAC and SIAC support the fact parties retain their right to appoint their own arbitrator. Retaining this freedom to make this decision is thus key.

But the fact that most parties do in fact exercise their right to appoint their own arbitrators does not make the decision any easier. For a "one-shot" player, the choice of arbitrator appointment can feel like a daunting "bet the farm" decision. An in-house counsel once explained that she would much rather the institution appoint the arbitrator because she did not want to be responsible for a decision that she felt she could not make in an informed manner. Unfamiliar with the forum and without the tools and information as to how to make such decisions, the "one-shot" player may regret the very reason why they chose arbitration in the first instance.

However, while arbitral institutions may often be well-informed and well-situated to appoint arbitrators, especially in the case of a dispute where "one-shotters" predominate, there is general agreement that the inequality between "repeat players" and "one-shotters" cannot be remedied by denying parties of the ability to choose their

---

7. Rogers at 105–106.
8. Peter Bert, "ICC Arbitrator Appointments: A First Look at the Data," Available at http://kluwerarbitrationblog.com/2016/09/13/icc-arbitrator-appointments-a-first-look-at-the-data/ (accessed Sep. 15, 2016).

arbitrator. As explained by Charles Brower and Charles Rosenberg in their article, "The Death of the Two-Headed Nightingale: Why the Paulsson-van den Berg Presumption That Party-Appointed Arbitrators Are Untrustworthy Is Wrongheaded":

> Parties will generally have greater faith in the arbitral process if they themselves are the creators of the tribunal that will judge them. There thus seems to be a close nexus between the perceived legitimacy of the international arbitration and the appointment of the arbitrators. Legitimacy of the proceedings may translate into respect for the arbitral award, regardless of the outcome. As well as respect for the ultimate enforcement proceedings, if needed at all. In other words, a losing party may be less likely to challenge the legitimacy of the decision-making process if that party played an intimate role in constituting the tribunal.[9]

Indeed, while Paulsson argues that the appointment of arbitrators is not a right, one needs not take it that far to still hold the concept of party-appointed arbitrators to be one of the key reasons parties continue to have faith in the system.[10] Done right, a party-appointed arbitrator gives parties a sense of ownership of the process as well as outcome, win or lose.

§2.03 THE PROBLEM AS FACED BY THE "ONE SHOT PLAYER"

If choice of arbitrator is a key inflection point in an arbitration, and if that is a choice that ought to be made by the parties, then it would seem reasonable to assume that there is likely no greater "repeat player" advantage (or "one-shotter" disadvantage) than at the time of arbitrator appointment. It may also seem reasonable to assume that players who are well-linked to the arbitration community might have extensive access to "soft" information about arbitrators will thus be better-equipped that their "one-shotter" peers when it comes to arbitrator selection.

In the 2010 Price Waterhouse Coopers/Queen Mary study, major corporations were asked whether they routinely gather information about potential arbitrators whom they may appoint to arbitrate potential disputes. Two-thirds responded that they did not as, on balance, the cost of doing so could not be justified given the unlikely chance of engaging in many arbitrations. Instead, they would prefer to rely on their external counsel for information about potential arbitrators when a dispute arose. Indeed, 68% of those surveyed said they did not feel they had sufficient information to make an informed choice. However, with the input of counsel, 67% felt that they were much better placed to decide on an appropriate arbitrator. The conclusion reached in this survey was that external counsel's views weigh heavily on the arbitrator appointment decision.[11]

---

9. Available at https://international-arbitration-attorney.com/wp-content/uploads/arbitrationlaw Charles_Brower_The_Death_of_the_Two-Headed_Nightingale_Speech_2.pdf (accessed Sep. 15, 2016).
10. Jan Paulsson, "Moral Hazard in International Disputes Resolution," Available at http://www.arbitration-icca.org/media/0/12773749999020/paulsson_moral_hazard.pdf (accessed Sep. 15, 2016).
11. Available at https://www.pwc.com/gx/en/arbitration-dispute-resolution/assets/pwc-international-arbitration-study.pdf (accessed Sep 15, 2016).

Thus, the true "one-shotter" issue would seem to be the perceived information advantage that parties who retain experienced repeat-player counsel may have in the arbitrator selection process versus parties who retain "one-shotter" counsel. To be fair, the extent to which counsel's "knowledge" of potential arbitrators actually constitutes a material advantage is not clear. Sometimes such players' information may be partial or subconsciously tainted by a prior experience with an arbitrator, such as a prior decision that was unfavorable to the player which may not have ended favorably for a client. Conversely, "repeat-players" may be a false sense of security that these arbitrators will perform their duties efficiently and effectively just because counsel knows the arbitrator, or has formed a superficial impression of their capabilities.

However, if we assume that "repeat-player" counsel's knowledge of the process at least creates the perception of an advantage, then this raises a potential issue for the perceived fairness of the arbitration system as a whole. If it is perceived that external counsel has a significant influence over arbitrator selection, and if it is also perceived that "repeat-player" counsel have an inherent knowledge advantage in that process, then a relatively small number of firms are likely to receive an increasingly disproportionate number of appointments, effectively making them "gatekeepers" to the arbitration process. Not only would this also tend to have the effect of increasing the risk that these firms develop relationships with certain arbitrators that may call into question those arbitrators' neutrality and objectivity, but it may also reduce the volume and diversity of the arbitrator pool.

The response to this issue may come from the user side. Clearly there is a demand for more information in order for the corporate counsel to play a greater role in the arbitrator appointment process. Moreover, such information, openly and available to all players, would lead to a more efficient process and one which may minimize potential challenge or enforcement issues. Suggestions that have been made to access more readily available include a Trip Advisor for arbitrators or other searchable engine for information.[12]

§2.04 WHERE DO WE GO FROM HERE?

It is here where institutions help to mitigate the "one-shotter" problem, not by taking on the responsibility of arbitrator appointment themselves, but rather by helping to fill this real (or perceived) information gap.

The traditional role of institutions in providing information on arbitrators and guidelines around the appointment process has focused on preventing biased arbitrators from being appointed, rather than on ensuring parties have objective information that may assist them in reaching an informed decision as to their choice of arbitrator. This injects a systemic imbalance of information into the process, as the

---

12. Ema Vidak-Gojkovic, Lucy Greenwood and Michael McIlwrath, "Puppies or Kittens? How to Better Match Arbitrators to Party Expectations," Manz Verlag 2016, Available at http://res.cloudinary.com/lbresearch/image/upload/v1460717417/puppies_or_kittens_a_modest_proposal_to_help_arbitrators_better_match_themselves_with_user_expectations_evg_lg_mm_for_aay_2015_153116_1150.pdf (accessed Sep. 15, 2016).

"knowledge"—whether actual or perceived—about the disposition of arbitrators and whether a given arbitrator is the "right" choice for a particular dispute rests principally amongst repeat players.

This need not be the case. Institutions have an opportunity to give real and objective data points through more vigorous vetting of arbitrators and then making those arbitrators' appointments public. In this later regard, ICC has taken the lead on this. And other institutions could easily follow suit. Not only does naming arbitrators lend towards transparency of institutional appointments but it also deepens and diversifies the pools of arbitrators. In Asia, where the pool of experienced arbitrators is still relatively limited (although growing), this service could be even more valuable than in more mature markets with a deeper pool of arbitrators. And, importantly, it would give "one-shot" players, more information, and thus, more of a fair shot. From the ultimate "repeat player" vantage point, institutions have insights into attributes arbitrator helpful in determining efficiency and ability to manage the arbitral process. Divulgence of such information would neither breach confidentialities nor raise any privacy concerns. Rather, the benefits served in providing valuable data points to all potential players would far outweigh on concerns. This, coupled with more vigorous vetting, would, bring light to the key decision users make in the arbitral process. The effect of such an effort would no doubt enhance the legitimacy of the process, giving more "one-shotters" the "repeat player" advantage.

CHAPTER 3
Third-Party Funding and the International Arbitrator

Louise Barrington

In 2008, soon after arriving at King's College Law School in London, I was casting about for a novel topic for a seminar for Arbitral Women. Having recently been intrigued by the concept during a conversation with a friend in the financial industry, I posted Third-Party Funding as the seminar theme and invited people to attend. Within twenty-four hours, a torrent of email from around the world flowed to the inbox: 'you can't do that, it's illegal, it's unethical, it's immoral.... it's *champertous*!' Despite that initial negativity, the ensuing discussion was provocative and instructive.

§3.01 WHAT IS THIRD-PARTY FUNDING?

A party (nearly always a claimant) secures a commitment from a funder who otherwise has no interest in the dispute, to pay the claimant's expenses, including legal fees, in return for a share of whatever amount may be awarded to the claimant in the litigation or arbitration. The share varies from 5% to 50%, depending on the parties involved, the merits and complexity of the case, and the chances of collecting. If the claimant loses, nothing is payable to the funder. In some cases the funder may pay an adverse costs award to the successful respondent.

§3.02 WHY ALL THE FUSS?

Champerty and maintenance are doctrines in common law jurisdictions, meant to discourage abuse of the legal system. Maintenance is the support of litigation by a stranger without just cause, which has the effect of inciting, provoking or encouraging frivolous litigation. Champerty is an aggravated form of maintenance. A stranger supports litigation in return for a share of the proceeds; if the claimant wins, the proceeds ('le champs' or field in pre-industrial times) is to be shared with the maintainer. This is known colloquially as 'buying into someone else's lawsuit'.

At common law, maintenance and champerty were both crimes and torts, as was barratry, the bringing of vexatious litigation. Champerty and maintenance are common law offences, so much of the original resistance to third-party funding appeared in the former British colonies. There does not seem to be a great deal of controversy about it in Europe, and in Asia it is still in its infancy. However, the principles found new relevance in debates over modern contingent fee agreements between lawyer and client and with respect to the assignment by a plaintiff of the rights in a lawsuit to someone with no connection to the case. In many jurisdictions champertous contracts can still be void for public policy or attract liability for costs.

As well as the danger that champertous contracts will encourage vexatious or frivolous lawsuits, the common fear expressed by opponents of third-party funding is that it cheapens 'justice' by reducing it to a tradeable commodity.

On the other hand, there is the access to justice argument. Resolving an international dispute through arbitration can be lengthy and prohibitively expensive. The stronger party may wage a war of attrition to discourage or defeat a less well-financed opponent. Turning to third-party funding for backing allows a claimant to bring an action to enforce rights which otherwise might have to be abandoned.

§3.03 WHO ARE THE FUNDERS?

In the 1994 *Ken-Ren* case,[1] the third party was in fact the mother company of the impecunious Ken-Ren. The case became famous when the respondent applied for security for costs in the UK courts, leading to a House of Lords decision that provoked discussion around the world and prompted a change in the law of England and Wales. But the controversy was not about the origin of the funding, but rather when should a tribunal or court order security for costs in an international arbitration, and under what circumstances.

The entity funding the arbitration may be, as in the *Ken-Ren* situation, a separate legal entity which has some relationship to the claimant. This type of arrangement seems uncontroversial, presumably because there is a chance the related company will somehow benefit from a win by the claimant. However, today's funders are just as likely to have no prior relationship at all with the claimant, and thus no interest in the outcome of the case, other than the potential cash payoff it represents. Several major insurance companies have ventured into third-party funding. Hedge funds may include third-party funding as part of their investment strategy, while others are dedicated funds, bringing investors together to invest in one or more suits and share the rewards.

Many funders are based in the UK, although there are also major players headquartered in the US, Europe, Australia, Hong Kong and Canada. Invest4Justice is a crowdfunding platform established in 2014 to allow litigation to be funded on a

---

1. *Coppee-Lavalin SA/NV v. Ken-Ren Chemicals and Fertilizers Ltd.*, [1994] 2 W.L.R. 631; [1994] 2 All E.R. 449.

contingent basis, with a fee or commission of only 4%. Some American funders use this platform.

In the words of Chris Bogart, CEO of Burford Capital, one of the largest funders, 'to focus on the identity of the funder rather than on the activity, and how it is conducted, is discriminatory.'

§3.04 WHO USES THIRD-PARTY FUNDING FOR ARBITRATION?

The trite answer is, 'we don't really know'. In a recent informal poll of thirty Toronto arbitrators, when asked if they had ever arbitrated a case where one party was backed by a third-party funder, only one individual raised his hand. The next question was whether anyone had acted as counsel in an arbitration where one party used a funder; one person said yes, in three of her own cases, but neither opposing counsel nor the arbitrator was aware of it. Both those responding qualified their answer with, 'at least, that is what we know about'. So those two lone examples may mean either that there is very infrequent use of third-party funding, or perhaps that they are the tip of an iceberg. In many cases a party simply does not disclose the existence of the funder.

Originally an impecunious plaintiff would turn to a third party so as to have access to the court or arbitrator. Today, perfectly solvent companies are using third-party funding as a risk-allocation technique, or simply to retain their own capital for running their business. As one funder reflected, it is probably an easier sell for a company's general counsel to persuade the CEO to embark on an arbitration if they are using someone else's money.

Most class actions could not get started without some form of third-party funding. Likewise, an investor initiating an investment treaty arbitration faces costly and drawn out proceedings which threaten to divert funds from the core business of the company. Investor-State arbitrations are notoriously expensive to run, but the resulting awards can be well worth the effort, with multi-million or even billion-dollar awards becoming commonplace. If the options are to write off a major loss or share a major gain, third-party funding makes sense, especially when there is an opportunity to insure against an expensive costs bill if the case goes awry.

Not every case will be funded. The funder will do due diligence to choose suitable cases to fund. Its business decision may include other considerations than the merits of the case. Diversification, to hedge against political or currency risks may lead a funder to favour one case over another. One funder says it funds one in twenty-five cases that come to it. That figure will vary among funders, and of course the cost of the funding may be a factor in whether it is worthwhile to the applicant to use it.

The would-be claimant shops around to find a funder who is willing to help for a reasonable share of the proceeds. One funder looks for a claim of at least GBP 10 million (*their* estimate, not the claimant's) and will then commit up to 10% of that value to funding the costs, in return for a percentage that varies according to the claimant, and the merits and the probability of collecting. Adequate funding allows claimant to hire experienced arbitration counsel, which is one important consideration when a funder is deciding where to put its money. Many funders use the 'return of three' mechanism to establish the share of the award they would expect to receive. For a claim of USD 20 million with USD 1 million in anticipated arbitration costs, a third-party funder would be expected to require at least a 15% stake in the amount awarded, in order to obtain a USD 3 million return. If the anticipated costs are USD 2 million, the stake would rise to 30%.

Funders do not insist on 'sure things', but usually do want at least a 50% chance of success. And the first thing they will look for is recoverability – if we get an award, can we turn the prospective award into money at the end of the road, or is this respondent likely to be insolvent or immune?

§3.05 WHAT CONCERNS MAY ARISE FROM THIRD-PARTY FUNDER INVOLVEMENT IN AN ARBITRATION CASE?

Aside from the champerty and maintenance considerations regarding the content of a funding agreement, will national courts enforce a funding agreement? In the French case of *Veolia v. Foris AG*,[2] the court was asked to enforce a claim against Foris which resulted from its funding of an Australian claim in an arbitration against respondent Veolia. The Australian was unsuccessful and Foris was ordered to pay Veolia's costs. The Court of First Instance granted enforcement, but its decision was quashed on appeal on other grounds. The Court of Appeal observed that, '…such agreements are *sui generis* and unknown in the European Union except in countries having a Germanic legal culture'. That said, there is no prohibition in law or in ethical rules in France against the practice.

Does the assignment of the award proceeds, or part of them, to a third party affect the standing of the claimant or the jurisdiction of the tribunal? This question was answered in the negative by the tribunal in the ICSID decision in case of *Teinver v. The Argentine Republic*,[3] who cited the principle of international adjudication that standing and jurisdiction issues are to be evaluated as of the date the arbitration is commenced, and subsequent events do not affect that evaluation.

The existence of a third-party funding arrangement may give the impression that the claimant is impecunious, triggering an application for security for costs, as in the *Ken-Ren* case above.

Does the knowledge that a funder has done due diligence change the respondent's evaluation of the merits? Some have suggested that knowing a claimant is backed by a funder may change the respondent's attitude toward the arbitration procedure, creating the impression of 'two against one'. Knowing that arbitration by attrition is not an option may encourage a recalcitrant respondent to settle.

But what about the arbitral tribunal? On the plus side, with backing, the claimant is likely to have engaged competent and experienced counsel, which generally makes for a smoother procedure. But a tribunal may be operating under the impression that

---

2. *Veolia v. Foris AG*, Cour d'appel de Versailles, CT 0012 du juin 2006.
3. *Teinver S.A., Transportes de Cercanías S.A. and Autobuses Urbanos del Sur S.A. v. The Argentine Republic*, ICSID Case No. ARB/09/1, para. 255.

the funder's financial backing signals the claimant is not alone in thinking it has a well-founded case.

Claimants should ensure that the funding actually exists as a firm commitment, not just 'we will get the funds for you'. Some funders find a claimant first, and then go into the market to bring together the investors to fund it. Or what happens if a funder terminates the agreement or runs out of money? As the financial dramas of the last decade have shown, even dealing with a 'name brand' insurance company or fund is no guarantee the funding will be available as promised. Some funders pull together a syndicate of other insurers to reinsure their exposure and spread the loss. But for the assisted party, it may mean an abrupt and unfortunate end to the case. A claimant whose financing has evaporated may be obliged to settle on unfavourable terms, after wasting the time and resources of both sides.

Confidentiality may be an issue. One of the main advantages of commercial arbitration is its privacy, and many arbitrations are confidential. A funder may require information on an ongoing basis, regarding not only the identity and circumstances of the case, but also about developments in the parties' relationship which could alter the outcome of the arbitration. A claimant may not be concerned by the divulgation of information to its funder, but how does one treat the respondent's objections? One counsel recalled a funder who insisted on attending the hearing to see how the arbitration was proceeding. It took some persuasion to convince him that his presence would be a distraction and unhelpful to the claimant presenting its case.

Depending on the arrangement, the funder may want access to information about the progress of the case, or insist on being consulted at critical moments. How much information and influence should a funder have, before it is seen to be usurping the functions of the party's counsel? Some funding agreements go further, with the funder wanting a say in the direction and management of the case, a practice termed 'officious meddling' by one Ontario judge. Without going to that extreme, most funders will have a 'mad clause' – an escape clause to deal with a material decline in the probability of success, a disappearing claimant who is no longer instructing counsel, or a respondent's bankruptcy. Some funders also include a provision that if the claimant settles for less than the claim, without consent of the funder, the funder is entitled to the agreed percentage of the original claim. This encourages the claimant not to capitulate, but if it does settle, the funder may end up getting the biggest piece of the settlement.

And what about the tribunal? One or all arbitrators may be operating under the impression that a funder's financial backing signals that the claimant is not alone in thinking its case is well founded. This could be an argument against disclosing the existence of a third-party funder to the tribunal. Tribunals should be aware though, that a funder does not necessarily insist on a 'watertight case', but will be satisfied with the risk if the chances of a win are 50:50.

The presence of a third-party funder may result in a challenge to the arbitrator on the basis of lack of independence or impartiality. Take for example a situation which often occurs with arbitrators who also act as counsel in arbitration cases. What if Arbitrator A in Case #1 where the claimant is backed by Funder, is also counsel for the claimant in Case #2, also backed by Funder? Surely this dual connection is enough to at least raise doubts as to A's independence.

Not all arbitrators welcome the advent of funders. In the ICSID case of *RSM v. St. Lucia*,[4] as the tribunal considered an application for security for costs, one arbitrator, in his assenting decision, called funders 'mercantile buccaneers in a gambler's nirvana where it is, "heads I win, tails I do not lose"'. This remark led the claimant to challenge him, arguing that he had pre-judged their willingness to pay an order for costs if it lost. The challenge failed, but cost months of delay and thousands of dollars. Perhaps just as important, it obscured the fact that the tribunal's decision to grant the order was probably an unfortunate one.

§3.06 SHOULD THE TPF BE DISCLOSED TO THE OPPOSING PARTY AND THE TRIBUNAL?

Some of these questions are moot if the tribunal does not know about the third-party funder behind the scenes. However, as the practice becomes more prevalent, transparency is becoming an issue, and arbitrators have to deal with it.

If the tribunal is awarding damages to compensate actual loss, with the knowledge that the proceeds of the award are to be shared with the funder, will it consider a more generous award? Can the funder's share of the award proceeds be considered a legal cost, producing a 'grossed-up' tally owed by the unsuccessful party at the end of the arbitration? This question may be dealt with by the law applicable to the merits, or if it is addressed, by the procedural law of the forum. In the English case of *Excalibur Ventures LLC v. Texas Keystone Inc and others* a third-party funder had to pay (limited) indemnity costs not for any improper action of its own, but because it backed a plaintiff's patently hopeless claim. In a case subject to English law, with an English seat, there is reason to suppose an arbitral tribunal could make a similar order.

Non-disclosure brings its own problems. Should the existence and identity of the third-party funder come to light part-way through the arbitration, a potentially dangerous situation occurs. How should an arbitrator react for example, if half-way through the case, it transpires that he or she has substantial shareholdings in the insurance company backing the claimant? With the current proliferation of challenges to arbitrators, this is a fire waiting to be ignited.

The new Canada-European Union: Comprehensive Economic and Trade Agreement (CETA) requires the existence and details of funding to be disclosed. Should all parties be obliged to disclose the existence of a funder at the beginning of the case, to allow for a full conflict check? Does disclosure give the impression the claimant is impecunious, triggering an application for security for costs? Many claimants and their funders are cautious about disclosure for various strategic or business reasons. The conversation continues about whether disclosure should be considered best practice or even mandatory, and if so what must be disclosed (the existence of the funding, the identity of the funder, the details of the funding contract?) and to whom (the opposing party, the tribunal, the arbitral institution?).

---

4. *RSM Production Corporation v. Saint Lucia*, ICSID Case No. ARB/12/10.

Should the funder be invited to sign on to an arbitration clause to the extent of assuming liability for any costs awarded to the opposing party? Some funders are happy to do this, but obviously it changes the price of the bargain. And how would such a promise be enforceable under the New York Convention?

In Canada, third-party funding is relatively new, and has been approved for class actions. In 2007, an Ontario judge noted that third-party indemnity (funding) agreements are now 'part of the landscape in class proceedings' and that 'jurisprudence must and has evolved' to respond to long and complex class proceedings.

Another Ontario Superior Court judge held such agreements are not per se[5] champertous, that the agreement in that case did not contravene public policy and that it was reasonable for the plaintiff to seek to protect itself against adverse costs awards whether the plaintiff was impecunious or not. In approving a third-party indemnity agreement, Justice Strathy considered the fairness and reasonableness of the funder's compensation, deciding that it was fair and reasonable.[6]

Ontario cases laid down basic principles for an acceptable funding agreement in Ontario courts, including:

- Non-interference by the litigation funder and no diminishment of either the plaintiff's right to control the litigation or the lawyer's duties to its client.
- Undertaking and duty of confidentiality by the litigation funder.
- Determination that the litigation funding is necessary to provide access to justice.
- Fair and reasonable financial terms.

But then came the *Bayens* case,[7] where the Ontario Superior Court of Justice approved the use of third-party funding subject to significant restrictions: disclosure of the funding agreement and approval by the court, with approval given only where the funder cannot interfere with the conduct of the proceedings or the lawyer/client relationship and *the funding is necessary to provide access to justice*.

Now these cases all concern state court litigation, and specifically class actions. The court got involved because of the certification process. In arbitration, there is no necessity to seek court approval, and as we have seen, funding may be totally invisible. There is no Canadian law specifically on funding for arbitration. However, one interesting recent Ontario case involved Reiner Shenk, a single Swiss plaintiff with no assets in Ontario, who was seeking to sue a large pharmaceutical company. Although there was no legal obligation to do so, the funder insisted that its agreement with Shenk be approved by the court.[8] Justice McEwen in the Ontario Superior Court refused to approve the agreement, under which the funder could have received 'the lion's share' of the proceeds, and would receive confidential information and documents. The agreement restricted Schenk's ability to instruct counsel; the funder had the option of terminating the agreement on seven days' notice and to refuse to provide future

---

5. *Metzler Investment GMBH v. Gildan Activewear Inc* [2009] Ont. Superior Court.
6. *Dugal v. Manulife Financial Corporation* [2011] Ont. Superior Court.
7. *Bayens v. Kinross Gold Corp* [2013] Ont. Superior Court.
8. *Schenk v. Valeant Pharmaceuticals et al.* [2015].

funding or to unilaterally revise the terms of the agreement if Schenk's costs exceeded the budget by 25%. Justice McEwen noted that his decision was without prejudice to Schenk bringing a further application for approval of a different funding agreement: 'I see no reason why such funding would be inappropriate in the field of commercial litigation. With that said, ...the prohibition on champerty and maintenance must be considered'. Otherwise, it is not really providing access to justice, but merely an attractive business opportunity to the funder, who never suffered the alleged wrong. Interestingly, Justice McEwen said that he would remain seized of the case, to consider another agreement with the same funder or another. He might well have said that court approval in the case of arbitration was unnecessary.

How relevant are these principles in an international arbitration? Should a tribunal involve itself in this kind of evaluation? Must an arbitrator respect these principles in an international case seated in Ontario? One might invoke public policy to justify such a constraint, but to do so could contravene the guiding principles of the Model Law and the New York Convention, both meant to harmonize international arbitration and minimize the effects of local laws in an international forum.

§3.07 ADDRESSING QUESTIONS AROUND THIRD-PARTY FUNDING

England and Wales were the first jurisdictions to address third-party funding with rules.[9] The Code of Conduct for Litigation Funders was published by the UK's Ministry of Justice in November 2011. The Association of Litigation Funders (the top seven funders in the UK are members, with associates from business, legal and academic spheres) self-regulates in line with the Code. The Code sets out the standards by which its members must abide, and covers key concerns, including capital adequacy of funders, reasonable grounds for approval of settlements and termination of the agreement, and maintenance of control of the case by the claimant.

Despite a recommendation of the November 2015 report of the ICCA-QMUL Task Force on Third Party Funding concluding that it is inappropriate to award funding costs, as they are not procedural costs incurred for the purpose of an arbitration, an English arbitrator ordered indemnity costs to a claimant, including the costs of litigation funding. On appeal, the respondent argued that the arbitrator lacked jurisdiction, but Justice Waxman Q.C. of the High Court decided that third party funding costs were indeed recoverable under Section 59(1)(c) of the 1996 Arbitration Act and article 31(1) of the ICC Rules, as "legal and other costs".

Hong Kong's Law Reform Commission in 2016 tabled the Arbitration and Mediation Legislation (Third Party Funding) (Amendment) Bill to ensure that third party funding of arbitration and mediation is not prohibited by the common law doctrine of maintenance and champerty, and to provide for related safeguards. The Bill received second reading before the Legislature in January 2017 so should be enacted before the end of the year. Briefly, the Bill provides standards for arbitrations taking

---

9. Australia too has made a number of attempts at regulating third-party funding. That experience is beyond the scope of this chapter.

place in Hong Kong to be included in an amendment to the Arbitration Ordinance, including:

- Capital adequacy;
- Confidentiality and privilege;
- Extent of extra-territorial application;
- Control of the arbitration by the funder;
- Disclosure of funding to the tribunal and other party;
- Grounds for terminating the funding agreement; and
- Complaints procedures.

§3.08 CONCLUSION

Third-party funding is still a novelty to most clients and their counsel and to many arbitrators. Without information about the frequency of disclosure it is difficult to know how arbitral tribunals might be influenced by it. But by raising questions about champerty and maintenance that probably many of us have never thought about since first year of law school, it is furthering debate about access to justice versus the monetization of justice.

Without statutory regulation in most jurisdictions, the oversight of third-party funding is usually left up to the courts in certifying class actions. Judges know that class actions are very expensive to run, but with high stakes and a great potential for high return, judges have permitted third party in a numerous cases. But in an arbitration, usually a private or even confidential matter, there will not necessarily be a state court judge to supervise. Nor will most parties regret this, having chosen arbitration as an alternative to court. What is appropriate in state court litigation may or may not provide a useful guide for claimants considering third-party funding for arbitration. With very little guidance and no international consensus visible, arbitrators dealing with funded cases may have to use not only their broad discretion, but also their good judgment.

For the future however, it seems that the development of third party funding is inevitable. In the words of a third-party funder: 'When we first started up, we heard two strongly worded reactions. On one side, 'this is terrible, it is turning justice into a new commodity market, on par with corn, or coal or pork bellies'. On the other, 'What's all the fuss? We have been using third-party funding for years, but never thought it necessary to mention it. Some of our best cases would never have made it to arbitration without financial assistance behind the scenes from a funder'.

CHAPTER 4
The Arbitrator Dr. Martin Regli: Pierre Karrer's *Alter Ego*

Klaus Peter Berger

§4.01 INTRODUCTION

My relationship with Pierre Karrer has always been very special. This is due to the way it all began in the early 1990s. At that time, my doctoral thesis on international commercial arbitration had just been published.[1] Even though a newcomer to the field, I had the aspiration to write a handbook that practitioners would read and use for their daily work. Not being a practitioner myself at that time, but an unknown university assistant, I had no idea whether this was just wishful thinking or a realistic perspective, until I found a letter from Pierre in my mail. Of course, I knew Pierre's name, but had never met him before. The text of the letter was short, but memorable: "At the beginning of a long train journey, I began to read your book and did not stop until the train had reached its final destination." I was happy and proud. For the first time, I had received an indication that a highly experienced and highly respected practitioner like Pierre Karrer had not only taken notice that my book was published, but had actually *read* it. Pierre and I had many other encounters at conferences and seminars, including the bi-annual ASA/DIS Practice Building Seminar in Badenweiler in the Black Forest, and at the Willem C. Vis Moot in Vienna. In light of this long history, it is not surprising that Pierre assumed a core role in a multimedia project on international alternative dispute resolution (ADR) which I developed with my academic team in the late 1990s. The fact that he participated in that project is yet another proof for Pierre's continued fascination and love for teaching the law and practice of international arbitration to newcomers in the field. The present contribution examines how Pierre—both as his

---

1. Klaus Peter Berger, *Internationale Wirtschaftsschiedsgerichtsbarkeit* (de Gruyter 1992); Klaus Peter Berger, *International Economic Arbitration* (Kluwer 1993, English version).

alter ego in the multimedia project and as himself in "real" arbitrations—approaches practical problems in the procedural management of international arbitrations.

§4.02 PIERRE KARRER'S ROLE IN THE MULTIMEDIA PROJECT: THE ARBITRATOR WHO PLAYS HIMSELF

After I had becom a professor, I taught courses on international arbitration, both in Germany and abroad. Very soon, I realized that there was a lack of practical teaching materials. There were many excellent handbooks on the market, as there are today. However, to get a profound understanding of the functioning of the arbitral process, knowing the black letter law was not enough. There are many things in international arbitration and ADR which one cannot learn by simply reading a handbook. This applies in particular to the advocacy, case management skills and other soft-skills required from a practitioner who wants to be successful in this field. The original idea behind the project was to provide the reader with a full and realistic picture of the arbitral process. It was clear that, in addition to the traditional written text, training and teaching aids, detailed contract documentation and the entire file of the arbitration, a vivid description of the oral hearing would be needed to introduce students and young practitioners to the practicalities and psychologies of the arbitration process. It was at that time that the idea to produce videos of the oral hearings which were part of the case study, including the examination of witnesses and a hearing on document production, was born.[2]

To do the videos, I needed legal practitioners, rather than professional actors, i.e., highly experienced arbitration lawyers who would share my enthusiasm for this idea.[3] In light of our long-standing relationship, it was only natural that I contacted Pierre. He immediately agreed to play Dr. Martin Regli, the arbitrator to be appointed by "Alpine Laseroptics Technologies (ALT)," the Swiss respondent in the case study which I had developed for the project.[4] I was extremely happy that with Pierre on board, I had a high caliber tribunal. The German Chairman ("Dr. Dieter Schmitz") was Martin Hunter, the other co-arbitrator, to be appointed by the Dutch claimant "Netherlands Transcontinental (NedTrans)," was German attorney-at law and well-known arbitration lawyer Hilmar Raeschke-Kessler. The in-house lawyer for claimant ("Pieter Stels") was played by Constantine Partasides; lead counsel for respondent was Claudia Kälin-Nauer ("Dr. Beate Mueller"). The videos were taken in a studio of the media department of Muenster University, where I taught at that time.

While I had written scripts for the actors, I did not want to bind them too much to a pre-formulated text. I wanted them to act and behave as if they were in a real arbitration. Therefore, the script contained many blanks and keywords instead of full text. That left enough flexibility for the actors. At the same time, however, it required

---

2. Klaus Peter Berger, *Private Dispute Resolution in International Business: Negotiation, Mediation, Arbitration* (3d ed., Kluwer 2015).
3. *See* the video-interview at www.private-dispute-resolution.com/8/concept-id24 (accessed March 20, 2017) for the teaching- and training-philosophy underlying the project.
4. Berger, *supra* n. 2, Case Study (Vol. I).

them to familiarize themselves with the case and the script to an extent which I was very hesitant to ask from such busy practitioners. Nevertheless, the video shoot went truly amazing and by far exceeded my expectations.[5] Everybody was extremely focused and professional. We even had a buffet lunch in the studio and did most of the videos in one single run. Essentially, we videotaped scenes from a two-day hearing in less than a day. I had the greatest admiration for the practitioners in the studio. They managed to forget the cameras, lights, set people, as well as the "director" with his assistant[6] around them. When the day was over and the actors had left Muenster, I sent an email to them thanking them for their support and their marvelous job as "actors" during the video session. Martin responded that there was no need to thank them, because they had not acted in the film studio in Muenster: "for us, it was just another ordinary day of business." Indeed, due to the fact that the scripts left freedom for each practitioner to adopt his own procedural management style, each fictional arbitrator in the videos is colored by the real arbitrator playing the part—Dr. Regli may thus be truly considered as Pierre's *alter ego*.

§4.03 1001 Q&AS: PIERRE KARRER'S ADAPTATION OF THE IDEA OF INTERACTIVE TEACHING AND TRAINING IN ARBITRATION

In 2014, Pierre Karrer once again revealed his enthusiasm for the practical teaching and training of students and young practitioners in the field of international arbitration by publishing his book "Introduction to International Arbitration Practice: 1001 Questions and Answers."[7] Rather than bringing out just another handbook, he decided to convey the know-how and tremendous practical experience he has accumulated over his unique career, spanning a period of more than four decades, in the form of a dialogue between an imaginary student asking questions to Pierre. Pierre explains this unusual approach in the preface to his book:

> The present book is for students and young practitioners of international arbitration. Nowadays, they have much better theoretical knowledge of the arbitration process, and far easier access to the sources of international arbitration law than today's seasoned arbitrators had at their age. But they are obviously still in the process of building up practical experience. This book tries to help them by summing up and updating life-time personal experience in the field, but in a simple, practical and commonsense fashion. Hence, questions and answers.

---

5. *See* for a report of the video shoot and photos from the set www.private-dispute-resolution.com /16/an_idea_becomes_reality-id12 (accessed March 20, 2017).
6. The assistant was Stefan Hoffmann, who also had an important role in the script; he played one of the witnesses, claimant's managing director Jan Bakker, who had negotiated the contract in dispute with his counterpart from respondent's side, ALT's sales manager Urs Stutz, who was played by Dr. Friedrich Blase. Stefan Hoffmann later used the project to teach a practice-building course for state court judges in Ulaanbaatar, Mongolia and acted as advisor to the Mongolian National and International Arbitration Court in relation to the implementation of Mongolian domestic arbitration laws.
7. Pierre A. Karrer, *Introduction to International Arbitration Practice: 1001 Questions and Answers* (Kluwer 2014).

> If one conducts an arbitration, one must institute a dialogue. This is a dialogue about instituting that dialogue.[8]

The last sentence tells us something about Pierre's philosophy of the arbitration process: rather than being a one-way communication process from the parties to the tribunal or *vice-versa*, he understands arbitration as a dialogue between parties and arbitrators aimed at achieving a fair, reasonable and just decision of the dispute that has arisen between them. Implementing such a dialogue-based concept of arbitration in actual practice requires proactive case management by the arbitrators:

> A party driven system [like arbitration] only works if the parties are driving in the same direction. A non-passive arbitrator should seek to steer the proceedings in the interest of all parties. The issue should not be what an individual party currently wants in the heat of combat but what [the parties] would have objectively wanted from a fair and efficient proceeding before the dispute commenced. A non-passive arbitrator can provide a fair and efficient proceeding through a steady hand and sharing his or her accumulated wisdom through an open dialogue with the parties.[9]

Understanding the arbitration process as a dialogue between tribunal and the parties may even proof fruitful beyond procedural management. It may result in reopening communication channels between the parties, assisting them in their efforts to reach an end without award, i.e., a settlement of the dispute, reached with or without the assistance of the arbitrators.[10] Dr. Regli's tribunal in the videos adopted a similarly proactive approach, which resulted in the suspension of the arbitration due to the fact that the parties resumed talks to settle the dispute amicably.

§4.04 TWO PROBLEMS AND THEIR SOLUTIONS BY DR. REGLI AND PIERRE KARRER

[A] Proactive Procedural Planning

Dr. Regli's tribunal in the multimedia project puts great emphasis on procedural planning. After discussion with the parties at a case-management telephone conference, it issues a rather detailed Procedural Order No. 1 (PO1), which is signed by the

---

8. Karrer, *supra* n. 7, xi.
9. Veit Öhlberger & Jarred Pinkston, "Iura Novit Curia and the Non-Passive Arbitrator: A Question of Efficiency, Cultural Blinders and Misplaced Concerns About Impartiality" in Christian Klausegger and others (eds), *Austrian Yearbook on International Arbitration 2016* 101, 115 (Manz 2016). Cf Klaus Peter Berger & J. Ole Jensen, *Due Process Paranoia and the Procedural Judgment Rule: A Safe Harbour for International Arbitrators' Procedural Management Decisions*, 32 Arbitration International 415 (2016).
10. Klaus Peter Berger, *Promoting Settlements in Arbitration: Is the "German Approach" Really Incompatible with the Role of the Arbitrator?*, 9 New York Dispute Resolution Lawyer 46 (2016); see also Hilmar Raeschke-Kessler, *Making Arbitration More Efficient: Settlement Initiatives by the Arbitral Tribunal*, International Business Lawyer 158 (2002); Bernd Ehle, "The Arbitrator as a Settlement Facilitator" in Olivier Caprasse (ed), *Walking a Thin Line: What an Arbitrator Can Do, Must Do or Must Not Do* 79 (Bruylant 2010).

chairman only.[11] In fact, the PO1 was "modernized," partly reformulated and made much more detailed from the second to the third edition of the project. Inspite of these changes, the PO1 is a far cry from the one contained in Pierre's book. That PO1 has almost 100 paragraphs, some of them being extremely detailed. In an effort to "organize the file as much as possible," Pierre's PO1 even contains instructions to the parties as to the exact identification and page numbering of evidentiary documents:

> Please put the date of the document near the top right-hand corner of the first page, using letters to indicate the month. Please use "Bates" numerator stamp for easy reference within an unpaginated document *before* copying.[12]

These instructions may seem overly detailed.[13] One may also question whether it is necessary to include in the instructions even the type of numerator to be used by the parties to number the pages of their documents.[14] However, this approach serves the very practical purpose of helping the tribunal to avoid problems which many arbitrators have faced in their practice with respect to the handling of voluminous documentary evidence submitted by the parties. Documents without page and paragraph numbers are difficult to quote from, not only during the hearing, but also in the final award. The videos of the hearing in the multimedia project reveal that Dr. Regli himself has his own "stamping routine" for documents submitted during the hearing. When confronted with such documents, he takes out his own stamp to immediately mark these documents with his name or another personal identifier. Apparently, he wants to avoid confusion within the tribunal "in the heat of the battle" as to which copy of a certain document belongs to which member of the tribunal. Everybody who has ever sat on a three-member tribunal knows that, especially in tight seating arrangements, this is not a purely theoretical scenario.

Behind this technical question lies a very important legal one: how should an international arbitral tribunal deal with the late submission of documents or other means of evidence, e.g., during the hearing? Again, Dr. Regli's tribunal is faced with such a scenario. Towards the end of the hearing, when counsel for respondent senses that her client might lose the case, she submits a motion on behalf of her client ALT to hear *"Professor Ylts,"*[15] a professor on international economic law, as an expert

---

11. The text of the order, together with all other orders and awards and the briefs submitted by the parties, is available as a pdf file on the USB Card which is part of the multimedia project, Berger, *supra* n. 2.
12. Karrer, *supra* n. 7, 297–298, Annex (L): Procedural Order No. 1, para. 31.
13. Pierre's PO1 even contains detailed instructions as to the quality of the binders to be used by the parties, Karrer, *supra* n. 7, 298, Annex (L): Procedural Order No. 1, para. 34: "Each binder should have a back, not just spirals. Please, *do not overload arch-folders* (they do not travel well)," emphasis in the original. In the experience of the present author, there are good reasons why a tribunal should make the parties aware of that problem.
14. The Bates Automatic Numbering-Machine or "Bates Stamper" is named after the late nineteenth century inventor Edwin G. Bates, *see* https://en.wikipedia.org/wiki/Bates_numbering (accessed May March 20, 2017).
15. The name *Ylts* was inspired by *Johnny Veeder* QC who has used this *alias* to review one of the present author's books as *Professor Dr. Ylts* (A. F-J. Ylts, *Das Neue Recht der Schiedsgerichtsbarkeit (The New German Arbitration Law)* edited by Klaus-Peter Berger, 14 Arbitration International 91–92 (1998)) and to publish a seminal one-page article as Professor Dr. Ylts, *The*

witness. After a brief consultation with his co-arbitrators, the Chairman indicates the tribunal's surprise at this request for expert evidence at such a late stage of the proceedings. At the end of the hearing, when the Chairman asks both counsel whether they have any objections against the conduct of the procedure by the Tribunal, both counsel express their satisfaction with the conduct of the arbitration so far. At the same time, however, counsel for respondent reserves her rights with respect to the tribunal's rejection of ALT's motion to hear the expert witness from London University. Pierre Karrer deals with this situation in his book and with ways to anticipate them through careful procedural management. Asked by the imaginary student what an arbitral tribunal can do to stay out of procedural trouble, Pierre responds:

> If a Party sees that it may lose, it sometimes tries to improve its position by last-minute offers of proof, particularly additional Party-appointed Experts' Reports or motions that the Arbitral Tribunal itself appoint an Expert. If the Arbitral Tribunal refuses, the Party will say that its right to be heard has been violated. This should be prevented in Procedural Order No. 1.[16]

While Dr. Regli's tribunal found no help for its decision in its PO1, Pierre has inserted a number of precautionary provisions in the text of his own PO1 to avoid such situations from the outset. They relate to the procedural effect of a cut-off date included in the provisional timetable. Notably, these provisions include a stipulation for cases in which no such specific cut-off date has been included in the timetable by the tribunal:

> 40. A deadline may be specifically set by the Arbitral Tribunal, after which no new factual documents will be admitted from the Parties, except as *nova* for cause shown by leave of the Arbitral Tribunal. If no specific deadline was set, the cut-off time will be at the time of the last main written submission (on the main claim and separately on the counterclaim) before the first Evidentiary Hearing (no new factual documents may be submitted with a skeleton submission, see above, paragraph 17). Sources of law may be submitted without leave at any time, even with Post-Hearing Briefs.
> [...]
> 44 The cut-off time for Witness Statements, Experts' Reports and motions to appoint a Tribunal-appointed Expert is the same as that for documents, above, paragraph 40.
> [...]
> 46. Party-appointed Experts' Reports (including Legal Expert Reports) shall be submitted as prescribed in the IBA Rules of Evidence (article 5.2) and above, paragraph 44.[17]

In addition to these provisions related to the effect of the cut-off date to be included in the provisional timetable, Pierre's PO1 also deals with situations in which

---

"Y2K Problem" and Arbitration: The Answer to the Myth, 16 Arbitration International 79–80 (2000) (with apologies in brackets: "It is regretted that for technical reasons publication of this article was rendered impossible"); in their review of this issue of Arbitration International, the editors of the ASA-Bulletin expressed "the hope that this is the last what we hear from this author about this topic" (18 ASA Bulletin 172 (2000)).

16. Karrer, *supra* n. 7, para. 105.
17. Karrer, *supra* n. 7, 300, Annex (L): Procedural Order No. 1.

the Parties disregard time-limits set by the tribunal and misuse the right to submit evidence for tactical reasons:

> In case a time limit is not respected by a Party, the Arbitral Tribunal shall, without further notice, be entitled to disregard any submission made by the Party after the expiry of the deadline. Last minute surprise submissions and evidence will be put unread into envelopes, and the envelopes will be sealed.[18]

It is important for the understanding of the effect of these provisions that they apply to both submissions concerning the claim and a possible counterclaim. Pierre rightly emphasizes the danger that a party might misuse its right to file a submission on the counterclaim as a disguised late submission on the claim:

> Here there is a special pitfall of which one must be wary. The temptation is great for a Party to present new arguments and new evidence on the main claim, under the guise of a last minute submission on a counterclaim. An Arbitral Tribunal is well advised to caution the Parties against such foul play, and to take precautionary measures against this.[19]

Dr. Regli's tribunal would probably have been authorized to make the same decisions even though his tribunal's PO1 did not contain such detailed provisions. Also, it is generally acknowledged today that arbitral tribunals are not bound by formal rules of evidence that apply in state court proceedings and enjoy broad discretion to admit or exclude evidence.[20] That discretion includes the right to reject further evidence without violating a party's right to be heard if the tribunal is convinced that it has received enough evidence on certain facts or that these facts are irrelevant for the decision of the dispute. This conclusion by the arbitral tribunal is not subject to a *de novo* examination by the state courts, e.g., in setting aside or enforcement proceedings.[21] However, having such provisions in the PO1, rather than relying on this settled case law, is an important case-management tool. It creates early transparency *vis-à-vis* the parties and serves to avoid misuse of procedural rights from the outset:

> To be able to stand firm against such procedural behaviour, the tribunal should clarify the rules of the game sufficiently as early as possible, so as to [prevent] a party from later claiming a "misunderstanding". It may be helpful to expressly mention certain matters such as that no new evidence may be submitted after a certain date, that extension requests will only be considered in exceptional

---

18. Karrer, *supra* n. 7, 293, Annex (L): Procedural Order No. 1, para. 8.
19. Karrer, *supra* n. 7, para. 403.
20. Gary B. Born, *International Commercial Arbitration*, 3238–3242 (2nd ed., Kluwer 2014).
21. *ABB AG v. Hochtief Airport GmbH and Athens International Airport S.A.* [2006] EWHC 388 (Comm) para. 67 ("It is not ground for intervention that the court considers that it might have done things differently"); also cf. *Pacific China Holdings Ltd (In Liquidation) v. Grand Pacific Holdings Ltd* [2012] 4 HKLRD 1; *Triulzi Cesare SRL v. XinyiGroup (Glass) Co Ltd* [2014] SGHC 220; BGH WM 1963, 944; BGH NJW 1966, 549; OLG München SchiedsVZ 2011, 230. See for a comprehensive review of pertinent case law Berger & Jensen, *supra* n. 9, 423–429.

circumstances, and that testimony of witnesses and experts at the oral hearing must be limited to issues already raised in their written submissions.[22]

Pierre Karrer shares this view and has included in his PO1 a clear message with respect to the tribunal's policy of handling extension requests from the parties and the misuse of the timetable as an instrument for tactical maneuvers:

> Time limits shall be extended only in exceptional circumstances. Any request for an extension must state until which date the extension is requested, why the extension is necessary and *why the request could not have been made earlier*. The Parties shall refrain from arguments based on an analysis of the Procedural Timetable and the absolute or relative length of time periods derived from it, or an extension of deadlines previously granted to their opponent.[23]

From the standpoint of proactive, anticipatory case management by the tribunal it is indeed essential for the acceptance by the parties of decisions made by the arbitrators in exercising their procedural discretion that the general approach which the tribunal intends to take in rendering such decisions throughout the proceedings does not come as a surprise to the parties. Often, parties select arbitrators precisely for his or her known (due to experience in previous proceedings or disclosure by the arbitrator[24]), proactive case-management philosophy, so they know or should know what to expect from him or her. Irrespective of these special scenarios, arbitrators should always make it clear from the outset of the proceedings that the tribunal intends to follow a proactive approach in conducting the proceedings, for example by discussing their approach at the case-management conference and/or inserting provisions to this effect in the PO1.

[B] The Pathological Arbitration Clause

Apart from applying their practical wisdom to the planning and management of the proceedings, both Pierre and his *alter ego* Dr. Martin Regli deal with a typical jurisdictional issue which arbitral tribunals face every now and then: the "pathological" arbitration clause.[25] This problem may be characterized as the downside of party autonomy. The arbitration agreement is the source of arbitral jurisdiction, the most visible expression of the autonomy of the parties, i.e., of their freedom to decide whether and how to arbitrate present or future disputes. At the same time, making use

---

22. Karl-Heinz Böckstiegel, "Case Management by Arbitrators: Experiences and Suggestions" in Gerald Aksen and others (eds), *Global Reflections on International Law, Commerce and Dispute Resolution: Liber Amicorum in Honour of Robert Briner* (ICC 2005) 115, 121.
23. Karrer, *supra* n. 7, 292–293, Annex (L): Procedural Order No. 1, para. 6 (emphasis in the original).
24. For example by way of publications etc., *see* Ema Vidak-Gojkovic, Lucy Greenwood and Michael McIlwrath, "Puppies or Kittens? How To Better Match Arbitrators to Party Expectations" in Christian Klausegger and others (eds), *Austrian Yearbook on International Arbitration 2016* (Manz 2016) 61, 67.
25. Born, *supra* n. 20, 770–788; Laurence Craig, William W. Park and Jan Paulsson, *International Chamber of Commerce Arbitration*, 127–135 (3d ed., Oceana 2000); cf Berger, *supra* n. 2, para. 16-3; Karrer, *supra* n. 7, paras. 120–138.

of that autonomy requires informed choices. Unfortunately, parties who want to arbitrate their disputes very often make such choices without possessing or having sought such information from arbitration experts. Pierre provides rather drastic examples which prompt the imaginary student to ask (in disbelieve): "have there really been cases like this?"[26] As an answer, Pierre cites the following real life examples:

> "Uncitral in Geneva" means Uncitral (the Arbitral Institution which is in Vienna) Arbitration Rules, seat of the arbitration Geneva. "Stockholm, Swiss" means Stockholm, Sweden. "Zurich, Sweden" means Zurich, Switzerland.[27]

It is indeed hard to believe that such examples exist in practice. However, when uninformed parties begin to draft their arbitration clauses rather than relying on the tried and tested model clauses of arbitral institutions, the outcome is unpredictable and the ultimate work product can be horrible and costly. In one of the most extreme cases, the parties even forgot to include the text of the arbitration clause in the final text of the contract before signing the document. A U.S. court then had to deal with the question whether the heading "Arbitration of disputes" *alone* suffices to assume that the parties had concluded an agreement to arbitrate their disputes.[28]

Dr. Regli's tribunal is faced with a different and very popular type of pathological clause, namely the wrong identification of the arbitral institution. While the claim is brought under claimant's standard forms which contain the regular model clause of the German Institution of Arbitration (DIS),[29] the respondent's standard terms refer to arbitration under "the Rules of the German Central Chamber of Commerce." Again, Pierre provides us in his book with some practical advice as to how to deal with such badly drafted arbitration clauses:

> Sometimes one can identify the Arbitral Institution all the same. In English, capitalization of a word points to institutional arbitration, since Arbitral Institutions have names that one normally capitalizes. One may then try to identify the Arbitral Institution that was meant. Some parts of the names of Arbitral Institutions are not specific and often wrongly translated, such as "institution", "Institute", "chamber", "commerce", and "trade". The word "international" does not necessarily point to the ICC since it is used by many other Arbitral Institutions as well. The words "court", "panel" and "college" are not helpful because they also apply in *ad hoc* arbitration.
>
> Sometimes there is a prominent Arbitral Institution in a particular city, and one can assume, if the name roughly fits that is the one that was meant. However, the mere *statistical* likelihood that a particular Arbitral Institution was meant should not be sufficient for it to be understood to have been chosen in this particular case.[30]

In Dr. Regli's arbitration, this practical advice would not have helped the tribunal. Since the arbitration clauses were contained in standard terms used by the

---

26. Karrer, *supra* n. 7, para. 128.
27. Karrer, *supra* n. 7, para. 127.
28. *Trimless-Flashless Design Inc. v. Thomas & Betts Corp.* 232 F.3d 890 (4th cir.) without published opinion. Full Text at 2000 U.S. App. LEXIS 26633.
29. The text of the model clause is available in various languages at www.disarb.org (accessed March 20, 2017).
30. Karrer, *supra* n. 7, para. 131 (emphasis in original).

parties to conclude the contract, the decisive question was one of contract formation under which the tribunal had to decide whether to apply the "knock out" doctrine. This doctrine is reflected in Article 2.1.22 UNIDROIT Principles of International Commercial Contracts (UPICC) and Article 2:209 Lando Principles. It is also accepted in international contract doctrine[31] and in domestic laws such as those of Germany, France and Austria[32] as well as—with modifications—in section 2-207 United States Uniform Commercial Code (UCC). In fact, comparative studies reveal a rather clear international trend in the direction of the "knock-out rule."[33] The effect of this doctrine would have been to eliminate the contradictory arbitration clauses from the contract. The result could have been a contract without an agreement to arbitrate. That would have left each party with the option to bring the dispute before a domestic court in the competent jurisdiction. However, such a result would not have been in line with the parties' initial intentions as expressed in the two arbitration clauses contained in their standard terms, i.e., their will to *arbitrate* future disputes. A more pragmatic result would thus have been to save the parties' principal agreement to arbitrate and to eliminate only the part of the parties' agreement on dispute resolution that refers to two different arbitral institutions, i.e., to assume an agreement on ad hoc arbitration in Germany. This is a result that Pierre also favors in his book when asked by the imaginary student whether to uphold a clause that refers to a non-existing arbitral institution:

> Even then, the Parties must be understood to have primarily chosen arbitration at the seat [...], and only secondarily the Arbitral Institution, and, in any event, not court litigation elsewhere. So this will be *ad hoc* arbitration at the chosen seat.[34]

But were the arbitration clauses in Dr. Regli's arbitration really contradictory? The reference to DIS-administered arbitration in Claimant's arbitration clause was unambiguous. Since an arbitral institution with the name "German Central Chamber of Commerce" does not exist, the true meaning of respondent's arbitration clause had to be determined by Dr. Regli and his two colleagues. To achieve this objective, they had to interpret the clause, taking into account all relevant circumstances and interests of the parties.[35]

In most modern jurisdictions, it is generally acknowledged today that the principle of presumptive validity of international arbitration agreements (*in favorem*

---

31. *See* Maria del Pilar Perales Viscasillas, *The Formation of Contracts and the Principles of European Contract Law*, 13 Pace International Law Review 371, 389 (2001); Burghardt Piltz, *Internationales Kaufrecht*, paras. 3-109, 3-111 (2nd ed., Beck 2008); Stefan Kröll and Rudolf Hennecke, *Kollidierende Allgemeine Geschäftsbedingungen in internationalen Kaufverträgen*, RIW 736, 741 (2001).
32. Ulrich G. Schroeter, "Commentary on Art. 19 CISG" in Ingeborg Schwenzer (ed), *Schlechtriem & Schwenzer Commentary on the UN Convention on the International Sale of Goods (CISG)*, para. 36 (4th ed., OUP 2016); *see* for German law BGH NJW 2002, 1651, 1653.
33. Ernst A. Kramer, '"Battle of the Forms"—eine rechtsvergleichende Skizze mit Blick auf das schweizerische Recht', in Pierre Tercier (ed.) *Festschrift für Peter Gauch* 493, 503 (Schulthess 2004).
34. Karrer, *supra* n. 7, para. 133.
35. *See* BGH NJW 2002, 1651, 1653 for the interpretation of conflicting standard forms in a contract that is subject to the CISG.

Chapter 4: The Arbitrator Dr. Martin Regli   §4.04[B]

validitatis) must be applied to the interpretation of an international arbitration agreement. According to this principle, an arbitration agreement should be construed in good faith[36] and in a way that upholds its validity.[37] This means that "doubts about the intended scope of an agreement to arbitrate are [to be] resolved in favour of arbitration."[38] This pro-arbitration approach or *"in favorem* presumption"[39] to the construction of arbitration agreements serves to enforce the common intention of the parties to have their dispute decided before an international arbitral tribunal:

> An agreement to arbitrate before a specified tribunal is, in effect, a specialized kind of forum-selection clause. [...] The invalidation of such an agreement [...] would not only allow the respondent to repudiate its solemn promise but would, as well, reflect a parochial concept that all disputes must be resolved under our laws and in our courts.[40]

The *in favorem* approach to the construction of arbitration agreements extends to the typical formula used in such clauses, stating that all disputes "arising out of," "arising under" and "in connection with" the contract shall be settled through arbitration. Instead of attaching different meanings to this terminology, the English House of Lords has made it clear in *Fiona Trust* that:

> the construction of an arbitration clause should start from the assumption that the parties, as rational businessmen, are likely to have intended any dispute arising out of the relationship into which they have entered or purported to enter to be decided by the same tribunal. The clause should be construed in accordance with this presumption unless the language makes it clear that certain questions were intended to be excluded from the arbitrator's jurisdiction.[41]

The quote from *Fiona Trust* shows that the *in favorem* principle is directly linked to the very fundament of the arbitration process: the consent of the parties to arbitrate. The *in favorem* presumption is thus one of the most essential principles of international arbitration law.[42] The *in favorem* approach is also a consequence of today's arbitration-friendly climate which is based on the understanding that dispute settlement by international arbitral tribunals has the same value and standing as adjudication before

---

36. *See* Decision on Jurisdiction, *Amco Asia Corp. et al. v. Republic of Indonesia*, ILM 1984, 351, 359 et seq.: "any convention, including conventions to arbitrate, should be construed in good faith, that is to say by taking into account the consequences of their commitments the parties may be considered as having reasonably and legitimately envisaged."
37. Nigel Blackaby and Constantine Partasides, *Redfern and Hunter on International Arbitration*, para. 2.28 (6th ed., OUP 2015); Craig, Park and Paulsson, *supra* n. 25, 43; Born, *supra* n. 20, 230–233; *see* generally TransLex Principle XIII.1.2, available at http://www.trans-lex.org/968902 (accessed March 20, 2017).
38. *Kaplan v. First Options of Chicago, Inc.*, 19 F.3d 1503, 1512 (3rd Cir. 1994); *see also Moses H. Cone Memorial Hosp. v. Mercury Constr. Corp.*, 460 U.S. 1, 24 (1983).
39. Born, *supra* n. 20, 1326, stating that "this type of presumption provides that a valid arbitration clause should generally be interpreted expansively and, in cases of doubt, extended to encompass disputed claims."
40. *Scherk v. Alberto-Culver Co.*, 417 U.S. 506, 519 (1974).
41. *Fiona Trust & Holding Corp v. Privalov* [2007] UKHL 40.
42. Jan Paulsson, *The Idea of Arbitration,* 300 (OUP 2013): "If we take this aspiration [to fulfil the very idea of arbitration as the binding resolution of disputes] as fundamental to the way we view, nurture, and control arbitration, it also appears to have a corollary. It is a simple principle,

domestic courts.⁴³ This means that a liberal way of construing arbitration agreements has to be pursued even in those cases where in general contract law the ambiguity could not be resolved through the application of traditional means of interpretation. It is for this reason that international arbitrators tend to adopt a liberal "pro-arbitration" approach in order to make sure that the will of the parties to arbitrate their disputes is not frustrated:

> The arbitrators have from the [arbitration] clause and the pleadings of the parties decided that both parties desire a settlement of disputes outside state jurisdiction. *That wish, expressed by both parties, has essentially determined the attitude of the arbitrators vis-à-vis the clause inserted into the contract. They felt an obligation to help the parties realize such a wish.*⁴⁴

In Dr. Regli's arbitration, the Tribunal realized that the German Federal Supreme Court has held that an arbitration agreement is not per se "incapable of being performed" (section 1032(1) German Arbitration Act) if the parties have inadvertently agreed to the jurisdiction of a non-existing arbitral institution. Rather, a supplementary interpretation of the clause is required in order to determine whether the parties have agreed to refer their disputes to arbitration under the rules of a specific existing arbitral institution.⁴⁵ This means that in Dr. Regli's case, the arbitral tribunal, in determining whether it has jurisdiction or not, needed to study carefully the wording of respondent's arbitration clause to determine the will of ALT as to the desired dispute resolution mechanism.

What is clear from the wording "German Central Chamber of Commerce" is that respondent ALT wanted *institutional* arbitration in *Germany*. The terminology used in its arbitration clause was used to denote an arbitral institution in Germany that is not associated with a particular branch of trade but which is independent and neutral because it is associated with the top organization of the German chambers of commerce. The "German Association for Industry and Trade" (*Deutscher Industrie- und Handelstag*, DIHT) functions as the representative association for all German chambers of commerce. In fact, it was renamed into the "German Association for Industry and Chambers of Commerce" (*Deutscher Industrie- und Handelskammertag*, DIHK)⁴⁶ in July 2001 in order to make that function more apparent to the public. From a functional perspective, the wording of the arbitration clause ("Central Chamber of Commerce") indicates that ALT wanted to select the arbitral institution that is associated with and endorsed by the "central" institution of the German chambers of

---

suggested as a lodestar for other social institutions, such as courts and legislatures, in their interaction with arbitrators: *consensual arrangements for the resolution of disputes should be presumed valid."*

43. Julian D. M. Lew, Loukas A. Mistelis & Stefan M. Kröll, *Comparative International Commercial Arbitration*, No. 7-61 with reference to the "pro-arbitration bias" expressed in such landmark decisions as *Mitsubishi Motors Corp. v. Soler Chrysler Plymouth Inc.*, 473 U.S. 614 (1985).
44. *Yugoslav Co. v. PDR Korea Co.*, Arbitration Court attached to the Chamber for Foreign Trade of the GDR, YCA 129, 131 (1983) (emphasis added).
45. BGH SchiedsVZ, 284, 285 (2011); *see also* OLG Frankfurt SchiedsVZ, 217, 218 (2007); OLG München SchiedsVZ, 159, 160 et seq (2012).
46. *See* the homepage of the *Deutscher Industrie- und Handelskammertag* at www.dihk.de (accessed March 20, 2017).

Chapter 4: The Arbitrator Dr. Martin Regli §4.04[B]

commerce. During its long history, dating back to 1920, the "German Institution of Arbitration" (*Deutsche Institution für Schiedsgerichtsbarkeit*, DIS) has always been and still is affiliated with the German chambers of commerce and with their head organization, the DIHK:

> DIS is today still closely connected to DIHK and the German chambers of industry and commerce. DIHK along with most chambers of industry and commerce supported the merger of DAS and the German Arbitration Institute [in 1992] and have transferred their arbitration services to the newly founded DIS to provide harmonized and improved arbitration services in Germany.[47]

For all these reasons, the Berlin Court of Appeal has held in two landmark decisions that the DIS may be regarded as the arbitral institution referred to in arbitration clauses that contain the wording used in respondents' arbitration clause.[48] The DIS Arbitration Rules have the "international spirit" required by the fact that the arbitration clause is contained in export conditions. The DIS Rules incorporate many of the provisions contained in the Tenth Book of the German Code of Civil Procedure, which is based on an international and widely accepted set of norms, the UNCITRAL Model Law.[49]

Consequently, Dr. Regli and his colleagues, in applying the *in favorem* rule of interpretation, construed respondent's clause as referring to arbitration to be administered under the DIS Arbitration Rules. Since Claimant's clause was the DIS standard model clause, there is no conflict between the two clauses. The parties have agreed to arbitration under the DIS Arbitration Rules. Consequently, there is no need to apply the "knock out" doctrine. The arbitral tribunal therefore confirmed its jurisdiction under the DIS Arbitration Rules in an "Interim Award on Jurisdiction"[50] pursuant to section 1040(3) of the German Arbitration Act which is signed by Dr. Regli and his two colleagues.[51]

While in the end, the legal reasoning was clear and Dr. Regli and his colleagues could confirm their jurisdiction, much time and money was wasted with this jurisdictional "intermezzo." This confirms a general experience that parties who negotiate a contract shy away from paying too much attention to the drafting of the dispute

---

47. Jens Bredow and Isabel Mulder, "Introduction DIS" in Karl-Heinz Böckstiegel, Stefan Michael Kröll and Patricia Nacimiento (eds), *Arbitration in Germany*, para. 3 (1st ed., Kluwer 2007, omitted from 2nd ed., Kluwer 2015).
48. *See* KG Berlin BB, Supp. No. 8, 13, 15 (2000); KG Berlin SchiedsVZ, 337 (2012) where the Court construed a clause that referred to the arbitration rules of the "German Chamber of Commerce" as referring to the DIS Arbitration Rules because it determined that the parties wanted to designate an arbitral institution that is expressly promoted by the DIHK and the DIS lists the DIHK as one of its members; *see* for a judgment of the Paris Cour d'Appel holding that an arbitration clause concluded decades ago and referring to the Arbitration Rules of the German Commission on Arbitration (DAS) must be interpreted to refer to the DIS Arbitration Rules, *SAS ADB v. Société Reo Inductive Components AG*, SchiedsVZ 238 (2012) with note Kühner, *ibid.*, 239 et seq; *see* for that problem Karrer, *supra* n. 7, para. 132.
49. KG Berlin BB, Supp. No. 8, 13, 15 (2000).
50. *See* for the qualification of such an award as a "Preliminary, Interim and Partial Award" Karrer, *supra* n. 7, para. 425.
51. The Interim Award is reproduced as a pdf-file on the USB-Card, which is part of the multimedia project, Berger, *supra* n. 2.

resolution clause. After all, the very fact that they conclude the contract shows that they anticipate a bright future of their mutual business relationship and do not want to think about future disputes:

> The business negotiators do not want the contract to be jeopardized by opening a discussion on hypothetical future disputes. For them, euphoric from the successful negotiations, which have usually involved mutual concessions, the coming into play of attorneys is as well received as that of Cassandra in Antiquity! Jurists, it is often thought, like insurance specialists, have a regrettable tendency to foresee the worst. So business negotiators often prefer not to listen to them or to ignore their somber predictions […] [As a result,] more often than not, there are too few lawyers in the beginning of the contract (negotiations) and too many at the end (litigation resulting from this contract)![52]

When asked by the imaginary student whether one should avoid the dangers of "midnight clauses" thrown into the contract at the last minute as the parties intend to toast the conclusion of their negotiations, Pierre echoes these concerns from his more than forty years of experience in international arbitration:

> Actual "midnight clauses" are rare, but many clauses are not well thought through. A phone call to an arbitration lawyer at the seat can help and will cost little. Fortunately, many disputes arise that will be solved amicably. Still, there are cases when the magic goes out of the relationship, and a clause that was lightly negotiated suddenly becomes important. Some mistakes that could easily have been avoided at the negotiation stage may then cost many millions. To be sure, by that time the person that negotiated the clause has long been fired or has retired, but the cost to the company may be huge.[53]

§4.05 CONCLUSION

Pierre Karrer's *alter ego* Dr. Martin Regli has many qualities which have made the real man one of the most respected figures in the world of international arbitration: proactive and anticipatory case management, a hands-on approach, always on top of the file and eager to find pragmatic solutions. In his book, Pierre shows us that in the real world of international arbitration, there are many more details and procedural scenarios that an arbitral tribunal needs to take care of at the outset and during the proceedings. Whether and to what extent the tribunal manages to cope with these problems ultimately depends on the experience, case management skills and natural authority of the arbitrator(s). This confirms the old adage according to which every arbitration is only as good as the arbitrator who conducts it: *Tant vaut l'arbitre, tant vaut l'arbitrage!*

---

52. Jean-Flavien Lalive, "Some Practical Suggestions on International Arbitration" in René-Jean Dupuy (ed), *Mélanges en l'Honneur de Nicolas Valticos: Droit et Justice*, 287, 288–289 (Pedone 1999).
53. Karrer, *supra* n. 7, para. 136.

CHAPTER 5
The Role of National Courts at the Threshold of Arbitration

George A. Bermann

§5.01 INTRODUCTION

A perennial, but still understudied, issue in international arbitration is the role of national courts *prior* to arbitration, and more particularly in deciding whether, how, and to what extent to refer parties to arbitration in the face of resistance by one of them. The matter is plainly a vital one in connection with the role of courts in international arbitration generally. Unless courts are prepared under appropriate circumstances to enforce agreements to arbitrate, there may be no arbitral proceeding in which courts may play a supporting role and no arbitral award to be recognized or enforced. There is in fact much less unanimity on the role of courts at the threshold of arbitration than during the arbitral proceedings themselves or in post-award phases. While jurisdictions certainly may vary as to the extent of judicial control in annulment actions, the New York Convention brings a high degree of consensus over the role of courts in the recognition and enforcement of foreign awards, despite the Convention receiving different interpretations in different countries.

The importance of the judicial role at the threshold of arbitration is only heightened by the fact that it is not only the courts of the arbitral situs that may decide whether or not to refer the parties to arbitration. The question whether to refer the parties to arbitration may come before *any* court, worldwide. Whenever a plaintiff institutes litigation—anywhere—the defendant may invoke an arbitration agreement as a basis for dismissal of the action in favor of arbitration in the arbitral situs.

§5.02 ON WHAT GROUNDS MIGHT AN APPARENT ARBITRATION AGREEMENT BE DENIED ENFORCEMENT?

The reported cases, as well as mere reflection, reveal a wide range of challenges that may be brought to the validity and enforceability of agreements to arbitrate. Commonly, a party institutes national court litigation over a claim that the defendant considers to besubject to a prior arbitration agreement between them—at which point the defendant invokes that agreement as the basis for dismissal of the action. If the plaintiff in turn is determined to have its claim remain in court, it will challenge the enforceability of the arbitration agreement, thus hoping to defeat the motion to dismiss.

It is not at all difficult to imagine the arguments that the plaintiff in national court litigation might make to discredit the arbitration agreement or its enforcement and thus remain in court.

The plaintiff may contend that no arbitration agreement was ever made, for example, on the ground that the offer to arbitrate was never accepted or that the agreement itself is a forgery. The plaintiff may assert that, even if the agreement was made, it is not a party to it. (It will ordinarily point out that it is a non-signatory of the agreement and maintain that the law does not permit disregarding that fact). It may also, while admitting that an agreement to arbitrate was made, challenge its validity, and thus its enforceability. (It may also seek to challenge the validity of the main contract containing the arbitration clause, but the notion of severability may get in the way of having that challenge heard and decided at the threshold.) Again, it may concede that an arbitration agreement was formed and is valid, but maintain that the dispute in question falls outside the scope of that agreement, so that a tribunal resolving the dispute would commit an excess of arbitral authority by resolving it. Further, the dispute in question may be one that is legally incapable of being arbitrated under the applicable law, despite the parties have agreed to arbitrate it. Enforcement of an arbitration agreement that was admittedly entered into may also be deemed offensive to public policy of the relevant jurisdiction.

All of these objections are essentially jurisdictional in nature in that they challenge the element of consent that is essential to international commercial arbitration.

But there are still other reasons why a court might be persuaded to deny effect to an apparent agreement to arbitrate, despite the presence of consent to arbitrate. The party invoking the agreement may have waived the right to arbitrate. (Most legal systems recognize waiver in this context.) It may have waited an unduly long time to commence arbitration, even possibly letting the statute of limitations pass. The party may have failed to comply with one or more conditions precedent to arbitration (such as mediation, conciliation or national court litigation for a specified period of time) and not be able to justify that failure. The dispute in question may already have been adjudicated by a court or arbitral tribunal so that it is res judicata. Other impediments to arbitration may well be imagined. These represent challenges to an arbitration agreement, not on the basis that an arbitral tribunal lacks authority (and thus lacks jurisdiction), but on the basis that the claim being asserted is, for one or another of these reasons, inadmissible.

The purpose of this presentation is to shed further needed light on the role of courts on what we might call this panoply of "threshold" issues.

§5.03 APPROACHES TO THE THRESHOLD ROLE OF NATIONAL COURTS

An examination of national practices shows that the role played by national courts at this early stage in the arbitral life cycle varies widely across jurisdictions. I describe here the spectrum and various positions that may be taken on it.

[A] Comprehensive Judicial Involvement at the Threshold

At one extreme lies the possibility of comprehensive judicial involvement at the stage of enforcing an agreement to arbitrate should the party against which it is invoked choose to challenge it. Under such an approach, parties would be entitled, should they so request, to a full judicial inquiry into the agreement's enforceability prior to the commencement of arbitration.

Article II of the New York Convention may be cited in general support of this approach, since it requires national courts to refer parties to arbitration only if they do not find the agreement to be "null and void, inoperative, or incapable of being performed." Some jurisdictions do permit parties to broadly challenge the enforceability of agreements to arbitrate at the threshold and enable courts to decide those challenges fully independently. Moreover, they draw no apparent distinction among the various challenges that may be advanced.[1]

Contrary to a common opinion, such jurisdictions are not necessarily hostile to arbitration, or even suspicious of it. But they do afford parties a right to have an arbitration agreement's enforceability determined initially and freely by a court if the party resisting enforcement so wishes. Such jurisdictions do not deny the *Kompetenz-Kompetenz* of the arbitral tribunal (i.e., they do not dispute the authority of tribunals to determine their own jurisdiction, if and when objections to their jurisdiction are raised), but they do not accord the tribunal what has come to be known as "negative" *Kompetenz-Kompetenz*, that is to say, a competence over arbitral jurisdiction that excludes any exercise of competence over arbitral jurisdiction by national courts on a pre-arbitration basis. Under "positive" *Kompetenz-Kompetenz*, arbitral tribunals may determine their own jurisdiction and thus their authority to adjudicate, but that authority does not displace the authority of courts to determine, if asked to do so, whether or not an arbitration agreement warrants enforcement.

On the other hand, allowing plenary judicial review of an arbitration agreement's enforceability at the outset risks imposing serious costs. It gives parties resisting arbitration a constant incentive to seek out a judicial forum and, in so doing, a judicial

---

1. *See*, for example, s. 1032(2) of the German Civil Procedure Code which provides that "[p]rior to the constitution of the arbitral tribunal, an application may be made to the court to determine whether or not arbitration is admissible."

determination that arbitration should not go forward. This could dangerously compromise some of arbitration's most essential rationales: speed, economy and avoidance of the procedural formalities associated with national court litigation.

[B] A "Hands-Off" Role for Courts at the Threshold

At the other extreme lie jurisdictions that insist on a complete absence of judicial involvement prior to, or during the pendency of, the arbitral proceeding. Under this view, the courts have no, or an exceedingly small, role to play in determining whether an arbitration agreement is worthy of enforcement. Should a party resort to court for a finding that an agreement to arbitrate should not, for one reason or another, be enforced, it will be told that decisions of that sort are reserved to the arbitral tribunal, at least until after the proceedings are over and an award has been rendered. The tribunal enjoys *Kompetenz-Kompetenz* in all its positive dimensions and in all its negative dimensions as well.[2]

It is difficult, though not impossible, for a State that is party to the New York Convention to deny national courts any role whatsoever in examining the enforceability of an arbitration agreement prior to arbitration, if asked to do so. As noted, Article II allows a court to find an arbitration agreement to be "null and void, inoperative, or incapable of being performed." This formula presupposes the possibility of at least some measure of inquiry into the arbitration agreement or its enforceability. Even more generally, it would not be logical for a court to refer parties to arbitration pursuant to an agreement to arbitrate without first finding some reason to suppose that the agreement proffered to it constitutes an arbitration agreement and that the party proffering it is a party to it.

The principal argument in favor of a "hands-off approach" is that it is essential to the efficacy of arbitration as a dispute resolution mechanism, due to the fact that parties resisting arbitration may go to great lengths to delay and possibly derail the arbitration. Eliminating virtually any judicial role at the threshold undoubtedly expedites the arbitral process.

Of course, the fact that a legal system bars courts from impeding enforcement of an agreement to arbitrate does not mean that the arbitral proceedings and arbitral award necessarily escape judicial review entirely. A legal system may confer both positive and negative *Kompetenz-Kompetenz* on an arbitral tribunal prior to arbitration, and still reserve to national courts broad authority, after the fact, to annul or deny enforcement of the resulting award.[3] The net effect of a regime that disallows pre-arbitration review of the arbitration agreement, but allows post-award review of it, is to ensure that agreements to arbitrate will virtually always be enforced even though the awards that result from the arbitral proceedings that follow will be subject to

---

2. *See* Gaillard & Banifatemi, *Negative Effect of Competence-Competence: The Rule of Priority in Favor of the Arbitrators*, in Gaillard & di Pietro (eds.), Enforcement of Arbitration Agreements and International Arbitral Awards: The New York Convention in Practice 257 (2008).
3. This is the French approach. *See*, e.g., Judgment of Oct. 6, 2010, Fondation Joseph Abela Family, 2010 Rev. Arb. 969 (French Cour de Cassation).

searching judicial review. Such a system may be regarded as "pro-arbitration," but it is certainly not highly "pro-award."

This demonstrates that, despite its emphasis on efficiency, a "hands-off" policy is not in all circumstances efficient. Clearly, a court may annul or deny enforcement of an award, after years have gone into an arbitral proceeding, on the basis of a ground (such as the invalidity of the arbitration agreement) that a court could have entertained at the threshold; had a court upheld the challenge at that stage, the resources devoted to the arbitration would have been spared.

[C]   Intermediate Positions on the Threshold Judicial Role

Legal systems at the extreme ends of the spectrum I have described prescribe for courts a highly well-defined threshold role. In both cases, parties to agreements to arbitrate enjoy the advantage of knowing well in advance that courts, as the case may be, have an exceptionally robust or barely any role to play before an arbitration has gotten underway. Both systems present manifest predictability advantages.

But it is possible for courts to adopt an intermediate position, that is to say, a position that aims at maintaining arbitration's efficacy without completely denying courts a policing role at the threshold of arbitration.

There are broadly four intermediate approaches that courts might adopt with this purpose in mind, and they are actually quite different, the one from the others. As will be seen, the ease and readiness with which agreements to arbitrate are given effect by the courts of a jurisdiction may depend on where between the ends of the spectrum I have described they happen to fall.

[1]   *Default Rule and Party Autonomy*

A first intermediate approach consists of positing the simple proposition that either of the extreme positions I have described entail "default rules" only. Under this view, the law prescribes a particular role, or non-role, for national courts at the threshold of arbitration, but recognize the parties' contractual freedom to vary that presumption.[4] An intermediate position of this sort is accordingly achieved not by finding a particular intermediate place on the spectrum, but by recognizing party autonomy to determine where that intermediate place will be.

This approach seeks to achieve predictability, in the form of a default rule, tempered by a showing of substantial respect for party autonomy. I identify this as a showing of substantial respect for party autonomy because one might well posit that the role of national courts at the threshold of arbitration is a matter of public policy that is not susceptible of modification by agreement between the parties. Under that view, parties may agree to arbitrate, as well as design the procedural contours of their

---

4. See *LG Caltex Gas Co. v. China Nat'l Petroleum Co.*, [2001] EWCA Civ. 788 (Eng. Ct. App.) (permitting parties by contract to vest in tribunals final decision-making over the question of arbitral jurisdiction); Judgment of May 26, 1988, 1988 NJW-RR 1526, 1527 (German Supreme Ct.) (same).

arbitration, but they may not determine themselves the proper role of courts in deciding whether an arbitration agreement will or will not be given effect.[5] Any intermediate approach that posits a default rule, but welcomes contractual departures from it, essentially rejects that view.

Recognizing party autonomy to confer authority on courts to determine the enforceability of arbitration agreements at the outset, when they would ordinarily lack that authority, or to deprive courts of authority to determine the enforceability of arbitration agreements at the outset, when they ordinarily enjoy plenary authority to do so, means that the position that a State has taken on that issue is not an unalterable one. But the fact remains that the State has staked out an extreme default position, and that the parties bear the onus of altering it, possibly by nothing less than clear and unmistakable evidence. It is questionable how often parties have this issue in mind at the time they insert an arbitration clause into the main contract and therefore how likely they are to exercise the party autonomy that they in principle enjoy.

[2] Heightening the Burden of Proof for Resisting Arbitration

A second intermediate approach is to permit courts to address challenges to the enforcement of an arbitration agreement at the outset, but to place a very substantial burden on the party resisting arbitration to demonstrate that the agreement should not be enforced. This could be achieved by announcing a presumption in favor of enforcement, but allowing that presumption to be overcome, but only with difficulty. The challenge for jurisdictions of this sort is to articulate a well-understood standard of proof for defeating enforcement of an agreement to arbitrate, so as to maintain at least some semblance of predictability, at least as to how the courts will go about exercising this threshold authority.

As is well known, French law allows a threshold judicial inquiry, but gives that inquiry an exceptionally narrow scope. Under French law, a court may, in principle, entertain a claim that an arbitration agreement is invalid or inapplicable, but in order for the challenger to prevail the invalidity or inapplicability of the agreement must be shown to be "manifest."[6] It is widely conceded that, in the face of so high a standard of proof, arbitration agreements are scarcely ever denied enforcement in France. As a result, parties are strongly disincentivized to seek denial of enforcement in the first place. If the barrier to getting judicial relief from a court is high enough, jurisdiction to determine arbitral authority for all practical purposes rests in the first instance exclusively with the arbitral tribunal itself.

Not all jurisdictions adopting an intermediate approach of this sort are as restrictive as the French. Thus, when Swiss courts examine an arbitration agreement prior to arbitration, they do so on what is considered to be a prima facie basis only.[7]

---

5. This is essentially the position taken by the U.S. Supreme Court on the question whether parties may by contract alter the annulment standards laid down in the Federal Arbitration Act. Hall Street Associates, L. L. C. v. Mattel, Inc., 552 U.S. 576 (2008).
6. See Decree no. 2011-48 of Jan. 13, 2011.
7. See, e.g., Judgment of Aug. 6, 2012, DFT 4A_119/2012, para. 3.2 (Swiss Fed. Trib.).

Presumably, even if it is not manifestly invalid or inapplicable, within the meaning of French law, it may still fail a test that requires a prima facie showing of enforceability.

The rationale in favor of an intermediate approach described in this section is that courts have a valuable function to perform in policing arbitration agreements prior to enforcing them, but that that function must operate within important limitations, lest agreements to arbitrate may be too easily frustrated and arbitration be deprived of its advantages.

This intermediate approach has considerable appeal. Placing the burden of avoiding an arbitration agreement on the party seeking to avoid it, and making that burden a serious one, is a way for a State to adopt a basically pro-arbitration stance, but one that is less than categorical. The courts of that State must of course establish a standard that captures this particular calibration, and then take care to employ it in a consistent and reasonably predictable fashion. That is not an especially easy task, but it is essential to this—as to any—intermediate approach.

[3]   Immediate Court Review of Arbitral Rulings on Jurisdiction

A third intermediate approach entails a very specific mechanism whereby an arbitral tribunal enjoys an exclusive first opportunity to determine the enforceability of an agreement to arbitrate, but its determination is subject to immediate "interlocutory" judicial review, i.e., review within a relatively short limitations period, resulting in a binding judicial determination of the matter. This approach is exemplified by the UNCITRAL Model Law.[8]

The appeal of this mechanism is clear. It gives only positive and not negative effect to the *Kompetenz-Kompetenz* principle in the first instance, but at the same time postpones judicial involvement until after the tribunal has had the opportunity to make its own determination of the matter. Such a mechanism presupposes a bifurcation of proceedings, in that the tribunal addresses the jurisdictional issue at the outset and renders a decision on that particular matter independent from any inquiry into the merits. The result is a partial award that is then itself judicially challengeable.

If the limitations period is a short one and the court acts promptly, this mechanism should not raise serious problems of delay. More importantly, it avoids the serious problem, raised by the "hands-off" approach, of postponing any judicial ruling on a challenge to the arbitration agreement until after the possibly lengthy arbitral proceedings have concluded and an award has emerged, with the attendant waste of resources if the award is annulled or widely denied enforcement.

The challenge is to determine the standard of review to be exercised by the courts on the occasion of this "interlocutory" review. Even UNCITRAL Model Law States differ in regard to the standard, with some taking the position that the court conducts

---

8. Article 16(1) of the UNCITRAL Model Law provides that "[t]he arbitral tribunal may rule on its own jurisdiction, including any objections with respect to the existence or validity of the arbitration agreement." However, Art. 16(3) provides that "any party may request, within thirty days after having received notice of that ruling, judicial review of the arbitrators' jurisdictional decision."

full, i.e., *de novo*, review[9] and others permitting a prima facie review only.[10] States may also make the standard of review vary according to the particular challenge at hand, for example, by showing greater deference to tribunals on the question of the scope of the arbitration agreement than on the agreement's existence or validity.[11]

This naturally brings us to a fourth intermediate approach.

[4] Distinguishing Among Challenges to the Arbitration Agreement

Still another intermediate approach consists of distinguishing among all possible objections to enforcement of an arbitration agreement, according to their nature, and determining that some are worthy of judicial control prior to arbitration, while others are not. For jurisdictions of this sort, the challenge lies precisely in making this delineation among challenges to the arbitration agreement and justifying why some challenges warrant threshold judicial review, if sought by a party resisting arbitration, while others do not.

The rationale in favor of this approach is that the strength of the case for allowing pre-arbitration review of an agreement to arbitrate varies with the objection that the party resisting arbitration happens to advance—that is to say, in effect, that some objections are more compelling than others. The former justify early judicial involvement, if sought, while the latter do not.

Legal systems that choose to treat different challenges to the arbitration differently, in so far as early judicial involvement is concerned, must establish criteria for making such a distinction. Among legal systems, support has grown for the distinction raised earlier between "jurisdictional" and "admissibility" issues.[12]

As noted, a jurisdictional issue is one on which the legal authority of an arbitral tribunal depends. Because arbitration is founded on party autonomy, the notion of legal authority in this context is intimately connected with the notion of party consent. For that reason, jurisdictional issues are widely viewed as *contractual* in nature. They include the following: Did the parties agree to arbitrate? Is the arbitration agreement entered into by the parties is valid? Does the dispute fall within the scope of the arbitration agreement to which the parties subscribed? Should a party that did not sign the arbitration agreement nevertheless be treated as contractually bound by it, so that it may be either a claimant or respondent in an arbitral proceeding based on that agreement?

---

9. *See* Gary B. Born, International Commercial Arbitration 1086 (2d ed. 2014), citing judicial decisions in, among other jurisdictions, Australia, New Zealand, England, Austria and Spain.
10. *See* Born, *supra* n. 9, at 1088, citing judicial decisions in, among other jurisdictions, Canada, India and Hong Kong. *See also* Bachand, *Does Article 8 of the Model Law Call for Full or Prima Facie Review of the Arbitral Tribunal's Jurisdiction?*, 22 Arb. Int'l 463 (2006).
11. *See*, e.g., *Rio Algom Ltd. v. Sammi Steel Co., Ltd.*, XVIII Y.B. Comm. Arb. 166 (Ontario Super. Ct. 1991).
12. *See* generally Jan Paulsson, *Jurisdiction and Admissibility*, in Global Reflections on International Law, Commerce and Dispute Resolution (*Liber amicorum* in honour of Robert Briner, ICC Publication 693 (November 2005).

While arbitral jurisdiction in international arbitration presupposes a firm contractual basis, the contract in question must in turn also be a *legal* one. Thus, even if parties choose to submit a category of disputes to arbitration, the law, for one reason or another, may not allow them to do so. Such disputes are considered to be "non-arbitrable." Similarly, even if the law as such does not prohibit arbitration of a given category of disputes, enforcement of a particular arbitration agreement may be thought offensive to public policy of the relevant jurisdiction. For these reasons, jurisdictional issues—i.e., issues of arbitral authority—have both a contractual and a legal dimension.

Unlike a jurisdictional challenge, an admissibility challenge questions not the authority of an arbitral tribunal to hear and decide a case, but rather whether a circumstance has arisen (or failed to arise) with the result that the tribunal should not exercise that authority with respect to the dispute at hand. Some examples of admissibility are always, or nearly always, recognized as such. If a statute of limitations on the underlying claim has elapsed, the claim should not in principle be entertained. If a party is found to have waived the right it now seeks to arbitrate, it is the exercise of arbitral authority that is challenged, not the authority itself. Much the same may be said about the failure of a party to satisfy certain preconditions to arbitration set out in the arbitration agreement itself, such as mediation or litigation for a period of time in national court. Arguably, res judicata is likewise an admissibility objection, since it raises a question about whether a claim should be heard, not about whether the arbitral tribunal has authority to entertain the claim.

Although in the U.S., the Federal Arbitration Act is silent on the matter, the Supreme Court has largely supported the notion that parties are presumptively entitled to access to courts on a pre-arbitration basis in order to raise jurisdictional challenges (such as the invalidity of the arbitration agreement), but not admissibility challenges (such as the failure of a party to satisfy preconditions to arbitration).[13]

The distinction between jurisdiction and admissibility is not without its critics, however. For example, one might say that if the underlying contract bars arbitration of a claim without a certain precondition having been satisfied, the tribunal lacks authority to conduct that arbitration unless and until the precondition has been satisfied. A similar argument may be leveled at the other objections commonly viewed as having an admissibility rather than a jurisdictional character. Second, as a practical matter, the immediate effect of a finding of inadmissibility is not all that different from a finding of lack of arbitral jurisdiction. In either case, the arbitration will not go forward.

Notwithstanding these critiques, there may be value in maintaining the jurisdiction/admissibility distinction for purposes of delineating those objections that courts will entertain if asked to do so prior to arbitration from those objections they will

---

13. *See*, e.g., *Howsam v. Dean Witter Reynolds, Inc.*, 537 U.S. 79 (2002). The U.S. Supreme Court does not employ the dichotomy between "jurisdictional" and "admissibility" issues, referring instead to issues of "substantive arbitrability" and "procedural arbitrability." *See* generally, Bermann, *The "Gateway" Problem in International Commercial Arbitration*, 37 Yale J. Int'l L. 1 (2012).

decline to entertain. In the first place, jurisdictional challenges, as noted, raise central issues of consent and legality. Did the claimant and respondent enter into an arbitration agreement (or may a non-signatory, by virtue of the applicable law, be legally treated as having done so)? Is the agreement to arbitrate, though entered into by the proper parties, invalid under the applicable law—in which case the agreement cannot legally support a finding of consent? Also, though the parties may have consented to arbitrate, they did not consent to arbitrate every imaginable dispute arising between them; they consented to arbitrate only those disputes encompassed by the particular agreement being invoked. If one accepts that consent lies centrally at the legitimacy of arbitration, then courts properly examine the reality of that consent, if it is plausibly called into question. Courts also properly ask whether consent, even if given, is legally effective, or whether principle of non-arbitrability or public policy gets in the way.

There is good reason why a party raising a jurisdictional objection to arbitration, as described here, should be entitled to have an objection of that sort addressed by an entity—a court—that would enjoy adjudicatory authority over the underlying claim if consent to arbitrate had never been given.

By contrast, a party may have waited too long to initiate arbitration or may have waived its right to arbitrate, or the claim may already have been adjudicated in a binding fashion and thus subject to res judicata, but in none of these situations is there ordinarily any doubt that an agreement to arbitrate a covered dispute was validly made. The only admissibility issue that could justifiably be viewed as jurisdictional in nature is failure to satisfy preconditions to arbitration. But in order to reach that result, a court would need to find that satisfaction of the preconditions is an element of the "acceptance" of the agreement to arbitrate, such that the offer cannot be accepted until that condition is fulfilled, rather than a mere procedural feature of the arbitral process.[14]

§5.04 CONCLUSION

The role that national courts play at the threshold of arbitration is anything but standard across jurisdictions. Jurisdictions have a wide range of choice. To the extent that they make a deliberate choice, they have at their disposal numerous considerations to take into account, the most important of which are arbitration's efficacy (in terms of facilitating arbitration's achievement of its core objectives) and its legitimacy (in terms of ensuring the adequacy of party consent on which arbitration depends). There is more than one way in which each of these twin objectives may be promoted and, no less important, more than one way to strike the balance between them.

Positions at the polar ends of the spectrum of judicial involvement are not especially attractive. A system that permits plenary judicial inquiries into all aspects of the enforceability of arbitration agreements prior to arbitration risks inviting costs, delays and judicial involvement in a very big way, contrary to arbitration's basic

---

14. The U.S. Supreme Court has declined, even in a treaty-based investment claim, to consider failure to meet preconditions to arbitrate as failure to effect acceptance of an offer to arbitrate. *BG Group PLC v. Republic of Argentina*, 572 U.S. __ (Mar. 5, 2014).

Chapter 5: The Role of National Courts at the Threshold of Arbitration   §5.04

premises. On the other hand, a system that treats access to a court for these purposes as wholly off-limits, irrespective of the seriousness of the challenge, risks exacting too great a price in terms of arbitral legitimacy. Efficacy may be achievable through less drastic means.

Of the four intermediate solutions that may be imagined, there are three, it seems to me, that commend themselves to policymakers, whether legislative or judicial.

A first such alternative is to permit judicial inquiry over a broad range of challenges, but at the same time place on the party making the challenge a substantial burden of proof. The task then is to identify the showing that the party resisting arbitration must make in order to succeed. This task is not insuperable. A usual means is to posit that arbitration agreements are to be enforced if there is any prima facie basis for enforcing them.

A second attractive solution is to give arbitral tribunals exclusive authority to make an initial determination of the enforceability of the arbitration agreement, but to subject the tribunal's determination in that regard to immediate interlocutory judicial review. Here, too, the system must define the courts' standard of review of the arbitral determination. And here too, the task is not insuperable.

A third, albeit more complex, solution is to draw a distinction among challenges to the enforceability of arbitration agreements between those that a court will entertain prior to arbitration if asked to do so and those that it will decline to entertain even if asked to do so. The viability of this alternative depends on the ability of a legal system to draw that line on a clear and principled basis. The distinction between jurisdictional and admissibility issues is a highly useful point of departure in this endeavor.

It should be noted in conclusion that these intermediate solutions are not mutually exclusive. The best possible solution may lie in a combination, such as one that adopts a system of interlocutory judicial review of a tribunal's initial jurisdictional determination (as in the second solution above), while also confining the court's involvement to issues of jurisdiction rather than admissibility (as in the third solution above). That said, there is no compelling reason why a legal system should prefer any one of these intermediate solutions over the others. Whatever solution or combination of intermediate solutions among these is adopted will strike a more appropriate balance between competing values than the solutions at either end of the spectrum can possibly achieve.

CHAPTER 6
Pierre Karrer

David J. Branson

There is always a beginning. I was there at Pierre Karrer's beginning as an international arbitrator in 1984. It was in Zurich, in the offices of his firm at the time, Pestalozzi, Lachenal Patry.

Charles Brower was our lead counsel and together we appeared in the firm's conference room where the tribunal was ready to receive us. Respondent's lead counsel was the very distinguished Paris lawyer, Jean Francois Prat. Pierre was the chair of this ICC arbitration which had been brought by an American company in the oil industry against a mid-east national oil company. Pierre's co-arbitrators were distinguished Professors, one American and the other from the country of the respondent.

Today, we would say those counsel and the members of the tribunal were well-known professional arbitration counsel and international arbitrators. But 1984 was an earlier, different time. No one was well known then—the field was new—we were all new.

In 1980, Charles Brower and I had been counsel to the Republic of Indonesia, in the International Centre for Settlement of Investment Disputes (ICSID) claim brought by Amco Asia. Though ICSID was established in 1965, Amco Asia was only the 10th claim registered with ICSID over that first twenty years. The London Court of International Arbitration's (LCIA's) international brand was not launched until 1985, when the LCIA Court became independent under the direction of Sir Michael Kerr. The first LCIA weekend meeting was held at the Selsdon Park Hotel in East Grinstead, better known as the locale for romantic weekends in Alan Ayckbourn's Norman Conquests. Perhaps twenty-five lawyers and arbitrators attended at the first Selsdon's weekend. Today, hundreds que for a place at the two Tylney Hall revivals. The American Arbitration Association reported it administered 30,000 arbitrations in 1980, but only 130 were international cases. The The International Court of Arbitration of the International Chamber of Commerce (ICC) reported 227 cases were filed in 1981.

Today, the ICC records over 800 cases per year. Hong Kong International Arbitration Centre (HKIAC) and Singapore International Arbitration Centre (SIAC) did not exist. Today those institutions report over 500 new arbitration filings per year.

The point is this—in 1980, there were 300 international arbitration cases filed per year, mostly in Europe. The field of arbitrators, generally appointed by the ICC, was small. Few were known to American practitioners. Pierre was just entering that arbitration world.

Over time, as the industry has grown, more and more lawyers have left their firms to open a practice as an independent arbitrator. Judges leave the bench. There was a time when an English law lord saw the appointment as one for life—today they leave the House of Lords to sit as arbitrators. But they all know, or soon learn, they enter a Darwinian world. Only the best survive over the years. Pierre Karrer has survived in that Darwinian world for forty years to become one of the best-known international arbitrators because he is one of the best international arbitrators.

International arbitrators cannot survive as repeat appointees without the blessings of those counsel and parties whose arbitrations they have chaired. Those blessings are not freely given—after all, in every case in which an arbitrator sits, 50% of those involved as a party or a counsel for a party lose the case. They are not always thrilled. Of course institutional approval is a necessity. The ICC Secretariat and Court of Arbitration review all awards, carefully. Those professionals are vigilant to make sure the arbitrator has written an award which will be enforceable. An arbitrator cannot survive in business in Europe without an ICC stamp of approval, and to maintain that approval for forty years is high praise from the most experienced institutional overseers in the world.

His talent became apparent to us when Charles Brower and I arrived at the offices of Pestalozzi in 1984.

We learned straight away that the Chair was in charge. Pierre Karrer has a presence that all leaders have—calm competence while imposing control. Leadership is given to some and it is apparent quickly. Without it, an arbitrator cannot survive in practice for long. The leadership displayed by arbitrators has to be of the velvet style. Counsel are often themselves used to leading and do not easily take to contradiction or confrontation. An arbitrator who appears to lead by arrogance or force will offend. Style matters. Pierre has the right style of leadership.

In 1999, Pierre published an article for the IFCAI Conference in New York. He titled it: "The Arbitrator's Role as Manager of the Process." It is a vital insight into his philosophy of the role of an arbitrator—a "manager of a process". I would suspect that no Judge sees her role in a courtroom in that light. Judges wield the power of the State, and thus, ultimately, the power to hold counsel or a party in contempt.

As Pierre recognized, arbitrators serve only with the consent of the parties. To have a successful arbitration, where each party and its counsel believes they were fairly heard and fairly judged, they must believe the arbitrator "listened" to them and allowed them to participate in setting the procedure and the rules for the proceeding. An arbitrator must fully embrace "party autonomy".

Pierre wrote that "all participants can contribute" in setting the procedure. He recognized the essential point that the arbitral process is one where "you have to work with people, quite different people." That requires empathy, sensitivity to the effect your words and decisions have on others. But that did not detract from the main point of his article—the process needs a "manager", and that person, he said, is the "presiding arbitrator, the natural project manager."

It sounds so simple, but Pierre had fifteen years' experience when he wrote this article. That experience prompted him to add: "You have to work with people. Very difficult people, sometimes." But it is wisdom to recognize that the arbitral process will often require the arbitrator to manage "very difficult people." To do so successfully for forty years is a rare talent indeed.

As I noted above, an international arbitrator who stays in the field for long, must have been exposed to ICC observation. Pierre said this in 1999: "With the officers of the institution the interaction should be close and trusting. They are professionals with a wide experience." The operative word is "trusting". That says a lot about Pierre's style in working with people—you should know how to trust them, not a quality all people possess.

He writes of the significant and important discussion on treating the parties "equally". A great arbitrator must demonstrate nuance in establishing a balance for the arbitration process. Pierre speaks to this by recognizing that a claimant will say a case is "straightforward", while a respondent will say it is "complex". Does equality demand each are allowed the same time on the clock? Pierre says holding time to a clock is better suited to sporting events. In a particularly astute passage, he says: "it is not always by treating people the same that you will treat them equally."

Pierre's discussion of the ideal interaction between the tribunal and the party representatives shows that he believes in "feedback", as he calls it, so that the parties will see that the Tribunal is listening to them. Without feedback, the representatives may belabor a point or go on to quickly. The manager needs to focus the flow of the presentation.

Pierre knew that the relationship with the co-arbitrators had to be managed like the other parts of the procedure. Pierre wrote that it was best for a tribunal to work together to write the award, "with drafting sessions preferably at the presiding arbitrator's office with the entire file available on the spot." This was at a time when a tribunal could not email their messages to each other (Fed Ex was incorporated in 1997; Google was incorporated in 1998, and thus in 1984, communication between our arbitral tribunal had to be in person, by fax or by phone.) In this case, one arbitrator filed a dissenting opinion. In reviewing the January 5, 1985 award in the case, I saw that the Tribunal noted there had been eight days of deliberation. One wonders if the eight days was spent at Pestalozzi, and was extended by the impending dissent. Pierre said that in dealing with a disappointed party-appointed arbitrator, it was important to manage that process as well so that the dissent will not hold up delivery of the award, by informing them when "the decision will be taken."

The case itself was complex because of a major disputed issue between the parties—alleged criminal behavior in the host country. The contract was for the operation of oil equipment for four years in a remote area. When the equipment had been imported into the host country, customs forms were completed listing every piece of equipment, by description and weight. Over the course of operations, equipment is used up or lost. Thus over four years, there was continuous replacement of equipment parts. At the conclusion of the contract, the American company had to pack the assorted equipment for export. The company used its water tanks as storage vessels in which to pack the equipment. When one water tank was being filled, a welder was sealing the door in place when the welding started a fire.

The local fire department responded and reported the fire up the chain of command. The tanks were all sealed and shipped to the port. Then Customs intervened. Alerted by the report from the fire brigade that parts were stored inside the water tanks, Customs opened them at the port and decreed the company was attempting to smuggle parts that it had not declared on custom's import forms. Customs froze the export process while a criminal proceeding was initiated in the criminal court. The American company was duly "condemned" and the equipment sat in the port for a year.

One of the main issues in the contract arbitration was whether the customer had agreed to pay the company per diem delay charges for each day the equipment was kept in port, or as the customer argued, the results of the criminal proceeding barred recovery under the contract.

In dealing with that issue, Pierre wrote a very modern, strong, pro-arbitration award.

The customer argued that the contract was expressly governed by the law of the host country. Under that law, criminal cases "take precedence over civil cases." The customer argued that the arbitral tribunal was therefore required to apply the decision of the criminal court which had condemned the American company "without reviewing in any way the judgment as to procedure or merits."

The Tribunal held that the Tribunal was not bound by the judgment of the criminal court. The majority explained: "The legal reasoning challenges the freedom of international arbitration in a new and dangerous manner....The Tribunal is of the opinion that whatever the law applicable to the procedure or the merits, whatever the law of the place of the arbitration, whether this law provides that criminal cases take precedence over civil cases or not, in an international arbitration no-one can take precedence over the arbitrators. The freedom of international arbitration requires it in an absolute manner."

But to be sure, the Tribunal noted there were others who believed the "freedom is not absolute." This was time of great debate about "delocalization" in the law of arbitration. The decades old territorial view of F. A. Mann was under attack by many international arbitration scholars and practitioners, such as Berthold Goldman, who wrote international arbitration was an "autonomous non-national system". Jan Paulsson had published "Arbitration Unbound" in 1981.

Pierre's majority then covered the other possibilities. The parties had agreed in the Terms of Reference that the ICC Rules and the Zurich Civil Code, the ZPO, applied to questions of procedure. It noted that the ICC rules guarantee the tribunal freedom to decide and the ZPO did not require application of a foreign criminal court judgment. In closing on this point, the Tribunal said: "the parties did not wish to force the arbitral tribunal to behave in all circumstances as a domestic court [of the host country]."

This was a "modern view" in 1984. It has stood the test of time.

Chapter 6: Pierre Karrer

There is one other important fact I learned at the hearing in Zurich in 1984. One of the witnesses was describing the need to protect metal equipment against the possibility of rust. This was apparently the explanation for why the welding caused a fire—oil or grease had been applied to the metal parts being stored. When the witness was being crossed examined on this point, Pierre interjected: "I understand this; all Swiss men keep rifles as part of our military duty and unless you oil your rifle, it will rust." Local knowledge is important!

The only more important report I can make about Pierre Karrer is that my wife and I have had the pleasure of listening to An Ming's music and enjoying Peking Duck with both in Hong Kong.

My best regards to one of the best—Happy Birthday Pierre.

CHAPTER 7
Is Efficiency an Arbitrator's Duty or Simply a Character Trait?

*Nadia Darwazeh**

The very first time I argued a case, it was before an ICC tribunal chaired by Pierre Karrer. The hearing was being held in Kathmandu, Nepal, which even by international arbitration standards is an extraordinary destination. Until only a few days before the hearing, we were unsure whether it would even go ahead because of active Maoist insurgence. However, Pierre, who is always focused on getting the job done and fearless as he is, confirmed that the hearing would take place as scheduled.

The morning of the first day of the hearing, the other guests at the hotel were ready to start their day of trekking and sightseeing. But instead of going to visit the temples of Bhaktapur or taking a flight over Mount Everest, we went into the conference room of the hotel to argue the case. That was the first time I met Pierre in persona. True to his Swiss sense of timeliness, Pierre was already in the conference room, fully prepared and equipped with a clock, pencil case and his ubiquitous stapler. He was ready to begin and exuded a sense of authority and experience, two key attributes for a good arbitrator.

It became clear very early on that Pierre has far more arbitrator attributes, one of them being that he is the embodiment of an efficient arbitrator. For instance, Pierre tailor-makes the proceedings for the arbitration and drives the proceedings forward without losing sight of the fact that it is the parties' process. What also makes Pierre an efficient arbitrator is that he does not hesitate to think "outside of the box" and to find pragmatic solutions to problems that arise. I remember, for instance, that a key witness in the case cancelled his attendance the very morning of the hearing by sending a fax

---

* Solicitor-Advocate (England & Wales) and Rechtsanwältin (Germany). Thanks are due to Mr. Adrien Leleu and Ms. Cécilia Miles, interns at Curtis, for their research assistance.

stating that he could not travel for health reasons. A debate ensued between counsel as to whether his witness statement should be disregarded or whether the hearing should be postponed. At this point, Pierre stepped in and suggested, as a first step, that I cross-examine the witness by telephone. While today it is more common to cross-examine witnesses remotely, fifteen years ago in 2001 a cross-examination by telephone was highly unusual. After the cross-examination, it became apparent that a face-to-face one would not be necessary and we were able to conclude the hearing the following day. This is one example among many that illustrates Pierre's willingness to adopt pragmatic and sometimes unorthodox solutions to ensure an efficient process.

So what makes an arbitrator efficient: is it mainly that he or she conducts the arbitration in a speedy manner or is it more than that? Does an international arbitrator actually have a duty of efficiency or is efficiency merely a character trait?

§7.01 DO ARBITRATORS HAVE A DUTY OF EFFICIENCY IN ARBITRATION?

When presenting the benefits of arbitration, the argument is often made that arbitration is an efficient process. But what exactly do we mean by "efficiency"?

Efficiency has its origin in the Latin term *"efficientia,"* which means "power to accomplish something." It reflects the idea of achieving a goal ("accomplish") by using energy ("power").

Today, efficiency is defined as the *"ability to do something or produce something without wasting materials, time, or energy"*[1] and as *"the good use of time and energy in a way that does not waste any."*[2] In the field of mechanics, efficiency is defined as the *"ratio of the useful work performed by a machine or in a process to the total energy expended or heat taken in."*[3]

If these definitions are applied in the context of arbitration, an efficient arbitrator could be defined as an arbitrator rendering a good award without wasting time or money. So do arbitrators have a duty of efficiency in international arbitration?

As early as 1938, the model law proposal prepared by UNIDROIT provided that if an arbitrator failed to act diligently, his or her appointment could be revoked by the parties.[4] Some authors have considered that an arbitrator's duty of efficiency, in the absence of express legal provisions, is at most a moral obligation.[5] Others have considered that the duty of efficiency is inherent to the arbitrator's mission with the disputing parties.[6] Professor Clay has gone so

---

1. The Merriam-Webster Dictionary, http://www.merriam-webster.com/dictionary/efficiency.
2. Cambridge dictionary, http://dictionary.cambridge.org/fr/dictionnaire/anglais/efficiency.
3. Oxford dictionary, http://www.oxforddictionaries.com/fr/definition/anglais/efficiency.
4. UNIDROIT Draft Uniform Law on Arbitration of 1938, Art. 14.
5. Jennifer Kirby, *Efficiency in International Arbitration: Whose Duty Is It?*, 32(6) JOURNAL OF INTERNATIONAL ARBITRATION 689 (Kluwer Law International 2015).
6. Christophe Seraglini and Jérôme Ortscheidt, DROIT DE L'ARBITRAGE INTERNE ET INTERNATIONAL (Lextenso 2013), at 283–284.

Chapter 7: Is Efficiency an Arbitrator's Duty or Simply a Character Trait?   §7.01

far as to consider the duty of efficiency to be part of a set of procedural *lex mercatoria*.[7]

Whether there is an inherent duty of efficiency or not, in practice, arbitrators will typically be bound by an obligation of efficiency because of the rules that are applicable to the arbitration.

For one, the law of the seat of arbitration (*lex arbitri*) may specify that the arbitrator should conduct the proceedings efficiently. The French Arbitration Law provides for instance for a duty of efficiency. It states in relevant part that: "*the arbitrators shall act with celerity and loyalty in the conduct of the proceedings.*"[8] Section 33(1)(b) of the English Arbitration Act 1996 also refers to such an express duty when it specifies that the arbitral tribunal shall "*adopt procedures suitable to the circumstances of the particular case, avoiding unnecessary delay or expense, so as to provide a fair means for the resolution of the matters falling to be determined.*"[9] However, it is more generally the case that the *lex arbitri* does not impose such a duty of efficiency on the arbitrator.

Indeed, most other arbitration laws, including the Model Law, are silent on the issue.

An arbitrator's duty of efficiency is more often entrenched in the institutional rules selected by the parties. Indeed, the main institutional rules bestow such an obligation on arbitral tribunals. For example Article 22(1) of the ICC Rules provides that:

> The arbitral tribunal and the parties shall make every effort to conduct the arbitration in an expeditious and cost-effective manner, having regard to the complexity and value of the dispute.

By the same token, Article 14(4) of the LCIA Rules specifies that:

> Under the Arbitration Agreement, the Arbitral Tribunal's general duties at all times during the arbitration shall include: a duty to adopt procedures suitable to the circumstances of the arbitration, avoiding unnecessary delay and expense, so as to provide a fair, efficient and expeditious means for the final resolution of the parties' dispute.

Article 17 of the UNCITRAL Rules also imposes a duty of efficiency on arbitrators:

> The arbitral tribunal, in exercising its discretion, shall conduct the proceedings so as to avoid unnecessary delay and expense and to provide a fair and efficient process for resolving the parties' dispute.

---

7. Thomas Clay, L'ARBITRE (Dalloz 2001), at 614.
8. French Arbitration Law, Art. 1464.
9. *See also* Swedish Arbitration Act, s. 21 ("*The arbitrators shall handle the dispute in an impartial, practical, and speedy manner.*"); Indian Arbitration Act, Preamble ("*Whereas the said Model Law and Rules make significant contribution to the establishment of a unified legal framework for the fair and efficient settlement of disputes arising in international commercial relations [...]*").

59

Similarly, Article 19(1) of the SIAC Rules states that:

> The Tribunal shall conduct the arbitration in such manner as it considers appropriate, after consulting with the parties, to ensure the fair, expeditious, economical and final resolution of the dispute.[10]

In addition, an arbitrator's duty of efficiency is also mentioned in several ethics guidelines for arbitrators, which have persuasive value.[11]

In many if not most cases, an arbitrator will therefore have a duty to conduct the arbitration efficiently and it is fair to say that such a duty is also in line with the parties' expectations.

§7.02 WHAT DOES IT TAKE FOR AN ARBITRATOR TO BE EFFICIENT?

Generally, efficiency is assimilated with the idea that arbitrators should act quickly in the arbitration.[12] Professor Clay considers that an arbitrator's duty of efficiency is to

---

10. *See also* Art. 13(1) of the HKIAC Rules ("[T]*he arbitral tribunal shall adopt suitable procedures for the conduct of the arbitration in order to avoid unnecessary delay or expense, having regard to the complexity of the issues and the amount in dispute* [...]") and Art. 13(5) of the HKIAC Rules ("*The arbitral tribunal and the parties shall do everything necessary to ensure the fair and efficient conduct of the arbitration.*"); Art. 19(2) of the SCC Rules ("*In all cases, the Arbitral Tribunal shall conduct the arbitration in an impartial, practical and expeditious manner, giving each party an equal and reasonable opportunity to present its case.*"); Art. 17(7) of the CRCICA Rules ("*The arbitral tribunal, in exercising its discretion, shall efficiently conduct the proceedings so as to avoid unnecessary delay and expenses that are likely to increase the costs of arbitration in an unjustified manner.*"); Art. 33.1 of the DIS Arbitration Rules ("*The arbitral tribunal shall conduct the proceedings expeditiously and shall render an award within a reasonable period of time.*").
11. Article 1 of the IBA Rules of Ethics for International Arbitrators 1987 states for example as a "*Fundamental Rule*" that: "*Arbitrators shall proceed diligently and efficiently to provide the parties with a just and effective resolution of their disputes...*". In the same way, Art. 8 of the Rules of Good Conduct for Proceedings organized by CEPANI provides that: "[b]*y accepting his appointment by CEPANI, the arbitrator undertakes to ensure that the Award is rendered as diligently as possible. This means, namely, that he shall request an extension of the time limit provided by the CEPANI Rules only if necessary or with the explicit agreement of the parties.*" See also ABA-AAA Code of Ethics for Arbitrators in Commercial Disputes, effective Mar. 1, 2004, Canon IV entitled "An arbitrator should conduct the proceedings fairly and diligently."
12. Bernard Hanotiau, *L'arbitre garant du respect des valeurs de l'arbitrage*, in GLOBAL REFLECTIONS ON INTERNATIONAL LAW, COMMERCE AND DISPUTE RESOLUTION, LIBER AMICORUM IN HONOUR OF ROBERT BRINER (ICC Publishing 2005), at 365 ("*The arbitrator shall ensure the expeditious conduct of the arbitral proceedings. From this standpoint, he must be prescriptive and proactive both with regards to his co-arbitrators and the parties: he shall make sure that reasonable but short deadlines prevail and are complied with, handle any of counsels' dilatory tactics, and try to deliver its procedural orders as well as the award in a short timeframe.*") ("*L'arbitre doit assurer un déroulement rapide de la procédure arbitrale. De ce point vue, il doit être directif et proactif, tant à l'égard de ses co-arbitres que des parties: veiller à faire prévaloir des délais certes acceptables mais courts, en assurer le respect, déjouer les manœuvres dilatoires des conseils, faire en sorte que ses ordonnances de procédure et sa sentence soient rendues dans les plus brefs délais.*"). *See also* Franz T. Schwarz and Christian W. Konrad, *The Vienna Rules: A Commentary on International Arbitration in Austria*, (Kluwer Law International 2009), p. 139 ("Justice delayed is justice denied, and the speed of arbitral proceedings has been termed one of arbitration's raisons d'être when compared to state court litigation.").

ensure that no more time than is necessary should be used for each stage of the proceedings.[13]

If time is surely an important factor to determine efficiency – it is by no means the only criteria that should be taken into consideration. As Pierre Karrer himself has pointed out:

> After all, if you want to be fast, you have to be efficient, and in order to be efficient, you have to do things well. Otherwise, haste makes waste.[14]

Indeed, in determining whether an arbitrator has lived up to his or her duty of efficiency, the quality of the proceedings and of the final award are equally key factors. If an arbitrator has conducted the proceedings quickly, but the award is ultimately unenforceable because of deficiencies that are a direct result of the *"haste,"*[15] then the arbitrator was not efficient and his or her *"haste* [indeed] *makes waste."*[16] While in recent years there has been attention focused on reducing time and costs in international arbitration – rightly so – it is important not to lose sight of the fact that the quality of the proceedings and of the award are at least of equal importance.[17]

In this context it is key to remember that the arbitration process is also about the parties' walking away from the proceedings feeling like they have been heard. If an arbitrator rushes through the arbitration, it can undermine the entire process and the parties' trust in the system. This does not mean that an arbitrator should agree to each and every request by a party for further submissions or concede each and every application. However, the arbitrator must ensure that the parties have had a reasonable opportunity to present their case.

In instances in which parties do not hesitate to obstruct the arbitration through what has become known as *"guerilla tactics,"* it can be particularly challenging for an arbitrator to be efficient. When confronted with such tactics, an arbitrator will have to pay particular attention to moving the proceedings forward and not wasting time. This will often require firm decisions by the arbitrators, whilst ensuring due process at the

---

13. Professor Clay provides the following definition of efficiency: "[t]*he arbitrator's duty to act with due diligence leads to the constant concern to prevent any stage of the arbitral proceedings from taking more time than necessary.*") (*"l'obligation de diligence de l'arbitre se traduit par le souci permanent de ne laisser à aucune étape de l'instance arbitrale plus de temps qu'il n'est nécessaire."*). Thomas Clay, L'ARBITRE (Dalloz 2001), at 615.
14. Pierre Karrer, *Why Speed is good for Arbitrators*, LIBER AMICORUM IN HONOUR OF MICHEL GAUDET (ICC Publishing 1999), at 135.
15. Indeed, a tribunal that is entirely focused on proceeding quickly with an arbitration may lose sight of the fundamental principals of due process and the parties' right to be heard.
16. Pierre Karrer, *Why Speed is good for Arbitrators*, LIBER AMICORUM IN HONOUR OF MICHEL GAUDET (ICC Publishing 1999), at 135; *see also* Frabricio Fortese, *Procedural Fairness and Efficiency in International Arbitration*, 3(1) GRONINGEN JOURNAL OF INTERNATIONAL LAW, at 116 (*"Efficiency is often assimilated with only cost and time efficiency, but the other side of the same coin is to gain the efficient proceedings without risking either the correct outcome of the due process."*).
17. As to the quality of the arbitration, *see* Jennifer Kirby, *Efficiency in International Arbitration: Whose Duty Is It?*, 32(6) JOURNAL OF INTERNATIONAL ARBITRATION (Kluwer Law International 2015), at 692 ("[M]*any parties would consider a quality arbitration to be one that results in an award that is both correct and enforceable. When an award is both correct and enforceable, this means that the arbitrator has managed to get to the right result while ensuring due process and otherwise avoiding any egregious procedural errors along the way."*)

same time. Bernardo Cremades gives the following perspective on an arbitrator's duty of efficiency in such cases:

> The arbitrators' duty to act with due diligence therefore requires taking a firm, intelligent and reasonable stand against any potential obstructionist tactics of the parties. The arbitrator has also the right and the duty to use all the means at his disposal in order to avoid the proceedings from being unnecessarily delayed or lengthened.[18]

The duty of efficiency is thus a balancing exercise between speed and getting it right:[19] it is not only about conducting the arbitration quickly (which often results in cost savings) – it is just as much about the quality of the service rendered.[20]

§7.03 WHAT ARE THE SANCTIONS IF AN ARBITRATOR BREACHES THE DUTY OF EFFICIENCY?

When arbitrators breach their duty of efficiency, they may be penalized in a number of ways. First and foremost, it is the arbitral institutions that are best placed to sanction such breach. The institution may decide, for instance, not to appoint such an arbitrator in future. Indeed, by virtue of the number of cases they handle, arbitral institutions have an unrivaled knowledge of who the efficient arbitrators are and who the inefficient ones are. The institutions can and should make use of that knowledge when appointing arbitrators. Indeed, during my time as Counsel at the ICC, there were several cases in which the ICC Court declined to confirm the nomination of an arbitrator based on its knowledge of previous egregious breaches of the efficiency duty of the arbitrator in question.

Once an arbitration is already ongoing, the institution may decide to replace an arbitrator, if the applicable rules foresee such a replacement procedure. Cases in which an arbitrator can be replaced include cases in which the arbitrator is very late in submitting an award for scrutiny, or once submitted, an award fails to meet quality

---

18. ("*Le devoir de diligence des arbitres exige donc une position ferme, intelligente et raisonnable face à l'éventuelle volonté obstructionniste des parties. L'arbitre a également le droit et le devoir d'utiliser tous les moyens à sa disposition pour éviter que la procédure soit retardée ou prolongée de façon non nécessaire.*") LIBER AMICORUM IN HONOUR OF MICHEL GAUDET (ICC Publishing 1999).
19. William Park, *Arbitrators and Accuracy*, 1(1) JOURNAL OF INTERNATIONAL DISPUTE SETTLEMENT 25 (2010).
20. It is interesting to note that an arbitrator's duty of efficiency is distinct from the duty to respect time limits. As such, an arbitrator may be very efficient in dealing with a complex case, but may fail, for example, to request an extension of time in an ad hoc arbitration. As a result, an award may be rendered after the deadline. In this case, as Yves Derains has pointed out, the arbitrator breached an essential duty but not the duty of efficiency: ("*The principle of expeditiousness is not to be confused with the duty to respect the time limit within which the award should be rendered. Arbitrators' failure to respect the time limit within which they must render the award constitutes a ground for annulment of the award but this is not a breach of the duty to act expeditiously.*") ("*Le principe de célérité ne se confond pas avec l'obligation de respecter le délai dans lequel doit être rendue la sentence. Le non-respect par des arbitres du délai dans lequel ils doivent remettre leur sentence constitue une cause de nullité de la sentence mais il ne s'agit pas là d'une violation de l'obligation de célérité.*"). Yves Derains, *Les nouveaux principes de procedure: Confidentialité, Célérité, Loyauté*, in LE NOUVEAU DROIT FRANÇAIS DE L'ARBITRAGE (Lextenso 2011).

Chapter 7: Is Efficiency an Arbitrator's Duty or Simply a Character Trait? §7.03

standards as it contains serious irregularities. Another example is the case in which a co-arbitrator repeatedly cancelled previously scheduled hearings at short notice without providing any valid justification thereof.[21]

The institution may also sanction inefficient arbitrators by cutting down on their fees. Earlier this year, the ICC published a note to parties and arbitral tribunals on the conduct of arbitrations which memorialized and specified the practice of sanctioning inefficient arbitrators by way of a reduction in fees:

> When the draft award is submitted after the time referred to in paragraph 43 above, the Court may lower the fees as set out below, unless it is satisfied that the delay is attributable to factors beyond the arbitrator's control.[22]

In this context, one has to bear in mind of course that an arbitrator's duty of efficiency is a best efforts obligation.[23] An arbitrator who is doing his or her best to conduct the proceedings efficiently, should in principle not be penalized because of delays in the proceedings.

The question of whether there was a breach of a duty of efficiency never arose with Pierre Karrer. Quite the contrary.

Indeed, many years after that first hearing in Kathmandu chaired by Pierre, I became Counsel at the ICC. During that time, I supervised a number of cases which had been dragging on for years and which were not being handled in an efficient manner by the arbitrators.

When the ICC considered replacing these arbitrators, Pierre immediately came to mind as an arbitrator who could take on these cases and conduct them efficiently. Thankfully he was always up for a challenge and agreed to step in on several cases, which were far from straightforward by any standard. He took control of the process, put the cases back on track and concluded them in an efficient manner. Whether he felt he had a duty to do so, I don't know. But what I do know is that efficiency is a trait of Pierre's character, so much so that one could even speak of "the Karrer benchmark" of an efficient arbitrator.

---

21. Nadia Darwazeh and Baptiste Rigaudeau, *Clues to Construing the New French Arbitration Law*, 28(4) JOURNAL OF INTERNATIONAL ARBITRATION (Kluwer Law International 2011), at 385–388, which also discusses various other examples.
22. Note to Parties and Arbitral Tribunals on the Conduct of the Arbitration under the ICC Rules of Arbitration, published on Feb. 22, 2016, para. 45.
23. Pierre Karrer, *Responsibility of Arbitrators and Arbitral Institutions*, THE LEADING ARBITRATOR GUIDE, at 161.

CHAPTER 8
The Role of Party-Appointed Arbitrators

Siegfried H. Elsing & Alexander Shchavelev

§8.01 INTRODUCTION

In international commercial arbitration it is customary to have three arbitrators on the tribunal.[1] Commonly, the two co-arbitrators in a tripartite tribunal are appointed or at least nominated by the parties.[2] The quality of an arbitration and the question whether, ultimately, the expected advantages and objectives sought by the parties are going to be obtainable and, ideally, fulfilled, is closely linked to the quality of the arbitrators.[3] It is an arbitrational truism that an arbitration is only as good as the arbitrators are.

In an article published not long ago Pierre Karrer retells the story of the so-called wine arbitrator, an entirely partisan party-appointed arbitrator who, despite his bias, may still be useful for he can at least be trusted with the decision to pick the wine at dinner.[4] In extreme cases, partisan co-arbitrators may cancel each other out and thereby de facto turn a three-member tribunal into a one-member tribunal in which the chair makes the award without listening to his colleagues.[5] Admittedly, we have

---

1. This is also the fall-back rule in the UNCITRAL Model Law which many national arbitration laws have adopted. *See* Art. 10(2) UNCITRAL Model Law on International Commercial Arbitration 1985 with amendments as adopted in 2006. Text available at http://www.uncitral.org/pdf/english/texts/arbitration/ml-arb/07-86998_Ebook.pdf (accessed 7 March 2017).
2. The term 'party-appointed' shall also include arbitrators nominated by a party and subsequently confirmed or appointed by the administering institution, *see* e.g., Arts 12(4) and 13 ICC Rules; Art. 7 LCIA Rules; Art. 5(1) Swiss Rules.
3. Pierre A. Karrer, *Introduction to International Arbitration Practice*, p. 61 (Kluwer Law International 2014); Alan Redfern, J. Martin Hunter, Nigel Blackaby and Constantine Partasides, *Redfern/Hunter on International Arbitration*, para. 4.13 (6th ed., Oxford University Press 2015).
4. Pierre A. Karrer, *One or Three Arbitrators? The More the Merrier, or Is Less More?*, 1 Y.B. Int'l Arb. 91, 93 (2010).
5. Cf. Alexis Mourre, *Chapter 20: Are Unilateral Appointments Defensible? On Jan Paulsson's Moral Hazard in International Arbitration*, in Stefan M. Kröll, Loukas A. Mistelis, et al. (eds.),

probably all encountered a biased party-nominated arbitrator once or twice. Fortunately, openly partisan arbitrators are rare. However, in the same article Pierre Karrer further states that co-arbitrators contribute relatively little to the decision-making even in the best of cases.[6] Why, then, is party-appointment still widely used and what is the role of party-appointed arbitrators in international commercial arbitration?

The focus of this paper is not the fundamental question of how the concepts of independence and impartiality apply to party-appointed arbitrators or the very legitimacy of composing the tribunal by unilateral appointment. In this respect, a few general observations suffice. After a quick look into the major institutional arbitration rules we will turn to the more practical aspects of a co-arbitrator's role during the various stages of the arbitral process.

§8.02 SOME NOTES ON GENERAL QUESTIONS

In recent years, criticism has been voiced by some of the most distinguished minds in the arbitration community arguing, in essence, that the established practice of party-appointed arbitrators is incompatible with the concept of impartial dispute resolution,[7] suggesting moving away from unilateral appointments.[8]

In fact, at first glance the mechanism of unilateral appointment seems to be incompatible with the arbitrator's duty to be and remain independent and impartial.[9] A closer look at the rationale behind unilateral appointments and proper understanding of independence and impartiality reveals, however, that this statement only holds true *if* the party-appointed arbitrator is partisan.

[A] The Right to Choose an Arbitrator

Jan Paulsson argues that 'there is no such right' to name one's arbitrator and that, 'if it existed, it would certainly not be fundamental'.[10] We strongly disagree. Arbitration

---

International Arbitration and International Commercial Law: Synergy, Convergence and Evolution, 381, 383 (Kluwer Law International 2011); previously published on Kluwer Arbitration Blog, 5 Oct. 2010, http://kluwerarbitrationblog.com/2010/10/05/are-unilateral-appointments-defensible-on-jan-paulssons-moral-hazard-in-international-arbitration/ (accessed 7 March 2017).

6. Karrer, *supra* n. 4, at 99.
7. Jan Paulsson, *Moral Hazard in International Dispute Resolution*, 25 ICSID Rev. 339 (2010); also available at http://www.arbitration-icca.org/media/0/12773749999020/paulsson_moral_hazard.pdf (accessed 7 March 2017); Albert Jan van den Berg, *Dissenting Opinions by Party-Appointed Arbitrators in Investment Arbitration*, in Mahnoush Arsanjani, et al. (eds.), Looking to the Future: Essays on International Law in Honor of W. Michael Reisman, 821 (Brill Academic 2011); *Id.*, *Charles Brower's Problem with 100 Per Cent – Dissenting Opinions by Party-Appointed Arbitrators in Investment Arbitration*, 31 Arb. Int'l 382 (2015).
8. Paulsson, *supra* n. 7, at 348; Juan Fernández-Armesto, *Salient Issues of International Arbitration*, 27 Am. U. Int'l L. Rev. 721, 726 (2012); less categorical van den Berg, *supra* n. 7, at 834.
9. Cf. Alfonso Gomez-Acebo, *Party-Appointed Arbitrators in International Commercial Arbitration*, paras 5–7 (Kluwer Law International 2016).
10. Paulsson, *supra* n. 7, at 348.

Chapter 8: The Role of Party-Appointed Arbitrators §8.02[A]

is adjudication by virtue of party autonomy.[11] It is a way of dispute resolution to which the parties may only resort if they so agree. Free choice not only of the method but also of the adjudicating body is the most distinctive feature and essential characteristic of arbitration compared to litigation in state courts.[12] Parties agree on arbitration precisely because they can choose their judges.[13] Some even call arbitrator appointment the 'ultimate form of forum shopping'.[14] Co-arbitrators are regarded as an essential means of ensuring the expert, efficient and internationally-neutral arbitral procedure which is a central object of the agreement to arbitrate.[15]

This basic right to appoint one's own arbitrator is the default position in UNCITRAL Model Law as well as in national arbitration laws of many countries,[16] and is acknowledged by institutional arbitration rules.[17] Hence, the agreement of the parties to arbitrate is the very source of their right to choose an arbitrator.[18] As explained in more detail below, selection of the 'own' arbitrator is also an integral part of fairness in international commercial arbitration.[19]

The value of the right to unilateral appointment is reflected in the fact that arbitration users not only feel comfortable with this system, but also in fact strongly support it. A survey conducted by the School of International Arbitration at Queen Mary University of London shows that the overwhelming majority of 76% of respondents favours the unilateral selection of co-arbitrators by the parties.[20] This figure is easily explained by the greater trust parties have in an arbitral process in which they have invested.[21] By appointing an arbitrator, they have a sense of proximity to the process.[22] Unilateral appointments give the parties the impression – justified or not – that they control the process; a feeling which they lack in state court litigation.

---

11. For a comprehensive analysis on party autonomy to select an arbitrator in international arbitration conventions, national arbitration laws and institutional arbitration rules cf. Gary B. Born, *International Commercial Arbitration*, pp. 1642 et seq. (2nd ed., Kluwer Law International 2014).
12. Born, *supra* n. 11, at 1638; Gomez-Acebo, *supra* n. 9, at 3-1.
13. Born, *supra* n. 11, at 1807.
14. Catherine Rogers, *A Window into the Soul of International Arbitration: Arbitrator Selection, Transparency and Stakeholder Interests*, 46 VUWLR 1179, 1179 (2015).
15. Born, *supra* n. 11, at 1809.
16. Article 11(3)(a) UNCITRAL Model Law; s. 1035(3) of the German Code of Civil Procedure (ZPO). Official English translation available at https://www.gesetze-im-internet.de/englisch_zpo/index.html (accessed 7 March 2017).
17. Article 12(4) ICC Rules; Art. 8(1) Swiss Rules; Art. 12(1) ICDR Rules; Art. 7 LCIA Rules; ss 6.2(5) and 12.1 DIS Rules.
18. Born, *supra* n. 11, at 1639; Charles N. Brower and Charles B. Rosenberg, *The Death of the Two-Headed Nightingale: Why the Paulsson-Van den Berg Presumption that Party-Appointed Arbitrators are Untrustworthy is Wrongheaded*, 29 Arb. Int'l 7, 9 et seq. (2013) including a retrospective overview.
19. Doak Bishop and Lucy Reed, *Practical Guidelines for Interviewing, Selecting and Challenging Party-Appointed Arbitrators in International Commercial Arbitration*, 14 Arb. Int'l 395, 428 (1998). *See* §8.04 [D] and [E].
20. Queen Mary University of London, *2012 International Arbitration Survey: Current and Preferred Practices in the Arbitral Process* 5–6 (2012), http://www.arbitration.qmul.ac.uk/docs/164483.pdf (accessed 7 March 2017).
21. Brower, Rosenberg, *supra* n. 18, at 18; Gomez-Acebo, *supra* n. 9, at 3–78.
22. Mourre, *supra* n. 5, at 384.

[B] On Independence and Impartiality

The criticism of unilateral appointment seems to be based on the (unspoken) presumption that a party-appointed arbitrator is per se partisan.[23] Yes, biased arbitrators are a problem, but not every party-appointed arbitrator is biased. From personal experience it is, in fact, a decreasingly small minority, at least in larger cases in international commercial arbitration. The number might be higher in investor-state disputes which seem to be the real catalyst for the aforementioned critiques. One might think of state-appointed co-arbitrators holding any kind of public office such as university professors or who are otherwise dependent on the mercy of that state.

Nonetheless, there is a virtually universal agreement in international commercial arbitration that each arbitrator has to be and must remain independent and impartial throughout the course of arbitration.[24] This fundamental principle is laid down in UNCITRAL Model Law and in all major institutional rules.[25] The reason for such requirement is to preserve the integrity of the arbitral process.[26]

The actual controversy, thus, concerns the precise content of what independent and impartial means. It is largely based on historically different concepts of the party-appointed arbitrator's role in national legal systems.[27] Thus, parties and arbitrators may understand impartiality and independence differently depending on their national background. Whereas it may well be true that on the part of parties' counsel there has been some convergent development in the understanding of a unilaterally appointed arbitrator's role,[28] at least in jurisdiction with a long standing tradition of partisan co-arbitrators little seems to have changed in the heads of the parties. In the US, historically, party-appointed arbitrators essentially competed for the vote of the chairperson or even openly supported the counsel of the appointing party. In domestic arbitration under the auspices of the AAA parties may still agree to use non-neutral arbitrators.[29] However, since 2004, party-appointed arbitrators have to be neutral by default.[30] Notwithstanding these developments, a US company will certainly not accept

---

23. Cf. Fernández-Armesto, *supra* n. 8, at 725: 'Party appointed arbitrators lead to situations which can only be described as miscarriages of justice and which undermine the legitimacy of arbitration'.
24. Born, *supra* n. 11, at 1761; Redfern, Hunter, Blackaby and Partasides, *supra* n. 3, at 4.75.
25. See e.g., Art. 12(2) UNCITRAL Model Law; Art. 11(1) ICC Rules; Art. 5.3 LCIA Rules; Art. 9(1) Swiss Rules; Art. 13(1) ICDR Rules; s. 15 DIS-Rules.
26. Born, *supra* n. 11, at 1762.
27. For a comprehensive analysis cf. Born, *supra* n. 11, at 1762 et seq.
28. Andreas F. Lowenfeld, *Chapter 3: Party-Appointed Arbitrator in International Controversies: Further Reflections*, in Lawrence W. Newmanand and Richard D. Hill (eds.), The Leading Arbitrators' Guide to International Arbitration, 41, 42 (2nd ed., Juris Publishing 2008).
29. So-called 'Canon X arbitrator', a term derived from the fact that ethical obligations of such arbitrators are set out in Canon X of the AAA Code of Ethics for Arbitrators in Commercial Disputes effective 1 March 2004. Text available at https://www.adr.org/aaa/ShowProperty?nodeId = /UCM/ADRSTG_003867 (accessed 7 March 2017).
30. Rules R-13(b) and R-18(b) of the AAA Commercial Arbitration Rules and Mediation Procedures. Text available at https://www.adr.org/aaa/ShowProperty?nodeId = /UCM/ADRSTG_004103& revision = latestreleased (accessed 7 March 2017).

(nor understand) that an arbitrator belonging to the same law firm as that company's counsel is appointed by a party adverse to one of its distant affiliates, even though this arbitrator is required to (and will) act independently and impartially.

Regardless of how the concepts of independence, impartiality, and neutrality[31] interplay,[32] it is generally accepted that no absolute impartiality/neutrality can reasonably be asked of an arbitrator.[33] Arbitrators are human beings shaped by their life experiences. To require complete absence of pre-existing philosophies is simply impossible. This applies equally to the presiding arbitrators as well as to his or her co-arbitrators. Hence, impartiality and neutrality do not exclude predisposition based on the respective arbitrator's legal perspective, academic writing, political views, and other such factors.[34] Predisposition or sympathy is often confused with bias or prejudice. They are not the same. The latter are adopted regardless of the merits of the particular case.[35]

§8.03 PARTY-APPOINTED ARBITRATORS IN UNCITRAL MODEL LAW AND INSTITUTIONAL RULES

A look into UNCITRAL Model Law, representative for many national arbitration laws, and into arbitration rules of some of the leading arbitration institutions reveals that these regulations barely expressly mention party-appointed arbitrators at all.

UNCITRAL Model Law confers one express power upon co-arbitrators: the appointment of the third arbitrator.[36] Institutional rules also contain provisions providing for co-arbitrators appointing, nominating, or at least participating in the selection of the chairperson or president of the tribunal.[37] An implied power of the co-arbitrators can be drawn from the second sentence of Article 29 UNCITRAL Model Law: co-arbitrators may delegate decisions on questions of procedure to the presiding arbitrator. Some institutional rules set out similar provisions.[38] In addition, the rules of LCIA and ICDR address the issue of (ex-parte) communication of a co-arbitrator with the parties.[39] Beyond that, UNCITRAL Model Law and institutional rules only refer to an arbitrator or the arbitral tribunal as a whole. Respective provisions on

---

31. Neutrality is sometimes regarded to be distinct from impartiality and shall mean the capability of the arbitrator to vote for the party with the better case. See Bishop, Reed, *supra* n. 19, at 399–400.
32. Cf. comprehensive analysis by Gomez-Acebo, *supra* n. 9, at 4–9 et seq.
33. Brower, Rosenberg, *supra* n. 18, at 17; Mohammed Bedjaoui, *The Arbitrator: One Man-Three Roles: Some Independent Comments on the Ethical and Legal Obligations of an Arbitrator*, 5 J. Int'l Arb. 7, 9 (1988).
34. Gomez-Acebo, *supra* n. 9, at 4–22.
35. Bishop, Reed, *supra* n. 19, at 396.
36. Article 11(3)(a) UNCITRAL Model Law.
37. Article 12(5) ICC Rules; Art. 8(2) Swiss Rules; s. 12.2 DIS Rules; Art. 13.5 LCIA Rules; Art. 13(6) ICDR Rules.
38. Article 14.6 LCIA Rules, Art. 31(2) Swiss Rules, Art. 29(3) ICDR Rule; s. 24.4 DIS Rules.
39. Article 13.5 LCIA Rules; Art. 13(6) ICDR Rules.

independence, impartiality, disclosure, and challenge;[40] conduct of the proceedings;[41] and making of the award[42] may serve as examples.

§8.04 PARTY-APPOINTED ARBITRATOR IN THE COURSE OF ARBITRATION

Despite this regulatory silence, party-appointed arbitrators are involved in the arbitral process throughout its entire term. In fact, they come into play at a very early stage and claimant's co-arbitrator before the arbitration even starts.

[A] Selection and Appointment

As outlined above, the ability to appoint an arbitrator who the party believes to be sympathetic to its case (but impartial) is one of the great strengths and benefits of tripartite commercial arbitration. Since the co-arbitrator is going to be one of three persons to hear and determine the case, a party naturally has some expectations which, as already mentioned, may differ depending on the party's national background. A common and unobjectionable goal is to have at least one 'chosen judge'[43] on the tribunal who will listen to, hopefully understand, if necessary, inform, and ideally persuade the others of the appointing party's case.[44] Appointing a particular arbitrator should at least not lower that party's chances to win. To accomplish this goal, ideally, parties (should) look for an arbitrator who will be receptive for the party's position, but still be open minded, and listened to and respected within the tribunal.[45]

Experience shows, however, that competence to appoint a proper arbitrator is less universal than one would hope,[46] particularly when less experienced parties (or counsel) are involved. The expectation that if you have retained one of the three arbitrators, he or she should be looking after your interests, still tends to lead parties to choose their arbitrator not on the basis of qualifications and integrity but rather advocacy skills and willingness to support the party's case.

There can be a significant difference between the role a co-arbitrator is expected to play by the appointing party and how this particular arbitrator understands his or her role. Hence, an arbitrator may find himself caught in between (ill-founded) expectations of the party and requirements of the applicable arbitration rules and his or her self-conception. This dilemma is reflected in the classic quote by Martin Hunter:

---

40. Articles 12–13 UNCITRAL Model Law; Arts 11 and 14 ICC Rules; Arts 5.3–5.5 and 10 LCIA Rules; Arts 9–11 Swiss Rules; Arts 13–14 ICDR Rules; ss 15, 16 and 18 DIS-Rules.
41. For example Arts 19(2), 24 and 26 UNCITRAL Model Law; Arts 22–25 ICC Rules; Arts 14, 19–22 LCIA Rules; Arts 15 and 22 Swiss Rules; Arts 20, 23 ICDR Rules; ss 24 and 27 DIS-Rules.
42. Article 31 UNCITRAL Model Law; Art. 32 ICC Rules; Art. 26 LCIA Rules; Arts 31–32 Swiss Rules; Arts 29–30 ICDR Rules; ss 33–34 DIS-Rules.
43. Bedjaoui, *supra* n. 33, at 8; Redfern, Hunter, Blackaby and Partasides, *supra* n. 3, at 4.16.
44. Redfern, Hunter, Blackaby and Partasides, *supra* n. 3, at 4.30. Questioning such 'duty of care' Gomez-Acebo, *supra* n. 9, at 5–14 et seq.
45. Lowenfeld, *supra* n. 28, at 43; Mourre, *supra* n. 5, at 385.
46. van den Berg, *supra* n. 7, at 386; Hans Smit, *The Pernicious Institution of the Party-Appointed Arbitrator*, Columbia FDI Perspectives. 33, (14 December 2010).

> When I am representing a client in an arbitration, what I am really looking for in a party-nominated arbitrator is someone with the maximum predisposition towards my client, but with the minimum appearance of bias.[47]

A less experienced arbitrator may assume, whether consciously or subconsciously, that partisanship, or at least being exceedingly obliged, is exactly what is expected by the appointing party and thus act accordingly. Ultimately, this may lead to an unintentional, but all the more burdensome double disadvantage of lacking experience coupled with detrimental bias. Hence, the selection of co-arbitrators and their role after appointment go hand in hand.[48] Appointing party and prospective arbitrator should have a clear understanding of the role to be filled. AAA Code of Ethics requires party-appointed arbitrators to determine their status 'as early as possible but not later than the first meeting of the arbitrators and parties'.[49] This seems to be too late. The nominee should know his or her role before accepting the nomination. An arbitrator is rarely appointed without prior contact. These pre-appointment contacts should not only be used by the party to get to know 'its' potential arbitrator but also by the approached to verify that party's expectations.

The types of pre-appointment contacts vary and may reach from a short e-mail or call to an extensive 'beauty contest'.[50] Whether and how a pre-selection interview is conducted should be left to the respective arbitrator's discretion.[51] In terms of content, both the nominee and the party should be very careful that the substance of the dispute is not discussed except in general terms and no questions are asked and/or answered to ascertain the nominee's views on points in issue.[52] In particular, the prospective arbitrator should never try to 'sell' himself or herself to the party.[53] The Chartered Institute of Arbitrators issued a comprehensive guideline on this matter.[54] If in doubt, it seems helpful to adopt the view of a party reviewing the matter after losing the arbitration.[55]

[B]   Disclosure

Once chosen by the party, a co-arbitrator is under a continuing duty to disclose any circumstances that may give rise to justifiable doubts as to his or her impartiality or

---

47. Martin Hunter, *Ethics of the International Arbitrator*, 53 Arb. 219, 223 (1987).
48. Andreas F. Lowenfeld, *Party-Appointed Arbitrator in International Controversies: Some Reflections*, 30 Tex. Int'l L. J. 59, 60 (1995); Born, *supra* n. 11, at 1683.
49. AAA Code of Ethics for Arbitrators in Commercial Disputes, *supra* n. 29, Canon IX.C.
50. Cf. anecdotal stories by Lowenfeld, *supra* n. 48, at 61 et seq.
51. Lowenfeld, *supra* n. 28, at 43; Antonio A. de Fina, *The Party Appointed Arbitrator in International Arbitrations – Role and Selection*, 15 Arb. Int'l 381, 392 (1999).
52. Born, *supra* n. 11, at 1685. For a critical view on the practice of ex parte communication *see* Gomez-Acebo, *supra* n. 9, at 5–33 et seq.
53. Lowenfeld, *supra* n. 48, at 62.
54. CIArb, Interviews for Prospective Arbitrators. Text available at http://www.ciarb.org/docs/default-source/ciarbdocuments/guidance-and-ethics/practice-guidelines-protocols-and-rules/international-arbitration-guidelines-2015/guideline-on-interviews-for-prospective-arbitrators.pdf?sfvrsn=16 (accessed 7 March 2017). The proposal in Art. 1(6) to record the interview in detail does not reflect current practice, cf. Born, *supra* n. 11, at 1686.
55. Born, *supra* n. 11, at 1687.

independence.[56] The obligation to disclose is an integral part of the concept of party-appointed arbitrators. Contrary to Jan Paulsson's notion,[57] unilateral appointment is not an appointment without the counterparty's agreement. Rather, by virtue of the agreement on unilateral appointment each party places confidence in the respective other party's choice or at least consents to the dispute being settled by that arbitrator. Hence, by not objecting to the respective other party's appointee both parties place their *mutual* confidence in the tribunal composed of the two co-arbitrators and the presiding arbitrator selected by them.[58] True consent requires full knowledge of the underlying facts. Therefore, it is not advisable for the prospective arbitrator to conceal potential problems. In fact, it is usually the concealment itself that turns out to be the problem at a later stage.[59] The golden rule here is: if in doubt, disclose.[60]

[C] Selection of the Chair

If co-arbitrators are appointed by the parties, they are usually also entrusted with the selection of the presiding arbitrator. By this parties obtain a further sense of proximity and 'control' over the arbitral process. We have seen earlier that this task is the only one expressly conferred upon co-arbitrators by arbitration laws and institutional rules. Some even say it is the most important function of party-appointed arbitrators.[61]

The chairperson determines the general style of the arbitration, both within the tribunal and vis-à-vis the parties. Hence, co-arbitrators are well advised not only to act as proxies and to go for a person favoured by the respective party but also to elect someone they will be able to work with properly. A prudent party should understand this. After all, it agreed on the selection of the chair by the co-arbitrators and not by the parties. Between the co-arbitrators, the selection of the chair should be a collaborative process.[62] A good method is to first determine abstract criteria and to then compile a (not necessarily ranked) shortlist. A suitable candidate should have appropriate expertise and practical experience in international arbitration, a juridical open-mindedness toward different legal cultures, and an international outlook.[63] In the course of the selection process it is common and generally accepted for co-arbitrators to confer with the parties in order to ensure that the appointee is acceptable to all

---

56. Cf. Art. 12(1) UNCITRAL Model Law. Exact wording varies, see Arts 11(2)–(3) ICC Rules; Arts 5.4–5.5 LCIA Rules; Art. 9(2) Swiss Rules; Art. 13(2)-(3) ICDR Rules; ss 16.1 and 16.3 DIS-Rules. A comprehensive assistance on the relevant circumstances is provided by the IBA Guidelines on Conflicts of Interest in International Arbitration (2014) Text available at http://www.ibanet.org/Publications/publications_IBA_guides_and_free_materials.aspx (accessed 7 March 2017).
57. Paulsson, *supra* n. 7, at 349 and 352.
58. Cf. Brower, Rosenberg, *supra* n. 18, at 13; *see also* Mourre, *supra* n. 5, at 384. Sceptical in this regard Gomez-Acebo, *supra* n. 9, at 5–6.
59. Bedjaoui, *supra* n. 33, at 16; Bishop, Reed, *supra* n. 19, at 396; Redfern, Hunter, Blackaby and Partasides, *supra* n. 3, at 4.79.
60. Bishop, Reed, *supra* n. 19, at 427.
61. de Fina, *supra* n. 51, at 382. *See also* Karrer, *supra* n. 4, at 98–99.
62. Bedjaoui, *supra* n. 33, at 16.
63. Bishop, Reed, *supra* n. 19, at 402.

concerned.[64] The optimal result of this process is going to be a mixed and, in the end, (internationally)-neutral panel capable of understanding both parties' positions and needs.[65]

[D] Pre-hearing Phase

Once the arbitration is underway, party-appointed arbitrators have to fulfil general duties that are imposed on them by virtue of the membership in the tribunal.[66] After all, arbitral tribunal, and this includes the co-arbitrators, is a service provider to the parties.[67] In addition, and more importantly, in the course of the arbitral proceedings party-appointed arbitrators are expected to act as guarantors of the nominating party's rights which requires active efforts by the co-arbitrators.[68] They have to make sure that the appointing party understands what the tribunal wants[69] and that it is granted a procedurally equal right to be heard.[70] This includes simple things such as indicating to the chairperson that a proposed deadline falls on a public holiday in that country.

The degree to which co-arbitrators are going to be involved in procedural issues primarily depends on the professionality of the chairperson. Occasionally, co-arbitrators are chosen due to their attitude regarding potentially controversial procedural issues such as the disclosure of documents. The task here is to work towards a mutually acceptable solution. Sometimes, particularly when they did not have a say in the selection process, co-arbitrators might be confronted with an inept chair requiring them to take action – of course as gently as possible – for their own benefit and the benefit of the parties.

In the course of arbitration co-arbitrators are unavoidably going to interact with their colleagues. Pierre Karrer advises party-appointed arbitrators to build up goodwill on the side of the presiding arbitrator.[71] This starts with small things such as timely reading of submissions in order to be able to react quickly to any proposals for further action circulated by the chair. With regard to the fellow co-arbitrator, AAA Code of Ethics calls for affording 'each other full opportunity to participate in all aspects of the proceedings'.[72] In any event co-arbitrators should be vigilant in terms of the behaviour of the other party appointee. But how should one react to misbehaviour? Even though

---

64. Redfern, Hunter, Blackaby and Partasides, *supra* n. 3, at 4.40; Lowenfeld, *supra* n. 48, at 64.
65. Cf. Gary B. Born, pp. 1669–1670.
66. *See* further on this matter Redfern, Hunter, Blackaby and Partasides, *supra* n. 3, at 5.43 et seq.
67. Klaus Peter Berger, *Chapter 2: The In-House Counsel Who Went Astray: Ex-Parte Communications with Party-Appointed Arbitrators*, in Domitille Baizeau and Bernd Ehle (eds.), Stories from the Hearing Room: Experience from Arbitral Practice – Essays in Honour of Michael E. Schneider, 7, 11 (Kluwer Law International 2015).
68. Born, *supra* n. 11, at 1811.
69. de Fina, *supra* n. 51, at 388.
70. Lowenfeld, *supra* n. 28, at 46.
71. Karrer, *supra* n. 3, at 180.
72. AAA Code of Ethics for Arbitrators in Commercial Disputes, *supra* n. 29, Canon IV.G.

it might feel natural, the opposing co-arbitrator should certainly not mimic such misbehaviour, in particular not employ the same partisanship, if detected.[73]

An even more delicate question is how concerns with regard to the other co-arbitrator's impartiality should be handled. Needless to say, actions of any kind should only be taken if there is sufficient proof.[74] A word to the chairperson is generally appropriate and will often suffice to secure one's own party's rights.[75] On the other hand, it is improper for the arbitrator to unilaterally communicate his or her concerns to the appointing party.[76] Initiating the challenge of a fellow arbitrator – if at all permissible[77] – should be the last measure to be taken. If the challenge fails the atmosphere within the panel will be tense. Appropriate and correct reaction to challenges by a party largely depends on the applicable procedure. Some institutional rules give other members of the tribunal the opportunity to comment,[78] others do not.[79] One should do no wrong by applying a no-comment policy.[80] However, taking a position might become inevitable if the tribunal is the first instance to decide on the challenge.[81] In turn, a challenged co-arbitrator should not resign, if the objection appears without merit, because the challenge itself may be a mere delaying tactic.[82]

The last issue concerns interaction between the arbitrator and the appointing party or its counsel. Any ex parte communication should cease immediately upon the selection of the presiding arbitrator.[83] Leaking any internal information to the appointing party significantly misbalances the arbitration and jeopardizes the fundamental right of the other party to equal treatment by the tribunal. This seems so self-evident that it is rarely addressed in applicable rules[84] and does not require any further comment at this point.[85]

[E] Hearing Phase

Most matters mentioned in the preceding section apply *mutatis mutandis* to the hearing phase. However, in a hearing room the tribunal, the parties and their experts and witnesses are brought together face-to-face in one place. Hearings are intense events and may be decisive for the final outcome of the dispute. Cultural and linguistic differences and deficiencies are much harder to compensate compared to written submissions. The task of party-appointed arbitrators is to ensure a fair hearing, in

---

73. Born, *supra* n. 11, at 1813–1814; Lowenfeld, *supra* n. 48, at 60 et seq.; Gomez-Acebo, *supra* n. 9, at 7–32.
74. Karrer, *supra* n. 3, at 79; de Fina, *supra* n. 51, at 384.
75. Lowenfeld, *supra* n. 28, at 43; Gomez-Acebo, *supra* n. 9, at 7–32.
76. de Fina, *supra* n. 51, at 384.
77. Pursuant to Art. 10.1 LCIA Rules a 'request of all other members of the Arbitral Tribunal' is required to initiate revocation proceedings.
78. Cf. Art. 14(3) ICC Rules.
79. Cf. Art. 14(2) ICDR Rules; Art. 10.4 LCIA Rules.
80. Karrer, *supra* n. 3, at 78.
81. Cf. Art. 13(2) UNCITRAL Model Law; s. 18.2 DIS Rules.
82. Redfern, Hunter, Blackaby and Partasides, *supra* n. 3, at 4.151.
83. Bishop, Reed, *supra* n. 19, at 426; Redfern, Hunter, Blackaby and Partasides, *supra* n. 3, at 4.72.
84. Cf. Art. 13.4 and para. 6 of the Annex to LCIA Rules; Art. 13(6) ICDR Rules.
85. *See* further Berger, *supra* n. 67.

particular, by acting as 'translators' of the respective party and by clarifying any misunderstandings that may arise during the hearing (for instance because of differences of legal practice, culture, or language) before they lead to injustice.[86]

In performing this task party-appointed arbitrators must be very careful not to appear as just another set of lawyers for the appointing party.[87] How far may they go? If a party-appointed arbitrator gets the impression that the appointing party's position or a witness testimony might be misunderstood by the rest of the tribunal it should not be regarded inappropriate for him or her to ask clarifying questions and to lead the party to the important issues.[88] Appropriateness of some sort of cross-examination of witnesses called by the non-nominating party will depend on whether the arbitration is of a more continental or US style type.[89]

[F]   Award Making

Up until this point, party-appointed arbitrators will focus their efforts on ensuring that 'their' party's arguments are heard and properly understood by fellow arbitrators. In the award-making phase, they should do their best in order to make sure that these arguments are also fully and seriously considered. Here, party-appointed arbitrators have to make up their minds on each question in issue and be advocates for their view (which must not necessarily be the view of the party which appoints them). Where the majority of the panel shows a tendency towards the other party they should play devil's advocates by means of constructive second-guessing.[90] By ensuring that the arguments and positions of the appointing party are completely and adequately dealt with, the party-appointed arbitrator makes a valuable contribution to the quality of the award even if he or she does not agree with the respective party. This is not a sign of partiality or bias. Except for a per se partisan arbitrator, party-appointed arbitrators advance a particular position not simply because that is the position of the appointing party. In fact, it is the other way around – that arbitrator was chosen because his or her views were considered sympathetic with the appointing party's case.[91]

Arbitral tribunals have to pass their judgment in accordance with the applicable law unless the parties have agreed on a decision *ex aequo et bono* or *as amiable compositeur*.[92] It is arguably rather unusual for all members of the tribunal to have firm views on all legal and factual questions in issue from the outset. The reality is that views are often formed as the arbitration proceeds. Hence, a party-nominated

---

86. Redfern, Hunter, Blackaby and Partasides, *supra* n. 3, at 4.30; cf. illustrative examples furnished by Lowenfeld, *supra* n. 48, at 66 and 67.
87. Cf. Art. 5.3 LCIA Rules: 'none shall act in the arbitration as advocate for or representative of any party'.
88. de Fina, *supra* n. 51, at 385; Lowenfeld, *supra* n. 28, at 44–45.
89. Lowenfeld, *supra* n. 28, at 44–45 regards questions designed to challenge the veracity or reliability of the witness to be improper.
90. Rogers, *supra* n. 14, at 1184–1185.
91. Cf. Gomez-Acebo, *supra* n. 9, at 3–72.
92. Cf. Art. 28 UNCITRAL Model Law.

arbitrator who is convinced of the merits of the case put forward by the appointing party can have a significant impact on the deliberations of the arbitral tribunal.[93]

These advantages are lost when the co-arbitrator is partisan on all issues. Advancing the position of one party over the other simply because that party has appointed him or her is even counter-productive. At this late stage of the proceedings, fellow arbitrators are arguably going to be rather reluctant to tackle this issue by any formal means. Hence, this arbitrator is simply going to loose credibility with the chairperson (and the other co-arbitrator),[94] most probably affecting not only the decision on the particular issue but the deliberative process altogether. This result would be particularly unfortunate when it is not a clean-cut case, either because the law is not settled or due to factual or evidentiary inconsistency.

In the course of deliberations reminders of the witnesses' cultural background may become necessary when the clinical transcript of the hearing is being reviewed by the tribunal. If co-arbitrators are chosen because of their particular knowledge in a field, they may also be asked to share this expertise within the tribunal. This is, however, rarely the case and fellow arbitrators lacking such knowledge are not likely to accept the advice at its face value.

The ultimate task of an arbitral tribunal is to render a decision. A significant majority of awards are unanimous. Unanimity does not necessarily have to go along with a compromise.[95] Predisposed (but impartial) party-appointed arbitrators will not let their sympathy rule over a good case and will decide in favour of the party with the better factual and legal position.[96] A party-appointed arbitrator may win on one argument and loose on another. It does not have to be a bazaar. Sometimes, however, for various reasons, it might become difficult to achieve a unanimous award. When this becomes apparent, presiding arbitrators could be tempted to look out for possible compromises. However, trade-offs for the mere sake of unanimity are most likely to result in undeserved benefits for the losing party. Unfortunately, some party-appointed arbitrators try to play this card.[97]

This leads us to the last issue we would like to address in this paper. What should a party-appointed arbitrator do if the majority is neither convinced by his or her arguments nor prepared for any kind of barter? It is sometimes said that a majority decision would appear less legitimate in the losing party's eyes[98] and dissenter should align[99] but ensure that the award addresses each of the losing party's arguments in a comprehensive way.[100] Others disagree.[101] If an arbitrator dissents, should he or she also deliver a dissenting opinion? The opinions are split again. One the one hand it is

---

93. Redfern, Hunter, Blackaby and Partasides, *supra* n. 3, at 9.115; Mourre, *supra* n. 5, at 385.
94. Redfern, Hunter, Blackaby and Partasides, *supra* n. 3, at 9.116.
95. Brower, Rosenberg, *supra* n. 18, at 25.
96. Bishop, Reed, *supra* n. 19, at 395.
97. Cf. Lowenfeld, *supra* n. 28, at 48; Paulsson, *supra* n. 7, at 353.
98. Paulsson, *supra* n. 7, at 11.
99. van den Berg, *supra* n. 7, at 385.
100. de Fina, *supra* n. 51, at 388.
101. Brower, Rosenberg, *supra* n. 18, at 41.

argued that separate opinions could undermine the authority of the tribunal, ultimately threatening the validity and enforceability of the award.[102] On the other hand, it has been suggested that dissents could strengthen the award, particularly if circulated in advance of the final decision.[103]

There seems to be no conclusive empirical evidence and it seems to be rather doubtful whether it really makes any difference whether the award was supported by the appointed co-arbitrator or is accompanied by a strident dissenting opinion. Admittedly, at least in international commercial arbitration the number of dissenting opinions is low. If issued, they are rarely an expression of an honest difference of opinion[104] but in fact seem to be targeted at saving one's face vis-à-vis the nominating party.[105] In the latter case, however, a dissent of any quality is certainly preferable to a potential alternative of leaking the result of deliberations to the appointing party breaching confidentiality of deliberations.

§8.05 CONCLUSION

One reason parties opt for arbitration is the ability to choose their judges. They trust that a tribunal composed of members chosen by them will resolve their dispute fairly and render a just decision. Partisan co-arbitrators are likely to do more harm than good and risk forfeiting this trust. In the long run, parties will not be prepared to pay and wait for an adjudication that they mistrust.[106] Although instances of bad party-appointed arbitrating continue to be reported, they remain exceptional and prove the rule that party-appointed arbitrators form an integral and valuable part of tripartite arbitral tribunals in international arbitration. Certain predisposition towards the nominating party's views does not affect an arbitrator's impartiality. Experienced and reputable international arbitrators are capable of safeguarding the appointing party's rights in the process leading to the decision and still exercise independent and impartial judgment.[107] Proper co-arbitrating will help a randomly selected group to become a team capable of living up to the parties' expectations.[108]

In an article published over fifty years ago Walther Habscheid noted that with co-arbitrators seeing a case from their respective perspective and the chairperson face on, the tribunal as a whole is more likely to arrive at a correct decision.[109] Proper understanding and execution of the role party-appointed arbitrators play on a tripartite arbitral panel will also help to strengthen the credibility, legitimacy, and reputation of

---

102. Redfern, Hunter, Blackaby and Partasides, *supra* n. 3, at 9.137; van den Berg, *supra* n. 7, at 387.
103. Brower, Rosenberg, *supra* n. 18, at 34.
104. If the tribunal is of a divided opinion on a question of law, the dissent seems to be better placed in an academic paper. This applies even more to a concurrent opinion.
105. Karrer, *supra* n. 4, at 97.
106. Fernández-Armesto, *supra* n. 8, at 721–722.
107. Mourre, *supra* n. 5, at 386; Born, *supra* n. 11, at 1813.
108. van den Berg, *supra* n. 7, at 385.
109. Walther Habscheid, *Das Problem der Unabhängigkeit der Schiedsgerichte*, NJW 5, 9 (1962).

arbitration beyond the arbitration community, which has attracted some undifferentiated criticism in the light of recent controversies over Investor-state dispute settlement.[110]

---

[110]. Cf. Jörg Risse, *Wehrt Euch endlich! Wider das Arbitration-Bashing*, SchiedsVZ 265 (2014); Jörg Risse, Nicolas Gremminger, *The Truth About Investment Arbitration (not only) under TTIP – Four Case Studies*, 33 ASA Bull. 465 (2015); Gloria Maria Alvarez, Blazej Blasikiewicz, et al., *A Response to the Criticism against ISDS by EFILA*, 33 J. Int'l Arb. 1 (2016).

CHAPTER 9
Concurrent Proceedings in Investment Arbitration

Emmanuel Gaillard

One of the most sensitive issues in contemporary international investment law is the issue of concurrent arbitral proceedings under more than one investment protection treaty which aim to protect the same interests and seek damages in respect of the same dispute. This phenomenon has become increasingly common in arbitral practice. It is a development that many States have perceived as unjust, as it requires them to face multiple arbitral proceedings where investors seek the same relief with respect to the same cause of action.

To date, arbitrators confronted with the issue of concurrent proceedings in investment arbitration have not been adequately equipped to fully address it. Such claims nonetheless present an important challenge for the investment treaty regime to react as a unified system.[1] A consistent approach to this issue is therefore essential. The alternative is the application of haphazard rules that may lead to incoherent or undesirable results.

Notwithstanding the clear practical implications of the issue at hand, there is also an essential theoretical dimension, namely, the ability of contemporary investment law to strike an appropriate balance between the protection of investors and the legitimate interests of States.[2] In an effort to identify this balance, this chapter addresses in detail the challenges arising from concurrent arbitral proceedings in international investment law (§9.01), and suggests potential solutions (§9.01).

---

1. *See*, on international law, J. Combacau, "Le droit international, bric-à-brac ou système?" ["International Law, Bric-a-brac or System?"], *Archives de philosophie du droit*, 31 (1986), p. 85.
2. On the need to find solutions which balance the investor's right to resolve disputes against the host State in a neutral forum while addressing existing shortcomings and imbalances of investor-State dispute settlement, *see* E. Gaillard, "Improving Investment Treaty Arbitration: Two Proposals," in *Liber Amicorum en l'honneur de William Laurence Craig* (2016), pp. 69–81.

§9.01 THE CHALLENGES ARISING FROM CONCURRENT PROCEEDINGS

The origins of the current trend – towards a plurality of arbitral proceedings initiated under different investment treaties for the benefit of the same interests – are easily identifiable ([A]). A brief analysis of the recent case law demonstrates that the problem of concurrent proceedings is not merely theoretical ([B]). This situation creates a structural disequilibrium in the investment law regime that unduly prejudices States and that must be remedied ([C]).

[A] The Origins of the Problem

The uneasy situation whereby a State is confronted with claims by investors seeking relief in multiple arbitral proceedings under different investment treaties is perfectly justified by rules and principles developed in arbitral case law. These rules and principles are perfectly justified when applied in individual cases. However, the combined exploitation of these rules may render the investor's claim or claims abusive or pathological.

The first of these principles is the rule developed in the arbitral case law that allows a shareholder of a local company to bring a claim against a State pursuant to a treaty signed between the shareholder's State of origin and the State hosting the investment, despite the fact that the direct victim of the host State's actions was the local company rather than the shareholder. Without this rule, today's phenomenon of concurrent proceedings would not have emerged. Case law arising out of the 2001 Argentine crisis offers numerous examples where shareholders of local companies were permitted to bring treaty claims against a host State for damages sustained by their local subsidiaries.[3] Given that most national laws prohibit shareholders from seeking compensation for damages suffered by companies in which they hold shares,[4] it is somewhat paradoxical that this principle has obtained the elusive status of a *jurisprudence constante* in investment law. The permissive stance towards shareholder claims is justified insofar as it can be established that the host State's impugned acts had a real impact on the shareholder claimant. This is the case, for instance, where the shareholder owns a majority or at least significant stake in the affected local company. However, where a shareholder holds only a minority stake in a local company, or where its investment was speculative or made subsequent to the impugned acts of the

---

3. *See e.g.,* CMS Gas Transmission Company v. Argentine Republic, ICSID Case No. ARB/01 /08, Decision on Jurisdiction of 17 July 2003, ¶ 48; Suez, Sociedad General de Aguas de Barcelona SA, and Vivendi Universal SA v. Argentine Republic, ICSID Case No. ARB/03/ 19, Decision on Jurisdiction of 3 August 2006, ¶ 49; Total SA v. Argentine Republic, ICSID Case No. ARB/04/01, Decision on Jurisdiction of 25 August 2006, ¶ 80; Impregilo S.p.A. v. Argentine Republic, ICSID Case No. ARB/07/ 1 7, Award of 21 June 2011, ¶ 138.
4. This paradox is highlighted by the comparative law study carried out by the OECD, D. Gaukrodger, "Investment Treaties as Corporate Law: Shareholder Claims and Issues of Consistency. A Preliminary Framework for Policy Analysis," OECD Working Papers on International Investment, No. 2013/3, OECD Investment Division, available on the website of the Organization.

Chapter 9: Concurrent Proceedings in Investment Arbitration   §9.01[A]

host State, arbitrators may need to reconsider the idea that a shareholder in a local company suffers the same damages as that company.

A more debatable trend in the arbitral case law is the application of this principle to the quantification of damages once a breach of the treaty by the host State has been established. Indeed, in a somewhat simplistic manner, case law has held that for quantum purposes, a shareholder should be treated like the local company on a *pro rata* basis according to its shareholding. In other words, a shareholder who holds 80% of the company's shares will be deemed to have suffered 80% of the damage suffered by the company, while a shareholder who holds 3% of the shares will be deemed to have suffered 3% of such damage.[5] A more nuanced approach to this issue is warranted. While a majority shareholder may control a company so as to channel benefits from the company in the form of dividends, the same is not necessarily true for a minority shareholder, whose position may vary depending on whether or not it has the ability to block a vote within the company. And for a very minor shareholder who exerts no influence over the company and who essentially relies on the value of the company's stock price, it is entirely artificial to assess damages based on the *pro rata* share of the company's damages. Moreover, in each of these circumstances, the effect of the actions of a host State on the company's creditors must also be taken into account for purposes of assessing quantum, particularly when assessing the "but for" scenario which aims to reconstitute what would have occurred in the absence of the State's wrongful acts. Indeed, it is important to recall that when a company avoids a loss, this does not necessarily mean that each of its shareholders consequently avoids a decrease in value proportional to their shareholding. Take, for example, the case of a deeply indebted company. The losses actually suffered by each of its shareholders can differ greatly from the amounts derived from a *pro rata* allocation of the company's damages. If tribunals consider that it is legitimate to protect a shareholder's right in and of itself for jurisdictional purposes, then they must also assess the impact on that specific right when determining the extent of the damages suffered. Thus, while the notion of protecting the shareholder of a company harmed by acts contrary to the host State's treaty obligations does not appear to be unfounded, it must also reflect the particularities of a given shareholder's situation. As tribunals become sensitive to the need for a more precise economic analysis, such realities will probably be increasingly taken into account.[6] In this sense, the rule allowing the protection of a shareholder impacted by State acts affecting its local subsidiary is in principle a legitimate rule.

The second rule that contributes to the problem of concurrent proceedings, and which may play a role in their increasing frequency, is the rule allowing a company controlled by shareholders of a certain nationality to be treated as possessing the same nationality as those shareholders for the purposes of a treaty-based claim. This "borrowing" of nationality based on control over the company applies both to a company constituted under the laws of the host State and the laws of a third State. The

---

5. *See* e.g., for an evaluation of the damage suffered by a 0.0032% shareholder based on the *pro rata* value of the company as a whole, *Quasar de Valores Sicav SA, Orgor de Valores Sicav SA, GBI 9000 Sicav SA and Alos 34 SL v. Russian Federation* (SCC), Award of 20 July 2012, ¶¶ 197 and 218.
6. *Compare with* Z. Douglas, "The International Law of Investment Claims," OUP, 2009, pp. 397 ff.

former hypothesis was envisaged as early as 1965 in Article 25(2)(b) *in fine* of the ICSID Convention, which provides that a "national of a Contracting State" for the purposes of the jurisdiction of the Centre includes "any juridical person which had the nationality of the Contracting State party to the dispute on [the] date [on which the parties consented to submit such dispute to conciliation or arbitration] and which, because of foreign control, the parties have agreed should be treated as a national of another Contracting State for the purposes of this Convention." Investment treaties negotiated subsequent to the ICSID Convention sometimes use this borrowing-of-nationality mechanism. By relying on this control test for nationality, a company incorporated outside the investor's State of origin, but which is directly or indirectly controlled by nationals of that State or by legal persons incorporated in that State, will be considered a national of the State of origin for the purposes of the treaty.[7] Some investment treaties expressly provide that a local subsidiary controlled by nationals of the State of origin automatically meets the conditions of the application of Article 25(2)(b) *in fine* of the ICSID Convention. A notable example is Article 26(7) of the Energy Charter Treaty of 1994:

> [a]n Investor other than a natural person which has the nationality of a Contracting Party to the dispute on the date of the consent in writing [to the arbitration] and which, before a dispute between it and that Contracting Party arises, is controlled by Investors of another Contracting Party, shall for the purpose of article 25(2)(b) of the ICSID Convention be treated as a "national of another Contracting State" and shall for the purpose of article 1(6) of the Additional Facility Rules be treated as a "national of another State".

These control-based definitions of a protected investor effectively allow the direct nationals of the State of origin and the entities they control (including, as the case may be, a local subsidiary) to benefit from both the substantive rights under a treaty as well as the procedural right to initiate arbitration proceedings in their own name pursuant to a treaty's investor-State dispute resolution clause.

Once again, there is nothing objectionable about this rule when it is applied in individual cases. Using the notion of control to determine the nationality of a company for the purposes of bestowing it with treaty-based protections simply acknowledges an economic reality; after all, control is a more legitimate criterion for determining the nationality of a legal entity than that of simple incorporation. Allowing the local company to file a claim in its own name is also a sound approach, as it avoids protecting only a portion of the company's shareholders while excluding from protection its local shareholders or those whose State of origin did not conclude a treaty with the host State. This approach also discourages shareholders of different nationalities from enforcing their rights before different arbitral tribunals based on different investment treaties. From the standpoint of procedural efficiency, therefore, the most cost-effective and fair approach is for the local company to borrow the nationality of its controlling shareholder(s) for the purposes of bringing an investment treaty claim. This is the reason that the drafters of the ICSID Convention conceived the rule under Article

---

7. *See* e.g., Art. I(b)(iii) of the Netherlands-Kazakhstan Treaty of 2002.

25(2)(b) *in fine* of the ICSID Convention at a time when claims by individual shareholders had not yet been envisioned. The rule initially gave rise to a handful of arbitral decisions,[8] and was then discarded in favor of claims by individual shareholders. It may however spark new interest should investment law become more concerned with economic realities rather than with formal criteria.

The local company's borrowing of nationality allows that company and the shareholder(s) whose nationality it borrows to bring a joint claim, on the basis of the same treaty, seeking damages for the consequences of a host State's violation of the treaty. Such joint claims are not objectionable, as they require the State to face a group of claimants before a single arbitral tribunal. Therefore, these claims do not raise the risk of inconsistent decisions by multiple tribunals, nor do they multiply the chances of investors to prevail before different tribunals in respect of the same claims.[9]

A different situation arises where a shareholder or a group of shareholders decide to exploit this nationality-borrowing mechanism, and opts to initiate two separate proceedings, i.e. one on behalf of the shareholder and another on behalf of the local company, both of which seek reparation for the same impugned actions of the host State. For reasons that will be analyzed further below, this situation may properly be considered abusive from the State's perspective. And, as will be explained, this situation is far from purely theoretical.

[B] Illustrations

The current landscape of international investment arbitration is becoming increasingly complex. Certain aspects of this complexity can be attributed to the manner in which treaties have been drafted.[10] In other cases, the complexity results from the temptation of litigants to exploit rules that were not conceived for the purposes for which they are now being invoked.

Two notable examples illustrate that the issue of concurrent proceedings initiated for the benefit of the same interests is not merely hypothetical.

The first example features the use of various investment treaties at different levels of the same chain of control of an investment. This example concerns the Egyptian company East Mediterranean Gas ("EMG"), which had been purchasing natural gas in Egypt from national companies EGPC and EGAS for transport to Israel. After the Arab Spring riots in Egypt caused disturbances on the gas pipeline linking Egypt to Israel and Jordan and EMG's gas supply contract was terminated, EMG and certain foreign

---

8. *See* E. Gaillard, "La jurisprudence du CIRDI" ["ICSID Case Law"], Pedone, 2004, pp. 59–62, 208–211 and 277–280.
9. On the practical interest of specifying in the request for arbitration who the affected parties are and in which proportions, *see Ioan Micula, Viorel Micula, SC European Food SA, SC Starmill SRL and AC Multipack SRL v. Romania*, ICSID Case No. ARB/05/20, Award of 11 December 2013, ¶¶ 1239–1248.
10. On the complexity of the mechanisms promoted by the EU as regards investment protection, *see* E. Gaillard, "L'avenir des traités de protection des investissements" ["The future of Investment Protection Treaties"], in C. Leben, *Droit international des investissements et arbitrage transnational [International Investment Law and Transnational Arbitration]*, 2015, p. 951.

shareholders of EMG initiated multiple arbitration proceedings against Egypt and the national gas companies. They accused Egypt of wrongfully performing and subsequently terminating the gas supply contract, even though the contract had been concluded by EGPC and EGAS and not the State itself, and of failing to protect the pipeline from terrorist acts.

The dispute gave rise to four parallel arbitrations featuring, to a large extent, the same witnesses and experts. The same facts were debated over the course of four hearings, each lasting two weeks, during which each of the tribunals addressed the same issues, examined the same documents and heard the same testimony. Two of these proceedings were brought on the basis of the gas supply agreement signed between EMG and the national Egyptian gas companies; the duplication between these two commercial arbitrations and the two arbitrations brought under investment protection treaties by EMG's shareholders is beyond the scope of the present article.[11] However, the two treaty-based arbitrations brought by EMG's shareholders were not only duplicative with the contract-based proceedings in which EMG seeks damages in relation to the same facts, but also duplicative as between one another.

Ampal-American Israel Corporation, an indirect 12.5% shareholder of EMG, pursued (with others) a claim against Egypt before an arbitral tribunal under the auspices of ICSID based on the 1986 US-Egypt BIT and the 1974 Germany-Egypt BIT.[12] At the same time, Ampal's direct subsidiary (as well as Ampal's ultimate controlling shareholder, Yosef Maiman and other companies under his control) brought a separate arbitration, for the benefit of the same 12.5% shareholding in EMG, in an UNCITRAL arbitration against Egypt based on the 1995 Poland-Egypt BIT.[13]

The claimants in both treaty-based proceedings did not hide that the damages they sought in each arbitration were for the loss of value of the same 12.5% shareholding in EMG and arose from the exact same facts. They argued, however, that neither of the treaties on which they relied, nor virtually any treaty that could be invoked by a shareholder at any level of their corporate chain, prohibits concurrent proceedings. This position ignores entirely that by bringing parallel claims in respect of the same facts and interests, the claimants were multiplying their chances of prevailing in the dispute, while leaving the State to bear the burden and risk of defending multiple proceedings initiated for the same purpose. In its Decision on Jurisdiction, the ICSID tribunal held that the parallel proceedings were "merely the result of the factual

---

11. As regards the articulation of proceedings based, on the one hand, on a treaty, and, on the other hand, on a contract, see e.g., I. Fadlallah, "La distinction 'Treaty claims – Contract claims' et la compétence de l'arbitre (CIRDI: Faisons-nous fausse route?)" ["The 'Treaty Claims – Contract Claims' Distinction and the Jurisdiction of the Arbitrator (ICSID: Are We in the Wrong?)"], Les Cahiers de l'Arbitrage, vol. III, July 2006, pp. 126–131; J. Crawford, "Treaty and Contract in Investment Arbitration," Arbitration International, 2008, ¶ 351. On parallel arbitral proceedings in general, see D. Mouralis, *L'arbitrage face aux procédures conduites en parallèle* [*Arbitration and Parallel Proceedings*], Université d'Aix-Marseille thesis, 2014.
12. *Ampal-American Israel Corporation et al. v. Egypt*, ICSID Case No. ARB/ 12/ 11. The US-Egypt treaty was signed on Mar. 11, 1986 and entered into force on Jun. 27, 1992. The Germany-Egypt treaty was signed on July 5, 1974 and entered into force on July 22, 1978. It has since been replaced by the 2005 Germany-Egypt treaty.
13. *Yosef Maiman et al. v. Egypt*, PCA Case No 2012-26. On the pressure consciously exercised on the State, see also "Yossi Maiman Threatens Egypt with $8b Lawsuit," Globes, May 31, 2011.

situation that would arise were two claims to be pursued before two investment tribunals in respect of the same tranche of the investment". Rather than dismissing the portion of the claims over which the UNCITRAL tribunal had already affirmed jurisdiction, the ICSID tribunal extended the claimants an opportunity to elect whether to pursue those claims in the ICSID proceedings or in the UNCITRAL proceedings.[14]

A second example illustrates the abusive use of treaty provisions that allow a local subsidiary to be considered a foreign national for the purposes of a treaty-based claim. As mentioned above, this control-based definition of nationality is found in Article 25(2)(b) *in fine* of the ICSID Convention as well as in certain other investment treaties. The example arose out of a dispute that followed Venezuela's nationalization of two glass production plants owned by local companies in which the Dutch company OI European Group BV ("OIEG") owned as much as 73% of the shares.

OIEG first filed an ICSID arbitration against Venezuela based on the 1991 Netherlands-Venezuela BIT, arguing that its investment – which consisted of shares which conferred it control over the companies which owned the plants – had been expropriated.[15] OIEG's locally incorporated subsidiaries subsequently initiated a second ICSID arbitration against Venezuela on the basis of the same treaty in their own name seeking damages for the expropriation of the plant.[16] Pursuant to the Netherlands-Venezuela BIT, the local subsidiaries were considered Dutch nationals because they are controlled by Dutch interests.[17] In the second arbitration, Venezuela requested that the arbitral tribunal stay the proceedings, arguing that they were duplicative given that they related to protection of the same interests. On September 23, 2013, the tribunal, by a majority, rejected this request. The two arbitrations therefore proceeded in parallel. OIEG ultimately prevailed in its claim against Venezuela,[18] while the local companies' claims are still pending.

[C]   **Analysis of the Difficulty**

A number of difficulties arise from the initiation of concurrent proceedings by investors in the same corporate chain pursuing the same interests.

The risks of inefficient use of resources and of contradictory awards are real, though not unique, to the problem of concurrent proceedings. For example, those same risks arise in the related but fundamentally different scenario in which claimants with different interests bring separate arbitrations against the same State on the basis of the same facts. It is often the case that the same measure of a host State affects a series of

---

14. *Ampal-American Israel Corporation et al. v. Egypt*, ICSID Case No. ARB/ 12/ 11, Decision on Jurisdiction, Feb. 1, 2016, para. 331.
15. *OI European Group BV v. Venezuela*, ICSID Case No. ARB/11/25. The Egypt-Poland treaty was signed on Jul. 1, 1995 and entered into force on Jan. 17, 1998. The Netherlands-Venezuela treaty was signed on Oct. 22, 1991 and entered into force on Nov. 1, 1993.
16. *Fabrica de Vidrios Los Andes, CA and Owens-Illinois de Venezuela, CA v. Venezuela*, ICSID Case No. ARB/ 12/2 1.
17. The Netherlands-Venezuela treaty was signed on 22 October 1991 and entered into force on 1 November 1993.
18. *OI European Group BV v Bolivarian Republic of Venezuela*, ICSID Case No ARB/11/25, Award, Mar. 10, 2015.

parties placed in the same position: the State may have given the same undertaking to different parties based on the same model contract, or – given that case law allows a shareholder in a local company to pursue a claim in its own name – multiple shareholders may have pursued the same State in relation to the same measure, each of them acting in their own interest on the basis of the treaty corresponding to their particular nationality. In these cases, the problems of duplicative proceedings and the multiplication of chances do not arise. However, such cases do implicate the risks of wasting State resources to defend multiple claims, as well as the risk of inconsistent decisions arising out of the same facts and claims. Treaty provisions allowing the State to require the constitution of a single arbitral tribunal to address all disputes stemming from the same facts provide the best solution to those concerns.

For example, Article 1117(3) of the North American Free Trade Agreement (NAFTA) allows the consolidation before the same tribunal of claims initiated by several shareholders or groups of shareholders based on the same State acts:

> [w]here an investor makes a claim under this Article and the investor or a non-controlling investor in the enterprise makes a claim under Article 1116 arising out of the same events that gave rise to the claim under this Article, and two or more of the claims are submitted to arbitration under Article 1120, the claims should be heard together by a Tribunal established under Article 1126, unless the Tribunal finds that the interests of a disputing party would be prejudiced thereby.

Likewise, Article 10.25 of the Central American Free Trade Agreement (CAFTA) provides for the consolidation of claims involving a common issue of law or fact or arising out of the same events or circumstances.

The same risks of wasted State resources and of contradictory decisions arise when different claims are being brought to protect the same interests. However, in these cases, they are compounded by additional risks, which are even more severe.

First, there is the obvious risk of double recovery. This risk exists whenever a subsidiary, whose compensation might ultimately be channeled up the corporate chain to its parent company, brings a claim while its parent company also pursues its own claim for damages that it incurred indirectly. It reasonable to assume that arbitrators seized of claims that may overlap with other claims will establish mechanisms to avoid double recovery. For example, arbitrators may specify in their award that any sum collected in another proceeding that indirectly benefits a claimant should be deducted from their own damages award.[19]

Rather, the most significant danger is the risk that investors who bring concurrent proceedings benefit from double or even multiple chances of prevailing in a dispute. A shareholder can bring a claim directly in its own name and in parallel, enjoy double,

---

19. *See* e.g., for such a mechanism, the Award of 9 October 2014 in *Exxon Mobil v. Venezuela* rendered by a tribunal composed of Gilbert Guillaume, President, Gabrielle Kaufmann and Ahmed El-Kosheri, providing that the award of damages is reduced by any amounts previously paid to the claimants' subsidiaries by the Venezuelan national companies further to parallel arbitrations based on contracts, *Mobil Corporation, Venezuela Holdings, BV, Mobil Cerro Negro Holding, Ltd., Mobil Venezolana de Petróleos Holdings, Inc., Mobil Cerro Negro, Ltd., and Mobil Venezolana de Petróleos, Inc. v. Venezuela*, ICSID Case No. ARB/07/27, Award of 9 October 2014, ¶¶ 378–381, 404(e).

triple, or even multiple chances of success by bringing claims through a subsidiary that it controls, or through a local company that can be deemed to be foreign for the purposes of investment protection. In the case of two parallel investment treaty arbitrations, there is no issue of double recovery if one of the tribunals constituted to hear the parallel claims rejects the claims. It is nonetheless unfair for the State to be required to assert the same defense before a second tribunal after it has already convinced the first arbitral tribunal of the merits of its position. This multiplication of chances gives an investor an unfair advantage, which is contrary to the fundamental principles of party equality in international arbitration, including from the standpoint of procedural justice and the equality of arms. It is clear, in practice, that an investor can multiply its chances of prevailing by setting up multiple arbitral tribunals composed of arbitrators that are more or less to its satisfaction. This procedural strategy is more than an insurance policy against the uncertainties surrounding the composition of arbitral tribunals. For instance, if three tribunals are constituted to hear the same dispute, then the State must convince six out of nine arbitrators in order to prevail, while the investor need only convince two arbitrators. Therefore, arbitrators who take into account only the need to prevent double – or multiple – recovery fail to address the profound procedural inequality that stems from allowing the investor to cease its claims whenever it emerges victorious, at whichever level in the chain of control, and to enjoy – if it does not prevail – a second, third or umpteenth chance in another proceeding. These ratchet-effect parallel proceedings present the most significant difficulty that confronts the investment arbitration system whenever many claims are brought in relation to the same facts and to protect the same interests, based on various treaties.

When envisioning potential solutions, it is necessary to take into consideration the procedural dimension of the injustice caused to the State by the strategies discussed above.

§9.02 THE POTENTIAL SOLUTIONS

Addressing the procedural inequality that results from the initiation of concurrent proceedings for the benefit of the same interests is more challenging *de lege lata* than *de lege ferenda*.

[A] *De lege lata*

The greatest difficulty in addressing concurrent proceedings confronts arbitrators who must apply early classical investment treaties, which lack provisions that may directly preempt the pursuit of multiple claims for the benefit of the same interests. Although these older treaties were not drafted with the intention of allowing parallel claims to proceed, they generally require only the satisfaction of the ordinary requirements for jurisdiction (an investor with the requisite nationality who owns a protected investment, etc.). If the claimant in each parallel proceeding can meet these formal requirements, the parent company will be able to present itself as a protected investor within the meaning of the treaty based on its own nationality, while its subsidiary may do the same under a separate treaty on the basis of its own nationality. Should the chain of controlled companies be longer, each company of the group will likewise, at least *prima facie*, meet the conditions for the application of the relevant treaty. As previously noted, only the concurrence of such claims proceeding in parallel is problematic, but not each claim taken individually. The difficulty is that the older generation of treaties lack specific provisions to limit the occurrence of such concurrent proceedings.

Arbitrators have several potential tools to address the problem of concurrent arbitral proceedings that are initiated to protect the same interests. *First*, they could focus on the conditions of their jurisdiction. In particular, arbitrators might consider whether the host State has consented to the protection of an investment indirectly held by a national of the other State party that is more directly held, in the chain of control, by a company of a different nationality. In other words, the question is whether, as a matter of jurisdiction, a company asserting a claim under a particular investment treaty – be it a classical treaty or a more modern treaty – on the basis of a given nationality may present the same investment as possessing another nationality for the purposes of the application of another investment protection treaty.

For example, consider an investment in Kazakhstan that is indirectly held by a French company but directly owned by its Dutch subsidiary (a wholly-owned subsidiary for the purposes of this example). The question that follows is whether the French investor may present the investment as French, in order to invoke the protection of the 1998 France-Kazakhstan BIT, at the same time that its subsidiary presents the investment as Dutch in order to invoke the 2002 Netherlands-Kazakhstan BIT. One could conclude that an indirect investment in Kazakhstan may be considered French based on the plain terms of the France-Kazakhstan BIT.[20] However, the question arises whether the indirect chain of ownership is broken if the investment is considered not as French, but as having the nationality of the entity that directly controls the investment. In fact, the decision to treat the investment as having the nationality of the directly controlling entity can only be taken with the assent of the parent company, i.e. the French company. In that case, a single investment is being presented as having a different nationality for the jurisdictional requirements of different treaties. Specifically, the Dutch subsidiary could not bring a claim against Kazakhstan pursuant to the Netherlands-Kazakhstan BIT without the consent or active participation of its parent company. Given these circumstances, the conditions of "investor" or "investment" under the treaty would not be met for the purposes of the arbitral tribunal's jurisdiction. This is because the interposition of nationality breaks the logic that would enable a finding that the French investor owns a protected investment in Kazakhstan, i.e., that the investment is French.

Another, more subjective, way of analyzing the issue involves a question of waiver, namely, whether the French investor's decision to direct its subsidiary to present the relevant investment as Dutch, for purposes of the Dutch-Kazakhstan BIT treaty, constitutes a waiver of its right to present the same investment as French for

---

20. *See* Art. 1(3) of the 1998 France-Kazakhstan BIT.

Chapter 9: Concurrent Proceedings in Investment Arbitration §9.02[A]

purposes of the France-Kazakhstan BIT. If one were to consider that the same investment may not have two different nationalities for the purposes of its protection under two different treaties, the decision to invoke the protection of one treaty could preclude the possibility of also invoking the benefit of another treaty through inconsistent claims. The principle of good faith or the principle of estoppel would support this analysis.

It remains problematic that classical investment treaties are silent on the issue of waiver. Furthermore, it must be noted that the problem itself originates in arbitral case law, specifically from awards which have held that the foreign shareholder of a domestic company that suffered damages due to actions of the host State in breach of the treaty may legitimately seek reparation of the damage that the shareholder has personally suffered as a result.[21] This case law has created the risk of multiple claims arising out of the same dispute. In reality, however, the direct victim of this action is in a better position than the indirect victim to demand reparation for the harm suffered. If the direct victim is able to assert its claims before an impartial adjudicative body that may uphold its rights, the indirect victim is not in a legitimate position to bring its own claim.

With these considerations in mind, it seems only appropriate that the case law should be altered in order to limit the most undesirable consequences of the principle. This fine-tuning could be based on the idea that, by inviting its subsidiary to bring a claim for damages before an arbitral tribunal constituted on the basis of a treaty, the shareholder has decided that its subsidiary's claim may replace the value it lost as a result of the impugned actions of the State against the subsidiary's assets. Therefore, the shareholder who would have kept its shareholding in the subsidiary intact would have no grievance to assert. For the purposes of jurisdiction – and without prejudice to the discussion on the notions of investor and investment – this approach would signify that advancing a treaty claim based on one nationality constitutes a waiver that precludes an investor's affiliates from invoking the protections of a different treaty using a different nationality.

Second, arbitrators could address the problem of concurrent arbitral proceedings by focusing on the requirements of standing and thus the admissibility of claims. Specifically, one could consider that a parent company lacks standing to pursue a claim for damages on behalf of its subsidiary if the parent lacks a right that is independent of its subsidiary, and has assented to its subsidiary's decision to assert its rights on the basis of a treaty. Indeed, the parent company does not suffer any harm if its subsidiary's claim is brought before an independent tribunal (rather than an organ of the defendant State) that applies standards similar to those that would have been applied by a tribunal seized of the parent company's claim under the treaty corresponding to the parent company's nationality.

Third, there is a potential argument, which could be advanced on the merits, that a parent company has not suffered any damage if it retained its shares in a subsidiary. Despite the fact that the value of those shares may have been affected by the impugned

---

21. *See supra.*

acts of the State, the subsidiary possesses a corresponding cause of action for the loss of value under an international treaty before an independent international tribunal.

This last approach is less satisfactory than the others, and does not put an end to a redundant claim brought by the entity with the most indirect connection to the dispute at the jurisdictional phase. Thus, it does not allow the State to avoid the burden of double or multiple proceedings. However, to the extent that this approach requires no more than ascertaining that the claimant company has retained its shareholding in the subsidiary that brought a claim before an independent tribunal, it could – for reasons of procedural efficiency – be considered as a preliminary objection and not, strictly speaking, as an argument on the merits.

Be it a question of jurisdiction, admissibility, or merits, the arbitral case law that has allowed the development of the shareholder's individual claims for damages suffered by its subsidiary, without measuring its full procedural consequences, should make the necessary adjustments to this rule, so as to prevent it from becoming an instrument for abuse of process by investors who are unconcerned with the integrity of the investment treaty system.

[B]   *De lege ferenda*

The possibility of triggering parallel arbitral proceedings for the benefit of the same interests under different treaties is probably one of the issues of contemporary investment protection law most in need of an urgent solution.

De lege ferenda, the simplest approach would be to introduce conditions accompanying the State's consent to arbitration in new investment protection treaties. Specifically, the State's consent would be subject to a waiver by the investor of any additional claim for reparation of the consequences of the same actions, be it on its own behalf or on behalf of any entity that it controls.

To that end, it would be sufficient to set up a mechanism modeled on the NAFTA and CAFTA clauses that require the investor to irrevocably waive any proceedings on the merits before domestic jurisdictions as a precondition to the admissibility of a claim founded on these instruments. Article 1121 of NAFTA provides that:

> 1. A disputing investor may submit a claim under Article 1116 to arbitration only if: […] (b) the investor and, where the claim is for loss or damage to an interest in an enterprise of another Party that is a juridical person that the investor owns or controls directly or indirectly, the enterprise, waive their right to initiate or continue before any administrative tribunal or court under the law of any Party, or other dispute settlement procedures, any proceedings with respect to the measure of the disputing Party that is alleged to be a breach referred to in Article 1116, except for proceedings for injunctive, declaratory or other extraordinary relief, not involving the payment of damages, before an administrative tribunal or court under the law of the disputing Party.

For its part, Article 10.18 of CAFTA provides that:

> 2. No claim may be submitted to arbitration under this Section unless: (a) the claimant consents in writing to arbitration in accordance with the procedures set

out in this Agreement; and (b) the notice of arbitration is accompanied, (i) for claims submitted to arbitration under Article 10.16.1(a), by the claimant's written waiver, and (ii) for claims submitted to arbitration under Article 10.16.1(b), by the claimant's and the enterprise's written waivers of any right to initiate or continue before any administrative tribunal or court under the law of any Party, or other dispute settlement procedures, any proceeding with respect to any measure alleged to constitute a breach referred to in Article 10.16. 3. Notwithstanding paragraph 2(b), the claimant (for claims brought under Article 10.16.1(a)) and the claimant or the enterprise (for claims brought under Article 10.16.1(b)) may initiate or continue an action that seeks interim injunctive relief and does not involve the payment of monetary damages before a judicial or administrative tribunal of the respondent, provided that the action is brought for the sole purpose of preserving the claimant's or the enterprise's rights and interests during the pendency of the arbitration.

These rules aim to prevent any duplication of treaty claims by the local company and by the shareholder whose investment consists of the shares held in that company. At the heart of these provisions lies the intention to preclude investors from obtaining multiple chances to succeed before different forums seized on different jurisdictional bases with respect to the same actions. In their current form, however, these provisions do not eliminate the risk that investors might bring multiple claims based on different treaties at different levels in the domestic company's chain of control. However, these provisions could easily be supplemented to eliminate such risk.

For example, there could be a requirement that a claimant who invokes a relevant treaty provides proof of waiver by all the entities it controls, of the benefit of any instrument of investment protection it may otherwise invoke to bring a claim in damages resulting from the specific actions of the host State. In this regard, the European Union, having inherited the competence to negotiate investment protection treaties for the Union as a whole since the Lisbon Treaty, has squarely addressed the problem in its recent treaties.[22] Pending a revision of existing treaties that do not feature this type of provision, the negotiation of an instrument that may be adopted by those States wishing to avoid situations of an investor having more than one chance to prevail under different treaties – based on the model instrument adopted by UNCITRAL on transparency[23] – would also be welcome.[24]

---

22. For instance, the recently concluded EU-Vietnam Free Trade Agreement provides for waiver of claims brought before a Tribunal insofar as a claimant acting on its own behalf or on behalf of a locally established company "may not submit a claim to the Tribunal if any person who directly or indirectly has an ownership interest in or is controlled by" the claimant or the locally established company, respectively, "has a pending claim before this Tribunal or any other domestic or international court or tribunal concerning the same measure as that alleged to be inconsistent with the provisions [of the treaty] and the same loss or damage, unless that person withdraws such pending claim." Finalized Draft EU-Vietnam Free Trade Agreement (2016), Chapter 8, chapter II, s. 3, Art. 8. *See also* Finalized Draft EU-Singapore Free Trade Agreement (2015), Chapter 9, s. A, Article 9.17; EU Commission Draft TTIP (2016), Trade in Services, Investment and E-Commerce, Chapter II, s. 5, Art. 14.
23. UNCITRAL Rules on Transparency in Treaty-based Investor-State Arbitration, Apr. 1, 2014.
24. For an UNCITRAL initiative to this end, see the reports of the 46th session (Jul. 8–26, 2013), §§ 129–133 and 311, and of the 47th sessions (Jul. 7–18, 2014), §§ 126 and 130.

The adoption of such provisions or agreements would erase the procedural injustice that follows from allowing different companies in the same chain of control to pursue, in parallel, different claims on the basis of different treaties to protect the same interests. This would undoubtedly contribute to reinforcing the legitimacy of the investment arbitration system as a whole.

CHAPTER 10
The Role of the Arbitrator in Energy Disputes

Robert Gaitskell Q.C. CEng.

§10.01 INTRODUCTION

The energy sector is fundamental to life as we know it. This is particularly so in the developed and mature economies in the northern hemisphere, but is also true, though to a lesser extent, even in the most undeveloped of nations.

The range of fuels that are embraced by the energy sector is steadily expanding. A century ago hydrocarbon fuels such as oil and gas were the predominant fuels in the developed world, while wood of various kinds was significant in impoverished nations. Now there is a kaleidoscope of energy sources to be considered, ranging from the traditional hydrocarbon suppliers mining coal or pumping oil and gas in conventional ways, through the relatively new procedure of fracking ('fracking'), particularly in the United States, and including traditional hydroelectric power, nuclear power plants and renewable sources such as wind, solar and wave power. The situation is complicated by developments within each of the above broad categories. For example, wind power has long been a feature on isolated farms in Africa, where a lone windmill often stands indolently still in the hot afternoon sun until periodically turning in a brief breeze to pump up water for thirsty cattle. Such wind power is now eclipsed by the monster wind turbines, both onshore and offshore, which proliferate throughout Europe, and particularly in the United Kingdom.

A number of the sources of energy are in a state of rapid development. For example, although nuclear fusion power plants have been in operation for half a century, the '*new kid on the block*' is the possibility of commercially available nuclear fusion power. Developments are coming at two ends of the spectrum: in France, at Cadarache, an international group, including every major nation with an interest in nuclear power, is funding the vast and exciting ITER F4E nuclear fusion prototype power plant. If all goes according to plan, this will in due course produce much cheaper, safer and more readily available nuclear power which will revolutionise the energy market, driving down prices significantly.

This rapidly changing and expanding energy sector is the environment within which an arbitrator practising in the field of energy disputes must operate. Consequently, there are a number of characteristics of the disputes encountered which tend to distinguish such cases from those in other commercial sectors. For example, energy arbitrations usually involve complex technical factual evidence, where detailed expert reports and oral evidence is essential. Further, it is often the case that a site visit to a remote hydroelectric dam or power station or oil refinery is required.

§10.02 TYPES OF ENERGY DISPUTES

The role of an arbitrator in an energy dispute is dictated by the precise nature of the dispute itself. The range is enormous. Each sector of the energy spectrum has its own characteristics and subtleties. For example, oil disputes come in a wide range of shapes and sizes. Upstream problems may include disputes about the search for oil or gas. Seismic prospectors in the North African desert, or marine seismic prospectors in boats off the West Coast of Africa are all dependent upon the support of the governments controlling the areas in which they work. If that support is withdrawn, whether because the government considers that the prospector is misbehaving or because the government is concerned about dissident activity in the area, the parties may resort to arbitration pursuant to the International Convention for the Settlement of Disputes (ICSID). This Convention became operational in 1966 and enables a private company, such as an oil prospector, to pursue an arbitration claim against a sovereign state. Similarly, should the state expropriate an oil refinery or drilling platform, arbitration under the ICSID procedure may be chosen as the route to redress for the aggrieved foreign company. Disputes also often arise in functioning oil fields, whether because the equipment malfunctions and the operator uses an arbitration clause in his agreement with the equipment manufacturer and supplier to seek compensation, or because the product of the oil field is being sold at an agreed rate when the market price collapses and the purchaser considers that taking the agreed volumes of oil at the agreed price will simply bankrupt it. The recent price collapse has led to premature terminations of a number of projects and the contractors concerned have turned to arbitration for redress.

This same range of possible disputes is replicated for each form of energy, whether hydroelectric or renewable or nuclear. The range is limitless, but in virtually every case there is a serious technical element. Energy sector disputes, other than straightforward differences about pricing mechanisms or the true construction of contractual terms, are very fact-heavy, involving substantial witness statements, as well as experts' reports, backed up by very substantial hearing bundles, and involving costs for each party well into the millions of US Dollars.

§10.03 OUTSET OF THE ARBITRATION

Since energy sector arbitrations generally arise from dispute resolution clauses drafted by experienced litigation lawyers, they usually include provision for an arbitration to be conducted under the rules of one of the major appointing bodies, such as the International Chamber of Commerce (ICC) in Paris, or the London Court of International Arbitration (LCIA), or similar bodies in Switzerland, Singapore and other major arbitration hubs. The arbitration clause will also identify the seat or place of arbitration, often a world centre such as London, Paris, Singapore or Miami. Also specified will be the law governing the arbitral procedure, and the substantive law governing the construction of the contract. These will often be the same.

Sometimes parties, when finalising a contractual deal late at night, omit to include within their arbitration clause key data such as that just described, or deliberately choose to specify UNCITRAL arbitration relying on the Model Law of the United Nations Commission on International Trade Law. Arbitrators generally look askance at an arbitration clause specifying an ad hoc arbitration, to be administered by the parties themselves, using the UNCITRAL procedure. This is because of the possibility that the arbitration will be unsettled by one or other party misbehaving in the absence of an overseeing administrative body to restrain them.

§10.04 CONDITIONS PRECEDENT TO ARBITRATION

It is becoming increasingly common for tiered dispute resolution clauses to be used in energy sector contracts. For example, a number of the standard forms produced by the Federation Internationale des Ingéniéurs-Conseils (FIDIC) include a dispute board procedure as a condition precedent to the commencement of arbitration. This obliges the party wishing to commence arbitration first to take the disputed matter to the contractual dispute board for an adjudication decision, and then to challenge that decision within the stipulated time. It is not uncommon for, say, a contractor being kept out of his money for work done on an oil refinery to hasten to arbitration without having fulfilled all the necessary preceding steps. Some multi-tiered clauses contain a series of graduated steps, commencing with negotiations between chief executive officers, then proceeding to mediation, then to adjudication (whether under a dispute board or not), all to be satisfied before arbitration may be commenced. The arbitrator may find that allegations about the failure to satisfy these earlier steps forms part of a challenge to his or her jurisdiction, and jurisdictional challenges of one kind or another are not uncommon. Thus, the jurisdictional challenge may have several limbs, including the failure to satisfy conditions precedent, as well as an assertion that a claim notice was not given within the contractually stipulated time, or that a statutory limitation period (which in some jurisdictions can be surprisingly short) has expired. Thus it is that before the substance of the dispute can be addressed the arbitrator may well find that a partial award dealing with a preliminary issue concerning jurisdiction will have to be produced. This both slows down the overall timetable for the arbitration, and increases costs for the parties.

§10.05 PROCEDURAL STEPS

Since many energy arbitrations take place on the basis of the ICC Rules, the arbitrators may often find that their first obligations after appointment are to produce the Terms of Reference and the First Procedural Order. These are generally finalised at the time of a first meeting, whether electronically by video-link or telephone, or physically in person. Energy disputes frequently involve parties in widely separately countries, with a Tribunal elsewhere, so that a physical meeting, often for only one or two hours, is a disproportionate use of costs. In these circumstances an electronic meeting has a substantial attraction. It is sometimes said that a physical meeting should be held whenever possible because this gives the warring parties an opportunity to consider settlement at an early stage. When the parties and Tribunal are collectively deciding upon the nature of the first meeting these factors will invariably be taken into account.

The arbitrator must also produce at this point the First Procedural Order. This can be conveniently achieved by asking the parties themselves to discuss the broad timetable they envisage, leading to a hearing. They will give the arbitrator their estimate of the length of hearing, and when they expect to be ready to hold it, and once that has been placed in everyone's diary the intermediate milestone steps leading to the hearing can be determined. Since energy disputes often involve substantial witness statements, relating a sorry tale of incompetence in construction work on an oil rig, or in installing sophisticated equipment in a power station, adequate time must be allowed within the timetable for these statements to be produced and for all the supporting documents to be located, since the statement will generally refer to them. Not only will the witness statements be lengthy, but there will often be a plethora of such statements. It is increasingly common practice for an arbitrator to suggest to the parties that each witness statement carries on its front page a photograph of the witness in question. This means that at the end of a long hearing, involving many witnesses, the Tribunal is able to recall easily the person who at the hearing gave the oral evidence supporting the statement.

§10.06 PLEADINGS OR MEMORIALS

Since energy arbitrations proliferate in both common law and civil jurisdictions, and the parties probably come from both backgrounds, at an early stage there needs to be agreement as to whether the common law preference for a series of pleadings (involving Statement of Claim, Defence and Counterclaim, Reply and Defence to Counterclaim, and a Reply to Defence to Counterclaim, followed by disclosure/discovery of documents) is to be adopted, or whether the memorial route (much more common in the civil law jurisdictions) is to be used. The latter procedure involves a much more comprehensive statement of each party's case at an early stage, accompanied by the relevant witness statements, correspondence, and, in some cases, experts' reports.

§10.07 EXPERTS AND THEIR REPORTS

As already noted, it is a common feature of energy arbitrations that experts and their reports play a significant role. There is a wide range of possible expert disciplines involved. Geologists may be concerned with the interpretation of seismic activity in the desert. Welding engineers may be called upon where pipe welding on oilrigs is in doubt. Geotechnical engineers may be crucial where a tunnel, for water feeding a hydroelectric turbine, has collapsed, and so on. An experienced energy arbitrator will have in mind a number of important considerations as regards the expert evidence. These include the following.

First, there needs to be control of the number and of the disciplines of the experts. The First Procedural Order should specify what each party considers to be the disciplines required. Thereafter, adding an expert from a further discipline will require leave. This prevents a party being taken by surprise close to the hearing by discovering that the other side has twice the number of experts, in a variety of novel disciplines, that he does not.

Secondly, once the experts have been identified the parties should agree, for each discipline, the precise questions they are to address. This avoids the problem, which will otherwise inevitably occur, of their reports being *'ships passing in the night'*, with one expert addressing a different series of questions from the other expert, so that the Tribunal is unaware of what each thinks about the other's views. This problem can be particularly acute in the case of programming/delay experts, where there is a range of possible analytical methods, and it is common for opposing experts to adopt different methods, even when addressing the same questions. Energy arbitrators are used to being faced with at least five commonly used delay analysis techniques:

(a) Impacted as-planned;
(b) Time impact analysis;
(c) Collapsed as-built/but-for analysis;
(d) Retrospective snapshot windows analysis/time slice;
(e) As-planned versus as-built windows analysis.

The Tribunal should give the greatest encouragement to the parties to find a consensus as to which method is to be employed by the experts. If each is insistent that it will use its own method, which is different from the other's method, then one solution can be for the Tribunal to ask that, having dealt with his own preferred method, the expert then goes on to comment in their report on the other expert's chosen method.

§10.08 'HOT-TUBBING' OF EXPERTS

For reasons that will now be explained, it is essential that well before the hearing the Tribunal makes plain to the parties whether or not there is to be concurrent expert evidence (colloquially known as 'hot-tubbing') or not, and, if so, the method to be used. It is becoming common in energy arbitrations for hot-tubbing in some form or another to be employed. Essentially, experts of like disciplines are put together in the witness box so that when they give their evidence the opposing expert or experts has the opportunity to challenge them immediately.

Two broad models are employed by Tribunals for the purpose of hot-tubbing. The first model involves the Tribunal itself effectively undertaking significant cross-examination of the experts. The author much prefers a second, quite different, model. In this procedure the advocates for the two parties carry out their cross-examination of the opposing experts in the normal way. Thereafter, the experts are put together in the witness box and the Tribunal has the opportunity to ask such questions of them collectively as it wishes. The advocates can then re-examine in the normal way. The first model has a number of potential problems. For example, the advocates may abdicate their conventional role and simply hand-over their experts for cross-examination by the Tribunal. The Tribunal itself is reluctant to cross-examine with any rigour because this can be perceived as bias, depending on the question. The result is that the experts are not properly challenged on their evidence, and the Tribunal is left with inadequate material to make the decisions it has to produce. There is also a problem with ill-matched experts, where one is bombastic (although not particularly knowledgeable), while the other is extremely knowledgeable but diffident in demeanour. In such a situation the bombastic expert may appear the most persuasive and so mislead the Tribunal.

§10.09 EXPERTS' MEETINGS AND REPORTS

When the First Procedural Order is being drawn up consideration should be given to the question of the production of the experts' reports and their meetings with their opposite numbers. Some Tribunals favour the experts' meetings before they produce their reports, so that the reports reflect what each expert has learnt in the meetings. Other arbitrators prefer that the reports come first, so that when the meetings take place they are informed by the earlier statement in print of what each expert considers to be the position. The author's own view is that meetings should precede reports, because otherwise there is a danger that once an expert has committed himself or herself in writing to a particular view they will be reluctant to depart from that view, since they might think this demonstrates a lack of conviction. By contrast, early meetings enable the experts to take account of the other experts' views as they develop and refine their own conclusions. This can help in narrowing the gap between the experts.

The Procedural Order ought also to include provision for a joint experts' report, which identifies areas of agreement and disagreement. This can be the most important document in the arbitration, since it focuses the Tribunal's attention on what is actually dividing the parties.

In the author's experience there can never be too many experts' meetings. Even after the joint report has been produced, a further meeting may well enable certain areas of disagreement to be reduced or refined. Prior to the joint report, there should ordinarily be the original report from each expert, followed by a reply report in which each expert has the opportunity to comment on what he has read in the other expert's report. It is not uncommon for an expert, having read his opponent's reply, to accept that a mistake has been made and to correct it, thereby reducing the area of disagreement. Often experts will represent the single largest element of cost expenditure for a party in an energy arbitration. Hence, finding methods of reducing the area of dispute between the experts can have a significant impact on the hearing costs incurred by each party.

§10.10 THE HEARING BUNDLE

It is not uncommon in energy arbitrations for the hearing bundle to run to many dozens of lever arch files. One way of reducing the number of files, and the costs associated with the production of the physical bundle, is to discuss with the parties a procedure whereby they produce a core bundle of what they consider to be the documents likely to be referred to at the hearing. These will generally include the documents identified by the witnesses in their statements, and by the experts in their reports, as well as the pleadings, the contract, manufacturing codes, etc. All the other documents produced by both sides can be put on an electronic storage device and made available to the Tribunal should it ever need to consult them, and be used, if necessary, at the hearing where a witness suddenly refers to a particular document. In such circumstances it can be called up from the electronic bundle on the electronic storage device and shown on a screen so that everyone is able to read it.

Sometimes Tribunals attempt to avoid paper bundles altogether and simply rely upon the electronic storage device and a lap top for the purposes of the hearing. The author does not favour this procedure because he ordinarily puts a yellow sticker on each document referred to at the hearing, identifying which witness referred to it. At the end of the hearing there emerges an annotated bundle which makes the production of the award much easier. Although there are various means by which electronic documents may be marked, in the author's experience marking them is not as convenient as marking a paper copy.

§10.11 THE PRE-HEARING SUBMISSIONS

The First Procedural Order should also include provision for pre-hearing submissions from both parties no less than one week prior to the hearing. This will give the Tribunal ample opportunity to digest the contents and refer to the many documents that will have been identified in the submissions.

These submissions should be accompanied by a running-order of witnesses, indicating roughly the time which the parties believe each will take. This running order enables the opposing side to plan its cross-examination sensibly.

A chronology and dramatis personae should ordinarily be produced by the parties and should accompany the Pre-Hearing Submissions. Not only will these be of benefit as the Tribunal reads into the case, but they are invaluable afterwards when the award is being produced.

§10.12 'CHESS-CLOCK' USAGE OF TIME

Since all involved, whether Tribunal or advocates or witnesses, are busy people, it is essential that there be firm control of the hearing period. If two weeks (a not uncommon period for an energy hearing) is the stipulated period, then the usual procedure is for each party to be allocated 50% of the time available, to use as it wishes. Thus, if the Claimant wishes to use time opening the case and elaborating on its pre-hearing submissions, followed by calling its evidence, and ending with lengthy closing oral submissions, that is a matter for the Claimant. The Respondent, for its part, may prefer to have a very short opening and closing, but to devote all the rest of its time to cross-examining the Claimant's witnesses. Again, that is entirely for the Respondent to decide.

Ordinarily, each party will appoint a timekeeper, and these persons will meet at each break in order to agree how much time each party has used from its allocation. If there is a dispute this can be immediately placed before the Tribunal for a decision. The parties need to agree amongst themselves how they will deal with time used by Tribunal interventions, or procedural applications (particularly those which fail) but which use up precious time.

In advance of the hearing, usually at the pre-hearing review, there should be agreement between the Tribunal and parties as to the detailed structure for each day. For example, if the hearing is to commence at 10:00 am and run until 1:00 pm, with an afternoon session of 2:00 pm to 5:00 pm, it is usual to have a fifteen minute coffee break in the morning and an equivalent tea break in the afternoon. All of this needs to be taken into account in determining precisely how long each party has.

§10.13 WITNESSES

Another matter that needs to be decided in advance of the hearing is how witnesses are to be treated. Are they to be sworn with the use of holy books? Are they simply to be affirmed? In the author's experience, in energy arbitrations it is not uncommon for the procedure to be adopted being that the Chairman of the Tribunal simply says to each witness, whether factual or expert, that they are expected to tell the truth, the whole truth and nothing but the truth, and if they fail to do this there may be legal consequences. If formal swearing is to be adopted, then it is usual for the parties to produce the necessary holy books, since only they will know the precise religions of their witnesses. In the Middle East certain forms of oath are compulsory.

Witnesses in energy disputes are often scattered about the globe. If the dispute is about, say, an oil seismic prospecting contract that was terminated prematurely, the witnesses will have moved from, say, the Middle East, to South America and Indonesia to work for other employers, who will be reluctant to release them to travel to, say, London, for a hearing. This raises the possibility of video, or even, Skype, cross-examination. There may also be translation/interpretation difficulties, because the energy industry is entirely global.

In energy arbitrations, where time is at a premium, it is not uncommon for the First Procedural Order to stipulate that witness statements will stand as evidence in chief, as will experts' reports. This saves much time at the hearing. When a witness is called there can, obviously, be an opportunity for the witness to identify the statements or reports produced by that witness and to confirm their veracity, and to make any necessary corrections. Thereafter, the witness is tendered for cross-examination. Re-examination is, in the usual way, restricted to dealing with points raised in cross-examination.

§10.14   POST-HEARING

In energy arbitrations, because of the wealth of evidence, particularly expert evidence, that needs to be adduced and assimilated, it is not unusual for the time to be used almost entirely for cross-examination of witnesses, with little time for opening or closing oral submissions. This means that the parties ordinarily wish to have an opportunity to produce post-hearing briefs. These should be produced soon after the hearing, so that memories have not faded.

It is not uncommon for reply post-hearing submissions to be produced, so that each party has the opportunity of responding to particular allegations made by the other side in their post-hearing briefs, where what is said is considered to be contrary to the evidence or law and hence unjustified.

In energy arbitrations the parties often ask the Tribunal, at the end of the hearing, for an indication of when the award will be complete. Obviously, where the administering body, for example, the ICC, has a procedure for scrutiny of a draft award, the time for this process needs to be factored into the overall timetable. Having such a target date for the Tribunal helps to ensure that the award is produced expeditiously.

§10.15   THE DRAFT AWARD

The draft Award should be produced as soon as possible after the receipt of any post-hearing submissions so that the evidence is fresh in the minds of the Tribunal. The draft is then submitted for scrutiny, where this is part of the stipulated procedure, and after approval and any necessary changes, may be returned to the administering body for formal issuance. A number of administrative bodies require that the draft award be produced within three months of the final submissions.

§10.16   CONCLUSION

The global nature and technical complexity of disputes in the fast-moving energy sector often generate hard-fought arbitrations. The Tribunals need to be prepared for these challenges, but in return are rewarded with fascinating cases.

CHAPTER 11
Annulled International Arbitral Awards and Remand: Can/Should the Same Arbitral Tribunal Take the Case Anew? A Short Analysis from a Swiss Perspective

Teresa Giovannini

The 27th Annual ITA (Institute for Transnational Arbitration) Workshop (Dallas, June 2015) was dedicated to the topic: *'Subconscious Influences in International Arbitration'*. Among others, the question of *'Subconscious influences in Arbitral Decision-Making'* was presented by prominent lawyers and psychologists, and in particular by Prof. Jeffrey Rachlinski, Professor of Law at Cornell Law School who also holds a BA, a MA and a PhD in Psychology. Prof. Rachlinski's research interests involve primarily the application of cognitive and social psychology to law with special attention to judicial decision-making.[1]

Based upon collected data from over 5,000 trial judges and 400 lawyers about how they make decisions, Prof. Rachlinski observes that the decision-making psychological mechanism shows that there are two ways that people make choices.

One is what psychologists like to call *'System One'*. *'System One is an intuitive way of making decisions, It is sort of deciding from the "gut". It is intuitive. It is associative. It is affective or emotional, and it produces rapid, confident judgments ... It is the confident system'*.[2]

'System Two' is *'more deliberative, more rule based, more calculating and mathematical'*.[3]

---

1. World Arbitration & Mediation Review, Institute for Transnational Arbitration, 2015, Volume 9, no. 4, pp. 356 and 357.
2. Jeffrey J. Rachlinski, in World Arbitration & Mediation Review, Institute for Transnational Arbitration, 2015, Volume 9, no. 4, p. 365.
3. *Ibid.*

As put by Prof. Rachlinski, *'You need System One'*, and people who are not very intuitive, who do not have strong emotional systems *'actually make terrible decision-makers'*.[4] The problem is that System One is *'happening without us knowing about it'*, which makes it a *'troublesome System because it is planting those illusions in your mind'*.[5]

In her commentary to these observations, Prof. Shari Seidman Diamond[6] noted that indeed, a *'number of studies ... show that judges as well as lay people are influenced by legally irrelevant information'*,[7] adding that *'when you hear something that is not consistent with a story that you believe to be true, you may not be hearing it. You may not be absorbing it. You may not be incorporating it into your deliberative process'*.[8]

This, in the author's opinion, explains why it is not possible for an individual or a tribunal to review and change a decision made on the merits of a dispute on the exclusive basis of a System Two Information, namely on the basis of a rule or an objective element that ought to be considered according to the set aside court judgment. System Two considerations, as we have seen, shall not and cannot alter System One results that, once reached, can hardly, even in the best good faith, be reconsidered. What is called in French *'l'intime conviction du Juge'* is reached once for all, and hardly ever be altered. And subjectively, as put by Andrew Foyle in his presentation to the ASA annual conference in Basel on 28 January 2011: *'The unsuccessful party will ... feel that a tribunal will inevitably feel it needs to defend and stand by the reasoning of its first award, so that the unsuccessful party will always be at a disadvantage in any arbitration before the same tribunal relating to future similar disputes.'*[9]

The Waivable Red List as per General Standard (4)(c) of the IBA Guidelines on Conflicts of Interests in International Arbitration[10] mirrors such concerns when stating that:

> '*A person should not serve as an arbitrator*' unless ' *all parties expressly agree that such person may serve as arbitrator despite the conflict of interest*'.

when:

> '*The arbitrator has given legal advice or provided an expert opinion, on the dispute to a party or an affiliate of one of the parties*' and/or

> '*The arbitrator had a prior involvement in the dispute*'.

The best illustration of arbitrators having given an opinion or having had a prior involvement in the dispute consists obviously in their having issued a final award on

---

4. Ibid., p. 366.
5. Ibid.
6. Professor of Law and Professor of Psychology, Howard J. Trienens and Northwestern University.
7. Shari Seidman Diamond, Institute for Transnational Arbitration, World Arbitration & Mediation Review, 2015, Volume 9, no. 4, p. 377.
8. Ibid., p. 381.
9. Andrew Foyle, *Extension and Resumption of the Arbitral Tribunal Function after the Final Award*, in Post Award Issues, ASA Special Series no. 38, 2011, pp. 113-115.
10. Adopted by resolution of the IBA Council on 23 Oct. 2014.

Chapter 11: Annulled International Arbitral Awards and Remand

the merits in that dispute. In line with the psychological process described above, the arbitrators indeed will be in the almost impossible position to have to decide anew and afresh the same dispute despite the fact that their intuition – on the basis of the same facts[11] – led them to decide 'from the gut' in a certain way.

This situation is echoed in and by the *functus officio* doctrine that dictates that:

> *'Once arbitrators have fully exercised their authority to adjudicate the issues submitted to them, their authority over those questions is ended, and the arbitrators have no further authority, absent agreement by the parties, to redetermine those issues'.*[12]
>
> *'The doctrine is based on the analogy of a judge who resigns his office and, having done so, naturally cannot rule on a request to reconsider or amend his decision. Arbitrators are ad hoc judges – judges for a case; and when the case is over they cease to be judges..., like Cincinnatus returning to his plow'.*[13]

This doctrine does not however prohibit a Tribunal from rectifying an error or from issuing an additional award on a question that has been omitted in the award, such steps not being equivalent or even comparable to revisiting a decision already made. Indeed, and to begin with, the Model Law[14] encompasses the *functus officio* doctrine as it contains a precise and structured system that provides that an arbitral tribunal loses its capacity to act in an arbitration after the final award has been rendered but in specific and *'carefully –defined exceptions for corrections and interpretation'*. Several national legislations have added to these exceptions the residual power of the tribunal to *'supplement'* the award to address omissions in the final award.[15]

In such a context, Article 34.4. of the Model Law provides that the court seized by a request to set aside an award may suspend those proceedings and remand the case to the arbitral tribunal for the latter to *'resume the arbitral proceedings or to take such other action as in the arbitral tribunal's opinion will eliminate the grounds for setting aside'*, which, as embodied in the national legislations (such as Article 1059.4 of the German Code of Civil Procedure) corresponds to the possibility for the arbitral tribunal to eliminate errors of mere form.

The 1996 English Arbitration Act goes somewhat further as it provides (beside the possibility for the arbitral tribunal – on its own motion or on a party's application – to correct, clarify or complete the award) for the court to remit the case to the tribunal for

---

11. The present study excludes the issue of revision of the awards based on new facts.
12. *T. Co Metals, LLC v. Dempsey Pipe & Supply*, 592 F. 3d 329, 342 (2d Cir. 2010), cit. in Gary Born, International Commercial Arbitration, Second ed., Wolters Kluwer, 2014, p. 3115.
13. *Glass Molders, Pottery, Plastics & Allied Workers Int'l Union, AFL-CIO, CLC, Local 182 B v. Excelsior Foundry Co.*, 56 F.3d 844, 846 (7th Circ. 1995), cit. in Gary Born, International Commercial Arbitration, Second ed., Wolters Kluwer, 2014, p. 3119.
14. As amended in 2006. Legislation based on Model Law has been adopted in seventy-two States in a total of 102 jurisdictions.
15. Gary Born, International Commercial Arbitration, Second ed., Wolters Kluwer, 2014, # 24.02 [B] [1], pp. 3117 and 3118, with reference to Model Law, Arts 33, 34(4); for a precise and detailed list of exceptions pursuant to some selected jurisdictions and arbitration rules, *see* Teresa Giovannini, *When do arbitrators become functus officio?*, in *Liber Amicorum en l'honneur de Serge Lazareff*, ed. A. Pedone, Paris, pp. 305 ff.

'*reconsideration in case a serious irregularity – procedural or substantial*' (section 68(3)). In the context of the *functus officio* doctrine, the English courts explain that:

> Once his final award is made ... the arbitrator himself becomes functus officious as respects all issues between the parties unless his jurisdiction is revived by the courts' exercise of its power to remit the award to him for his reconsideration.[16]

Specifically, and as put by prominent legal scholars:

> 'With regard to the effect of the annulment on the arbitrators, the short answer will generally be that the tribunal is functus officio *and an annulment does not change this or bring the tribunal back into legal existence (...)*'. Thus 'when *an award is annulled* ... *in most jurisdictions a new tribunal must be constituted*'.[17]

Apparently however Switzerland's approach is different. According to the same author:

> Unusually, the Swiss Law on Private International Law provides that, when an award is annulled, it is remitted to the former tribunal for further proceedings.[18]

Swiss legal writers indeed explain that: '*If the Swiss Federal Tribunal as the competent judicial authority concludes that the motion to set aside is well-founded, it is basically only empowered to annul the challenged award and remand the case to the arbitral tribunal for a new decision*',[19] being specified in that regard that '*the petitioner may in principle only request that the challenged award be set aside and that the case be remanded to the arbitral tribunal for a new decision*'.[20]

With the utmost respect, the author is bound to object to such statements as:

(i) With respect to the law, Article 191 of the PIL Act merely refers to Article 77 of the Law on the Federal Tribunal of 17 June 2005 that provides for the exclusion of Article 107.2 PIL Act to the extent that the latter entitles the Federal Tribunal to decide on the merits of the case by itself. As put by the legal commentators to the Law of 17 June 2005 indeed (in free translation):

> If the award is affected by a heavy defect as foreseen by Article 190 al. 2 PIL Act, it is only permitted to the state court to annul the award. The recourse can therefore only be aimed at the annulment, total or partial, of the award. Any other conclusion is not admissible. The jurisprudence has set only one exception to this principle: the

---

16. Ex multis: *Fidelitas Shipping Co. v. V/O Exportchleb* [1965] 1 Lloyd's Rep. 223, 231 (English Ct. App.), cit. in Gary Born, International Commercial Arbitration, Second ed., Wolters Kluwer, 2014, p. 3116.
17. Gary Born, International Commercial Arbitration, Second ed., Wolters Kluwer, 2014, (C), p. 3392, and references.
18. *Ibid.*, with reference to Art. 191 of Swiss Law on Private International Law; Judgment of 2 May 2012, DFT 4A_14/2012/DFT 138 III 270; Berti & Schnyder, in S. Berti et al., (eds), *International Arbitration in Switzerland*, Art. 191, # 28 (2000).
19. Bernhard Berger & Franz Kellerhals, *International and Domestic Arbitration in Switzerland*, 2nd ed, Sweet and Maxwell, Stämpfli, 2010, # 1825, p. 643.
20. *Ibid.*, # 1827, p. 643.

Federal Tribunal can state itself the jurisdiction or the lack thereof of the arbitral tribunal.[21]

(i) Thus, the issue under Article 191 PIL Act is not the remand, but the Federal Tribunal power (or lack thereof) to decide itself in case of annulment of an arbitral award.
(ii) The Swiss Federal Tribunal constantly affirms that, as a consequence of the *'nature cassatoire'* of the set aside proceedings, i.e., the ability to 'break' or 'annul' international arbitral awards as per Article 190 PILS, it has no authority to remand the case to the arbitral tribunal and any conclusion aimed at obtaining such remand is inadmissible.[22]

The conclusion therefore is clear that not only is there no legal provision entitling the Federal Tribunal to remit a case after annulment of an international final arbitral award to the arbitral tribunal that issued that award, but also, due to the *nature cassatoire* of the recourse under Article 190 PIL Act, such possibility is excluded.

Thus the only legal route left for considering that the arbitral tribunal that issued an award on the merits then set aside could decide anew the same dispute would consist in denying the *functus officio* doctrine and effect on an annulled award. This is precisely the solution adopted by the Swiss Federal Tribunal that – in its decision of 2 May 2012 mentioned by Gary Born[23] – set out the principle as follows (in free translation):

> *In theory, it is true, as the applicant emphasizes, that under the maxim lata sententia judex desinit esse judex, a judge is no longer competent to hear a matter once he has rendered his judgment in the sense that he may no longer modify it ...: What applies to a judge also applies to an arbitrator, whether it be in international or domestic arbitration: the award is final as soon as it is communicated (Art. 190 PILS), at which point it produces the same effects as a court judgment which has entered into force (Art. 383 Code of Civil Procedure). Thus, once the final award has been rendered, the arbitral tribunal's competence ceases and it becomes functus officio, notwithstanding certain exceptions .... The formal res judicata of the award (or its formal 'Rechtskraft' in German), which arises once it is communicated and which triggers the material res judicata (or its material 'Rechtskraft') ceases if the award is annulled after a specific recourse under Article 77(1) of the Law on the Federal Tribunal .... In such a situation, the legal situation corresponds to that which existed before the communication of the final award to the parties. Through the annulment, the parties are once again in the situation where they are awaiting*

---

21. Bernard Corboz, Alain Wurzburger, Pierre Ferrari, Jean-Maurice Frésard, Florence Aubry Girardin, ... # 83, pp. 632 and 633: '*Si la sentence rendue est affectée d'un vice grave prévu par l'article 190 al.2 LDIP, il est seulement permis au tribunal étatique d'annuler la sentence. Le recours ne peut donc tendre qu'à l'annulation totale ou partielle de la décision attaquée. Toute autre conclusion est irrecevable. La jurisprudence n'a fait qu'une seule exception à ce principe: le Tribunal fédéral peut lui-même constater la compétence ou l'incompétence du tribunal arbitral...*'.
22. DFT of 9 Feb. 1999, 4 A_400/2008, cons. 3.2. *in fine*; DFT of 7 Mar. 2003, 4P_250/2002, cons. 1.3.
23. *Supra* n. 18.

a final award which will determine their dispute and which will end the pending arbitral proceeding. As for the arbitrators who managed this proceeding, their mission is not accomplished or, if one considers that it was temporarily, it is reactivated. It is therefore not illogical to consider, in such a situation, that the arbitral tribunal which had rendered the award which was later annulled and which is responsible for rendering a new award, was never functus officio ... or it was only so during the time between the communication and the annulment of the award. ....[24]

One notes, first, that the allegation that the formal and material res judicata (*'force jugée matérielle and formelle'*) disappear in case of annulment of the award is debatable since, as put by Article V.1 *(e) of the New York Convention, 'recognition and enforcement of the award **may** be refused'* (emphasis added) in case of annulment of the award. And it is common knowledge that an award set aside by the Court of the seat can be recognised and enforced in another country and therefore be held as vested with res judicata effect.

Secondly and more generally, the Swiss Federal Tribunal supports its 'unusual' approach to the *functus officio* doctrine in setting forth that: *'the solution according to which in case of annulment of an award, the Arbitral Tribunal already in charge of the dispute remains competent to render the new award is approved by the entire doctrine'*[25] and refers in that regard to the Swiss leading legal authorities who however do not propose an independent and reasoned opinion in that regard, but merely refer to the Federal Tribunal's jurisprudence that however is foreign to the issue at stake.

The Swiss Federal Tribunal thus refers in particular to:[26]

---

24. DFT 138 III 270: *'D'un point de vue théorique, il est exact, comme le souligne la recourante, qu'en vertu de l'adage lata sententia judex desinit esse judex, le juge est dessaisi de la cause à partir du moment où il a rendu son jugement en ce sens qu'il ne peut plus modifier celui-ci ...: Ce qui vaut pour le juge vaut aussi pour l'arbitre, dans l'arbitrage international comme dans l'arbitrage interne: la sentence est définitive dès sa communication (art. 190 al. 1 LDIP), moment à partir duquel elle déploie les mêmes effets qu'une décision judiciaire entrée en force et exécutoire (art. 387 CPC). Ainsi, la sentence finale rendue, le tribunal arbitral voit sa compétence s'éteindre et devient functus officio, sous réserve de diverses exceptions .... La force de chose jugée formelle (formelle Rechtskraft) qu'emporte la communication de la sentence et qui confère à celle-ci l'autorité matérielle de la chose jugée (materielle Rechtskraft) cesse si la sentence est annulée à la suite d'un recours extraordinaire au sens de l'art. 77 al.1 LTF .... Dans une telle hypothèse. La situation juridique équivaut à celle qui existait avant la communication de la sentence finale aux parties. Par l'effet de l'annulation, ces dernières sont de nouveau dans l'attente d'une sentence finale qui tranchera leur différent et mettra un terme à la procédure arbitrale pendante. Quant aux arbitres ayant conduit cette procédure, leur mission n'est pas achevée, ou, si l'on considère qu'elle l'a été temporairement, elle est réactivée. Il n'est donc pas illogique d'admettre, dans un tel cas, que le tribunal arbitral qui a rendu la sentence annulée et qui est chargé d'en rendre une nouvelle n'a jamais été functus officio ... ou ne l'a été que durant la période qui s'est écoulée entre la communication et l'annulation de la sentence ...'.*
25. DFT 138 III 270, cons. 3.1.3: *'la solution voulant qu'en cas d'annulation d'une sentence, le Tribunal arbitral déjà saisi du litige reste compétent pour rendre la nouvelle sentence est approuvée par l'ensemble de la doctrine'*.
26. DFT 138 III 270, cons. 3.1.1.

- Berger/Kellerhals[27] who affirm that *'If the Federal Tribunal admits the motion to set aside and thus annuls the challenged award, it is the same arbitral tribunal that shall decide the case anew, unless the award was annulled on the grounds or irregular composition of the arbitral tribunal'*.[28] This affirmation however is exclusively based upon two decisions of the Federal Tribunal, namely DTF 117 II 94[29] that deals with jurisdiction,[30] and therefore is foreign to the issue at stake here of the setting aside of an award on the merits, and DTF 112 IA 344 relating to Article 40 of the Concordat[31] that does not exist anymore and is not mirrored in the PIL Act.
- Kaufmann-Kohler/ Antonio Rigozzi[32] who explain that *'except in the cases where the recourse is admitted on the basis of Article 190 al. 2 let. A PIL Act,*[33] *it will be the same arbitral tribunal (Berger/Kellerhals, n. 1654, p. 579 and references)'*.[34] In other words, these legal authors do not propose any independent reasoning as compared with the authors they referred to, the reasoning of which – as we have seen - is based on decisions that are foreign to the very issue discussed here.
- Poudret/Besson[35] sustain that *'The setting aside of the award in whole or in part leads to the case being sent back to the same arbitral tribunal for a new decision rendered in accordance with the terms of the Federal Tribunal'*, and thus *'A remittal of the case to the arbitrators will remain the rule in Switzerland if the application to set aside the award is granted, except for the cases where the jurisdiction is at stake and where the Swiss Federal Tribunal can determine itself this question'*.[36] Now the only basis for such conclusions consists in the DFT 102 I a 493[37] that relates to the Concordat again, precisely to the provision addressing the remittance to the lower state authority that decided the set aside in the first place. Such a provision does not exist in the PIL Act and cannot therefore serve as a basis for this affirmation.

It results from the above that remittance upon annulment of an arbitral award to the arbitral tribunal that has decided a dispute in the first instance finds no legal basis and no independent doctrinal support, on the one hand, and requires an 'unusual'

---

27. Bernhard Berger & Franz Kellerhals, *International and Domestic Arbitration in Switzerland*, 2nd ed, Sweet and Maxwell, Stämpfli, 2010.
28. *Ibid.*, # 915a and # 1654.
29. That also constitutes the basis for Jermini's position: Cesare Jermini, *Die Anfechtung der Schiedssprüche im Internationalen Privaterecht*, Schulthess, # 681 and note 2386, p. 336.
30. Bernhard Berger & Franz Kellerhals, *International and Domestic Arbitration in Switzerland*, 2nd ed, Sweet and Maxwell, Stämpfli, 2010, # 565, note 436 and # 674, note 44.
31. *Ibid.*, # 804, note 30.
32. Gabrielle Kaufmann-Kohler &Antonio Rigozzi, *Arbitrage International, Droit et pratique à la lumière de la LDIP*, 2ème ed., Editions Weblaw, Bern, 2010.
33. That is for irregular composition of the Arbitral Tribunal.
34. Gabrielle Kaufmann-Kohler & Antonio Rigozzi, *Arbitrage International, Droit et pratique à la lumière de la LDIP*, 2ème ed., Editions Weblaw, Bern, 2010, # 778a, p. 484, note 567.
35. Poudret & Besson, *Comparative Law of International Arbitration*, 2nd ed., Sweet and Maxwell, 2007.
36. *Ibid.*, # 835, p. 776.
37. *Ibid.*, # 835, note 423, p. 776.

approach to the *functus officio* doctrine, in other words that such doctrine would not survive the annulment, on the other hand.

Be that as it may, and as a result of the Swiss jurisprudence's creation of a remand, the question naturally arises of the independence and impartiality of the arbitrators that have to decide twice on the same dispute, a solution apparently prohibited by the IBA Guidelines mentioned unless both Parties agree otherwise.

The Swiss Federal Tribunal has been confronted with this concern as a basis for a request to set aside an award under Article 190 al. 2 let. a PIL Act on some occasions. After having once and for all established that the guarantee of independence and impartiality as per Article 30 al.1 of the Federal Constitution applies also to international arbitration,[38] the Federal Tribunal declared in 2010 (in free translation):

> *The fact that a judge has already acted in a case may cast doubt of partiality. The concurrence of the functions is then admissible only if the judge, in participating in prior decisions related to the same case, has not already taken position on given issues so that he does not seem exempted of prejudgment and therefore that the fate of the dispute seems already decided.*[39]

Then, obviously not satisfied with this criterion that might logically lead to the conclusion that an annulled award on the merits, namely on all the issues put to the tribunal,[40] cannot be decided again by the same individual (s), the Federal Tribunal introduced in a further decision a distinction in the characterisation of the annulled award between '*procedural errors or materially erroneous decision*'[41,42] that '*are not sufficient to give rise to the appearance of bias of an arbitrator or arbitral tribunal, unless there have been particularly grave or repeated errors constituting a manifest violation of his obligations*'[43] for thereafter concluding in that specific case that: '*the violation of the party's right to be heard found in the decision of the Federal Tribunal dated 26 May 2010 [rendered in the same case] manifestly does not appear as an error so grave as to trigger a signal of bias*'.[44]

Thus, and beside the difficulty of drawing the line, the Swiss Federal Tribunal seems to consider the question of independence and impartiality raised by the fact that the very same arbitral tribunal whose award on the merits has been annulled will be

---

38. For example DFT of 10 Jun. 2010, 4A_458/2009, cons. 3.1.
39. *Ibid.*, cons. 3.3.3.2: '*Le fait qu'un magistrat a déjà agi dans une cause peut éveiller un soupçon de partialité. Le cumul des fonctions n'est alors admissible que si le magistrat, en participant à des décisions antérieures relatives à la même affaire, n'a pas déjà pris position au sujet de certaines questions de manière telle qu'il ne semble plus à l'avenir exempt de préjugés et que, par conséquent, le sort du procès paraît scellé*'.
40. The issue of addendum to an award in connection with an omitted issue is not at stake in the present study.
41. '*fautes de procédure ou décision matériellement erronée*'.
42. Being emphasised that none of these two grounds is listed in Art. 190.2 PIL Act.
43. '*ne suffisent pas à fonder l'apparence de prévention d'un arbitre ou d'un tribunal arbitral, sauf erreurs particulièrement graves ou répétées constituant une violation manifeste de ses obligations*'.
44. DFT of 27 Jun. 2012, 4A_54/2012, cons. 2.2.3: '*...la violation du droit d'être entendu retenue dans l'arrêt du Tribunal fédéral du 26 mai 2010 [rendu dans la même affaire] n'apparaissant manifestement pas comme une erreur si grave qu'un signe de prévention doive en être déduit...*'.

competent to decide anew the same dispute in light of the prevention or bias possibly shown by the same tribunal during the first arbitral proceedings.

But this is not the question put in the decision of 27 June 2012 analysed here: indeed, alike in the decision of 2 May 2012,[45] the issue at stake consists in the lack of independence and impartiality of the arbitral tribunal as a result of having to decide twice the same dispute on the merits, and not on the question as to whether the arbitral tribunal was independent and impartial in the arbitration proceedings then set aside, thus in the first arbitration proceedings.

The conclusion to be drawn from this brief study is – in the opinion of the author – unequivocal: there is no court power in Switzerland to remand an international arbitral award, and the fact that the same arbitral tribunal decides anew the same dispute after the annulment of an award on the merits of a dispute goes against the principle of independence and impartiality embedded in Article 30 of the Swiss Constitution and is clearly mirrored in the waivable red list of IBA Guidelines on Conflicts of Interest.

Besides, the possibility for the arbitral tribunal to decide twice on the same dispute is held by the international arbitration community to be contrary to the *functus officio* doctrine.

By disregarding these rules, one ignores the importance of System One by considering System Two as the relevant and decisive factor in the decision-making process. As set forth by Albert Einstein, *'the intuitive mind is a sacred gift and the rational mind is a faithful servant. We have created a society that honours the servant and has forgotten the gift'*.

---

45. *Supra* n. 19.

CHAPTER 12
Foreign Mandatory Norms in Swiss Arbitration Proceedings: An Approach Worth Copying?

Daniel Girsberger

§12.01 INTRODUCTION

The question under what circumstances mandatory norms of a state other than the state whose law has been chosen by the parties to apply to the substance of the dispute (often called the '*lex causae*') has been one of the most intensely discussed and debated academic topics for the past two decades worldwide. Many articles and doctoral or even professorial theses have been written, and many more will doubtlessly be written in many jurisdictions. It would therefore be brazen if not illusionary to cover even only part of this vastly debated topic in one short article. A similar problem must have arisen to Pierre Karrer when he accepted to be the commentator of Article 187 of the Swiss Private International Law Act (hereinafter 'SPILA') in the prestigious 'Basler Kommentar'. Yet he mastered to address the problem meaningfully on only ten pages,[1] and many practitioners and academics have profited from that commentary for their work, which is often cited in numerous publications, awards and decisions.

---

1. Pierre Karrer, in: Basler Kommentar, Internationales Privatrecht, Art. 187 paras 230–289, 1973–1984 (Honsell Heinrich/Vogt Nedim Peter/Schnyder Anton K./Berti Stephen V. (eds.), 3d ed., Basel, Helbing Lichtenhahn Verlag 2013) (cited as *BSK IPRG-Author*).

§12.02 MANDATORY NORMS IN STATE COURT LITIGATION VIS-À-VIS ARBITRATION

[A] State Court Litigation

I will limit my remarks to mandatory rules or norms (often also referred to as '*lois de police*' or '*lois d'application immédiate*') that national or regional legislators wish courts or arbitral tribunals to consider even though the parties to a contract have chosen another law to apply to the merits of their dispute. Today, it appears largely undisputed that *state courts* may or must, under certain circumstances, apply such norms or at least take them into account.[2] This approach is now codified in various jurisdictions around the world including Switzerland.[3]

Whether and if so *arbitral tribunals* should follow the same or a similar approach has been widely discussed, and no unanimity exists to this day.[4] In fact, there is so much controversy that the drafters of the recently adopted Hague Principles on Choice of Law in International Commercial Contracts[5] were forced to leave the issue open.[6]

The relevant provision of *Swiss law applying to state courts* is Article 19 of the SPILA, which reads as follows:

(1) If, pursuant to Swiss legal concepts, the legitimate and manifestly preponderant interests of a party so require, a mandatory provision of a law other than

---

2. Symeonides, Symeon C., Codifying Choice of Law Around the World: An International Comparative Analysis, 299 ff. (New York, Oxford University Press 2014).
3. *Id.*, at 302 ff.
4. For an overview, see, e.g., Born, Gary B., International Commercial Arbitration, 2691 ff. (2d ed., Alphen aan den Rijn, Wolters Kluwer Law & Business 2014); Blackaby Nigel/Partasides Constantine/Redfern Alan/Hunter Martin, Redfern and Hunter on International Arbitration, paras 3.128 ff. (6th ed., Oxford, Oxford University Press 2015); Daniel Girsberger/Nathalie Voser, International Arbitration – Comparative and Swiss Perspectives, paras 1373 ff. (3d ed., Zürich/Basel/Genf, Schulthess 2016); Wilkens, Jonas Philipp, Eingriffsnormen im Gesamtsystem der internationalen privaten Schiedsgerichtsbarkeit, 252 ff., with various references (Dresden, TUD press Verlag der Wissenschaften 2012).
5. Principles on Choice of Law in International Commercial Contracts as adopted by the Hague Conference on Private International Law on 19 March 2015, https://www.hcch.net/en/instruments/conventions/full-text/?cid=135 (accessed 4 Apr. 2016).
6. Article 11 of the Principles reads as follows: – Overriding mandatory rules and public policy (*ordre public*):

   '1. These Principles shall not prevent a court from applying overriding mandatory provisions of the law of the forum which apply irrespective of the law chosen by the parties.
   2. The law of the forum determines when a court may or must apply or take into account overriding mandatory provisions of another law.
   3. A court may exclude application of a provision of the law chosen by the parties only if and to the extent that the result of such application would be manifestly incompatible with fundamental notions of public policy (*ordre public*) of the forum.
   4. The law of the forum determines when a court may or must apply or take into account the public policy (*ordre public*) of a State the law of which would be applicable in the absence of a choice of law.
   5. These Principles shall not prevent an arbitral tribunal from applying or taking into account public policy (*ordre public*), or from applying or taking into account overriding mandatory provisions of a law other than the law chosen by the parties, if the arbitral tribunal is required or entitled to do so.'

that designated by this Act may be taken into account if the circumstances of the case are closely connected with that law.

(2) In deciding whether such a provision must be taken into account, its purpose is to be considered as well as whether its application would result in an adequate decision under Swiss concepts of law.

According to the case law of the Swiss Federal Supreme Court (hereinafter 'FSC')[7] and related doctrine, the following key conditions must be fulfilled in order for a provision of a foreign law to be considered pursuant to Article 19 SPILA:

- Intention of the foreign state to apply the respective provision in a mandatory manner due to its purpose;
- Close nexus between the case at hand and the law of the state whose mandatory norms are in question;
- Interests [of one party[8]] which, from a Swiss perspective, are obviously worth of protection and prevailing.

Following the Swiss FSC, such consideration entails a judgment of value: The interest to apply the foreign mandatory legal provision(s) must be worth being protected also from a Swiss legal perspective and clearly prevail over the interest to apply the *lex causae*. In other words, consideration must be given to the purpose of the foreign mandatory law, and the consequences of its extraordinary application. In state court proceedings, this appreciation must be made in accordance with the fundamental values of Swiss law. It is sufficient that the purpose of the foreign mandatory norm is in conformity with Swiss and international concepts. The taking into consideration of legal provisions of a third, foreign state must allow to achieve a result that takes into account the consequences of those legal provisions on the legal relationship in question and the situation of the party concerned in a manner that is in conformity with the concepts of Swiss law.[9]

[B] Arbitration

Chapter 12 SPILA on international arbitration does not contain express rules on mandatory norms and further limits to a party choice of substantive law, as opposed to Articles 18 and 19 SPILA. While Chapter 12 is formally a part of the SPILA, it is to be understood and interpreted as an instrument that stands alone,[10] and therefore, as a

---

7. See, e.g., Decision of the Federal Supreme Court (hereinafter '*DFSC*') 136 III 392 of 29 Jun. 2010, with further references.
8. The Federal Supreme Court has left open the (disputed) question of whether or not the application should be in the interest of one party. See DFSC 136 III 392, cons. 2.3.3.1.
9. DFSC 138 III 489, cons. 4.4.; DFSC 136 III 392, 398, cons. 3. See also Frank Vischer, in: Zürcher Kommentar zum IPRG, Art. 19 paras 1 ff. (Girsberger Daniel/Heini Anton/Keller Max/Kren Kostkiewicz Jolanta/Siehr Kurt/Vischer Frank/Volken Paul (eds.), 2d ed., Zürich/Basel/Genf, Schulthess 2004) (cited as *ZHK-Author*); BSK IPRG-Mächler-Erne/Wolf-Mettier, *supra* n. 1, Art. 19 paras 12 ff.
10. Berger Bernhard/Kellerhals Franz, International and Domestic Arbitration in Switzerland, para. 87 (3d ed., Berne, Stämpfli 2015); BSK IPRG-Hochstrasser/Fuchs, *supra* n. 1, Einl. 12. Kap. para. 202; Jermini Cesare/Bernardoni Nicola, Chapter 1, Part II, Domestic Arbitration under the New Swiss Code of Civil Procedure, para. 2, in: Arbitration in Switzerland, The Practitioner's

principle, the general provisions of the SPILA (Article 1–Article 31) do not directly apply to international arbitration.[11] Notwithstanding, the issue whether and if so under which circumstances a Swiss arbitral tribunal (i.e., an arbitral tribunal having its seat in Switzerland) is obliged to apply foreign mandatory law irrespective of the parties' choice of law, is very much debated.[12] In particular, whether Article 19 SPILA also applies to Swiss arbitration proceedings directly or by analogy, has not been solved so far.[13]

[1]   Swiss FSC

In a decision of 30 December 1994, the Swiss FSC approved of the prevailing opinion that Article 19 SPILA does not bind an arbitral tribunal in case of a choice of law clause, to apply a law other than the *lex causae*.[14] However, in a decision of 28 April 1992 already,[15] the Swiss FSC had set aside an award based on Article 190(2)(b) of the SPILA (in connection with Article 187[1] of the SPILA) on the grounds that the arbitral tribunal had wrongly declined jurisdiction to determine the validity under the then governing Article 81 of the EU Treaty of the contract in dispute. Thus, according to the Swiss FSC, an arbitral tribunal has *jurisdiction to examine* the validity of a contract pursuant to European competition law, even though arbitrators do not act as authorities of an EU Member State.[16] However, in a later decision of 13 November 1998, the Swiss FSC held that an award which does not take European competition law into account is not contrary to public policy pursuant to Article 190(2)(e) of the SPILA. It found that it was doubtful whether national or European rules of competition law are part of the fundamental legal or moral principles recognized by all 'civilized' states, thus concluding that their violation should not be considered automatically to be contrary to public policy.[17] In an even more recent decision of 8 March 2006, the Swiss FSC stated that there was no longer room for doubt that the provisions of competition law do not belong to international public policy, i.e., to the broadly recognized values

---

Guide (Arroyo Manuel (ed.), Alphen aan den Rijn, Wolters Kluwer Law & Business 2013) (cited as Arroyo-Author); Kaufmann-Kohler Gabrielle/Rigozzi Antonio, International Arbitration Law and Practice in Switzerland, para. 1.91 (Oxford, Oxford University Press 2015).
11. See Berger/Kellerhals, *supra* n. 10, para. 87; Besson, in Arroyo (*supra* n. 10), Chapter 2, Part I, Salient Features and Amenities of Chapter 12 PILS, para. 12.
12. For an overview, see Girsberger/Voser, *supra* n. 4, para. 1394.
13. See, e.g., BSK IPRG-Karrer, *supra* n. 1, Art. 187 para. 263. Pierre Karrer himself rejects an application (even if only by analogy) of Art. 19 SPILA and votes for an ad hoc approach which takes account of the particular circumstances. See also Kaufmann-Kohler/Rigozzi, *supra* n. 10, paras 663 ff.; Hochstrasser, Daniel, Public and Mandatory Law in International Arbitration, in: Towards a Uniform International Arbitration Law, IAI Series on International Arbitration, 18, 24 ff. (Schlaepfer Anne Véronique/Pinsolle Philippe/Degos Louis (eds.), Berne, Stämpfli 2005). Similar debates exist for arbitration outside Switzerland. See, e.g., from a German point of view, Wilkens, *supra* n. 4, 253 ff.
14. DFSC of 30 Dec. 1994, 13 ASA Bull. 225, 225 (1995).
15. DFSC 118 II 193, cons. 5.
16. It should be noted, however, that this decision related to a matter in which the governing law was the law of an EU Member State, which necessarily incorporates EU law as an inherent part, i.e., it was not an issue of mandatory laws of a third state.
17. DFSC 4P. 199/1998 of 13 Nov. 1998, cons. 1b bb; confirmed in DFSC 128 III 234, cons. 4c.

which, according to the prevailing opinion in Switzerland, should be the basis of any legal system.[18] Consequently, the Swiss FSC found that a breach of such a provision does not fall within the scope of Article 190(2)(e) of the SPILA. As to other mandatory rules of third countries, the Swiss FSC has not issued a clear opinion so far.

However, it appears established that Article 187 SPILA, which is the relevant provision on the law governing the substance of Swiss arbitration proceedings, unequivocally reflects the paramount principle of party autonomy in international arbitration.[19] This appears to be a strong indication that any limitations to the principle of party autonomy in arbitration must be considered with caution, in particular where the parties have expressly chosen the law applicable to the substance of their dispute.[20] This interpretation is corroborated by both the wording and the drafting history of Article 187 SPILA,[21] and also by the fact that the parties, unlike in state court proceedings, may authorize the tribunal to decide *ex aequo et bono* (Article 187(2) SPILA), thereby dispensing it from considering any specific law.[22]

However, a long-debated question is whether and if so, there must be any connection of the dispute with Switzerland where the parties have chosen the seat of the arbitral tribunal to be, combined with a choice of Swiss law to govern the substance of their transaction. The majority view is that no such connection is required, and that the parties do not act against the principle of good faith when doing so.[23] Indeed, it appears now to be established that Switzerland may be chosen without any further connection as a neutral place of arbitration, and Swiss law as a neutral law, where the parties to the transaction are located in different jurisdictions.[24] This may be different where the parties and the transaction in question are all connected to one single state,

---

18. DFSC 132 III 389, cons. 3.
19. Article 187 SPILA reads as follows:

    1 The arbitral tribunal shall decide the dispute according to the rules of law chosen by the parties or, in the absence of such a choice, according to the rules of law with which the case has the closest connection.
    2 The parties may authorize the arbitral tribunal to decide *ex aequo et bono*.

20. DFSC 136 III 392, 398, cons. 2.2 *in fine*; ZHK-Vischer, *supra* n. 9, Art. 19 para. 33; Dasser, Felix, Rechtswahl im schweizer Recht, in: Rechtswahlklauseln, 30. Tagung der DACH in Berlin vom 6. bis 8. Mai 2004, 39 ff., 61 f., with further references in n. 60 (DACH Schriftenreihe, Berlin/Zürich 2005). The same opinion prevails internationally. See, e.g., s. 11.17 of the preliminary commentary to the Revised Hague Principles on Choice of Law in International Commercial Contracts, http://www.hcch.net/upload/wop/princ_com.pdf (accessed 4 Apr. 2016), sec. 11 .17: '[T]he exceptional nature of the Article 11 [on public policy and overriding mandatory rules] qualifications to party autonomy should caution against the conclusion that a particular provision is an overriding mandatory provision in the absence of clear words to that effect.'
21. Courvoisier, Matthias, In der Sache anwendbares Recht vor internationalen Schiedsgerichten mit Sitz in der Schweiz, 372, with references in paras 1734 f (Zürich, Schulthess 2005).
22. *Id.*, at para. 1733.
23. This view corresponds to a global trend. See, e.g., the Hague Principles on Choice of Law in International Commercial Contracts, which are stating: '*No connection is required between the law chosen and the parties or their transaction.*'
24. Kaufmann-Kohler/Rigozzi, *supra* n. 10, para. 7.12; DFSC 91 II 44, cons. 5.

therefore lacking any international element.[25] Any theory of mandatory norms in Swiss arbitration should carefully examine these prerogatives in a particular case.

[2]   'Swiss' Arbitral Awards Addressing the Issue

Pierre Karrer noted in his commentary that he had no knowledge of any Swiss (or other) arbitration awards which considered mandatory norms of a state other than that of the chosen state.[26] However, there exist a few published Swiss awards in this context, and there are undoubtedly further unpublished awards dealing with the issue.[27] The majority of the published awards have referred to Article 19 SPILA in their findings, without, however, always clearly distinguishing whether it should apply directly, by analogy, or as a mere source of inspiration:

- In ICC Award Nr. 6294 of 1991,[28] an Arbitral Tribunal sitting in Zurich had to decide a dispute between a German main contractor and a Hungarian subcontractor relating to construction works in the (then) Federal Republic of Germany. The German respondent argued that although the parties had selected Swiss law as the substantive law applicable to their contract, the contract was null and void as it was intended to circumvent German mandatory provisions of a public law nature on work permits. However, the Arbitral Tribunal denied the application of German overriding mandatory law (which would have led to invalidity of the contract), arguing that the contract had been performed by both parties and that the interest of one of the parties to have their contract annulled appears to consist in escaping its obligations vis-à-vis the other party, and that such interest cannot be protected both taking into account the prerequisites of Article 19(2) SPILA and the overarching principle that prohibits a *venire contra factum proprium*, i.e., that no-one may act in contradiction to his own previous conduct.[29]

---

25. See, e.g., with regard to 'domestic' arbitration in Switzerland and a choice of a completely unrelated foreign law: Daniel Girsberger, in: Basler Kommentar zur schweizerischen Zivilprozessordnung, Art. 381 paras 10a and 10b (Spühler Karl/Tenchio Luca/Infanger Dominik (eds.), 2d ed., Basel, Helbing Lichtenhahn Verlag 2013). With regard to a party choice of law subject to state court proceedings, i.e., absent an arbitration clause, see, e.g., Symeonides, *supra* n. 2, 116 ff., 116 at para. 44.
26. BSK IPRG-Karrer, *supra* n. 1, Art. 187 para. 250: ‚Ist es aber für ein Schiedsgericht möglich, trotz einer Rechtswahl (bei subjektiver Anknüpfung) Eingriffsnormen, die einem *anderen* Recht zugehören, anzuwenden oder bloss zu berücksichtigen, als dem von den Parteien gewählten? In der schweizerischen Schiedspraxis sind (noch) keine Fälle publiziert, wo ein Schiedsgericht so entschieden hat ('ratio decidendi'). Auch in der ausländischen Schiedspraxis ist kein solcher Fall bekannt.'
27. I acted as co-arbitrator in at least two proceedings, one of them an ICC proceeding, in which the issue arose.
28. ICC Award Nr. 6294 (1991), Journal de Droit International (Clunet) 1991, 1050–1052.
29. *Id.*, at 1052: 'L'intérêt de l'une des parties de voir annuler ledit contrat ne peut aujourd'hui résider que dans la tentative de se libérer d'obligations non honorées à l'égard de l'autre partie … Même sans cette condition expressément stipulée à l'article 19 [2] de la LDIP, le refus de prestation de la partie astreinte à des obligations apparaîtrait comme abusif en application du principe d'interdiction du venire contra factum proprium.'

Chapter 12: Foreign Mandatory Norms in Swiss Arbitration Proceedings §12.02[B]

- Similarly, a sole arbitrator in an ICC case of 1989[30] referred to Article 19 SPILA in the context of corruption: A service contract for which the parties had chosen Swiss law to apply had been concluded between a Swiss company and an off-shore company to facilitate a government contract of the state of X. The Swiss party later alleged that the contract was void, among others because the law of X prohibited such types of contracts. The Arbitral Tribunal shortly analysed whether the prerequisites of Article 19 SPILA were met and found in the negative because there existed no close ties with the law of X.[31]
- In ICC Case 9333 of 1998,[32] a sole arbitrator was asked by the French Respondent to apply the US Foreign Corrupt Practices Act to non-US subsidiaries of US corporations. Respondent had become part of that US group of companies, and refused to pay the outstanding part of a commission to a Moroccan broker, allegedly in order to prevent violating the Foreign Corrupt Practices Act. The parties had chosen Swiss law to apply, and the place of arbitration was in Geneva. The sole arbitrator examined, among others, Article 19 SPILA and left open whether or not it applied, directly or by analogy, because he found that the Foreign Corrupt Practices Act did not apply to non-US subsidiaries of US corporations.
- Another typical example regarding the application of mandatory law other than the *lex causae* or *lex arbitri* is ICC case No. 8528 of 1996.[33] The arbitral tribunal was confronted with a Turkish statute that it considered internationally mandatory and which required the mandatory involvement of a Turkish entity in a Joint Venture Agreement between otherwise non-Turkish parties, including the exclusive right of the Turkish entity to obtain tax benefits from the Turkish State. The tribunal found that the Turkish statute must be applied irrespective of the parties' choice of Swiss law governing the Joint Venture Agreement. The award is an excellent example for a careful analysis of Article 19 SPILA, which the Arbitral Tribunal applied, even though it did not distinguish whether it applied directly or only by analogy.[34]
- Two of the published awards were made by the CAS in Lausanne and dealt with sports disputes. In both matters, the panel had to determine whether the UEFA had breached overriding European Union law. In both cases, they referred to Article 19 SPILA and found that the overriding mandatory law had to be considered.[35]

---

30. *Société K. Ltd. v. Société M. SA (1989)*, in: 11 ASA Bull. 216, 216–250 (1993).
31. *Id.*, at 232. The Tribunal also remarked that the parties hat not invoked the nullity of the contract on this basis, *id.*, at 233. On the similar issues that arose in the famous *Hilmarton v. OTV* dispute, see BSK IPRG-Karrer, *supra* n. 1, Art. 187 paras 242 and 244.
32. *Monsieur X v. société L, Final Award*, ICC Case No. 9333, 1998, 19 ASA Bulletin 757–780 (1999), paras 12.3 and 12.4.
33. YCA XXV, 2000, 341–354.
34. *Id.*, at paras 28–39, 346–348.
35. *Celtic Plc v. Union of European Football Associations (UEFA)*, Award, CAS Case No. 1998/O/201, 7 Jan. 2000, in Matthieu Reeb (ed.), Digest of CAS Awards II 1998–2000 (2002), 106–121, 110 (mandatory EU law on the freedom of movement of sports professionals, as specifically reflected in the ECJ's Bosman case: Reference to Art. 19 SPILA in para. 4); *AEK Athens and Slavia Prague*

- Finally, in an award in ad hoc proceedings in Switzerland of 2005,[36] the Arbitral Tribunal was confronted with an agreement on the division of a future estate for which the parties who were all residents or nationals of Belgium and Spain had chosen Swiss law to apply. In a dictum, the Arbitral Tribunal excluded the application of Article 19 SPILA because of the lack of a manifest and preponderant interest to apply the mandatory law of another state as required by this provision.[37]

§12.03 IS THERE A COMMON DENOMINATOR?

When analysing these few published arbitral awards and the practice of the Swiss Supreme Court, they all have in common (and confirm Pierre Karrer's findings[38]) that arbitral tribunals have been extremely cautious when considering applying mandatory rules of other states than those providing the *lex causae* or the *lex arbitri*. This approach has been consistent at least when the parties had chosen Swiss law to apply to the substance of their contract. So far, not even the argument of 'fraus legis' (which is one of the exceptions accepted by the majority of commentators including Pierre Karrer)[39] has been upheld in those arbitral and challenge proceedings, not even in ICC Award Nr. 6294 of 1991(*supra* n. 28), where the arbitral tribunal closely analysed the issue.[40] This result indeed mirrors the practice of Swiss state courts regarding Article 19 SPILA, although there have been situations where a contrary decision would have been conceivable.[41] As Pierre Karrer points out, often, the application of mandatory norms will be excluded because the parties fail to prove that they constitute internationally mandatory norms.[42]

Where the parties had not specifically chosen Swiss law to govern their contract, arbitral tribunals have at least considered and in certain cases even applied mandatory norms of the European Union despite their findings that Swiss law governed the merits of the dispute (see the awards referred to *supra*, n. 35).

Nevertheless, there has been a clear tendency to at least examine the prerequisites for the application of third-state mandatory rules as embodied in Article 19 SPILA directly or by analogy, and the Swiss Supreme Court has even found that an arbitral

---

v. UEFA, CAS 98/2000 of 20 Aug. 1999: in Matthieu Reeb (ed), Digest of CAS Awards II 1998-2000 (2002), 38, paras 10–12.
36. Ad hoc Tribunal, *Madame X v. Madame Y* of 19 Jun. 2005, in: 24 *ASA* Bulletin 471, 471–481 (2006).
37. *Id.*, at 476: '*Les parties ayant choisi de soumettre leur convention au droit suisse, c'est à la lumière de ce droit que les diverses clauses doivent être examinées, ce d'autant plus que l'interdiction des pactes sur succession future est critiquée dans les pays qui la maintiennent et que la tendance est plutôt de revoir ou d'assouplir ces interdictions. Dans ces conditions, il n'y a pas d'intérets légitimes ou manifestement prépondérants pour exiger de prendre en compte une disposition impérative de droit étranger [n. 20, referring to Art. 19 SPILA].*'
38. BSK IPRG-Karrer, *supra* n. 1, Art. 187 para. 250.
39. BSK IPRG-Karrer, *supra* n. 1, Art. 187 para. 253.
40. ICC Award Nr. 6294 (1991), Journal de Droit International (Clunet) 1991, 1050–1052.
41. See, e.g., DFSC 136 III 392 of 29 Jun. 2010, with further references.
42. BSK IPRG-Karrer, *supra* n. 1, Art. 187 para. 232.

tribunal is not only competent, but obliged to undertake such an analysis in a given case (*supra*, at n. 16).

§12.04 IS THE SWISS APPROACH A RECOMMENDABLE MODEL?

The question whether the approach taken by Swiss courts and – sporadically by Swiss arbitral tribunals – may serve as a model for arbitral tribunals elsewhere cannot be solved without looking at what approach has been taken in the past by arbitral tribunals elsewhere. This task cannot be accomplished in a short article. Fortunately, there have been research studies published in the form of doctoral theses which have undertaken to collect the relevant information for this purpose.[43]

They confirm that while there is no one method for solving the problem of third-state mandatory norms, any approach must take account of those factors enunciated in Article 19 SPILA as applied, mutatis mutandis, to international arbitration. I therefore believe that the approach taken by Article 19 SPILA provides an excellent guideline,[44] provided however that the specificities of international arbitration are taken into account, in particular the fact that arbitral tribunals have no forum, and that therefore, no specific connection of the dispute with the seat of the arbitration or an examination of preponderant interests of Switzerland are required.[45] Within these limits, Article 19 SPILA, in my opinion, reflects a careful and balanced test even for arbitration tribunals that, if it were not codified, would most probably escape many arbitrators' attention when reflecting over a dispute for which Switzerland has been selected as the place of arbitration. The (admittedly rather scarcely published) awards of arbitral tribunals sitting in Switzerland appear to be a welcome proof of this assumption.

---

43. See, e.g., Siwy Alfred, Mandatory Rules in International Commercial Arbitration, in: Austrian Yearbook on International Arbitration 2012 (Klausegger et al. (eds)), 165, 176 ff.; Wilkens, *supra* n. 4.
44. That is the only point in which I respectfully disagree with Pierre Karrer and certain Swiss commentators, BSK IPRG-Karrer, *supra* n. 1, Art. 187 para. 263; *id.*, The Position of the Arbitration Chapter in Switzerland's Private International Law Codification, 7 ASA Bulletin 13, 20 (1989).
45. Unfortunately, an opportunity was missed when the recently published Hague Principles on Choice of Law in International Commercial Contracts (*supra* n. 5) left the issue open with regard to arbitration. It is noteworthy that Art. 11 of the Hague Principles on Choice of Law on mandatory norms and public policy (*supra* n. 6) is the only provision in the Principles which distinguishes between state court litigation and arbitration, in that it does not go as far as to formulate its own rules regarding the competence of arbitral tribunals to apply mandatory law of a state other than that of the *lex causae*.

CHAPTER 13
The Arbitrator's Duty of Efficiency: A Call for Increased Utilization of Arbitral Powers

Philipp Habegger

§13.01 INTRODUCTION

The international arbitral process seeks to achieve many goals. The objective of obtaining dispute resolution procedures that allow speedy and efficient results constitutes one of the main reasons why parties agree to international arbitration. For this aim international arbitration is also designed to avoid formalities and technicalities associated with national litigation systems. International business *'trades the procedures and opportunity for review of the courtroom for the simplicity, informality, and expedition of arbitration'*.[1]

In recent times, criticism has mounted that the arbitral process has lost the informality and expedition that once characterized it. Indeed, although the 1999 IBA Rules on the Taking of Evidence in International Commercial Arbitration were already issued with a view *'to conduct the evidence phase of international arbitration proceedings in an efficient and economical manner'*[2] and to promote the 'pro-active' arbitrator,[3] it appears that in most instances the structure of arbitral proceedings is almost entirely determined by agreements between the parties with little intervention from the arbitrators. However, in the author's experience, parties and their external and

---

1. *Mitsubishi Motors Corp. v. Soler Chrysler-Plymouth*, Inc., 473 U.S. 614, 628 (U.S. S.Ct. 1985).
2. *Ibid.*, Foreword.
3. The 1999 IBA Rules of Evidence for that purpose 'encouraged [the arbitral tribunal] to identify to the Parties, as soon as it considers it to be appropriate, the issues that it may regard as relevant and material to the outcome of the case' (Preamble item 3) and empowered the tribunal to 'determine the admissibility, relevance, materiality and weight of evidence' (Art. 9(1)).

in-house legal counsel do not address frequently the criticism of the process in their own choices. In particular, over-cautiousness and risk aversion of counsel and in-house counsel more often than not lead the parties to agree on excessively lengthy and burdensome procedures. In addition, frequent trepidation of arbitrators to question or even reject joint procedural proposals by the parties has significantly contributed to the current unsatisfactory state of affairs.

Pierre A. Karrer, our friend and colleague to be honoured by this *liber amicorum*, has always struck the author as an arbitrator blessed with not only a wealth of creative procedural *savoir faire*, but also with a gentle robustness in asserting his (better) procedural ideas in the face of procedural agreements of parties. In each instance, he asserted his views in the best interests of the parties and in the proper exercise of the procedural powers given to him.

This contribution submits that the modern arbitrator should be more robust in his or her attempts to seek assertively to dissuade the parties from inefficient procedures. It is suggested that for these purposes the starting point for discussion at any case management conference should be the minimal due process requirements and that parties should be required to justify the need to go beyond them. Looking first at the legal basis for the international arbitrator's duties and rights concerning the efficient conduct of proceedings (§13.02), the article then examines the interplay between the principles of party autonomy and the arbitrators' powers and discretion in establishing the procedural framework (§13.03). It then explores the limitations on the arbitrators' discretion set by mandatory law (§13.04). Section §13.05 provides a few examples of procedural milestones where the approach may lead to time and cost savings, before the final conclusion is reached (§13.06).

§13.02 LEGAL BASIS FOR ARBITRATOR'S DUTIES AND RIGHTS CONCERNING EFFICIENCY

Neither the New York Convention, nor virtually any national arbitration legislation expressly addresses the question of the international arbitrator's relationship with the parties.[4] The focus is rather on the parties' rights, particularly vis-à-vis one another, and not on the arbitrator's own rights and obligations. Institutional arbitration rules also contain only isolated provisions addressing the arbitrator's status, rights and obligations.[5]

---

4. For instance, the UNCITRAL Model Law is completely silent on the status of arbitrators and the relationship between arbitrators and parties. There are only indirect references in the Model Law to the arbitrators' obligations and responsibilities, as well as to their rights. These provisions are limited to the arbitrators' obligations of independence and impartiality, disclosure and procedural fairness during the course of the arbitration (Arts 12, 14, 18 UNCITRAL Model Law).
5. They usually just prescribe a number of aspects of the arbitral procedure relating to the arbitrators, thereby imposing various obligations on the arbitrators, such as, e.g., maintaining their independence and impartiality, complying with specified timetables (Arts 11 UNCITRAL Rules; 11(2), 24, 30 ICC Rules; 5(3) LCIA Rules), fixing the arbitrators' remuneration (Arts 41 UNCITRAL Rules; 37(1) ICC Rules; 28(1) LCIA Rules), maintaining confidentiality (Arts 44 Swiss Rules; 30 LCIA Rules), etc.

Under the arbitrator's contract, the arbitrator undertakes to perform specific functions vis-à-vis the parties in return for remuneration, cooperation and defined immunities.[6] The terms of the arbitration agreement between the parties also have important consequences for the arbitrator[7] and are incorporated into the arbitrator's contract, because they prescribe the mandate that the arbitrator agrees to undertake when accepting his or her appointment.[8]

Where the parties have agreed to institutional arbitration, the institutional rules are incorporated into the arbitrator's contract in the same manner as in the arbitration agreement between the parties.[9] A contract is formed between the arbitrator and the institution,[10] which, *inter alia*, involves the arbitrator's undertaking to conduct the arbitration in accordance with the institution's rules. The arbitration agreement, the arbitrator's contract, and the arbitral institution's contract with the parties and the arbitrator respectively, all work together in regulating the conduct of the various participants in the arbitration.[11]

It is also clear that fundamental aspects of the relationship between the arbitrator and the parties are the result of a non-contractual legal status recognized by national laws as inherent in the concept of the adjudicative function of an 'arbitrator'. Indeed, the arbitrator's central obligation is to resolve the parties' dispute in an adjudicatory manner.[12] This duty usually entails the obligations to not only act fairly and impartially towards the parties, to grant them an opportunity to present their respective cases, but also to act expeditiously.[13] Most national arbitration laws,[14] and institutional rules,[15] impose the same or similar obligations. While rather directed at the conduct of the arbitral proceedings than at the arbitrators' contractual responsibilities towards the parties,[16] the adjudicative function introduces aspects of mandatory law, which cannot be altered by contract.

Under some arbitration laws, the arbitrator's duty to conduct an arbitration with expedition is made express or at least generally accepted.[17] The arbitrator's obligations

---

6. G. Kaufmann-Kohler & A. Rigozzi, International Arbitration, Law and Practice in Switzerland, §§ 4.186, 4.192–4.195 (Oxford 2015).
7. For example, the definition of the scope of the arbitrators' jurisdiction, the seat or the language of the proceedings.
8. G. Born, International Commercial Arbitration, § 13.03[B] (2d ed., Kluwer 2014).
9. *Ibid.*, §13.03[B], §13.04[B].
10. Fouchard, Relationships Between the Arbitrator and the Parties and the Arbitral Institution, in ICC, The Status of the Arbitrator 12, 23 (ICC Ct. Bull. Spec. Supp. 1995).
11. G. Born, International Commercial Arbitration, §13.03[D] (2d ed., Kluwer 2014).
12. Fouchard, Relationships Between the Arbitrator and the Parties and the Arbitral Institution, in ICC, The Status of the Arbitrator 12 (ICC Ct. Bull. Spec. Supp. 1995); G. Kaufmann-Kohler & A. Rigozzi, International Arbitration – Law and Practice in Switzerland, § 4.188 (Oxford 2015).
13. G. Kaufmann-Kohler & A. Rigozzi, International Arbitration – Law and Practice in Switzerland, § 4.188 (Oxford 2015).
14. *See* e.g., Arts 18 UNCITRAL Model Law; 1510 French Code of Civil Procedure; 182(3) Swiss PIL and 29(1) and (2) Swiss Federal Constitution; Sect. 33(1)(a) English Arbitration Act 1996.
15. *See* e.g., Arts 17(1) UNCITRAL Rules, 22(4) ICC Rules, 15(1) Swiss Rules, 14(1) LCIA Rules, 16(1) ICDR Rules.
16. G. Born, International Commercial Arbitration, § 13.04[A] (2d ed., Kluwer 2014).
17. *See* e.g., Art. 14 UNCITRAL Model Law, Sect. 33(1)(a) English Arbitration Act 1996; Mabillard, in Basler Kommentar zum Internationalen Privatrecht, Art. 185 PIL n. 9 (3d ed., Helbling 2000).

include the duty to comply with both the general requirements of expedition and efficiency, as well as with specific time deadlines imposed by applicable institutional rules or national law, or by the parties' arbitration agreement.

However, an arbitrator is also contractually entitled to the parties' good faith and cooperation in resolving their dispute expeditiously. This is a fundamental aspect of the parties' agreement to arbitrate[18] and the arbitrator's contract.[19] A failure to fulfil these obligations of cooperation is also a breach of the party's (or parties') commitments towards the arbitrator.[20]

§13.03 PARTY AUTONOMY VERSUS ARBITRATOR'S DISCRETION IN DETERMINING EFFICIENT PROCEDURES

The New York Convention emphasizes the central role of the parties' autonomy to fashion the arbitration procedure, and provides for the non-recognition of awards following proceedings that failed to adhere to the parties' agreed procedures.[21] Most arbitration legislation equally guarantees parties the freedom to agree mutually on the procedural rules governing the conduct of the arbitration, subject only to limited mandatory restrictions of national law.[22] A decision of the Swiss Federal Tribunal thus concluded that Swiss arbitration law *'leaves the determination of the arbitral procedure to the parties' autonomy'*.[23]

[A] Arbitral Tribunal's Objections to Parties' Procedural Agreements

Difficult issues arise in cases where an arbitral tribunal does not wish to accept a procedure agreed upon by the parties, for instance where the tribunal considers that the parties' agreed procedure is inefficient. In these instances, there is obvious tension between the parties' procedural autonomy and the arbitrators' mandate to conduct the arbitral proceedings efficiently. Thus, the question arises whether the tribunal has the authority to reject the parties' agreement and impose different procedures that it considers appropriate.[24]

An arbitrator has the right, and arguably the obligation, to seek assertively to dissuade the parties from inefficient procedures, including by requiring direct

---

18. G. Born, International Commercial Arbitration, §§ 8.02[A]–[B] (2d ed., Kluwer 2014).
19. *Ibid.*, § 13.06[B]. See also Art. 15(7) Swiss Rules: *'All participants in the arbitral proceedings shall act in good faith, and make every effort to contribute to the efficient conduct of the proceedings and to avoid unnecessary costs and delay'* and C. Jermini & A. Gamba, Swiss Rules of International Arbitration, Art. 15 n. 26 (T. Zuberbühler & C. Müller & P. Habegger (eds.), 2d ed., Schulthess/Juris 2013) (*'applies to both the arbitral tribunal and the parties'*).
20. G. Born, International Commercial Arbitration, § 13.06[B] (2d ed., Kluwer 2014).
21. Article V(1)(d) New York Convention.
22. Article 19(1) UNCITRAL Model Law provides that *'[s]ubject to the provisions of this Law, the parties are free to agree on the procedure to be followed by the arbitral tribunal in conducting the proceedings'*. The same is held in Art. 182(1) Swiss PIL.
23. Decision of 12 Mar. 2003, DFT 4P.2/2003 cons. 3.
24. Veeder, Whose Arbitration Is It Anyway: The Parties or the Arbitration Tribunal – An Interesting Question?, in The Leading Arbitrators' Guide to International Arbitration 347 (L. Newman & R. Hill (eds.), 2d ed., Juris 2008).

communications with the parties' officers (as distinguished from the parties' external counsel).[25] The arbitrator may also call upon the parties to honour their obligations to cooperate with the tribunal in fashioning an efficient procedure.[26]

It is stated that parties do not frequently refuse to accept the arbitrator's procedural proposals, and insist upon proceeding with their agreement.[27] It is also said that it is relatively unusual that the arbitrators will disagree sufficiently seriously with the parties' agreed arbitral procedures that they will overrule that agreement. It is also held that it is even more unusual that, when arbitrators seek to do so, the parties (and the tribunal) will not agree on alternative procedural arrangements that satisfy all concerned.[28] While this may be empirically correct, the author suspects that this infrequency rather is the result of arbitrators' trepidation in making their own procedural proposals or in seeking assertively to dissuade the parties.

If the arbitrators fail to persuade the parties to accept their proposed procedures, however, the arbitrator is generally bound to comply with the terms of the parties' arbitration agreement, *'including the parties' agreement concerning procedural aspects of the arbitration'*,[29] save where that agreement violates applicable mandatory law[30] or where the parties have agreed (in institutional rules or otherwise) to grant the arbitrators the authority to override their joint procedural agreements.[31]

Very exceptionally, an arbitrator may also resign as a consequence of an unforeseen change in the arbitration post-appointment, such as a serious and unforeseeable increase in the workload resulting from the arbitration as a consequence of the parties' agreement, or, the failure of the parties to cooperate with the arbitrator's efforts to conduct the arbitration in an efficient manner.[32] However, the arbitrator is not entitled to reject that procedure and to conduct the arbitration in accordance with his or her own conception of what is appropriate.[33]

[B] Institutional Rules Giving Priority to Party Autonomy in Matters of Procedure

One element of the parties' procedural autonomy is the freedom to agree to arbitration pursuant to institutional arbitration rules.[34] In agreeing to arbitrate in accordance with

---

25. Article 24(4) ICC Rules; ICC Commission Report on Controlling Time and Costs in Arbitration, no. 30 (2d ed. 2012).
26. *See* above p. 3.
27. G. Born, International Commercial Arbitration, § 13.04[B] (2d ed., Kluwer 2014).
28. *Ibid.*, § 13.04[B].
29. M.J. Mustill & S.C. Boyd, The Law and Practice of Commercial Arbitration in England, 282 (2d ed., 1989) ('*[I]f the parties decline to take his advice [regarding arbitral procedures], he should yield. He is, after all, no more than the agreed instrument of the parties*').
30. *See* below p. 6.
31. *See* below p. 5.
32. G. Kaufmann-Kohler & A. Rigozzi, International Arbitration – Law and Practice in Switzerland, § 6.64 (Oxford 2015).
33. G. Born, International Commercial Arbitration, § 13.04[B] (2d ed., Kluwer 2014).
34. *See* e.g., Art. 182(1) Swiss PIL.

a set of institutional rules, the parties consent to the procedural and substantive provisions of those rules. Most of these rules acknowledge the parties' autonomy and allow parties to adopt such procedures as they choose. For instance, Article 19 ICC Rules provides that:

> the proceedings before the arbitrator shall be governed by these Rules, and, where these Rules are silent, by any rules which the parties or, failing them, the arbitral tribunal may settle on, whether or not reference is thereby made to the rules of procedure of a national law to be applied to the arbitration.

The wording of this provision suggests that any procedural stipulation of the parties prevails over a procedural direction of the arbitral tribunal. Hence, under the ICC Rules, absent resignation, the arbitrator is generally required to give effect to the parties' agreements regarding arbitral procedures, even if he or she considers them inefficient.

[C] Institutional Rules Limiting Party Autonomy on Matters of Procedure

Where institutional rules include some form of mandatory provisions which impose limitations on the parties' future exercise of their procedural autonomy, arbitrators may be granted the power to determine the arbitral procedure, even in the face of agreements between the parties on specific procedural matters,[35] including for the purpose of ensuring an efficient arbitral procedure.

For instance, while affirming the principle of party autonomy, including by permitting modification of the UNCITRAL Rules themselves,[36] Article 17(1) UNCITRAL Rules provides that:

> [t]he arbitral tribunal, my conduct the arbitration in such manner as it considers appropriate, provided that the parties are treated with equality and that at an appropriate stage of the proceedings each party is given a reasonable opportunity of presenting its case. The arbitral tribunal, in exercising its discretion, shall conduct the proceedings so as to avoid unnecessary delay and expense and to provide a fair and efficient process for resolving the parties' dispute.

Hence, considerations of efficiency are accorded identical status as mandatory requirements of equal treatment and due process.[37] As the procedural requirements imposed by mandatory law are exceptional,[38] this means that for most procedural matters arising in the course of the arbitration, the arbitral tribunal retains the ultimate authority to prescribe the arbitral procedures, including where the parties have agreed otherwise.

When the parties so cede their procedural authority to the arbitrators and once a tribunal is constituted, and an arbitrator contract formed, the tribunal's procedural

---

35. *See* e.g., Arts 17(1) UNCITRAL Rules, 15(1) Swiss Rules, 14(1) LCIA Rules, 16 ICDR Rules.
36. Article 1(1) UNCITRAL Rules.
37. G. Born, International Commercial Arbitration, § 15.03[C] (2d ed., Kluwer 2014).
38. *See* below pp. 5–6.

authority cannot be revoked or altered by either one party unilaterally or by both parties acting jointly; rather, such a change requires the consent of the arbitrators.[39]

§13.04 MANDATORY PROVISIONS AND ARBITRATORS' DISCRETION IN DETERMINING EFFICIENT PROCEDURES

The tribunal's discretion to adopt procedures (absent contrary agreement), is subject to the mandatory requirements of applicable law. However, applicable mandatory law imposes only very limited and general guarantees of procedural fairness and regularity. Usually, these guarantees are limited to a duty to treat the parties equally and to afford them the right to be heard.[40]

These mandatory procedural protections may conflict with the objective of efficiency. However, it is not per se incorrect to afford priority to considerations of efficiency over the parties' right to be heard. The protections are not rooted in a particular national legal tradition. Rather, they are – together with party autonomy – akin to a universal charter for arbitral procedures.[41] Thus, national courts have almost always permitted the use of arbitral procedures devised by the arbitrators provided that those procedures are applied equally and afford a minimal level of procedural rights.

Indeed, mandatory law or public policy do not impose some positive rules, but are specific protections aimed at preventing a fundamentally unfair procedure from being imposed by the arbitral tribunal:[42]

> 'It should be underlined that *procedural public policy* will constitute only a simple exclusion provision namely that it will merely have a protective function and *will not generate any positive rules*. This is because the legislature did not desire that procedural public policy should be extensively interpreted and that there should arise a code of arbitral procedure to which the procedure, as freely selected by the parties, should be subjected.' (emphasis added)

Hence, in most jurisdictions, the right to be heard in international arbitration does not impose any comprehensive definition of the parties' procedural rights. Indeed, doing so would mean disregarding the inevitable involvement of parties from different legal systems.

---

39. G. Born, International Commercial Arbitration, § 15.03[C] (2d ed., Kluwer 2014); *contra*: G. Kaufmann-Kohler & A. Rigozzi, International Arbitration – Law and Practice in Switzerland, § 6.63 (Oxford 2015) stating that considering that Art. 182(1) Swiss PIL does not provide that procedural agreements are irrevocable, parties can revoke the delegation contained in Art. 15 Swiss Rules.
40. Articles 18 UNCITRAL Model Law ('*[t]he parties shall be treated with equality and each party shall be given a full opportunity of presenting his case*'), 182(3) Swiss PIL ('*Whatever procedure is chosen [by the parties and/or tribunal], the arbitral tribunal shall ensure equal treatment of the parties and their right to be heard in an adversary procedure*').
41. G. Born, International Commercial Arbitration, § 15.04[B][1] (2d ed., Kluwer 2014).
42. Decision of the Swiss Federal Tribunal of 30 Dec. 1994, published in 13 ASA Bull. 217, 221.

§13.05 ARBITRATORS' EXERCISE OF POWER AND DISCRETION: A SHIFT IN APPROACH IN CASE MANAGEMENT

Parties in practice often do not agree in advance on detailed procedural rules for their arbitration. Instead, their agreement to a set of institutional rules will supply only a broad procedural framework. Thus, if the chosen institutional rules delegate the powers in matters of procedure to the tribunal, the procedural conduct of international arbitrations is largely in their hands.

It is said that *'[a] tribunal's selection of one approach to procedural matters, rather than another, will as a practical matter be influenced significantly by the need for evidentiary inquiry in particular cases, the parties' respective backgrounds and desires with regard to procedural matters, the applicable law and the nature of the dispute.'*[43]

It is submitted here that – looking at procedure solely from the perspective of efficiency – discussions at a case management conference or a procedural hearing[44] should take another starting point, namely that the right to be heard does not generate any positive rule and that parties therefore have to justify a request for any specific rule. In particular, the right to be heard generally does not include,[45] *inter alia*, (a) arbitral procedures of a party's home jurisdiction or based on 'international soft law', (b) unlimited time to prepare or present a party's case, (c) bifurcation of issues, (d) document production, (e) witness evidence and a hearing,[46] (f) written submissions (let alone of a specific number or in a specific sequence), and (g) verbatim transcripts and post-hearing briefs.

Parties and counsel will at the initial case management conference, of course, hardly agree to a procedure which does not include most of these procedural steps. Also, when they have a joint idea as to what would constitute a fair and efficient procedure, an arbitral tribunal should be reluctant to override this idea. This is because at the outset of an arbitration, the parties have greater familiarity with the dispute. However, from the perspective of the arbitrators' duty to conduct the arbitration efficiently, it does not seem justified to automatically give broad deference to the parties' choices,[47] not the least in light of the risk aversion of many counsel which frequently is the major impediment to the efficient structuring of arbitral proceedings. However, the more the arbitration progresses and the arbitrators' knowledge of the case increases, the more robustness arbitrators should show in asserting their ideals of an efficient procedure.[48]

---

43. G. Born, International Commercial Arbitration, § 15.07[D][1] (2d ed., Kluwer 2014).
44. *See* e.g., Arts 24(1) and (3) ICC Rules, 15 Swiss Rules, 17(2) UNCITRAL Rules.
45. For a list see G. Born, International Commercial Arbitration, § 15.04[B][3] (2d ed., Kluwer 2014).
46. Provisions like Arts 24(1) UNCITRAL Model Law, 17(3) UNCITRAL Rules and 25(2) ICC Rules providing for a mandatory hearing if a party so requests are at odds with the principle that procedural public policy does not generate any positive rule and constitute an unjustified concession to certain legal traditions. *Contra*: G. Born, International Commercial Arbitration, § 15.08[AA][1] (2d ed., Kluwer 2014).
47. *Contra*: *Ibid.*, § 15.03[C].
48. *Ibid.*, § 15.03[C].

Chapter 13: The Arbitrator's Duty of Efficiency   §13.05[C]

[A]   Application of IBA Rules and Other 'Soft Law'

Despite the absence of a 'standard' procedural approach in international arbitration, there have been efforts to develop uniform principles concerning some of the basic aspects of the procedure, the prime example being the IBA Rules on the Taking of Evidence in International Arbitration. They *'are intended to provide an efficient, economical and fair process for the taking of evidence in international arbitrations, particularly those between Parties from different legal traditions.'*[49] As such they are a blend of different legal traditions. However, blending hardly ever contributes to efficiency. If the parties are from the same legal tradition, arbitrators should therefore not accept widely used 'international soft law' as a starting point for discussion on aspects of procedures, not even for guidance. The better and more efficient way is to discuss and adopt solutions known to the parties' common legal culture.

[B]   Time to Prepare a Party's Case

The tribunal must take account of the nature and requirements of the dispute when establishing a procedural timetable. However, a tribunal may wish to take into account and notify the parties even prior to the case management of any default time-limits provided for in the chosen institutional rules for the submission of written statements.[50] Having agreed to these rules, the parties should be required to present substantiated reasons for requesting longer periods of time. The tribunal may also advise the parties that they are expected to work on their first submissions even before all procedural modalities as to their format have been determined. The tribunal can then take into account any time that has elapsed since this notification, when fixing the time-limits for first submissions.

[C]   Bifurcation of Issues

The efficient organization of the parties' presentation of disputed issues sometimes occurs by identifying preliminary issues, whose resolution will avoid wasted effort and expense. These include jurisdictional issues, choice of law and statute of limitations questions and separation of liability and damages. However, the decision on bifurcation depends on speculative assumptions about the likely outcome of the preliminary issue. This makes it difficult to justify bifurcation and potential delay in the complete resolution of the parties' dispute. Moreover, bifurcation imposes delays in the resolution of some issues, which can only be justified on the basis that expenses would be wasted in litigating those issues, which might become moot or irrelevant following

---

49. 2010 IBA Rules of Evidence, Preamble.
50. Articles 25 UNCITRAL Rules, 23 Swiss Rules.

decisions on other issues.[51] Tribunals should therefore only provide for bifurcation *'when doing so may genuinely be expected to result in a more efficient resolution of the case'*.[52]

[D] Document Production

'There is no automatic right to disclosure or discovery in international arbitration'.[53] Hence, arbitrators should inquire whether parties really anticipate to be in need of document production in order to be able to present their cases. To the extent that any document production will be allowed, it is more efficient to make it dependent on more stringent requirements than in the IBA Rules of Evidence,[54] such as, e.g., with regard to the necessary degree of specification of the requested document. It is also more efficient not to provide in the timetable for a specific time window for document production. Proceeding in that manner usually has the effect of reducing the number of (overreaching) document production requests and enhances the efficiency of proceedings.

[E] Witness Evidence and Hearings

In order to reduce costs and save time, tribunals should consider dispensing with oral hearings, even when requested by one party.[55] Hearings are expensive and time-consuming. From an efficiency perspective, dispensing with the oral hearing is not only *'acceptable in small cases, where expectations regarding cost or timing are paramount, and the consequences of ill-informed decisions tolerable.'*[56] A tribunal may always refuse to hear evidence on particular issues, including when they are irrelevant or when the evidence would be duplicative. As was stated by the Swiss Federal Tribunal:[57]

> The arbitral tribunal may refuse to hear evidence without violating the right to be heard if the evidence is improper to base its decision, if the fact to be proved is already established, if it is without pertinence or also when the tribunal, by assessing the evidence in advance, reaches the conclusion that its mind is already made up and that the result of the evidentiary procedure requested could not alter it.

---

51. G. Born, International Commercial Arbitration, § 15.07[R] (2d ed., Kluwer 2014).
52. ICC Commission Report on Controlling Time and Costs in Arbitration, no. 30 (2d ed., 2012); Appendix IV lit. a) ICC Rules.
53. G. Born, International Commercial Arbitration, § 15.08[D] (2d ed., Kluwer 2014).
54. Except may be for well-substantiated fraud cases where the documentary evidence by nature rather is in the respondent's possession, custody or control.
55. ICC Commission Report on Controlling Time and Costs in Arbitration, no. 35 (2d ed., 2012).
56. G. Born, International Commercial Arbitration, § 15.08[AA][1] (2d ed., 2014).
57. Decision of 7 Jan. 2011, DFT 4A_440/2010 cons. 4.1.

In this context, it is appropriate to mention the general preference for documentary evidence in international arbitrations.[58] Indeed, unless the contents of a contemporaneous document are said not to correctly reflect a communication, understanding, etc., witness evidence often adds little if not no value to the meaning of the document on its face. Hence, based on their power to decide on the relevance and materiality of (witness) evidence,[59] and their duty to conduct the proceedings efficiently, arbitrators should assess carefully whether witness testimony is reasonably capable of altering their minds in light of the documentary evidence before them and to play the significant role it sometimes effectively does.

If (some) witness evidence is to be taken, arbitration is more efficient when the arbitrators actively seek to elucidate the relevant disputed allegations of fact to counsel prior to the hearing, rather than merely evaluating what the parties choose to present at the hearing.[60]

[F] Written Submissions

During the course of most international arbitrations, the parties will file written submissions to further substantiate their initial submissions, such as the request for arbitration and the answer to the request for arbitration. Some national laws and institutional rules provide default rules regarding written submissions, usually providing for a statement of claim and a statement of defence.[61] Note, however, that the institutional rules in question leave it to the discretion of the arbitral tribunal to decide whether any further written submissions should be filed beyond these submissions.[62] The arbitrators are not required to decide at the initial case management conference whether such further written submissions will be permitted. Indeed, not only do parties agreeing to these rules have to accept that there is no *eo ipso* entitlement to a second round of submissions, the arbitral tribunal will also be in a better position to assess whether it shall require further submissions from the parties after receipt of the first round of submissions. An ancillary benefit of proceeding in this manner is that the parties' first submissions tend be more detailed and complete than if the parties know in advance that they will be granted a 'second bite at the apple'. Moreover, even if the initial timetable only provides for a single exchange of submissions and that is not changed later, arbitrators will afford the opportunity for comments on one or more specific issue if the right to be heard so requires. Hence, there is considerable potential

---

58. D. Caron & L. Caplan, The UNCITRAL Arbitration Rules, A Commentary, pp. 566–567 (2d ed., Oxford 2013); T. Zuberbühler & D. Hofmann & C. Oetiker & T. Rohner (eds.), IBA Rules of Evidence: Commentary on the IBA Rules on the Taking of Evidence in International Arbitration, 29 (Schulthess 2012).
59. Articles 27(4) UNCITRAL Rules, 24(2) Swiss Rules, 9(1) 2010 IBA Rules on the Taking of Evidence.
60. S. Elsing, Procedural Efficiency in International Arbitration: Choosing the Best of Both Legal Worlds, 2011 Schieds VZ 114, 123.
61. Articles 23 UNCITRAL Model Law, 20 and 21 UNCITRAL Rules, 18 and 19 Swiss Rules.
62. Articles 24 UNCITRAL Rules, 22 Swiss Rules.

in structuring the proceedings more efficiently by not allowing two exchanges from the outset without infringing the parties' due process rights.

Pre-hearing written submissions are almost invariably sequential, with the claimant making the first submission. However, this may be inefficient in certain circumstances. If the burden of proof for the main contested facts rests on the respondent, it may make more sense for the arbitral tribunal, even against the usual preference of the parties, to request the respondent to file the first submission. Only this will enable the claimant to understand what the crucial arguments against its otherwise uncontested claims and the supporting evidence are and will only then allow the claimant to present its claim in a meaningful fashion.[63]

Simultaneous filings in the early stages of the case do not always run the risk of 'two ships passing in the night'. The risk is inexistent in the case of a counterclaim or set-off defence which is disconnected from the claim. Requiring the respondent to file its statement of counterclaim or statement of set-off defence at the same time as the claimant files its statement of claim considerably shortens the overall duration of the proceedings in these instances. Again, arbitrators should not be shy of imposing such solutions against the will of the parties in appropriate circumstances.

[G] Post-hearing Briefs

From a cost and efficiency perspective, verbatim transcripts followed by post-hearing briefs only make sense for significant evidentiary hearings and where the size of the case justifies the costs.[64] In smaller cases, a tape-recording or video-recording may by far suffice for the purpose of retaining a record.

For short hearings and small cases, the costs for post-hearings briefs tend to be disproportionate to their benefits. Not only do they increase the costs (both legal and for court reporters) given that they will be prepared after the transcript of the hearing has been circulated, they also lead to considerable delay. For hearings of up to about two days, counsel may be expected to present oral closing statements at the end of the hearing, with virtually no or only a short delay.[65] If the presiding arbitrator then secures the availability of the arbitral tribunal for immediate deliberations and award drafting while the panel's recollection of witness evidence is fresh and the record fully mastered, considerable cost and time savings can be achieved.

---

63. Examples: (i) The respondent's only (or main) argument of defence is the nullity of the contract based on allegations of corruption. The respondent bears the burden of substantiating and proving the corruption allegations. (ii) The claimant claims its fees under a contract for works terminated by the respondent. The respondent argues that it terminated for cause and that therefore no fees are owed. The respondent bears the burden of proof that the requirements for a termination for cause were met.
64. D. Caron & L. Caplan, The UNCITRAL Arbitration Rules, A Commentary, 610 (2d ed., Oxford 2013).
65. G. Born, International Commercial Arbitration, § 15.08[EE] (2d ed., Kluwer 2014).

§13.06 CONCLUSION

With the criticism as to costs and delay in international arbitration mounting, tangible actions of arbitral institutions in addressing the problem, much to the writer's regret, have more or less been limited to increasing the pressure on arbitrators.[66] There is, however, no reason for arbitrators to complain. Arbitrators should be delighted to learn that they are deemed best placed to reduce cost and delay[67] and take the challenge and do things differently and more efficiently.[68] This will likely involve an increased utilization of the arbitrators' powers in shaping the procedure.

And, as an arbitrator, when next confronted with criticism of a user about cost and delay in international arbitration, do not forget to mention that you wished you had been more assertive in dissuading the parties and their counsel when they last proposed an inefficient procedure ... .

---

66. Communiqué of the International Court of Arbitration of the International Chamber of Commerce dated 5 Jan. 2016, www.iccwbo.org/News/Articles/2016/ICC-Court-announces-new-policies-to-foster-transparency-and-ensure-greater-efficiency/.
67. D. Jones, Improving Arbitral Procedure: Perspective from the Coalface, in Stories from the Hearing Room: Experience from Arbitral Practice, p. 92 (Kluwer 2015) with reference to White & Case and Queen Mary University, 2010 International Arbitration Survey.
68. Geisinger, President's Message, 34 ASA Bull. 3 (2016).

CHAPTER 14
Latin and International Arbitration

Kaj Hobér

§14.01 *EXORDIUM*

When the German Civil Code of 1896 entered into force in 1900 that year could be said to mark the end of Roman law as directly applicable law in a national jurisdiction. Modified forms of Roman law continue even today to have a certain degree of authority, for example in South Africa and Sri Lanka, where it is usually referred to as Roman-Dutch law. Until 1900 Roman law had exercised an enormous influence on most legal systems. In fact, Roman law plays a unique role in the history of our civilization. So does Latin. For centuries Latin was the *lingua franca* of international relations and commerce. Private letters and official documents were drawn up in Latin. Legal rules, principles and maxims were derived from Roman law and were interpreted and further refined by medieval jurists. It is no exaggeration to qualify Latin as the *lingua franca* also of law and lawyers throughout our history.

Roman law was studied in the universities of Europe. University trained lawyers were active in courts and chancelleries. They exerted a far-reaching influence on the development of legal concepts and doctrine throughout Europe. Less so in England. In this way Roman law became one of the foundations of the civil law system. The influence of Roman law in England was more limited, primarily because of the early rise of a national legal profession and the development of a national common law. Until the introduction of the 1999 Civil Procedure Rules, however, Latin and Roman law terminology seems to have been used frequently in English courts.

Interestingly enough, in the field of public international law, jurists coming from the common law system seem to be inclined to adopt Roman law concepts and ideas in search of solutions, or reasonable approaches, to international law problems. More so than colleagues from civil law jurisdictions where the influence of Roman law has been much stronger.

Although the grammatical structure of Latin is rather complicated, Latin is a clear and practical language. Latin is usually terse and to the point. The linguistic and grammatical exactness of Latin is perhaps one reason why it has been used by lawyers – and indeed by other learned men and scientists – for centuries. Ever since Linnaeus published his *Systema naturae* in 1735, and *Species plantarum* in 1753, botanists, for example, have been happy to classify in Latin.

The purpose of this contribution is not to analyze Roman law, nor Latin from a linguistic perspective. No. The purpose is simply to try to create a harbinger of joy for the person in whose honor this *Liber Amicorum* is published. Although Dr. Karrer is a prominent modernizer of international arbitration – indeed a trailblazer – he is also a traditionalist, illustrated, *inter alia*, by his interest in and love for Latin and Roman law. This contribution will allow him to enjoy Latin legal terminology – randomly and very unscientifically selected – before it becomes as rare as hen's teeth. The focus is on terminology used in, or relevant to, international arbitration.

§14.02 LEGIS ACTIO

It could perhaps be said that arbitration is a more civilized form of court litigation. Some observers would probably throw in a *veto* and say that international arbitration today is increasingly becoming like litigation in national courts. One fundamental difference between arbitration and litigation is that arbitration is based on the agreement between the parties. The arbitration agreement – *compromissum* – is the *condicio sine qua non* for any arbitration.

Another necessary ingredient in any arbitration is the decision-maker, the *arbiter*. There are a number of rules and regulations which the decision-maker must comply with. Of central importance is the principle *nemo iudex esse in propria sua causa* which reflects the duty of arbitrators to be impartial. If an arbitrator fails to observe this principle, a resulting award may be set aside. This is also the case if an arbitrator has violated the principle *audiatur et altera pars*. All parties to an arbitration must be given the opportunity to present their respective cases.

Since arbitration is based on the agreement of the parties, the mandate of an arbitrator is determined by the parties in their agreement. That is why *extra compromissum arbiter nihil facere potest*. Should an arbitrator go beyond his mandate, this may also lead to the annulment of the award.

The ultimate task of the arbitrator is to decide the dispute before him. To do so, he will usually need to identify a law to apply, unless the parties have explicitly authorized him to decide *ex aequo et bono*. The parties will often have identified the applicable law in the disputed contract. In such cases the arbitrator will have to apply the *lex contractus*. With respect to procedural matters arising during the arbitration he will resort to the *lex arbitri* which is to be distinguished from the *lex fori*. Where the parties have not chosen the law in the contract, the arbitrator may have a difficult time identifying the law to be applied to the merits of the dispute. Depending on the nature of the dispute he may have to apply the *lex loci contractus*, the *lex loci solutionis*, the *lex rei sitae* or the *lex loci delicti commissi*.

When ruling on the issues before him, the *arbiter* will be guided by the arguments on fact and on law presented by the parties. Some arbitrators, however, seem to adhere to the principle *iura novit curia* and thus apply the law, or rules of law, they find applicable based on the facts presented by the parties. This principle, which is applied in court proceedings in many civil law jurisdictions, can lead to surprising results for both parties to an international arbitration. Generally speaking, an international arbitration should strive to avoid surprises.

The arguments of each party are usually presented by an *advocatus* whom the other party will often refer to as the *advocatus diaboli*, even though he or she may have nothing to do with the beatification or canonization process in the Roman Catholic Church.[1] Most arbitrators wish that the *advocati* comply with the golden rule of advocacy *rem tene verba sequentur*, such that the focus is put on the relevant issues. In fact most *advocati* do. Even if that exceptionally is not the case, the *arbiter* must have an open mind and remember that *interdum stultus bene loquitur*. The important thing for the decision-maker is to understand the *crux* of the matter. The parties are expected to instruct the *advocati* such that arguments are presented in a *bona fide* manner, without resorting to any *ad hominen* arguments. When arguments are presented *de bene esse*, the decision-maker is mostly left in the dark as to the significance of the argument.[2]

When it comes to resolving the dispute the *arbiter* must find a solution. It could be in the form of an *aurea mediocritas*, but a decision must be rendered. The *arbiter* cannot hide behind *non liquet*.[3] In preparing his decision the *arbiter* must make sure that he is not acting in violation of the principle of *res iudicata* and *lis pendens*. This is often easier said than done since these fundamental principles – globally accepted as they are – are understood and applied differently in different jurisdictions.

In preparing his *arbitrium* the decision-maker must focus on the *petita(ae)* and *causa(ae) petendi* presented by the parties. Based thereon he must identify the *ratio decidendi* leading to his conclusions, and make sure to distinguish between the *ratio decidendi* and any *obiter dicta*. While the *advocati* usually refer extensively to previous *arbitri* – some *arbitri* would say *ad nauseam* and in a *non sequitur* fashion – the *arbiter* must not forget that there is no principle of *stare decisis* in international arbitration.

At the conclusion of a hearing, the parties will usually ask the *arbiter* when they can expect to receive the *arbitrium*. The prudent *arbiter* will say "as soon as possible", but leave it *sine die*.

§14.03 IUS CIVILE ET IUS COMMERCII

Most disputes that go to international arbitration arise out of contracts or treaties. Both called *pactum* in Latin. One of the central tenets in any legal system is *pacta sunt servanda*. It is an absolutely necessary cornerstone for any kind of economic and

---

1. This is the context in which the concept of *advocatus diaboli* was introduced.
2. It literally means "concerning well being". For an entertaining attempt to explain what it means in a legal context, *see* Gray, Lawyer's Latin. A vade-mecum (2006) 46.
3. This must of course be distinguished from *non licet*, which means "it is not allowed".

commercial transaction, as well as for orderly international relations. A rather more cynical – or realistic? – approach was reportedly – jokingly? – taken by President de Gaulle. In a speech in 1965 he said: "Les traitées, voyez vous, sont comme les jeunes filles et comme les rose; ça dure ce que ça dure".[4]

As long as the agreement is not a *pactum turpe* the *arbiter* will need to interpret and apply it. This presupposes that the *pactum* is not void *ab initio*, *ex nunc* or *ex tunc*. He must also keep in mind that *pactum tertiis nec nocent nec prosunt*.

Experience shows that it is not humanly possible to draft a contract which excludes the need for interpretation. No matter how detailed a contract is, there will always be aspects of it which must be interpreted. When the contract, or the provision in question, has been drafted by the opposite party, *advocati* will usually try to rely on the *contra proferentem* principle to argue that any ambiguity and consequences flowing from it, must be construed against the party having proffered it. Another rule of contract interpretation which may be relevant is *expressio unius est exclusio alterius* which could be helpful when a contract specifically lists or identifies objects or events. In the same vein the *advocatus sedulus* might rely on *generalia specialibus non derogant*, a principle which might be helpful also when interpreting statutes. Otherwise, in this context, *advocati* often rely on *lex posterior derogat priori*, or even *ex abundanti cautela* that *cessante rationae legis, cessat lex ipsa*.

When the buyer in a transaction alleges that the seller has breached the contract and therefore requests *lucrum cessans* as well as *damnum emergens*, the seller would probably simply say *caveat emptor*! The buyer might respond that the seller has guaranteed that the products be of certain quality, but, alas, *falsus in uno, falsus in omnibus*. If the seller had acted *ultra vires* the buyer should perhaps have understood that *vestigia terrent*.[5] He may, then, with a sigh of resignation say: *deo volente* I ask for a *quantum meruit* order.

§14.04 IUS GENTIUM

Ius gentium is a very distant relative to modern day public international law. The first beginnings of modern public international law are often ascribed to Grotius and his book *De jure belli ac pacis* published in 1625. One of the fundamental principles of international law is that *par in parem non habet imperium* which is one of the building blocks for the principle of sovereign immunity. Refinement and modernization of this principle have led to the distinction between *acta iure gestionis* and *acta iure imperii*. The principle of sovereign immunity plays no role, however, with respect to the jurisdiction of an arbitral tribunal because it does not and cannot, exercise governmental authority. Another fundamental principle which historically was of central importance was the idea of *comitas gentium* as a guiding rule for orderly international

---

4. "Treaties, you see, are like young girls and roses; they last while they last", quoted from Gray, *supra* n. 2, at 102.
5. From Aisopo's fabel, when the fox having been invited to the lion's den saw that all traces lead to, but none from, the den.

relations, to be taken into account, for example, in the exercise of a sovereign's *ius protectionis*.

A regrettable, but unavoidable, distinctive feature of international law is the focus on *bellum*. An important distinction is to be made between *ius ad bellum* and *ius in bello*. In modern times the *ius in bello* is to a large extent regulated in the so-called Geneva Conventions adopted in the 1940s following World War II. *Ius ad bellum*, to the extent it exists at all in modern public international law, seems to spur a never-ending hunt for a *casus belli* among states which for various reasons have an interest in using force in international relations.

Another constant feature of international law is the focus on *terra*. Even though we seldom speak of *terra incognita* or *terra nullius* today, territorial disputes arise on a fairly regular basis. Acquisition of territory can take place in different ways, for example, via *usucapio*, *occupatio* or *possessio longi temporis*, provided certain requirements are met. Territory may also be ceded, whereby one must keep in mind that *nemo dat quod non habet*. When states emerge from the dissolution of other larger states, or entities, the principle of *uti possidetis*[6] may be helpful in determining the extent of sovereignty by maintaining earlier administrative boundaries.

International law is manifested in *pacta* and international custom. The latter is formed on the basis of *usus* of states provided there is *opinio iuris sive necessitatis*. The threshold is high for state practice to be accepted as customary international law. This is also the case with respect to *ius cogens*.

International law disputes which go to arbitration almost without exception turn on the interpretation of *pacta*. The rules of treaty interpretation are found in the Vienna Convention on the Law of Treaties.[7] In addition to the rules laid down in Articles 31 and 32 of the Vienna Convention, other general interpretative principles may become relevant such as in *dubio mitius*, or *a contrario*. Other such principles are *expressio unius exclusio alterius*[8] and *eiusdem generis*, the latter essentially saying that one can only compare apples with apples.

In disputes before *arbitri* it is not unusual that the claimant will seek to achieve *status quo ante* and argue that *rebus sic stantibus*. To achieve this the arbitral tribunal may need to order *restitutio in integrum*.

§14.05 CONCLUSIO

Dixi!
Sit iucundus tibi dies!

---

6. The full text of the edict issued by the Roman *praetor* is "*uti possidetis, ita possidetis*" which literally means "as you possess, so you posses".
7. May 22, 1969, 1155 UNTS 331.
8. See p. 140, *supra*.

CHAPTER 15
The Angelic Arbitrator Versus The Rogue Arbitrator: What Should an Arbitrator Strive to Be?

Günther J. Horvath

§15.01 INTRODUCTION

Arbitration as an institution and dispute resolution mechanism has undergone many changes over time.[1] These transformations have also impacted the role and obligations associated with the powers and duties of the arbitrator. Arbitrators were traditionally regarded as "grand old men," but have since evolved into a new generation of technical experts that are members of an elite and skilled group.[2] Traditionally, fairness and industry knowledge were the cornerstones and key characteristics of arbitral awards, while modern times have seen an increased emphasis placed on the legal analysis and reasoning of awards.[3] The change in the global climate has also played a major role in affecting the current duties and obligations attributed to arbitrators. Globalization has seeped into every aspect of international trade and relations, including the legal world. The current legal environment has witnessed the creation of large, multi-office global law firms with far-reaching international networks,[4] as well as the development of small specialized arbitration boutiques, which are currently *en vogue*.

These global changes have caused the role of the arbitrator to become less clear than ever before. The once straightforward and uncomplicated duties and obligations

---

1. Susan D. Franck, *The Role of International Arbitrators*, 12 ILSA J. Intl. & Comp. L. 499, 499–500 (2006).
2. *Ibid.* at 500.
3. Susan D. Franck, *supra* n. 1, at 504.
4. Anne Marie Whitesell, *Independence in ICC Arbitration: ICC Court Practice Concerning the Appointment, Confirmation, Challenge and Replacement of Arbitrators*, Independence of Arbitrators – ICC ICArb. Bull. 7, 8 (2007 Special Supplement).

that accompanied less complex and extensive cases have long since seen their day. Arbitration is an ever-evolving landscape of growing diversity and complexity of disputes, parties, and counsel – and the role and duties of arbitrators is not immune to this changing landscape. This article seeks to examine two categories that arbitrators fall into, either intentionally or by chance, the angelic (ideal) arbitrator and the rogue (train wreck) arbitrator. We then suggest a third alternative category of arbitrator that is more realistic and something every arbitrator should strive to reach: the enlightened arbitrator.[5]

§15.02 THE ANGELIC ARBITRATOR: THE IDEAL

"Have no fear of perfection – you'll never reach it." ~ Salvador Dalí

The ideal arbitrator regards himself as a superhuman efficiency machine who provides the parties with optimal assistance to best serve their interests. This arbitrator strives for perfection in all aspects of his duties and obligations, regardless of the circumstances and extent of his other obligations.

The duty of an arbitrator to render an impartial decision, and thereby an enforceable award, is crucial to the arbitral process.[6] This requirement is often described as being self-imposed by the arbitrator because it involves an internal mental process.[7] The requirement that an appointed arbitrator be an impartial adjudicator is widely reflected in both institutional rules and national laws,[8] but the perfect arbitrator takes these general guidelines one step further. This arbitrator believes that he can apply logical and analytical skills in the evaluation of the dispute without the faintest taint of bias or prejudice for or against a particular party or line of reasoning, i.e., he believes that he is not laden with dormant or subconscious feelings of bias or preference. The question of impartiality is particularly controversial and problematic in the context of the selection of a party-appointed arbitrator. Parties will often strategically select an arbitrator that is somehow predisposed to rule in their favor by virtue of education, beliefs, nationality, environment, etc. However, the angelic party-appointed arbitrator believes himself to be immune to the influences of a legal background or any personal affinity between himself and the party or counsel appointing him. That said,

---

5. This paper deals exclusively with commercial arbitration and does not address the role of arbitrators in investment arbitration.
6. Remarks for Discussion by Dr. Günther J. Horvath, *The Selection of Arbitrators*, CILS Intl. Constr. L. & Dispute Res. (Salzburg, Jun. 19–21, 1998).
7. Alfonso Gomez-Acebo, *Party-Appointed Arbitrators in International Commercial Arbitration*, Intl. Arb. L. Lib. 34, 74 (Kluwer Law International 2016). *See also* Julian D. M. Lew, Loukas A. Mistelis and Stefan Michael Kröll, *Comparative International Commercial Arbitration*, para. 11–19 (Kluwer Law International 2003).
8. The requirement that an appointed arbitrator be an impartial adjudicator is widely reflected in institutional rules and national laws alike. The ICC Rules of Arbitration (2012), Art. 11(1) requires that "Every arbitrator must be and remain impartial and independent of the parties involved in the arbitration." *See also* UNCITRAL Rules (2010), Art. 12.1; LCIA Rules (2014), Arts. 5.4 and 10.1; Swiss Rules of International Arbitration (2012), Arts. 9.2 and 10.1; HKIAC Rules (2013); Austrian Arbitration Law (2006), Art. 588; French CCP (2011), Arts. 1456 and 1506.2.

there is a danger to approaching impartiality with such self-conviction of neutrality. As a human being, such an arbitrator would likely be suppressing the biased and partial emotions, even if in truth they are minimal. This unknown or suppressed bias and prejudice might ultimately have an unfair effect on his reasoning and consequently unfairly impact the final award.

In a similar manner, an angelic arbitrator will remain completely independent during and after the proceedings. As is the case with the duty of impartiality, the duty of independence is another obligation that is universally represented at both domestic and international levels.[9] It goes without saying that any direct relationship between an arbitrator and one of the parties to the dispute would negate his independence and require him to abstain from presiding over the dispute. However, the ideal arbitrator would disclose all circumstances that "connect" him in any way to a party, although there is a general perception in international arbitration that this is not absolutely necessary.[10]

The ideal arbitrator gives the parties to a dispute the impression that he has no other pending cases – he is continuously available and always has the time to invest in any and all procedural or substantive issues in a prompt manner. For example, this arbitrator takes a proactive approach to the entire proceeding by familiarizing himself with the facts and issues of the case early on rather than waiting until the parties themselves have submitted multiple lengthy pleadings and gone through extensive discovery and disclosure. The same applies in particular to the arbitrator's approach to the hearing, this ideal arbitrator takes the time to read the expert reports so instead of asking irrelevant, off-topic questions, he can narrow down the topics and questions to the most relevant issues. The flawless arbitrator will ensure an efficient and economic conduct of the proceedings by implementing a strict imposition of time limits that compel focused work. This arbitrator will also not be hesitant to impose such time limits, i.e., have no hesitation in using the allocation of costs to sanction dilatory tactics nor will he be irresolute to interrupt the most eloquent advocate during a cross-examination.[11]

The desirable arbitrator in a tripartite tribunal will manage to keep the panel focused and ensure that the other arbitrators are attentive to the relevant law and applicable facts. This super being will mediate between the other two arbitrators, involve them in lengthy discussions of the relevant legal and factual issues, and yet still challenge a perspective offered by one or other tribunal member.[12] If there was such a thing as a perfect human being, this could potentially reflect the reality. However, it

---

9. *See also supra* n. 8.
10. Gomez-Acebo, *supra* n. 7, at 84. Furthermore, an arbitrator might be disappointed if parties would use this extensive disclosure to make tactical challenges (with sometimes surprising outcomes).
11. Arthur L. Marriott, *The Arbitrator's Responsibilities for the Proper Conduct of Proceedings*, 10 ICCA Congress Ser. 80, 81 (2001).
12. In the 2010 *International Arbitration Survey: Choices in International Arbitration conducted by the Queen Mary School of International Arbitration*, http://www.arbitration.qmul.ac.uk/docs/123290.pdf (accessed May 1, 2016), respondents emphasized the importance of arbitrators' soft skill, which they categorized as the "ability to work well with the other members of the panel, the parties and their layers and generally adopt a helpful and friendly demeanor".

will not be possible to keep all tribunal members focused at all times. Tribunals are often made up of arbitrators who do not speak the same native language, which can lead to misunderstandings and important issues getting lost in translation. Furthermore, they can also stem from entirely different legal backgrounds or simply have very dissimilar personalities, which would make an arbitrator's desire to manage and focus the panel, albeit an exemplary goal, highly unrealistic.

The ideal arbitrator always has the interests of the parties at heart. Thus, he would periodically inquire whether the parties are interested in settlement and whether the arbitrator can assist, e.g., in the form of mediation. This arbitrator would facilitate the parties' better understanding of each other's case by forcing them to reassess and re-evaluate their respective positions intermittently.[13] The problem here is that the angelic arbitrator may unintentionally assume that settlement is always in the best interest of the parties and thus something they always desire and strive for. However, not all parties may want this. In some cases, parties may have conducted obligatory or voluntary settlement negotiations for a long time before the commencement of an arbitration, and then an arbitrator's constant inquiry as to a potential settlement of the dispute would be perceived as negative and pushy. This behavior might even draw the arbitrator's independence and impartiality into question – what motives he might have for overzealously advocating for a settlement agreement.

In the final stages of an arbitration, the divine arbitrator would conduct his deliberations promptly following the oral hearing and begin drafting the award at an early stage,[14] thereby ensuring a quick award turnaround time.[15] However, in the real world, arbitrators are often in back-to-back hearings, which makes the immediate deliberation post-hearing very difficult and often impossible. Furthermore, the too early drafting of the award can lead to excessively long documentation of the background of the proceedings and procedural history, which are not a vital aspect of the award and result in unnecessary paper production and increased costs for the parties – after all, length does not stand for platinum quality.

If we lived in a perfect world the roles and duties of an arbitrator would be a lot easier!

§15.03 THE ROGUE ARBITRATOR: THE TRAIN WRECK

"Commend a fool for his wit, or a rogue for his honesty and he will receive you into his favor." ~ Henry Fielding

As a result of the increased workload and pressures exerted on arbitrators in the current commercial arbitration climate, arbitrators may be tempted to cut corners. However, if an arbitrator goes down this path, scrimping here and saving there, he may

---

13. Marriott, *supra* n. 11, at 81.
14. *See* generally Elliott Geisinger, *President's Message: A 'Clarion Call' Seconded*, 33:4 ASA Bull. 731, 731–739 (2015).
15. VIAC Rules Art. 32 – the VIAC Rules have a requirement to include a time period when an award can be expected.

end up systematically and gravely violating the most fundamental principles of procedural fairness, due process, impartiality and professional ethical obligations, not to mention the integrity of the arbitral process as a whole.

This type of arbitrator may, for instance, not pay particular care or attention to the expenses and costs of the proceedings, and, costs are one of the major user dissatisfactions in international arbitration.[16] By not tailoring the proceedings to the particularities and needs of each individual case,[17] the arbitrator may – albeit unconsciously – be increasing the cost of the arbitration for the parties and not providing the parties with the "service" they are entitled to.

An arbitrator who meets counsel for his appointing party at a conference and casually discusses an issue in relation to the pending proceedings could be on a slippery slope to displaying bias in favor of that party. By engaging in ex-parte communications, the arbitrator is not only breaching his confidentiality obligations but could potentially be jeopardizing the entire arbitral proceeding. Any party-appointed arbitrator that shows himself to be partial to the party that appointed him will lose credibility forever. The validity of the award would consequently be at risk,[18] and the pool of evidence would risk corruption, which may be irreversible. It may be near impossible to establish the extent to which the other members of the tribunal have been tainted by the new matters. Often no replacement arbitrator can remedy the problem as the waters have effectively been poisoned. In extreme cases, a party could even argue that due to a material breach the arbitration agreement has ceased to apply.[19]

Another roguish arbitrator character is the one who pawns off his functions and duties to an arbitral secretary or other third-party assistant. This arbitrator may not consciously be doing so, but it does not change the effect that such actions would have. The arbitral secretary's role will generally begin with simple administrative tasks, drafting emails to the parties, coordinating times for the case management conference, and other tasks of this nature. However, with the increasing workload of the chair, the administrative secretary reads and monitors submissions, provides the chair with summaries, and thereby indirectly influences the thought process of the chair. Slowly but surely this results in the arbitral secretary participating in deliberations of the tribunal and thereafter writing substantive parts of the award of his own initiative. The process of deciding and writing the award is one of the most sacred duties assigned to an arbitrator – it represents the culmination of all the time, effort and thought invested in the proceedings. Arbitral secretaries writing substantive parts of awards with no management or guidance are not completely unheard of. In the *Sachar v. Robot to* case, rogue arbitrators (albeit non-legal professionals) hired a third-party lawyer to draft the

---

16. Ema Vidak-Gojkovic, Lucy Greenwood and Michael McIlwrath, *Puppies or Kittens? How to Better Match Arbitrators to Party Expectations*, Austrian Yearbook on Intl. Arb. 61, fn 2 (2016).
17. Geisinger, *supra* n. 14.
18. Ahmed S. El-Kosheri and Karim Y. Youssef, *The Independence of International Arbitrators: An Arbitrator's Perspective*, Independence of Arbitrators – ICC ICArb. Bull. 43, 49 (2007 Special Supplement).
19. Alison Ross, *"Poisoned waters": Croatia's stance on the Sekolec scandal*, http://globalarbitrationreview.com/journal/article/34069/poisoned-waters-croatias-stance-sekolec-scandal (accessed May 5, 2016). While this example stems from an investment dispute, it cannot be excluded that an arbitrator could engage in such behavior in a commercial dispute.

award on their behalf.[20] Other far from angelic figures have crossed the line of delegable duties and allowed a third-party assistant to draft legal reasoning and substantive parts of the award without any supervision or direction from the tribunal.[21]

An arbitrator who has a tendency to be a rogue runs the risk of completely losing control of himself and truncating the arbitral tribunal by refusing to participate in deliberations or resigning at a critical juncture. Such behavior can bring an arbitral tribunal to a halt and entirely frustrate the proceedings.[22] Some institutional rules allow such truncated arbitral tribunals to proceed to an award without one active member.[23] In the case of an ad hoc arbitration, an appointing authority and/or tribunal must decide, without specific authorization, how to deal with an obstructive arbitrator.[24] The enforceability of such awards rendered under these conditions is another matter entirely: it may damage the arbitral process as a whole, jeopardize the entire profession or as some scholars put it, damage a whole "industry".

§15.04 THE ENLIGHTENED ARBITRATOR: WHAT AN ARBITRATOR SHOULD STRIVE TO ACHIEVE

"Your own Self-Realization is the greatest service you can render the world." ~
Ramana Maharshi

Between the non-existent perfect scenario represented by the angelic arbitrator, and the contradictory scenario represented by the sly and sometimes corrupt rogue arbitrator, there is a realistically attainable scenario represented by the enlightened arbitrator.

The enlightened arbitrator should possess the widely accepted minimum qualities that are associated with his role as a service provider, which include but are not limited to personal competence, intelligence, diligence, availability and integrity. The latter qualities are self-explanatory. Furthermore, this arbitrator should possess the

---

20. Dmytro Galagan and Patricia Zivkovic, *The Challenge of the Yukos Award: an Award Written by Someone Else – a Violation of the Tribunal's Mandate?*, http://kluwerarbitrationblog.com/2015/02/27/the-challenge-of-the-yukos-award-an-award-written-by-someone-else-a-violation-of-the-tribunals-mandate/ (accessed May 9, 2016).
21. While this example stems from an investment dispute, an arbitrator in a commercial dispute could also engage in such behavior. Alison Ross, Russia attacks Yukos awards, http://globalarbitrationreview.com/journal/article/34373/russia-attacks-yukos-awards/ (accessed May 9, 2016). Martin Valasek, assistant to the tribunal in the famous Yukos cases, has been accused of drafting the award. Although the tribunal has denied such allegations, writing expert Carole Chaski concluded that Valasek was responsible for drafting 79% of the preliminary objections section, 65% of the liability section and 71% of the damages section. This is further supported by the disproportionate amount of hours Valasek billed compared to any of the arbitrators, compounded by the fact that two other assistants were responsible for all administrative and logistical work. (The award has since been overturned by the Dutch court on procedural grounds for lack of jurisdiction).
22. Gary Born, *International Arbitration: Law and Practice*, 141 (2d ed., Kluwer Law International 2015).
23. ICC Rules, Art. 15(5); LCIA Rules, Art. 12(1).
24. Born, *supra* n. 22, at 142.

nationality, arbitration experience, linguistic abilities, industry knowledge and legal qualifications that are required on an individual case-by-case basis.[25]

In addition to these arguably minimum requirements that an enlightened arbitrator should possess, the author believes that there are certain personal characteristics that are essential when adjudicating an arbitration: self-confidence, firmness, practicability and reasonableness. These qualities play a vital role in making an arbitrator the "enlightened" one.

First, an arbitrator should be confident enough to craft proceedings in a truly specific way because every arbitration is unique. Every arbitral dispute is a different beast, demanding different procedures that require an arbitrator to be innovative in his approach to case management – not an easy task in the conservative field of dispute resolution.[26] An enlightened arbitrator will be able to recognize when a specific case does not necessarily require the standard template Procedural Order No. 1 but will discuss the specific requirements of the case with parties, and will have the confidence to implement the rules specifically crafted for that case.[27]

Second, the enlightened arbitrator should not be a pushover – he should use a firm hand when dealing with the parties. This is especially important in an arbitration climate where so-called *guerrilla tactics*[28] are on the rise.

Third, the enlightened arbitrator should take a practical approach to all procedural and substantive matters, including the length of submissions. International commercial arbitration is constantly under attack for producing excessive unnecessary volumes of paper, and a capable arbitrator can implement page limits and other procedural instruments to keep this under control.

Fourth, an enlightened arbitrator would reasonably encourage the parties to be concise and to the point in the use of their time in both written submissions and at the oral hearing. This arbitrator would further be reasonable with regard to important aspects of the proceeding: reasonable when dealing with parties, witnesses and experts, reasonable when deliberating with the arbitral tribunal, reasonable with setting time limits and granting time extensions, and reasonably ruling on discovery requests.

All of these qualities imply that the enlightened arbitrator takes his duties seriously and, by definition, fulfills these duties himself. The enlightened arbitrator is aware that trying to be perfect would likely overwhelm him and hurt the arbitral process and the interest of the parties as a whole. Consequently, this arbitrator will avail of any assistance, e.g. in the form of an arbitral secretary, in a manner that does not violate his mandate. The enlightened arbitrator will utilize the tribunal secretary to assist with administrative functions, as well as legal research or managing correspondence between the parties and the tribunal, and even help draft parts of the award (for instance the procedural history) under the direct supervision and direction of the

---

25. Gary Born, *International Commercial Arbitration: Commentary and Materials*, 1389 (2d ed., Kluwer Law International 2001).
26. Vidak-Gojkovic, Greenwood and McIlwrath, *supra* n. 16, at 18.
27. *See* generally Geisinger, *supra* n. 14.
28. Stephan Wilske and Günther J. Horvath, *Guerilla Tactics in International Arbitration*, Intl. Arb. L. Lib. 28 (Kluwer Law International 2013).

arbitrator.[29] This arbitrator is fully conscious that such support from an administrative secretary will only enhance the efficiency of the proceedings.

In addition to the several important and somewhat obvious qualities outlined above, an enlightened arbitrator distinguishes himself from the angelic and rogue arbitrator by approaching the crucial obligations of impartiality, independence and disclosure in a different and arguably more effective and fair manner.

Take for instance the requirement of impartiality – this obligation is often described as requiring "that an arbitrator neither favors one party nor is predisposed as to the question in dispute. In so far as this is a state of mind it is a fairly abstract and subjective standard which is hard to prove."[30] The enlightened arbitrator will take this vague standard and recognize that he is human, prone to bias or affinity for certain beliefs or backgrounds he may share, and be self-aware. This self-awareness of bias, in some instances could be harmful and in others harmless, but will enable the arbitrator to most accurately assess whether he is capable of acting neutrally and impartially over a specific dispute; and if he is not, then he will have the awareness and foresight to refuse appointment. Furthermore, once appointed, the enlightened arbitrator will not demonstrate impartiality to the party that nominated him, or he will risk losing credibility and putting the validity of the award at risk.[31] He will at the same time not overcompensate by being biased *against* the party that appointed him – such an attitude is likely to cause as much damage as showing too much favor.

The requirement of independence, on the other hand, may appear to be straightforward, but in practice there is no clear-cut approach. The enlightened arbitrator is a human being and not a computerized program or machine. It is not reasonably feasible to be thoroughly independent with no link to any party, entity, or counsel. There is a difference between consciously and purposefully showing and feeling bias in favor of the party that selected you, versus simply feeling some overall general sympathy for the plight or situation of that party.[32] The business, legal, educational or cultural background of the enlightened arbitrator might be the same as that of the party appointing him, but the existence of such commonalities will not negate his neutrality to the extent that he cannot objectively analyze and evaluate the merits of the dispute.

In this context of independence, the question of what an arbitrator must disclose to avoid breaching his duty remains, for practical purposes, exposed to some degree of uncertainty.[33] In the international commercial arbitration climate, i.e., a world of globalized business and legal services, quite a significant number of actors are acquainted with one another in some manner or other, causing the lines to become blurred.[34] The enlightened arbitrator will rationally use all the tools at his disposal –

---

29. Gary Born, *International Commercial Arbitration*, 1999 (2d ed., Kluwer Law International, 2014).
30. Lew, Mistelis and Kröll, *supra* n. 7, at para. 11-11.
31. El-Kosheri and Youssef, *supra* n. 18, at 49.
32. M. Hunter and J. Paulsson, *A Code of Ethics for Arbitrators in International Commercial Arbitration?*, 13 Arb. 153 (1985).
33. Some of the rules foresee disclosure obligations relating to matters that would call into question impartiality e.g., UNCITRAL Rules Art. 9; ICC Rules Art. 7.2; LCIA Rules Art. 5.3.
34. Whitesell, *supra* n. 4, at 8-9.

conflict checks through electronic software searches - to ensure that he is made aware of any link that might be too direct or close to be appropriate. At the same time, this arbitrator is aware that he does not need to go overboard by disclosing every possible distant and indirect link to all of the parties, counsel or entities associated with them – at the end of the day in most small knit national legal communities everyone is somehow acquainted. He is aware that that is an unrealistic feat, and an unnecessarily time consuming one. He is ultimately aware that the most important aspect of disclosure is not the existence of professional or individual relations, but the declaration of such relations. After all, "…it is secrecy that is problematic".[35]

§15.05 CONCLUSION

The increased complexity of the legal world, combined with the increased express and explicit authority granted to modern day arbitrators, has placed a higher burden of responsibility on the office of the "service-provider" arbitrator in commercial arbitration. It is becoming more difficult for arbitrators to fulfill their role at the same high level of intellectuality and efficiency as they once used to. Workloads are reaching almost insurmountable proportions as complex cases are often accompanied by extensive discovery requests and the delegation or sharing of duties is frowned upon.

An arbitrator who strives to fulfill the ideal role of a perfect arbitrator, although admirable, is setting himself up to fail. It is unrealistic to believe that this already demanding and complex role of service provider can be fulfilled at a level of perfection. Striving to attain such a level is only fraught with problems and possible negative consequences. At the same time, arbitrators have been known to cut corners and fall into a "rogue" pattern due to the overwhelming workload and extensive legal and ethical duties that the role requires him to fulfill.

Ultimately, arbitrators are human and the best possible "service provider" they can realistically strive to be is the enlightened arbitrator. This is the arbitrator who possesses the basis personal characteristics and skills necessary to work on the specific case. In a globalized commercial arbitration climate this role of an enlightened arbitrator is certainly not an easy one. As a result of the changing times arbitrators have been increasingly granted more authority and power in proceedings. However, this increased authority goes hand in hand with more responsibility. The exercise of arbitral power also requires restraint.[36] Now more than ever arbitrators have to recognize and acknowledge their human failings and natural faults particularly in relation to the requirements of impartiality and independence. While the enlightened arbitrator may make the best efforts to rectify such failings, if they cannot, they must act in the best interests of the parties and acknowledge this.

---

35. Kosheri and Youssef, *supra* n. 18, at 48.
36. Marriott, *supra* n. 11, at 83.

CHAPTER 16
Assessment of Future Damages in Arbitration

Hans van Houtte

Pierre Karrer has been a "companion de route" for many years. When we first met, I do not remember, but we have spent many hours together. Moreover, we both enjoy The Hague, my actual residence, where he has lived for many weeks and became a fluent Dutch speaker. It is therefore a pleasure to contribute to his *liber amicorum*.

My contribution could have covered "mass claims processes," an experience we both have in common, as Pierre has been a Member of the German Property Claims Commission[1] and has studied one of the few mass claims processes I have been involved in.[2]

However, not many readers would be interested in a contribution on past mass claims processes, which are moreover very contextual and ephemeral. Fortunately, we both are also interested in other topics which may carry a broader interest, such as decision standards in arbitration and efficient conduct of arbitration proceedings. Hence, this brief note on the assessment of future damages in arbitration.[3]

---

1. P. Karrer, Innovation to Speed Mass Claims: the Work of the Property Claims Commission of the German Foundation "Remembrance, Responsibility and Future", 5 *Journal of World Investment & Trade*, (2004) 57–62; P. Karrer, Mass Claims Proceedings in Practice: a few lessons learned, 23 *Berkeley Journal of International Law*, (2005) 463–473. P. Karrer, Mass Claims to provide Rough Justice: the Work of the Property Claims Commission of the German Foundation "Remembrance, Responsibility and its Future", in Grenzüberschreibungen: Beiträge zum Internationalen Verfahrensrecht und zur Scheidsgerichtbarkeit, *Festschrift für P. Schlosser*, 2005.
2. P. Karrer, ed., The Claims Resolution Process in Dormant Accounts in Switzerland, ELSA Conference 1999.
3. For a general background on future damages, *see* i.a. A. Pinna, *La Mesure du Préjudice contractuel*, L.G.D.J. 2007; M. Kantor, *Valuation for Arbitration Compensation Standards, Valuation Methods and Expert Evidence*, Kluwer 2008 and S. Ripinsky and K. Williams, *Damages in International Investment Law*, BILC 2008.

The damages claimed in many arbitrations do not only concern past damages, i.e., damages which already have occurred, but also future damages, which have not yet been concretized when the request for arbitration is filed.

This paper will first discuss the conceptual framework of future damages (I). Thereafter some practical aspects of the arbitral determination of future damages will be mentioned (II).

§16.01 CONCEPTUAL FRAMEWORK

[A] Future *Lucrum Cessans* and *Damnum Emergens*

Future damages are damages which are expected to occur but have not yet been concretized. They often relate to "lost profits" (*"lucrum cessans"*), i.e., profits which are lost because of a breach of contract, and which often not only relate to the period between the breach and the decision on compensation but also to the future period, stretching beyond the date of the decision. From the perspective of the arbitrator, the latter lost profits concern "future" damages. Similarly losses (*"damnum emergens"*) because of a breach of contract can be suffered before as well as after the decision. The latter compensation likewise concerns "future" damages.

[B] Time Span of Future Damages

The time span of the future damage which will have to be evaluated, has to be established.

The period of future harm is sometimes clearly delimited from the outset. This is, for instance, the case in a situation where non-performance or defective performance is only temporary (e.g., when the contract thereafter resumes its normal course and is once again expected to generate regular profit); or when a contract for an indefinite period has been terminated with a shorter notice than what the contract or the law provides for. The period after the award where the contract should have continued under the regular notice period, will be the relevant time span to assess future damages. Similarly, when a contract for a definite period of time was illegally terminated, the relevant time span to assess future lost profits runs between the date of the award and the end of the contract term. Long-term supply contracts, which are prematurely ended in an early stage of their life, may thus give rise to future damages extending for years, but never for longer than the original end date of the contract.

On the contrary, it also may happen that the time span for future damagesremains vague. For instance, in case of non-delivery in breach of contract of a machine, license or know-how, which would allow the purchaser to manufacture much-sought-after items, the purchaser will be unable to produce these items and will forfeit substantial profit therefrom. For how long profit will be lost, is hard to tell. Much depends also on how long the lost market would have been lucrative. Besides, while substantial profits may be lost at the outset, the loss of profit will water-down with time and become more hazardous to evaluate. Therefore, for the sake of simplicity, the future-damage- time span is often limited to the period of most substantial damage.[4] Similarly, although profits lost because of expropriation may span over many decades, the lost profits are generally assessed for only a few years after the expropriation.

[C] Forecasting and Probability

Assessment of future damage requires macro- and micro-forecasting. On the macro-level, general parameters, such as the evolution of the relevant market and of the economy as a whole, have to be evaluated. The micro-level requests a forecast of the specific prospects of claimant, such as its evolving profitability, cost structure, business model and specific position in the relevant market.

An arbitrator can only grant compensation for future damages when he can draw "sufficient" certainty from the forecast. A counter-factual analysis may give him thereby some support. For such analysis, he needs to determine the (extra) profits which would have been made and the costs which would have been avoided if the contract had been performed correctly.

A counter-factual analysis starts generally from the Claimant's operations before the breach and projects a fictive future on the basis of these operations. Of course, what happened in the past is not guaranteed to continue in the future as well. Nevertheless, past operations remain the best available basis to construe future potential. In all events, projections should be made with appropriate prudence and restraint. An annual sales increase in a given year because of exceptional circumstances does not allow projecting a same increase to the next year, even less year after year.

In brief, while one can never be 100% certain about the future, certainty is replaced by probability.

[D] Different Levels of Certainty

Forecasting future damages is inevitably guesswork. Nevertheless, certainty still plays a role therein.

The first instance, where certainty is required concerns the causality between the breach of contract and the future damage. To what extent such causation can be established depends much on the required "threshold" of certainty. Damages, which can be established with "sufficient" certainty, can be fully compensated in spite of a remaining small cloud of doubt whether the estimate is correct. When on the other hand, there is no "sufficient degree of certainty" to establish the actual amount of damage the arbitrators have full discretion to assess the future damage.

In brief, even when there is a limited risk that the assessed amount is not correct, full compensation for future damages can be granted. However, when the probability lowers to – let us say –80% – the certainty seems no longer sufficient and the evaluated amount should be multiplied by the probability that the assessment is correct. Finally,

---

4. However, if the purchaser is in a position to acquire a replacement, from a third party, the time span ends when the replacement becomes effective.

when it is even not certain whether the breach of contract would entail *any* damage at all, in many legal systems no compensation can be granted. Under other legal systems, such situation may, however, give rise to compensation for "loss of a chance" (*"perte d'une chance"*). For such loss of a chance, the maximum amount should be multiplied by the probability of the occurrence of.

The UNIDROIT Principles on International Commercial Contracts very well formulate the difference scenario's in its Article 7.4.3 (*Certainty of harm*):

(1) Compensation is due only for harm, including future harm, that is established with a *reasonable degree of certainty*
(2) Compensation may be due for the loss of a chance in proportion to the probability of its occurrence.[5]
(3) Where the amount of damages cannot be established with *a sufficient degree of certainty*, the assessment is at the discretion of the court.

§16.02 PROCEDURAL ASPECTS

[A] "Mind the Gap"

The evaluation of future damages is completely based upon estimates. The further the estimates stretch into the future, the more hazardous they become.

All parameters to be used being guesswork by definition, the arbitrator should endeavor to make guesswork an educated operation and counsel have the duty to help him thereby. However, counsel, unfamiliar with economic assessments and prognoses, would lack credibility when they themselves engage in complicated forecasts of future damages. Therefore, they often involve evaluation experts, very often from larger accounting firms. However, unfortunately, their involvement is too often not as efficient as it could be. In many arbitration proceedings, the respective experts for claimant and respondent are frequently the proverbial "ships passing in the night" radically criticizing the assumptions and findings from the other and expanding their own assumptions and findings, but not allow to link and bridge their respective opinions. Sometimes, the respondent's expert even limits him/herself to break down the findings of the claimant's expert without elaborating any alternative evaluation. The reason for the unbridgeable gap are not only the genuinely different opinions experts have on the specific issues (i.e., what experts are for and different opinions can be very enlightening). More problematic is the fact that, at the instructions of counsel who engaged them, they address different questions and even start from different facts. Sometimes for strategic reasons experts do not dwell on a line-of-reasoning, which their instructing counsel excludes to consider. For instance, a claimant, may ask its expert not to envisage the possibility of "loss of a chance" out of fear that the tribunal, following that path, would grant less compensation.

---

5. The Comment illustrates that "the owner of a horse which arrives too late to run in a race, as a result of delay in transport cannot recover the whole of the prize money, even though the horse was the favourite", but may only receive the hypothetical maximum loss multiplied by the probability of the chance coming about."

Whatever the reason may be, the gap between the claimant's and respondent's estimates of future damages is substantial and does not facilitate the arbitrator's task. A recent study found that in ninety-five arbitration proceedings, the respondent's expert only came out at 13% of the amount claimant asked for. As the above-mentioned study concluded: "given the huge disparity in the parties' relative positions, tribunals have a difficult job to determine an appropriate amount of damages to award."[6]

[B] How to Bridge the Gap?

The tribunal should make sure that the experts address the same set of questions. To that end, it may already include these questions in the Terms of Reference, or in a Procedural Order before the hearing.

In order to obtain a fruitful exchange and dialogue among the experts, the tribunal may also invite the experts to submit – after having filed their separate expert statements – a joint report in which they address each other's arguments and assumptions and indicate their points of agreement. Another possibility is to have the experts jointly examined at the hearing after each of them presented its own evidence and was cross-examined.

In order to make sure that the experts discuss the same factual scenario, the tribunal may impose the scenario– or alternative scenarios – which the experts have to analyze. Very often, the tribunal will not have sufficient insight into the relevant facts, to construe the relevant scenario(s) in an early stage of the proceedings. However, these scenarios may take form with the exchange of briefs and pleadings. Therefore, the tribunal will be in a better position at the end or after the hearing to construe the scenario(s) which the experts have to analyze in Post-Hearing submissions.

If feasible, and with the agreement of the Parties, the tribunal may – at the hearing or thereafter – even requisition the parties' experts and convert them into "tribunal experts". Although all experts have a duty to enlighten the tribunal with their "sincere belief", party-appointed experts are under the instructions of the instructing counsel and work from the data submitted by counsel. As tribunal experts, on the other hand, they are solely under the instructions of the tribunal and have to take into account the facts and assumptions, submitted by the tribunal. The transparency of the process is important. When the parties' experts are requisitioned by the tribunal and testify at the hearing, the questions put to them and their answers will be known by the parties present at the hearing. More delicate, however, are the communications between tribunal and these experts after the hearing. In my view, such communications should not take place behind the parties' back and the latter should be copied, be able to submit their remarks and give their input as well.

---

6. *See* 2015 – International Arbitration Damage Research – Closing the Gap between Claimant and Respondent, p. 2., Price Waterhouse Cooper, www.pwc.com.

[C] The Manageable Excel Sheet

Expert reports on future damages with their many documentary exhibits, statistics and, excel sheets, look solid. However, forecasts remain hazardous and subjective. In spite of their solid appearances, the elaborated and precise calculations of experts are often built on quicksand. Huge amounts claimed for future damage have often shaky foundations. Therefore, tribunals should critically examine the parameters on which the experts base their calculations, whereby the input from the other party's experts may be helpful.

For strategical reasons, however, Claimant's experts sometimes opt to submit their conclusions "*en bloc*" in order to put the tribunal before the choice – "take it or leave it" – between their damage evaluation or nothing. Arbitrators may avoid this pitfall by requesting experts to submit excel sheets where all relevant parameters for their future damage evaluation (e.g., projected profit rates, turn-over, discount rates, relevant period, interest rates) can be changed and with the data in the summary excel sheet, referring to underlying cells to be opened with the mere click of a mouse. Whenever arbitrators then agree with the report's methodology (or part of it) but disagree with how specific parameters have been filled in, they themselves can change these parameters accordingly and arrive at the correct amount of compensation.

[D] The Future Shrinks

With the passage of time, future damages become past damages. What was a claim for future harm when the request for arbitration is filed, may have become a claim for past damages at the hearing. Arbitrators should avoid unnecessary speculation. They should therefore allow parties to update the evidence and replace forecasts by actual data –even after the hearing. Post-hearing submission of new evidence should, however, be subject to a contradictory debate between the parties, either by correspondence, post-hearing briefs or, if necessary, by way of a dedicated (teleconference) hearing.

[E] Recurrent or Continues Future Damages

Whenever the future harm stretches over a very lengthy period, a tribunal may exceptionally in a partial award grant compensation for "past" harm and postpone the compensation of future harm to a later date when future costs and lost profits have become "past" damages as well. Of course, much depends on the time span for future damage to become past damage and on the willingness of the arbitrators (and at least one of the parties) to replace a final "once-and-for-all" compensation for past and future harm by consecutive partial compensation(s). Indeed, it may be quite inconvenient for a case to remain on the docket until all "future" harm lies behind. Moreover, an arbitration panel may not want to keep jurisdiction for too long. In that event, the arbitrators may consider to render in a first stage a partial award on the merits and to grant further compensation some time later in one or more consecutive awards for future damage which has concretized since then. Another solution could be that the arbitrators decide the merits but limit their grant of compensation to "past" damages, allowing the parties to start new proceedings on future harm once it will have crystallized.

However, arbitrators should not readily dodge their judicial responsibilities and avoid assessment of future damages because such assessment would become more comfortable at a later moment. The business community is not well served by arbitrators who shy away from setting disputes – even if that would require reasonable forecasts about future damages. Nevertheless, in some exceptional situations, the evaluation of future damages may have become so hazardous that it does no longer fit with the judicial function.

For instance, some years ago, an ICSID Tribunal, which I chaired, had to assess the profits lost on an oil concession for another thirty-two years. Exploitation, although still feasible, was set to become less lucrative because of contract infringements by Canada. Assessment of lost profits till 2036 would require to forecast for twenty years, not only the evolution of production costs and volume, but also demand for oil, sales prices, exchange rates, technological evolution, etc. The Tribunal found that it could not with "reasonable certainty" forecast these critical variables (which, besides, had much fluctuated in the past so that predictions became even more whimsical). It concluded that "[t]he evaluation of future damages for such a long period is extremely hazardous and it does not, on balance, seem to us that the estimates are more probable than not."[7] The Tribunal accordingly only granted compensation for past lost profit (running until 2012) and hinted that future lost profits might be open for compensation at some point in the future when they had become "fully ascertainable and actual".[8] In fact, the next "slice" of future damages, covering the period 2012–2015, which in the meantime became "past" damage, was recently claimed.[9]

In the event of recurrent or continuing future damages, arising out of a past or continuing breach, it may be appropriate for a tribunal to grant only compensation for past damages and leave the future open. Besides, not deciding future damages may be an incentive for the respondent to remedy the breach.

---

7. *Mobil Investments Canada Inc. and Murphy Oil Corporation v. Canada*, ICSID ARB (AF) 07/4, May 22, 2012, para. 477.
8. *Idem*, para. 476.
9. *Mobil Investments Canada v. Canada*, ICSID 15/6.

CHAPTER 17
The Problem of Undisclosed Assistance to Arbitral Tribunals

Benjamin Hughes

§17.01 INTRODUCTION

The role of tribunal secretaries in international commercial arbitration has been the subject of much discussion and debate among arbitration practitioners in recent years. While it is widely accepted that administrative secretaries may be appointed to assist arbitral tribunals in large and complex international arbitrations, considerable disagreement exists as to the proper scope and nature of such assistance. Some insist that the tribunal secretary should play a very limited role, performing only logistical and administrative or secretarial tasks. Others argue for a more robust role which would allow the tribunal secretary to conduct legal research, provide summaries of the facts and the submissions of the parties, and even participate in the tribunal's deliberations or draft non-dispositive portions of the award.[1]

Regardless of one's views on the acceptable scope of a tribunal secretary's activities, however, it should not be controversial to say as a preliminary matter that no tribunal secretary should be appointed without the knowledge of the parties. This is reflected in the Administered Arbitration Rules (2013) of the Hong Kong International Arbitration Centre (the "HKIAC Rules"), which provide that an arbitral tribunal may appoint a tribunal secretary only after consulting with the parties.[2] The HKIAC also issued a set of "Guidelines on the Use of a Secretary to the Arbitral Tribunal" effective

---

1. For excellent discussions of these issues, *see* Constantine Partasides, "The Fourth Arbitrator? The Role of Secretaries to Tribunals in International Arbitration" in *Arbitration International*, Vol. 18, No. 2 (2002); Michael Polkinghorne and Charles B. Rosenberg, "The Role of the Tribunal Secretary in International Arbitration: A Call for a Uniform Standard" in *Dispute Resolution International*, Vol. 8, No. 2 (October 2014).
2. *See* HKIAC Administered Arbitration Rules (2013), Art. 13.4.

as of June 1, 2014 (the "HKIAC Guidelines"), perhaps the most comprehensive treatment of the subject by any arbitral institution.[3] The HKIAC Guidelines provide that an arbitral tribunal may appoint a tribunal secretary only after informing the parties of its intention to do so, providing the parties with the proposed secretary's CV and declaration of independence and impartiality, and allowing the parties an opportunity to comment, unless the parties agree otherwise.[4] In addition, the HKIAC Guidelines contain provisions for a party to raise an objection with respect to the independence or impartiality of a tribunal secretary.[5]

Several leading arbitral institutions go one step further, requiring the informed consent of the parties prior to the appointment of a tribunal secretary. For example, in 2012 the Secretariat of the ICC International Court of Arbitration issued a "Note on the Appointment, Duties and Remuneration of Administrative Secretaries" (the "ICC Note"), which requires the arbitral tribunal to inform the parties prior to taking any steps to appoint an administrative secretary. The tribunal must submit the proposed secretary's CV to the parties, together with a declaration of impartiality and independence and an undertaking by the proposed secretary to act in accordance with the ICC Note. The tribunal must also make it clear to the parties that they may object to the proposed secretary, and a secretary may not be appointed if a party has raised an objection.[6] Likewise, in 2015 the Singapore International Arbitration Centre issued Practice Note PN-01/15 9493942108 "On the Appointment of Administrative Secretaries" (the "SIAC Note"), which provides that "[n]o administrative secretary may be appointed without the consent of all parties to the arbitration."[7] Finally, the LCIA has published on its website (under "Frequently Asked Questions") a brief statement to the effect that a tribunal secretary may be appointed "provided that the parties agree, and subject to the usual conflict checks."[8] In addition, the LCIA issued its "Notes for Arbitrators" in June 2015 (the "LCIA Note"), which provides that the tribunal may appoint a tribunal secretary "subject to the express written agreement of the parties."[9]

These requirements seem to reflect a consensus which has emerged in the international arbitration community. In a 2012 survey conducted by the Young ICCA Task Force for the Appointment and Use of Arbitral Secretaries ("ICCA Task Force"), a majority of respondents (72.4%) favored requiring party consent for the appointment of tribunal secretaries. In a follow up survey conducted in 2013, a majority of respondents agreed that: (i) tribunal secretaries should be formally appointed with the knowledge of the parties (74.7%); (ii) the consent of the parties should be obtained prior to the appointment of a tribunal secretary (76.9%); and (iii) the consent of the parties to a particular candidate proposed as tribunal secretary should be required

---

3. Available at http://www.hkiac.org.
4. *Id.*, para. 2.3.
5. *Id.*, paras. 2.7–2.9.
6. ICC Note, s. 1 (Appointment). Available at http://www.iccwbo.org.
7. SIAC Note, para. 3. Available at http://www.siac.org.sg.
8. *See* http://www.lcia.org//Frequently_Asked_Questions.aspx#Secretaries.
9. LCIA Note, para. 68. Available at http://www.lcia.org.

(75.8%).[10] Among the first recommended "Best Practices for the Appointment and Use of Arbitral Secretaries" in the *Young ICCA Guide on Arbitral Secretaries* (the "ICCA Guide") is that "[a]n arbitral secretary should only be appointed with the knowledge and consent of the parties."[11]

It nevertheless remains the case, as noted in the ICCA Guide, that "some arbitrators are habitually assisted by arbitral secretaries without any formal appointment process, or, in some circumstances, without identifying these assistants to the parties."[12] Obviously, the use of undisclosed assistance by arbitrators is difficult if not impossible to quantify or substantiate. However, anecdotal evidence and experience suggests that it remains a widespread practice, despite the ICCA Guide's warning that this practice should be avoided "in order to promote transparency and protect the legitimacy of the international arbitration process."[13]

In discussing this issue with colleagues, it seems that most have encountered this problem but are somewhat reluctant to raise it in a public forum (much less in writing). One colleague called it "the elephant in the room," while another even advised against writing this article. Obviously, raising the issue with respect to any particular arbitrator would be extremely uncomfortable to say the least. For the avoidance of doubt, it is not the intention of this brief note to call into question the integrity of any individual arbitrator(s), but rather to stimulate an open discussion of a widespread practice which should be addressed in order to maintain the confidence of parties in the international arbitration system.

§17.02 THE PROBLEM

It is easy to see why the use of undisclosed assistance by arbitral tribunals undermines the legitimacy of the arbitration process. Where a tribunal secretary has been appointed with the informed consent of the parties or after consultation with them, the parties have information about, and the opportunity to comment on or consent to, the secretary's access to confidential information, independence and impartiality, role in the arbitration, and remuneration. All of these issues will be discussed to some degree with the parties prior to the appointment of the secretary, and are often regulated by the rules or guidelines of the relevant arbitral institution. Where assistance to the tribunal is not disclosed, the parties obviously have no opportunity to understand or have any input with respect to these factors, or even know that they may be at issue.

[A] Confidentiality

Where the parties have agreed or the arbitral rules provide that the arbitral proceedings shall be confidential, it would not seem permissible for the arbitral tribunal to share

---

10. International Council for Commercial Arbitration, *Young ICCA Guide on Arbitral Secretaries*, ICCA Reports No. 1, Mar. 12, 2014, pp. 5–6.
11. *Id.* at p. 5.
12. *Id.*
13. *Id.*

any information regarding the arbitral proceedings with an undisclosed assistant. For example, Rule 39 (Confidentiality) of the SIAC Rules provides that an arbitrator "shall at all times treat all matters relating to the proceedings and the award as confidential. The discussions and deliberations of the Tribunal shall be confidential." Where a tribunal secretary is appointed, the same duty of confidentiality applies to the secretary. However, as noted above, the SIAC Practice Note provides that no tribunal secretary may be appointed without the consent of the parties. Where an assistant has not been disclosed to the parties, it goes without saying that no such consent is possible. The assistant is therefore not properly appointed as a tribunal secretary and is merely a third party, to whom the tribunal is not permitted to disclose any information relating to the proceedings.

It may be suggested that confidentiality is not an issue where a law firm partner makes use of an associate in the same firm, because the duty of confidentiality extends to all members of the firm. After all, partners often share confidential information with associates in order to enable them to assist the partner with his work. However, a law firm partner acting in the capacity of an arbitrator is not working for a client who has engaged the firm. The law firm has not been appointed as the arbitrator. Rather the individual partner has been appointed *intuiti personae*, as an individual who must perform his or her duties personally.[14]

Further, where an arbitral tribunal is required to maintain confidentiality, this duty normally extends to any tribunal secretary, expert or other person appointed by the tribunal. As noted above, this is the case under Rules 39 of the SIAC Rules. The SIAC Note also requires the tribunal secretary to execute a declaration of independence, impartiality and confidentiality prior to appointment.[15] Likewise, the HKIAC Guidelines provide that "[a] tribunal secretary is under an obligation to maintain the confidentiality of the arbitration and any decisions made by the arbitral tribunal unless the parties agree otherwise."[16] The Best Practices set forth in the Young ICCA Guide also recommend that tribunal secretaries be bound by the same duties of confidentiality and privacy as applicable to the arbitral tribunal.[17] However, as a practical matter it is difficult to see how an assistant lurking in the shadows unbeknownst to the parties can be held accountable for a breach of confidentiality, much less be held to a higher standard of confidentiality and privacy than the very arbitrator who has improperly disclosed confidential information to such an assistant.

[B] Independence and Impartiality

However limited the role of the tribunal secretary may be with respect to substantive matters, there remains the justified fear that any bias on the part of the secretary may

---

14. Pierre Tercier, "The Role of the Secretary to the Arbitral Tribunal" in Lawrence Newman and Richard Hill, *The Leading Arbitrators' Guide to International Arbitration*, Juris Publishing 2014, p. 537; Polkinghorne and Rosenburg, *supra* n. 1, p. 109.
15. SIAC Note, *supra* n. 7, para. 4.
16. HKIAC Guidelines, *supra* n. 2, para. 3.7.
17. ICCA Guide, *supra* n. 10, pp. 8, 10–11.

Chapter 17: The Problem of Undisclosed Assistance §17.02[C]

taint the proceedings in some way.[18] For this reason, most institutions which contemplate a role for a tribunal secretary also provide that the secretary must at all times be independent and impartial with respect to the parties. For example, the ICC Note provides that tribunal secretaries "must satisfy the same independence and impartiality requirements as those which apply to arbitrators under the Rules."[19] As noted above, the ICC Note also requires the secretary to submit a declaration of independence and impartiality prior to appointment.[20] Likewise, the SIAC Note also requires a tribunal secretary to execute a declaration of independence and impartiality prior to appointment.[21] The HKIAC Guidelines go even further, requiring a declaration of independence and impartiality, including disclosure of any circumstances likely to give rise to justifiable doubts as to the secretary's impartiality or independence, and providing procedures for the challenge and potential removal of a tribunal secretary where a party raises an objection with respect to the secretary's impartiality or independence.[22] The Best Practices set forth in the Young ICCA Guide also provide that a tribunal secretary should be independent, impartial and free of any conflicts of interest, but puts the onus on the tribunal to confirm these fact to the parties. The Best Practices also provide that the parties should be given an opportunity to object to the appointment.[23]

It goes without saying that it is not possible for the parties to confirm the independence or impartiality of an undisclosed assistant to the tribunal, nor is it possible for them to consent or object to his or her involvement in the case. This certainly undermines the integrity of the proceedings, even where the assistant has no conflicts of interest. It is not sufficient, as I have heard suggested on occasion, that a conflict check may have been undertaken at the firm in which both the appointed arbitrator and the undisclosed assistant work. While it is important for the arbitrator to confirm that there are no conflicts within his or her law firm with respect to the parties to the arbitration, the individual (and not the law firm) has been engaged as the arbitrator. It is entirely possible for there to be no circumstances giving rise to justifiable doubts as to the independence or impartiality of one member of a law firm, while another member of the same firm may have a clear conflict of interest.

[C]   Role in the Arbitration

As noted at the outset, there has been considerable debate as to the permissible role of tribunal secretaries. Leading arbitral institutions have addressed this issue in their practice notes and guidelines on tribunal secretaries, confirming a general consensus that secretaries should perform primarily administrative tasks, and should not be involved in the decision-making of the tribunal. For example, the ICC Note provides that a tribunal secretary may perform such organizational and administrative tasks as

---

18. Partasides, *supra* n. 1, pp. 148–151.
19. ICC Note, *supra* n. 6, para. 1.
20. Id.
21. SIAC Note, *supra* n. 7, para. 4.
22. HKIAC Guidelines, *supra* n. 2, pars. 2.2, 2.7–2.10.
23. ICCA Guide, *supra* n. 10, pp. 7–10.

transmitting documents and communications on behalf of the tribunal, organizing and maintaining files and documents, organizing hearings and meetings, attending hearings, meetings and deliberations, taking notes and keeping time, conducting legal or similar research, and proofreading and checking citations, dates and cross-references in procedural orders and awards, as well as correcting typographical, grammatical or calculation errors.[24] The ICC Note unequivocally prohibits the delegation of any essential function of the tribunal to a tribunal secretary:

> Under no circumstances may the Arbitral Tribunal delegate decision-making functions to an Administrative Secretary. Nor should the arbitral tribunal rely on the Administrative Secretary to perform any essential duties of an arbitrator. The Administrative Secretary may not act, or be required to act, in such a manner as to prevent or discourage direct communications among the arbitrators, between the Arbitral Tribunal and the parties, or between the Arbitral Tribunal and the Secretariat. A request by an Arbitral Tribunal to an Administrative Secretary to prepare written notes or memoranda shall in no circumstances release the Arbitral Tribunal from its duty to personally to review the file and/or to draft any decision of the Arbitral Tribunal.[25]

The HKIAC Guidelines likewise provide that "the arbitral tribunal shall not delegate any decision-making functions to a tribunal secretary, or rely on a tribunal secretary to perform any essential duties of the tribunal."[26] A similar list of administrative functions which may be undertaken by the tribunal secretary is also included. The HKIAC Guidelines also provide for additional tasks which the tribunal secretary may perform, "provided that the arbitral tribunal ensures that the secretary does not perform any decision-making function or otherwise influence the arbitral tribunal's decisions in any manner." These include conducting legal research, checking the legal authorities cited by the parties to ensure they are the latest authorities on a matter, researching discrete questions relating to factual evidence and witness testimony, preparing case law summaries, preparing memoranda summarizing the parties' respective submissions and evidence, attending the deliberations of the tribunal and taking notes, and preparing drafts of non-substantive letters and non-substantive parts of the tribunal's order, decisions and awards.[27]

Commentators generally agree that tribunal secretaries may be engaged in tasks beyond the merely clerical or administrative, so long as they are not involved in the decision-making of the tribunal (thereby becoming the famous "fourth arbitrator").[28] This consensus is reflected in the 2013 survey of arbitration practitioners conducted by the ICCA Task Force, which found that a majority of respondents (75.0%) believed that a tribunal secretary should be qualified as a lawyer (indicating that the secretary should perform more than simply administrative duties), but an even larger majority (83.5%) felt that the tribunal secretary should not participate in the tribunal's deliberations.[29]

---

24. ICC Note, *supra* n. 6, para. 2.
25. *Id.*
26. HKIAC Note, *supra* n. 2, para. 3.2.
27. *Id.*, para. 3.4.
28. *See* Partasides, *supra* n. 1, p. 161. Polkinghorne and Rosenberg, *supra* n. 1, pp. 124–127.
29. ICCA Guide, *supra* n. 10, p. 3.

The Best Practices set forth in the ICCA Guide suggest that "[w]ith appropriate direction and supervision by the arbitral tribunal, an arbitral secretary's role may legitimately go beyond the purely administrative."[30] However, this role should not extend to participation in the decision-making process of the tribunal, drafting substantive portions of the award, or otherwise assuming the essential duties of an arbitrator.

Where assistance to an arbitrator is not disclosed, the arbitrator is in effect representing that he or she is not receiving any such assistance at all. Thus, any work performed by the undisclosed assistant is de facto claimed as work performed by the arbitrator personally. This is inherently troubling. It is also difficult under these circumstances to exclude the possibility that an undisclosed assistant to an arbitrator is performing substantive work, including becoming involved in decision-making and drafting of dispositive portions of the award, which should be personally performed by the arbitrator.

Moreover, this practice begs the question of why the assistance of an associate or other assistant is not being disclosed. If the role of the assistant is consistent with the accepted role of a tribunal secretary, there would seem to be no reason why such assistance could not be disclosed. It may be that undisclosed assistants in international arbitrations are being used for purposes not contemplated by the various guidelines applicable to tribunal secretaries. A few possible examples could include: (i) assistants to individual co-arbitrators, regardless of whether there is a tribunal secretary appointed to assist the tribunal, (ii) the use of assistance in excess of the accepted limits applicable to tribunal secretaries in order to enable busy independent arbitrators to accept more appointments, or (iii) the use of undisclosed associates by law firm partners to enable the partner to accept appointments without impinging on time required for more remunerative counsel work for clients. None of these scenarios inspire confidence in the system of international arbitration.

[D] Remuneration

One of the most troubling aspects of the use of undisclosed assistants to arbitral tribunals is the question of remuneration. Where the tribunal is paid on an *ad valorem* basis, such as under the ICC Rules or the SIAC Rules, perhaps no particular problem arises. Presumably, the assistant would be paid from the fees paid to the arbitrator or the tribunal, which are not significantly affected by the number of hours billed. However, where the tribunal is paid on an hourly basis, how are the hours of an undisclosed assistant to be compensated? For example, in the context of a law firm, it seems unlikely that all of an associate's time spent on an arbitration would simply be written off. Would the partner appointed as arbitrator simply appropriate the hours billed by the associate? Or would some calculation be applied to reduce the partner's billing rate and/or number of hours in order to avoid overcharging the parties? How

---

30. *Id.*, p. 11.

can such a formula be arrived at? The ethical landmines and potential for mischief are obvious.

§17.03 THE SOLUTION?

The obvious solution to the problem of undisclosed assistance to arbitrators is for arbitrators to be required to disclose any such assistance to the parties and the arbitral institution (where applicable). In other words, any assistance to an arbitrator, beyond the services of a professional secretary (such as word processing, calendaring, or making travel and other logistical arrangements), should be treated in the same manner as a tribunal secretary in terms of disclosure to, and consent of, the parties.

There are several simple ways to accomplish this without promulgating yet another set of guidelines. For example, existing arbitral rules (or notes or guidelines) could: (i) define tribunal secretaries to include any person who provides any assistance to any member of the arbitral tribunal, other than professional secretarial services such as word processing, calendaring, or making travel and other logistical arrangements; (ii) provide that the provisions relating to tribunal secretaries also apply to any other person providing assistance to any member of the tribunal; or (iii) require arbitrators to sign a statement, perhaps integrated into a standard statement of independence and impartiality, undertaking to make a disclosure (and obtain consent, where applicable) prior to using any assistance in the performance of his or her duties as arbitrator.

It may be fairly said that arbitrators are effectively already under an obligation to disclose any assistance they intend to receive. However, there is something to be said for an explicit rule or guidance. It may also be argued that this modest solution ultimately depends entirely upon the integrity and self-policing of the arbitrators. That is true, but so do many if not most of the rules and guidelines applicable to arbitrators. As Professor Partasides has put it: "[t]he reliance of the system of arbitration on the integrity of the arbitrator is after all as pervasive as it is unavoidable."[31] And further:

> The system should not be fashioned by fear of the irresponsible, for they can undermine any safeguard. Rather, it should be designed with the overwhelming majority in mind: those who are concerned to fulfil their mandate responsibly.[32]

I am confident that very few if any of our colleagues in the field of international arbitration would accept appointment under rules which explicitly require the disclosure of any assistance to the arbitrator, or sign an undertaking to disclose any such assistance, and then proceed to violate that trust.

---

31. Partasides, *supra* n. 1, p. 160.
32. *Id.*, p. 157.

CHAPTER 18
Standard of Proof for Challenge Against Arbitrators: Giving Them the Benefit of the Doubt

Michael Hwang SC & Lynnette Lee

§18.01 INTRODUCTION

An arbitrator must be independent and impartial. This is a universal principle applicable to any arbitrator.[1] However, a universal acceptance of a principle does not always mean a universal interpretation of its rules.

The test for bias has seen its variations in jurisdictions all over the world. That said, many countries have incorporated the UNCITRAL Model Law's ('Model Law') standard of 'justifiable doubts' under Article 12(2) as part of the *lex arbitri* of the jurisdiction.

Article 12(2) is in the following terms:

> 'An arbitrator may be challenged only if circumstances exist that give rise to *justifiable doubts* as to his impartiality or independence, or if he does not possess qualifications agreed to by the parties.' (emphasis added)

Even then, it is important to appreciate the varying tests used in national arbitration laws, which not only operate in ad hoc arbitration with a seat in that

---

1. This universality of the independence and impartiality is in the context of international arbitration. *See* e.g., Julian DM Lew, Loukas A. Mistelis, and Stefan M. Kröll, *Comparative International Commercial Arbitration* (Kluwer Law International 2003) 95: The '*Magna Carta*' of International Commercial Arbitration has two main rules: (1) due process and fair hearing; and (2) the independence and impartiality of arbitrators; Sam Luttrell, *Bias Challenges in International Commercial Arbitration: The Need for a 'Real Danger' Test* (Kluwer Law International 2009) 1–2: *Nemo debet esse judex in propria causa*, meaning every man has a right to an impartial (and independent) adjudicator.

country, but also inadvertently influence the finding of bias while national courts are applying the 'justifiable doubts' standard.[2] Perhaps this could be attributed to the fact that 'justifiable doubts' is an abstract concept itself that is open to numerous interpretations.

Nevertheless, a lack of clarity surrounding the meaning of the term was the main reason why the Original 2004 IBA Working Group for the Guidelines on Conflicts of Interest ('the Original Working Group') introduced a practical definition of 'justifiable doubts' under General Standard 2(c).[3] Since its introduction in 2004, the IBA Guidelines on Conflicts of Interest in International Arbitration ('2004 IBA Guidelines'[4]) have been widely referred to before arbitral tribunals as well as national courts in various jurisdictions.

Prior to the main discussion, it is important to distinguish between *apparent* and *actual* bias, even though this paper will not deal with the latter issue at length.[5] The fundamental distinction is that apparent bias focuses on the *appearance* of bias rather than whether the bias *actually* exists.[6] This affects the nature of the test, since apparent bias is judged *ex-ante* and actual bias is judged *ex-post*. In other words, independence (apparent bias) is judged prospectively, and impartiality (actual bias) is judged retrospectively. The hypothetical nature of this *ex-ante* test is the cause for much difficulty in interpretation. Against this backdrop, the paper will later address some criticisms directed at the 2004 IBA Guidelines by Gary Born.

The discussion over the applicable standard of proof for challenging arbitrators will be broadly divided into three main sections:

(a) This paper will first consider various competing tests for apparent bias across academic commentaries and several jurisdictions to reflect a spectrum of varying thresholds for challenging arbitrators. (section §18.02).
(b) More specifically, this paper will interpret the applicable standard of proof under General Standard 2(c) of the IBA Guidelines in the light of the origins and aims of the IBA Guidelines, concluding that this standard refers to 'more than 50% probability'. This paper will also consider Born's critique of the General Standard 2(c) definition of 'justifiable doubts' against the intent and

---

2. See *HSMV Corp. v. ADI Ltd.*, 72 F. Supp. 2d 1122 (C.D. Cal. 1999), where the court purported to apply Art. 12(2) Model Law, which was applicable in that case, but went on to expound on the 'evident partiality' common law principles common in the US.
3. To be discussed in detail later in this paper.
4. This discussion will refer to both the 2004 and the 2014 versions of the IBA Guidelines. The changes made to the 2014 version are not substantial, but they will be highlighted in the text where appropriate. The 2014 version of the IBA Guidelines will be referred to as '2014 IBA Guidelines'.
5. There appears to be only one reported English case where an arbitrator was removed for actual bias. See *Re Catalina (Owners) and Norma MV (Owners)* (1938) 61 Ll L Rep 360, where the arbitrator questioned the credibility of evidence submitted by witnesses of Portuguese descent based on their ethnicity during the course of the proceedings. He was overheard saying, '*The Italians are all liars in these cases and will say anything to suit their book. The same thing applies to the Portuguese [directly then referring to the two Portuguese who had given evidence on July 13].*'
6. Jeffrey Waincymer, *Procedure and Evidence in International Arbitration* (Kluwer Law International 2012) 294.

discussions of the Original Working Group when the 2004 IBA Guidelines were drafted.[7] (section §18.03).

(c) Finally, this paper will address Born's critique of disclosure requirements under General Standard 3 and the Orange List of the IBA Guidelines. (section §18.04).

This explanation of the inner workings of the Original Working Group will enhance one's understanding and employment of soft-law instruments like the IBA Guidelines.

§18.02 THE STANDARD OF PROOF FOR CHALLENGING ARBITRATORS

[A] Standard of Proof Spectrum for Challenging Arbitrators

There are various formulations of the test to challenge arbitrators across different jurisdictions and rules. We will begin by exploring the most commonly used 'justifiable doubts' test as set out in the Model Law followed by other formulations of the test for bias. While all these tests are focused on establishing apparent bias,[8] they differ in terms of the requisite standard of proof in assessing the merits of a challenge. In other words, particular facts and circumstances may be relevant in two tests, but a difference in the threshold required may result in contrasting findings of bias.[9]

[1] Academic Commentaries

In common law jurisdictions, various tests for bias include the 'reasonable apprehension' test,[10] the 'real possibility' test,[11] the 'real danger' test,[12] and the 'evident

---

7. The nineteen members of the Original Working Group for the 2004 IBA Guidelines were Henri Alvarez, Canada; John Beechey, England; Jim Carter, U.S.; Emmanuel Gaillard, France; Emilio Gonzales de Castilla, Mexico; Bernard Hanotiau, Belgium; Michael Hwang, Singapore; Albert Jan van den Berg, Belgium; Doug Jones, Australia; Gabrielle Kaufmann-Kohler, Switzerland; Arthur Marriott, England; Tore Wiwen Nilsson, Sweden; Hilmar Raeschke-Kessler, Germany; David W Rivkin, U.S.; Klaus Sachs, Germany; Nathalie Voser, Switzerland (Rapporteur); David Williams, New Zealand; Des Williams, South Africa; and Otto LO de Witt Wijnen, The Netherlands (Chair). In 2012, the IBA Guidelines were reviewed by the expanded Conflicts of Interest Subcommittee, chaired by David Arias and later co-chaired by Julie Bédard, with the review process led by Pierre Bienvenu and Bernard Hanotiau. This revised version was later published as the 2014 version of the IBA Guidelines.
8. *Waincymer* (n. 7) 295.
9. *See* e.g., Edmund-Davies LJ in *Metropolitan Properties Co (FGC) Ltd v. Lannon and ors* [1969] 1 QB 577 (CA) 606: '[...] the different tests, even when applied to the same facts, may lead to different results is illustrated by *R v Barnsley Licensing Justices* itself.'
10. This test is from the judgment of Lord Hewart CJ in *R v. Sussex Justices, Ex p McCarthy* [1924] 1 KB 256 (KB).
11. This test is from the decision of the House of Lords in *Porter v. Magill* [2001] UKHL 67, [2002] 2 AC 357 (HL).
12. This test is from Lord Goff of Chieveley, in *R v. Gough* [1993] AC 646 (HL).

partiality' test.[13] Even among academics, there are differences in interpreting the applicable standard of proof for bias.

For one, Waincymer concludes that the applicable standard of proof depends on the likelihood of doubt – whether *'there may be doubts, there are likely to be doubts, or there would be doubts'*[14] – superimposing these distinctions on the following standards: the 'reasonable apprehension' test, the 'real possibility test' and the 'real danger' test.[15]

Born interprets the standard of justifiable doubt as *'a real, serious possibility that the arbitrator lacks independence and impartiality.'*[16] (emphasis added) Born adds that *'this standard of proof should require more than a 5%, 10% or 20% chance of bias, … where there is a realistic (or "justifiable") possibility that an arbitrator genuinely lacks impartiality or independence.'*[17] (emphasis added)

He reaches this conclusion by focusing on *'the existence of risks or possibilities of partiality, rather than requiring a certainty or probability of partiality.'*[18] Born also rejects a *'more likely than not standard [which] introduces unacceptable risks in (inevitable) cases of erroneous analysis of the underlying conflict.'*[19] He explains that the relatively lower standard of 'realistic possibility' is to maintain *'the integrity of the arbitral tribunal and arbitral process, particularly given the extremely limited review available for substantive or procedural errors by the arbitrators.'*[20]

In contrast, Luttrell contends otherwise, that this lower standard has precipitated the rise of *'the Black Art of tactical challenges [–] unsuccessful, often frivolous challenges that attempt to disqualify or remove arbitrators for trivial interests, associations, and events.'*[21] Instead, Luttrell calls for a higher standard found in the 'real danger' test, rejecting the 'reasonable apprehension' and 'real possibility' tests.[22]

Finally, Moses' interpretation of the applicable standard of proof is that it *'requires more than the mere possibility that the circumstances in questions could create doubts about impartiality and independence'*.[23] Moses also cites General Standard 2(c), *'justifiable doubts are those that would persuade a reasonable third party that the arbitrator might make a decision based on factors other than the merits of the case.'*[24] (emphasis added) In this case, Moses is supportive of a threshold in between 'mere possibility' and 'likelihood'.

---

13. This formulation is from the United States of America as stated in the Federal Arbitration Act ('FAA') 9 USC §10(a)(2).
14. *Waincymer* (n. 7) 294.
15. *Ibid.*, 295.
16. Gary B. Born, *International Commercial Arbitration* (2nd edn Kluwer Law International 2014) 1779.
17. *Born* (n. 17) 1779.
18. *Ibid.*, 1778.
19. *Ibid.*, 1779.
20. *Born* (n. 17) 1779.
21. *Luttrell* (n. 1) 278.
22. *Ibid.*, 278–279.
23. Margaret L. Moses, *The Principles and Practice of International Commercial Arbitration* (2nd edn CUP, Cambridge 2012) 137.
24. *Ibid.*

[2] Arbitral Rules

Most of the arbitral institutions have adopted the standard of 'justifiable doubts' from the Model Law.[25] For one, Article 10(3) of the LCIA Rules states that an arbitrator may be challenged where *'circumstances exist that give rise to justifiable doubts as to his impartiality or independence.'* Article 14(1) of the ICDR Arbitration Rules contains the same wording, as do other arbitral rules.[26]

In contrast, Article 57 of the ICSID Convention, which only governs arbitrations between investors and states while administered by ICSID states that an arbitrator may be disqualified *'on account of any fact indicating a manifest lack of the qualities required by paragraph (1) of Article 14.'* (emphasis added) paragraph 1 go on to list some qualities including 'independent judgment'.[27]

This standard of 'manifest lack' imposes a high evidentiary threshold, where challenges can only be brought on *facts* rather than *inference*,[28] and there is *'a real risk of lack of impartiality based on those facts (and not any mere speculation or inference)'*[29] (emphasis added). However, that tribunal also opined that the threshold is whether there is *'reasonable doubt'*.[30] While the 'manifest lack' standard is comparatively higher than the 'justifiable doubts' test, which is based on inferences, rather than facts, the inclusion of 'reasonable doubt' puts into question whether this threshold is on par with White J's interpretation of 'evident partiality'.[31]

[3] National Arbitration Laws

While drafting the 2004 IBA Guidelines, the Original Working Group submitted thirteen National Reports from the following jurisdictions: Australia, Belgium, Canada, England, France, Germany, Mexico, the Netherlands, New Zealand, Singapore, Sweden, Switzerland and the United States. The jurisdictions that have not adopted the Model Law nonetheless reflect a similar standard for challenging arbitrators. The standards adopted by various national jurisdictions are set out as follows.

In England, section 24(1)(a) of the English Arbitration Act 1996 provide that an arbitrator may be removed if *'circumstances exist that give rise to justifiable doubts as to his impartiality'*. This standard has been interpreted as facts leading a 'fair-minded and reasonable observer' to conclude that there is a 'real possibility' of bias.[32]

In Sweden, section 8 of the Swedish Arbitration Act 1999 ('SAA') indicates a lower threshold than IBA Guidelines: *'an arbitrator shall be discharged if there exists*

---

25. See above, §18.01 for Art. 12(2) of the Model Law.
26. Other arbitral institutions i.e., SCC, SIAC and HKIAC also adopt a similar 'justifiable doubts' test.
27. Article 14(1) of the ICSID Convention.
28. Lucy Reed, Jan Paulsson and Nigel Blackaby, *Guide to ICSID Arbitration* (Kluwer Law International 2010) 134.
29. *Compañía de Aguas del Aconquija SA & Vivendi Universal v. Argentine Republic*, ICSID Case No ARB/97/3, Decision on the Challenge to the President of the Committee (3 Oct. 2001), 17 ICSID Review–FILJ (2002) 180 para. 25.
30. *Compañía de Aguas del Aconquija SA & Vivendi Universal* (n. 30) 181 para. 28.
31. See §18.02[A][3] for analysis of 'evident partiality' test used in the US.
32. See *A and Ors v. B and X* [2011] EWHC 2345 (Comm).

any circumstance which may diminish confidence in the arbitrator's impartiality.' (emphasis added) The SAA also provides a non-exhaustive list of such circumstances.

In Switzerland, arbitral proceedings are governed by Chapter 12 of the Federal Private International Law Act ('PILA'). Similar to the Model Law, Article 180(1)(c) PILA prescribes a 'legitimate doubts' standard of proof. Here, Liebscher has suggested that *'a bare minimum of independence'* will be sufficient.[33]

The United States has adopted the test of 'evident partiality',[34] leaving the courts to articulate the applicable standard of proof. Unfortunately, courts have experienced much difficulty in establishing a uniform standard, as illustrated in the seminal case of *Commonwealth Coatings Corp. v. Continental Casualty Co.*[35] In that case, Justice Black and Justice White adopted differing thresholds. While the former called for a lower threshold requiring *'arbitrators [to] disclose to the parties any dealings that might create an impression of possible bias'*,[36] (emphasis added) the latter articulated a much higher evidentiary threshold, where *'a reasonable person, considering all of the circumstances, would have to conclude that an arbitrator was partial to one side'*.[37] (emphasis added)

This divergence in opinion has led some courts to apply Justice Black's view,[38] with others relying on Justice White's standard.[39] In relation to the latter standard, Kantor has noted that this is higher than Article 12(2) Model Law and General Standard 2(c) 2004 IBA Guidelines.[40] Luttrell also comments that Justice White's standard comes *'very close to a requirement that actual bias be shown'*.[41] The authors believe that the jury is still out, and the applicable standard hinges on the view which the particular court decides to adopt.

France does not have a statutory duty of independence or impartiality, but such challenges can be made under the general test for partiality, where the threshold is 'reasonable doubt'.[42] This objective test has been applied with a relatively high evidentiary threshold, and will normally fail unless a 'definite risk' of partiality is

---

33. Christoph Liebscher, *The Healthy Award: Challenge in International Commercial Arbitration* (Kluwer Law International 2003) 191, cited in *Luttrell* (n. 1) 110.
34. FAA 9 USC §10(a)(2).
35. 393 U.S. 145 (1968).
36. *Commonwealth Coatings* (n. 36) 148–150.
37. See *NGC Network Asia v. PAC Pacific Group International, Inc.*, 511 F. Appx. 86, 88 (2d Cir. 2013).
38. See e.g., *New Regency Prods., Inc. v. Nippon Herald Films, Inc.*, 501 F.3d 1101 (9th Cir. 2007); *Montez v. Prudential Sec., Inc.*, 260 F.3d 980 (8th Cir. 2001); *Olson v. Merrill Lynch, Pierce, Fenner & Smith, Inc.*, 51 F.3d 157, 160 (8th Cir. 1995).
39. See e.g., *AIMCOR v. Ovalar Makine Ticaret ve Sanayi, A.S.*, 492 F.3d 132 (2d Cir. 2007); *Freeman v. Pittsburgh Glass Works, LLC*, 709 F.3d 240 (3d Cir. 2013); *Bapu Corp. v. Choice Hotels International, Inc.*, 371 F. Appx. 306 (3d Cir. 2010); *ANR Coal Co. v. Cogentrix of NC, Inc.*, 173 F.3d 493 (4th Cir. 1999); *Morelite Constr. Corp. v. N.Y.C. Dist. Council Carpenters' Benefit Funds*, 748 F.2d 79 (2d Cir. 1984).
40. Mark Kantor, 'Arbitrator Disclosure: An Active But Unsettled Year' [2008] Int ALR 11, 25, cited in *Luttrel* (n. 1) 153.
41. *Luttrell* (n. 1) 153.
42. See *Luttrell* (n. 1) 78–80; Otto LO de Witt Wijnen and others, 'Background Information on the IBA Guidelines on Conflicts of Interest in International Arbitration' (2004) 5(3) Bus. L. Int'l 433, 440–441. See e.g., Cass Civ 1, 16 Mar. 1999, *Etat du Qatar v. Société Creighton*, 96-12748, Rev Arb 1999, 308.

proven.[43] Further, Article 341 of the New Code of Civil Procedure exhaustively sets out the factual circumstances under which a challenge may be brought. That said, Article 341 is not as thorough as the general test of 'reasonable doubt'.[44]

Apart from adopting the Model Law as its *lex arbitri*, Hong Kong has kept in step with the common law rules applied in England, relying on the *Porter v. Magill*[45] standard of 'real possibility' in *Suen Wah Ling v. China Harbour Engineering Co.*[46]

In India, section 12 of the Arbitration and Conciliation Act, 1996 incorporates the Model Law test of 'justifiable doubts'. Similarly, the courts have applied an evidentiary threshold *'judged from a healthy, reasonable and average point of view and not on mere apprehension of any whimsical person.'*[47] (emphasis added).

In Singapore, developments of the test for bias have generally followed developments in English law. First, the 'reasonable suspicion' standard was laid out in *Turner (East Asia) Pte Ltd v. Builders Federal (Hong Kong) Ltd.*[48] After some doubt,[49] this was later confirmed by Judicial Commissioner Sundaresh Menon (as he then was) in *R v. Re Shankar Alan s/o Anant Kulkarni.*[50] In that case, he distinguished the 'real likelihood' standard – which requires a sufficient degree of possibility – from the 'reasonable suspicion' standard, where it is sufficient *'that a reasonable number of the public could harbour a reasonable suspicion of bias even though the court itself thought there was no real danger of this on the facts.'*[51] (emphasis added) Considering these authorities, Luttrell also comments that this standard closely resembles *'the Sussex Justices reasonable apprehension'* standard of proof.[52]

[4] Standard of Proof Spectrum

Overall, the various standards of proof, as mentioned earlier, can be illustrated on a spectrum below:

---

43. *Luttrell* (n. 1) 80.
44. *Ibid.*, 79.
45. *Porter* (n. 12).
46. [2007] BLR 435 (CA).
47. *International Airports Authority of India v. KD Bali & Anor* 1988 (2) SCC 360.
48. [1988] 1 SLR(R) 483, [1988] SLR 532 (HC).
49. A year before *Re Shanker*, in *Tang Kin Hwa v. Traditional Chinese Medicine Practitioners Board* [2005] 4 SLR(R) 604, [2005] SGHC 153 (HC), Judicial Commissioner Andrew Phang (as he then was) likened this test to the standard of 'real likelihood', commenting *obiter*, that *'there appears ... to be no difference in substance between the "reasonable suspicion of bias" and "real likelihood of bias" tests'* (at [39] of the judgment). However, Judicial Commissioner Sundaresh Menon disagreed, giving his analysis as seen above.
50. [2007] 1 SLR(R) 85 (HC).
51. *Re Shanker* (n. 51) [75] (Menon JC as he then was).
52. *Luttrell* (n. 1) 179–180.

§18.02[A]   Michael Hwang SC & Lynnette Lee

Lower threshold
may

● possible/ reasonable apprehension

● real possibility[53]/ realistic possibility (Born)/ evident partiality (Black J)/ reasonable suspicion

● real likelihood/ legitimate doubts[54]/ more likely than not/ justifiable doubts
likely

● manifest lack

● real danger/ definite risk/ reasonable doubt/ evident partiality (White J)
Higher threshold
would

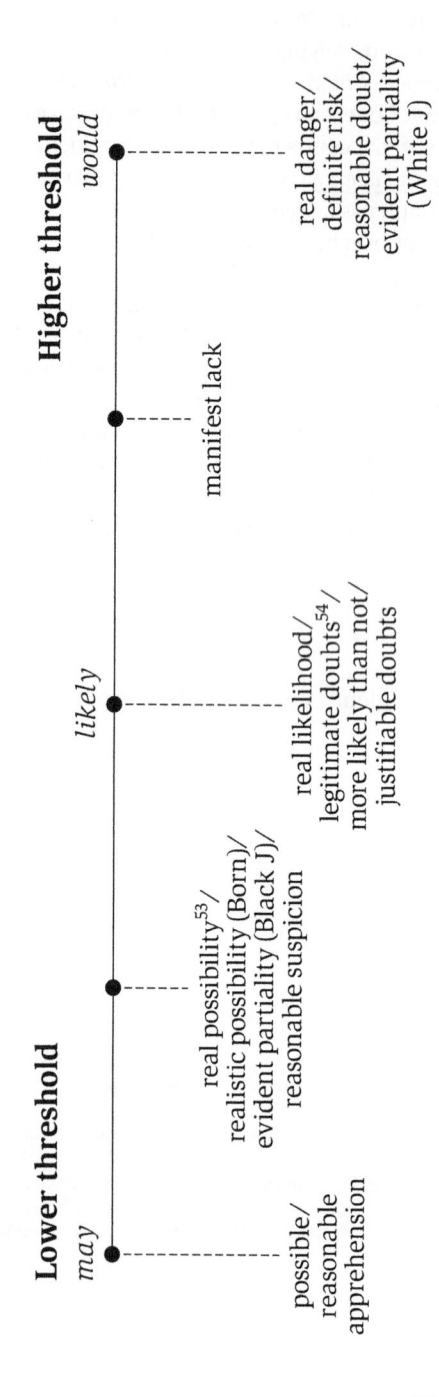

53. See *Luttrell* (n. 1) 39, where Luttrell states that 'real possibility' confers a higher standard of proof than 'reasonable apprehension' because "[w]hile a suspicion (or apprehension) may be reasonably founded insofar as it has been formed in the mind of a person as a result of his or her exercise of the faculty of reason, the facts upon which the suspicion is based may not necessarily interact to produce the result that the apprehended outcome is a real possibility."
54. Even though different terms have been used, the 'legitimate doubts' test in practice means the same thing as the 'justifiable doubts' test since the since the term 'justifiable doubts' in Art. 12(2) of the Model Law is translated into '*doutes légitimes*' ('legitimate doubts') in the official French version.

§18.03 APPLICABLE STANDARD OF PROOF FOR THE 'JUSTIFIABLE DOUBTS' TEST UNDER THE IBA GUIDELINES[55]

Using the 'justifiable doubts' test as a starting point, this raises the issue of what the term means. General Standard 2(c) of the 2014 IBA Guidelines identifies[56] and addresses this issue by defining 'justifiable doubts':

> 'Doubts are justifiable if a reasonable third person, having knowledge of the relevant facts and circumstances, would reach the conclusion that there is a *likelihood* that the arbitrator may be influenced by factors other than the merits of the case as presented by the parties in reaching his or her decision.'[57] (emphasis added)

The key question here is: What doubts would justify the removal of an arbitrator?

[A] The Intentions of the Original Working Group for the Definition of 'Justifiable Doubts'

[1] *The Interpretation of 'Likelihood'*

The standard of 'likelihood' refers to one that is 'more likely than not' i.e., 'more than 50% probability'. In my view, the words *'there is a likelihood that the arbitrator may be influenced by factors other than the merits of the case'* are simply to focus the inquiry on the litmus test of independence. The question that must be asked at the time the objection is raised is: what do we know of this arbitrator that might lead us to the conclusion that he is more likely than not to depart from the straight and narrow? Facts will be placed before the body which has to decide on the challenge, and those facts can be of any nature but, so long as that conclusion is reached, it follows that the arbitrator was *likely* to base his decision on other factors rather than the evidence and law placed before him.

[2] *Best International Practice*

This interpretation of General Standard 2(c) accurately reflects the rationale and aims of the IBA Guidelines: to explore various jurisdictions and practitioners' experiences in order to find the best international practice. In fact, this goal is achieved by balancing

---

55. This section has been solely authored by Dr Michael Hwang SC.
56. Part I: General Standards Regarding Impartiality, Independence and Disclosure, Explanation Part (c) to General Standard 2 of the 2014 IBA Guidelines, which deliberately highlights that the '[l]aws and rules that rely on the standard of justifiable doubts often do not define that standard. This General Standard is intended to provide some context for making this determination.' Note that the 2004 edition has the same explanation as well, with very similar wording.
57. The version in the 2004 IBA Guidelines is very similar, except that *'having knowledge of the relevant facts and circumstances'* is replaced with *'informed'*. That said, both wordings essentially set the same requirement.

the various interests of the parties, their counsel, arbitrators and arbitration institutions.[58]

While the Original Working Group knew that this was a noble endeavour to strive for, this often meant finding a compromise of contrasting standards in reality.[59] One example is the contrast between the vastly different approaches adopted by Born and Luttrell. On one hand, Born espouses the lower standard, a 'real, serious possibility', in order to maintain the integrity of the arbitral process and tribunal. On the other hand, Luttrell calls for a higher 'real danger' standard because of the rise of insubstantial and frivolous challenges that tribunals and courts face. Luttrell's stance is also reflected in Germany's interpretation of the 'justifiable doubts' test, where a high threshold of 'grave and obvious partiality or dependence' is required, especially when setting aside an award.[60] German courts' aversion to finding arbitrator bias is due to its policy preference in *'upholding the certainty of the arbitral bargain and process'*.[61]

With that in mind, the difference between their views depends on the values to be emphasised. While Born focuses on the integrity of the arbitral process, Luttrell stresses the importance of its efficiency. Even though both standards have individual merit, they are also mutually exclusive because they sit at diverging ends of the spectrum, prioritising one interest over another. Hence, the 'more than 50% probability' interpretation reflects a fair compromise between terminal ends of the spectrum. While it does not accommodate the interests of everyone involved, this balanced approach reflects the preferred approach to the issue of 'justifiable doubts'.

[B] General Standard 2(c): The Explanation of 'Justifiable Doubts'

Born has recently made a series of strong criticisms against the 2004 IBA Guidelines.[62] This is not the place for a full critique of Born's views. However, as I was one of the original nineteen members of the Working Group that created the 2004 IBA Guidelines, it may be useful for the international arbitration community to understand how certain key concepts in these Guidelines were conceived.

---

58. See para. 4 of the Introduction to the IBA Guidelines in either the 2004 or the 2014 version.
59. *de Witt Wijnen* (n. 43) 435 fn 5, where the Original Working Group had different perspectives on many issues but ultimately agreed that the final draft was the best practice available.
60. *See* BG decision dated 4 Mar. 1999, ZIP 859 (1999). *See also* the decision of the Hanseatic OG (Hamburg) of 3 Apr. 1975 (II YB Comm Arb. 241), where the award was set aside on public policy grounds because of the arbitrator's consideration of ex parte communications, cited in *Luttrell* (n. 1) 104.
61. *Lew* (n. 1) 314, cited in *Luttrell* (n. 1) 104.
62. *See Born* (n. 17) pp. 1841–1865, 1906–1907. It should be noted that his criticisms are against the original 2004 version, which has been modified and reissued in the current 2014 edition. However, given Born's deep-seated scepticism of the value of the IBA Guidelines, it is unlikely that he would change his opinion of the 2014 version.

[1] The 2004 and 2014 Versions of General Standard 2(c)

To put things into context, I would like to highlight the changes that have occurred between both versions of General Standard 2(c) of the IBA Guidelines. The 2004 version is as follows:

> 'Doubts are justifiable if a reasonable and *informed* third party would reach the conclusion that there was a likelihood that the arbitrator may be influenced by factors other than the merits of the case as presented by the parties in reaching his or her decision.' (emphasis added)

This has been slightly amended in the 2014 version:

> Doubts are justifiable if a reasonable [*omitted*] third person, [*having knowledge of the relevant facts and circumstances*], would reach the conclusion that there is a likelihood that the arbitrator may be influenced by factors other than the merits of the case as presented by the parties in reaching his or her decision.

There is effectively no difference between the two versions.

[2] Born's Critique

Born's complaint is as follows:

> [T]he elaboration of the 'justifiable doubts' formula contained in General Standard 2(c) appears to be unduly expansive, prescribing a materially stricter approach to the concepts of impartiality and independence than that under the UNCITRAL Model Law (and many other national arbitration statutes): the likelihood that an arbitrator '*may*' be '*influenced*' by factors other than the merits of the parties' cases would, if taken literally, disqualify most arbitrators in most cases.[63]

His contention is made on the following grounds:

> Any decision-maker, no matter how independent and impartial, not only 'may' be, but inevitably is, 'influenced' by factors other than the merits of the parties' cases – including his or her legal training, philosophical approach towards law and business, cultural and national characteristics, and countless other factors. The general formula set forth in General Standard 2(c) ignores these realities, instead prescribing a standard of independence and impartiality that, read literally, is more demanding than that under many national laws and institutional rules. In addition, General Standard 2(c) also fails to provide a means of distinguishing between those external influences on an arbitrator which are acceptable and those which are not.[64]

[3] Born's Alternative: A Higher Threshold?

Born's solution is as follows:

---

63. *Born* (n. 17) 1843–1844.
64. *Ibid.*, 1844.

The better approach would be to redraft General Standard 2(c) so as not to depart from the existing standard of impartiality and independence in the Model Law (and many other jurisdictions), and instead to focus the standard on the risk that an arbitrator will in fact base his or her conclusion on considerations other than an independent evaluation of the evidentiary record and the applicable law. This formulation would introduce a higher standard of causality (an arbitrator basing a conclusion, as compared to being influenced) and a more useful effort to define improper external factors (by recognizing that the arbitrator inevitably brings a personal background and legal training to evaluation of the record and the law).[65]

[4] Origins of General Standard 2(c)

In order to properly assess the validity of Born's criticisms, let me first explain the origin of General Standard 2(c). When the Original Working Group began to draft the Guidelines, it was quickly accepted that the benchmark for the test of conflicts of interest would be the Model Law standard of independence and impartiality. I then pointed out to my colleagues that neither the Model Law nor any of the other laws or rules which adopted the same criterion of 'justifiable doubts' as to independence and impartiality defined the test for when such doubts would arise. I therefore submitted the first draft version of General Standard 2(c), which was worked on by several other pens before emerging in its final form in the 2004 IBA Guidelines. My strong feeling was that it was essential for the 2004 IBA Guidelines (if they were to be of real assistance to the international arbitration community) to give a tangible and workable guideline which would be the litmus test in any challenge to an arbitrator.

I agree with Born that the emphasis in General Standard 2(c) should be on the duty of the arbitrator to decide the case purely on the merits of the case as presented by the parties. That is the litmus test of whether or not an arbitrator has been faithful to his duty. Born objects to the words, *'there is a likelihood that the arbitrator may be influenced by factors other than the merits of the case'*,[66] and he suggests an alternative formula which will *'focus the standard on the risk that an arbitrator will in fact base his or her conclusion on considerations other than an independent evaluation of the evidentiary record and the applicable law.'*[67] (emphasis added) I tend to agree that this might be an improvement in wording, but not necessarily for the reasons he advances.

[5] The Litmus Test of Independence

Born argues that it is wrong to bar an arbitrator on the basis that he is influenced by other factors, and I acknowledge that every arbitrator is unique, and will consequently be influenced by his or her own set of circumstances. That said, these factors on their own do not matter, so long as the arbitrator follows the narrow path of deciding the

---

65. *Born* (n. 17) 1844.
66. *Ibid.*, 1843-1844.
67. *Ibid.*, 1844.

case on the merits as presented (including an independent evaluation of the evidentiary record and the applicable law as expounded by Born).

When testing the independence of an arbitrator (impartiality only capable of being tested based on the actual conduct of the arbitrator in acting after appointment), parties do not normally question arbitrators on their education, race, religion or political views. There are of course cases where such issues might be relevant in testing independence (and/or impartiality) because the issue is whether or not a conflict of interest exists (which is typically judged in relation to the relationship between the arbitrator and one of the parties). This might lead to a predisposition in favour of that party, and not on the arbitrator's background,[68] affiliations[69] or beliefs[70] outside of the issues in the case at hand. To the extent that certain cases might raise questions concerning these factors, they tend to be questions or challenges based on *issue* conflicts rather than conflicts of *interest*.

As mentioned before, the words *'there is a likelihood that the arbitrator may be influenced by factors other than the merits of the case'* are simply to focus the inquiry on the litmus test of independence. It is uncontroversial that one arbitrator can be very different from another in terms of the factors mentioned by Born, and these factors are to be put aside for the purposes of deciding a case (unless there is evidence to suggest that these factors should not be disregarded in terms of assessing the independence and/or impartiality of the arbitrator).

[6] Application of General Standard 2(c)

The only relevant criteria when determining a case should be:

(a) What are the facts? and
(b) What is the applicable law?

Indeed, if the arbitrator follows the test according to how the parties have presented them, and not based on speculation or independent inquiry by the tribunal, the problem of *'other factors'* will disappear.

The formula under General Standard 2(c) is meant to elaborate and clarify the meaning of the critical term 'justifiable doubts' in the Model Law. If a reasonable and informed third party (or, as in the 2014 version, one *'having knowledge of the facts and circumstances'*) would reach a conclusion that it is *likely* (meaning a greater than 50% possibility) that the arbitrator is not going to decide the case solely on the merits based on proven facts and applicable law, then that would be a proper ground for challenge, regardless of the exact reason for the departure from this norm.

---

68. For example, whether the arbitrator went to the same exclusive school as one of the parties.
69. For example, whether the arbitrator and one of the parties are both members of the same exclusive society like the Freemasons.
70. For example, whether the arbitrator and one of the parties are both members of a relatively small religion like the Jehovah's Witnesses.

In short, the difference between Born and myself might be only semantic. At the same time, it must be remembered that this test is normally applied *before* an arbitrator's appointment is confirmed by an institution (or very shortly after appointment if no independent confirmation is required), and before he has commenced his duties. At that stage, it is difficult to apply Born's test that the alleged disqualifying matters should be judged on the basis of *actual causality*; instead decisions have to be made only on the basis of *forecasts* based on the objective evidence of likely bias or prejudice available at that stage (rather than on any overt acts of bias or prejudice).

Personally, at the time I drafted them, I intended the words *'influenced by factors other than the merits of the case...'*[71] to indicate where the straight and narrow path lay, and thus anything that led the arbitrator to stray from that path must be considered 'other factors'. I was not thinking of the personal makeup of the arbitrator in terms of the factors described by Born, but rather factors indicating potential bias, i.e., the examples given in the Red and Orange Lists (which are nearly all based on a prior or current relationship with one of the parties rather than issue conflict).

§18.04 DISCLOSURE REQUIREMENTS UNDER THE IBA GUIDELINES[72]

[A] General Standard 3: Disclosure Requirements

The debate over the applicable standard of proof for challenging arbitrators inexorably spills over to what arbitrators are required to disclose upon appointment. I will now address two main issues: disclosure requirements in this section and the Orange List in the following section. In particular, I will compare Born's critique of these areas with the findings of the Original Working Group.

[1] *Disclosure Requirements under General Standards 3(a) and 3(c) of the 2004 IBA Guidelines*

General Standard 3(a)[73] of the 2004 IBA Guidelines states:

> If facts or circumstances exist that may, in the eyes of the parties, give rise to doubts as to the arbitrator's impartiality or independence, the arbitrator shall disclose such facts or circumstances to the parties, the arbitration institution or other appointing authority (if any, and if so required by the applicable institutional rules) and to the co-arbitrators, if any, prior to accepting his or her appointment or, if thereafter, as soon as he or she learns about them.

---

71. General Standard 2(c), Part I: General Standards Regarding Impartiality, Independence and Disclosure, 2004 IBA Guidelines.
72. This section has also been solely authored by Dr Michael Hwang SC.
73. The 2014 version is almost identical to the 2004 version with the omission of *'to'* in *'and [to] the co-arbitrators'*.

General Standard 3(c)[74] of the 2004 IBA Guidelines provides a further obligation in case of doubt:

> Any doubt as to whether an arbitrator should disclose certain facts or circumstances should be resolved in favour of disclosure.

[2] Born's Critique: Excessive Disclosure Requirements

Born attacks General Standards 3(a) and 3(c) on the grounds that such requirements are unduly excessive and inconsistent with the generally accepted standard under the Model Law and other national jurisdictions because the 'justifiable doubts' test for bias is an objective and not subjective test.[75]

[3] Universal Acceptance of the IBA Guidelines

Again, it must be understood how these Guidelines came into being. There was a debate within the Original Working Group as to whether the test for disqualification should be objective or subjective, with the consensus being in favour of objectivity. Nevertheless, it was eventually agreed that, for purposes of disclosure, a subjective test should be adopted. This was so that the IBA Guidelines as a whole would be acceptable to the ICC, which has, since time immemorial, relied on a subjective test for disclosure for potential conflicts of interest according to the expectations of the parties, rather than those of a reasonable and informed third party.[76]

In contrast, it was agreed that the test for disqualification should be stated as objective; hence the viewpoint of a *'reasonable third person, having knowledge of the relevant facts and circumstances'*[77] being adopted as the overriding criterion. This explains the apparent contradiction between the tests for disqualification and disclosure. I should also point out that the ICC test of 'the eyes of the parties' is only applicable at the disclosure stage and is not the test for ultimate denial of confirmation or removal.[78] However, on the basis that no express standard for actual disqualification is stated in the ICC Rules, it cannot be said that there is any contradiction between the IBA Guidelines and the standards prevailing at the ICC.

---

74. The sentence in the 2004 version is identical to the one in the 2014 version, save for the fact that it was renumbered as 3(d) in the 2014 version.
75. *Born* (n. 17) 1844–1845.
76. *See* Art. 11(2) of the ICC Rules 2012: *'disclose…any facts or circumstances which might be of such a nature as to call into question the arbitrator's independence in the eyes of the parties'*.
77. General Standard 2(b), Part I: General Standards Regarding Impartiality, Independence and Disclosure, 2004 IBA Guidelines.
78. As ICC decisions on disqualification have historically been taken by the votes of the members of the ICC Court without publishing any reasons for the decision, it is difficult to generalise about the exact formula applied in ICC cases, until recently. Since 2016, the ICC has introduced a system whereby parties may apply for the grounds of a decision of a challenge.

[B] Circumstances to Disclose under the IBA Guidelines

[1] The Orange List 2004 IBA Guidelines

The purpose of the Orange List is outlined in the IBA Guidelines as follows:

> The Orange List is a non-exhaustive enumeration of specific situations which (depending on the facts of a given case) in the eyes of the parties may give rise to justifiable doubts as to the arbitrator's impartiality or independence. The Orange List thus reflects situations that would fall under General Standard 3(a), so that the arbitrator has a duty to disclose such situations.[79]

[2] Born's Critique

Born attacks the Orange List as giving rise to a presumption of disclosure,[80] and thus '*a basis of disqualification*' for any of the circumstances mentioned in that list.[81] His view is predicated on the use of language relevant to the standard of disqualification and authorities which have '*cited Orange List items in considering applications to disqualify arbitrators (or annul awards) on grounds of arbitrator independence or impartiality.*'[82]

[3] The Concept of Subjective Relevance

This was certainly not the intention of the Original Working Group. As explained in the immediately following paragraph of the 2004 IBA Guidelines:

> '[S]uch disclosure should not *automatically* result in a disqualification of the arbitrator; no presumption regarding disqualification should be arise from a disclosure. The purpose of the disclosure is to inform the parties of a *situation* that they may wish to explore further in order to determine whether objectively – ie, from a reasonable third person's point of view having knowledge of the relevant facts – there is a justifiable doubt as to the arbitrator's impartiality or independence. If the conclusion is that there is no justifiable doubt, the arbitrator can act.'[83] (emphasis added)

The 2014 version of the same provision has a slightly expanded wording, but, for the purposes of this discussion, its intent is substantially the same. It provides:

> '[d]isclosure does not imply the existence of a conflict of interest; nor should it *by itself* result either in a disqualification of the arbitrator, or in a presumption regarding disqualification. The purpose of the disclosure is to inform the parties of a *situation* that they may wish to explore further in order to determine whether objectively – that is, from the point of view of a reasonable third person having knowledge of the relevant facts and circumstances – there are justifiable doubts as

---

79. Paragraph 3, Part II: Practical Application of the General Standards, 2004 IBA Guidelines.
80. *Born* (n. 17) 1849.
81. Ibid., 1850.
82. Ibid., 1849–1850.
83. Paragraph 4, Part II: Practical Application of the General Standards, 2004 IBA Guidelines.

to the arbitrator's impartiality or independence. If the conclusion is that there are no justifiable doubts, the arbitrator can act.'[84] (emphasis added)

Evidently, the objective of the Orange List is to encourage relatively full disclosure and possible conflicts of interest beyond the call of duty because of the concept of subjective relevance. Disclosure would at least give the opposing party an opportunity to seek clarification and information about potential conflicts of interest. If the answers given by the putative arbitrator satisfy the hypothetical reasonable and informed third party that the circumstances disclosed would not jeopardise his independence, then any challenge or objection made by the opposing party should then be withdrawn or dismissed.

In practice, the system has worked relatively well. The ICC does not recognise the binding authority of the IBA Guidelines because the criteria for disqualification are governed by its own rules. Nevertheless, it does take into account arguments from either party based on the Guidelines in objections to appointment as well as in applications for removal.

[4] Comparison with ICC Guidance Note on Disclosure Requirements

In February 2016, as part of its updated practice note ('ICC Guidance Note'),[85] the ICC outlined specific circumstances which may raise the question of independence and/or impartiality. While there are many overlaps between the 2014 IBA Guidelines and the ICC Guidance Note, e.g. the requirement to state the identity of the law firm, ongoing duty to disclose, and other factors, there are also key differences between the two regimes.

It is notable that the 2014 IBA Guidelines only imposes a three-year limitation on the arbitrator's involvement with one of the parties,[86] but the ICC Guidance Note requires disclosure without any time limit.[87] On a broader view, the ICC continues to employ a wholly subjective test, without the 'traffic-light' system of the 2014 IBA Guidelines. On the one hand, the ICC imposes stricter requirements of disclosure than the 2014 IBA Guidelines because of the test's subjective nature and lack of time limits. On the other hand, the fact that there is no traffic-light system in the ICC Guidance Note makes it more liberal than the IBA Guidelines because there are no strict obligations. This is not the time or place to go into a detailed comparison of the two lists, except to say that international standards of disclosure will continue to evolve as the international arbitration community begins to use the ICC Guidance Note more frequently.

---

84. Ibid.
85. See International Chamber of Commerce, 'Note to Parties and Arbitral Tribunals on the Conduct of the Arbitration under the ICC Rules of Arbitration' http://res.cloudinary.com/lbresearch/image/upload/v1456236629/note_to_parties_and_arbitral_tribunals_on_the_conduct_of_arbitration_22_231116_1410.pdf accessed 8 Jul. 2016 ('ICC Guidance Note').
86. See Art. 3.1, Orange List, Part II: Practical Application of the General Standards, 2014 IBA Guidelines.
87. Paragraph 20, 'Section A – Statement of Acceptance, Availability, Impartiality and Independence, Part III – Arbitral Tribunal', ICC Guidance Note (n. 85).

§18.05 CONCLUSION

My conclusions can be summarised as follows.

(a) Across the various thresholds outlined by different national and academic standards, one underlying thread is the difficulty in establishing with surgical precision the applicable standard of proof. However, as mentioned earlier, much of the difficulty is attributed to the fact that we are trying to gauge the *appearance* of bias – which requires a hypothetical enquiry – rather than *actual* bias.

(b) This obfuscation provides more impetus for tribunals to apply the IBA Guidelines, which not only seek to reflect best international practice, but also focus on a centred approach i.e., the 'likelihood' standard, which lies at the heart of any analysis of conflict of interest under the Guidelines.

(c) Born's critique of the 2004 IBA Guidelines are understandably predicated on a textual analysis of the IBA Guidelines, as he would not have had access to the intentions of the Original Working Group. I therefore hope that this explanation will have given some insights as to some of the underlying premises that underpinned the 2004 IBA Guidelines (and, to a lesser extent, the 2014 IBA Guidelines), which might help the international arbitration community to understand them better. That said, the fact that such a distinguished practitioner and scholar as Born can arrive at a very different understanding of the meaning of seemingly controversial sections of the IBA Guidelines may be cause to review the wording yet again.

This article has demonstrated that, in international arbitration, challenges against arbitrators are not as straightforward as many would expect, since there is no universal consensus on the basis of 'justifiable doubts', and the applicable standard of proof.

Against this context, this is precisely what the IBA Guidelines seek to do – provide an international consensus. More fundamentally, they strike a balance between the rights of parties to participate in the appointment of the tribunal and the integrity of the tribunal. Its significance in the international arbitration community lies in preserving the reputational integrity of arbitral tribunals – the trust of the international community that decisions are made by independent tribunals. If that confidence begins to erode, then the attractiveness of arbitration as a forum for dispute resolution will diminish along with it.

CHAPTER 19
The Use of Experts in International Arbitration

Neil Kaplan CBE QC SBS

It is a great honour and a privilege to offer this modest piece on the occasion of Pierre Karrer's 75th birthday.

I first met Pierre in Japan at the ICCA Congress in 1986. We had just set up the Hong Kong International Arbitration Centre and I was keen to get his views on what we should be doing. He was of course most helpful, and he must have been one of the first virtually full time arbitrators I ever met.

Pierre has a justifiable reputation for academic excellence, but this is combined with arbitral efficiency to which I wish to add some thoughts in the context of expert witnesses.

When I started at the Bar, the use of experts was limited. Today, no case is without its experts and the whole issue has become complex and has added considerably to the cost involved and the length of hearings as well as the length of, and delay in, publication of awards.

We need a new protocol to deal with experts and I set out my proposals in this article.

§19.01 TRIBUNAL OR PARTY-APPOINTED EXPERT?

Whereas the civil law/common law has been dissipated somewhat in the practice of international arbitration, the differences can still be stark in relation to the approach to the use of experts.

In terms of procedural rules, national legislations are often silent about the use of experts in international arbitration. However, it is interesting to observe how courts use experts in different countries.

In the United Kingdom for instance, court-appointed experts are more and more common and this is seen as a way to reduce costs. However, most parties still prefer to choose and use their own experts.

The same trend can be observed in Canada. Some provinces, such as Ontario and British Colombia, have even adopted specific codifications stating that, once appointed, experts must acknowledge in writing that they are exclusively obliged to the court.[1]

Civil law countries often favour court-appointed experts rather than parties-appointed experts. However, this trend is evolving. For instance, a report on the rules and practice of experts in the European Union shows that most systems *'involve the parties in the process of appointing the expert'*.[2] Among the countries covered by the study, half of them use partyappointed experts.[3]

As for international arbitration, it is commonly accepted that both the tribunal and the parties are allowed to use the services of experts.

Article 25.3 of the ICC rules goes beyond that and provides that the parties' *and also any other person'* have the right to appoint an expert. The arbitral tribunal is obviously allowed to appoint an expert, but only after having consulted the parties (Article 25.4). However, the vast majority of cases involve party-appointed expert.

Also, most systems put a strong emphasis on preserving the equality between the parties. Both parties must have the same opportunity to submit expert evidence and to cross-examine experts from the opposing side.

The ICC rules on expertise (ICC Expert rules) also provide that the expert should sign a declaration of independence.

The IBA rules touch upon the issue of expertise and allow the Parties and the tribunal to appoint an expert.

One well appreciates the reasons why on the whole Counsel prefer to have their own experts. They are, of course, fearful of losing control of the expert process if the tribunal appoints its own expert. The SACHS protocol was an attempt to find a compromise to the two extreme views.

It arose in a construction dispute between two large construction companies resident in the same State. The final account issues had been festering for a considerable time and various attempts at expertise had not succeeded. The claimant commenced an ICC arbitration and when the tribunal met with the parties it was agreed that the tribunal would attempt to find two independent experts who, if approved by the parties, would undertake the work of preparing a detailed and substantial joint report itemizing what happened on site during the period of construction. The tribunal found two such experts who were approved by the parties. They then began the task of putting together this joint report. In the protocol it was agreed that the experts could ask the parties for documents and comments at any stage. On most occasions, the

---

1. See 'Role of expert witnesses in litigation and arbitration', a discussion between J. Reynard, D. Malcolm and C. Hine. (Tenonhttp://www.financierworldwide.com/role-of-expert-witnesses-in-litigation-and-arbitration/#.VqmjzcreMxE).
2. A. Nuée, 'Civil-Law Expert Reports in the EU: National Rules and Practices' (2015), Europa, pp. 19–20.
3. *Id.*

experts were able to deal with the parties themselves who willingly provided the material requested. On some occasions, the tribunal met with the parties and the experts to deal with more contentious issues. Eventually, the experts prepared a draft report of some substance which was submitted to the tribunal and the parties. There was then a hearing at which both sides had an opportunity to question the experts and to suggest how the report might be varied. The experts then went away with their cross-examinations in mind and prepared a final report which was submitted to the tribunal.

Finally, there was a hearing at which both parties made submissions as to the correct approach by the tribunal as to the adoption of the written report. It is fair to say that the tribunal relied heavily on the experts' report bearing in mind the way in which it had been compiled in a consensual manner, but the tribunal did not accept every recommendation and independently arrived at a final award.

This turned out to be somewhat of a slow process, which in part was caused by the seeming lack of urgency on the part of the parties. It was certainly an expensive exercise, but had the parties had their own experts, the costs may not have been materially less.

This approach deserves further consideration in appropriate cases.

§19.02 NO EXPERT TESTIMONY WITHOUT LEAVE OF THE TRIBUNAL

The first Procedural Order (PO) should state that *'no expert evidence shall be adduced without leave of the Tribunal'*.

This is an important police power that controls everything thereafter as will be seen.

The first PO should then go on to state:

If any party wishes to adduce expert testimony it shall:

(a) inform the Tribunal and the other party (s) of the name of the expert, the firm for which the expert works and the discipline of the testimony sought to be adduced.

The sooner the identity and discipline are known the better for all. I have had a case where the parties did not share this information with the result that they both engaged the same firm, one using Hong Kong office and the other the Singapore office. This would not have happened if this simple precaution had been obeyed.

It is essential for the tribunal and other party to know the disciplines involved. One party might want to call an expert to opine on a matter solely within the province of the tribunal, for example a former judge perhaps to interpret the contract, or a policeman to discuss credibility of witnesses where criminal conduct may be involved. The tribunal can stamp on this at the earliest opportunity.

Once the tribunal has granted leave to adduce expert testimony, it should arrange a meeting in person if possible – or by video if not – to establish the relationship with the tribunal. The tribunal needs to get across to the expert that they are the tribunal's expert regardless of who is paying them. Mere written acknowledgment that they understand this is not enough. A relationship has to be established. The tribunal should make clear that they have access to the tribunal at any time if problems arise. Furthermore, meetings with the experts should be built into the tribunal's schedule in order to update on progress and underscore that they are truly working for the tribunal.

In complex cases where there are several experts preparing reports, it is often helpful if the President of the Tribunal has regular telephone conference calls with the experts to ensure that their work is on track, that there will be no delays and that they all have the materials they need upon which to base their expert opinions. This relationship with the presiding arbitrator helps to cement the relationship between the Tribunal and the experts and helps to distance them slightly from the party for whom they are providing expertise.

§19.03 INSTRUCTIONS

At a very early stage in this process, the experts have to inform the tribunal precisely what questions they have been asked to advise on and whether and if so, what assumptions have they been instructed to work on. This is crucial because if the experts are asked different questions there will inevitably be different answers, which will not assist the tribunal. Similarly, if experts are asked to make different assumptions then their results will inevitably be different, as they will be shooting at different targets. Again, this is an area where the tribunal might need to step in to ensure the target is the same.

§19.04 REPORTS

The first PO should specify that the expert's reports should be kept as short as possible and should contain an executive summary. Reports of experts of like discipline should be exchanged on a without prejudice basis, and a reasonable time thereafter these experts should have a without prejudice meeting in order to attempt to reduce or clarify their differences. After this meeting, they should be required to prepare a joint report setting out the matters upon which they agree, as well as the matters upon which there is no agreement and the reasons for such disagreement.

At this stage, after making any necessary amendments to their draft reports, they can then sign and serve their final reports.

This procedure, which has been in use for some time, does have the benefit of reducing and clarifying issues. It will be even more useful when the experts are answering the same questions. There is nothing wrong in an expert being told to make an assumption, provided this is disclosed and the expert provides an alternative view lest the assumption be not accepted by the tribunal.

§19.05 EARLY OPENING AND EXPERT PRESENTATION

I believe that the move to written pleading at the expense of oral advocacy has gone too far. In the 1960s, in most common law countries the judge would not be in charge of a case since inception. Rather, he would receive the case fairly shortly before the hearing. Case management, such as it was, would be handled by Masters who specialized in procedure. The result of this was that the judge knew virtually nothing before the case started. In these circumstances, counsel's oral opening was crucial. A skilful opening was often the key to success. The end of the opening should have been the high water mark of any case. It could only get worse from thereon.

But today, both in court and especially in arbitration, we see lengthy submissions, detailed witness statements with exhibits attached, complex expert reports often running to hundreds of pages, skeleton openings, and long and detailed written closings. The documents served on the tribunal prior to the hearing are often contained in several large boxes of A4 binders.

The big fallacy in all this is that it is physically and mentally impossible for anyone to understand and digest all this material without assistance. Instead, having served all this material, the hearing starts with a brief introduction followed by the cross examination of the first witness.

I do not advocate a return to the old days of solely oral argument. However, I do believe that there is a suitable compromise. That lies in the early opening of a case.

After the first round of pleadings, witness statements and experts' reports have been served, the tribunal should convene a hearing at which counsel presenting the case should appear and be prepared to open the case orally to the tribunal. They should take the tribunal to the relevant parts of the contract or treaty and advance their case by reference to the evidence filed to date. They should introduce the tribunal to the relevant correspondence. They should also outline their legal submissions.

I have suggested that this should take place after the first round of pleadings. It may take place later if there is sufficient time before the hearing. The optimum time is about six months before the main hearing.

The advantage of this procedure is that it assists in getting the whole tribunal up to speed. It enables the tribunal to ask questions, to raise questions relating to missing witnesses, and to assist in attempting to reduce or refine the issues. In this way, questions raised by the tribunal will not take any party by surprise on the first day of the hearing and there will be plenty of time to deal with any such issues.

Further, at this early opening all experts should give a brief presentation of their report.

All of this will have the effect of informing the tribunal's final preparation for the main hearing.

To those who say that this procedure only serves to increase the cost I respond by pointing out the following:

- This procedure helps to achieve a quicker and better award.
- It helps ensuring that all three members of the tribunal are on top of the issues.
- It obviates the need for fuller openings at the hearing and may lead to avoiding skeleton openings.
- It provides an opportunity for the tribunal and counsel to meet early, and may lead to a refining of issues if not the compromising of some.

§19.06 POST-HEARING

A not infrequent scenario is the following. There are two experts on quantum. They disagree on height points. These points have a substantial bearing on quantum. No problem arises if the tribunal agrees with one expert on all height points. But what if the tribunal agrees with one expert on four points and the other on four points? Unless the tribunal are given a programme to work out the final figure, they will be lost as to the correct answer on the basis of their findings.

A sensible way to deal with this situation is to ask the parties to agree that after the written closings are submitted both these experts become the tribunal's experts, and they help the tribunal work out a figure on the basis of the tribunal's findings.

This procedure has worked well. However, it needs the agreement of the parties and the experts. Furthermore, the experts have to agree to the utmost confidentially, and must have no further contact with their former client, save of course to submit fee notes that the parties will have agreed to discharge.

In cases where this approach has been used it has proved to be most effective. Freed of instructed assumptions and acting on the tribunal's direction the experts have been quick to agree the appropriate figure and all necessary interest calculations. Unfortunately, it is difficult for the tribunal to work with the experts before the tribunal has decided certain key points. An example would be from what date damages should be calculated. Is it date of breach or date of award? Findings such as this can have enormous consequences to the bottom line. Also in looking to the future, the experts need to be guided by the tribunal as to the future factual scenario upon which they can base their calculations.

As was stated at the beginning of this article, the amount and complexity of expert evidence especially in relation to damages can impact substantially on the length and cost of a case and can thereby impact on the length of time it takes a tribunal to render its award. Accordingly, any steps that can be taken before, during and after the hearing that can reduce or control these factors is worth very careful consideration. Even if the parties will not agree to tribunal-appointed experts, it is still crucial for tribunals to exercise more control over party-appointed experts.

Hopefully, the above proposals will go some way to achieving this.

CHAPTER 20
How Far Should an Arbitrator Go to Get it Right?

Jennifer Kirby

A few years ago, I attended a meeting of international arbitration lawyers. The lawyers had gathered to hear presentations from accounting experts who regularly give opinions as to the quantum of damages in international cases. The experts, hoping to sell their services, told war stories to demonstrate their knowledge and expertise. One of these stories still sticks in my mind.

The expert described a large, complex case where an arbitral tribunal received wildly divergent quantum opinions from the parties' experts. In its award, the tribunal noted this and stated that it considered that both quantifications were wrong. Rather than attempting to arrive at an amount of damages it considered correct, however, the tribunal stated that it considered it had to choose between the two incorrect figures from the parties' experts. So it picked one. And that became its award.

Admittedly aghast, I said, 'That's absurd. The tribunal should have determined an amount of damages it considered correct. And if the arbitrators felt they didn't have enough information to do so, they should have used their broad powers under the rules to get whatever information they needed.'

Silence. Now it was the lawyers who were aghast. Finally, one of them, who appeared to voice what was in the minds of all, said that the tribunal did the right thing. To do otherwise would be to help one party at the expense of the other and that wouldn't be fair.

Gulp.

So how far should an arbitrator go to get it right?

To 'get it right' an arbitrator does not have to find The Truth. As Rusty Park has observed, 'Accuracy in arbitration means something other than absolute truth as it might exist in the eyes of an omniscient God.'[1] Some of the questions arbitrations throw up lend themselves to clear, discrete answers – *Did the agent receive his commission?* – while others do not – *What is the appropriate discount rate?* At their worst, arbitrations can present intractable questions of perception like W.E. Hill's famous drawing of 'My Wife and My Mother-in-Law'[2] (see Figure 20.01) and require the arbitrator to decide whether it is one or the other.

Figure 20.01   My Wife and My Mother-in-Law

Still, in most cases, certain answers are better than others, even if *the* answer proves illusive. Being human, the arbitrator necessarily operates within these limits. To get it right, an arbitrator has to render an award that 'rests on a reasonable view of what happened and what the law says'.[3] And he has an obligation to do so. It's part of the job.

Parties do not submit disputes to international arbitration to get them resolved any old which way. If that's what they wanted, they could flip a coin.[4] Instead, in choosing international arbitration, parties usually choose to (1) spend significant time and money[5] (2) to tell their stories in detail[6] to (3) three independent and impartial

---

1. William W. Park, *Arbitrators and Accuracy*, 1(1) J. Int'l Dis. Settlement 25, 26 (2010) (explaining that, in 'examining the competing views of reality proposed by each side, arbitrators aim to get as near as reasonably possible to a correct picture of those disputed events, words, and legal norms that bear consequences for the litigants' claims and defenses').
2. Hill's drawing first appeared in *Puck* magazine on 6 Nov. 1915.
3. Park, *supra* n. 1, at 27.
4. *Ibid.* at 33.
5. *See* Robert B. Kovacs, *Efficiency in International Arbitration: An Economic Approach*, 23(1) Am. Rev. Int'l Arb. 155, n. 3 (2012) (cataloguing the 'growing chorus of discontent from the users or "consumers" of international arbitration regarding the time (and associated cost) it takes to conduct international arbitrations').
6. It is common for parties to submit comprehensive written statements of claim, defence, reply and sur-reply. Along with these, parties also typically submit several witness statements apiece, as well as scores of exhibits. And the hearing itself can often last several days, with the parties filing further written submissions thereafter.

Chapter 20: How Far Should an Arbitrator Go to Get it Right?

people[7] who are (4) required to decide the dispute pursuant to applicable rules of law[8] in (5) a reasoned award that explains how they arrived at their decision.[9] Parties choose all this because they want an award that is not only final and binding but right, and that is what arbitrators should deliver. That their award cannot usually be challenged for getting it wrong only heightens their obligation to get it right.[10]

To that end, all modern international arbitration rules give arbitrators broad powers to get the factual and legal information they need to take correct decisions. Arbitrators can generally order the parties to produce documents, question witnesses, conduct site visits, inspect property, engage factual and legal experts to assist them and otherwise establish procedural rules that allow them to get material information.[11] That arbitrators *can* use these powers to reach the right result cannot be gainsaid. The question is whether they *should*.[12]

The lawyers at the meeting thought not. This may be because all of them were American and the adversarial system is deeply engrained in American legal culture. In its raw form, the adversarial system leaves it to the parties to investigate and present evidence and argument before a passive decision-maker, who merely listens to both sides and renders a decision based on what he has heard.[13] If the parties have failed to

---

7. School of International Arbitration, Queen Mary, University of London & White & Case, *2010 International Arbitration Survey: Choices in International Arbitration* 25 (2010) (finding that '73% of respondents [had] a general preference as to the number of arbitrators, of which 87% [preferred] three arbitrators'); *see also 2014 ICC Statistical Report*, 1 ICC Dispute Resolution Bull. 7, 12 (2015) (indicating that over 60% of cases are heard by three-member arbitral tribunals). Whether having three arbitrators instead of one actually leads to more accurate decisions is an open question. Jennifer Kirby, *With Arbitrators, Less Can Be More: Why the Conventional Wisdom on the Benefits of Having Three Arbitrators May Be Overrated*, 26(3) J. Int'l Arb. 337 (2009).
8. *See*, e.g., ICC Arbitration Rules (as of 1 Jan. 2012) ('ICC Rules'), Art. 21(1); International Centre for Dispute Resolution (ICDR) International Arbitration Rules (as of 1 Jun. 2014) ('ICDR Rules'), Art. 31(1); LCIA Arbitration Rules (as of 1 Oct. 2014) ('LCIA Rules'), Art. 22.3; Arbitration Institute of the Stockholm Chamber of Commerce Arbitration Rules (2010) ('SCC Rules'), Art. 22(1); Arbitration Rules of the Singapore International Arbitration Centre (as of 1 Apr. 2013) ('SIAC Rules'), Art. 27.1; UNCITRAL Arbitration Rules (as revised in 2010) ('UNCITRAL Rules'), Art. 35(1). If parties were not concerned about having their disputes correctly decided at law, they could 'give someone a blank check to decide "in equity" without reference to law' (Park, *supra* n. 1, at 33), but parties rarely do this.
9. ICC Rules, Art. 31(2); ICDR Rules, Art. 30(1); LCIA Rules, Art. 26.2; SCC Rules, Art. 36(1); UNCITRAL Rules, Art. 34(3). And parties who elect ICC arbitration further choose to have the ICC Court scrutinize both the form and substance of the award before it is notified to the parties. ICC Rules, Art. 33. The value of the scrutiny process cannot be overstated. *See* Gustav Flecke-Giammarco, *The ICC Scrutiny Process and Enhanced Enforceability of Arbitral Awards*, 24(3) J. Arb. Stud. 47, 56–69 (2014).
10. Jennifer Kirby, *What Is an Award, Anyway?*, 31(4) J. Int'l Arb. 475, 478–480 (2014).
11. *See*, e.g., ICC Rules, Arts 19, 22, 25; ICDR Rules, Arts 20, 21, 25; LCIA Rules, Arts 14, 21–22; SCC Rules, Arts 19, 29; SIAC Rules, Arts 16, 23–24; UNCITRAL Rules, Arts 17, 27, 29.
12. Phillip Landolt, *Arbitrators' Initiatives to Obtain Factual and Legal Evidence*, 28(2) Arb. Int'l 173, 175 (2012) (doubting that 'in most cases the parties seek an award corresponding to any objective standard of correctness of fact and law beyond what the parties themselves submit').
13. Ellen E. Sward, *Values, Ideology, and the Evolution of the Adversary System*, 64(2) Ind. L.J. 301, 302 (1989).

give the decision-maker the information he needs to render a correct decision, it is right and proper for him to render an incorrect one.[14]

American 'baseball arbitration' – so called because it is used to resolve disputes over the salaries of professional baseball players – embraces this approach to dispute resolution whole hog. In baseball arbitration, each side submits a proposed monetary award to the tribunal. After hearing the parties, the tribunal must choose one of the proposed awards without modification. Structured this way, each party has an incentive to submit a reasonable proposed award in the hope that the tribunal will select it. But it also leaves the parties room to be as wrong as they want to be. If no party submits a reasonable proposed award, the tribunal still has to choose one and issue an award that is unreasonable on its face.[15] While this may suit enthusiasts of the adversarial system, it has yet to catch on as a method for resolving international commercial disputes.[16]

As its name suggests the adversarial system is not an end in itself. It is rather a system that is designed to get at the truth and produce fair outcomes. The extent to which it actually does this – and does it with reasonable efficiency – is debatable.[17] Whatever its merits, however, the adversarial system is not the system parties sign up for when they agree to resolve disputes through international arbitration. What parties sign up for is a system that gives arbitrators broad powers to get the information they consider they need to take their decisions. That an arbitrator's exercise of those powers may run counter to the adversarial system is accordingly neither here nor there.

This is not to say that an arbitral tribunal would be right to use its powers to run the proceedings in an inquisitorial fashion. Parties generally want and expect to investigate the facts, research the law, select and develop the arguments they wish to make and present their cases to the tribunal as they see fit.[18] As a consequence, in

---

14. For avoidance of doubt, to the extent the tribunal in the opening anecdote thought that it would act outside the scope of its mission (*ultra petita*) if it awarded damages in an amount that neither party had advocated, it was mistaken. An arbitrator may award damages in an amount that neither party advocated, provided the amount awarded is not more than the amount sought.
15. Jeff Monhait, *Baseball Arbitration: An ADR Success*, 4 Harv. J. Sports & Entm't L. 105, 119–120, 132–133, 140 (2013).
16. This could be changing, however. See ICDR Final Offer Arbitration Supplementary Rules (Also referred to as Baseball or Last Best Offer Arbitration Supplementary Rules) (effective 1 Jan. 2015). For now, though, in an effort to avoid the sorts of unreasonable decisions baseball arbitration permits, many arbitral rules provide that awards are to be made by majority or, where there is no majority, by the chairman alone. ICC Rules, Art. 31(1); LCIA Rules, Art. 26.5; SCC Rules, Art. 35(1); SIAC Rules, Art. 28.5. Absent such a provision, co-arbitrators can stake out extreme positions (e.g., on the quantum of damages) and force the chairman to choose between them to make a majority and issue an award. With the power to decide alone, the chairman remains at liberty to decide the case correctly. And, knowing this, the co-arbitrators are less likely to engage in partisan conduct. Yves Derains & Eric A. Schwartz, *A Guide to the ICC Rules of Arbitration* 306–307 (2d ed. 2005). But cf. ICDR Rules, Art. 29(2) (requiring that awards be by majority); UNCITRAL Rules, Art. 33(1) (same).
17. Sward, *supra* n. 13, at 355 (finding that, even in the United States, '[a]dversarial ideology has failed' and the judicial system 'is transforming itself into a more inquisitorial, less individualistic methodology').
18. Landolt, *supra* n. 12, at 211 (noting that if 'parties are not submitting certain factual evidence, not making certain legal arguments, or not relying on certain legal authorities, they may have a legitimate reason not to do so').

Chapter 20: How Far Should an Arbitrator Go to Get it Right?

practice, a tribunal should usually exercise its powers to seek further information at the margins – to clarify factual and legal issues the parties have raised and fill gaps in the record the parties have already fleshed out. And it should usually only do so when it considers it necessary to correctly resolve the dispute the parties have submitted.[19] An international arbitration is generally not an occasion for arbitrators to indulge idle curiosity or investigate novel theories of recovery or defence that no party has raised.[20] Their aim should be to narrow the scope of the parties' problems, not broaden it.

Even this restrained approach can draw objections, however. In one of my cases as sole arbitrator, the parties' submissions failed to provide me all of the material provisions of the applicable law. The claimant, who was not represented by counsel, had provided me none. The respondent had provided me an obviously curated set of provisions that, taken out of all context, appeared to go in its favour. When I asked the parties to submit the missing provisions, the respondent objected that I had to make due with the provisions it had already provided. To request anything further, it contended, would help the claimant and therefore violate due process.

Arbitrators should generally not seek to help one party over another, even to 'level the playing field'.[21] Seeking to help one party over another is arguably inconsistent with an arbitrator's due process obligation to treat the parties equally and may well invite accusations of bias. But an arbitrator should not be deterred from seeking the information he needs to correctly resolve a case just because that information may weigh in favour of one of the parties' positions. In requesting such information, the arbitrator is not seeking to help one party over another. He's trying to reach the right result. The right result will necessarily go in favour of one party and against the other, but that fact alone does not convert an arbitrator's request for further information into a due process violation.[22]

Still, the line an arbitrator has to walk can sometimes be fine. The claimant bears the burden of proving its claims. If it fails to produce sufficient evidence to do so, it will often be most appropriate for the arbitrator to simply dismiss the claims. But the burden of proof is a blunt instrument, and it is not always entirely clear how it should

---

19. *Ibid.* at 199–214 (advocating that arbitrators exercise restraint where their powers to seek further information are concerned).
20. One potential exception concerns issues of international public policy. An arbitrator should be alert to such issues and raise them with the parties if necessary to ensure that his award is not set aside on public policy grounds. International Law Association (ILA), *Report on Ascertaining the Contents of the Applicable Law in International Commercial Arbitration* ('ILA Report') 21 (2008) (considering that, when a dispute may implicate mandatory public policy norms, an arbitrator has 'more freedom to probe, to set the agenda, and to drive the development of the legal analysis'); ILA Resolution No. 6/2008 ('ILA Resolution'), Recommendation 13. But it is important not to get carried away. Awards that implicate international public policy are rare, and court decisions setting awards aside on public policy grounds are even rarer. As a consequence, it is seldom helpful for an arbitrator to go running after public policy issues the parties have not raised.
21. *But see* Landolt, *supra* n. 12, at 217–218 (considering that it may be appropriate for an arbitrator to take a more proactive role in seeking information where a party is financially unable to put on its case or does not appear at all).
22. *Ibid.* at 191–192 (noting than an arbitrator does not fail to treat the parties equally in requesting further information – even information that affects the outcome – provided he would have requested the information no matter which party benefitted).

cut. While the claimant bears the burden of proving its claims, each party generally bears the burden of proving the facts it relies upon to support its claim or defence.[23] This can lead to finger pointing as to where the relevant burden lies. And it usually lies nowhere where questions of law are concerned.[24]

This is because the content of the law applicable to the merits of the dispute is not normally considered a fact that a party must prove.[25] But neither is it something the arbitrator necessarily knows. Indeed, he frequently does not know it.[26] He must apply it, however.[27] And that implies that he has an obligation to learn it.[28] In most cases, he can satisfy that obligation by reading the parties' submissions. But where this is not the

---

23. See, e.g., UNCITRAL Rules, Art. 27(1) (providing that '[e]ach party shall have the burden of proving the facts relied on to support its claim or defence').
24. Landolt, supra n. 12, at 221 (noting that '[i]n arbitration there is no rational basis for placing a burden of proof on any party as to the ascertainment of the law').
25. International arbitration avoids debates about whether the content of the applicable law should be treated as a question of fact or law and adopts a pragmatic approach. In this regard, it is for the parties to establish the content of the law applicable to the merits. But the arbitrator has the power, though not the obligation, to conduct his own research. If he does so, he should give the parties an opportunity to comment on the results. And if the content of the applicable law is not established with respect to a specific issue, the arbitrator may apply to such issue any rule of law he deems appropriate. Gabrielle Kaufmann-Kohler, *The Governing Law: Fact or Law? – A Transnational Rule on Establishing Its Content, Best Practices in International Arbitration*, ASA Special Series No. 26 79, 84 (2006); ILA Report, supra n. 20, at 22 (considering that arbitrators 'should inquire about the applicable law within the general parameters of the arbitration defined by the parties and, considering costs, time and relevance of issues, may conduct their own research, provided the parties are given an opportunity to be heard on material that goes meaningfully beyond the parties' submissions'); ILA Resolution, supra n. 20, Recommendations 5–8, 11, 15. It bears emphasizing that, where an arbitrator does his own research, it is mission critical that he give the parties an opportunity to comment on the results. Failing to do so may well leave the award open to set aside on due process grounds. See, e.g., *Engel Austria GmbH v. Don Trade*, Cour d'appel [CA] [regional Court of Appeal], Paris, pôle 1, ch. 1, 3 Dec. 2009, case no. 08/13618 (setting aside an award that turned on an issue of Austrian law, where the award stated that the parties had not had an opportunity to address the issue).
26. While it may be appropriate under the principle *jura novit curia* to presume that national judges know the law of their respective jurisdictions, there is no reason to presume that an arbitrator knows the law applicable to the merits of the parties' dispute. See Gabrielle Kaufmann-Kohler, *The Arbitrator and the Law: Does He/She Know It? Apply It? How? And a Few More Questions*, 21(4) Arb. Int'l 631 (2005) (noting that she has resolved disputes under Argentinean, Colombian, English, Egyptian, French, German, Greek, Hungarian, Korean, Lebanese, Liberian, Moroccan, Polish, Portuguese, Sudanese, Thai, Tunisian, Turkish and Venezuelan law – none of which she knows). *But see* Bernhard Berger & Franz Kellerhals, *International and Domestic Arbitration in Switzerland* 373–375 (2d ed. 2006) (explaining that the *jura novit curia* principle applies to arbitrations seated in Switzerland).
27. See supra n. 8.
28. ILA Report, supra n. 20, at 6 (noting that, in cases to be decided at law, 'arbitrators are duty bound to apply the relevant law' and therefore often 'must become educated in a law that they may not be expert in and may never before have even considered'). Despite this, most arbitral rules do not expressly empower arbitrators to seek information about the content of the applicable law. The LCIA Rules are a notable exception. LCIA Rules, Art. 22.1(iii) (empowering the arbitral tribunal to 'conduct such enquiries as may appear ... necessary or expedient, including whether and to what extent the Arbitral Tribunal should itself take the initiative in identifying relevant issues and ascertaining relevant facts and the law(s) or rules of law applicable to the Arbitration Agreement, the arbitration and the merits of the parties' dispute'). That this power falls within the broad powers arbitral rules generally grant arbitrators (*see supra*

case, he should not throw up his hands and render an award he considers wrong, but rather seek the information he needs to decide the case correctly.

Doing this often requires tact, skill and some modicum of courage. A tribunal that decides a case based wholly on the parties' submissions – no matter how misguided or incomplete – usually runs little to no risk that its award will be set aside. The arbitrator's duty to get it right is not an enforceable one. Some arbitrators doubtless take comfort in this. Here's to one who doesn't.

---

n. 11), however, cannot be gainsaid. ILA Report, *supra* n. 20, at 16 (noting that the determination of the contents of the applicable law is 'by and large procedural and thus governed by [the] broad discretionary powers of arbitral tribunals' that give them freedom that is 'largely unfettered').

CHAPTER 21
Sanctioning of Party Conduct Through Costs: A Reconsideration of Scope, Timing and Content of Costs Awards

Richard Kreindler & Mariel Dimsey

It is within the discretion of the arbitral tribunal, subject to agreement by the parties, to fix the costs of the arbitration between the parties as the tribunal considers appropriate. While it is often not consciously reflected upon or expressly addressed, including in the formulation of awards, an arbitral tribunal may base its decision as to allocation of costs in whole or in part on the conduct of the parties in the underlying arbitration.

In this regard, a tribunal may consider "sanctioning" a party for conduct considered unbecoming, dilatory, disruptive or otherwise worthy of rebuke in the arbitration. What is the scope of the relevant conduct, the timing of costs sanctions, and the form and content of a costs award for sanctions?

§21.01 SCOPE OF COST-RELEVANT CONDUCT

A starting point for analysis of cost-relevant conduct is the principle that the parties to an arbitration are to conduct themselves in good faith.[1] This extends not only to raising of a claim, but also to conduct during the proceedings. Even considering the standard

---

1. *See* Preamble No. 3 to the IBA Rules on the Taking of Evidence in International Arbitration ("The taking of evidence shall be conducted on the principles that each Party shall act in good faith ..."); *see also* e.g., Bernardo Cremades, "Good Faith in International Arbitration" (2012) 27(4) *American University International Law Review* 761 et seqq.; Colin Y.C. Ong & Michael Patrick O'Reilly, *Costs in International Arbitration* (Singapore/Malaysia/Hong Kong: LexisNexis, 2013), pp. 76–77; Art. 15(7) Swiss International Arbitration Rules (2012); Art. 1464 French Arbitration Law, Decree of Jan. 13, 2011.

of good faith, conduct for which an arbitral tribunal can impose sanctions is not limited to clear examples of bad faith or misconduct.

There are other reasons for which arbitral tribunals may choose to allocate costs so as to constitute a "sanction" based on conduct. The 2012 ICC Commission Report on Controlling Time and Costs in Arbitration provides useful examples of behavior – assessed against a standard of reasonableness rather than good faith – which could result in costs sanctions: "Unreasonable conduct could include: excessive document requests, excessive legal argument, excessive cross-examination, dilatory tactics, exaggerated claims, failure to comply with procedural orders, unjustified applications for interim relief, and unjustified failure to comply with the procedural timetable."[2]

Intentional misconduct, fraud or bad faith may serve as a basis, even the "sole" basis,[3] to sanction a party in costs.[4] Blatant refusal to comply with an order of the tribunal, willfully misstating the facts, withholding evidence, and similar activity are examples of possible bad faith or misconduct which could be taken into consideration when awarding costs.[5] In investment treaty-based arbitration, the practice of allocating costs for bad conduct is well documented[6] and reflected in recent case law. In the case of *Europe Cement Investment & Trade S.A. v. Republic of Turkey*, decided under the ICSID Additional Facility Rules,[7] the tribunal awarded the (victorious) respondent all of its costs for the following reasons: "… where the Tribunal has reached the conclusion that the claim to jurisdiction is based on an assertion of ownership which the evidence suggests was fraudulent, an award to the Respondent of full costs will go some way towards compensating the Respondent for having to defend a claim that had no jurisdictional basis and discourage others from pursuing such unmeritorious claims."[8] The effect of the costs award was then not to "sanction" the claimant, but to "compensate" the respondent and, potentially, to deter future unmeritorious claims.

Contrasted with this reasoning is *Plama v. Bulgaria*,[9] in which the respondent prevailed on the merits. The tribunal awarded the respondent its full costs, and evidently took into account the additional costs incurred by the respondent due to the claimant's failure to disclose certain matters in the jurisdictional phase. The driving factor behind its award of costs against the claimant was stated to be to penalize it for

---

2. ICC Commission Report on Controlling Time and Costs in Arbitration (2012), para. 82. *See also* Art. 37(5) ICC Arbitration Rules, which authorizes the tribunal, when making decisions on costs, to take into account "the extent to which each party has conducted the arbitration in an expeditious and cost-effective manner."
3. ICC Commission Report on Decisions on Costs in International Arbitration (2015), para. 78.
4. *See* e.g., ICC Final Award No. 4629 (1989) in Albert Jan van den Berg (ed.), (1993) XVIII *Yearbook of Commercial Arbitration* 11.
5. *See* generally ICC Commission Report on Decisions on Costs in International Arbitration (2015), paras. 78–85, Appendix A, I No. 5.
6. *See* e.g., Stephan Schill, "Cost-Shifting, Arbitration Risk and Effective Compliance" (2006) 7 *Journal of World Investment and Trade* 653, for an extensive discussion of cases concerning this issue.
7. *Europe Cement Investment & Trade S.A. v. Republic of Turkey*, ICSID Case No. ARB(AF)/07/2, Award dated Aug. 13, 2009.
8. *Europe Cement Investment & Trade S.A. v. Republic of Turkey*, ICSID Case No. ARB(AF)/07/2, Award dated Aug. 13, 2009, para. 185.
9. *Plama Consortium Limited v. Republic of Bulgaria*, ICSID Case No. ARB/03/24, Award dated Aug. 27, 2008.

fraudulent misrepresentation in obtaining the investment in Bulgaria.[10] Thus the tribunal took into account not only the conduct during the arbitral proceedings, but also conduct leading to the dispute. Similarly, in *World Duty Free Co. Ltd. v. Republic of Kenya*, rather than awarding costs based on "success" the tribunal apportioned costs equally to penalize the respondent host state for what was held to be corrupt behavior in the underlying relationship.[11]

In terms of *other cost-relevant conduct*, it is also conceivable that conduct that does not amount to bad faith may serve as a basis for exercise of discretion to allocate costs. Distinguishing between bad faith conduct and "other" conduct can be justified: in cases of bad faith, allocation of costs may reflect elements of "penalty" and "compensation," while the allocation of costs in the situations below suggests a predominance of compensatory elements. The conduct outlined below, while not *mala fides*, generally serves to increase the legal fees and overall costs of arbitration for both parties[12] and provides further examples of improper behavior justifying an award of costs.

General dilatory conduct has been found to warrant an award of costs. Such conduct could include failure to comply with deadlines, failure to produce documents when required, failure to sign terms of reference and revisiting matters already decided by the tribunal.

Moreover, an award of costs may result from *overzealousness* in the presentation of a party's case, including presenting the case in excessive length.[13] Other cases of an excess of "zeal" may include the incurring of unnecessary costs in the evidentiary process, failing to observe page limits, and generally generating a greater volume of pleadings or evidence than might reasonably be regarded as necessary. Overzealousness could also consist of putting the other party to proof due to a refusal to admit certain facts or issues which were manifest. The rationale behind a costs award here is thus more compensatory than penal, as the "needless" defense of issues which could easily have been proved lead to negative cost implications. Conversely, withholding evidence that could conclusively destroy the basis for a claim until the oral hearing can also flow into allocation of the costs of arbitration.[14]

Furthermore, a *deliberate inflation of claims* may be taken account of in a costs award. In such cases, the award may similarly have more of a "compensatory"

---

10. *Plama Consortium Limited v. Republic of Bulgaria*, ICSID Case No. ARB/03/24, Award dated Aug. 27, 2008, para. 322.
11. *See World Duty Free Co. Ltd. v. Republic of Kenya*, ICSID Case No. ARB/00/7, Award dated Oct. 4, 2006; *see also* ICC Final Award No. 6248 (1990) in Albert Jan van den Berg (ed.) (1994) XIX *Yearbook of Commercial Arbitration* 124.
12. *See also* in this respect Noah Rubins, "The Allocation of Costs and Attorney's Fees in Investor-State Arbitration" (2003) *ICSID Review* 109 at 127.
13. *See* Michael W. Bühler & Thomas H. Webster, *Handbook of ICC Arbitration: Commentary, Precedents, Materials* (U.K.: Thomson/Sweet & Maxwell, 2008), paras. 37–106.
14. *See* ICC Final Award No. 14108 (year unknown) in Albert Jan van den Berg (ed.) (2011) XXXVI *Yearbook of Commercial Arbitration* 135 at para. 264.

element, since in institutional arbitration an inflated claim may lead to an unnecessarily high advance on costs.[15] Certain ICC tribunals have held that while the claimant prevailed on the merits, it had inflated its claim and should not recover the full amount of the advance on costs.[16] The inflated complexity or quantum of a claim may also prompt a respondent to spend more on its defense. If the claim is inflated in this sense, the unnecessary inflation may have caused the respondent's legal costs, at least in part. Even if the claimant prevails, the tribunal could award that portion of the legal costs caused by the excessiveness of the claim.[17] Deciding what that "portion" is will frequently be a challenge for the tribunal.

In addition, an interesting aspect of party conduct that may have relevance for a costs award is the *failure to accept a settlement offer*. It is open to debate whether a settlement offer exchanged between the parties in confidence may be brought to the tribunal's attention to demonstrate that the tribunal did not award more than the settlement offered.[18] The tribunal then has the discretion to decide whether pursuit of the case after the settlement offer was, in effect, wasted. As a preliminary point, there must be a legal basis for waiving the confidentiality of the settlement offer, and this basis can be found in certain common law jurisdictions.[19] Absent such basis, evidence of the settlement offer will generally not be admissible. At the same time, the shortcomings of considering settlement offers are evident. The tribunal may be called upon to assess when particular findings were made. The tribunal may have made findings affecting the outcome of the case *after* a settlement offer was made which it would have been unable to make earlier. Thus the settlement offer may have been premature in terms of the reasoning required to reach the amount, but nevertheless correct in light of the amount ultimately awarded. Also, provided the party has rejected a settlement offer and proceeded in good faith on the strength of its case, it may be unfair to "punish" such good faith efforts by an award on costs.

Related to but distinguishable from the topic of settlement is the *abandonment of claims* in an arbitration. Claimant is entitled to make out its case as comprehensively and as early as appropriate. Indeed certain legal cultures encourage and expect a "front-loading" of a party's presentation of facts, evidence and law which contrasts with the bare-bones "notice pleading" approach prevalent among certain U.S. practitioners. Yet that front-loading may carry with it the risk that claims are later abandoned as the evidence becomes clearer and the legal arguments more developed. It generally

---

15. Although in ICC arbitration this would usually be accounted for in the total costs of the arbitration.
16. *See* ICC Final Award No. 5726 (1992), (1993) 4 *ICC Court of International Arbitration Bulletin* 35.
17. *See* the general discussion on this point in Jeffrey Waincymer, *Procedure and Evidence in International Arbitration* (Alphen aan den Rijn: Kluwer Law International, 2012), p. 1224.
18. *See* generally ICC Commission Report on Decisions on Costs in International Arbitration (2015), paras. 94–100, specifically para. 97 concerning ways in which a confidential settlement offer can be used without prejudicing the arbitral tribunal's decision on the merits of the case.
19. *See* the discussion in Jeffrey Waincymer, *Procedure and Evidence in International Arbitration* (Alphen aan den Rijn: Kluwer Law International, 2012), pp. 1225 et seqq., which refers to the New Zealand Arbitration Act (1996) as an example.

cannot be expected that a respondent bear the costs of claims unnecessarily defended.[20] Thus in the investment case of *Piero Foresti et al. v. Republic of South Africa*,[21] the claimants abandoned certain claims before unilaterally applying for discontinuance. The tribunal considered these factors relevant in making its order that the claimants pay a portion of the respondent's costs on the basis that the claimants were in a position to "avert the need for some part of the Parties' expenditure."[22]

Finally, there is acknowledgement that it is not only the conduct of a party, but also *conduct of counsel* or legal representatives that may have relevance to allocation of costs.[23] The 2013 IBA Guidelines on Party Representation in International Arbitration authorize the tribunal to have regard to a party *representative's* misconduct in awarding costs: "… the Arbitral Tribunal, as appropriate, may … (c) consider the Party Representative's Misconduct in apportioning the costs of the arbitration, indicating, if appropriate, how and in what amount the Party Representative's Misconduct leads the Tribunal to a different apportionment of costs."[24] It is important to distinguish awarding costs against a party expressly based on its representative's conduct from sanctions directed at the representative personally.[25] The "personal" sanctioning of party representatives warrants a cautious approach. Several factors are to be taken into account in assessing the consequences of a party representative's conduct, including whether an arbitral tribunal has authority over a party's representative.[26] For example, at least some U.S. case law, while acknowledging the prerogative of arbitral tribunals to sanction parties, has been less willing to uphold awards in which counsel of record were sanctioned.[27]

---

20. *See* e.g., Colin Y.C. Ong & Michael Patrick O'Reilly, *Costs in International Arbitration* (Singapore/Malaysia/Hong Kong: LexisNexis, 2013), p. 64.
21. *Piero Foresti et al. v. The Republic of South Africa*, ICSID Case No. ARB(AF)/07/1, Award dated Aug. 4, 2010.
22. *Piero Foresti et al. v. The Republic of South Africa*, ICSID Case No. ARB(AF)/07/1, Award dated Aug. 4, 2010, para. 132.
23. *See* e.g., Charles N. Brower & Stephan W. Schill, "Regulating Counsel Conduct before International Arbitral Tribunals" in Pieter H. F. Bekker, Rudolf Dolzer and Michael Waibel (eds), *Making Transnational Law Work in the Global Economy* (2010), pp. 501 et seqq.; Günther J. Horvath, Stephan Wilske & Niamh Leinwather, "Countering Guerrilla Tactics at the Outset, Throughout and at the Conclusion of the Arbitral Proceedings" in Günther J. Horvath & Stephan Wilske (eds), *Guerrilla Tactics in International Arbitration* (Alphen aan den Rijn: Kluwer Law International, 2013), pp. 48–50.
24. Similarly, Art. 18.6 LCIA Arbitration Rules (2014) allows a party's legal representative to be sanctioned for its conduct, although the authority to impose a costs sanction is not specifically referred to.
25. *See* Lucy Reed, "Sanctions Available for Arbitrators to Curtail Guerrilla Tactics" in Günther J. Horvath & Stephan Wilske (eds), *Guerrilla Tactics in International Arbitration* (Alphen aan den Rijn: Kluwer Law International, 2013), p. 101.
26. *See also* Günther J. Horvath, Stephan Wilske & Niamh Leinwather, "Countering Guerrilla Tactics at the Outset, Throughout and at the Conclusion of the Arbitral Proceedings" in Günther J. Horvath & Stephan Wilske (eds), *Guerrilla Tactics in International Arbitration* (Alphen aan den Rijn: Kluwer Law International, 2013), pp. 48–50.
27. *See* e.g., *Interchem Asia 2000 v. Oceana Petrochemicals*, 373 F.Supp.2d 340 (2006), 352 et seqq., making a clear distinction between sanctions on a party and sanctions on that party's representative.

§21.02 TIMING OF COSTS SANCTIONS

It is apparent that the prevailing approach, also in the context of awards sanctioning parties in costs, is to await the end of the case to make an award of costs, which is usually embedded in the final award overall. Criticism has been voiced of this approach of deciding on allocation of financial burden at a time when, for many arbitrators, an appreciation of the work and time involved in particular phases of the proceedings may have been dulled by the passage of time.[28] Dilatory or unnecessary applications of a party may have been "forgotten" by the time the arbitral tribunal addresses the issue of costs, or their evaluation may have submerged in the overall evaluation of the case.

Perhaps in part as a result of this phenomenon, parties are often confronted with costs awards which are sparely, broadly and generally worded, and which fail to set out at all or with any appreciable precision the allocation of costs for individual phases of the proceedings. This approach arguably results in a not insignificant financial burden to a party which, at an earlier stage, may have been the victim of unnecessary or other obstructive behavior that with the passage of time has "gone under." On the other hand, what is unnecessary or obstructive may become apparent only with the benefit of time and the tribunal's growing appreciation of the material and relevant issues. Accordingly, the extent to which the passage of time is the bane or the boon of any petition for costs based on conduct will depend on the particular case.

Another point in time at which costs orders could be made is at the time of any interim award. While arbitral tribunals do not usually make interim costs awards at this time, there is nothing to stop them from reaching an interim ruling on the issue.[29] If tribunals do decide to order costs at an interim stage, care must be taken, in the context of enforcement, to ensure that such costs order is contained in a reasoned award.[30]

The notion of an "Instant Costs Order" has been discussed, whereby tribunals make orders as to costs as and when the cost-inducing activity occurs. Such order can flow into the final decision on costs. One of the advantages of such an order during the proceedings could be to act as an incentive or a reminder to the parties to reconsider the introduction of dilatory applications and to minimize document production requests. It is also considered that such an order would increase transparency and signal to the parties an awareness as to costs by the tribunal.[31] Indeed Article 37(3) of the ICC

---

28. See also Niuscha Bassiri, "The Instant Cost Order", Kluwer Arbitration Blog, Oct. 19, 2010.
29. For some reservations as to interim awards on costs, see Colin Y.C. Ong & Michael Patrick O'Reilly, *Costs in International Arbitration* (Singapore/Malaysia/Hong Kong: LexisNexis, 2013), p. 63.
30. See CIArb Practice Guideline 9: Guideline for Arbitrators on Making Orders Relating to the Costs of the Arbitration, 5.8.4, 5.8.5.
31. Niuscha Bassiri, "The Instant Cost Order", Kluwer Arbitration Blog, Oct. 19, 2010. Other similar suggestions include running a "balance sheet" of anticipated costs assessments, see Lucy Reed, "Sanctions Available for Arbitrators to Curtail Guerrilla Tactics" in Günther J. Horvath & Stephan Wilske (eds), *Guerrilla Tactics in International Arbitration* (Alphen aan den Rijn: Kluwer Law International, 2013), p. 99; and giving an "indication", see Colin Y.C. Ong & Michael Patrick O'Reilly, *Costs in International Arbitration* (Singapore/Malaysia/Hong Kong: LexisNexis, 2013), p. 63.

Arbitration Rules is supportive of the concept that costs orders can be made at any time during the proceedings.[32] And the AAA Commercial Arbitration Rules (2013) R-23 provides: "The arbitrator shall have the authority to issue any orders necessary [...] and to otherwise achieve a fair, efficient and economical resolution of the case, including, without limitation ... (d) in the case of willful non-compliance with any order issued by the arbitrator, drawing adverse inferences, excluding evidence and other submissions, and/or *making special allocations of costs or an interim award of costs* arising from such non-compliance [...]."[33]

This approach has considerable appeal. It has the advantage that the tribunal is not likely to "forget" the costs implications of certain phases due to the written record that it will have established through the Instant Costs Order(s). It would also have the effect of sensitizing parties to the (cost) consequences of their actions and requests as and when they occur and even prompt them to re-think certain requests on the basis that they may trigger a Costs Order against them.

§21.03 FORM AND CONTENT OF COSTS SANCTIONS

There is extensive discussion on whether costs orders should be made as orders or as awards. To the extent that a "typical" form can be discerned from current practice, costs decisions seem to be a hybrid. They are often contained in final arbitral awards (whether on the merits or finally denying jurisdiction), thereby forming part of such awards. Consequently, the costs sections of awards are able to be enforced in the same way as the findings on the merits;[34] moreover, the view is generally held that costs orders will not be enforceable *unless* contained in an award.[35] On the other hand, unlike the rest of the award, costs awards quite often are not truly "reasoned", but simply set out the allocation without further comment, and thus might be regarded on this basis as more akin to an "order."

With respect to content, as stated above, costs findings are generally attributed the character of an "award" although they often lack reasoning. This lack of reasoning is often a product of express tribunal direction. Tribunals frequently request costs submissions to be made without detailed submissions and supporting exhibits, indeed sometimes even restricted in the first instance to a mere tally of costs claimed.

Depending on the circumstances, without comprehensive submissions on the factual and even legal basis for the costs claimed – including their reasonableness and their nexus to the necessary pursuit of the case – it can be difficult for a tribunal to write

---

32. Article 37(3) ICC Arbitration Rules reads as follows: "At any time during the arbitral proceedings, the arbitral tribunal may make decisions on costs, other than those to be fixed by the Court, and order payment."
33. Emphasis added.
34. Indeed, often enforcement or annulment actions do pertain to the decision on costs in the final award, see in the U.S. award vacatur context *Interchem Asia 2000 v. Oceana Petrochemicals*, 373 F.Supp.2d 340 (2006); *ReliaStar Life Insurance Co. v. EMC National Life Co.*, 564 F.3d 81 (2d Cir. 2009); *Century Indem. Co. v. AXA Belgium*, 2012 WL 4354816 (S.D.N.Y.); *Gen. Sec. Nat'l Ins. Co. v. Aequicap Program Admin.*, 785 F.Supp.2d 411 (S.D.N.Y. 2011).
35. *See* CIArb Practice Guideline 9: Guideline for Arbitrators on Making Orders Relating to the Costs of the Arbitration, 5.8.1.

a truly "reasoned" costs award. The deficits in reasoning or motivation of many sparely worded costs awards are all the more problematic insofar as the costs claim is often a highly significant component of the overall financial burden for one or both sides.[36]

Costs awards sanctioning a party must be reasoned and be based on reasonably detailed submissions. It is also the prerogative of parties to draw the tribunal's attention to conduct which they believe ought to be considered in the rendering of a costs award.[37] The tribunal should rely on its prior instructions putting the parties on advance notice that costs sanctions could be imposed, then outline the conduct found to have taken place, and finally justify why a party is being sanctioned and for a specific amount. Interim "instant" costs orders pertaining to certain phases of the arbitration and having the benefit of "recency" may aid the reasoning of a (final) costs award. A reasoned costs award is not only part of the obligation to ensure due process, but also comprises part of the tribunal's duty to render an enforceable award. Notably, the requirement that costs decisions be reasoned is set out explicitly in Article 28.4 of the LCIA Rules (2014): "[a]ny decision on costs by the Arbitral Tribunal shall be made with reasons in the award containing such decision."[38] This should be seen as applying all the more so to awards in which a party is sanctioned for its conduct, since the award will need to withstand the scrutiny of the parties (and potentially an annulment or enforcement court).[39]

§21.04 CONCLUSION

Arbitral tribunals have the authority to allocate costs based on parties' conduct in the arbitral proceedings which, depending on the circumstances, can amount to a "sanction" for improper conduct. Such authority is increasingly set out expressly in institutional rules and other relevant instruments.

Yet the power to sanction is not unfettered, and mandates that the arbitral tribunal inform the parties of the intended approach as early as appropriate in the proceedings. Consideration should also be given in this context to the potential utility of cost orders "along the way" in the arbitration, which can maintain the tribunal's and the parties' awareness of the consequences of their conduct on an ongoing basis.

The "sanctioning" of parties for conduct in arbitral proceedings should not be burdened with negative connotations but rather, viewed positively, and can be used as an effective tool in international arbitration to control proceedings and to ensure that one of the primary aims of arbitration, namely that of efficiency, is achieved to the greatest extent possible.

---

36. *See also* in this respect Colin Y.C. Ong & Michael Patrick O'Reilly, *Costs in International Arbitration* (Singapore/Malaysia/Hong Kong: LexisNexis, 2013), p. 62.
37. *See* Günther J. Horvath, Stephan Wilske & Niamh Leinwather, "Countering Guerrilla Tactics at the Outset, Throughout and at the Conclusion of the Arbitral Proceedings" in Günther J. Horvath & Stephan Wilske (eds), *Guerrilla Tactics in International Arbitration* (Alphen aan den Rijn: Kluwer Law International, 2013), pp. 48–50.
38. *See also* s. 52(4) English Arbitration Act (1996).
39. *See also* the discussion in Colin Y.C. Ong & Michael Patrick O'Reilly, *Costs in International Arbitration* (Singapore/Malaysia/Hong Kong: LexisNexis, 2013), pp. 60–63.

CHAPTER 22
Promoting Settlements in Arbitration: The Role of the Arbitrator

Stefan Kröll

§22.01 INTRODUCTION

Arbitration is commonly defined as a "a process in which the parties agree to refer their disputes to one or more neutral persons (arbitrators) in lieu of the court system for judicial determination with a binding effect."[1] It has an adjudicative nature and the primary task of an arbitrator is to decide the dispute and render an enforceable award. By contrast the facilitation of settlement is generally considered to be the realm of mediation or conciliation. The 2002 UNCITRAL Model Law on International Commercial Arbitration defines conciliation as a "process... whereby parties request a third person... to assist them in their attempt to reach an amicable settlement of their dispute." It then states that the conciliator "does not have the authority to impose upon the parties a solution of the dispute." While it is uncontested that mediators or conciliators cannot render an enforceable award the question of whether and to what extent the arbitrator can or even should promote a settlement between the parties is less clear. The arbitrator's role in seeking an amicable settlement is one of the topics where the cultural divide between the various systems is still very apparent.[2] While parties and arbitrators coming from a common law background have traditionally been reluctant to fully embrace an active role for an arbitrator in the parties' search for a settlement, the "Germanic" and Chinese tradition has been very much in support of

---

1. Julian D.M. Lew, Loukas A. Mistelis & Stefan Kröll, *Comparative International Commercial Arbitration*, paras. 1-5 (2003).
2. Gabrielle Kaufman-Kohler, *When Arbitrators Facilitate Settlement: Towards a Transnational Standard*, 25 Arbitration International 187, 189 (2009).

such a role.[3] Even if the Chinese case discussed below is an extreme – and probably not appropriate – example of how far some arbitrators will go in order to facilitate a settlement between the parties, arbitrators with a "Germanic" background are generally known for their willingness to take an active role in encouraging parties to seek a settlement which often goes beyond what their common law colleagues are used to or consider advisable.

Unfortunately, I never had the pleasure to sit with Pierre Karrer in a real arbitration but I know him primarily from his participation in the Willem C. Vis International Commercial Arbitration-Moot.[4] Thus, I have to rely on hearsay in assuming that his way to approach the issue is more influenced by his Swiss origin, his education in the "Germanic" legal system and his close ties with the Chinese culture than by his considerable experience in the common law world. That conclusion is also supported by the Rules and Recommendations issued by the CEDR Commission on Settlement in International Arbitration.[5] Pierre had been one of the members of this high-profile Commission set up in 2007 by the Centre for Effective Dispute Resolution to investigate the issue and to draft rules addressing the various concerns existing. I hope that his interest in the topic has not been vanished since then.

In the following, after a short overview on the different approaches in practice, the individual steps suggested in the CEDR-Rules which may be taken by an arbitrator will be analyzed in detail and against the background of the "Germanic" practice.

§22.02 OVERVIEW OF THE DIFFERENT APPROACHES IN PRACTICE

The divergence in approach to the problem which can be found in practice is enormous. One end is marked by an attitude following the traditional approach adopted by judges in England. The latter is best captured in the following statement by Francis Bacon, historically one of the most influential jurists in England, in his essay "Of Judicature":

> The parts of a judge in hearing are four: to direct the evidence; to moderate length, repetition or impertinency of speech; to recapitulate, select and collate the material points of that which hath been said; and to give the rule or sentence. Whatsoever is above these is too much; and proceedeth either of glory, and willingness to speak, or of impatience to hear, or of shortness of memory, or of want of a staid and equal attention.[6]

---

3. *See* CEDR Commission on Settlement in International Arbitration, *Final Report November 2009*, paras. 2.2 and 2.3, https://www.cedr.com/about_us/arbitration_commission/Arbitration_Commission_Doc_Final.pdf (accessed Sep. 22, 2016).
4. For details about the Moot *see* https://vismoot.pace.edu/ (accessed Sep. 22, 2016).
5. *See* CEDR Commission on Settlement in International Arbitration, *Final Report November 2009*, https://www.cedr.com/about_us/arbitration_commission/Arbitration_Commission_Doc_Final.pdf (accessed Sep. 22, 2016).
6. Francis Bacon, *Of Judicature,* in: *The Essays* (1601), available at https://ebooks.adelaide.edu.au/b/bacon/francis/b12e/essay56.html (accessed Sep. 22, 2016).

Notwithstanding that the statement is 400 years old and concerns the position of judges and not arbitrators, the underlying thinking has been the basis of the "adversarial system" as developed in the common law world. Despite all recent changes in the civil procedure rules it still influences the expectation of the parties from the common law world and the approach arbitrators of such a background have adopted.[7] That is well evidenced by the findings of a recent empirical study conducted by the College of Commercial Arbitrators and the Straus Institute for Dispute Resolution amongst leading arbitrators in the US.[8] Out of the 134 individuals who replied to the questionnaire sent to 225 leading arbitrators in the US more than 50% were not concerned at all with settlement options.[9]

The authors of the study furthermore state that despite the rising importance of settlements in the arbitration practice:

> many experienced arbitrators apparently do not perceive their arbitral role as extending to the promotion of settlement. The roots of such perceptions are unclear, but may in some cases reflect an all-consuming focus on the arbitrator's adjudicative function. This focus may be reinforced by the sense of discomfort some may feel about shifting to a facilitative role, either because it requires different skills and a different mindset, or because it is viewed as incompatible or even detrimental to the arbitral role. (As we will see, however, it is possible for arbitrators to play a role in settlement without actively facilitating or mediating.) For some, a perhaps-unconscious motivation to ignore opportunities to promote settlement may lie in the desire to maintain sufficient hours of commercial arbitration work in an increasingly competitive environment (footnotes omitted).[10]

This finding is in line with my own experience. Whenever I have advocated at conferences, lectures or in cases a more active role of the arbitrator in reaching a settlement the feedback I received from colleagues with a common law background was at best cautious. I was often told by them that the approach suggested was very interesting and definitively had its benefits. In their view it was, however, no proper arbitration but a different form of dispute resolution, at best med-arb.

The other end of the spectrum is marked by the approach adopted by the arbitral tribunal in a Chinese case under the Rules of the Xian Arbitration Commission (XAC) where members of the tribunal switched roles from arbitrators to mediators and back to arbitrators, often referred to as Arb-Med.[11] The approach was considered to be

---

7. For some of the changes in the US and the UK see Gabrielle Kaufman-Kohler, *When Arbitrators Facilitate Settlement: Towards a Transnational Standard*, 25 Arbitration International 187, 191 seq. (2009).
8. Thomas Stipanowich & Zachary P. Ulrich, *Commercial Arbitration and Settlement: Empirical Insights into the Roles Arbitrators Play*, 6 Penn State Yearbook on Arbitration and Mediation 1 (2014).
9. *Ibid*. p. 19 seq.
10. *Ibid*. p. 6 seq.
11. *See* Friven Yeoh & Desmond Ang, *Reflections on Gao Haiyan – of "Arb-Med", "Waivers" and Cultural Contextualisation of Public Policy Arguments*, 29 Journal of International Arbitration 2012, 285; for a more detailed discussion of the new SIAC-Arb-Med-Arb Protocol allowing for a comparable procedure see below, Reeg, *Should an International Arbitral Tribunal engage in Settlement Facilitation?*, § 27.03.

acceptable by the courts in Xian, as can be deduced from the enforcement decision by the Hong Kong Court of Appeal.[12] In the arbitration, which concerned the alleged invalidity of the sale of shares in a company, the Arbitral Tribunal after a first hearing had taken the decision to suggest to the parties to mediate the dispute which the parties agreed to do. According to the applicable arbitration rules the Arbitral Tribunal was empowered to "conduct mediation at any time before the rendering of an award." Furthermore, the rules provided that the "mediation may be proceeded simultaneously between both parties or with one party separately" and that the "mediator may put forward a mediation resolution plan for the parties' reference." The Arbitral Tribunal additionally decided to make a settlement proposal to the Parties and entrusted the arbitrator appointed by the seller and the Secretary General of XAC to contact the Parties with the proposal. In the case of the seller, the proposal was sent by the office of the Secretary General. In relation to the buyer, the arbitrator selected and the Secretary General met with a person close to the buyer for diner at the Shangri-La, transmitted the proposal and asked the third party to "work on" the buyer to reach a settlement. Pursuant to the proposal the contracts were to be treated as valid but the buyer was to pay RMB 250 million. As both parties rejected the proposal and no settlement could be reached a second hearing was held. In its award the tribunal dismissed the claim for performance of the buyer holding the contracts to be invalid but recommended that the seller should pay an economic compensation of RMB 50 million. The buyer then applied to the Xian courts to have the award set aside *inter alia* for serious procedural mistakes and "favouritism and malpractice" evidenced by the Arbitral Tribunal and XAC. The court in Xian refused to set aside the award holding that the participation of the Secretary General in the mediation efforts in the Shangri-La was in line with the procedural rules and the mere fact that the final award differed completely from the settlement proposal made before was not sufficient to prove that the Secretary General manipulated the award.[13] In the subsequent enforcement proceedings initiated by the seller in Hong Kong the High Court at first instance came to the opposite conclusion and rejected enforcement finding that there was an appearance of bias.[14] The Court of Appeal, however, declared the award enforceable, primarily because it considered that the buyer had waived its rights to complain about the conduct of the settlement effort. As an auxiliary argument the court also came to the conclusion that, contrary to the findings of the High Court, the conduct of the Arbitral Tribunal did not give rise to an impression of apparent bias. The court did only address the issue of whether the mediation was conducted properly or in a way to raise concerns about the impartiality of the mediators. By contrast, the arbitrator's involvement in the mediation process or that only one member of the Arbitral Tribunal participated in the mediation and that he was one of the party appointed arbitrators did

---

12. *See Gao Haiyan and Another v. Keeneye Holdings Ltd. And Another* (HKCA, 2011).
13. *See* para. 39, *Gao Haiyan and Another v. Keeneye Holdings Ltd. And Another* (HKCA, 2011).
14. *See* the summary in the judgment of the CA at paras. 71 et seq., *Gao Haiyan and Another v. Keeneye Holdings Ltd. And Another* (HKCA, 2011); *see also* Friven Yeoh & Desmond Ang, *Reflections on Gao Haiyan – of "Arb-Med", "Waivers" and Cultural Contextualisation of Public Policy Arguments*, 29 Journal of International Arbitration 2012, 285 (287).

not raise concerns with the court. Addressing the appropriateness of the failed mediation, the court rejected the findings of the High Court stating:

> With respect, although one might share the learned Judge's unease about the way in which the mediation was conducted because mediation is normally conducted differently in Hong Kong, whether that would give rise to an apprehension of bias, may depend also on an understanding of how mediation is normally conducted in the place where it was conducted.[15]

Between these two extremes but much more to the proactive side, are the CEDR Recommendations and Rules for the Facilitation of Settlement in International Arbitration. The purpose of the high-profile CEDR Commission for Settlement in Arbitration was "to review the current practice regarding the promotion of settlement by international arbitral tribunals and come up with recommendations to improve this aspect of the process for end users."[16] On the basis of the assumption that often a negotiated settlement is the most cost efficient and effective solution to the parties' problem, the Commission prepared Recommendations and Rules which are intended to be a kind of best practice on how to approach the issue. According to the introduction of the Rules, they are designed to increase the chances of settlements in international arbitration by outlining in particular the "steps which Arbitral Tribunals are to take (and are not to take) with a view to facilitating settlement by the Parties." Article 5 lists the steps an arbitrator may take to facilitate settlements. It provides the following under the heading of "Facilitation of Settlement by Arbitral Tribunal":

1. Unless otherwise agreed by the Parties in writing, the Arbitral Tribunal may, if it considers helpful to do so, take one or more of the following steps to facilitate a settlement of part or all of the Parties' dispute.
1.1. provide all [p]arties with the [a]rbitral [t]ribunal's preliminary views on the issues in dispute in the arbitration and what the [a]rbitral [t]ribunal considers will be necessary in terms of evidence from each [p]arty in order to prevail on those issues;
1.2. provide all [p]arties with preliminary non-binding findings on law or fact on key issues in the arbitration;
1.3. where requested by the [p]arties in writing, offer suggested terms of settlement as a basis for further negotiation;
1.4. where requested by the [p]arties in writing, chair one or more settlement meetings attended by representatives of the [p]arties at which possible terms of settlement may be negotiated.[17]

The recommendation to take proactive steps is subject to the general principle, set out in Article 3.1 that in assisting the Parties with a settlement, the Arbitral Tribunal shall not knowingly act in such a way that would make its award susceptible to a successful challenge.

---

15. Paragraph 112, *Gao Haiyan and Another v. Keeneye Holdings Ltd. And Another* (HKCA, 2011).
16. *See* CEDR Commission on Settlement in International Arbitration, *Final Report November 2009*, para. 1.5, https://www.cedr.com/about_us/arbitration_commission/Arbitration_Commission_Doc_Final.pdf (accessed Sep. 22, 2016).
17. *Ibid.* Art. 5.

That raises the question whether some of the steps recommended potentially "make the award susceptible to a successful challenge." In their analysis of the CEDR Rules and Recommendations Nappert and Flader criticize *inter alia* that the rules do not take into account "psychological components" such as that settlement facilitation might be perceived as "incompatible with the arbitrator's duty of impartiality, as illustrated by the concern that settlement facilitation could be seen as encouraging pre-judgment on certain issues."[18]

§22.03 CONNECTION WITH OTHER DEVELOPMENTS IN INTERNATIONAL ARBITRATION PROCEDURE

Any evaluation of these concerns must consider the general developments in international arbitration practice and the broader discussion about efficiency and economy in arbitration. Both are closely intertwined with the question of whether an arbitrator shall take an active role in promoting settlements.[19]

One of the hallmarks of international arbitral procedure is its flexibility, resulting from the important role accorded to party autonomy. Within the very broad limits imposed by the few mandatory requirements of due process the parties – or failing an agreement by the parties the arbitrators – are generally free to adopt a procedure which takes into the account the needs of each particular case. Naturally, the procedure finally adopted is affected by the procedural backgrounds of the parties, their lawyers and the members of the tribunal. Despite all flexibility and the different starting points of parties and arbitrators used to a more adversarial style of conducting proceedings and those used to a more inquisitorial style, the last decades have seen the gradual development of an "internationalized" or "harmonized" procedure. It is based on elements coming from the various systems and is encapsulated in the numerous IBA rules and guidelines.[20]

Notwithstanding the infinite variations possible and required by the specific needs or the dynamics of each case, a widely held understanding about the major procedural steps in an arbitration has developed over time. Parties normally set out their case in one or several rounds of written submissions. These contain, as far as possible and practical, the relevant evidence either in form of attached documents, witness statements or expert reports or at least offers to provide the relevant statements and reports to support the factual allegations made in the submissions. The purpose of

---

18. Sophie Nappert & Dieter Flader, *A Psychological Perspective on the Facilitation of Settlement in International Arbitration – Examining the CEDR-Rules*, p. 3, published in Journal of International Dispute Management 8/2011, available at: http://ssrn.com/abstract=1863843 (accessed Sep. 22, 2016); *see also* Thomas Stipanowich & Zachary P. Ulrich, *Commercial Arbitration and Settlement: Empirical Insights into the Roles Arbitrators Play*, 6 Penn State Yearbook on Arbitration and Mediation 1, 15 (2014).
19. For the connection with the topic of efficiency and costs *see also* Gabrielle Kaufman-Kohler, *When Arbitrators Facilitate Settlement: Towards a Transnational Standard*, 25 Arbitration International 187, 188 (2009); Thomas Stipanowich & Zachary P. Ulrich, *Commercial Arbitration and Settlement: Empirical Insights into the Roles Arbitrators Play*, 6 Penn State Yearbook on Arbitration and Mediation 1, 5 (2014).
20. Gary Born, *International Commercial Arbitration*, § 15.07 [D][3] pp. 2207 et seq. (2nd ed., 2014).

the evidentiary hearing is to present the previously offered evidence directly to the tribunal and to allow the arbitrators to evaluate it. The effect of this now prevailing framework of international arbitration is that already before the oral hearing most of the information available has been presented to the tribunal. As a consequence, international arbitration proceedings are much more frontloaded than traditional court proceedings in the common law world.

In parallel to this development, major users have complained that arbitration has largely lost its attraction as a cost and time-efficient dispute settlement mechanism. Instead, arbitration proceedings have turned into "off-shore" litigation mirroring court proceedings with lengthy submissions, expensive document production phases and arbitrators unwilling to take decisions to speed up the proceedings. There have been clear statements by users that they would move away from arbitration to other forms of dispute resolution should these problems not be addressed.[21] Practice and the arbitration institutions have taken that criticism seriously and have launched initiatives trying to remedy the problem. The best known of these activities is probably the brochure published by the ICC originally in 2007 about "Techniques for Controlling Time and Cost in Arbitration."[22] Its central elements have, in their revised version, become part of the ICC-Arbitration Rules. Appendix IV of the Arbitration Rules now provides a list of case management techniques to be employed by tribunals to "ensure that time and costs are proportionate to what is at stake in the dispute." Without going into any further detail, the common theme of these suggestions is that the tribunal should take an active role in structuring the proceedings in a time and cost efficient way. Thereby, the ICC suggestions reflect a general tendency in arbitration, but also in procedural law, which makes a proactive arbitrator or judge more acceptable to the common law world.[23]

§22.04 THE POSITION TAKEN BY ARBITRATION LAWS AND RULES ON SETTLEMENT FACILITATIONS

One of the reasons why the arbitrator's role in promoting settlement is controversial is that the statutory provisions offer very little guidance. They often contain rules that

---

21. See the comments by inhouse lawyers of Siemens, Paul Hobeck, Volker Mahnken & Max Koebke, *Time for Woolf Reforms in International Construction Arbitration*, 11 (2) IntALR 84 (2008); Thomas Stipanowich, *Reflections on the State and Future of Commercial Arbitration: Challenges, Opportunities, Proposal*, Columbia American Review of International Arbitration 25, (2014); see also Queen Mary University of London, PriceWaterhouseCoopers, *2013 International Arbitration Survey: Corporate Choices in International Arbitration, Industry Perspectives 2013*, pp. 6, 8, 21, 22, where time and costs are consistently cited by users as their biggest concerns in connection with arbitration, https://www.pwc.com/gx/en/arbitration-dispute-resolution/assets/pwc-international-arbitration-study.pdf (accessed Sep. 22, 2016).
22. ICC Arbitration Commission, *Report on Techniques for Controlling Time and Costs in Arbitration*, http://www.iccwbo.org/Advocacy-Codes-and-Rules/Document-centre/2012/ICC-Arbitration-Commission-Report-on-Techniques-for-Controlling-Time-and-Costs-in-Arbitration/ (accessed Sep. 22, 2016).
23. Hilmar Raeschke-Kessler, *The Arbitrator as Settlement Facilitator*, 21 Arbitration International, 523, 524 (2005).

once a settlement has been reached it can be turned into an award on agreed terms.[24] By contrast, the question whether the arbitrator should or at least can take actions to facilitate such a settlement is rarely addressed at all.[25] Notable exceptions, influenced by the Chinese tradition, are the arbitration laws of Singapore[26] and Hong Kong[27] which explicitly regulate the case that the arbitrator is acting also as a mediator. By contrast the arbitration laws in the other most popular jurisdictions for arbitration[28] as well as the UNCITRAL Model Law are silent upon the issue. In the few jurisdictions where the issue is addressed the solution is that if the Parties have empowered the tribunal to do so it may use mediation techniques to promote settlements. In this regard, the International Commercial Arbitration Act of British Columbia adopts an interesting position. It states in section 30 (1):

> It is not incompatible with an arbitration agreement for an arbitral tribunal to encourage settlement of the dispute and, with the agreement of the parties, the arbitral tribunal may use mediation, conciliation and other procedures at any time during the arbitral proceedings to encourage settlement.

The provision seems to make a distinction between general efforts to encourage settlements on the one hand and the use of "mediation, conciliation and other procedures" to encourage settlements on the other hand. The former are considered to be authorized by an ordinary arbitration agreement while the latter requires an express additional agreement of the parties.

A comparable rule but with a different emphasis is found in the Arbitration Act of Ontario where section 35 states:

> The members of an arbitral tribunal shall not conduct any part of the arbitration as a mediation or conciliation process or other similar process that might compromise or appear to compromise the arbitral tribunal's ability to decide the dispute impartially.

A comparable situation exists as far as the arbitration rules are concerned. In the above references example from China the Rules of XAC provided in Article 36 that subject to the parties' consent the Arbitral Tribunal was empowered to "conduct mediation at any time before the rendering of an award".

---

24. See for example Art. 30 UNCITRAL Model Law; Sect. 51 English Arbitration Act 1996.
25. For a more complete analysis see the "Table of existing Provisions on settlement in Arbitration" attached as Appendix 4 to CEDR Commission on Settlement in International Arbitration, *Final Report November 2009*.
26. There ss 16(3) and 17 International Arbitration Act expressly provide for the appointment of a conciliator and the possibility to become an arbitrator as well as for the arbitrator to act as conciliator.
27. Section 33 Arbitration Ordinance 2011.
28. According to a study of the School of International Arbitration and White & Case in 2010 the preferred seats of arbitration are in the following jurisdictions: England, Switzerland, France, Japan, Singapore and the US, Queen Mary University of London, White & Case, *2010 International Arbitration Survey: Choices in International Arbitration*, pp. 17 et seq. https:// http:// www.arbitration.qmul.ac.uk/docs/123290.pdf (accessed Sep. 22, 2016).

That may be one of the reasons why the chairman of the XAC apparently had no objections against one of the arbitrators getting involved in a mediation with ex parte communication with one of the parties.

The majority of other rules is silent upon the issue. One of the few institutions which explicitly requests the arbitrator to take up a facilitative role for settlements is the German DIS. Section 32.1 of the DIS-Rules provides under the heading of settlements:

> 32.1: At every stage of the proceedings, the arbitral tribunal should seek to encourage an amicable settlement of the dispute or of individual issues in dispute.

No such provision can be found in the rules of the other leading arbitration institutions in the countries belonging to the "Germanic" family of laws, i.e., Austria and Switzerland. And also in Germany the question has arisen whether section 32.1 DIS-Rules should be kept in the new version of the DIS-Rules. The discussion in the context of the DIS-rules revision raises, however, a much broader issue of whether such an approach is potentially conflicting with basic tenets of arbitral proceedings or is even commendable.

These concerns are also apparent in the suggestions for case management techniques in Appendix IV of the ICC-Arbitration Rules. There, steps to facilitate the settlement of a dispute are mentioned as a possible case management technique, "provided that any effort is made to ensure that any subsequent award is enforceable in law." A comparable caveat is contained in the UNCITRAL Notes on organizing Arbitral Proceedings, which has, however, evolved from the original version of 1996 to a second version in 2016. While the 1996 version, referring to the different approaches in different jurisdictions, stated that a "tribunal should only suggest settlement negotiations with caution",[29] the version adopted in 2016 contains a much less restrictive guidance. If the applicable law permits the arbitral tribunal to facilitate a settlement "it may, if so requested by the parties, guide or assist the parties in their negotiations."[30]

§22.05 DETAILED EVALUATION OF THE DIFFERENT MEASURES SUGGESTED

[A] Information About Preliminary Views on the Issues in Dispute in the Arbitration and the Evidence Needed

The first instrument to promote settlements suggested in the CEDR-Rules is information about preliminary views of the relevant issues in dispute and the evidence needed. The underlying idea is that such indications by the arbitral tribunal help the parties to

---

29. UNCITRAL Notes on Organizing Arbitral Proceedings, para. 47 (1996); https://www.uncitral.org/pdf/english/texts/arbitration/arb-notes/arb-notes-e.pdf (accessed Sep. 22, 2016).
30. 2016 UNCITRAL Notes on Organizing Arbitral Proceedings, para. 74 http://www.uncitral.org/pdf/english/texts/arbitration/arb-notes/arb-notes-2016-e-pre-release.pdf, (accessed Sep. 22, 2016).

re-evaluate their case in light of the tribunal's indications. Parties tend to focus on the positive aspects of their case and may therefore have wrong ideas about the strength of their case. Such misperceptions are often a major obstacle to all settlement efforts. They render the gap existing between the expectations of one party and the proposals by the other party non-bridgeable. The hope is that the tribunal by indicating which issues it considers to be important helps the parties to get a more realistic understanding of the strengths and weaknesses of their case and thus narrows the gap between the respective positions to such a degree that it can be bridged in subsequent negotiations.

For parties and lawyers trained and operating in the German system such information about preliminary views and the evidence needed are very familiar as they constitute standard practice in the state courts. In court proceedings in Germany, the court prepares and structures the evidentiary hearing by issuing a *Beweisbeschluss* (order to take evidence). It sets out in detail for which controversial facts the court intends to hear witnesses or take other forms of evidence. The order is based on the so-called *Relationstechnik* which constitutes an integral part of the post university legal education in Germany preparing law students for practice. The purpose of this technique is to concentrate the taking of evidence to those facts in dispute between the parties which would affect the outcome of the case. It involves a three-step process and is based on a strict distinction between law and facts as well as one fundamental rule often described by the Latin term of *iura novit curia*: The parties have to plead only the facts while the judge knows the law. Before the judge can apply the law he or she has first to determine from the eventually opposing pleadings of the parties what the facts of the case are. In doing so the judge will first analyze the whole case on the assumption that the facts as pleaded by the Claimant are correct. The judge who is not bound by the Claimant's pleading on the law will apply the rules which he or she considers relevant to those facts and determine whether or not the Claimant has the claim raised on the basis of such rules. If not, the claim is rejected as non-conclusive. If the claim exists, the judge will in a second step analyze whether the Respondent has a defense against such claims if one assumes that the facts as pleaded by the Respondent are correct. If not, the claim is granted without any taking of evidence even if the facts alleged between both parties differ. If the Respondent has a defense on the basis of the facts as pleaded by itself, the judge determines in a third step which of the various facts on which the parties differ is relevant for the outcome.[31]

In Germany, the judge's determination of the further evidence needed is based on a full pleading of the case by the parties in ideally two rounds of written submissions. Consequently, there is no danger that the judge will pre-judge the case.

That would have been different under the "notice pleading" which was typical for the proceedings in the common law world for a long time. There, the parties only gave a rough outline of the case and presented the details in a longer oral hearing. In such

---

31. For a more detailed description of the method, *see* Monika Anders & Burkhard Gehle, *Das Assessorexamen im Zivilrecht*, pp. 3 et seq. (12th ed., 2015); for an English language summary of the German *Relationstechnik see* James Maxeiner, *Guiding Litigation: Applying Law to Facts in Germany* in: Common Good Forum – The Boundaries of Litigation: A Forum Addressing the Alignment of Civil Justice with Social Goals, pp. 9 et seq. (2008), http://papers.ssrn.com/sol3/papers.cfm?abstract_id=1230453 (accessed Sep. 22, 2016).

a scenario, a judge could be considered to prejudge the case if he or she determined on the bases of the limited information provided by the parties before the oral hearing which additional information would be needed. Consequently, the concern about pre-judgment in my experience is primarily raised by lawyers educated in the common law world.

In international arbitration, as described above, there has been a growing practice over the years to front-load the proceedings and to give more weight to the parties' submissions. Nowadays, they are often hundreds of pages long and set out all details of the case. The relevant documents are attached to such submissions and the witnesses have described in their written statements in detail what they are going to say. Such submissions, including the documents attached should have been read by the arbitrator before any evidentiary hearing. The primary purpose of the hearing is to verify the credibility of the evidence submitted, in particular where the parties have conflicting submissions, and to clarify open issues. It is normal that an arbitrator after reading through the submissions, documents and witness statements has formed an at least preliminary view about questions he or she considers relevant for the decision of the case and which of the offered witnesses or experts should be heard or which documents have to be discussed. Informing the parties about these preliminary views is therefore not prejudging the case. At that stage, parties have had the opportunity to present their case and are not expected to present additional evidence. The purpose of the hearing is primarily to evaluate and test the evidence offered. Information about the arbitrator's preliminary thinking which of the controversial facts are in his or her view relevant for the case helps, first, to streamline the process of taking evidence. The parties can concentrate on those facts the tribunal considers relevant. Second, such early indications give the parties the chance to see where the tribunal may have misunderstood their submissions or where, at least in the parties' view, it has not given sufficient weight to certain suggestions. It grants the party the opportunity to clarify the relevant issue in the oral hearing and in particular during the opening statement.

The above considerations are confirmed by the latest version of the IBA Rules on Taking Evidence in International Arbitration. They provide in paragraph 3 of the new included Article 2 as follows:

> 3. The Arbitral Tribunal is encouraged to identify to the Parties, as soon as it considers it to be appropriate, any issues:
>   (a) that the Arbitral Tribunal may regard as relevant to the case and material to its outcome; and/or
>   (b) for which a preliminary determination may be appropriate.

The previous version of the Rules had already contained a comparable encouragement but only in the Preamble and not in the body of rules.

Taking into account the particularities of international arbitration, the suggested identification of the relevant issues which have to be proven at the evidentiary hearing should normally merely indicate the broad topics which to be addressed in the oral hearing. It should not be as specific and prescriptive a *Beweisbeschluss* in German court proceedings. The latter defines the specific facts which have to be proven, lists the evidence which is examined for that and leaves no room for additional evidence. That may be possible in a purely national setting with parties and lawyers coming from the same legal and cultural background. In an international setting a tribunal should consider that the likelihood of having misunderstood the parties' submissions and not properly evaluated it may be much larger. Parties should be given the opportunity to remedy these misunderstandings in the oral hearing. In particular, opening statements may provide the parties with an opportunity to emphasize issues which the tribunal has not properly evaluated and to present them in a different manner in an effort to convince the tribunal about their relevance.

[B] Preliminary Non-binding Findings on Law or Fact on Key Issues in the Arbitration

The second possible tool to facilitate a settlement suggested in the CEDR-Rules, i.e., a preliminary non-binding finding on law or facts on key issues, is largely based on the same ideas and principles as the first. The parties should be informed where the tribunal stands presently in its decision-making process. That may help the parties to re-evaluate their case and reach a settlement in light of the looming decision by the tribunal. The underlying idea is again to inform the parties about the present status of the internal and ongoing decision-making process which is made transparent to parties hoping to encourage them to settle. The comparability of the underlying ideas and of the way of operating of the first and the second tool may also be the reason why the CEDR-Rules – as for the first tool – do not require an express written authorization by the parties for such a way of proceedings. That distinguishes it from the other two tools suggested in the rules.

The second tool, however, goes one-step further than the first instrument, in so far as the arbitrator informs the parties already about certain findings of the tribunal. These must obviously be based on an evaluation of the legal reasoning or the evidence presented to the tribunal. Unlike the first instrument suggested, preliminary non-binding findings could be presented at two different stages of the proceedings. First, after the written submissions have been made, but before an evidentiary hearing. Informing the parties about preliminary non-binding findings instead of merely indicating what the tribunal considers relevant before the evidence is properly taken is only appropriate if the tribunal has formed already a fairly firm view about factual and legal positions which is not dependent on the subsequent taking of evidence, as the latter may either be irrelevant for that issue or obviously not convincing. Second, and that is probably the prevalent situation in practice, such findings can be presented at the end of or after such an evidentiary hearing taking into the account the tribunal's preliminary evaluation of the evidence presented to it. In that case, the parties may only hope to change the tribunal's evaluation by their post-hearing briefs or, in case that is possible, through additional evidence offered.

At first sight, there should be no objection against such an approach. Conceptually, the members of the tribunal are in principle again not doing more than merely communicating to the parties the present and preliminary status of their decision-making process. That process takes place anyway but is normally not made known to the parties until the final award. No arbitrator reads submissions or participates in an evidentiary hearing without forming at least a preliminary view about what he or she has read or has been presented. Thus, it is difficult to see how an information about the conclusions reached until a given time results in prejudging the case or affecting the independence or impartiality of the tribunal. Post hearing briefs are generally not intended to adduce new evidence which the arbitrator has not yet seen. Their purpose is to comment on the evidence presented at the oral hearing. Consequently, preliminary findings presented after an evidentiary hearing are not expressed before the tribunal has seen all evidence but with the knowledge of all evidence presented. Furthermore, as it is made clear that the tribunal informs only about its preliminary views the parties may have the chance to change that view through their subsequent submissions as they would have, if the view had not been expressed.

A closer look at the practical effects of such preliminary findings on the further conduct of the tribunal's decision-making process reveals, however, that the situation may not be that clear. In practice, an arbitrator who has formed a preliminary view on one issue and has communicated it to the parties is generally less inclined to change that view in light of subsequently presented evidence or arguments than an arbitrator who has not communicated the preliminary view to the outside. It is natural to search primarily for arguments supporting the view expressed than to admit that the preliminary evaluation was "wrong" and had to be revised. That is even more so as such a change of view will often result in the allegation that the final decision constitutes a surprise to the party which relied on the preliminary evaluation and has thus not provided additional arguments to support and strengthen the tribunal's preliminary evaluation. That risk may be aggravated by the concerns that in giving preliminary evaluations in order to facilitate settlements arbitrators are influenced not solely by objective legal consideration but instead also take into account settlement considerations. There are regularly issues, where the arbitrators are not yet completely certain which alternative they adopt and where their decision could be influenced by considerations of which of the alternatives makes a settlement more likely.

In light of these considerations – and in so far deviating from the CEDR-Rules – a tribunal should only engage in openly communicating its preliminary findings if it has been explicitly authorized in writing by the parties. Notwithstanding the fact that conceptually the tribunal is only making the present status of its decision-making process transparent to the parties, such a communication may affect the process in such a way that it should be authorized by the parties.

There is also a second reason why a general submission to the CEDR-Rules before or at the time the arbitration is initiated should not be considered sufficient. There may be occasions where – in the view of at least one party – a communication of the tribunal's preliminary findings does not facilitate a settlement but makes it more difficult. A party may be more inclined to compromise and to accept when it is not certain about its legal situation than after finding its legal views endorsed by the tribunal's preliminary evaluation.

[C] Suggested Terms of Settlement as a Basis for Further Negotiation

The first two means of settlement facilitation suggested by the CEDR-Rules are obviously much closer to an early neutral evaluation than to a proper mediation. They are definitively no Arb-Med or Med-Arb but are part of the task of the arbitrator.

The third and the fourth tool suggested in the CEDR-Rules are conceptually of a different character than the first two instruments. The tribunal is no longer only informing the parties about a process which is clearly part of its adjudicative task but potentially engages in a different task, i.e., that of regulating the parties' future cooperation. Consequently, the CEDR-Rules require an express written authorization by the parties before the tribunal can perform such a task, which is not covered by the original arbitration agreement.

The suggestion may be made primarily on the basis of a preliminary finding which the tribunal has communicated to the parties. In several of my own arbitrations the parties, after having received a preliminary evaluation, have explicitly asked for such a proposal to start the negotiation process, so no party had to struggle with the tactical advantages or disadvantages of making the first offer.

In most of my cases, the settlement terms suggested by the tribunal have been influenced not only by the preliminary evaluation and the underlying purely legal considerations. They were merely the starting point from which the terms suggested were developed. In addition, other considerations of a more economic nature have often played a role, such as the ability of the debtor to comply with an award or the terms of a settlement, the threats of insolvency or long-lasting set aside or enforcement proceedings in case a non-consensual award is rendered.

There have also been cases where such economic considerations truly formed the basis for settlement proposals. In these cases, it was clear that an award based on purely legal considerations ordering the debtor to pay the full amount due under the contract would not be enforceable or at least its enforcement would be fairly difficult. Thus, the settlement proposal was much lower than what would have been due on the basis of our preliminary evaluation based on purely legal considerations, often coupled with the condition that in case of non-performance of the settlement a higher amount would have to be paid.

If the terms for the settlement suggested can be explained by the arbitral tribunal in a rational way, in particular, why other factors than the possible legal outcome were taken into account, the proposal can hardly lead to an appearance of bias which would require an arbitrator to step down or even justify a successful challenge. Thus, such proposals if covered by an advance written submission of the parties should not pose any problems from the legal side.

Irrespective of that, the question arises whether such proposals are advisable. There is no doubt that a proposal by a "true" conciliator or mediator which had a proper insight into the parties' real interests underlying the dispute may be more effective. It can take into account numerous factors which are not known and have not been disclosed by the parties to the arbitrator. Parties are understandably more reluctant to be completely open to a person which will have to decide the case if no settlement can be reached than to a proper mediator which lacks such power.

Nevertheless, according to my experience, there is a considerable benefit of such proposals if the parties cannot agree on proper mediation.

[D] Chair Settlement Meetings Attended by Representatives of the Parties at Which Possible Terms of Settlement May Be Negotiated

The last tool suggested by the CEDR Rules to facilitate settlements, i.e., to chair settlement meetings, is the one which comes closest to the task of a mediator. To what extent an arbitrator becomes a mediator depends largely on what is understood by "chairing". Based on a narrow interpretation the arbitrator would merely be presiding over negotiations by allocating speaking time to the parties or summarizing their proposals.

To be truly efficient "chairing" requires, however, more than that. The arbitrator must also structure the proceedings, overcome impasses and eventually use mediation tools to create a settlement friendly atmosphere, including caucusing. Thus, in the Chinese example given above, the arbitrator truly assumed the task of a mediator for a certain time, meeting separately with one party or a person affiliated with it. Notwithstanding the wide use of Arb-Med in China,[32] there are justifiable doubts whether the arbitrator is the right person to act as a mediator. It is very likely that the parties will even in their ex parte communication consider that the mediating arbitrator has to decide the case should they be unable to reach a settlement. Thus, they may not communicate their true interests to the mediating arbitrator with the same frankness as they would do that to a proper mediator. At the same time, the arbitrator has to ensure that any award rendered is not taking into account information disclosed ex parte and not subsequently included into the arbitral proceedings.

Even if both parties attend the settlement negotiations and no ex parte communications occur, already a broadly understood management of these proceedings is never free from the risk, that one of the parties considers it to be unfair and in favor of the other party. Thus, if no settlement can be reached it could in a worst-case scenario result in the subsequent challenge of an arbitrator. In addition, there is always the risk that a party may feel coerced into settling when the initiative comes from the very person who may later has to decide the dispute if a settlement fails.

§22.06 CONCLUSION

The developments of the recent decades in arbitration, in particular the growing support for a proactive role of arbitral tribunals, have largely removed any eventually existing legal objections against arbitrators taking an active role in facilitating settlement. In light of the extensive written submissions preparing evidentiary hearings which are now prevailing in international arbitration proceedings, informing the parties about elements or the preliminary stages of the tribunal's decision-making

---

32. Gabrielle Kaufman-Kohler & Fan Kun, *Integrating Mediation into Arbitration: Why It Works in China*, 25 Journal of International Arbitration 479 (2008).

process cannot be equated with a prejudgment of the case or raise concerns as to the independence of the tribunal.

Today, the question of whether an arbitrator can take steps to facilitate a settlement is no longer one of legal powers but more of an arbitrator's perception of his or her role. It is beyond doubt that unlike a mediator or conciliator an arbitrator has been given the power by the parties to adjudicate their dispute by a final and binding award. The only question is whether an arbitrator considers his or her task to be limited to the adjudication of the dispute or whether the arbitrator assumes that the primary objective of the parties submitting to arbitration was to have their dispute resolved.[33] In the latter case, the mere fact that by opting for arbitration the parties wanted to make sure that at the end of the process the dispute is solved by a final and binding adjudication, if no other way is successful, does not mean that no other means should be tried. Arbitrators who have a broad understanding of their task approach it from the beginning with the mindset of a dispute resolver, so no change of mindset is required when moving from settlement facilitation to adjudication.[34]

In all other matters I have discussed with Pierre he has always favored broad and holistic views over narrow understandings. Thus, I would be surprised if that were different in relation to the role of an arbitrator. I hope that in the years to come I get the chance to verify my assumptions and Pierre sees the CEDR-Rules developing into the new transnational standard requested by one of the chairpersons of the CEDR-Committee. *Ad multos annos.*

---

33. Gabrielle Kaufman-Kohler, *When Arbitrators Facilitate Settlement: Towards a Transnational Standard*, 25 Arbitration International 187, 188 seq (2009).
34. The required change of mindset is one of the psychological concerns raised by Sophie Nappert & Dieter Flader, *A Psychological Perspective on the Facilitation of Settlement in International Arbitration – Examining the CEDR-Rules*, p. 3, published in Journal of International Dispute Management 8/2011, available at: http://ssrn.com/abstract = 1863843 (accessed Sep. 22, 2016).

CHAPTER 23
The Role of Individuals in International Arbitration

Werner Melis

I want to thank the editors of this book for their brilliant idea to edit this book of friends and to invite me to make a contribution. This gives me the opportunity to express my sincere thanks to Pierre Karrer for decades of good co-operation and personal friendship. We met first long time ago and kept in touch continuously. I can, therefore, confirm that Pierre has made valuable contributions to international arbitration worldwide and particularly to his country, Switzerland, as one of the first places for international arbitral proceedings. I remember with pleasure an arbitration under his chairmanship in Paris more than twenty years ago which gave me and my colleague arbitrators the privilege to see Disneyland Paris in another way than normal visitors do.

Pierre's professional performance is a good proof that individual persons have always played a determinative role in the establishment of international arbitration as it stands now. I will, therefore, devote my contribution to this subject. Arbitration as such has a long history. As an example Article 270 of the 'General Rules of the Court' of the Habsburg Empire 1781 state that 'the disputing parties are free to agree upon an arbitratior...'. This provision was of course meant for local ad-hoc proceedings only. For international commercial arbitration, as we understand it now, attempts to find common international solutions have been made in the interwar period, as the Protocol on Arbitration Clauses 1923 and Convention for the Execution of Foreign Arbitral Awards 1927. However, due to the international finance crisis international arbitrations have rarely taken place. The turning point was after the Second World War the Convention on the Recognition and Enforcement of Foreign Arbitral Awards 1958 (New York Convention), particularly Article V which has practically limited the grounds for refusal of enforcement of awards to formal grounds, thus avoiding the repetition of proceedings on the merits of a case in the enforcement proceedings.

The negotiations of this convention lasted quite some time. This gave the negotiators of the participating states the possibility to establish good relationships and friendships with other colleagues. A group of them met regularly at the Relais de Chambésy, a restaurant close to the negotiating place at the United Nations Office at Geneva. They initiated the Club de Chambésy with Professor Pieter Sanders, Jean Robert and others. This Club de Chambésy was also the start of the International Council for Commercial Arbitration (ICCA) which has celebrated 2013 its 50th anniversary. Its Governing Board can still be considered as a 'Club of friends', persons who play a role in international arbitration. ICCA-Congresses have largely contributed to the development of international arbitration worldwide and continue to be the most important events for the presentation of and the exchange of views about new ideas.

Coming back to the late Seventies and early Sixties, it must also be said that the then existing arbitral institutions were mostly arbitration courts attached to the Chambers of Commerce in the capitals of countries which had originally been set up for the decision of local disputes between members. Also the then existing Court of Arbitration at the International Chamber of Commerce in Paris (ICC), which is legally an association under French law, was established for the decision of disputes between the members of the association, i.e. the National Committees of the ICC. As a consequence, the Secretary General of this Court was the Head of the Legal Department of the ICC, then Mr Frederic Eisemann, and the financial matters, as arbitrators and administrative fees and expenses were handled by the Administrative Department of the ICC. It is largely the merit of Mr Eisemann and other negotiators of the New York Convention that the ICC Court of Arbitration has been used for international arbitration and has become worldwide the most important international institution in this field. Just a short story from the early 1960s for the understanding of the situation at this time. Mr Eisemann asked the Austrian National Committee of the ICC to propose a name for a sole arbitrator in a dispute between a French Claimant, a German Respondent, place of Arbitration Heidelberg, French law applicable, French as language of the proceedings and a marginable amount in dispute. As then Secretary of the Austrian National Committee of the ICC I was unable to find a person which the necessary qualifications to accept the mandate for the proposed fee. The same happened apparently in other National Committees which had also been asked for a proposal. To my surprise, Mr Eisemann asked me to do the job and proposed my President to suggest my name, what he successfully did. After the end of the proceedings at my next visit of the ICC, the Head of the Administrative Department gave me a bill of exchange for my fees in French francs which I discharged at the next bank. The amount of my fees enabled me to invite a friend to a good fish restaurant in Paris for dinner. This was the start of my career as an international arbitrator. For persons who are familiar with the present size of the administration of the ICC Court of Arbitration, this story sounds probably like a joke.

Another meeting opportunity for international arbitration practitioners were the negotiations for the UNCITRAL Arbitration Rules 1976 in which many of them from all parts of the world participated as members of the national teams of their respective countries. This gave the opportunity to become acquainted with persons working in this field and to establish personal relationships and even friendships which were very

Chapter 23: The Role of Individuals in International Arbitration

helpful for the work in the professional field. This useful co-operation continued with the negotiations for the UNCITRAL Model Law on International Commercial Arbitration 1985 at which many of the negotiators of the UNCITRAL Arbitration Rules participated. This is in my opinion also the reason why some texts of the UNCITRAL Arbitration Rules have been literally taken over in the UNCITRAL Model Law. This co-operation still continues and UNCITRAL meetings concerning international arbitration are always also considered as useful meeting opportunities for practitioners working in this field.

After the Second World War, Europe got divided in east and west. The so-called eastern countries, members of the Council for Mutual Economic Assistance (CMEA) established already 1958 in General Conditions of Delivery of Goods between the Organizations of the Member Countries of the CMEA a system of compulsory arbitration for all disputes arising from contracts governed by these General Conditions between economic organizations of member countries, to the exclusion of the jurisdiction of the courts of law. This system worked satisfactorily mainly with arbitration courts at the Chambers of Commerce in the capitals of the member countries. As a result of this, all eastern countries disposed of experienced practitioners who handled all these cases. For so-called east-west arbitrations the practice developed to settle east/west commercial disputes by arbitration in so-called neutral third countries' as Switzerland, Sweden and Austria, by ad hoc but preferably by institutional arbitration. This situation was also the reason for the setting up of the Vienna International Arbitral Centre (VIAC) 1975. However 'east/west-cases' were also handled by the arbitration courts in other western or also in CMEA-countries. As a result of this personal relationship between practitioners from east and west were very important for the satisfactory handling of such cases. Particularly practitioners from the eastern countries needed to be sure that the confidentiality of open internal discussions would be respected. Here again, common negotiations at UNCITRAL working groups and also ICC A-Congresses were very useful for this purpose. For my part I can say that I was able to establish good personal relationships with all my eastern colleagues and that this has also been very useful for my work. It is interesting to note that most administrators of eastern arbitration courts could continue their work after the fall of the iron curtain.

Good personal contacts between administrators of internationally active arbitral institutions on a worldwide basis have always been very helpful for the daily work. Such institutions may consider themselves as competitors in the market, but there are always cases, where parties considering an arbitration agreement in a contract will prefer to have a possible arbitration at an arbitral institution in a third country and not at the place of business of one of the partners of the contract. In such cases arbitral institutions in the country of one of the parties are often asked for advice. Such advice can be given provided that the addressees know not only the arbitration rules of the proposed arbitral institution but also the persons who handle it then. For this reason I have almost always accepted to serve as an arbitrator under the rules agreed by the relevant parties last not least in order to see how cases are in practice administered by the relevant institutions. In addition, it is not always easy for an arbitral institution to find suitable persons for default appointments of arbitrators who speak the necessary language(s), have knowledge of the applicable law and have possibly knowledge of other particularities of a reference. Also in such situations good personal relationships with the colleagues in other arbitral organizations have always been very helpful.

The key individuals in international arbitration are, of course, the arbitrators. According to all laws and arbitration rules in the world they have to be independent and impartial. Within these limits, they can master-tailor the proceedings according to the requirements of the reference in ad-hoc-arbitrations which are, however, rather rare in international arbitrations. In institutional international arbitrations and in ad-hoc-arbitrations under the UNCITRAL Arbitration Rules, the applicable procedural provisions cover now practically the whole arbitral proceedings. However, the way how the arbitrators apply the applicable rules and how they communicate with the parties or their representatives can still influence the proceedings in a positive or in a negative way. Parties to an arbitration should take this into consideration when they have to agree upon a sole arbitrator. In arbitrations with a panel of three arbitrators it is particularly the presiding arbitrator who has the power to determine the proceeding according to the requirements of the case. It is normally up to the party-appointed arbitrators to agree upon a chairperson who is acceptable for both of them.

To sum up: I hope that in the future many 'Pierre Karrers' will be available as potential arbitrators for international arbitrations.

CHAPTER 24
The Pre-hearing Checklist Protocol: A Tool for Organizing Efficient Arbitration Hearings

*Michael Moser**

§24.01 INTRODUCTION

The most important date in the calendar of an arbitration is the hearing. Months, and sometimes even years, of preparations precede the convening of the hearing. Hundreds and thousands of pages of materials are collated. Witnesses and experts are prepared. Counsel tune their instruments and sharpen their swords.

Often lost in the shuffle in the weeks leading up to the hearing is the simple fact that a smooth and efficient hearing depends on planning and preparation – not just for the legal case but for the hearing itself. Much 'day one' wrangling between counsel over procedural and logistical issues can be avoided if they are addressed and dealt with in a direct and transparent manner well before the hearing begins.

This article offers some practical solutions to dealing with common procedural issues which can be conveniently resolved prior to the hearing. After summarizing some key points for consideration as part of the pre-hearing planning process, the article provides a sample Pre-Hearing Checklist which it is hoped might cover off the most important pre-hearing procedural matters to be resolved in advance of a hearing.

---

* An earlier version of this article appeared in the Journal of International Arbitration. Thanks are due to Mark Tushingham for his assistance.

§24.02 PRE-HEARING PLANNING: KEY POINTS FOR CONSIDERATION

[A] Dates and Venue

The first two points to clarify are the dates and venue of the hearing, both of which may have shifted over time. In the weeks leading up to the hearing, the parties will be in a better position to know whether they will need more or less time than an earlier procedural order may have envisaged. Arbitrators will wish to confirm that the hearing venue has been booked, that breakout rooms have been organized and that the venue is large enough to accommodate the hearing. Now is time to pin these matters down.

[B] Attendees

It is generally desirable to obtain a list of persons who will be attending the hearing. This will include confirmation of legal teams, parties, interpreters, court reporters and whether LiveNote/Transcend or equivalent software is available for the purposes of the hearing transcript. In addition, visas or work permits may be needed for persons to attend the hearing. These matters should be clarified in advance to avoid any last-minute surprises.

[C] Hearing Schedule

The parties will have generally given an estimate of the duration of any hearing at an early stage of the arbitration when the procedural timetable is being fixed. These estimates may have changed after pleadings and evidence has been exchanged. Issues which were once in dispute may no longer be contested. New issues may arise out of the production of documents and witness testimony.

Parties will need to work together to formulate a realistic schedule for the hearing, including the total hearing time to be allocated between each party, the duration of submissions and the duration of cross-examination and re-examination for each witness. If one party has more witnesses than the other party (or if one party requires witness testimony to be interpreted into the language of the arbitration) then a purely equal allocation of hearing time may not be appropriate.

These matters will need to be discussed between counsel and, if necessary, brought to the Tribunal's attention for a ruling. In addition, it will be necessary to obtain an indication of the general sitting hours each day, the number of breaks and the time for lunch. Ultimately, the aim is to develop a daily plan for the hearing even if this may only be indicative. Much will depend on how time will be allocated – and whether a 'chess clock' or some other process will be used. Agreeing a protocol on the allocation of hearing time can be useful.

[D] Pre-hearing Items

Hearing bundles will generally be provided according to the preferences of the parties and the arbitral tribunal (e.g., the sizes and format of hard copies and electronic copies on a USB drive). Items such as a statement of agreed facts, chronologies and a list of dramatis personae can be helpful, especially in factually complex cases. Parties should be encouraged to prepare an agreed list of issues or, if they cannot agree, submit their own individual lists. Finally, deadlines for the exchange of written opening submissions should be fixed. Provision should also be made for the some of the above hard copy items to be given to the court reporters to assist them in their preparation for the hearing.

[E] Order of Play, Witnesses and Sequestration

The 'order of play' of the hearing – the order and length of oral submissions, the order of witnesses and how they will be heard ("live" or via video) are also important matters which need to be clarified before the hearing commences. Sequestration of witnesses should also be addressed.

There is no general consensus on whether, and if so when, sequestration orders should be made in international arbitration to exclude witnesses of fact from the hearing room until they have given their evidence. Different approaches are often taken depending upon the seat of the arbitration and the traditions and expectations of the parties and the arbitral tribunal.

If a sequestration order is made, practical difficulties can sometimes arise if party representatives are also called to give evidence as witnesses of fact. These issues will need to be considered before the hearing and it may be necessary to schedule the testimony of party representatives before the testimony of other witnesses of fact. Again, it may be helpful to agree on a sequestration protocol in this regard well before the hearing convenes.

[F] Interpretation

Witnesses in international arbitration frequently give evidence in a language other than the language of the arbitration. Consideration must therefore be given to the interpretation of their oral testimony into the language of the arbitration. For example, suitably qualified and experienced interpreters will need to be found. Parties will also need to decide which interpretation method to use (e.g., consecutive interpretation, simultaneous interpretation or a hybrid approach).[1]

---

1. See generally ICCA Drafting Sourcebook for Logistical Matters in Procedural Orders (ICCA, The Netherlands, 2015) at 17–18.

[G] Post-hearing Submissions and the Award

The tribunal will wish to know before the hearing whether the parties will want to make oral closing submissions at the end of the scheduled hearing or whether they would prefer to submit post-hearing briefs.

In addition, it will be important for the tribunal to be made aware of any special requirements that may apply regarding the award. These may include timing requirements, signing and notary formalities, whether certified translations will be required and other matters.

§24.03 THE PRE-HEARING CHECKLIST PROTOCOL

One way to ensure that all of above points are well taken care of is to build into the procedural timetable provision for a Pre-Hearing Checklist Protocol. This involves the following:

(1) Preparation of a checklist of items to be considered and addressed by the parties prior to the beginning of the hearing.
(2) Circulation of the checklist to the parties several weeks before the hearing.
(3) The parties are then invited to confer on the various issues and items set out in the checklist and to provide their responses (as in a Redfern Schedule) in reply by a fixed date.
(4) In the event of substantial disagreement between the parties, the Tribunal will then convene a telephone conference with counsel for the parties to resolve outstanding differences well before the hearing.

A sample checklist is set out below.

PRE-HEARING CHECKLIST
FOR THE ORAL HEARING FIXED FOR ___

The Parties are invited to confer on the points listed below, take the actions indicated and provide a status report to the Tribunal on or before _____ . A Pre-hearing procedural telephone conference will be convened, if necessary, on _____ to deal with unresolved matters or other issues that require the Tribunal's intervention.

I. THE HEARING

- The Hearing will take place between [*dates of hearing*] in [*city/country*].
- The venue for the Hearing shall be _____ [or] Parties to advise the venue for the hearing by _____.

[The Tribunal prefers [venue] for reasons of convenience]

- The daily schedule during the Hearing shall be from --- a.m. to --- p.m. and from ---- p.m. until --- p.m. (approximately) with a short break of 15 minutes in each of the morning and afternoon sessions.
- The Parties are requested to agree upon and submit an agreed hearing schedule (indicating the order and timings for the Parties' oral opening submissions, the witness testimony and oral closing submissions) by _____.

[A draft hearing schedule is included as Appendix A]

- The Tribunal invites the Parties to submit a list of attendees at the Hearing (including legal counsel, party representatives and witnesses) by _____.
- How will total hearing time be allocated between the Parties? Do the Parties wish to adopt a formal 'chess clock' or 'guillotine' approach?

[A draft protocol on the allocation of hearing time is included as Appendix B]

- The Parties shall make arrangements for:
  - Hearing room and break-out rooms at the Hearing venue for the Parties and the Tribunal for the entire period of the Hearing;
  - Interpreter(s) for witnesses and/or experts, to the extent necessary;
  - Court reporter(s) (with LiveNote or equivalent and PC terminals for each member of the Tribunal and for the witness/interpreter, as well as the Parties); and
  - Projectors, screens, etc. as required.

II. SCOPE OF THE HEARING

- The scope of hearing shall include: [Respondents' jurisdictional objections / Claimant's claims / Respondent's counterclaims / liability and quantum etc.].

III. ITEMS TO BE PROVIDED BEFORE THE HEARING

- Not later than _____, the Parties shall provide to the Members of the Tribunal the following:
- Agreed Chronology of Principal Facts.
- Agreed List of Issues to be determined by the Tribunal.
- Copies of the Hearing Bundle in A5 double-sided print format, including the following:
  - Evidence Documents in chronological order;
  - Pleadings and Memorials;
  - Witness Statements of Fact (including exhibits);
  - Expert Reports (including exhibits);
  - Procedural Orders;
  - Authorities Relied Upon;
  - Material Party/Party correspondence; and

- Technical documents
- A USB stick containing the Hearing Bundle (as above).
- The Parties shall also provide the court reporter(s) with relevant documents in order to allow them to familiarize themselves with the case.

[The Arbitral Tribunal suggests doing so by ____]

IV. PRE-HEARING WRITTEN SUBMISSIONS

- Pre-hearing Opening Written Submissions shall be exchanged between the Parties and served on the Tribunal on ____ .

V. ORAL OPENING STATEMENTS

- Will there be Opening Statements?
    [The Tribunal suggests that each side present Opening Statements on the first day of the Hearing of no more than two hours for each side. In their Opening Statements, each Party should succinctly explain its case (including its claimed relief) in opposition to the other Party's case and indicate how the oral testimony of the witnesses may support its case or contradict the other Party's case. The Parties are also encouraged to identify which matters are common ground or (if once disputed) which matters are no longer in dispute]
- Do the Parties intend to provide anything in writing to accompany their Oral Opening Statements (for example, outlines, skeletons, summaries, demonstrative exhibits, power point presentations)?
    [As a general principle, neither Party shall present any new documents at the Hearing. However, demonstrative exhibits may be presented by a Party using documents submitted earlier and each shall be affixed with the prefix 'C' for the Claimant and 'R' for the Respondents. If demonstrative exhibits are used by a Party, a hard copy of such exhibit shall be provided by the Party submitting such exhibit to the other Party and to each Member of the Tribunal no later than ____]

VI. WITNESSES

- As a general principle, the procedure for hearing oral witnesses at the Hearing shall be as follows:
    - Factual witnesses should not be examined-in-chief for more than ten minutes, without prior permission from the Tribunal. The Tribunal may limit the examination-in-chief of an expert witness, in further consultation with the Parties.

- The scope of the re-examination shall be limited to matters that have arisen in the cross-examination.
- The Tribunal has the right to examine all witnesses at any time and to interject questions during the examinations by counsel for the Parties. Nonetheless, the Tribunal will endeavor to save its principal questions to a time following that witness' re-examination; and in that event, the Tribunal would seek to ensure that each Party shall have an opportunity to examine a witness on matters arising from questions by the Tribunal.
- The Tribunal shall have complete control over the procedure in relation to any witness giving oral evidence, including the right to recall a witness and the right to limit or deny, on its own motion or at the request of a Party, the right of a Party to conduct any examination-in-chief, cross-examination or re-examination if it appears to the Tribunal that such examination or evidence is unlikely to serve any relevant purpose.

- What are the names of all witnesses and experts appearing? Will all be appearing 'live' at the Hearing? Will any be appearing via video?
- The cross-examining party shall provide an estimate of the time required for cross-examination of each witness and expert in the draft hearing schedule referred to paragraph 4 above.
- What is the scope of the cross-examination of each witness and expert?
- The cross-examining party shall provide an estimate of the time required for cross-examination of each witness and expert by _____.
- Do the Parties foresee sequestration of fact witnesses? If so, to the extent relevant, do the Parties foresee examining Party representatives before other fact witnesses? What sequestration orders should the Tribunal make?
- [A draft sequestration protocol is included as Appendix C]
- Can any of the factual or expert witnesses be usefully heard together (that is, 'witness conferencing')? If so, what is the protocol that is to be adopted?
- Will witnesses give oral evidence in a language other than the language of the arbitration? If so, what arrangements have been made in relation to the interpretation of testimony? Will the testimony be interpreted consecutively, simultaneously, or will a hybrid approach be adopted?

VII. AT THE HEARING LOGISTICS

- The Parties shall arrange for access to an assistant throughout the Hearing to deal with problems with projectors, microphones, photocopying and other matters.
- The Parties shall arrange for coffee and tea service during the Hearing breaks.
- The Parties shall provide at the Hearing:
  - Four full copies (that is, one for each member of the Arbitral Tribunal, as well as one clean witness set) in A5 format of the Hearing Bundle; and
  - Six full copies (that is, one for each member of the Tribunal, one for the witness, and two for the opposing side) of cross-examination bundles

containing the documents (which must be from the documents already filed) which counsel intends to use in his/her cross examination of a particular witness.

VIII. CLOSING STATEMENTS

- Will the Parties wish to make oral Closing Statements at the end of the Hearing?

IX. POST-HEARING BRIEFS

- Further directions in respect of Post-hearing Briefs will be made in consultation with the Parties at the close of the Hearing.

X. AWARD(S)

- Are there any formal or timing requirements for the issuance of the Award?

§24.04 CONCLUSION

The Pre-Hearing Checklist can provide arbitrators with a useful tool for ensuring that important procedural issues are addressed well in advance of the substantive hearing. Of course, the specific contents of the checklist can be tailored to the needs of each case as many items could be added (or deleted from) the sample set out above. But by adopting the approach recommended in this article, both the tribunal and the parties will be able to save valuable time at the inception of the hearing without being diverted by procedural 'loose ends'.

Chapter 24: The Pre-hearing Checklist Protocol

APPENDIX A: DRAFT HEARING SCHEDULE

	Day 1	Day 2	Day 3	Day 4	Day 5
AM	Claimant's Opening (2.5 hours)	Claimant's Witness 1	Claimant's Witness 3	Respondent's Witness 2	Witness Conference (Legal Experts)
PM	Respondent's Opening (2.5 hours)	Claimant's Witness 2	Respondent's Witness 1	Respondent's Witness 3	

	Day 6	Day 7
AM	Witness Conference (Quantum Experts)	Claimant's Closing (2.5 hours)
PM		Respondent'sClosing (2.5 hours)

APPENDIX B: DRAFT HEARING TIME PROTOCOL[2]

(1) [Option 1] Each Party shall have an equal amount of time to present its case. [Option 2] The amount of time allocated to each Party during the oral hearing shall be determined by the Tribunal based upon the relevant factors, including the number of witnesses for each side and the interpretation of the testimony of witnesses into the language of the arbitration.

(2) Unless otherwise directed by the Tribunal, time shall be deducted from a Party's total allocated hearing time as a result of that Party:
   (a) Making oral submissions (including opening and closing statements);
   (b) Examining a witness (irrespective of who proposed the witness, but subject to adjustment upon application in the event of insistent unresponsiveness or translation delays);
   (c) Making an objection which ultimately proves unjustified (thus, an unsuccessful objection is generally to be charged against the Party who made it, and a successful objection against the Party who resisted it);
   (d) Arriving late; and
   (e) Setting up displays while the Tribunal is sitting.

(3) Unless otherwise directed by the Tribunal, time spent interpreting the testimony of a witness into the language of the arbitration shall be deducted from the total hearing time of the Party who called the witness to give evidence.

(4) Unless otherwise directed by the Tribunal, time shall be deducted equally from all Parties' remaining time as a result of:
   (a) Interventions by the Tribunal lasting more than 10 minutes;

---

2. This protocol is adapted from the *ICCA Drafting Sourcebook for Logistical Matters in Procedural Orders* (ICCA, The Netherlands, 2015) at 13 (available at < http://www.arbitration-icca.org/media/3/14314586363730/icca_reports_2_final.pdf >).

(b) A procedural application;
(c) Caucuses between the Parties while the Tribunal is sitting; and
(d) Time incurred through no fault of the Parties.
(5) Each Party shall nominate a timekeeper to keep a daily record of the time taken by each Party. The timekeepers shall communicate their records to the Tribunal Secretary at the end of each hearing day. The Tribunal Secretary shall also keep a daily record of the time taken by each party and communicate this record to the Parties' timekeepers.
(6) In the event of a dispute between the time records of the Parties' timekeepers and the time records of the Tribunal Secretary, the Tribunal Secretary's time record shall be final.
(7) If the Tribunal Secretary is not present on a hearing day, the Parties' timekeepers shall communicate their records to the Tribunal Secretary on the next hearing day. Any disagreement shall be dealt with outside sitting hours wherever possible and referred to the Tribunal only as a last resort.

APPENDIX C: DRAFT SEQUESTRATION PROTOCOL[3]

(1) The Tribunal hereby orders that all witnesses of fact shall be sequestered. Such witnesses shall have no access to any fact witness testimony given by other witnesses testifying in the proceedings until after such witness has provided his or her own oral testimony.
(2) For the avoidance of doubt, the Tribunal's sequestration order means that:
   (a) Witnesses of fact must not have access to any transcript, live audio feed or recording of the testimony given by witnesses of fact testifying in these proceedings until after the witness of fact has provided his or her own oral testimony; and
   (b) Witnesses of fact must not discuss any testimony, any part of the transcript, any live audio feed or any recording of the hearing, with any other witness of fact in these proceedings until after the witness has provided his or her own oral testimony.
(3) Counsel for each party shall use their best efforts to ensure compliance with this sequestration order and shall inform the fact witnesses for its respective clients about the terms of this ruling and the need to fully respect the terms of this ruling.
(4) The terms of this ruling shall apply equally to any fact witness who is also a party representative of either party. In general, party representatives shall give evidence before other witnesses of fact.
(5) The terms of this ruling do not apply to opening statements by either Party, or to any other aspect of the hearing that does not involve fact witness testimony.

---

3. I am grateful to Gary Born of Wilmer Hale for permission to reproduce this Draft Protocol.

CHAPTER 25

About Procedural Soft Law, the IBA Guidelines on Party Representation and the Future of Arbitration

Alexis Mourre[*]

Arbitration is fundamentally the exercise of a human freedom. And because it rests so intensely on party autonomy, it has developed a culture that is instinctively adverse to regulation. Any attempt to regulate provokes the fear that the inherent flexibility of this private means of resolving disputes will be affected, that the ability of parties and arbitrators to agree on the best suited rules for each single case will be hampered, and that the arbitral procedure will degenerate in the use of boilerplate, standard documents, each of which will be ill-adapted to the particular needs of each single case.

It could certainly be conceived that certain human activities entirely dispense with any form of regulation or legislation, other than a limited number of principles of natural law such as good faith and *pacta sunt servanda*. However, as soon as any human activity touches upon the general or public interest, the situation changes entirely. The banking sector is a useful comparison. It has undergone, in the 1980s and 1990s, a huge process of deregulation that has arguably been one of the causes of the 2008 financial crisis. But no one has ever suggested that the sector could or should be unregulated. In fact, there is no such thing as an "unregulated bank". Nor could there be. Banks are institutions to which the government has granted the power to create money. Obviously, no government would grant anyone – least of all a profit-seeking company – the power to create as much money as it wants without any rules or controls. And if any such completely insane thing would happen, the immediate result would be the collapse of the entire banking system. That was perfectly understood by Walter Bagehot almost 150 years ago: "*the peculiar essence of our financial system is an*

---

[*] The author thanks Julie Esquenazi, Attorney at Law, for her valuable help in researching this topic and the drafting of this paper. This paper was drafted in May 2006.

unprecedented trust between man and man: and when that trust is weakened by hidden causes, a small accident may greatly hurt it, and a great accident for a moment may almost destroy it".[1]

The same applies to arbitration. Exactly as the financial system, the system of arbitration rests on the trust of the public. While banks have privatized monetary creation, arbitration is the privatization of another important sovereign function: the administration of justice. And exactly like the banking system needs to be seen as sound and reliable in its functions of collecting savings and lending money to economic actors, for arbitration to survive, it must be seen by its stakeholders as a fair, reliable, and predicable system of justice. In finance, lack of trust will provoke a run on deposits, and ultimately a krach. Likewise, if trust in arbitration disappears, parties will turn to other ways of resolving their disputes, States will tighten their controls, so as to make it useless, and arbitration will ultimately disappear.

Something close to a krach is happening under our eyes in investor-State arbitration. The backlash against investment arbitration was certainly predictable. It is essentially the byproduct of a change in paradigm in the world economy, with the end of the powerful trend towards ever more globalization as a driver for the development of exchanges, the return of nationalism and isolationism on the global stage, and the resulting increasing opposition to free trade agreements. It is also the result of our own failure to communicate, and we have also seen how political propaganda can prevail over technical arguments that are generally carefully framed and reasonable, but also at times arrogant and complacent. Be it as it may, the question is whether the same backlash can happen to International Commercial arbitration. The answer depends on whether the arbitration community will be able to ensure that arbitration continues to enjoy the trust of the public, of States and of judges as a fair, legitimate and efficient means of resolving international disputes. This is by no means a given, in a world that has become more complex than it ever was, where communications are instantaneous, and the public's watch upon arbitration is decupled by the increased sensitivity to issues of ethics, transparency and accountability.

Self-regulation, from that perspective, is not part of the problem. It is an indispensable part of the solution. And it would be meaningless if it failed to address the question of what ethical standards and rules apply to counsel and to arbitrators. While, however, the ethics of arbitrators is already the subject matter of meaningful regulation, this is not the case for counsel. Arbitrators are subject to disclosure duties that are defined and enforced based on texts such as the IBA Guidelines on conflicts on interest in arbitration and the recent ICC Guidance Note on conflicts of interest (which is incorporated in the ICC Note to Parties and Arbitral Tribunals). Counsel conduct, to the contrary, was entirely unregulated at the transnational level until when the matter was taken up by the IBA in 2008,[2] and addressed by Doak Bishop in his opening lecture

---

1. Walter Bagehot, *Lombard Street: A Description of the Money Market* (1873).
2. In 2008, the IBA Arbitration Committee formed a Task Force on Counsel Ethics in International Arbitration "to focus on issues of counsel conduct and party representation in international arbitration that are subject to, or informed by, diverse and potentially conflicting rules and norms" (*See* the Guidelines Preamble).

Chapter 25: About Procedural Soft Law, the IBA Guidelines

at the ICCA congress in Rio.[3] In 2014, after a remarkably open and transparent consultation process, the IBA finally adopted the IBA Guidelines on Party Representation. This initiative was timely, and it certainly helped to prevent initiatives, such as that of the CCBE,[4] which would have been fundamentally at odds with fundamental principles of arbitration as a private and transnational justice and would have ended up in imposing on arbitration rules drawn from court procedures.[5]

Codification of arbitration law is a healthy phenomenon. It is an evolution towards more predictability and more consistency of a global system of justice that cannot be left to local idiosyncrasies, and which needs to reach a common framework that is acceptable to all players. The development of soft law is an element of objectivation of arbitration that is such as to increase the confidence in, and the acceptability of, the process.

The development of soft normativity in arbitration is also the expression of the strength of what Gabrielle Kaufmann-Kohler calls the epistemic arbitration community, a community that shares the same interests and expertise.[6] The epistemic community is multifaceted: it is composed of the legal profession, of scholars, of arbitral institutions and professional organizations. As Gabrielle Kaufmann-Kohler puts it: *"through a process of intellectual cross-fertilization, these actors play a dominant role in shaping the transnational consensus on arbitration law and practice"*.[7] The development of soft law in arbitration illustrates the vitality of the epistemic community and the cross-fertilization between its different components, practitioners, arbitral institutions and professional organizations. And this is a particularly fertile, dynamic and positive process, because it combines compilation of existing practices and innovation by the elaboration of new rules. This is how arbitration progresses and evolves.

Two frequently heard arguments against the development of soft law in arbitration are its non-democratic nature, and the fact that it would be incompatible with independent thinking.

What, however, is a "democratic" rule, as opposed to the purportedly "undemocratic" soft law? The answer can only be a statute adopted by Parliament, or a rule passed by a democratically elected government. The criticism of soft law is therefore bound to fall into one of the following two extreme propositions: ethics in arbitration should either be regulated by Statute or remain entirely unregulated. A middle ground

---

3. Doak Bishop, *Adocacy and Ethics in International Arbitration: Ethics in International Arbitration* in Albert Jan van den Berg (ed.) Arbitration Advocacy in Changing Times, ICCA Congress Series 2010, pp. 383–390.
4. The CCBE (*Conseil Consultatif des Barreaux Européens*) Code of Conduct was originally adopted at the Council of Bars and Law Societies in Europe (CCBE), Plenary Session on Oct. 28, 1998. It was subsequently amended in 1998, 2002 and 2006.
5. Article 4.5 of the draft CCBE Code of Conduct provided that "the rules governing a lawyer's relations with the courts apply also to the lawyer's relations with arbitrators". The full text of the Code of Conduct can be accessed at: http://www.ccbe.eu/fileadmin/user_upload/NTCdocument/EN_CCBE_CoCpdf1_1382973057.pdf.
6. Gabrielle Kauffman-Kohler, *Soft Law in International Arbitration: Codification and Normativity*, 1 J. Int'l Disp. Settlement (2010), pp. 283–299, at 295.
7. Ibid.

consists in criticizing the process that is followed to elaborate arbitration soft law rather than soft law itself. It is accordingly suggested that soft law is elaborated behind closed doors by individuals who have no legitimacy to elevate themselves as legislators for the entire arbitration community. These individuals, to employ the words of Toby Landau, would be the new clergy of arbitration.[8]

This idea of a lack of legitimacy has been presented in its most polemic form by Felix Dasser in an article against the Guidelines on Party Representation published by the Swiss Arbitration Association.[9] In describing the process of discussion and adoption of the IBA Guidelines within the IBA, he writes that *"the opinion of the IBA Arbitration Committee members at large was not really welcome"*, and that *"many, if not most, members of the Arbitration Committee at large realized what was cooking only after the IBA Guidelines had been published in their name"*, to then conclude that *"the IBA Guidelines were drafted by a small circle within the IBA with the membership at large having no real say in the drafting"*.[10] This description of the process that was followed by the IBA is of course entirely inaccurate. The suggestion of a subversion of the IBA by a small, secretive leadership to the detriment of its membership at large is pure fantasy. There were not one, but two, public consultations on the draft IBA Guidelines, which were public rather than limited to the 2,700 members of the arbitration committee. In addition, the Guidelines were adopted by the IBA Council, which is composed of authorized representatives of more than 190 professional bars spanning 160 different jurisdictions. This hardly corresponds to a secret complot.

This, however, begs a more general and interesting question on the legitimacy of rule-making by professional bodies. Each institution certainly has its own internal politics, which can influence its internal dynamics. Membership can vary widely from one institution to another. But at the end of the day, legitimacy essentially rests on three factors: experience, inclusiveness and internationality.

It is first of all necessary that soft law be elaborated by an organization with sufficient representativity and experience in rule making. The IBA, of course, has this kind of experience, but others do as well, such as ICCA or the Chartered Institute. Second, the process has to be inclusive, in the sense that the arbitral community needs to be consulted as widely as possible. Third, any rule-making exercise needs to reflect the wide cultural diversity of the arbitral community, so that the final product will not be perceived as an expression of a particular legal culture as opposed to another.

This particular point has given rise to debate as far as the Party Representation Guidelines are concerned, some having suggested that it was essentially an import from the Anglo-Saxon legal culture. This criticism is, I believe, misconceived.

To say that soft law needs to reflect cultural diversity does not in fact mean that it should be a patchwork of measures coming in equal measure from the civil law and

---

8. Lecture by Toby Landau at the opening of the MIDS session in September 2014 (which can be accessed at: http://www.mids.ch/the-program/media-publications/lectures/academic-year-2014-2015/lecture-landau-2014.html).
9. Felix Dasser, *A Critical Analysis of the Guidelines on Party Representation* in D. Favalli (ed.) The Sense and Non-Sense of Guidelines, Rules and Other Para-regulatory Texts in International Arbitration, ASA Special Series No. 37, 2015, pp. 33–62.
10. *Ibid*, pp. 35–36.

the common law culture, or – even worse – a superposition of civil law and common law recipes. Such a sandwich would be highly difficult to digest, and it would be of little use and only add to the complexity of arbitration. What neutrality means is something else: it means that the process leading to the adoption of a given set of rules needs to have been open, neutral, and inclusive, and that the final work product is therefore acceptable by both civil lawyers and common lawyers, even though it may ultimately draw more from one side than from the other.

And why should we not, in achieving this result, draw particular inspiration from one legal culture, if what we learn from it is valuable? After all, the duty to arbitrate in good faith was advocated in 2001 by Johnny Veeder, an English Barrister.[11] Should we for that reason reject the principle as alien to arbitration? The idea that counsel has duties not only to its client, but also to the court, is also an Anglo-Saxon idea. Should it be rejected because of that? The duty of candor, the idea that lawyers should not misrepresent the truth to the judge, is again an idea that comes from the Anglo-Saxon culture, a great culture that has given us the Magna Carta and due process of law. Do these great principles cease, because they come from the Anglo-Saxon culture, from being highly civilized ideas that will help the culture of dispute resolution progress in the right direction? When we, civil lawyers, made the argument that U.S. style discovery is inefficient and ill-adapted to arbitration, we were right, and we essentially prevailed. The same can be said for depositions. Why should we not be able to accept that the oldest legal tradition in the world has something good to tell us?

Michael Schneider has embarked in a more subtle attack against soft law, an attack that is dangerous because it uses the powerful weapon of humor. He published, in the Liber Amicorum to Serge Lazareff, an article which title was *"The Essential Guidelines for the Preparation of Guidelines, Directives, Notes, Protocols, and Other Methods Intended to Help International Arbitration Practitioners to Avoid the Need for Independent Thinking and to Promote the Transformation of Errors into Best Practices"*.[12] Any good politician knows the golden rule: *"mettons les rieurs de notre côté"*. Serge Larareff also applied it when he compared soft law to a disease, the *"regulatory pruritus"* – the *prurit règlementaire* –.[13] The underlying idea behind the humor has been well expressed by Matthieu de Boisséson in a recent article:[14] arbitration is not a technique; it not a science; it is not a professional practice that should be regulated. Arbitration is an art, and because it is an art, any form of rules, guidance or guidelines will prejudice the inherentcreativity of the artist-arbitrator.

Such a proposition would of course seem odd in any service industry other than arbitration. What should we think of a banker pretending that, because he or she is an

---

11. V.V. Veeder Q.C., "The 2001 Goff Lecture: The Lawyer's Duty to Arbitrate in Good Faith" 18 Arb. Int'l (2002), pp. 431–451.
12. Michael Schneider, *"The Essential Guidelines for the Preparation of Guidelines, Directives, Notes, Protocols, and Other Methods Intended to Help International Arbitration Practitioners to Avoid the Need for Independent Thinking and to Promote the Transformation of Errors into Best Practices" in* Laurent Lévy and Yves Derains (dir.), *Liber Amicorum en l'honneur de Serge Lazareff*, Pedone 2011, 563–567.
13. Serge Lazareff, "Avant Propos: Le bloc note de Serge Lazareff" in Alexis Mourre (dir.) Les cahiers de l'arbitrage Volume III (2006), pp. 5–15, at 9.
14. Mathieu de Boisséson, "La 'Soft Law' dans l'arbitrage", 3 Paris J. Int'l Arb. (2014), pp. 519–523.

artist – and after all, why should finance not be an art as much as arbitration? – he or she should be left undisturbed, unregulated, free to develop and sell those sophisticated financial products that have led the world economy to the brink of collapse in 2008? And surely, when a party selects an arbitrator, it does not look for an artist, but for a practitioner that will conduct a fair, legitimate and predictable process of law.

Does soft law reduce independent thinking, as posited by Michael Schneider? His fear is that soft law, by progressively acquiring a certain degree of normativity, will end up by limiting the liberty of the arbitrator.[15] What is at stake here is therefore not soft law in itself, but the soft normativity that it may acquire. It can be responded to that, however, that the starting point remains that notes and guidelines do not have normative value, or at least that they do not have full normative value.[16] They are no more than tools that arbitrators and parties – precisely by exercising their liberty – may decide to use or not.

There has been, in this regard, some level of discussion concerning the first IBA Party Representation guideline. That guideline provides that: *"The Guidelines shall apply where and to the extent that the Parties have so agreed, or the Arbitral Tribunal, after consultation with the Parties, wishes to rely upon them after having determined that it has the authority to rule on matters of Party representation to ensure the integrity and fairness of the arbitral proceedings"*.[17] This particular provision has sometimes been interpreted as imposing the Guidelines on the parties irrespective of their choice.[18] This is incorrect. What it in fact says is that the Guidelines will apply if the parties so chose, or if the arbitral tribunal decides that there is some other basis for them to apply. That other basis cannot be the Guidelines themselves, for they are not mandatory. But the Tribunal may well find, for reasons extraneous to the Guidelines, that it has inherent powers to deal with issues of counsel conduct. In that case, the Tribunal may resort to the Guidelines. This does not in any manner alter the non-binding nature of the Guidelines.

It may well be that guidelines may acquire, with time, some level of normativity. What that means is that, because of the general recognition that a given set of rules enjoys, parties and arbitrators will apply them because they feel that they are best practices and will therefore feel compelled to apply them. This, arguably, is the case of the IBA Rules on the Taking of Evidence, a set of rules that is now almost universally endorsed by parties and arbitrators. Equally, the IBA Guidelines on Conflicts of Interest are generally referred to by arbitrators in making their disclosures, and by parties, institutions and even national courts, in dealing with challenges. Even if the parties do not expressly make reference to them in their agreement, they have become standard practice.

In a decision of March 22, 2008, the Swiss Federal Court defined as follows the soft normativity of the Guidelines on Conflicts of Interests: *"Such Guidelines do not*

---

15. Michael E. Schneider, *supra* p. 567.
16. Gabrielle Kauffman-Kohler, *supra* at 285.
17. *See* Guideline 1 of the IBA Guidelines on Party Representation, the text of which can be accessed at: http://www.ibanet.org/Publications/publications_IBA_guides_and_free_materials.aspx.
18. Felix Dasser, *supra* at 38.

have the force of law; they are nonetheless a valuable tool, capable of contributing to harmonize and unify the standards applied in the field of international arbitration to conflicts of interest issues, and one that will undoubtedly exert influence on the practice of arbitral institutions and courts. These Guidelines state general principles".[19] This proposition also applies to the IBA Rules on the Taking of Evidence, with the difference that arbitral institutions and national courts apply the IBA Guidelines on Conflicts of Interest in dealing with challenges and setting aside actions, while the IBA Rules on the Taking of Evidence are applied by arbitrators in the conduct of the arbitration. It is therefore the arbitral tribunal that will judge whether the IBA Rules can be applied in absence of an express choice of the parties. The Arbitral Tribunal's freedom to apply soft law rules remains unaltered.

Another criticism against soft law lies in the risk that, because of the multiplication of guidelines and other soft law rules, the arbitral process will somewhat become less flexible. As Gabrielle Kauffmann-Kohler observed: *"even though the law may be soft, flexibility is traded with predictability"*.[20] It is however doubtful that it is really so. To the contrary, the existence of soft law instruments is an element of additional flexibility for arbitral tribunals and parties. It is in fact extremely difficult for an arbitral tribunal, in front of a disagreement between parties from different legal cultures, to invent a solution out of the blue. The risk of seeming arbitrary is always there.

In absence of a soft law instrument, the parties will therefore argue on the basis of the procedural law in force at the seat of the arbitration, or they will seek to apply their own national procedural rules. As Rusty Park rightly said in his Freshfields lecture of 2002: *"the benefits of arbitrator discretion are overrated; flexibility is not an unalloyed good, and arbitration malleability often comes at an unjustifiable cost"*.[21] Parties expect a measure of ordered procedure as an element of equal treatment and due process, and most of the times, they do not welcome arbitrators behaving as some sort of absolute king, imposing rules of its own making that they did not expect. Being able to resort to pre-established soft law rules that the arbitral tribunal will be free to adapt to the specificities of each case is a much more satisfactory solution.

Another frequently heard criticism is that rules and guidelines would be disruptive because they risk provoking skirmishes and unnecessary procedural incidents.[22] As far as the IBA Party Representation Guidelines are concerned, it has been said that counsel willing to disrupt the arbitration would instrumentally accuse the other of having misbehaved, for the sole purpose of distracting its opponent party from the preparation of the case.[23] The dishonest counsel would rely on the Guidelines to harass its honest opponent. It has also been said that the very existence of a set of rules such

---

19. Decision of the Swiss Federal Court of Mar. 22, 2008, 26 ASA Bull. 565 (2008).
20. Gabrielle Kauffman-Kohler, *supra* at 298.
21. William W. Park, "The 2002 Freshfields Lecture – Arbitration's Protean Nature: The Value of Rules and the Risks of Discretion", 19 Arb. Int'l 279 (2003), at 283.
22. *See* Toby Landau's Lecture, *supra*.
23. Michael E. Schneider, "President's Message Yet Another Opportunity to Waste Time and Money on Procedural Skirmishes: The IBA Guidelines on Party Representation", 31(3) ASA Bull. (2013), pp. 497–500.

as the IBA Rules on the Taking of Evidence of the IBA Guidelines on Conflicts could give rise to challenges whenever such rules are not applied.[24]

As far as the first of these two arguments is concerned, there is no evidence that the adoption of guidelines or soft law rules has resulted in more incidents in the arbitral proceedings. The proposition is in fact counter-intuitive, for it would make much more sense to believe that the *absence* of transnational rules setting a common ground between the parties is a source of unnecessary conflicts. As to the second proposition, it is rather circular, for to suppose that an award could be challenged because procedural rules were not applied or misapplied supposes that such rules have acquired normative value and have in fact ceased to be soft law. There is no known example of a court having set aside an award because the arbitral tribunal failed to properly apply soft law.

Toby Landau has developed another line of criticism against soft law in occasion of his MIDS lecture in 2014: the harmonization of practices and their codification in soft law instruments would lead to a one size fits all approach, to the detriment of diversity. And by going into unnecessary details, soft law would freeze arbitration law by codifying it at the level of micromanagement.[25]

These arguments have some force. Inevitably, with the elaboration of soft law, comes a convergence in practices that favors the emergence of common responses to common problems. While this may be to the detriment of the diversity of legal practices, it is to the advantage of predictability. But again, the proper question is: are we not overrating diversity? Is there real value in each party playing by different rules?

Soft law has the advantage of answering that question by establishing a common playing field. And, by so doing, it is an element of appeasement and simplification, for in absence of uniform rules, any procedural disagreement will inevitably be resolved by resorting to a rule that is closer to one party, to the dissatisfaction of the other. In absence of a transnational soft law rule, parties would spend a huge amount of time arguing, at times in an unnecessary bitter way, about procedural issues that may not even arise if the tribunal is able to place both parties on the same ground at the outset by referring to an accepted common set of rules.

The questions that are addressed by the IBA Rules on the Taking of Evidence and by the IBA Guidelines on Party Representation are not questions of micromanagement.[26] These are important questions, each of which can derail an arbitration if they are not properly dealt with. And in absence of pre-established rules, they cannot be properly be dealt with in a consistent manner by thousands of tribunals across the globe, composed of arbitrators of different cultures and immensely diverse experience and background.

The absence of transnational rules is a cause for inconsistencies, and it is also a source of imbalances between the parties. Party equality is a cornerstone of international arbitration. But are the parties really placed on an equal foot if one of them knows the unwritten rules of the game, while the other does not? Is there real party

---

24. Gerald Philipps, "Is Creeping Legalism Infecting Arbitration?" 58 Disp. Res. J. (2003), pp. 37–42.
25. Toby Landau's MIDS Lecture, 2014. *supra*.
26. *ibidem*

equality if one of the parties knows what the expectations of the tribunal are while the other ignores them? Written rules ensure transparency and equality. They allow counsels who are not as versed as others in the intricacies of arbitration to know what is expected from them and how the other party will behave.

Most of the criticism against procedural soft law in arbitration is directed against the IBA Party Representation Guidelines, and it is fair to address these specifically.

The question that the Guidelines address is a fundamental one: what are the rules applying to counsel in an arbitration seeking to discharge its duty to achieve procedural fairness towards the arbitral tribunal and the other party? Is it conceivable that arbitration as a global system of international justice has no clear answer to that question? Leaving the answer to professional bar rules is highly problematic for a number of reasons. First, the delays and complications that inevitably arise from parallel proceedings before arbitral tribunals and professional bodies. Second, the differences between rules applying to different counsel in the arbitration. And, finally, because professional bar rules are ill-adapted to arbitration. Only transnational rules adapted to the practice of international arbitration can answer these questions.

It has in this regard been said that the Guidelines would overstep the prerogatives of professional bars and circumvent public policy rules applying to registered lawyers. There is however a fundamental difference between the role that is ascribed to the arbitral tribunal by the Party Representation Guidelines and that of a Bar council. The IBA Party Representation Guidelines are strictly limited to matters pertaining to the conduct of the procedure. They do not include anything, for example, about attorney's fees or attorney-client relationship. Every single issue that is dealt with in the Guidelines pertains to the preservation of the integrity and fairness of the proceedings.

As such, these issues can and should be dealt with by arbitral tribunals, and that is by no means inconsistent with the functions that are reserved to professional bars. The IBA Party Representation Guidelines can also protect counsels against local bar rules that may be at odds with arbitration practice. For example, in 2008, an advocate was pursued before the Paris Bar Council for having prepared a witness in an arbitration procedure, and the French arbitration community had to explain that this was indeed the practice in international arbitration.[27] Had the Guidelines been available then, such a disciplinary procedure might not have been initiated.

The starting point is that arbitral tribunals have the power to deal with matters of counsel conduct, insofar as measures are necessary to ensure the integrity of the arbitral proceedings. The ICSID Arbitral Tribunal in *Hvratska* was right in considering that "*as a judicial formation governed by public international law, the Tribunal has an inherent power to take measures to preserve the integrity of its proceedings*", which entails the power to exclude a newly introduced counsel from a hearing when his representation of a party would create a situation of conflict of interest such as to

---

27. Following this disciplinary procedure, the Paris Bar Council adopted a resolution on Feb. 26, 2008 which allowed French counsels to prepare a witness in international arbitration procedures (*Bulletin du Barreau de Paris*, 4 mars 2008, n°9).

imperil the constitution of the tribunal.[28] We do not see any reason, though, why the same proposition should not be true in commercial arbitration. Depriving the arbitral tribunal of such powers would have highly undesirable consequences. The Swiss Arbitration Association (ASA) has, in April 2014, adopted a position in this regard and decided that *"It is not the role of arbitrators to enforce standards and ethical rules of professional conduct. No responsibility for the enforcement of such standards should be placed on the arbitrator".*[29] Such a proposition would however not only prevent a tribunal from preserving the integrity of the tribunal in case of the late introduction of counsel creating a conflict of interests, but also from taking any measure dealing with a professional misconduct that is such as delaying or obstructing the arbitration.

The Swiss Arbitration Association has also proposed to create an international arbitration ethical bar council.[30] Two observations need to be made in this respect. First, the legitimacy of such a body would be doubtful for arbitration does not have an organized bar. Even we imagined that the most relevant arbitration professional bodies, such as the IBA and ICCA, as well as the main global arbitral institutions, would sign up to it – which is at best doubtful –, it would still not have the necessary legitimacy to regulate counsel conduct for many counsel acting in international arbitrations would not be members of such bodies and many international arbitrations would not be conducted under the rules of the institutions having signed up to the ASA initiative. Second, even assuming that it could have the necessary legitimacy, the creation of such a body would be undesirable anyway, for it would add to the complexity and uncertainties of the current situation by adding a third layer of jurisdiction, on top of the arbitral tribunal itself and local bars. The risk of delays and concurrent proceedings would therefore be multiplied.

A better solution is the adoption by arbitration institutions of rules addressing counsel conduct. This is what the London Court of International Arbitration (LCIA) has done.[31] The risk, however, is that this will lead to the multiplication of different standards, which is not desirable. In addition, any set of rules dealing with these issues needs, in order to preserve legal certainty, to have a sufficient level of specificity. Institutions can also endorse the IBA Guidelines or incorporate them into their rules. This is what the Australian Centre for International Commercial Arbitration (ACICA)

---

28. As in the Hvratska case. *See Hrvatska Elektroprivreda DD v. The Republic of Slovenia* (ICSID Case No. ARB/05/24), Order Concerning the Participation of Counsel of May 6, 2008.
29. The ASA position on the IBA Guidelines on Party Representation in International Arbitration can be accessed at: http://www.arbitration-ch.org/pages/en/publications/conference-and-position-papers/index.html.
30. ASA President's Message, *Counsel Ethics in International Arbitration—Could one Take Things a Step Further*, September 2014. The full text can be accessed at http://www.arbitration-ch.org/pages/en/asa/asa-president-messages/index.html.
31. The new LCIA Arbitration Rules, which entered into force on Oct. 1, 2014, have included provisions regulating counsels' conduct in the arbitration procedure. *See* Annex to the LCIA Rules – Guidelines for the Parties' Legal Representatives, which can be accessed at www.lcia.org.

has done in its 2016 Rules, by including a provision requiring each party to use its best endeavors to ensure that its legal representatives will comply with the Guidelines.[32]

The latter solution is preferable in order to address the difficulties pertaining to the regulation of counsel conduct in international arbitration is the adoption of universally recognized soft law rules. The IBA Guidelines on Party Representation will achieve that purpose once arbitral practice will have endorsed them with sufficient consistency. A recent Kluwer survey shows that 11.1% of respondents declare that they use the Party Representation Guidelines regularly, and 36.5% occasionally,[33] which is a promising start.

The IBA Guidelines on Party Representation will serve yet another purpose, which is purely educational. There are many jurisdictions across the globe where there is not yet a structured arbitration bar, where newcomers are knocking at the door of arbitration, new arbitral institutions are being created, and where an arbitral community will soon emerge. By disseminating the Guidelines in these countries, the idea will progress that arbitration has rules of its own, and that counsel have a series of duties that are different from those applicable before a local court.

As to the merits, the ASA acknowledges that *"most of the Guidelines are not objectionable"*.[34] Criticism focuses on two specific provisions of the Guidelines, however.

The first are those provisions which direct a party representative to inform its client of the need to preserve documents or to comply with an order to produce (Guidelines 12–17). The ASA sees those provisions as an inappropriate *"interference with attorney-client privilege"*, because they would imply for the Arbitral Tribunal to look into the relationship between counsel and its client.[35] The Guidelines, however, expressly reserves attorney-client privilege.[36] But this is not the fundamental question: the fundamental aim of the Guidelines is of course not to have arbitrators inquire into the correspondence between counsel and its client. The aim is different: it is to make sure that a party is made aware by its counsel of certain duties that are incumbent upon it in order to comply with the Tribunal's orders and directions. Because many counsels would be reluctant to educate their clients to what may be perceived by them as measures adverse to their interests, the Guidelines will help them by providing a basis for compliance with the Tribunal's orders.

---

32. *See* Rule 8.2 of the ACICA 2016 Rules: "Each party shall use its best endeavours to ensure that its legal representatives comply with the International Bar Association Guidelines on Party Representation in International Arbitration in the current version at the commencement of the arbitration".
33. Results of the Survey on the Use of Soft Law Instruments in International Arbitration (conducted between February and March 2014). The Survey aimed at exploring the use of different instruments: the IBA Rules on the Taking of Evidence, the IBA Guidelines on Conflict of Interest, the IBA Guidelines on Party Representation, the UNIDROIT Principles for International Commercial Contracts, Lex Mercatoria, and CIArb Guidelines and Protocols. The results of the survey are available at: http://kluwerarbitrationblog.com/2014/06/06/results-of-thesurvey-on-the-use-of-soft-law-instruments-in-internationalarbitration.
34. *See* the ASA position on the IBA Guidelines on Party Representation in International Arbitration, *supra.*, at ¶ 4.
35. *Ibid*, at ¶ 4.1.
36. Guideline 15 of the IBA Guidelines on Party Representation.

The other provision that was harshly criticized by the ASA is Guideline 12, relating to the preservation of documents. The ASA considers that this leads to *"expand the duties of the parties concerning document production beyond the scope of the IBA Rules on evidence"*.[37] Guideline 12, however, only invites counsel to inform its client of the need, once an arbitration has started, and insofar as it is likely to involve document production, to preserve documents that may be relevant and material. It does not and cannot have any effect on the scope of document production orders made under the IBA Rules on Evidence.

Arbitration is not an art. It is an industry that fulfills one of the most important functions that one could imagine in a society. That of rendering justice. It plays a vital role in international trade, resolving disputes involving billions of Dollars and strategic interests of States and State entities around the globe. The ICC alone administers cases involving amounts in dispute on top of USD 280 billion. Arbitration is as such under public scrutiny as it never was in the past. It is simply inconceivable that the different aspects of the arbitral procedure – disclosures, counsel conduct, the taking of evidence are only some of these aspects – remain unregulated. Rules can come from institutions, but there is limit to what institutions can regulate. There is therefore a vacuum that can either be filled by soft law or by States. The former proposition is of course much preferable. Soft law has the immense advantage of flexibility. It is well adapted, because it emanates from the arbitration community, to the special needs of the arbitral procedure. It is also much simpler than regulation emanated by States. The three IBA booklets: Rues on Evidence, Guidelines on Conflicts and Party Representation Guidelines represent a mere sixty-four pages in total. Is this the intolerable overregulation of international arbitration that some critics complain of? The adoption by internationally recognized professional bodies such as the IBA of carefully drafted, simple, clear and flexible soft law rules is an indispensable part of the effort or fairness and legitimacy that commercial arbitration needs to make in order to avoid the fate of investment arbitration.

---

37. ASA's position on the IBA Guidelines on Party Representation, *supra.*, at ¶ 4.2.

CHAPTER 26
Arbitration and Fine Dining: Two Faces of Efficiency
*William W. Park**

Tout ce qui est excessif devient insignifiant.** Charles Maurice de Talleyrand-Périgord,
Prince de Talleyrand.

§26.01 THE PARTIES' LEGITIMATE EXPECTATIONS

[A] Rival Goals

Aiming to provide fine dining, a restaurant chef will pay attention to several goals, not all of which marry well one with another. Guests must not wait too long for their meal. Yet a good dish often takes time to prepare. The wine list should offer quality and choice, but without being pretentious or overpriced.

Shortcomings in any one area could turn dinner into disappointment. Few points will be scored if tasty cuisine arrives two hours late, even assuming the customer has not departed in the interim. Prompt service will rarely save bad food. The evening would be ruined by a chef who had become preoccupied with any single aspect of fine dining, to the exclusion of the others.

To amplify Talleyrand's observation, the excessive may become not only insignificant, but also counterproductive. Too much emphasis on speed can affect food preparation. An obsession with preparation upsets timely service. Either way, the customer leaves with a grievance.

---

* Copyright ©William W. Park, 2016. Helpful research assistance was provided by Maria Slobodchikova.
** "The excessive becomes insignificant."

Like most analogies, comparisons between arbitration and dining will limp badly. Few business managers relish a lawsuit in the way they enjoy an evening with friends at a good restaurant. Yet like dining, arbitral proceedings implicate proportionality and balance among a multitude of factors which can make the experience better or worse.

As we shall explore in a moment, several elements play key roles in evaluation of any arbitration: accuracy, enforceability cost and speed.[1] An inevitable tension exists among these fundamentals. Decisions reached quickly and cheaply will not do an arbitrator much honor if wrong on the substantive merits. A correct result provides little satisfaction to a prevailing party if refused recognition because the arbitrators denied due process or exceeded their jurisdiction.

Many discussions of arbitration focus on efficiency in its slimmest sense, isolating speed and economy from the other elements necessary for the legitimacy of the process. Time and cost are portrayed as enemies, rather than trade-offs in the pursuit of a fair process leading to an accurate and enforceable result.

In this connection, arbitration is often painted as having been infected with poor case management making the process too much like litigation. Critics say that arbitration has lost the "quick, cheap and cheerful" tone that made it popular back when commercial men (as they inevitably were in those days) visited a warehouse to sniff the corn before lunch, then retired to deliberate with a good bottle of Bordeaux before meeting the parties that afternoon to scold the seller for failing to deliver "Grade A" grain.

Today however, economic disputes rarely yield themselves to the clarity of old-fashioned grain purchases in an imagined golden age of simple arbitration. Although there may be some relatively simple questions (analogous to an umpire calling a baseball player "out" as he slides into home plate), many more will require serious expert testimony on accounting, legal or engineering matters; they may relate to lost profits, competition, taxation, capitalized expenditures or power plant operation. Controversies may involve long-term energy supply, bio-technology licenses and multi-party construction projects. Dramatically changed circumstances may be invoked as a defense to contract performance. Or one side may seek to pierce the corporate veil between a modestly capitalized subsidiary and its better-funded parent.

When international elements infuse arbitration, choice-of-law analysis will often play a key role in proper decision-making. For such cases, finding the right answer in a fair fashion may not always be cheap and quick. Unless arbitrators have prejudged the questions presented to them (hardly a recipe for good proceedings) answering complex questions usually takes time.[2]

---

1. For a list of other arbitrator attributes which play into the mix of good (or bad) arbitration, *see* Thomas Clay, *L'Arbitre est-il un être normal?*, in L'EXIGENCE DE JUSTICE: MÉLANGES EN L'HONNEUR DE ROBERT BADINTER 225 (Dalloz 2016).
2. One recalls the Latin maxim *Veritas filia temporis* (truth is the daughter of time) attributed by a second century Roman grammarian to an unnamed predecessor. "Alius quidam veterum poetarum, cuius nomen mihi nunc memoriae non est, Veritatem Temporis filiam esse dixit." (Another ancient poet, whose name I have forgotten, said that Truth was the daughter of Time.) Aulus Gellius, Noctes Atticae, XII.11.7.

To some extent, arbitration has become a victim of its own success, as the arbitral process moves beyond the simplicity of earlier days, finding acceptance as a commercially preferred path to decide significant business disputes. Expectations of procedural simplicity often breed disappointment in the context of adjudicatory reality.

In the best of all possible worlds, experienced arbitrators will find ways to meet all goals with equal robustness. Yet the best of all words frequently eludes us, thus requiring occasional compromise and concession, a matter to which we shall now turn in greater detail.

[B] Four Aspirations

In his novel *The Three Musketeers*, Alexander Dumas features a trio of brave comrades who sought to guard their king and serve the queen, all the while living by the motto "All for one, one for all." Similarly, the aspirations of a good arbitrator comprise three core goals: accuracy, fairness and efficiency, which find themselves joined by a fourth objective: an enforceable award. Together these duties join in service to a relatively predictable and neutral dispute resolution process promoting the type of economic cooperation enhanced by reliable vindication of *ex ante* expectations.

The first aim of arbitration must be accuracy in the sense of "getting it right" when determining the facts and applying the law. Award accuracy implicates fidelity to the text of the contract and the context of the relevant bargain. The arbitrator should aim to get as near as reasonably possible to an understanding of what actually happened between the litigants and how the pertinent legal norms apply to the controverted events.[3] Not an absolute truth as might exist in the mind of an omniscient God; but rather a reasonably correct picture of the controverted events, words, and norms that affect claims and defenses. The good arbitrator recognizes that although a perfect understanding of disputed facts often proves elusive, some answers are more correct than others.

Second, the process must be fair. In the context of arbitration, the capacious notion of "fairness" incorporates several elements: to hear before deciding, often called "due process" or "natural' justice" in the Anglo-American legal world, and *principe du contradictoire* in Francophone legal systems; to respect the contours of arbitral jurisdiction, whether by reason of the relevant contract or some public policy constraint; and to remain impartial and independent. Litigants should expect a decision by arbitrators who avoid pre-judgment, remain unbiased and demonstrate respect for the limits of their authority, whether fixed by contract, statute or treaty.

---

3. That awards are not generally subject to judicial review for inaccuracy per se in no way diminishes an arbitrator's duty to seek the right result. Arbitration would be a poor form of justice if the process aimed only at satisfying minimum standards for judicial annulment. In modern arbitration law, the limitations on grounds for judicial review (which generally do not include mistake of law or fact as such) derive from respect for the parties' bargain to have the merits of their dispute decided by an arbitrator rather than a judge. *See* generally, William W. Park, *Explaining Arbitration Law*, in Defining Issues in International Arbitration: Celebrating 100 Years of the Chartered Institute of Arbitrators 7 (Julio César Betancourt, ed. 2016).

Third, arbitrators should aim to avoid undue time and cost, with the devil in the detail surrounding the adjective "undue." One person's delay might be another's due process. As discussed shortly, the efficiency of an arbitration in the narrow sense (low cost and high speed) must be evaluated against broader notions of efficiency related to the choice of procedures appropriate to the case at hand.

Readers of *The Three Musketeers* will remember that the novel's three initial heroes (Athos, Porthos and Aramis) found themselves joined by a fourth comrade named d'Artagnan, a poor but courageous nobleman from Gascony who hoped to enter the King's Guards and fight beside his friends. Likewise, the catalogue of arbitrator duties includes an additional aspiration: the award should be enforceable.

Enforceability, the "fourth musketeer" of arbitral duties, touches the interaction of arbitrators and courts, implicating vigilance in promoting an arbitral process that leads to something more than a mere piece of paper. Prevailing litigants expect arbitrators to avoid grounds for annulment or non-recognition by judicial authorities called to review the award.[4] Award defects which taint enforceability would normally include breach of due process, excess of authority, and disregard of mandatory legal norms.

Any thoughtful observer will note that these four aspirations of a good arbitrator will often conflict with one another. Granting an opportunity for more testimony, or additional document production, might enhance procedural fairness, perhaps also furthering substantive accuracy by providing the arbitrator supplemental information on which to base a decision. Yet the potential benefit comes at a cost: delay and extra expense. In turn, any attempt to economize by denying more testimony or document production could lead to challenge of the award by the aggrieved party.

When alternatives seem finely balanced, how does an arbitrator proceed? Does a thumb on the scale tilt for fairness and accuracy, or for efficiency? To these matters we shall now turn.

§26.02 CONTEMPLATING ALTERNATIVES

[A] Efficiency from Two Perspectives

In its popular usage, efficiency has come to mean doing things quick and cheap. A process tends to be perceived as efficient if the expense is low and the speed is high.

In arbitration, this narrow definition sometimes runs counter to broader notions of efficiency that implicate effective case management. Arbitrators are expected to craft processes appropriate to the circumstances and proportional to what is at stake. Except for lawyers with a very bad case, arbitration rarely wins accolades for being effective

---

4. This duty of enforceability has been underscored in institutional arbitration rules. Article 35 of the ICC Rules provides: "In all matters not expressly provided for in these Rules, the [ICC] Court and the Arbitral Tribunal shall ... make every effort to make sure that the Award is enforceable at law." Likewise, the LCIA Rules provide in Art. 32.2: "In all matters not expressly provided for in these Rules, the LCIA Court, the Arbitral Tribunal and the parties shall ... make every reasonable effort to ensure that an award is legally enforceable."

when the proceedings go so fast that the arbitrators lack an adequate opportunity to appreciate evidence and argument. Nor would the prevailing party consider a proceeding efficient if the award ends up being annulled for lack of due process. By contrast, a fair process will usually be accepted as legitimate, even by the side receiving the rough side of the award.

Saving time and money (the narrower sense of efficiency) constitutes a means to an end, not the goal itself. The ultimate objective of good case management lies in fixing a process that suits the case.[5] Like the restaurant chef in our opening scenario, arbitrators can spoil things by acting so rapidly as to serving bad food even if arrives quickly.

Seen in this larger context, the juxtaposition of fairness and efficiency may prove a false conflict. Fairness requires some measure of efficiency, since justice too long delayed becomes justice denied. Likewise, without fairness an arbitral proceeding would hardly be efficient, since it would fail to deliver a key element of the desired product: a sense that justice had been respected.

A paradigm articulation of this tension presents itself in section 33(1) of the 1996 English Arbitration Act, which directs arbitrators to: (i) act fairly and impartially as between the parties, giving each party a reasonable opportunity of putting his case and dealing with that of his opponent; and (ii) adopt procedures suitable to the circumstances of the particular case, avoiding unnecessary delay or expense, so as to provide a fair means for the resolution of the matters falling to be determined.[6]

These competing directives provide convenient hooks for counsel to hang procedural arguments, either for or against applications to bifurcate, to compel disclosure, or to move deadlines. However, they contain little inherent guidance on how the arbitrator should weigh competing aims, a nuanced task which generally benefits from an experience level sufficient to guide the tribunal on shared expectations of fairness in the community of arbitration users. Promoting an optimum administration of justice often proves to be an art more than a science, with a delicate counterpoise among aims such as speed, economy, accuracy, fairness and enforceability.

[B] Costs and Benefits

[1] *The Last Bad Experience*

Rightly or wrongly, much current commentary puts the spotlight on efficiency in its narrow sense, as related to time and cost. Less thought seems to be given to broader

---

5. In this connection, *see* generally Fabien Gélinas & Clément Camion, *Efficiency and Values in the Constitution of Civil Procedure*, 4 (Issue 2) INT'L J. PROCEDURAL L. 202 (2014). In both commercial settings and investor-state disputes, serious public interests are implicated by reliability, in the sense of promoting positive economic cooperation.
6. On the interaction between an arbitrator's discretion to craft proceedings and the elements of due process in the context of the 1996 Act, *see* William W. Park, *Two Faces of Progress: Fairness and Flexibility in Arbitral Procedure*, 23 ARB. INT'L 499 (2007).

contexts in which speed and economy can operate to the detriment of due process, accuracy and enforceability.[7]

One reason might be that basic fairness has become a "given" to be assured by the judicial supervision of curial courts monitoring the integrity of arbitral proceedings at the time an award receives confirmation or recognition.[8] In addition, the details of each dispute must be considered when questioning the accuracy of an award or the proportionality of a procedural measure.

By contrast, complaints about time and cost require less robust analysis. The confidentiality of proceedings makes it difficult to discuss details about alternative ways to do things, or the optimum paths to equilibrium among various elements of legitimate decision-making. Although thoughtful arbitrators make efforts to "square the circle" so as to reconcile these multiple conflicting goals, the reality of the conflicting tensions often dictates a result that disappoints the seekers of both curves an right angles.

As in many areas of life,[9] the lodestar for evaluating arbitration often resides in some recent bad experience that overshadows other more positive incidents.[10] The business manager who sees her case as wrongly decided will sense grievance that annulment actions cannot be filed for a simple mistake of fact and law, but lie only for breach of due process or excess of authority. By contrast, the corporate executive who just prevailed in an arbitration will likely feel frustrated that the losing side gets any right of court recourse at all, providing a second bite at the apple even for limited grounds. One lawyer feels aggrieved at failure to get an order for fuller document production, to obtain the hoped-for "smoking gun" that will destroy an adversary's case. By contrast, the recipient of the same discovery order will complain about the overly generous scope of the order that results in senseless waste of time and money combing company files.

---

7. A 2010 study by the Corporate Counsel International Arbitration Group found that 100% of corporate counsel think arbitration takes too long, and 69% think it costs too much. Lucy Reed, More on Corporate Criticism of International Arbitration, Kluwer Arbitration Blog (Jul. 16, 2010), http://kluwerarbitrationblog.com (blaming delays in arbitral proceedings on the limited availability of top-tier arbitrators and their "excessive concern for due process"). Another study, co-sponsored by a major law firm and a London university, suggested that 50% of the participating respondents were dissatisfied with the performance of arbitrators in international arbitration. *See 2010 International Arbitration Survey: Choices in International Arbitration*, White & Case LLP and School of International Arbitration (Queen Mary, University of London) (2010). The study follows an earlier survey sponsored by PriceWaterhouseCoopers.
8. Some scholars argue that there has been an overreaction to the prospect of award vacatur. *See* Klaus Peter Berger & J. Ole Jensen, *Due Process Paranoia and the Procedural Judgment Rule: A Safe Harbor for Procedural Management Decisions by International Arbitrators*, 32 ARB. INT'L 415 (2016).
9. The pattern does not limit itself to arbitration. In most supermarket suggestion boxes, complaints seem to outnumber compliments. Disappointed shoppers unable to find just the right brand of mustard usually feel more aggrieved, and thus are moved to express themselves. On the other hand, relatively few customers fill in such forms to express delight at finding the other thirty-six items on their shopping list.
10. Many thanks to my friend Jim Carter for introducing this insight, albeit in a slightly different format.

Complaints about the efficiency of arbitration often follow similar lines. A claimant will remember that the case did not move as quickly as hoped, failing to recollect that its lawyers agreed to arbitrate in a country known for interventionist judicial proceedings. A respondent will complain about the high cost of having to defend against a meritless claim, forgetting that the proceedings were prolonged because its legal team insisted that without extensive document production their rights would be prejudiced.

[2]   Hard Choices

[a]   Contract Drafting

Reacting against bad experience sometimes runs in tandem with forgetfulness about our own role in making hard choices. Human nature being what it is, some critics of arbitration (and of arbitrators) forget that time and expense often derive from the very procedural features the parties adopted in an effort to enhance fairness and accuracy.

With a few keystrokes of the computer, contract drafters could adopt some simple adjustments to the standard arbitration clause that would substantially reduce the duration of proceedings and the money spent on legal fees. These changes might: (i) provide for one rather than three arbitrators; (ii) ban document production; (iii) limit the size and number of briefs; and (iv) stipulate awards without detailed reasoning. The critics of undue time and cost might also lobby for legislation to eliminate annulment of awards at the arbitral seat, leaving the only judicial recourse at the place of enforcement itself.[11]

Each innovation, however, would carry its own cost, drawing understandable resistance from large segments of the arbitration community. Three arbitrators make for a more rigorous process, as do comprehensive written reasons explaining the legal and factual underpinnings of a decision.[12] Document production reduces the possibility of an unjust result by enhancing the prospect that arbitrators will receive a fuller record, including previously undisclosed letter or emails unfavorable to one side's position. Thorough memorials enhance rigorous analysis. And the right to challenge a defective award where rendered presents the paradigm example of competing costs and benefits. A motion to vacate might add expense just after the award has been made; but even more money may be needed to challenge a procedurally defective award in multiple enforcement actions around the world.[13]

The chief downside of any over-simplification lies in the risk of diverting attention and thoughtful reflection from genuine quandaries that reside in the many

---

11. The late Professor Fouchard (among others) proposed such legislation two decades ago. See generally Philippe Fouchard, *La Portée internationale de l'annulation de la sentence arbitrale dans son pays d'origine*, 1997 REV. ARB. 329.
12. More than once, arbitrators have found that initial conclusions "just won't write" during the award drafting exercise.
13. For a further discussion of such choices, see Jennifer Kirby, *Efficiency in International Arbitration: Whose Duty Is It?*, 32 J. INT'L ARB. 689 (2015).

procedural choices which implicate finely balanced costs and benefits. To bring the debate back to what actually goes on in real-life proceedings, it may be helpful to consider some of the common questions that resist facile analysis and blanket responses.

[b] A Laundry List of Dilemmas

The situations listed below exemplify some of the dilemmas facing arbitrators in complex cases. Although perfect answers may prove elusive, some solutions will be better than others in accommodating efficiency and fairness:

- Document production. A request for information exchange implicates time, money and energy. However, losing the case by reason of not getting a key exhibit can be much worse. The arbitrator's dilemma lies in making decisions about relevancy and materiality before a case is fully understood.
- Reconsideration. Following a decision on document production, a dissatisfied party may seek reconsideration and ask for additional material to be disclosed. An automatic refusal to consider the request may result in injustice. Considering the application will in any event require time. If the motion is found to have merit, an order is made to produce additional documents, deadlines may need to be adjusted to take into account the time for one side to produce more documents and for the other side to study the material before the next submission. The addition of days given to the requesting party will likely trigger a call for "equal time" by the other side, sometimes putting hearing schedules in jeopardy.
- Bias. Challenges for arbitrator bias prove disruptive to timetables. Yet even less attractive would be a system with no mechanism to monitor the arbitrator's impartiality and independence.
- Hidden financiers. Concern about arbitrator conflict may lead to requests for disclosure of third-party funders. Addressing the request will take time, and may meet the objection, "What you don't know can't hurt you." Denying the application has its own costs. If it transpires that an arbitrator had links with the person paying bills for the prevailing party, the integrity of the process (if not the validity of the award) would doubtlessly be called into question, regardless of what the arbitrator actually knew at the time.
- Bifurcation. Deciding an issue on a preliminary basis (whether related to jurisdiction or liability) can add time and cost. However, a system would be quite unattractive if respondents were always forced to engage high-priced experts to present testimony before arbitrators who clearly lack authority, or where no breach of contract had occurred. The appropriateness of bifurcating some questions depends on a fact-specific analysis, implicating factors that include whether one question will remain so intertwined with another as to

make a separate hearing duplicative. Analogous concerns arise with respect to summary judgments (dispositive motions) on questions that can be decided without an evidentiary hearing.

[c]   Institutional Rules

Arbitral institutions often join the chorus of characterizing time and cost as enemies. Yet most institutions recognize the trade-offs inherent in speed and economy. The ICC Rules, for example, require arbitrators "to conduct the arbitration in the expeditious and cost-effective manner"[14] while at the same time imposing at least two additional stages of arbitration: signing of Terms of Reference and scrutiny of an award by the ICC Secretariat.[15]

Most institutional rules impose reasoned awards (which can enhance both rigor and transparency) notwithstanding the time taken to provide explanations of a decision when three arbitrators might disagree on the reasoning even if not on the result.

The International Chamber of Commerce requires "Terms of Reference" on the assumption that an early effort to refine the claims and counterclaims will assist the arbitral process. Yet in many cases, the need to draft such terms blocks a case from proceeding without time-consuming administrative steps.[16]

The Stockholm Chamber of Commerce (SCC) rules require a final award within six months from referral of the dispute to the arbitral tribunal, presumably to foster efficiency, even though this deadline normally proves quite out of the question for "big ticket" cases raising complex legal and factual questions.[17] Still the SCC routinely requires the arbitral tribunal and counsel to make a reasoned award for an extension, even when the deadline falls before presentation of evidence or argument.

Some institutions require arbitral awards to be witnessed or notarized. At the same time, from a concern about award enforceability, the institution will deny a three-member tribunal the right to execute an award in counterparts. The result may be an unattainable and contradictory effort to produce an electronic copy of an award for purposes of speed (to meet an enforcement deadline) while at the same time insisting that all three arbitrators execute the same signature page with the same witnesses or notarizations.

---

14. Article 22(1) of the ICC Rules of Arbitration.
15. Articles 23(1) and 33 of the ICC Rules of Arbitration.
16. Although an outright refusal of a party to sign the Terms of Reference would lead the ICC to step in and approve the Terms, the delay may be due not to any refusal to participate, but because one side misunderstands the process, or because the ICC differs from the arbitral tribunal on what should be included in the Terms. Article 23(3) of the ICC Rules provides, "If any of the parties refuses to take part in the drawing up of the Terms of Reference or to sign the same, they shall be submitted to the Court for approval. When the Terms of Reference have been signed ... or approved by the Court, the arbitration shall proceed."
17. Article 37 of the SCC Arbitration Rules.

§26.03 THE ENFORCEMENT STAGE

[A] The Law of Arbitration

Arbitral awards do not normally become unenforceable simply because they are wrong, or because the process has been long and costly.[18] However, award annulment or non-recognition could be the destiny of an arbitrator's decision reached through proceedings that constituted a serious departure from fundamental rules of basic procedural fairness.[19]

In most modern legal systems, the law of arbitration (as distinct from the specific legal rules applied to decide a particular dispute) comprises statutes, cases and treaties to guide the interaction between arbitrators who decide cases and judges who review awards.[20] This legal structure includes two distinct limbs. First, parties should be held to their bargains to arbitrate. Second, the courts and institutions which enforce the commitment to arbitrate must also monitor the basic integrity of the arbitral process, so as to enhance the prospect that cases will be heard by fair individuals who listen before deciding, stay within their mission, and respect the limits of relevant public policy.

A certain irony exists in penalties for breach of an arbitrator's duty to provide fair hearings. The sanction of award annulment falls not so much on the arbitrator who breached his duty,[21] but rather on the prevailing party which must suffer annulment of an award that implicated a breach of procedural integrity.

[B] The Arbitral Seat: Conflict in Action

The arena of judicial review, in France and in England, provides an opportunity to explore some of the tensions among different duties of an arbitrator. As illustrated below, deciding quickly and cheaply can sometimes run afoul of due process; and fidelity to the parties' contract can occasionally conflict with mandatory norms of an enforcement action.

---

18. *See*, e.g., Federal Arbitration Act § 10; Art. 1520 of the French *Code de procédure civile*; Art. 52 of the ICSID Convention of 1965.
19. Indirectly of course, sanctions for violation of due process will promote accuracy, by encouraging arbitrators to listen to both sides before deciding, thus augmenting the information available to the decision-making process.
20. International disputes usually implicates more than one jurisdiction and therefore require thoughtful arbitrators to take into account several sets of arbitration laws. In particular, arbitrators may need to reconcile arbitration regimes of the seat of arbitration with the arbitration laws of a country where award's enforcement will be sought.
21. Even if they may suffer loss of reputation, offending arbitrators can benefit from immunity notwithstanding having violated their duty of basic procedural integrity. In one case, a sole arbitrator failed to disclose a romantic relationship with the sister of respondent's counsel. Immunity was upheld even though the award had been vacated. *See La Serena Properties v. Weisbach*, 186 Cal. App. 4th 893, 112 Cal. Rptr. 3d 597 (Cal. Ct. App. 2010).

[1] New Theories and Due Process

In each of the cases discussed below, experienced tribunals sitting in France rendered thoughtful awards that were later vacated because the efficiency of their proceedings failed to provide adequate opportunity for counsel to comment on relevant legal theories.

[a] Caribbean Niquel

In 2010, the Paris *Cour d'appel* decided the case of *Caribbean Niquel v. Overseas Mining*,[22] which implicated the parties' rights to address new legal theories in a context that pitted the aim of efficiency against the goal of due process. After a Cuban mining venture had gone sour, arbitrators sitting in Paris awarded the claimant USD 45 million on a theory of "lost chance" (*la perte de chance*), even though the parties had argued a theory of quantum based on lost profits (*le gain manqué*). One can well imagine that arbitrators would not find it satisfying to apply a "lost profits" theory with respect to a mine that had not yet become operative.[23]

The *Cour d'appel* vacated the award for violation of provisions in the *Code de procédure civile* related to the right to be heard (*principe de la contradiction*[24]) and procedural public policy (*ordre public procédural*).[25] Although not questioning the assumption that arbitrators know the law (often expressed as *jura novit curia*) the French court found it unacceptable that an award should rest on a method of damages calculation that counsel had not had an adequate opportunity to address.

The decision carries its own problems, providing a stark example of the difficulty faced by arbitrators seeking to balance their various duties, with each alternative likely to spring its own special trap. Imagine that the arbitrators in *Caribbean Niquel*, in the midst of their deliberations, had re-opened the proceedings to set a briefing schedule on the new legal theory of lost chance. There would have been moaning all around about added expense and delay.

Had the tribunal raised with counsel the new theory earlier, the tribunal might have been perceived as lacking even-handedness. The respondent could have said, with some justification: "You arbitrators are acting as advocates, signaling that

---

22. *La Société Commercial Caribbean Niquel v. La Société Overseas Mining Investments Ltd.*, Paris Court of Appeals, 1st Chamber, 08/23901, Mar. 25, 2010.
23. Indeed, the tribunal held that calculating the lost economic benefit was too uncertain, whereas calculating the value of the chance to take advantage of an economic opportunity could "undeniably" be evaluated. The tribunal therefore based the reasoning in its award on the legal theory that the party should be compensated for the economic value of the lost opportunity.
24. The oft-used term *"principe du contradictoire"* has been memorialized in the *Code de procédure civile* as the *"principe de la contradiction"*.
25. As in force at the time of the *Cour d'appel* decision, these provisions were contained in Art. 1502 of the *Code de procédure civile*, which provided *inter alia* as follows: "L'appel de la décision qui accorde la reconnaissance ou l'exécution n'est ouvert que dans les cas suivants: 4° Lorsque le principe de la contradiction n'a pas été respecté; 5° Si la reconnaissance ou l'exécution sont contraires à l'ordre public international." A 2011 decree moved these two clauses to Art. 1520 of the state statute, albeit with the same formulation.

claimant's chances of success will increase with a pleading amended to include new damages theories."

Finally, it would have been equally problematic for the arbitrators to decide the case without consideration of the "lost chance" measure of damages. The tribunal would face the unattractive choice between granting an award simply for lost profits, yielding an incorrect amount, or denying recovery entirely, which would have penalized an otherwise meritorious claim.

An arbitrator's attempt to improve proceedings from one perspective can make things worse from another angle. Enhancing efficiency can reduce fairness and accuracy. To complicate matters further, the concepts of fairness, accuracy, efficiency and enforceability are not monolithic. Each notion includes multiple obligations. Tensions thus exist not only among those four goals, but also within each of the various distinct yet related duties which in practice often compete one with another. As noted, suggesting counseling an opportunity to address a new legal theory promotes the parties' right to be heard, but perhaps at the expense of exposing arbitrators to a charge of being biased.

[b] De Sutter v. Madagascar

The tensions within the set of duties guiding arbitrator comportment presented themselves again in France a half-dozen years later, following an award rendered pursuant to the bilateral investment treaty between the Republic of Madagascar and the Belgium-Luxembourg Economic Union. In *De Sutter et al. v. Madagascar,* an ICC award had been rendered in favor of Belgian textile manufacturers that had suffered damage due to labor strike at the factory, which as it happened accompanied a *coup d'état* in Madagascar.[26]

When a Madagascar insurer refused to reimburse the investors for the damage, a lower court in Madagascar rendered a judgment in favor of the Belgian investor, finding the loss covered by the policy as having originated from labor unrest rather than riot of a political nature. Later, the execution of that decision was suspended by Madagascan authorities, triggering the arbitration under the investment treaty, which permitted selection of the ICC Rules to govern the procedure.

According to the sole arbitrator, the Madagascan court's decision to suspend execution of the judgment's execution derived not from the interests of justice, according to applicable law, but because the insurance company was owned by the Madagascar government. Consequently, the treaty had been breached in respect of its third Article, including *inter alia* the duty to accord fair and equitable treatment to investors. So far, so good.

As in *Caribbean Niquel,* the difficulty came in the way the arbitrator characterized damages. The request for capital and interest (the amount granted by the Madagascar court) had been rejected by the arbitrator as outside treaty coverage, given

---

26. Cour d'Appel de Paris, Arrêt du 16 Mars 2016, Pole 1 – Chambre 1, RG 14/ 19164. The underlying award had been rendered under the ICC Rules (as permitted by the treaty) by an eminent Paris-based American arbitrator.

that the underlying claims were still pending and thus precluding expropriation as such.

Under the circumstances, however, the arbitrator ordered payment of an amount equal to interest (at the legal rate in Madagascar) running from the date of the 2012 local court judgment through June 2014, shortly before the award was issued. The arbitrator determined this amount as fair compensation for gain to which claimant had been entitled but was unable to enjoy ("*bénéfice dont PGM n'a pu profiter*") due to the suspension.

The Paris *Cour d'appel* vacated the award pursuant to Article 1520(4) of the French *Code de procédure civile* which as mentioned earlier addresses breach of the right to be heard, referred to as *principe de la contradiction* in the French text. Through a multitude of those clauses which provide such difficult reading for common law jurists, each introduced by the rhetorical device *considérant que* ("considering that"), the Court seemed to reason that the arbitrator could not, without inviting comment by counsel, substitute an amount of damages during the period of suspension in Madagascar for the sum actually requested by the claimants.[27]

Contrary to what William Shakespeare suggested about a rose by any other name smelling as sweet,[28] allocation of the interest under a different label (in substance taken from the claimants' original request) was deemed unsatisfactory to the reviewing French court. The case underscores the frequent overlap between a simple mistake (normally unreviewable under modern arbitration statutes) and matters of due process, with the latter (like excess of authority) remaining grounds for annulment.

[2] Cost Allocation and Contract Terms

To explore how one set of arbitral duties may collide with another, few examples serve better than the norms for cost allocation in England, which in some instances prove at odds with fidelity to the parties' agreement, as well as the requirements for award enforcement in other fora.

The 1996 English Arbitration Act invalidates pre-dispute agreements to allocate arbitration costs "in any event."[29] In advance of the dispute, parties may not by contract forbid an arbitrator from taking into account who won and who lost when allocating costs.[30] The provision casts a wide net, serving not only as an anti-abuse mechanism to prevent "you-pay-in-any-event" clauses from discouraging claims by

---

27. The total amount requested by claimant initially had come to approximately EUR 5.8 million, while the interest element (characterized as "*bénéfice*" in the award) came to EUR 691 thousand.
28. William Shakespeare, Romeo and Juliet, Act II, Scene 2.
29. Section 60, Arbitration Act of 1996: "An agreement which has the effect that a party is to pay the whole or part of the costs of the arbitration in any event is only valid if made after the dispute in question has arisen." Section 61 goes on to set forth the general principle that "costs should follow the event except where it appears to the tribunal that in the circumstances this is not appropriate in relation to the whole or part of the costs". This standard, however, is made subject to the parties' agreement otherwise, which in context with s. 60 would be an agreement after the dispute has arisen.
30. To be clear, the statute does not impose the English "costs follow the event" rule in all events, but simply invalidates pre-dispute attempts to eliminate the arbitrator's discretion to consider

weaker parties, but also catches otherwise reasonable arrangements among sophisticated business managers.

Promoting award enforceability by complying with English law remains a problematic proposition in an international case. Consider what an arbitrator should do in the following situation.

The parties have decided to arbitrate in England, but also subjected their contract to the law of New York. The contract contains an explicit provision that in any arbitration the two sides will split arbitrator compensation on a 50/50 basis. Even more significant from a financial perspective, the agreement says each side covers its own arbitration-related legal expenses.

Flouting clear contract language on cost allocation would comply with English law.[31] However, to disregard the contract, which requires each side to bear its own expenses, might well (and not unreasonably) appear as an excess of authority to a New York court called to enforce an award costs. Disregard of contract terms would also be less than appealing from the perspective of accurate implementation of the parties' agreement.[32]

What is a conscientious arbitrator to do? Remain faithful to the parties' agreement? Respect the procedural law at the arbitral seat? Or look to the laws to be applied by the enforcement court in New York? Occasionally, nuanced approaches to award may provide an exit from this particular quandary. However, the dilemma demonstrates again how the achievement of counterpoise among rival goals remains an enduring challenge of arbitration policy and practice.

§26.04 GOOD PRACTICES

In arbitration, the elusiveness of counterpoise among rival goals should not be surprising. Vigorous discussion also exists on the optimum way to conduct court proceedings, both on a comparative level (considering different national systems) and as between positions taken by different scholarly camps and judicial circuits in a single country.

---

who won and who lost in fixing obligations for items such as attorneys' fees and amounts paid to the arbitrators and the arbitral institution.
31. Presumably, s. 68 of the 1996 Act ("serious irregularity causing substantial injustice") permits judicial action to correct an arbitrator's failure to respect s. 60.
32. A landmark decision of the U.S. Supreme Court implicated a similar dilemma, albeit with respect to substantive norms rather than procedure. See *Mitsubishi Motors v. Soler Chrysler-Plymouth*, 473 U.S. 614 (1985). An agreement involving a Japanese auto manufacturer and an American dealer provided for application of Swiss law by arbitrators in Japan, a choice explained by the existence of a Swiss affiliate of a joint venture company in the distribution chain. Ordering arbitration, the Court warned that American antitrust law must be considered in connection with any counterclaim, despite the contractual choice-of-law clause. *Mitsubishi* footnote 19 suggests a "prospective waiver" doctrine that would invalidate choice-of-law agreements that operated to waive a right to pursue American remedies. Moreover, the so-called second look doctrine in *Mitsubishi* warned that American courts would exercise their power at the award enforcement stage to "ensure that the legitimate interest in the enforcement of the antitrust laws [of the United States] had been addressed".

To take an illustration, arbitrators often struggle with the wisdom of granting "dispositive motions" (equivalent to "summary judgment" in some legal systems) dismissing a claim at the outset of an arbitration pursuant to a preliminary ruling, without full consideration of testimony.[33] Such applications may be permitted pursuant to the express or implied terms of institutional rules,[34] and on occasion pursuant to the terms of the parties' agreement.[35]

The appropriateness of ending the arbitration before a full hearing will depend on the factual configuration of the case.[36] In some instances, the equivalent of a summary judgment rule in arbitration may have unintended consequences, adding rather than reducing cost.[37]

---

33. *See* e.g., *Bucheit Int'l Ltd. v. Overseas Private Inv. Corp (OPIC)*, AAA Case No. 50T 195 00361 03 (2004), with a summary judgment motion granted under AAA Commercial Rules Art. 30(b). *See* Robert O'Sullivan, "Motion Practice in Arbitration", in *International Commercial Dispute Resolution*, 39 INT'L LAWYER 235, at 239–241 (Mark A. Garfinkel ed. 2005). *See also* James H. Carter, *Dispositive Motions in International Arbitration and the Role of U.S. Court*, in INTERNATIONAL ARBITRATION: CONTEMPORARY ISSUES 39 (24th Sokol Colloquium, Univ. Virginia, ed. J.N. Moore 2013).
34. *See* e.g., AAA Commercial Arbitration Rules, Art. 30(b), providing that an arbitrator, exercising his or her discretion [may] direct the parties to focus their presentations on issues the decision of which could dispose of all or part of the case. Compare 2012 ICC Arbitration Rules providing that "in order to ensure effective case management, the arbitral tribunal, after consulting the parties, may adopt such procedural measures as it considers appropriate, provided that they are not contrary to any agreement of the parties." *See also* 2014 LCIA Rules Art. 14.4 a duty to adopt procedures suitable to the circumstances of the arbitration, avoiding unnecessary delay and expense, so as to provide a fair, efficient and expeditious means for the final resolution of the parties' dispute.
35. *See* decision *Travis Coal Restructuring Holdings LLC v. Essar Global Fund Limited*, [2014] EWHC 2510 (Comm), involving an application to enforce in London an award made in New York, opposed in part on the grounds that the arbitrators had exceeded their authority in making an award pursuant to a request for summary judgment. The opinion by Mr. Justice Blair noted *inter alia* that the relevant contract provided that "the arbitrators shall have the discretion to hear and determine at any stage of the arbitration any issue asserted by any party to be dispositive of any claim or counterclaim, in whole or part, in accordance with such procedure as the arbitrators may deem appropriate, and the arbitrators may render an award on such issue."
36. In Travis Coal (*infra*), the court went into detail on the facts of the dispute, which implicated a complicated share purchase transaction, with a guarantee of the sale purchase price contained an ICC arbitration clause providing for proceedings seated in New York. After failure to make payments, an arbitral tribunal issued an award in favor of the beneficiary of the guarantee. Although ultimately adjourning the enforcement action pending resolution of an annulment motion before courts in New York, the learned judge expressed serious doubts about success of the application to vacate. He noted that in fact the arbitral tribunal had moved beyond a simple summary judgment process, and actually heard testimony on key questions of fraud. The court also emphasized the context of the case, citing the award, "As a commercial center, New York is even more rigorous in expecting that parties that have given a written guarantee of performance – in which they waive certain defenses and disclaim certain subjects of reliance – will promptly honor their commitments".
37. In 2006 the ICSID Arbitration Rules were amended to add provision for a preliminary objection that a claim is "manifestly without legal merit". Doubtlessly intended to make proceedings more efficient by allowing a hopeless case to be put to rest early, some observers express concern that the rule encourages Respondent's to file such complaints as a matter of course, inserting an unnecessary procedural step. Article 41(5), ICSID Arbitration Rules.

In national court proceedings, analogous questions arise about when to allow claims to be dismissed early in the proceedings. The questions usually work themselves out in connection with broader policy discussions by legislatures or courts about litigation costs and social justice. Some legal systems authorize summary judgment for specific types of transactions, particularly with respect to financial instruments.[38]

The stakes may differ as between judicial and arbitral proceedings, since court judgments remain appealable on the substantive merits of the decision, while arbitration awards normally do not. Thus, the results of "getting it wrong" may prove more dramatic for an arbitrator's decision than for that of a judge.

In some legal systems, deeper social and economic issues work themselves into what at first blush appear to be relatively formalistic pleading requirements, particularly with respect to rules on dismissal of complaints for failure to state a claim. Standards have fluctuated with respect to rival concern about litigation expense, on the one hand, and access to justice, on the other.

Liberal federal practice in the United States long allowed "notice pleading" under which courts allowed an action to proceed as long as the trial judge could construe a complaint to state some semblance of a case.[39] Later, experience with the high cost of discovery led the U.S. Supreme Court to raise the bar by interpreting the law to require enough facts to state a claim to relief "plausible on its face."[40] The approach was later refined to require courts in essence to apply their experience to screen out weak claims, a task that sometimes carries political overtones.[41]

---

38. *See* e.g., French Nouveau code de procédure civile (NCPC), Art. 1405(2) (formerly Code de commerce, Art. 641), granting French courts the power to issue a payment order (*injonction de payer*) with respect to promissory notes and other negotiable instruments.
39. Under Rule 8(a)(2) of the Federal Rules of Civil Procedure, a complaint need include only "a short and plain statement of the claim showing that the pleader is entitled to relief". The U.S. Supreme Court once construed this rule to preclude complaints from being dismissed "unless it appears beyond doubt that the plaintiff can prove no set of facts in support of his claim which would entitle him to relief." *Conley v. Gibson*, 355 U.S. 41 (1957).
40. *Twombly v. Bell Atlantic Corp*, 550 U.S. 544 (2007) involved a putative class action for alleged market allocation by cable companies in violation of American competition law. The mere fact of competitors acting in the same fashion ("conscious parallelism") would normally be insufficient to state a claim for violation of the Sherman Act. Some "plus factor" must indicate an anti-competitive agreement. In *Twombly*, the Second Circuit Court of Appeals held the complaint could not be dismissed unless "no set of facts" would permit plaintiffs to demonstrate collusion rather than coincidence. The U.S. Supreme Court reversed, citing concerns about litigation expense which required a pleading of enough facts to state a claim that is "plausible on its face."
41. *Twombly* was followed by *Ashcroft v. Iqbal*, 556 U.S. 662 (2008), where a detainee's complaint was dismissed for failed to plead sufficient facts to state a claim for purposeful discrimination. A Pakistani Muslim claimed mistreatment while held for terrorist connections after improperly obtaining a Social Security number. Following release, the detainee alleged racial and religious bias by the FBI Director and former U.S. Attorney General, seeking relief for violations of various Constitutional rights. In a 5-4 decision, the U.S. Supreme Court reversed a lower court decision refusing to dismiss the claim. The Court found a plausible explanation for the detention, other than purposeful targeting of Arabs and Muslims. According to the Supreme Court majority, a non-discriminatory aim to detain illegal aliens with terrorist connections might, in the post-9/11 world, produce a disparate but incidental impact on Arabs and Muslim. This alternative explanation meant that the complaint failed to plead sufficient facts to state a claim for purposeful discrimination.

Whether conducted by courts or by arbitrators, decisions on dispositive applications and motions to dismiss claims will usually elude "black letter" rules. Instead, such measures put a premium on understanding the nuances of how procedural principles interact with rival concerns about cost and justice.

§26.05 COUNTERPOISE AND COMMON SENSE

An oft-quoted line from the philosopher Francis Bacon suggests, "If a man will begin with certainties, he shall end in doubts; but if he will be content to begin with doubts, he shall end in certainties."[42] Careful observers will note how the proposition proves overbroad in both its limbs. Some individuals end their intellectual pilgrimages as self-assured as they began, while others retain doubts all along the way.

Despite its extravagant nature, the aphorism points to the rewards of a healthy humility which, in arbitration as elsewhere, often leaves sounder analysis in its wake. In the real-life drama of high stakes arbitration, tensions among legitimate adjudicatory aims often resist facile resolution. Hearing additional testimony may enhance fairness at the expense of speed and economy. An arbitrator's suggestion that counsel consider a new legal theory might promote an accurate result, but at the risk of creating perceptions of arbitrator bias. Willingness to reconsider discovery rulings could yield helpful documents, while at the same disrupting a delicate briefing timetable and jeopardizing hearing dates.

Beginning with too much certainty about questions like those outlined above, some arbitrators (like some scholars, judges, lawyers and list-serve pundits) may later find themselves blindsided by facts indicating a different direction of analysis. An affirmation that some conclusion "surely must be the case" can add rhetorical punch, but at the cost of producing an astigmatic vision of costs and benefits. Particularly in international arbitration, more than one path may prove useful to resolve a procedural dilemma.

In some instances, one course of conduct commends itself over alternatives. In other cases, rivalry among various goals may prove more troublesome, with competing options neither better nor worse than one another, just different. Compromise and open-mindedness, more than dogma or ideology, usually remain the touchstone for sound counterpoise among aspirations to accuracy, fairness, efficiency and enforceability,[43] with good judgment rather than cleverness proving the hallmark of an effective arbitrator.

---

42. Francis Bacon, OF THE PROFICIENCE AND ADVANCEMENT OF LEARNING, DIVINE AND HUMAN (1605). The careful reader will note the shift from "will" to "shall" in each half of the sentence, perhaps suggesting that wilful insistence on being right ultimately leads to self-doubt, while an intentional openness to ideas yields confidence in the end.
43. For perspectives with an alternative emphasis, *see* Richard Weisberg, IN PRAISE OF INTRANSIGENCE: PERILS OF FLEXIBILITY (2014); William W. Park *Arbitration's Protean Nature: The Value of Rules and the Risks of Discretion* (2002 Freshfields Lecture), 19 ARB. INT'L 279 (2003). As in so many questions, arguments often turn on examples and contexts considered.

CHAPTER 27
Should an International Arbitral Tribunal Engage in Settlement Facilitation?

Axel Reeg

The author vividly and gratefully remembers many an appearance of Pierre Karrer, the famous Swiss international arbitrator, at conferences, meetings and workshops, way back in the last decade before the millennium, when the author was aspiring to make his first steps into the world of international arbitration. Pierre Karrer's presentations, statements and his kind and welcoming attitude towards the youngsters in the arbitral community have always been an example to be followed. In particular, it has been Pierre Karrer's structured approach to the management of cases in international arbitration which have impressed and influenced the author. Hence, this contribution in honour of Pierre Karrer has certainly been inspired by some of the *stimuli* for further thought set by Pierre Karrer.

Engaging in settlement facilitation, for an international arbitral tribunal, may be a tricky issue. It may result in disaster if overly active arbitrators pushing hard for a settlement are successfully challenged and the tribunal falls apart. It may also earn praise by and lead to satisfaction of the parties with the performance of the tribunal in cases where it facilitates a solution both parties can live with well rather than rendering an award which produces a full victory for one side and a full defeat for the other party.

While common law based arbitration practitioners are traditionally rather and, in many cases, extremely reluctant to even consider the idea of the tribunal engaging in settlement facilitation, their civil law based counterparts are much more open to it and, as in the case of Germany, they are often even embracing the idea by making settlement facilitation an obligation of the tribunal. This article will briefly contrast the differences of the approaches (§27.01), discuss whether settlement facilitation by an international arbitral tribunal is admissible or even desirable (§27.02), touch on hybrid dispute resolution models (§27.03) and then endeavour to establish some pre-conditions for this activity of arbitrators which goes beyond their genuine task to resolve a dispute by rendering a decision (§27.04) followed by a brief summary (§27.05).

§27.01 IS SETTLEMENT FACILITATION BY ARBITRATORS VIABLE?: THE COMMON LAW AND THE CIVIL LAW PERSPECTIVES

Many civil law jurisdictions are open towards settlement facilitation in civil litigation and, consequently, in arbitration if administered under the rules of an institution based in their jurisdiction. The most prominent example may be Germany where settlement facilitation is even made a duty of the arbitrators. Article 32.1 of the 1998 Arbitration Rules of the German Institution for Arbitration (DIS),[1] applicable also for international arbitration disputes, makes that very clear:

> At every stage of the proceedings, the arbitral tribunal should seek to encourage an amicable settlement of the dispute or of individual issues in dispute.

While such a mission of the arbitral tribunal may not have been established so vigorously in Switzerland, Austria and, among others, also the Czech Republic,[2] these jurisdictions are known for having a similar settlement facilitation culture as Germany.

Hence, in such jurisdictions, settling a dispute within an arbitration and not in a separate mediation process is perceived as normal. Parties would generally expect having a settlement discussion with the arbitral tribunal. They are, often and depending on the case, even likely to be disappointed when a tribunal would not approach the issue of settling the matter. For them, this is part of the normal course of the process.

In contrast, in common law countries, settlement facilitation by the arbitral tribunal is not perceived as a natural element of dispute resolution in an arbitration case. Rather to the contrary, it is traditionally seen as something that the arbitral tribunal should avoid engaging in. A common law trained arbitrator would see his paramount duty in the rendering of a judgment or an arbitral award, following, of course, a series of proceedings during which the arbitrator's principal duty is safeguarding the procedural rights of the parties with as little intervention in the action as possible. Such an arbitrator would not engage in a discussion on the merits of the case, he would rather sit and hear what Counsel and the witnesses have to say. Hence, common law trained arbitrators shy away from the mention of a settlement and common law trained Counsel do not wish any arbitrator to start a discussion of a settlement. Following this tradition, parties in common law jurisdictions share the expectation that the tribunal would intervene as little as possible in the proceedings and would certainly not promote a settlement of the matter before rendering an award. They would be taken by surprise if an arbitrator were to do so and would at least

---

1. The DIS Arbitration Rules are currently undergoing a revision with revised rules expected to be presented in 2017. While the result of the revision is open, the likelihood of the DIS completely abandoning the idea of settlement facilitation within an arbitration seems to be quite low.
2. Vid. Olik/Cáp, Comparison of Settlement Efforts by Arbitrators and Mediators, Arbitration, Vol. 82, No. 3 (2016) 250–253 (251), (Chartered Institute of Arbitrators), with reference to the Czech Arbitration Act and the Rules of the Czech Arbitration Court.

wonder whether he is pre-determined in his assessment if not consider challenging the appointment of such an arbitrator.[3]

Is a new transnational standard evolving?

From time to time, in the international arbitration community, there are voices appearing who advocate in favour of allowing settlement facilitation[4] and some institutions even actively promote this idea.

The most prominent institution, in this respect, is the London-based Center for Effective Dispute Resolution (CEDR) which, in 2009, has published Rules for the Facilitation of Settlement in International Arbitration.[5] These Rules have adopted some features of the German approach towards settlements in arbitration such as the idea of the tribunal providing the parties early on with its views on the issues in dispute.[6]

The ICC International Court of Arbitration contemplates the facilitation of a settlement in the context of an ongoing arbitration as something to be dealt with separately in another type of proceedings and not within the arbitration. This can be concluded from sections 41 and 42 of the ICC Report on 'Techniques for Controlling Time and Costs in Arbitration', published in 2012.[7] It may be noted, however, that the 2012 version of the report, in contrast to its first edition published in 2009, contains (in the second phrase of its new section 42) at least a timid approximation towards the idea of a tribunal intervening, at the request of the parties, in the facilitation of a settlement.

Along the same lines, the UNCITRAL Notes on Organizing Arbitral Proceedings, in section 72 of their new 2016 version,[8] are alluding to the idea of settlement facilitation by the arbitral tribunal, making, however, several (sensible) caveats.

The idea that an arbitration tribunal may or even should offer the parties its active assistance in reaching a settlement of their dispute,[9] is, however, still far from penetrating the common law part of the International Arbitration Community.[10]

---

3. Vid. Reeg, The New Arb-Med-Arb Protocol of the Singapore International Arbitration Centre -Can It Help Overcome the Settlement Dilemma in Cross-Cultural Arbitration Cases? IWRZ (Zeitschrift für Internationales Wirtschaftsrecht) 2015, 15–18.
4. Vid. Raeschke-Kessler, The Arbitrator as Settlement Facilitator, Arbitration International (LCIA), Vol. 21. No. 4 (2005), 523–536, with an illustrative example of how settlement facilitation may be performed.
5. http://www.cedr.com/about_us/arbitration_commission/Rules.pdf, accessed 20 Sep. 2016.
6. Vid. Art. 5.1.1 of the CEDR Rules for the Facilitation of Settlement in International Arbitration.
7. ICC Commission on Arbitration, Report on Techniques for Controlling Time and Costs in Arbitration, published in 2012 and available at: http://www.iccwbo.org/Advocacy-Codes-and-Rules/Document-centre/2012/ICC-Arbitration-Commission-Report-on-Techniques-for-Controlling-Time-and-Costs-in-Arbitration/, accessed 20 Sep. 2016.
8. United Nations Commission on International Trade Law (UNCITRAL), 2016 UNCITRAL Notes on Organizing Arbitral Proceedings, Pre-Release Publication http://www.uncitral.org/pdf/english/texts/arbitration/arb-notes/arb-notes-2016-e-pre-release.pdf, accessed 20 Sep. 2016.
9. For a similar suggestion see *Raeschke-Kessler, supra* n. 4, 523–536.
10. This is evidenced, *inter alia*, by the new Arbitration Rules of the Chartered Institute of Arbitrators, effective as of 1 Dec. 2015, which do not address the issue of a settlement other than as a reason for the termination of the proceedings, vid. Chartered Institute of Arbitrators, Arbitration Rules of the Chartered Institute of Arbitrators http://www.ciarb.org/docs/default-source/ciarbdocuments/arbitration/ciarb-arbitration-rules.pdf?sfvrsn=14 accessed 20 Sep. 2016.

§27.02 IS SETTLEMENT FACILITATION BY INTERNATIONAL ARBITRATION TRIBUNALS DESIRABLE?

When filing a request for arbitration, the underlying aim of a party in dispute with another party is, in the first place, to obtain a favourable decision and a title which can be executed against its opponent. Such opponent, in turn, will target at a dismissal of the claim and, in case it brings a counter-claim, at a decision awarding the counter-claim. So far, so good. The arbitrators, *audiatur et altera pars*, will invite the opponent to respond to the claim and to the counter-claim. While, perhaps, in some rare cases, in view of the claim (and the counter-claim) and the response(s) thereto, the legal conclusions may be clear, reality shows that, in most cases, at this point in time, the dispute resolution process will only start. A second and often a third round of submissions will occur, document production requests will be made, witness statements and expert opinions be prepared and sometimes lengthy hearings will take place with witnesses and experts being examined and cross-examined, closing and post hearing statements filed or even orally presented followed by submissions on cost. Not rarely, the help of state courts is applied for by the parties or even by the tribunal. Subsequently, and if the award is not honoured voluntarily, the matter passes on to the recognition, enforcement and setting-aside stages.

Following these procedures, dispute resolution by arbitration, may turn into a rather lengthy and also quite costly exercise. The original target of having a dispute expeditiously resolved by learned experts, may become hard to reach. Some of the described procedural operations, at times, may turn into defeating the overall purpose of arbitration. As a result, users of commercial arbitration are becoming increasingly dissatisfied[11] with this development as they only obtain the final result of the dispute resolution at a late point in time and at a high cost which is often perceived as disproportionate in relation to the value of the issue at stake. Hence, the users are frequently looking for quicker ways to take the dispute forward and, above all, to bring it to an end such that they can again use their resources for the pursuit of their pure business interests.

There may be cases which parties, for some reasons, need to have decided upon, as a matter of principle or because the decision as to whether a disputed approach of their doing business is legally admissible or not. A vast portion of disputes, however, does not necessarily call for a black and white decision. Many disputes do not arise out of only one party infringing the rights of the other one. Often enough both parties, to some extent, have contributed to one side suffering damages or to causing a default of an obligation. Such cases may be better, more quickly and less costly resolved by a settlement.

Another group of disputes may occur in the context of an ongoing business relation. The resolution of the problem by an award creating a looser versus winner situation may not help the business relation at all and be even counterproductive for its future success.

---

11. Vid. *inter alia*, Hohbeck/Koebke/Mahnken, Schiedsgerichtsbarkeit im internationalen Anlagenbau – ein Auslaufmodell? SchiedsVZ 2007, 225.

While parties, and often also their Counsel, in view of the subjective view immanent to their position in the dispute, should almost naturally be convinced of having a case, a sole arbitrator or a three arbitrator panel, having read a complete statement of claim and a complete statement of defence, with some deliberation, would almost inevitably have some degree of an idea of where the case is likely to go or, at least, which are the critical points for either party to eventually succeed with their claim or their prayer to dismiss such claim. This puts the arbitrators in a privileged position giving them a panoramic and above all more objective view of the success chances of either side.

In summary, there is: (i) a substantial group of cases calling for settlement rather than for a decision; and (ii) an interest of many users of arbitration to avoid lengthy and costly proceedings. And, provided the arbitrators are on top of the case, there is one or, in the case of a three arbitrator panel, there are three well qualified learned persons, more often than not selected by the parties, having an objective perspective of the issues at stake, who may act as born guides for the parties to lead them in finding a settlement. As a result, facilitating settlements of disputes by arbitrators offers response to a need of the users by those who have been called to decide on the dispute and therefore best know its legal implications and the success chances of the parties without the need of seeking recourse in mediation.

Thus, in general, the clear answer to the question is that, for a large group of disputes, settlement facilitation by arbitrators may be a desirable option.

§27.03 ARE HYBRID DISPUTE RESOLUTION MODELS TRULY AN ALTERNATIVE?

Let us, however, pause for a moment. The concern of common law based members of the international arbitration community, which makes them oppose so much the idea of settlement facilitation in arbitration, is that the arbitrator, called to decide the case but, however, engaging in settling it, may become biased and, if no settlement is reached, can no longer be sufficiently neutral to objectively pass a decision of the dispute. Often, the perspective of common law based arbitrators makes them confuse settlement facilitation with mediation. Mediation, however, is not only fundamentally different from arbitration but also quite different from settlement facilitation in arbitration. Mediation, as such, includes the balancing of the parties' expectations and aspirations and, almost as a defining element, caucusing, i.e., the holding of separate meetings with either party. This, however, is something innately inadmissible in arbitration. The borderlines between arbitration and mediation are not always absolutely clear.

Mediation, certainly in response to arbitration and court litigation having become too costly and too lengthy in the eyes of many users, has evolved as an attractive alternative option for many parties who have substituted arbitration clauses by provisions establishing mediation as the means of resolution of disputes arising out of the contractual relation. Mediation, however, implies the willingness of an approximation of the parties towards a consensual solution to the dispute. If there is no such consensus or if one party obstructs the approximation process, a mediation exercise may eventually leave the parties without a solution and with their dispute unresolved. Another shortcoming of mediation is, in the absence of binding rules and legislation to that end, the lack of enforceability of the obligations the parties forming part of the mediated result.

With a view to overcoming these shortcomings and deficiencies of mediation, hybrid forms of dispute resolution have developed. The most common of these approaches is the med-arb formula. In a nutshell, med-arb dispute resolution clauses have parties agree to start attempting the reach an agreement within a mediation process which, if a resolution of their dispute in such process fails, then provides for the transformation of the dispute resolution into a classic arbitration. At first sight, this formula looks promising and persuasive. It implies, however, two serious downsides: First, it does not resolve the enforceability issue that arises if a party refrains from complying with its obligations contained in the mediated agreement on the resolution of the dispute. Secondly, and more importantly, if the mediation part of the process fails, one wonders whether the unsuccessful mediator/arbitrator(s) can act as arbitrators in the subsequent arbitration part of the process. Having tried to mediate the dispute, the mediators-become-arbitrators will, as a result of caucusing with either party, have intrinsic knowledge not only of the matter in dispute as such but also of the internal perspectives and views of the parties, of which the other parties will not know. This disqualifies them much more to act as arbitrators in the subsequent arbitration as compared to an arbitrator who has unsuccessfully tried to facilitate a settlement of the parties in a pure arbitration. Hence, the risk of bias is clear and even the idea of a waiver of a challenge of such a mediator when he then becomes the arbitrator, may be questionable. The solution of choice is that the mediator(s) cannot be the arbitrator(s) in the same case. This, in turn, means that the parties need to appoint a new set of dispute resolvers, i.e., the arbitrator(s) and a new procedural timetable has to be established. This duplication makes the process complicated, lengthy and costly. In other words: it may defeat the purpose of avoiding the perceived disadvantages of arbitration. It does therefore not come as too much of a surprise that med-arb approaches, on a global perspective, have not been too successful.

The Arb-Med-Arb Protocol of the Singapore International Arbitration Centre (SIAC) in conjunction with the Singapore International Mediation Centre (SIMC) (AMA-Protocol)[12] was designed to overcome some of these deficiencies. The basic idea is rather simple: The resolution of a dispute is started, by virtue of an arbitration clause referring it to arbitration under the SIAC Arbitration Rules, by the filing of an Arbitration Notice with SIAC. After the arbitration process has started, the arbitration tribunal is validly constituted and both the Notice of arbitration as well as the Response to the Notice of arbitration have been submitted, the matter will automatically be referred to mediation under the SIMC Mediation Rules and the arbitration proceedings be stayed. The mediation shall be conducted during a given period. The mediator(s)

---

12. Vid. Singapore International Mediation Centre/Singapore International Arbitration Centre, SIAC-SIMC Med-Arb Protocol http://simc.com.sg/siac-simc-arb-med-arb-protocol/ accessed 20 Sep. 2016.

shall not be identical with the arbitrators of the arbitration tribunal in place, such that the impartiality of all dispute resolvers engaged in the matter is conserved. If the mediation is successful, the parties may request the arbitration tribunal already in place to issue an award by consent following the terms of the mediated agreement making it enforceable under the 1958 New York UN-Convention. If the mediation is not or not entirely successful, the parties can ask the matter to be re-transferred to the arbitration tribunal already in place in order to resolve the matter by rendering an award.

This simple formula is complemented by seamless processing of the file from SIAC to SIMC and back and by the single filing fee for matters brought before the SIAC under the AMA Protocol.

The AMA Protocol may be noteworthy for its creativity in overcoming some shortcomings of classic med-arb approaches. It also may help, to some extent, overcome the common law-civil law settlement dilemma in cross-cultural arbitrations.[13] It does, however, still suffer from one major deficiency: Parties may end up needing two sets of disputes resolvers: the arbitrators and the mediators.

It is therefore worthwhile examining the conditions for settlement facilitation within an arbitration.

§27.04 PRE-CONDITIONS FOR SETTLEMENT FACILITATION BY INTERNATIONAL ARBITRATION TRIBUNALS

There are fundamental and, in my view, indispensable pre-conditions for settlement facilitation by an arbitral tribunal and there are other conditions which may, at times and as the case may develop, be foregone but which, in most instances, will be, if met, helpful and favourable for the reaching of a settlement. The following are among those pre-conditions which are indispensable:

(1) First and most fundamentally: The arbitrators must not engage in settlement facilitation insofar any of the parties is opposed to it.
(2) Settlement facilitation by the arbitral tribunal must never include caucusing. Otherwise settlement facilitation will turn into mediation.
(3) The arbitrator(s) should, in general, be pro-active case managers and they must be aware of what the parties have brought forward for their case, i.e., they must have read and reflected on the submissions of the parties. They should constantly be on top of the case as it develops. Ideally, the arbitrator(s) take the trouble of an ongoing preliminary case assessment whenever a new submission comes in. *Böckstiegel* has very instructively described this approach calling the instrument he uses for this exercise 'Tribunal Working Paper'.[14]

---

13. Vid. Reeg, *supra* n. 3, p. 18.
14. Vid. Böckstiegel, Party Autonomy and Case Management – Experiences and Suggestions of an Arbitrator, SchiedsVZ 2013, 1, 5; and also Elsing, Procedural Efficiency in International Arbitration: Choosing the Best of Both Legal Worlds, SchiedsVZ 2011, 114, 123.

(4) Settlement discussions involving the tribunal can only start after a full statement of claim and a full statement of defence have been submitted.
(5) Any attempt of a settlement facilitation by the arbitrator(s) has to be stopped as soon as any party so requests.
(6) In case a settlement is reached, the arbitral tribunal should offer to issue an award by consent following the terms of the mediated agreement making it enforceable under the 1958 New York UN-Convention.

Apart from these fundamental pre-conditions, there are other circumstances which should but not necessarily need be in place for a success of the settlement attempts and, also, for avoiding challenges of the tribunal.

(1) At the outset of the arbitration, in a case management conference, in the Procedural Order No. 1, or perhaps even in the rules of the relevant arbitration institution, parties should be required to submit, in their statement of claim, all facts and all evidence they plan to be relying on. This applies, *mutatis mutandis*, to the statement of defence. Such frontloading of the proceedings with fully-fledged statements of claim and of defence is crucial for allowing settlement facilitation by the arbitral tribunal.
(2) The arbitral tribunal may ask the parties at the very beginning of the proceedings whether they wish the arbitral tribunal to engage in settlement facilitation at all, notwithstanding the possibility for the parties to ask the arbitrators to do so at any later point in time of the proceedings.
(3) Also at the outset of the arbitration, the arbitral tribunal should ask the parties to waive any right to challenge the arbitrators for their attempts to facilitate a settlement and unless the arbitrator(s) would infringe any of the compulsory pre-conditions as established in paragraphs 1 to 5 above.
(4) Settlement facilitation attempts are helped, prior to starting them, by identifying the factual and legal issues at stake.
(5) The arbitrators should deliberate on the merits of the claim based on fully-fledged statements of claim and of defence. This implies, it cannot be stated often enough, an ongoing analysis of the merits al through the proceedings.[15]
(6) Any settlement facilitation attempts should be preceded by a tentative discussion of the merits[16] with the parties and their Counsel.
(7) Settlement facilitation attempts may also be made in respect of a part of the issues at stake.

---

15. See pre-condition number 3 above and Böckstiegel's suggestion of keeping a Tribunal Working Paper.
16. For the proposal of a discussion of the merits of the case between the tribunal and Counsel vid. Risse, Ten Drastic Proposals for Saving Time and Cost in Arbitration, Arbitration International (LCIA), Vol. 29. No. 3 (2013), 453–466, Proposal Seven, 461–462.

§27.05 SUMMARY

The above reflections show that settlement facilitation should be seen as a natural part of arbitration not only in those jurisdictions where it already is common practice or even a mandatory duty of the arbitrators to sound out the perspectives for a settlement and the parties' expectations in this respect but also in jurisdictions which, so far, have not been feeling comfortable in attributing the role of a settlement facilitator to an arbitrator. If properly done, settlement facilitation should not contravene the idea that an arbitrator's task is primarily to decide on a dispute, i.e., to render an award. Allowing settlement facilitation rather widens the role of the arbitrator towards a dispute resolver without making him a mediator.

Settlement facilitation by arbitral tribunals also responds to an expectation of users. They do not necessarily and in all instances, need to attain an award. Their prime interest is having their dispute resolved expeditiously. This target may often be reached more quickly, more easily, at lower cost and more sustainably by a settlement of the matter rather than by a lengthy arbitration ending with an award.

Settlement facilitation helps avoiding the duplication of efforts, time and cost caused by hybrid approaches. If it fails, the arbitral tribunal may still render an award.

Hence, settlement facilitation by arbitrators, if done properly, may help overcome the deficiencies of arbitration, above all in terms of cost and time involved.

CHAPTER 28
Time Limits in International Arbitral Proceedings

Klaus Sachs & Tom Christopher Pröstler

Traditionally, one of the most cited advantages of international arbitration is that it is faster than state court proceedings. However, this notion has apparently lost appeal. Today, many users of international arbitration criticise the ever-increasing length of arbitral proceedings. In the most recent Queen Mary International Arbitration Survey, only 10% of participants stated that speed was one of the most valuable characteristics of international arbitration, while 36% stated that the lack of speed was one of the worst.[1]

In order to meet the demand for faster dispute resolution, a number of arbitral institutions, including the Swiss Chambers' Arbitration Institution (SCAI), German Institution of Arbitration (DIS), Hong Kong International Arbitration Centre (HKIAC), and Singapore International Arbitral Centre (SIAC), have introduced special rules for 'expedited proceedings'. Other institutions like the International Chamber of Commerce (ICC) have time limits for passing awards in their regular rules and are working on making these time limits more effective.

In contrast, the time limits set for procedural steps in arbitral proceedings have received relatively little attention. These time limits are normally determined by the parties and arbitrators in a procedural timetable at the onset of the proceedings and, if required, are extended during the proceedings. In their sum, these time limits account for the longest part of arbitral proceedings. Thus, by setting, keeping and enforcing them, parties and arbitrators can considerably contribute to expediting arbitrations.

---

1. International Arbitration Survey: Improvements and Innovations in International Arbitration, pp. 6–7 (2015), www.arbitration.qmul.ac.uk/docs/164761.pdf.

In this article we will explore how effective time limits can help regain speed as one of the key advantages of international arbitration. We will first discuss the different ways in which procedural time limits can be established (at §28.01 below). We will then evaluate what constitutes 'right' time limits and the risks of overly long or overly short time limits (at §28.02 below). Finally, we will discuss the possible consequences and sanctions if time limits are violated (at §28.03 below).

§28.01 ESTABLISHING TIME LIMITS

Time limits can be determined by the tribunal, agreed by the parties, or established by the consent of parties and arbitrators. Furthermore, time limits can be set by an arbitral institution or by applicable law.

[A] Tribunal Determination

Modern arbitration rules and laws give tribunals wide discretion to determine the arbitral process.[2] This includes the power to determine procedural time limits.[3] In addition, arbitration rules include specific references to tribunals' power to determine time limits.

Many arbitration rules require the tribunal to establish a 'procedural' or 'provisional timetable', which sets out the time limits for the arbitration.[4] The rules generally require that the tribunal establishes the procedural timetable at an early stage of the arbitration,[5] that it consults the parties before doing so,[6] and that it provides the timetable to the parties and administrating institution.[7] For example, Article 24(2) ICC Rules provides that the timetable should be established as a result of the case management conference held between the tribunal and parties at the onset of the arbitration. Arbitration rules further give tribunals the power to fix time limits for

---

2. For example Arts 19, 22(2) ICC Rules, Art. 15(1) Swiss Rules, § 24.1 DIS Rules, Art. 13.1 HKIAC Rules, Rule 16.1 SIAC Rules, Art. 17(1) UNCITRAL Rules, Art. 19(2) UNCITRAL Model Law. Born, *International Commercial Arbitration* vol. II, § 15.03 (2nd ed., 2014); Girsberger/Voser, *International Arbitration: Comparative and Swiss Perspectives*, para. 897 (3rd ed., 2016); Poudret/Besson, *Comparative Law of International Arbitration*, paras 532 et seq. (2nd ed., 2007).
3. cf. Born, *International Commercial Arbitration* vol. II, § 15.08[P] (2nd ed., 2014); Girsberger/Voser, *International Arbitration: Comparative and Swiss Perspectives*, para. 928 (3rd ed., 2016); Reiner/Aschauer, *ICC Rules*, para. 444, in: Schütze (ed.), *Institutional Arbitration: Article-by-Article Commentary* (2013).
4. For example Art. 24(2) ICC Rules, Art. 15(3) Swiss Rules, Art. 13.2 HKIAC Rules, Art. 17(2) UNCITRAL Rules.
5. Article 15(3) Swiss Rules: 'early stage', s. 5.1 DIS Supplementary Rules for Expedited Proceedings '[a]t the onset of the proceedings'; Art. 13.2 HKIAC Rules: 'early stage', Art. 17(2) UNCITRAL Rules: '[a]s soon as practicable'.
6. Article 15(3) Swiss Rules: 'in consultation with the parties', Art. 13.2 HKIAC Rules: 'in consultation with the parties', Art. 17(2) UNCITRAL Rules: 'after inviting the parties to express their views'.
7. For example Art. 24(2) ICC Rules, Art. 15(3) Swiss Rules, Art. 13(2) HKIAC Rules, Art. 17(2) UNCITRAL Rules.

written submissions (including the statements of claim and defence),[8] hearings[9] and the production of evidence.[10]

The establishment of a comprehensive procedural timetable at the onset of proceedings is an important case management tool for tribunals. The early determination of the procedural time limits allows the parties and the tribunal to accommodate the arbitration in their own schedules and influences the volume of parties' submissions. As such, an early, well-coordinated timetable can do a lot to expedite arbitral proceedings.

While rarely expressly stated in arbitration rules or laws, based on their general procedural discretion, tribunals also have the power to amend procedural time limits previously determined by them, if and when this becomes necessary.[11] An exception is Rule 24.1 SIAC Rules, which gives tribunals the power to 'extend or abbreviate any time limits provided ... by [the tribunal's] directions'. Furthermore, Article 24(2) ICC Rules indirectly refers to tribunals' power to modify time limits by stating that 'any modifications' to the original procedural timetable must be communicated to the parties and the ICC Court.

Thus, time limits determined by tribunals remain flexible and can be adapted by tribunals even where one or all parties do not agree. Tribunals can therefore amend such time limits where a party requests an amendment for valid reasons, but the other party nevertheless refuses.

[B] Parties' Agreement

The discretion of tribunals to determine the arbitral process is limited by the overriding principle of party autonomy.[12] Pursuant to this principle, parties can agree on the procedural rules, including time limits applicable to their arbitration, with binding effect.[13] If a tribunal conducts an arbitration in violation of procedural rules agreed by the parties, it may violate party autonomy, possibly overstepping its jurisdiction and endangering the validity of an award.[14]

---

8. For example Arts 18(1), 19(1), 23 Swiss Rules, § 9 DIS Rules (only for Statement of Defence), Arts 16.1, 17.1, 21 HKIAC Rules, Rules 17.2, 17.3, 17.4, 17.6 SIAC Rules, Arts 20.1, 21.1, 25 UNCITRAL Rules.
9. For example Art. 26(1) ICC Rules, Art. 25(1) Swiss Rules, Art. 22.4 HKIAC Rules, Rules 21.2 SIAC Rules, Art. 28(1) UNCITRAL Rules.
10. For example Art. 24(4) Swiss Rules, Art. 27(1) UNCITRAL Rules.
11. cf. Girsberger/Voser, *International Arbitration: Comparative and Swiss Perspectives*, para. 963 (3rd ed., 2016).
12. Born, *International Commercial Arbitration* vol. II, § 15.02[E][1] (2nd ed., 2014); Poudret/Besson, *Comparative Law of International Arbitration*, para. 531 (2nd ed., 2007), referring to the exceptions to this general rule under Italian and Swedish arbitration law.
13. Born, *International Commercial Arbitration* vol. II, § 15.02 (2nd ed., 2014); Girsberger/Voser, *International Arbitration: Comparative and Swiss Perspectives*, para. 889 (3rd ed., 2016); cf. also Art. 19 ICC Rules.
14. Born, *International Commercial Arbitration* vol. III, § 15.02[E][1], § 25.04[C][5], § 25.04[D][3] (2nd ed., 2014); Borris/Hennecke, *Article V*, paras 232–233, in: Wolff (ed.), *New York Convention: Commentary* (2012).

With regard to procedural time limits this is an undesirable consequence, as, in contrast to most procedural rules, time limits often need to be amended throughout arbitrations. If amendments of procedural time limits were only possible by party agreement, fast and flexible reactions to changed circumstances could be prevented and parties seeking to stall arbitral proceedings would be equipped with additional weapons.[15]

In most cases this consequence will not be intended by parties at the time they agree time limits. Rather, by concluding an arbitration agreement, parties have expressed their overriding objective to resolve their disputes by arbitration. Generally, this objective also includes the intention to submit the dispute to effective and expeditious proceedings.[16] Time limits which can only be amended by party agreement would endanger this objective. Thus, unless the circumstances provide the contrary, when agreeing on time limits, parties will generally not intend to prevent tribunals from later amending these time limits, if and when this becomes necessary.

An exception may be time limits specifically targeted at the tribunal, such as time limits for rendering the award. In such cases, circumstances may well show that parties intended these time limits to bind the tribunal. Thus, depending on the gravity of the violation, there may be grounds for the cancellation of the award.[17] However, even in these situations courts are reluctant to cancel awards, considering that this would necessarily mean to delay the resolution of the relevant dispute even further.[18]

Some arbitral rules include provisions intended to guard against a binding effect of time limits agreed by the parties. For example, Article 17(2) UNCITRAL Rules provides that tribunals may 'extend or abridge any period of time ... agreed by the parties'. Where parties have agreed on arbitration rules containing a respective provision, this is another strong indication that the parties do not intend party agreed time limits to bind the tribunal.[19] However, as the binding nature of such a provision itself derives from the parties' (earlier) agreement on the applicable arbitration rules, such a provision remains subject to change by the parties' (successive) agreements. Accordingly, such a provision is no absolute protection against an adverse interpretation if later circumstances so permit.

---

15. Cf. also Böckstiegel, *Case Management by Arbitrators: Experiences and Suggestions*, pp. 120–121, in: Aksen/Böckstigel et al., *International Law, Commerce and Dispute Resolution: Liber Amicorum in honour of Robert Briner* (2005).
16. cf. Wilske, *Legal Challenges to Delayed Arbitration Awards*, 6(2) Contemp. Asia Arb. J. 153, 175-16 (2013).
17. Bahrain Court of Cassation, *Action No. 433/2003* (17 Nov. 2003); Belgian Court of Cassation, *Case No. C.08.0028.F/1* (5 May 2009); Indian Supreme Court, *NBCC Limited v. JG Engineering Pvt Ltd* (2010) 2, SCC 385; Tunisian Court of Appeal, *Case No. 134* (3 Dec. 2002); cf. also Wilske, *Legal Challenges to Delayed Arbitration Awards*, 6(2) Contemp. Asia Arb. J. 153, 168–171 (2013).
18. Swiss Federal Tribunal, *Case No. 4P.14/2004* (16 Mar. 2004) 22 ASA Bull. 770; US District Court for the Eastern District of Tennessee, *Dean Witter Reynolds, Inc. v. McCoy*, 853 F. Supp. 1023 (E.D. Tenn. 1994) U.S. Court of Appeals for the Third Circuit, *PaineWebber Inc. v. Hofmann*, 984 F.2d 1372 (3d Cir. 1993); cf. also German Federal Court of Justice, *Case No. III ZR 12/87* (14 Apr. 1988) BGHZ 104, 178; Wilske, *Legal Challenges to Delayed Arbitration Awards*, 6(2) Contemp. Asia Arb. J. 153,i 168–171 (2013).
19. Born, *International Commercial Arbitration* vol. II, § 15.03[C] (2nd ed., 2014).

In order to prevent uncertainty, parties should thus clearly indicate when they intend to bind the tribunal to agreed time limits and when not. The latter is best done by phrasing communications on procedural time limits as requests to the tribunal even where these have been previously discussed and agreed inter partes. Further, as explained below, where terms of reference are agreed at the beginning of an arbitration a provision discharging the binding effect of party agreed time limits on the tribunal can be included.

[C] Terms of Reference

Terms of reference serve to provide a framework for an arbitration and, *inter alia*, set out its 'procedural parameters'.[20] Pursuant to Article 23(1)(g) ICC Rules the terms of reference in ICC arbitrations must include the 'particulars of the applicable procedural rules'. The terms of reference are signed by the parties and arbitrators, and – in case of ICC arbitration – approved by the ICC Court. Determinations made therein are binding for tribunals.[21]

In order to preserve procedural flexibility, it is therefore not advisable to include the procedural timetable or other time limits in the terms of reference.[22] Instead, the terms of reference can be used to strengthen procedural flexibility by expressly stating the tribunal's right to amend time limits were necessary. This may include a provision similar to Article 17(2) UNCITRAL Rules granting the tribunal the power to, where necessary, amend party agreed time limits.

[D] Arbitral Institutions and Rules

Time limits can also be determined by arbitral institutions. They can be directly prescribed in the institution's arbitration rules or the arbitration rules can give the institution's organs the power to fix time limits. Arbitration rules stipulate time limits for a number of procedural steps. These include time limits for filing the answer to a request for arbitration,[23] the submission of counterclaims,[24] the reply to

---

20. Fry/Greenberg/Mazza, *The Secretariat's Guide to ICC Arbitration*, para. 3-827 (2002); Poudret/Besson, *Comparative Law of International Arbitration*, para. 575 (2nd ed., 2007).
21. Poudret/Besson, *Comparative Law of International Arbitration*, para. 576 (2nd ed., 2007).
22. Cf. Fry/Greenberg/Mazza, *The Secretariat's Guide to ICC Arbitration*, paras 3-855 to 3-857 (2002).
23. For example 5(1) Article ICC Rules, Art. 3(7) Swiss Rules, Art. 5.1 HKIAC Rules, Rule 4.1 SIAC Rules, Art. 4(1) UNCITRAL Rules. Article 9 DIS Rules leaves it to the tribunal to determine the time limit for the statement of defence, which is Respondent's first substantial submission under these rules.
24. For example Art. 5(5) ICC Rules, Art. 3(10) Swiss Rules, Art. 5.4 HKIAC Rules. Art. 10 DIS Rules gives tribunals discretion to decide the admissibility of a counterclaim. Rules 4.2 and 17.3 SIAC Rules allow respondents to submit counterclaims with their response to the notice of arbitration and, if such an early submission is not made, leave it to the tribunal to determine the time limit for the counterclaims. Article 4(2)(e) UNCITRAL Rules allows respondents to submit counterclaims with their response to the notice of arbitration and, if such an early submission is not made, Art. 21(3) UNCITRAL Rules gives tribunals discretion to decide the admissibility of a counterclaim.

§28.01[D]

counterclaims,[25] the nomination or appointment of arbitrators,[26] and the request for the correction or interpretation of an award.[27]

As is obvious from the examples above, main areas for time limits determined in arbitral rules are the time limits for the initial submissions in an arbitration and for constituting the arbitral tribunal. As such, these time limits ensure a fast and efficient commencement of arbitral proceedings. Furthermore, time limits determined by arbitration rules concern the time after the award has been rendered. These time limits require that any corrections or interpretations to an award are requested instantly or not at all. Thus, the time limits provide fast legal certainty as to the exact content of an award.

In some cases, arbitration rules will only determine default time limits, subject to amendment by tribunals. Default time limits are most common for parties' written submissions. Their purpose is to benchmark a 'normal' time limit and to guide arbitrators, counsel and parties in establishing an efficient procedural timetable. As default time limits are normally comparatively short,[28] their guidance may serve to prevent overly long time limits.

Some arbitration rules also stipulate a maximum length for the arbitration itself or for the tribunal's preparation of the award. For example, Article 30 ICC Rules provides that tribunals are generally to render their final award within six months from the conclusion of the terms of reference. Since the 2012 ICC Rules, the ICC Court has the power to deviate from this default time limit and fix a time limit based on the procedural timetable determined by the tribunal following the case management conference. Thus, the ICC Court can now take into account the scope and complexity of a case and set an appropriate time limit. The ICC Court may further extend the original time limit for the rendering of the award if this becomes necessary.

Similarly, rules on expedited procedures include time limits for the rendering of the final award. Article 42(1)(d) Swiss Rules, Article 41.2(f) HKIAC Rules and Rule 5.2(d) SIAC Rules require an award to be made within six months from the date the file was transmitted to the tribunal (SCAI and HKIAC) or the date the tribunal was constituted (SIAC). Under all three rules, the institution may extend this time limit in 'exceptional circumstances'. Section 1.2 DIS Supplementary Rules for Expedited Proceedings requires the award within six months for a sole arbitrator and nine months for a three-member tribunal. Pursuant to section 6.1 of said Rules, these time limits may be modified by parties or, if there is good cause, by tribunals. However, once a tribunal is constituted, parties require its consent for modification.

Time limits for the arbitration as a whole or for the final award are intended to increase overall procedural efficiency by motivating tribunals to conduct the proceedings in an expedited way and, most importantly, prepare awards in the shortest

---

25. For example Art. 5(6) ICC Rules.
26. For example Art. 12(2), (3) ICC Rules, Arts 7, 8 Swiss Rules, §§ 12, 13, 14 DIS Rules, Arts 7, 8 HKIAC Rules, Rules 7.2, 8.2, 9 SIAC Rules, Arts 8, 9 UNCITRAL Rules.
27. For example Art. 35(1), (2) ICC Rules, Arts 35, 36 Swiss Rules, §§ 37.2, 37.3 DIS Rules, Arts 37, 38 HKIAC Rules, Rule 29 SIAC Rules, Arts 37, 38 UNCITRAL Rules.
28. Regularly the default time limit for written submissions is between thirty and forty-five days.

appropriate time. The effectiveness of such time limits has been questioned, especially where no direct remedies exist to sanction their violation. Nevertheless, their psychological effect should not be underestimated. In addition, the ICC as the primary institution using such time limits has reworked its sanctions regime in this regard.[29]

Further, arbitration rules regularly determine that the organs of the institutions can amend the time limits fixed in their rules. In fewer cases, this power is also given to parties. SCIA, HKIAC and SIAC each include a general rule allowing their organs to amend time limits fixed in their rules.[30] In the ICC Rules, this power is regularly stated in connection to the specific time limits.[31] By giving their own organs the power to amend the time limits fixed in their arbitration rules, arbitral institutions safeguard the flexibility of arbitral proceedings.

Article 38(1) ICC Rules grants parties the power to shorten the time limits stipulated in the ICC Rules. In case a tribunal has already been constituted, this is only possible with the tribunal's approval. Article 38(2) ICC Rules then grants the ICC Court the power to extend any time limit abridged by parties, if it deems this necessary for it or tribunals to fulfil their responsibilities. This provision is interesting, as it apparently states the obvious. As discussed above, party autonomy allows parties to determine the time limits for their arbitration. In principle, such party determined time limits also bind administrating arbitral institutions. However, arbitral institutions offer their administrative services in respect of a specific set of rules, normally their own arbitration rules.[32] Any deviation by the parties from binding provisions, including time limits, contained in the relevant arbitration rules, thus contradicts the conditions of the institution's offer to administer proceedings. In such cases, institutions may choose not to administer the proceedings, leaving the parties with a defunct arbitration agreement. As a consequence, mandatory time limits stipulated by an arbitral institution in or based on its arbitral rules are effectively binding for parties choosing these rules.

[E] Arbitration Laws

Finally, time limits can be established by arbitration laws. Similar to arbitration rules, arbitration laws may fix specific time limits or give independent institutions or state organs the power to determine them.

Arbitration laws may determine time limits for procedural steps for ad-hoc arbitrations conducted in their jurisdiction. Similar to arbitration rules, such time limits often refer to the initiation of an arbitration, including the appointment of arbitrators,[33]

---

29. *See* further below.
30. Article 2(2) Swiss Rules, Art. 2.4 HKIAC Rules, Rule 2.5 SIAC Rules.
31. For example Arts 4(4), 7(1), 11(2), 12(5), 13(3), 23(2), 30(1), 30(2), 36(6), 38(2) ICC Rules.
32. The HKIAC expressly offers its services either as administrative institution under its own HKIAC Rules or as appointing authority under the UNCITRAL Rules.
33. For example Art. 11(3) UNCITRAL Model Law, Art. 11(3) Singapore Arbitration Act, § 1035 German Code of Civil Procedure, ss 11(1), 11(2), 11(3) Hong Kong Arbitration Ordinance.

or the correction and interpretation of awards.[34] Mostly, such time limits are non-mandatory and can be amended by the parties.

Arbitration laws may also determine time limits for arbitrations as a whole or the rendering of awards by tribunals. Most arbitration laws do not contain such time limits. However, exceptions include the arbitration laws of Belgium, Brazil, Delaware, Egypt, India, Quebec, Spain, Taiwan and Turkey.[35] In France, such time limits exist for domestic arbitrations.[36]

Mandatory law limits party autonomy.[37] Thus, mandatory statutory time limits have to be adhered to in arbitral proceedings and their violation may infringe the validity of awards.[38] Where they exist, mandatory statutory time limits for the arbitration or award should be taken seriously.[39] Most arbitration laws including such time limits allow parties, or even tribunals, to derogate from the time limits – a possibility which should be used where appropriate.

In addition, arbitration laws regularly stipulate the time limits for submitting challenges and enforcement requests to the competent courts following the rendering of awards by tribunals. However, technically these are not procedural time limits regarding the arbitration, as they actually concern following state court proceedings.

§28.02 FINDING THE 'RIGHT' TIME LIMIT

Time limits are a central tool for making arbitral proceedings expeditious and efficient. However, to fulfil this purpose, time limits need to have the right length. What then is the 'right' length for time limits in international arbitration and what are the dangers of overly long or short time limits?

[A] Overly Long Time Limits

If overly long time limits are fixed, the overall duration of arbitrations increases. This is in itself undesirable as it deprives parties of a key arbitration benefit, i.e., expeditious dispute resolution. The negative effect of overly long time limits even potentiates itself in additional procedural inefficiencies, inflated legal costs and unnecessary accumulation of contractual payments, damages or interest. In extreme cases, overly long time limits can even constitute a violation of procedural public policy and thereby frustrate arbitral proceedings as a whole.

---

34. For example Art. 33 UNCITRAL Model Law, Art. 19B(2) Singapore Arbitration Act, § 1058 German Code of Civil Procedure, s. 69 Hong Kong Arbitration Ordinance.
35. Articles 1680(3), 1713(2) Belgian Code of Civil Procedure, Art. 23 Brazilian Arbitration Act, s. 5808 Delaware Rapid Arbitration Act, Art. 45 Egyptian Arbitration Act, s. 29A(1) Indian Arbitration Act, Art. 642 Quebec Code of Civil Procedure, Art. 37(2) Spanish Arbitration Act, Art. 10(B) Turkish International Arbitration Act, Art. 21 Taiwanese Arbitration Act.
36. Article 1463 French Code of Civil Procedure.
37. Born, *International Commercial Arbitration* vol. II, § 15.04[B] (2nd ed., 2014); Girsberger/Voser, *International Arbitration: Comparative and Swiss Perspectives*, paras 900 et seq. (3rd ed., 2016).
38. Born, *International Commercial Arbitration* vol. III, § 25.04[D][3] (2nd ed., 2014).
39. cf. Wilske, *Legal Challenges to Delayed Arbitration Awards*, 6(2) Contemp. Asia Arb. J. 153, 159, 160 (2013).

If intervals between different procedural steps are too long, arbitrators, counsel and party representatives will inevitably lose detailed case knowledge,[40] thereby requiring additional review times prior to submissions, hearings, procedural requests and decisions. Where large corporations and/or law firms are involved, this drain of case knowledge may be increased by changes of personnel, especially at the more junior levels. The same may apply regarding tribunal secretaries or case handlers at administrating institutions. Such brain drain can considerably hamper the effective conduct of arbitral proceedings, infringe the quality of decisions and inevitably leads to longer review times.

There is also a general correlation between the length and the costs of an arbitration. If the length is not due to the complexity or size of the dispute, but rather due to overly long time limits, cost increases may not be proportionate. As stated above, long time limits require longer review times for arbitrators, counsel and parties to recall necessary case knowledge or for new personnel to familiarise themselves with the case. Also, if counsel are left with overly long time for the preparation of written submissions, the scope of submissions may increase without the actual content following suit. The same may apply to the preparation of document requests, expert reports, witness statements, cross-examinations, oral submissions and other procedural steps. Consequently, counsel, arbitrators and experts may spend more time and effort on a case than necessary, appropriate or justifiable. Such excessive efforts also mean excessive costs.

Further, overly long time limits may increase the amounts of contractual payments, damages or interest owed by the losing party. Considering the amounts at stake in high profile international arbitrations, even increasing the time for which pre-award interest is owed can drastically increase a losing party's payment obligations. The financial effect is even greater where outstanding contractual payments or damages increase with time due to parties' unsettled legal relationships.

In many cases the losing party will have to bear the consequences of overly long time limits. However, overly long time limits may also deprive an ultimately successful party of benefits that cannot be adequately remedied. For example, business opportunities or good will may be lost. In extreme cases, overly long time limits may even prevent parties from receiving justice, if they run out of money to continue proceedings or if damage irreversibly perpetuates itself during proceedings. In such extreme cases, overly long time limits may result in a violation of procedural public policy. One element of procedural public policy recognised in many jurisdictions is the right to justice.[41] This right is violated when the duration of proceedings factually prevents a party from pursuing its rights ('justice delayed is justice denied').[42]

---

40. cf. Wilske, *Legal Challenges to Delayed Arbitration Awards*, 6(2) Contemp. Asia Arb. J. 153, 156 (2013).
41. Haas, *Part 3: New York Convention*, Art. V, para. 109, in: Weigand (ed.), *Practitioner's Handbook on International Arbitration* (2002).
42. cf. Wilske, *Legal Challenges to Delayed Arbitration Awards*, 6(2) Contemp. Asia Arb. J. 153, 179 (2013).

[B] Overly Short Time Limits

Overly short time limits can also lead to undesirable results. If unrealistically short, time limits can provoke later requests for their extension. If granted, such requests can throw off the procedural timetable and ultimately lead to longer and less efficient proceedings.[43]

If tribunals enforce overly short time limits, they may deprive parties of a reasonable opportunity to present their case. The right to present one's case is also an integral part of the procedural public policy recognised throughout jurisdictions and is expressly protected under Article V(1)(b) New York Convention.[44] It follows that any award issued on a procedural timetable that did not allow one of the parties to present its case, may be set aside at the place of arbitration or may be denied enforcement.

[C] The 'Right' Time Limits

In conclusion, both overly long and overly short time limits should be avoided, especially in their most extreme forms. Instead, time limits should be long enough to duly accomplish the procedural steps they regulate, but not so long as to allow slack or proliferation.

Beyond the time limits surrounding the initiation of arbitral proceedings and for corrections and interpretations of awards, there can be no 'one fits all' approach. Rather, in determining time limits, the factual and legal circumstances of the case have to be taken into account. In addition, procedural timetables should include a reasonable reserve in order to allow (smaller) amendments of time limits which may become necessary throughout the ongoing proceedings.

§28.03 CONSEQUENCES OF BREACHING TIME LIMITS

Most tribunals and parties in international arbitrations adhere to time limits. However, if parties and tribunals choose to ignore time limits, the necessity of effective sanctions may arise.

[A] Sanctions Against Parties

If parties breach time limits stipulated in arbitration rules, the sanctions will most often follow from said rules. Parties that do not nominate or appoint arbitrators in time lose

---

43. Reiner/Aschauer, *ICC Rules*, para. 444, in: Schütze (ed.), *Institutional Arbitration: Article-by-Article Commentary* (2013).
44. United Nations Convention on the Recognition and Enforcement of Foreign Arbitral Awards (New York, 1958).

their right to make the nomination or appointment.[45] In case respondents fail to submit answers to a request for arbitration, tribunals can render default awards.[46] Counterclaims may be excluded if they are not filed in time,[47] and corrections or interpretations of awards are not possible after the time limit for their request.[48]

The sanctions tribunals can impose if parties fail to adhere to time limits are less obvious. However, if applied, these sanctions can also have a strong effect.

[1] Extensions for Non-dilatory Parties

First, tribunals can award extensions to the non-dilatory party equivalent to the delay caused by the dilatory party. In most cases, such an extension is commanded by procedural fairness and will work less as a sanction against the dilatory party than as a compensation for the non-dilatory party. However, tribunals may choose to subtract the time extensions awarded to both parties from the time limits for the dilatory parties' following submissions. Thereby, tribunals can preserve the overall length of proceedings and the key dates in the procedural timetable, including hearing dates, while sanctioning dilatory parties. Where appropriate and within the boundaries of procedural fairness, tribunals can also grant longer extensions to non-dilatory parties.

[2] Exclusion of Submissions

Second, tribunals can exclude late submissions. This sanction may impact dilatory parties' right to present their case and should therefore be exercised with care. Tribunals should take into account whether the dilatory party had or has any other opportunity to present the submission's content, albeit not in as much detail or in such a convenient time, and whether the submission's exclusion would impede the non-dilatory party's case or defence.[49] Further, tribunals should give ample warning before dismissing submissions and, if parties present reasons for a late submission, should properly weigh these reasons in their decisions.[50]

[3] Adverse Cost Decisions

Third, tribunals can take breaches of time limits into account in their cost decisions. Most arbitration rules give tribunals the power to take into account the circumstances

---

45. For example Arts 12(2), 12(3), 12(4) ICC Rules, Arts 7(4), 8(4) Swiss Rules, § 12, 13 DIS Rules, Arts 7, 8 HKIAC Rules, Rules 7.1, 8.2, 9.1, 9.2 SIAC Rules, Arts 8, 9 UNCITRAL Rules, Art. 11(3) UNCITRAL Model Law, Art. 9A(2) Singapore Arbitration Act, § 1035(3) German Code of Civil Procedure.
46. For example Art. 5(2) ICC Rules, Art. 28(1) Swiss Rules, § 30.1 DIS Rules, Art. 26(2) HKIAC Rules, Rule 17.9 SIAC Rules, Art. 30(1) UNCITRAL Rules, Art. 25 UNCITRAL Model Law, § 1048(2) German Code of Civil Procedure, s. 53 Hong Kong Arbitration Ordinance.
47. cf. Fry/Greenberg/Mazza, *The Secretariat's Guide to ICC Arbitration*, para. 3-175 (2002).
48. Fry/Greenberg/Mazza, *The Secretariat's Guide to ICC Arbitration*, para. 3-1268 (2002).
49. Scherer, *Article V*, paras 172–173, in: Wolff (ed.), *New York Convention: Commentary* (2012).
50. Scherer, *Article V*, para. 172, in: Wolff (ed.), *New York Convention: Commentary* (2012).

of the case when allocating arbitration costs.[51] Article 37(5) ICC Rules specifies that this also includes 'the extent to which each party has conducted the arbitration in an expeditious and cost-effective manner'.[52] Other arbitration rules are less explicit. Nevertheless, tribunals are generally allowed to take parties' conduct into account when allocating costs, including whether a party adhered to time limits.

[B] Sanctions Against Arbitrators

[1] Loss of Jurisdiction

Arbitration laws may provide that tribunals which do not pass an award within the time limits prescribed by mandatory law lose their jurisdiction.[53] Due to its severity, this sanction may be described as effective. However, it will likely hit the parties, or at least the otherwise successful party, harder than the dilatory tribunal.[54] Thus, some arbitration laws moderate this sanction by subjecting it to the decision of state courts[55] or by allowing state courts to extend the relevant time limits,[56] each upon a party's request. Nevertheless, arbitration laws imposing such strict sanctions have to be taken seriously by both tribunals and parties.[57]

Tribunals may also lose jurisdiction if they breach time limits for awards or arbitrations stipulated in arbitration rules or arbitration agreements. However, some arbitration rules expressly state that if the time limits for an arbitration or award are exceeded, tribunals do not lose jurisdiction.[58] In the absence of such provisions, courts are nevertheless less stringent on infringements of time limits not resulting from mandatory law. In most cases, delays of a few days, weeks or in some cases even months,[59] have not led to awards being set aside or declared unenforceable. In their decisions, courts have weighed the parties' interest in receiving a binding result from their arbitration against their interest in keeping with the relevant time limits, in most cases finding for the former.

---

51. For example Art. 37(5) ICC Rules, Art. 40(1) Swiss Rules, § 35.2 DIS Rules, Art. 33.2 HKIAC Rules, Rule 31.1 SIAC Rules, Art. 42(1) UNCITRAL Rules.
52. Cf. also Fry/Greenberg/Mazza, *The Secretariat's Guide to ICC Arbitration*, para. 3-799 (2002).
53. Born, *International Commercial Arbitration* vol. III, § 25.04[D][3] (2nd ed., 2014).
54. Wilske, *Legal Challenges to Delayed Arbitration Awards*, 6(2) Contemp. Asia Arb. J. 153, 178 (2013).
55. For example Art. 45 Egyptian Arbitration Act.
56. For example Art. 21 Taiwanese Arbitration Act.
57. cf. Wilske, *Legal Challenges to Delayed Arbitration Awards*, 6(2) Contemp. Asia Arb. J. 153, 159, 160 (2013).
58. For example s. 6.2 DIS Supplementary Rules for Expedited Proceedings.
59. Swiss Federal Tribunal, *Case No. 4P.14/2004* (16 Mar. 2004) 22 ASA Bull. 770; US District Court for the Eastern District of Tennessee, *Dean Witter Reynolds, Inc. v. McCoy*, 853 F. Supp. 1023 (E.D. Tenn. 1994) U.S. Court of Appeals for the Third Circuit, *PaineWebber Inc. v. Hofmann*, 984 F.2d 1372 (3d Cir. 1993); cf. also German Federal Court of Justice, *Case No. III ZR 12/87* (14 Apr. 1988) BGHZ 104, 178.

Chapter 28: Time Limits in International Arbitral Proceedings   §28.03[B]

[2]   Replacement of Arbitrators

Under both arbitration rules and laws dilatory arbitrators may be replaced.[60] The wording of the relevant provisions differs, with some simply stating that an arbitrator can be removed if she/he 'fails to act', while others explicitly refer to arbitrators failing to 'act without undue delay' or to fulfil their 'functions ... within the prescribed time limits'. Some arbitration rules, including the ICC, Swiss and SIAC Rules, give the administering institution the power to remove dilatory arbitrators on its own initiative. Other rules, including the DIS, HKIAC and UNCITRAL Rules, and the UNCITRAL Model Law require a challenge by a party.

If an arbitrator is replaced, certain procedural steps will generally have to be repeated in order to allow the replacement arbitrator her/his own view on the case.[61] This in particular concerns oral hearings, including witness examination. Replacing dilatory arbitrators can therefore result in considerable delays and additional costs. Nevertheless, it can be a viable option where no procedural steps have to be repeated (e.g., where only written submissions were exchanged) or where the expected future delay caused by the dilatory arbitrator is greater than the delay of repeating the relevant procedural steps. In certain circumstances, repetitions may also be avoided by concluding an arbitration with a truncated tribunal.[62]

[3]   Written Report by Arbitrators

Pursuant to section 6.2 DIS Supplementary Rules for Expedited Proceeding, if an arbitration is not concluded within the time limits fixed in the Rules, tribunals have to inform the DIS and the parties in writing of the reasons in writing. This sanction mainly aims at the psychological effect of such a written report. However, unsatisfactory reasons or a refused report may also result in the DIS and parties not appointing concerned arbitrators in the future.

[4]   Reduction of Tribunals' Fees

Finally, the fees of dilatory tribunals may be reduced. This is only possible where the necessary rules and mechanisms are in place. In ICC arbitrations, tribunals' fees are fixed at the end of the proceedings by the ICC Court. Pursuant to Article 37(2) ICC Rules, when fixing the fees, the ICC Court may take into account the 'exceptional circumstances of the case'. It is the established practice of the ICC Court to use this

---

60. For example Art. 15(2) ICC Rules, Art. 12(1) Swiss Rules, § 19.1 DIS Rules, Art. 11.6 HKIAC Rules, Rule 14.2 SIAC Rules, Art. 12(3) UNCITRAL Rules, Art. 14(1) UNCITRAL Model Law. Fry/Greenberg/Mazza, *The Secretariat's Guide to ICC Arbitration*, para. 3-798 (2002).
61. Girsberger/Voser, *International Arbitration: Comparative and Swiss Perspectives*, paras 798–801 (3rd ed., 2016); Poudret/Besson, *Comparative Law of International Arbitration*, para. 435 (2nd ed., 2007).
62. For example Arts 15(5) ICC Rules, Art. 13(2)(b) Swiss Rules, Art. 12.2(b) HKIAC Rules, Rule 14.2 SIAC Rules, Art. 14(2)(b) UNCITRAL Rules.

power to sanction dilatory tribunals.[63] While in the past this practice was exercised on a case-by-case basis, as of January 2016, the ICC Court has given itself a guiding policy.[64] The Court now expects tribunals to submit draft awards to its scrutiny within three months for three-member tribunals and within two months for sole arbitrators, starting from the last substantive hearing or written submission, whichever is later. If tribunals fail to meet these time limits, the Court will reduce the otherwise appropriate fees by 5% to 10% for awards submitted within seven months, by 10% to 20% for awards submitted within ten months and by 20% or more for awards submitted more than ten months after the last substantive hearing or written submission. Where the circumstances of the case demand, the Court will derogate from these time limits and reductions. Additionally, the Court may increase the fees for tribunals which handle a case in an extraordinarily expeditious manner.

Most other arbitral institutions do not have similar practices. In most cases tribunals' fees are determined at the beginning of the proceedings either with reference to a value-based table of fees or by setting an hourly rate for the arbitrators. Also, many arbitration rules leave it to tribunals to fix the final amount of their fees at the end of the proceedings.[65]

Even where the organs of an administrating institution are involved in the final determination of tribunals' fees, this power rarely allows the reduction of tribunals' fees.[66] Rule 32.1 SIAC Rules determines that the SIAC Registrar can increase fees beyond the fees scheduled in exceptional circumstances. A corresponding power to reduce fees is not stipulated. The HKIAC also has the power to increase tribunals' fees pursuant to Article 10.3(c) HKIAC Rules, while a corresponding power to reduce fees is missing. Article 38(a) and section 2.3 of Annex B of the Swiss Rules give the power to increase tribunals' fees to tribunals themselves, provided that there are exceptional circumstances and that the SCAI Court has approved. Again, there is no power to reduce fees.

In theory, it is possible for parties to agree on a mechanism reducing the fees of a dilatory tribunal in their arbitration agreement. However, such an agreement would entail the danger of enforcing reductions where these are not appropriate. In ICC arbitration, the fee reductions are decided by the ICC Court, i.e., by a highly experienced body which is independent of the parties and the tribunal, and which has an in-depth insight into the respective proceedings. In making its decision, the ICC Court is guided, but not bound, by the published sliding scale described above. Thus, the ICC Court can adapt its decision as necessary based on the circumstances of the case. Any mechanisms stipulated in an arbitration agreement would necessarily lack such a high

---

63. Fry/Greenberg/Mazza, *The Secretariat's Guide to ICC Arbitration*, paras 3-1454 to 3-1457 (2002); Wilske, *Legal Challenges to Delayed Arbitration Awards*, 6(2) Contemp. Asia Arb. J. 153, 162 (2013).
64. ICC press release of 5 Jan. 2015 'ICC Court announces new policies to foster transparency and ensure greater efficiency' (www.iccwbo.org/News/Articles/2016/ICC-Court-announces-new-policies-to-foster-transparency-and-ensure-greater-efficiency).
65. For example Art. 38(a) Swiss Rules, § 40.2 DIS Rules, Art. 40(1) UNCITRAL Rules.
66. Next to the ICC, exceptions included the Arbitration Institute of the Stockholm Chamber of Commerce (Art. 2(4) Appendix III SCC Rules).

profile decision-making body. Consequently, including such an inflexible sanction mechanism may reduce the willingness of qualified arbitrators to take a case, and lead tribunals to rush awards, thereby possibly reducing quality and precision.

§28.04 CONCLUSION

Time limits are an effective tool for making arbitrations more expeditious. They enable the fast appointment of tribunals and start of proceedings, they secure that procedural steps are conducted contiguously and without undue delay, and they promote a speedy and final award. However, they can only accomplish these tasks if they are fixed and handled effectively. In order to accomplish this, the following points should be considered:

- Time limits should be flexible. One arbitration is not like the other and arbitrations develop during the course of proceedings. Time limits that are non-amendable by tribunals, administrating institutions or other independent bodies should thus be avoided. This especially applies for time limits agreed by parties. Parties that cooperate at the onset of proceedings may be less cooperative further down the procedural road and may refuse to amend time limits where this is objectively necessary. While in most circumstances good arguments will speak against the binding nature of such time limits, these arguments may not always be heard. Moreover, the flexibility of time limits for arbitrations as a whole or arbitral awards is also important. Such time limits can have positive, disciplinary effects on parties and arbitrators. However, if they remain non-amendable where modifications are objectively necessary, time limits may put entire proceedings in vain, thereby serving neither parties nor justice.
- Time limits should permit due accomplishment of the procedural steps they regulate, without allowing slack or proliferation. Both overly long and overly short time limits should be avoided. While the negative consequences of overly long time limits are mostly straightforward, too short time limits can also lead to delays. This is especially the case where they provoke extensions, thus rendering the procedural timetable ineffective and necessitating short-term rescheduling of hearings or other major procedural steps.
- Time limits should be given effect by tribunals, institutions and parties alike. Tribunals should only grant extension requests if these are actually justified and they should not flinch from sanctioning violations of time limits. As shown above, a rich repertoire of sanctions exists and, as demonstrated elsewhere,[67] the probability of awards being set aside or refused enforcement due to tribunals' stringent handling of proceedings is slight. Arbitral institutions

---

67. For example Gerbay, *Due Process Paranoia*, http://kluwerarbitrationblog.com/2016/06/06/due-process-paranoia.

should continue on developing new tools and strategies increasing the speed of arbitrations, and they should not hesitate to adopt such tools and strategies that have proven themselves, even where these were developed by others. Finally, parties should assist tribunals in establishing reasonable but concise procedural timetables, treat extension requests with restraint and hold their counsel to act accordingly.

CHAPTER 29
Mandatory Private Treaty Application? On the Alleged Duty of Arbitrators to Apply International Conventions

Ulrich G. Schroeter

§29.01 INTRODUCTION

International arbitration, an institution that *Pierre Karrer* has shaped and influenced through his practical work as a leading international arbitrator as well as through his scholarly writings,[1] aims at the peaceful settlement of disputes by practical, foreseeable and reasonably fast decisions,[2] thereby eventually serving the development of international trade.[3] The creation of uniform commercial law by way of international conventions is driven by a very similar aim, namely the removal of legal barriers in and the promotion of the development of international trade through the adoption of uniform rules governing international contracts.[4] International arbitration and uniform law conventions generally act in a complementary manner by following reasonably consistent policy norms,[5] one as a means of international dispute settlement, the other

---

1. Recently in particular Pierre A. Karrer, *Introduction to International Arbitration Practice – 1001 Questions and Answers* (Kluwer 2014).
2. See Karrer, *supra* n. 1, Questions 946 and 974.
3. See the Preamble of the European Convention on International Commercial Arbitration, done at Geneva on 21 Apr. 1961.
4. See the Preamble of the United Nations Convention on Contracts for the International Sale of Goods, done at Vienna on 11 Apr. 1980 (CISG).
5. On the CISG see Jeffrey Waincymer, 'The CISG and International Commercial Arbitration: Promoting a Complimentary Relationship Between Substance and Procedure', in Camilla B. Andersen and Ulrich G. Schroeter (eds.), *Sharing International Commercial Law Across National Boundaries* (Wildy, Simmonds & Hill 2008) 582–599; Jean Thieffry, 'Arbitration and the New Rules Applicable to International Sales Contracts under the United Nations Convention', *Arbitration International* 4 (1988) 52 et seq.

by creating an international 'level playing field' in the law governing the merit of disputes.

[A] A Duty of Arbitrators to Apply International Conventions?

In practice, uniform law and international arbitration usually coincide without difficulties.[6] Only occasionally, their interaction gives rise to more intricate questions. One of them is: Do arbitrators have a duty to apply international conventions? A significant number of authors indeed believe that such a legal obligation exists and have in particular argued for a duty of arbitrators to apply the 1980 Vienna Convention on Contracts for the International Sale of Goods (CISG)[7] and the 1980 Rome Convention on the Law Applicable to Contractual Obligations.[8] The same argument could be made for most other uniform private law conventions.

If the just-mentioned view is correct, it would result in what the title of this contribution refers to as 'mandatory private treaty application'. Under a duty of arbitrators to apply international conventions, treaty law would influence – some may say: disturb – the determination of the law applicable in everyday commercial arbitrations. The consequences could be far-reaching, indicating that the discussion is not merely *l'art pour l'art*: First, international conventions usually define autonomously *when* they are to be applied, and the provisions governing their applicability are often less flexible than arbitration laws that give arbitrators much discretion in determining the law to be applied to the merits. The unclear and disputed role of treaty reservations in arbitrations[9] would result in additional complexity. A generally framed duty to apply conventions could furthermore conflict with the more delicate and

---

6. See e.g., ICC Award 9887/1998, *ICC International Court of Arbitration Bulletin* 11:2 (2000) 109, 110: 'The 1980 United Nations Convention on Contracts for the International Sale of Goods (Vienna Convention) enjoys a strong recognition in the arbitration practice ...'; see also Andrea Giardina, 'International Conventions on Conflict of Laws and Substantive Law', in Albert Jan van den Berg (ed.), *Planning Efficient Arbitration Proceedings/The Law Applicable in International Arbitration* (Kluwer 1996) 459 et seq.
7. Bernard Audit, *La vente internationale de marchandises* (LGDJ 1990) 22; Christoph Benicke, 'Art. 1 CISG', in *Münchener Kommentar zum Handelsgesetzbuch* (3rd ed, Beck 2013) para. 41; Franco Ferrari, 'The CISG's Sphere of Application: Articles 1–3 and 10', in Franco Ferrari, Harry Flechtner and Ronald A. Brand (eds.), *The Draft UNCITRAL Digest and Beyond* (Sellier European Law Publishers 2004) 55 et seq; Sebastian Knetsch, *Das UN-Kaufrecht in der Praxis der Schiedsgerichtsbarkeit* (Peter Lang 2011) 41 et seq.; Ulrich Magnus, 'Art. 1 CISG', in *J. von Staudingers Kommentar zum Bürgerlichen Gesetzbuch mit Einführungsgesetz und Nebengesetzen: Wiener UN-Kaufrecht (CISG)* (Sellier – de Gruyter 2013) para. 120.
8. Mary-Rose McGuire, 'Grenzen der Rechtswahlfreiheit im Schiedsverfahrensrecht? Über das Verhältnis zwischen der Rom-I-VO und § 1051 ZPO', *Zeitschrift für Schiedsverfahren* (2011) 257, 262 et seq.; Gerhard Wagner, 'Rechtswahlfreiheit im Schiedsverfahren: Ein Probierstein für die juristische Methodenlehre', in Peter Gottwald and Herbert Roth (eds.), *Festschrift für Ekkehard Schumann zum 70. Geburtstag* (Mohr Siebeck 2001) 535, 554–556.
9. Considering reservations as potentially relevant for arbitrators: Alexis Mourre, 'Application of the Vienna Sales Convention in Arbitration', *ICC International Court of Arbitration Bulletin* 17:1 (2006) 43, 48; Georgios C. Petrochilos, 'Arbitration Conflict-of-Laws Rules and the 1980 International Sales Convention', *Revue Hellénique de Droit International* 52 (1999) 191, 199–200.

much-disputed conditions of the impact of mandatory laws in arbitrations.[10] Second, international conventions often include rules on *how* they are to be applied, Article 7(1) of the CISG and Article 18 of the Rome Convention being prominent examples. As these provisions provide legally binding principles for the conventions' interpretation and application,[11] they would affect an arbitrator's application of law to the merits of the dispute. Third, conflict-of-laws conventions sometimes subject the parties' choice of law to stricter limitations than arbitration laws that e.g., allow a choice of mere 'rules of law'.[12] Fourth, some conventions address issues of fact-finding often regarded as 'procedural' in nature, as e.g., the admissibility of certain means of evidence[13] or the burden of proof[14] – matters also covered by arbitration laws, but in a potentially different way. And fifth, some conventions (notably the CISG) have even been interpreted as governing typical arbitration matters, as e.g., the formation of arbitration agreements or their form.[15] If arbitrators were legally bound to apply these conventions, collisions with stricter or less strict provisions in arbitration laws would be difficult to avoid.

In short, treaty law would affect arbitration practice in every commercial arbitration cases that happen to fall into an international convention's sphere of application. International arbitrators would become private decision-makers with 'treaty-strings' attached.

[B] Treaty Law and Arbitration Practice: Differences in General Approach

The present contribution will try to clarify whether such an arbitrators' duty does exist, and what legal source it could arise from. As these questions reside at the intersection of treaty law and the law of international commercial arbitration, additional complexity is caused by these two areas typically employing different approaches in addressing legal problems: For treaty lawyers, the treaty is the natural starting point from which to evaluate its effect on persons and institutions, or the treaty's relationship to other legal rules and instruments. This 'treaty-centric' approach can be traced to the rule of

---

10. See e.g., Pierre Mayer, 'Mandatory Rules of Law in International Arbitration', *Arbitration International* 2 (1986) 275.
11. On Art. 7(1) of the CISG Ingeborg Schwenzer and Pascal Hachem, 'Article 7', in *Schlechtriem & Schwenzer Commentary on the UN Convention on the International Sale of Goods (CISG)* (4th ed., Oxford University Press 2016) para. 7; on Art. 18 of the Rome Convention Bernhard Rudisch, 'Artikel 18', in Dietmar Czernich and Helmut Heiss (eds.), *EVÜ – Das Europäische Schuldvertragsübereinkommen* (Orac 1999) para. 3.
12. On Art. 3 of the Rome Convention Giardina, *supra* n. 6 at 465; McGuire, *supra* n. 8 at 258.
13. See Art. 11 second sentence of the CISG.
14. For the international prevailing view under the CISG see Ingeborg Schwenzer and Pascal Hachem, 'Article 4', in *Schlechtriem & Schwenzer Commentary, supra* n. 11, para. 25. For a more sceptical position see Peter Schlechtriem and Ulrich G. Schroeter, *Internationales UN-Kaufrecht* (6th ed., Mohr Siebeck 2016) para. 211.
15. See the extensive case law and scholarly writings listed by Stefan Kröll, 'Arbitration and the CISG', in Ingeborg Schwenzer, Yesim Atamer and Petra Butler (eds.), *Current Issues in the CISG and Arbitration* (Eleven International Publishing 2013) 59, 71 et seq. and by Ulrich G. Schroeter, 'Intro to Arts 14–24', in *Schlechtriem & Schwenzer Commentary, supra* n. 11, paras 16 et seq.

customary international law[16] expressed in Article 27 of the 1969 Vienna Convention on the Law of Treaties, according to which '[a] party may not invoke the provisions of its internal law as justification for its failure to perform a treaty' – if no provisions of domestic law, arbitration-related or otherwise, can lawfully affect the performance of a treaty, it has to be the treaty itself determining how and by whom it needs to be performed.

In contrast, arbitration law and practice naturally takes as its starting point the arbitration agreement[17] that has been described as the 'foundation stone' of modern international arbitration.[18] Accordingly, the arbitration agreement is the first point of reference in identifying the legal rules that an arbitral tribunal has to apply throughout the arbitration, possibly to be supplemented by the *lex arbitri* (that, in some cases, may also set boundaries for the admissible content of arbitration agreements[19]). The instinctively different starting points of treaty lawyers and arbitration lawyers has been the source of some misunderstandings in the past, and calls for a new approach that combines the two perspectives.

§29.02 DUTY OF ARBITRATORS TO APPLY INTERNATIONAL CONVENTIONS RESULTING FROM THE CONVENTIONS THEMSELVES?

The defining characteristic of the view alleging an arbitrator's duty to apply international conventions[20] is that it, expressly or implicitly, derives this duty from the conventions themselves, independent of the parties' choice or the rules governing the respective arbitration. This approach conforms to the usual, 'treaty-centric' focus in international uniform law, but increases the risk of conflicting with arbitration principles. The central question is therefore whether such a duty follows from international conventions, and why.

[A] Wording of International Conventions

The first point of reference must be the international conventions' wording. Do they explicitly or implicitly name arbitral tribunals as addressees of their provisions, thereby providing a basis for an arbitrator's duty to apply their rules? On rare occasions, explicit provisions of this sort have indeed been proposed during the preparation of uniform law conventions. An early example can be found in Article 3 of the International Law

---

16. Kirsten Schmalenbach, 'Article 27 VCLT', in Oliver Dörr and Kirsten Schmalenbach (eds.), *Vienna Convention on the Law of Treaties – A Commentary* (Springer 2012) para. 5.
17. ICC award 1512/1970, V *Yearbook Commercial Arbitration* (1980) 174, 176; Mourre, *supra* n. 9 at 43; Jeffrey Waincymer, *Procedure and Evidence in International Arbitration* 52 (Wolters Kluwer 2012); Waincymer, *supra* n. 5 at 589.
18. Nigel Blackaby, Constantine Partasides, Alan Redfern and J. Martin Hunter, *Redfern and Hunter on International Arbitration* (6th ed., Oxford University Press 2015) at para. 1.38.
19. See Karrer, *supra* n. 1, Question 86.
20. See *supra* at §29.01[A].

Association's 1928 Draft of an International Convention for the Unification of certain Rules relating to the Conflict of Laws as regards Contracts of Sale:[21]

> If and insofar as arbitrators have to give decisions according to the law governing the contract, arbitrators shall, subject to Art. 4 [ordre public], apply this Convention.

Unfortunately, and as far as could be ascertained, neither this provision nor any similar draft provision ever became part of actual treaty law.[22] The international conventions currently in force are less clear in specifying their addressees, and provisions referring to arbitrators are few and far between.

[1] Substantive Law or Conflict-of-Laws Conventions

The CISG refers to arbitrators twice, although merely in passing: In its Article 45(3), it stipulates that '[n]o period of grace may be granted to the seller by a court *or arbitral tribunal* when the buyer resorts to a remedy for breach of contract.'[23] Article 61(3) of the CISG contains a mirror-image provision for contract breaches by the buyer. While both provisions indicate that the Sales Convention contemplates its application by arbitral tribunals,[24] they do not address why an arbitral tribunal is applying the Convention, but rather presuppose that it does. By extension, Articles 45(3), 61(3) of the CISG also say nothing about an arbitral tribunal's duty to apply the CISG. This is confirmed by the fact that Article 28 of the CISG only limits the obligation of courts to apply certain provisions of the CISG ('… a court is not bound to enter a judgement for specific performance unless the court would do so under its own law …'), but not of arbitral tribunals. The limited scope of Article 28 of the CISG has sometimes been explained by an oversight of the CISG's drafters,[25] and authors argue that it should apply to arbitral tribunals by analogy.[26] However, its wording could also be due to arbitral tribunals being under no obligation to apply the Sales Convention in the first place. At best, it therefore appears unclear whether the CISG's wording says anything about arbitrators' intended duty to apply this convention.

Other substantive law or conflict-of-laws conventions lack any explicit reference to arbitrators, thus arguably providing no indication that their drafters contemplated an arbitrator's duty to apply them. In contrast, some authors draw exactly the opposite

---

21. Text reprinted in Anton von Sprecher, *Der internationale Kauf: Abkommen und Abkommensentwürfe zur Vereinheitlichung der Kollisionsnormen des Kaufvertrags* (Polygraphischer Verlag 1956) 133.
22. For express provisions on arbitrators in conventions on the carriage of goods that, however, belong to a different category of rules see *infra* at §29.02[B][2].
23. Emphasis added.
24. Kröll, *supra* n. 15 at 61; Petrochilos, *supra* n. 9 at 192.
25. See Pilar Perales Viscasillas and David Ramos Muñoz, 'CISG & Arbitration', in Andrea Büchler and Markus Müller-Chen (eds.), *Private law: national – global – comparative. Festschrift für Ingeborg Schwenzer zum 60. Geburtstag* (Stämpfli 2011) 1355, 1365–1366.
26. Beate Gsell, 'Artikel 28', in Heinrich Honsell (ed.), *Kommentar zum UN-Kaufrecht* (2nd ed., Springer 2010) para. 8; Markus Müller-Chen, 'Article 28', in *Schlechtriem & Schwenzer Commentary*, *supra* n. 11, para. 8.

conclusion and argue that an international convention's silence about arbitral tribunals should not be read as arbitrators not being among their addressees: They regard uniform private law conventions as primarily directed at private parties, so that a distinction between courts and arbitral tribunals would supposedly not make sense.[27] To the same end, it could be pointed out that arbitral awards have the same *res judicata* effect between parties as final and binding court judgments[28] and that arbitral tribunals accordingly fulfil a task similar to that of state courts; a similarity in function that would militate in favour of a similar treatment in law.

In spite of these arguments, it is submitted that conventions making no mention of arbitrators should not be read as nevertheless (implicitly) imposing an application duty on them,[29] for at least two reasons: First, it is reasonable to assume that their drafters were aware of arbitration as a well established means of private dispute settlement and the significant freedom traditionally granted to arbitrators in determining the law to be applied to the merits – should conventions have aimed at inferring with this freedom, one would expect a sufficiently clear indication of this aim. Second, a number of international conventions on the carriage of goods have long contained explicit provisions in this regard,[30] allowing the *argumentum e contrario* that conventions that remain silent in this matter are most likely not directed at arbitrators.

[2] Arbitration Conventions

As far as international conventions unifying aspects of arbitration law are concerned, their wording is similarly not indicative of an arbitrator's obligation to apply these conventions. This is relatively clear in case of the 1958 New York Convention,[31] which from the outset is only addressed to state courts in Contracting States of that convention.[32] The wording of its Article I(1) ('This Convention shall apply to the recognition and enforcement of arbitral awards ...') makes this sufficiently clear, given that both recognition and enforcement require a state's authority, which private

---

27. McGuire, *supra* n. 8 at 262; also Wagner, *supra* n. 8 at 555 (both on the Rome Convention of 1980).
28. See e.g., § 1055 of the German Civil Code of Procedure.
29. Thomas Pfeiffer, 'Neues Internationales Vertragsrecht – Zur Rom I-Verordnung', *Zeitschrift für Europäisches Wirtschaftsrecht* (2008) 622, 623; Stephan Wilske and Lars Markert, '§ 1051 ZPO', in Vorwerk & Wolf (eds.), *Beck'scher Online-Kommentar ZPO* (21ed., C.H. Beck July 2016) para. 3.
30. See in detail *infra* §29.02[B][2].
31. Convention on the Recognition and Enforcement of Foreign Arbitral Awards, done at New York on 10 Jun. 1958.
32. ICC award 5730/1988, *Journal du droit international* 117 (1990) 1029, 1033; Julian D.M. Lew, Loukas A. Mistelis and Stefan M. Kröll, *Comparative International Commercial Arbitration* (Kluwer 2003) para. 6-48; Pierre Mayer, 'L'application par l'arbitre des conventions internationales de droit privé', in *L'internationalisation du droit: Mélanges en l'honneur de Yvon Loussouarn* (Dalloz 1994) 275, 278; Reinmar Wolff, 'Article II', in Reinmar Wolff (ed.), *New York Convention* (Beck Hart Nomos 2012) para. 187. But see Cour d'appel Paris, 20 Jan. 1987 – *Bonmar Oil NV v. Entreprise Tunisienne d'Activités*, XIII *Yearbook Commercial Arbitration* (1988) 466, 469; Albert Jan van den Berg, 'Should an International Arbitrator Apply the New York Arbitration Convention of 1958?', in Jan C. Schultsz (ed.), *The Art of Arbitration: Liber Amicorum Pieter Sanders* (Kluwer 1982) 39 et seq.

arbitral tribunals do not possess. That arbitrators frequently take the New York Convention's rules on form requirements for arbitration agreements (Article II) and on reasons for non-enforcement (Article V) into account is driven by their aim (and, under certain arbitration rules, obligation to make every effort[33]) to render an enforceable award, but is not due to the convention being directly addressed at them.

At first sight, the matter is different in case of the 1961 European Convention[34] that contains a number of provisions explicitly outlining arbitrators' tasks and obligations,[35] as e.g., its Article IV(3) ('... the necessary steps shall be taken by the arbitrator(s) already appointed ...').[36] Nevertheless, the European Convention cannot count as support for a duty of arbitrators to apply conventions,[37] because it does not list arbitrators as addressees of its provisions, but as their subject matter. Put differently: Arbitral tribunals are to the 1961 European Convention what sellers and buyers are to the 1980 Vienna Sales Convention. As a result, the convention is not applied *by* them, but *to* them, and therefore provides no help in answering the general question investigated here.

[B] Addressees of the Obligation to Apply International Conventions Under Treaty Law

As the wording of most international conventions provides limited assistance in identifying their addressees, it is appropriate to look next to general treaty law for guidance.

[1] International Uniform Private Law Conventions in General

From the perspective of treaty law, it is quite clear that arbitral tribunals are not legally bound by international conventions, because of a simple formal reason: They are not organs of a state party to a convention.[38] In support, one may look to the fundamental principle of *pacta sunt servanda* as laid down in Article 26 of the 1969 Vienna Convention on the Law of Treaties: 'Every treaty in force is binding upon the parties to it and must be performed by them in good faith.' By limiting every treaty's binding

---

33. Article 42 of the 2017 ICC Rules. See Pierre A. Karrer, 'Must an Arbitral Tribunal Really Ensure that its Award Is Enforceable?', in *Global Reflections on International Law, Commerce and Dispute Resolution: Liber Amicorum in Honor of Robert Briner* (ICC Publishing 2005) 429–435.
34. *Supra* n. 3.
35. Dominique T. Hascher, 'European Convention on International Commercial Arbitration of 1961: Commentary', XXXVI *Yearbook Commercial Arbitration* (2011) 504, 512.
36. Further provisions of this category are Arts V and VII of the European Convention.
37. With a different reasoning also Mayer, *supra* n. 32 at 278–279.
38. Gustav Flecke-Giammarco and Alexander Grimm, 'CISG and Arbitration Agreements: A Janus-Faced Practice and How to Cope with It', *Journal of Arbitration Studies* 25(3) (2015) 33, 46 et seq.; André Janssen and Matthias Spilker, 'The Application of the CISG in the World of International Commercial Arbitration', *Rabels Zeitschrift für ausländisches und internationales Privatrecht* 77 (2013) 131, 137; Mayer, *supra* n. 32 at 282, 284; Petrochilos, *supra* n. 9 at 195, 208; Nils Schmidt-Ahrendts, 'CISG and Arbitration', *Belgrade Law Review* LIX (2011) 211, 214; Ingeborg Schwenzer and Pascal Hachem, 'Intro to Arts 1–6', in *Schlechtriem & Schwenzer Commentary*, *supra* n. 11, para. 11.

force to 'the parties to it' and the obligation to perform the treaty in good faith to 'them' (the parties), Article 26 makes clear that treaties merely create obligations for states and, by association, their organs, namely state courts. As arbitral tribunals in the field of commercial arbitration are private creations, this indicates that international conventions due to their treaty nature are not addressed to them.

[2] In Particular: Conventions on the Carriage of Goods

The position that conventions do generally not intend to create obligations for arbitrators is further supported by the particular wording of conventions in the area of transport law, notably the international carriage of goods. Conventions in this area differ in an important regard from uniform law conventions that respect party autonomy,[39] because they establish mandatory rules for contracts of carriage that cannot be excluded or modified by parties to such contracts.[40] The purpose of this strict regulatory approach is to prevent an unwelcome 'competition through contract conditions' between carriers that would undermine the uniform effect of the conventions in this area.[41] Accordingly, they explicitly declare contractual stipulations that would directly or indirectly derogate from their provisions to be null and void.[42] Among their mandatory provisions are also – somewhat unusually – provisions expressly addressing the admissibility of arbitration agreements.[43] One of them – Article 33 of the CMR – reads:

> The contract of carriage may contain a clause conferring competence on an arbitration tribunal if the clause conferring competence on the tribunal provides that the tribunal shall apply this Convention.

The purpose of Article 33 of the CMR is to make sure that arbitral tribunals acting in place of a state court will also apply the Convention.[44] In light of this goal, the provision has been construed strictly, requiring that the arbitration agreement must

---

39. See *inter alia* Art. 6 of the CISG.
40. Roland Loewe, 'Commentary on the Convention of 19 May 1956 on the Contract for the International Carriage of Goods by Road (CMR)', *European Transport Law* 11 (1976) 311 para. 292; Malcolm A. Clarke, *International Carriage of Goods by Road: CMR* (Informa 2009) para. 92: 'matter of public policy'; Harald de la Motte & Jürgen Temme, 'Vor Art. 1', in Karl-Heinz Thume (ed.), *CMR* (3rd ed., Deutscher Fachverlag 2013) para. 10. See also the critical remarks by Jan Ramberg, 'Freedom of Contract in Maritime Law', in Alexander von Ziegler (ed.), *Internationales Recht auf See und Binnengewässern: Festschrift für Walter Müller* (Schulthess 1993) 171, 179–184.
41. Oberster Gerichtshof, *Transportrecht* (2010) 383; Loewe, *supra* n. 40 at para. 292; Reinhard Th. Schmid, 'Art. 41', in Thume, *supra* n. 40, para. 3.
42. Article 32 first sentence of the 1929 Warsaw Convention for the Unification of Certain Rules Relating to International Carriage by Air; Art. 41(1) of the CMR; Art. 22(5) of the 1978 United Nations Convention on the Carriage of Goods by Sea (Hamburg Rules); Art. 34(4) of the 1999 Montreal Convention for the Unification of Certain Rules for International Carriage by Air.
43. Article 33 of the CMR; Art. 22(4), (5) of the Hamburg Rules; Art. 34(3), (4) of the Montreal Convention. Similar, but less clear Art. 32 second sentence of the 1929 Warsaw Convention: arbitration clauses are allowed 'subject to this Convention'.
44. Roland Loewe, 'Die Bestimmungen der CMR über Reklamationen und Klagen', *Transportrecht* (1988) 309, 319.

specifically oblige the arbitrators to apply the CMR.[45] If this requirement is not met, the arbitral clause is null and void according to Article 41(1) of the CMR,[46] thus rendering an award unenforceable according to Article V(1)(a) of the 1958 New York Convention. For the purposes of the present contribution, it is important that Article 33 of the CMR also clarifies another matter: The assumption implicitly underlying its *raison d'être* is that arbitral tribunals originally are under no obligation to apply the CMR, so that a written contract clause providing that the tribunal shall apply the CMR is needed in order to guarantee its application. Article 33 of the CMR accordingly calls upon the parties to contracts of carriage to create a contractual duty for arbitrators to apply a treaty where no such duty exists under the treaty itself. This indirectly confirms that the general position suggested earlier[47] must be correct, as provisions of this type[48] would otherwise be superfluous.

[3]   In particular: European Union Treaties

One could believe that the addressees of the EU Treaties may have to be determined differently, given that the European Court of Justice (ECJ) has traditionally held that the EEC Treaty 'by contrast with ordinary international treaties' has 'created its own legal system which [...] binds both [the Member States'] nationals and themselves',[49] and more recently has even spoken of 'the constitutional architecture [...] intended by the framers of the Treaties now in force'.[50] Do the EU Treaties therefore differ from traditional uniform law conventions by also addressing arbitral tribunals?

This was one of the questions put to the ECJ in the famous *Eco Swiss* case, when the Dutch Supreme Court asked *inter alia* whether arbitrators are required to apply Article 85 of the (then) EC Treaty.[51] While the ECJ did not answer this question,[52] Advocate General Saggio opined that the argument for extending the obligation to apply EC Treaty provisions to arbitrators 'could not be based purely and simply on Article 5 of the Treaty, which, as we know, is addressed only to the Member States and cannot therefore of itself operate to impose obligations on arbitrators.'[53] It is therefore recognized today that also the EU Treaties are not directly addressed to arbitral tribunals, even if the seat of the respective arbitration is located in an EU State.[54] The

---

45. Arrondissementrechtbank Rotterdam, *European Transport Law* 6 (1971) 273; Cour d'appel Paris, *Bulletin des Transports* (1979) 440; Clarke, *supra* n. 40 at para. 47; Klaus Demuth, 'Art. 33', in Thume, *supra* n. 40, para. 3; Loewe, *supra* n. 44 at 319.
46. Oberster Gerichtshof, *Transportrecht* (2010) 383; Clarke, *supra* n. 40 at para. 47; Demuth, *supra* n. 45 at para. 4a; Loewe, *supra* n. 40 at para. 271; Schmid, *supra* n. 41, para. 27.
47. *Supra* at §29.02[B][1].
48. See *supra* n. 43.
49. European Court of Justice, Case 6/64 – *Costa v. ENEL*, *European Court Reports* (1964) 585, 593.
50. European Court of Justice, Joined Cases C-402/05 P and C-415/05 P – *Kadi v. Council and Commission*, *European Court Reports* (2008) I-6351 para. 202.
51. Such was the interpretation of the question posed by Advocate General Saggio, Opinion in Case C-126/97 – *Eco Swiss v. Benetton International*, *European Court Reports* (1999) I-3057, I-3064.
52. European Court of Justice, Case C-126/97 – *Eco Swiss v. Benetton International*, *European Court Reports* (1999) I-3079 para. 42.
53. Advocate General Saggio, *supra* n. 51 at I-3068.
54. Lew, Mistelis and Kröll, *supra* n. 32 at paras 18–76.

EU Treaties, in particular their provisions on anti-competitive agreements, may be applicable in arbitrations because of their nature as mandatory provisions,[55] but such an application would not depend on their legal nature as treaty provisions. In any case, arbitral tribunals will have an incentive to take into account EU Treaty provisions in order to render an enforceable award, given that state courts in EU States are under an obligation to consider whether an arbitral award made is contrary to Article 101 of the TFEU – a point that will be further addressed below.[56]

[C] Conclusion and a General Suggestion

For the reasons presented above, international conventions do not create any duty for arbitrators to apply their rules. Although most conventions' wording is at best inconclusive in this respect,[57] treaties are generally addressed to states and their organs (notably courts) only,[58] and not to arbitral tribunals. Most importantly, this conclusion respects the fundamental nature of arbitral tribunals as private institutions[59] that treaty law does not seek to disturb. Indeed, it seems justified to assume a general rule according to which international conventions unifying private or commercial law do not require their application by arbitral tribunals, but rather respect the long-standing particular nature of arbitration as a private means of dispute settlement that has traditionally been governed by principles different from those applicable in state courts.

Nevertheless, this result does not necessarily mean that an arbitrator's duty to apply international conventions cannot flow from other legal sources. These sources will be investigated next.

§29.03 THE *LEX ARBITRI* AS SOURCE OF AN ARBITRATOR'S DUTY TO APPLY INTERNATIONAL CONVENTIONS?

One alternative source of an arbitrator's legal duty to apply conventions is the *lex arbitri*, i.e., the law of the country in whose territory the arbitration takes place.[60] (*Pierre Karrer* prefers a narrower meaning of the term, translating *lex arbitri* as the law at the seat dealing with the relationship between the arbitral tribunal and the state courts at the seat *(Schiedsverfassungsrecht)*.[61]) In modern arbitration laws, the *lex arbitri* – understood in a broader sense – is the law in force at the (juridical) seat of the arbitration.[62]

---

55. Lew, Mistelis and Kröll, *supra* n. 32 at paras 18–76; Waincymer, *supra* n. 17 at 1037.
56. *Infra* at §29.05[B].
57. *Supra* at §29.02[A].
58. *Supra* at §29.02[B].
59. *Triulziu Cesare SRL v. Xinyi Group (Glass) Co. Ltd.*, [2014] SGHC 220 para. 163: '… arbitral tribunals, private institutions that are not bound by the CISG, … '.
60. On this definition of *lex arbitri*, see Redfern and Hunter, *supra* n. 18 at para. 3.34.
61. Karrer, *supra* n. 1, Questions 666–669 and 989.
62. Redfern and Hunter, *supra* n. 18 at para. 3.51.

Against this background, an obligation of arbitrators to apply an international convention in force at the seat of the arbitration would arise if the *lex arbitri* would require arbitrators to identify and apply the applicable substantive law in the same manner as a judge in a state court of this country. And indeed, such was the position half a century ago, when the Institut de Droit international included the following rule in its Resolution on 'Arbitration in Private International Law' adopted in 1957:

> Les règles de rattachment en vigeur dans l'Etat du siège du tribunal arbitral doivent être suivies pour déterminer la loi applicable au fond du litige.[63]

Ten years later, *F.A. Mann* similarly wrote:

> Just as the judge has to apply the private international law of the forum, so the arbitrator has to apply the private international law of the arbitration tribunal's seat, the *lex arbitri*. Any other solution would involve the conclusion that it is open to the arbitrator to disregard the law.[64]

Under this approach, the *lex arbitri* would require arbitral tribunals to also apply international conventions to which the seat state of the arbitration has acceded. The reason is that conventions' provisions defining a particular convention's applicability – Article 1(1) of the CISG being a prominent example – are unilateral conflict-of-laws rules[65] and would accordingly be subject to the requirement described above. Arbitral tribunals with their seat in a convention's Contracting State would thereby be equated to state courts of that state.[66]

Today, this view has lost most (although not all) of its followers. For some time now, the position has prevailed that an arbitration seat's rules of private international law are not binding for arbitrators,[67] because an arbitrator, unlike a state court, does not have a forum.[68] Due to their private nature, arbitral tribunals are not created by states; states merely provide the legal framework within which arbitral tribunals operate.[69] In theory, the legal framework of the *lex arbitri* could impose the conflict-of-laws rules designed for state courts also on arbitral tribunals, but domestic legislators generally refrain from doing so. One of the clearest indications are the specific conflict-of-laws rules for arbitration proceedings that exist in many domestic laws today, often modelled on Article 28 of UNCITRAL's Model Law on International Commercial Arbitration. Accordingly, there is generally no duty for arbitrators to apply

---

63. Institut de Droit international, Résolution 'L'arbitrage en droit international privé', Session d'Amsterdam – 1957, in *Tableau des Résolutions Adoptées (1957–1991)* (1992) 237, Art. 11(1).
64. F.A. Mann, 'Lex Facit Arbitrum', in Pieter Sanders (ed.), *International Arbitration: Liber Amicorum for Martin Domke* (Nijhoff 1967) 157, 167.
65. See Schlechtriem and Schroeter, *supra* n. 14 at para. 39.
66. In favour of this approach regarding the CISG Benicke, *supra* n. 7 at para. 41.
67. Emmanuel Gaillard and John Savage (eds.), *Fouchard Gaillard Goldman on International Commercial Arbitration* (Kluwer 1999) para. 1541; Emmanuel Gaillard, 'The Role of the Arbitrator in Determining the Applicable Law', in: Lawrence W. Newman and Richard D. Hill (eds.), *The Leading Arbitrators' Guide to International Arbitration* (Juris 2004) 185; Mayer, *supra* n. 32 at 276; Mourre, *supra* n. 9 at 47; Petrochilos, *supra* n. 9 at 198; Redfern and Hunter, *supra* n. 18 at para. 2.80.
68. Kröll, *supra* n. 15 at 64; Mayer, *supra* n. 32 at 282; Mourre, *supra* n. 9 at 43.
69. Kröll, *supra* n. 15 at 64.

international conventions under modern domestic arbitration laws.[70] From a typical *lex arbitri*'s perspective, arbitral tribunals *may* therefore apply conventions, but do not have to. It is accordingly at best imprecise when arbitrators write that they apply e.g., the Vienna Sales Convention 'according to' Article 1(1)(a)[71] or Article 1(1)(b) of the CISG,[72] because Article 1(1) of the CISG in its entirety is only addressed to courts in Contracting States.[73]

§29.04 INTERNATIONAL CONVENTIONS AS PART OF THE *LEX CAUSAE*

The usual basis on which the application of international conventions by arbitrators rests is therefore neither the convention itself nor a convention-specific application requirement by the *lex arbitri*, but rather the parties' choice of law and the general, non-convention-specific rules of the *lex arbitri* about the law to be applied to the merits of a dispute. Arbitral awards that have so applied international conventions are legion[74] and will not be reported here in detail. With regard to the arbitrators' duty to apply a given convention, two situations can be distinguished: Where the parties to the arbitration have chosen the respective *lex causae*, a duty of the arbitral tribunal to apply an international convention arises from this party agreement[75] if the choice therein refers to a convention as applicable 'rules of law', as 'general principles of international law', the *lex mercatoria* or similar, or – probably most often – as an integral part of the domestic law of a state that has ratified the convention. Where the parties have not chosen the law applicable to the merits and the determination of the *lex causae* is left to the arbitrators, arbitrators may well decide to apply an international convention,[76] either through a *voie directe*, by considering a convention to be an expression of trade usages, by a *voie indirecte* or as part of a domestic law. The discretion granted to arbitrators in this context under most arbitration rules and laws makes it difficult to speak of a 'duty' to apply the convention, at least until the tribunal has made its choice. In any of the above cases, the source of such a duty is either the parties' or the arbitral tribunal's choice, but not the convention itself.

---

70. On the CISG Filip De Ly, 'The Relevance of the Vienna Convention for International Sales Contracts: Should We Stop Contracting it Out?', *Business Law International* 4 (2003) 241, 242; Janssen and Spilker, *supra* n. 38 at 139; Schmidt-Ahrendts, *supra* n. 38 at 214.
71. See Tribunal of International Commercial Arbitration at the Russian Federation Chamber of Commerce and Industry, 3 Mar. 1997, CISG-online No. 1298; CIETAC Award, 10 Dec. 2003, CISG-online No. 1546; and many more.
72. See ICC award 7585/1994, *Journal du droit international* 122 (1995) 1015; Schiedsgericht der Handelskammer Hamburg, *Recht der Internationalen Wirtschaft* (1996) 766; and many more.
73. Accord in regard of Art. 1(1)(a) of the CISG Janssen and Spilker, *supra* n. 38 at 137; Petrochilos, *supra* n. 9 at 195; Schwenzer and Hachem, *supra* n. 38 para. 21; but see in regard of Art. 1(1)(b) of the CISG Janssen and Spilker, *supra* n. 38 at 139; Kröll, *supra* n. 15 at 64–65.
74. See on the application of various conventions Giardina, *supra* n. 6 at 467 et seq.; on the application of the 1980 Vienna Sales Convention Kröll, *supra* n. 15 at 61 et seq.; Mourre, *supra* n. 9 at 43 et seq.; Petrochilos, *supra* n. 9 at 196 et seq.
75. Loukas Mistelis, 'CISG and Arbitration', in André Janssen and Olaf Meyer (eds.), *CISG Methodology* (Sellier 2009) 375, 382.
76. According to Mistelis, *supra* n. 75 at 388, in 57% of published arbitral awards applying the CISG the Convention was applied as choice of the arbitral tribunal.

§29.05 DUTY OF STATE COURTS TO APPLY INTERNATIONAL CONVENTIONS WHEN REVIEWING ARBITRAL AWARDS?

A final question concerns setting-aside or enforcement procedures in state courts. In such a context, courts – that, when located in Contracting States of an international convention, are under an obligation to apply its rules – are called upon to decide whether to set aside an arbitral award or to declare it enforceable. Assuming that the arbitral tribunal at hand has failed to apply an applicable convention in making the award, may or must the state court take this factor into account?

[A] Perspective of Arbitration Law

The question is important because under modern laws on arbitration, state courts generally have no authority to vacate an arbitral award or refuse its enforcement because the arbitral tribunal has failed to apply a convention in deciding the merits of the dispute. Such a degree of scrutiny is considered a *révision au fond* that arbitration laws do not allow,[77] irrespective whether the substantive law misapplied were provisions of an international convention. It is a more difficult question whether the non-application of a convention by an arbitral tribunal even escapes the control by state courts where the parties had explicitly chosen the convention as the applicable law: While some read the ground for refusing enforcement in Article V(1)(d) of the 1958 New York Convention – that 'the arbitral procedure was not in accordance with the agreement of the parties' – as not covering violations of party choices about the law to be applied to the merits,[78] others consider it a ground for refusal when the arbitrator has ignored the parties' choice of law by applying a different substantive law than the one chosen.[79] The dispute is interesting because provisions like Article 33 of the CMR,[80] which require the arbitration agreement to explicitly provide that 'the tribunal shall apply this Convention', were apparently so designed in order to ensure that an award may be set aside if the arbitral tribunal fails to apply the CMR.[81] Under current arbitration laws, this goal is not necessarily reached – a result that may be explained by the developments in the law of arbitration since the adoption of the CMR in 1956, when not even the 1958 New York Convention yet existed.

[B] Compatibility with Treaty Law

From the treaty law perspective, it could theoretically be argued that a state court's obligation to apply a convention also extends to setting-aside or enforcement

---

77. Fouchard Gaillard Goldman, *supra* n. 67 at paras 661 et seq., 688; Waincymer, *supra* n. 17 at 1264.
78. Fouchard Gaillard Goldman, *supra* n. 67 at paras 1701 et seq.
79. Christian Borris and Rudolf Hennecke, 'Article V', in Wolff, *supra* n. 32 para. 337; Kröll, *supra* n. 15 at 65.
80. *Supra* at §29.02[B][2].
81. Loewe, *supra* n. 40 at para. 271: '... probably admitted under all national legislations on arbitral procedure ...'; Loewe, *supra* n. 44 at 319; in agreement Clarke, *supra* n. 40 at para. 47.

procedures in that court, as such procedures are nowhere expressly excluded from a Contracting State's application duty. In addition, it could be said that by allowing arbitral tribunals to decide disputes falling into the substantive scope of international conventions, a state merely suspends the performance of its own application duty until the setting-aside or enforcement stage, but cannot completely neglect it.

However, these arguments must fail, because they overextend a state party's obligations arising from uniform law conventions. Given that – according to the reasoning developed earlier[82] – international conventions of this type implicitly respect arbitration's autonomy as a private dispute settlement mechanism, it would be contradictory to measure the results of this mechanism (the awards) against a standard designed for state courts. An exception only applies to European Union law, in respect of which the ECJ has ruled in *Nordsee*[83] and *Eco Swiss*[84] that, where questions of European law arise in an arbitration, ordinary courts may have to examine those questions during review of the arbitration award or upon any other form of action or review available under the relevant national legislation. This stricter standard of review has its roots in the particularities of the EC/EU Treaties that 'by contrast with ordinary international treaties' have created their 'own legal system'.[85] The resulting division of tasks shifts responsibility for the review downstream, namely to the courts in EU Member States, rather than upstream, to arbitral tribunals.[86] It exceptionally requires courts to second-guess arbitrators' application of fundamental provisions of the TFEU,[87] but is not capable of being extended to 'ordinary' uniform law conventions.

§29.06 CONCLUSION

In conclusion, it can be confirmed that arbitrators are indeed under a duty to apply international conventions in deciding the merits of the disputes presented to them. However, this duty does not flow from the respective conventions themselves, because these are addressed merely to state courts as organs of a convention's state parties. International conventions, being treaties under public international law, implicitly tolerate and respect arbitral tribunals and their nature as private institutions. An arbitrator's duty to apply conventions is therefore a duty created and designed by the parties through their arbitration agreement, either directly (by choosing a convention

---

82. *Supra* at §29.02[C].
83. European Court of Justice, Case 102/81 – *Nordsee v. Reederei Mond*, European Court Reports (1982) 1095 para. 14.
84. European Court of Justice, *supra* n. 52 at para. 32.
85. European Court of Justice, *supra* n. 49 at 593.
86. Advocate General Wathelet, Opinion in Case C-567/14 – *Genentech v. Hoechst*, ECLI: EU:C:2016:177 para. 60.
87. See recently European Court of Justice, Case C-567/14 – *Genentech v. Hoechst*, ECLI: EU:C:2016:526, where the interpretation of Art. 101 of the TFEU by the sole arbitrator was confirmed.

as the applicable law) or indirectly (by vesting the arbitral tribunal with determining the rules of law applicable to the merits). For arbitrators, treaty application is accordingly only mandatory if the legal arbitration framework says so, resulting in a peaceful coexistence of treaty law and arbitration practice.

CHAPTER 30
The CISG in International Arbitration

Ingeborg Schwenzer & Florence Jaeger

§30.01 INTRODUCTION

At first, it might be surprising what the CISG[1] and international arbitration have in common. While the CISG is considered substantive law, arbitration is qualified as procedural law. However, both have greatly facilitated international trade during the last twenty to thirty years by harmonising and unifying the applicable law.[2] Predictability as one of the most important factors for parties in international trade has been considerably increased.

Today, the CISG is applicable in eighty-five States, nine of the ten most influential trade nations are Member States.[3] Thus, it potentially covers more than 80% of global trade.[4] This international success is further underlined by the fact that during the last twenty years most of the national and international reform or legislative projects used the CISG as a starting point.[5] To name a few recent developments; the reform of the

---

1. The United Convention on Contracts for the International Sale of Goods (1980) (CISG).
2. Cf. Jeffrey Waincymer, *The CISG and International Commercial Arbitration: Promoting a Complimentary Relationship Between Substance and Procedure*, 582, 583, 584 (C. Andersen & Schroeter, Sharing International Commercial Law across National Boundaries, Festschrift for Albert H. Kritzer on the Occasion of his Eightieth Birthday, London: Wildy, Simmonds & Hill, 2008). For further shared characteristics Morten Fogt, *The Interaction and Distinction Between the Sales And Arbitration Regimes – the CISG and Agreements or Binding Practice to Arbitrate*, 26 Am. Rev. Int. Arb. 365, 385 et seq. (2015).
3. *See* for the current number of contracting states, http://www.uncitral.org/uncitral/en/uncitral_texts/sale_goods/1980CISG_status.html (accessed 11 May 2016).
4. Nils Schmidt-Ahrendts, *CISG and Arbitration*, Belgrade L. Rev. 3, 211, 220 (2011).
5. Cf. the reform of the German law of obligations; the Dutch Wetboek; the sales law of the Slavic countries and of the OHADA States; the former socialist States as well as the subsequent States of the former Soviet Union, Yugoslavia and the Czechoslovakia. The CISG has also strongly influenced the contract law of Japan and South Korea, but even more so the new Chinese contract law; one exception is Turkey. A similar tendency can be made out with international rules: the

Spanish Commercial Code, the Argentinian and the Hungarian as well as the Korean and Japanese Civil Code. If one was to resort to the term of *lex mercatoria*,[6] the CISG would undoubtedly constitute the core of its contractual rules.[7]

A comparable story of worldwide success is the development of international arbitration.[8] The New York Convention (NYC) is applicable in 156 countries[9] and the UNCITRAL Model Law was implemented in seventy-two countries encompassing more than 100 jurisdictions.[10] In the last twenty years the number of arbitration proceedings has tripled. Today, it can be well assumed that 60% of all international contracts contain an arbitration clause, whereas the likelihood increases even more with a rising in contract volume.[11] Consequently, in practice significant international disputes are no longer litigated before state courts.[12] Remarkably, while traditional arbitral institutions in Western countries experience a certain stagnation of the number of arbitral

---

UNIDROIT Principles for International Commercial Contracts (PICC) and the Principles of European Contract Law (PECL). For further evidence, see Ingeborg Schwenzer, *Schlechtriem & Schwenzer: Commentary on the UN Convention on the International Sale of Goods*, Art. 35 para. 4 (6th ed., Oxford: Oxford University Press, 2013); Ingeborg Schwenzer & Pascal Hachem, *The CISG – A Story of Worldwide Success*, 119, 123 et seq. (Kleinemann, CISG Part II Conference, Stockholm: Iustus Forlag, 2009).

6. Reflecting the critical views Klaus Peter Berger, *The Creeping Codification of the Lex Mercatoria*, 32, 33 (The Hague: Kluwer Law International 1999) and regards *lex mercatoria* in general; *see also* Nigel Blackaby, Constantine Partasides, Alan Redfern & Martin Hunter, *Redfern and Hunter on International Arbitration*, paras 3.167 et seq. (6th ed., Oxford: Oxford University Press, 2015).
7. Pilar Perales Viscasillas & David Ramos Muñoz, *CISG & Arbitration*, 1366, 1359 (Büchler & Müller-Chen, Private Law – national – global – comparative, Festschrift für Ingeborg Schwenzer zum 60. Geburtstag, Berne: Stämpfli, 2011); Gustav Flecke-Giammarco & Alexander Grimm, *CISG and Arbitration Agreements: A Janus-faced Practice and How to Cope with It*, 25 J Arb. Stud. 33, 47 (2015). Mainly the *lex mercatoria* is seen in the PICC und PECL, see Ingeborg Schwenzer, Pascal Hachem & Christopher Kee, *Global Sales and Contract Law*, para. 3.73 (Oxford: Oxford University Press 2012); Blackaby, Partasides, Redfern & Hunter, *supra* n. 6, at paras 3.167 et seq., particularly at paras 3.183 et seq.; PICC und PECL draw their basis strongly from the CISG, *see* Ingeborg Schwenzer, *Uniform Sales Law – Brazil Joining the CISG Family*, 21, 22 (Schwenzer, Pereira & Tripodi, A CISG e o Brasil, São Paulo: Marcial Pons, 2015).
8. Ingeborg Schwenzer & Claudio Marti Whitebread, *Legal Answers to Globalization*, 1, 2 et seq. (Schwenzer, Atamer & Butler, Current Issues in the CISG and Arbitration, The Hague: Eleven International Publishing, 2014).
9. Convention on the Recognition and Enforcement of Foreign Arbitral Awards (New York, 1958), for the current status, *see* http://www.uncitral.org/uncitral/en/uncitral_texts/arbitration/NYConvention_status.html (accessed 11 May 2016).
10. UNCITRAL Model Law on International Commercial Arbitration (1985), with amendments of 2006, for the current status, *see* http://www.uncitral.org/uncitral/en/uncitral_texts/arbitration/1985Model_arbitration_status.html (accessed 11 May 2016).
11. Stefan Vogenauer, *Civil Justice Systems in Europe*, 2008, Questions 49.1 and 51.1, https://www3.law.ox.ac.uk/themes/iecl/pdfs/Oxford%20Civil%20Justice%20Survey%20-%20Summary%20of%20Results,%20Final.pdf (accessed 11 May 2016); Ingeborg Schwenzer & Christopher Kee, *International Sales Law – The Actual Practice*, 29 Penn St. Int'L. Rev. 425, 446, 447 (2011); Schwenzer & Marti Whitebread, *supra* n. 8, at 1, 2.
12. As a result, different States try to make their national litigation more attractive for international disputes by establishing specialised courts, cf. particularly Singapore International Commercial Court; cf. for Germany Landgericht Mannheim (Regional Court), proceedings in English at the Chamber of Commerce.

proceedings, it is increasing immensely in Asia[13] and new arbitration institutions are founded particularly in Latin America, Africa and the Arabic States.

In arbitral practice the CISG is often applied.[14] This is closely related to the international composition of the arbitral tribunal which possesses comprehensive practical comparative legal experience and is therefore accustomed to bridge the differences arising out of different legal traditions.[15] In that regard, the CISG serves as a very successful compromise between the continental European and Anglo-American legal backgrounds.[16]

Numerous scholarly writings discuss the application of the CISG by arbitral tribunals. In addition to theoretical questions such as the application and interpretation of the CISG by arbitral tribunals, there are also a number of writings shedding light on the practical perspective to illustrate how often the CISG is applied in arbitration. The analysis showed that approximately 25% of all published CISG cases were rendered by arbitral tribunals.[17] Bearing in mind how little arbitral awards are published in general, it can be assumed that a majority of proceedings dealing with the CISG take place before arbitral tribunals and not national courts.

From the wide range of interesting issues, the following two questions are being discussed: (1) When is the CISG applied in arbitral proceedings? (2) Can the CISG be applied to the arbitration clause?

§30.02 CISG AS SUBSTANTIVE LAW

[A] Preliminary Remarks

According to Article 1(1) CISG the CISG applies if the parties have their seat in two different contracting states or the applicable rules of private international law lead to the application of the law of a Contracting State. The CISG thereby determines its sphere of application autonomously. Due to obligations arising out of international law this is binding for national courts.[18] Arbitral tribunals, however, as a private dispute resolution instance chosen by the parties, are not bound by these international law

---

13. Cf. the statistics by the China International Economic and Trade Arbitration Commission (CIETAC) http://cietac.org/index.php?m=Page&a=index&id=40&l=en (accessed 11 May 2016); cf. also statistics by the Hong Kong International Arbitration Centre (HKIAC), http://220.241.190.1/en/hkiac/statistics (accessed 11 May 2016).
14. See on this Stefan Kröll, *Arbitration and the CISG*, 59, 61, 62 (Schwenzer, Atamer & Butler, Current Issues in the CISG and Arbitration, The Hague: Eleven International Publishing, 2014), who could even make out a pro-CISG attitude by the arbitrators based on a case study – in 57% of the analysed cases the CISG was chosen by the arbitral tribunal. Similarly Loukas Mistelis, *CISG and Arbitration*, 373, 388 (Janssen & Olaf, CISG Methodology, Munich: Sellier 2009).
15. Likewise Schmidt-Ahrendts, Belgrade L. Rev. 3, 211, 220 (2011); Kröll, *supra* n. 14, at 59, 69.
16. Schwenzer, *supra* n. 7, at 21, 36 f.
17. Schmidt-Ahrendts, Belgrade L. Rev. 3, 211, 213 (2011); Kröll, *supra* n. 14, at 59, 61.
18. Burghard Piltz, *Internationales Kaufrecht*, § 2 para. 6 (2nd ed., Munich: Beck 2008); Kröll, *supra* n. 14, at 59, 62 et seq.; Alexis Mourre, *Application of the Vienna International Sales Convention in Arbitration*, ICC ICArb. Bull. 17, 43 (2006).

obligations.[19] As there is no *lex fori* for arbitral tribunals comparable with the one for national courts, they are not requested to abide by the private international law rules.[20] It is rather the law at the seat of arbitration according to which the arbitral tribunal has to determine the applicable substantive law.[21] Subsidiarily, the arbitral rules chosen by the parties are to be applied.[22]

Recent developments in international arbitration show a remarkable congruence. Primarily, the arbitral tribunal decides the dispute according to the law chosen by the parties.[23] Today, such a choice of law is considered to be a direct choice of a substantive law of the selected state excluding its rules of international private law.[24] In absence of such a choice of law some of the national arbitration statutes still refer the arbitral tribunal to the rules of international private law.[25] According to a more modern view, the arbitral tribunal shall directly apply the law which is most closely connected to the dispute.[26] This approach is also mirrored by the most important arbitration rules.[27] In general, it is internationally recognised that in addition to the law of a state, rules of law, i.e., soft law, may be applied.[28]

[B] Choice of Law by the Parties

Nowadays the overwhelming majority of jurisdictions acknowledges the possibility of the parties to choose the applicable law at least for arbitral proceedings.[29] The Hague

---

19. Pierre Mayer, *L'application par l'arbitre des conventions internationales de droit privé*, 275, 287 (Loussouarn, L'internationalisation du droit, Paris: Dalloz 1994); also Schmidt-Ahrendts, Belgrade L. Rev. 3, 211, 214 (2011).
20. Kröll, *supra* n. 14, at 59, 64; cf. also Mourre, ICC ICArb. Bull. 17, 43, 46 (2006), especially at 44 regarding the parties' choice of law, which bases on party autonomy and thereby excludes the provision of conflict law in Art. 1(1)(b) CISG.
21. Kröll, *supra* n. 14, at 59, 64; Blackaby, Partasides, Redfern & Hunter, *supra* n. 6, at paras 3.213 et seq.; Gary Born, *International Commercial Arbitration*, 525 et seq. (2nd ed., Alphen aan der Rijn: Kluwer, 2014) with further references.
22. Blackaby, Partasides, Redfern & Hunter, *supra* n. 6, at paras 3.50 et seq.; cf. the concrete example of § 23 DIS-Arbitration Rules 98; Art. 17(1) ICC Arbitration Rules; Art. 22.3 LCIA Rules; Art. 28(1) AAA Rules; Art. 35(1) HKIAC Rules; Art. 24(1) SCC Rules; Art. 24(2) Vienna Rules und Art. 33 Swiss Rules; *see* also Art. 35 UNCITRAL Arbitration Rules.
23. Germany: § 1051(1) s. 1 CCP; Switzerland: Art. 187(1) PILS; United Kingdom: English Arbitration Act 1996, s. 46(1)(a).
24. *See* § 1051(1) s. 2 German CCP; English Arbitration Act 1996, s. 46(2).
25. English Arbitration Act 1996, s. 46(3); *see* also in Art. 28(2) UNCITRAL Model Law.
26. Germany: § 1051(1) CCP; Switzerland: Art. 187(1) PILS.
27. Article 33(1) Swiss Rules; §§ 23.1, 23.2 DIS-Arbitration Rules 98; Art. 21(1) ICC Arbitration Rules, which do not focus on the *closest connection* but on the law which the arbitral tribunal determines to be the most *appropriate* law.
28. English Arbitration Act 1996, s. 46 (1)(b); § 1051 German CCP includes explicitly *rules of law*; Joachim Münch, *Münchener Kommentar zur Zivilprozessordnung*, § 1051 para. 14 (Krüger et al., 4th ed., Munich: Beck, 2013); explicitly in the Introduction I.18 und Art. 3 The Hague Principles on Choice of Law in International Commercial Contracts; however, arbitration clauses are excluded from their scope pursuant to Art. 1(3)(b); further *Geneviève Saumier*, 40 Brook. J. Int'l L. 1, 18 et seq. (2014); Frank Vischer, Lucius Huber & David Oser, *Internationales Vertragsrecht*, paras 114 et seq (2nd ed., Berne: Stämpfli, 2000).
29. *See* Gary Born, *International Arbitration and Forum Selection Agreements*, 167, 168 (4th edn, Alphen aan der Rijn: Kluwer, 2013).

Chapter 30: The CISG in International Arbitration §30.02[B]

Principles on Choice of Law in International Commercial Contracts first adopted in 2015 affirm this principle and will attribute even greater importance to it in the future. In practice, in more than 70% of all international contracts parties embrace this possibility to conclude a choice of law clause.[30]

In general, the parties simply choose the law of a particular state without further specifications, for example clauses like 'This contract is governed by Swiss law'. In such a case it is questionable whether the parties have exclusively chosen the Swiss Code of Obligations as non-harmonised Swiss law or also the CISG, since Switzerland is a contracting state of the CISG.

National courts have repeatedly discussed the question, whether the choice of the law of a contracting state constitutes an opting-out of the CISG according to Article 6 CISG. There is agreement that the choice of the law of a contracting state by itself cannot be interpreted as an exclusion of the CISG.[31] Rather, further specifications are required, for example, 'the law of the State X excluding the CISG', 'the Swiss Code of Obligations' or 'application of Articles 184 et seq. of the Swiss Code of Obligations'.[32]

However, this case law cannot be directly applied to Article 6 CISG in arbitral proceedings. It derives from the national courts' obligation by international law to apply the CISG in case the preconditions of Article 1(1) CISG are met. A national court has to decide in a second step, if there is a valid opting-out according to Article 6 CISG at hand. Since the arbitral tribunal – as already mentioned – is not bound by Article 1(1) CISG, it is not requested to assess opting-out of the CISG, but to establish its application.[33] This is achieved by interpretation of the parties' choice of law clause. It remains questionable, whether this interpretation is conducted in accordance with the non-harmonised domestic law or Article 8 CISG.[34] Despite existing differences between domestic principles of interpretation and Article 8 CISG, the result of interpreting choice of law clauses in international settings might hardly ever lead to diverging results.[35] After all, it is decisive what reasonable parties intended by agreeing on a

---

30. Vogenauer, *supra* n. 11, Questions 15 et seq., https://www3.law.ox.ac.uk/themes/iecl/pdfs/Oxford%20Civil%20Justice%20Survey%20-%20Summary%20of%20Results,%20Final.pdf (accessed 11 May 2016). Cf. further Schwenzer, Hachem & Kee, *supra* n. 7, at paras 5.21 et seq.
31. CISG Advisory Council, Opinion No. 16, Rapporteur Spagnolo, *Exclusion of the CISG under Article 6*, n. 4.2; Waincymer, *supra* n. 2, at 582, 595.
32. See also Born, *supra* n. 29, at 167; Mourre, ICC ICArb. Bull. 17 (2006), 43, 44, 45.
33. Schwenzer & Hachem, *Schlechtriem & Schwenzer Commentary on the Convention on the International Sale of Goods (CISG)*, Art. 6 para. 13 (Schwenzer, 4th ed., 2016).
34. In favour of an application of Art. 8 CISG, *Chateau des Charmes Wines Ltd. v. Sabate USA Inc., Sabate S.A.*, 9th Cir., 5 May 2003, CISG-online 767; OLG Stuttgart, 15 May 2006, CISG-online 1414; OLG Düsseldorf, 30 Jan. 2004, CISG-online 821; CISG Advisory Council, Opinion No. 16, *supra* n. 31, n. 3.6 et seq.; Schmidt-Kessel, *Schlechtriem & Schwenzer Commentary on the CISG* (2016), Art. 8 para. 5. Critical Waincymer, *supra* n. 2, at 582, 586, 587.
35. With a comparison of §§ 133, 157 German CC also the BGH, VIII ZR 125/14, 25 Mar. 2015, CISG-online 2588, n. II.2.a).

specific clause.[36] For this evaluation, the principles developed under Article 6 CISG can be applied by analogy.[37]

When parties choose the law of a Contracting State, it has to be emphasised that the CISG is an integral part of this law and is, furthermore, the law that particularly applies to international contracts.[38] Moreover, as mentioned above, the CISG presents modern regulations tailored to international legal transactions.[39] By contrast, most of the domestic legal systems are not only outdated, but also exclusively focusing on domestic matters. Further, their provisions – contrary to the CISG – do not always balance the interests of both parties.[40] Finally, for reasonable parties it makes sense to choose a national law even when they are not opting-out of the CISG. As it is well known, the CISG does not govern all questions related to a sales contract. Accordingly, these questions are governed by the subsidiarily applicable law.[41]

By means of a choice of law clause parties can also agree on the CISG to govern disputes not ordinarily covered by the CISG (opting-in).[42] Under these circumstances it is not considered as national law; however, as demonstrated above, it is for the arbitral tribunals to decide on the application of rules of law in addition to the national law chosen by the parties. In that case the CISG contains rules of law.[43] Opting into the CISG is advisable especially for framework contracts, in which the performance of services is outweighing the sales obligations of the parties and hence would not be covered by the CISG according to Article 3(2) CISG.

[C] Applicable Law in Absence of a Choice of Law Clause

As demonstrated above, different approaches are still present in different national arbitration statutes.[44] If the arbitral tribunal needs to follow the conflict of law rules in order to determine the applicable law,[45] it is decisive whether they refer to the law of a contracting state. In this case, the CISG can be applied without any difficulty.

If the applicable national arbitration statute refers the arbitral tribunal to determine the applicable substantive law according to the closest connection test or the most

---

36. For a comparative approach, see Schwenzer, Hachem & Kee, *supra* n. 7, at paras 26.10 et seq.: it becomes evident that in fact a multitude of jurisdictions already apply the standard of *a reasonable person in the shoes of the recipient* to the interpretation, moreover there is a tendency in the same direction in a few Civil law jurisdictions, see particularly para. 26.12.
37. Cf. for the general principles Schwenzer & Hachem, *Schlechtriem & Schwenzer Commentary on the CISG* (2016), Art. 6 paras 12 et seq.; CISG Advisory Council, Opinion No. 16, *supra* n. 31, at n. 3.1 et seq.
38. Piltz, *supra* n. 18, at § 2 para. 6; cf. Franco Ferrari, *Kommentar zum Einheitlichen UN-Kaufrecht*, Art. 6 para. 7 (Schwenzer, 6th ed., Munich: Beck, 2013) with further references.
39. Waincymer, *supra* n. 2, at 282, 283, 284.
40. Waincymer, *supra* n. 2, 282, 284, 285.
41. See also Waincymer, *supra* n. 2, at 282, 298.
42. Mourre, ICC ICArb. Bull. 17, 43, 46 (2006).
43. Mourre, ICC ICArb. Bull. 17, 43, 46 (2006).
44. Article 17(3) ICC Arbitration Rules; Art. 28 UNCITRAL Model Law; Art. 33 UNCITRAL Arbitration Rules.
45. English Arbitration Act 1996, s. 4(5) and Art. 28(2) UNCITRAL Model Law.

suitable law,[46] this will frequently lead to the application of the CISG.[47] Primarily, this will be the case when both parties have their places of business in contracting states.[48] The CISG was further applied to contracts between parties from non-contracting states, when arbitral tribunals found that the CISG represents international trade[49] or is part of the *lex mercatoria*.[50] Bearing in mind that – as shown above – the CISG served as a blue print for most modern law revisions,[51] this reasoning seems to be justified.

§30.03 CISG AS THE LAW APPLICABLE TO THE ARBITRATION CLAUSE

[A] General Remarks Regarding the Applicable Law to the Arbitration Clause

Only very few national arbitration legislation contain an explicit regulation regarding which law governs the arbitration clause.[52] There is consensus that the law explicitly chosen by the parties is decisive.[53] Moreover, in absence of a choice of law some national arbitration statutes revert back entirely to the law of the seat of arbitration;[54] on the basis of the validation approach others either declare the *lex causae* or the law at the seat of arbitration to be applicable.[55]

Also in scholarly writings there is consensus about the parties' possibility to choose the applicable law.[56] The revised arbitration rules of the Hong Kong International Arbitration Centre (HKIAC) even include such a choice of law in their model clause.[57] Nevertheless, parties make use of this possibility very rarely,[58] even though – as shown above – the choice of the substantive law for the main contract is common

---

46. Born, *supra* n. 21, at 517, 518.
47. Also international conventions may be considered, such as Art. 4 Rome I Regulation.
48. Differentiating Kröll, *supra* n. 14, at 59, 64; also in case law represented, ICC case 8962 (1997); ICC case 7331 (1994); ICC case 7531 (1994); ICC case 7844 (1994), cited in: Mourre, ICC ICArb. Bull. 17, 43, 47 (2006).
49. Cf. Mourre, ICC ICArb. Bull. 17, 43, 49 (2006) with further references., also with reference to ICC case 8501 (1996) in fn. 34.
50. Similarly Mourre, ICC ICArb. Bull. 17, 43, 49, 50 (2006), who notes that arbitrators attribute a great importance to the great number of contracting states, critical towards the application of the CISG as *lex mercatoria*; ICC case 6281 (1989), cited in: Arnaldez, Derains & Hascher, *Collection of ICC Arbitral Awards* 1991-1995, 409 (Paris: Kluwer, 1997): *universal* impact of the CISG.
51. See *supra* n. 5.
52. As for example Switzerland: Art. 178(2) PILS as a conflict of law rule with an *alternative character*; *see* in absence of a choice of law in Austria: § 35(2) PILA, where the law of the party performing the characteristic performance is decisive; cf. Dietmar Czernich, *Das auf die Schiedsvereinbarung anwendbare Recht*, SchiedsVZ 181, 185 (2015).
53. Czernich, SchiedsVZ 181, 183 (2015) (Austria: § 35(1) PILA); *Tamil Nadu Electricity Board v. St-CMS Electric Co. Pvt. Ltd.* [2007] EWHC 1713 (Comm); *Braes of Doune Wind Farm (Scotland) Ltd. v. Alfred McAlpine Business Services Ltd.* [2008] EWHC 426 (TCC).
54. Turkish International Arbitration Act, Art. 4; Swedish Arbitration Act 1999, s. 48.
55. As for example Art. 178(2) Swiss PILS.
56. Born, *supra* n. 21, at 472 et seq., 478 with further references.
57. As an option the following wording is suggested: 'The law of this arbitration clause shall be ...'.
58. Klaus Peter Berger, *Re-Examining the Arbitration Agreement*, 301, 302 (van den Berg, International Arbitration 2006: Back to Basics?, ICCA Congress Series Vol. 13, Alphen aan der Rijn: Kluwer, 2007).

practice. Only in exceptional cases its interpretation will show that the parties' also intended to apply the choice of law to the arbitration clause in the contract.

Highly disputed is the question, which law applies to the arbitration clause in absence of any choice of law by the parties regarding the arbitration agreement. One author is of the opinion that he can make out up to nine different theories in international practice.[59] Even though this number seems fairly high, at least three main approaches can be clearly distinguished.

The majority of scholars in arbitration primarily advocate the application of the law of the seat of arbitration.[60] This reasoning relies on the *doctrine of separability*.[61] Accordingly, the validity of the arbitration agreement and the main contract are to be assessed on an independent basis; the invalidity of the main contract generally does not affect the validity of the arbitration agreement.[62] Equally, notwithstanding an avoidance of the main contract the arbitration agreement is upheld.[63] Today, this *doctrine of separability* is widely accepted in international arbitration.[64] The CISG, too, acknowledges the *doctrine of separability*, as it explicitly states in Article 81(1) CISG that the avoidance of a contract does not affect the dispute resolution clause.[65]

In case law, however, there are many examples that the law applicable to the main contract has also been applied to the arbitration agreement without a detailed reasoning.[66] English courts traditionally tended to reach this conclusion if the parties made an explicit choice of law for the main contract.[67] The *doctrine of separability* shall

---

59. Marc Blessing, The Law Applicable to the Arbitration Agreement, 168, 169, 170 (van den Berg, Improving the Efficiency of Arbitration Agreements and Awards: 40 Years of Application of the New York Convention, ICCA Congress Series Vol. 9, The Hague: Kluwer, 1999).
60. Berger, *supra* n. 58, at 301, 320 with further references.
61. Born, 26 SacLJ 814, 818 (2014); Czernich, SchiedsVZ 181, 182 (2015): so called *Trennungsprinzip* in Austria; so called *Autonomiegrundsatz* in Germany and in Switzerland, Münch, *Münchener Kommentar zur ZPO* (2013), § 1040 paras 8 et seq. for Germany; Dieter Gränicher, *Basler Kommentar zum Internationalen Privatrecht*, Art. 178 paras 89 et seq. (Honsell et al., 3rd ed., Basel: Helbing Lichtenhahn, 2013) for Switzerland.
62. Gränicher, *Basler Kommentar IPRG* (2013), Art. 178 para. 90 f.; for Austrian law Czernich, SchiedsVZ 2015, 181, 182 with further references; Lawrence Collins et al., *Dicey, Morris and Collins on Conflict of Laws* vol 2, para. 16-008 (15th ed., London: Sweet & Maxwell 2012).
63. Cf. Gränicher, *Basler Kommentar IPRG* (2013), Art. 178 paras 84, 85.
64. *See* § 1040(1) German CCP; Art. 178(3) Swiss PILS; English Arbitration Act 1996, s. 7; Art. 16(1) First Schedule Singapore International Arbitration Act (CAP. 143A, rev 2002); Art. 16(1) UNCITRAL Model Law; as regards wide recognition Gränicher, *Basler Kommentar IPRG* (2013), Art. 178 para. 89. As an independent agreement also laid down in Art. II NYC.
65. Janet Walker, *Agreeing to Disagree: Can We Just Have Words? CISG Article 11 and the Model Law Writing Requirement*, 25 J. L. & Comm. 153, 163 (2005–2006); *see* the decision by the International Commercial Arbitration Court at the Chamber of Commerce and Industry of the Russian Federation, 13 Jun. 2000, CISG-online 1083, n. 3.1.
66. *Motorola Credit Corp. v. Uzan*, 2d Cir, 22 Oct. 2004, 388 F.3d 39, 51; accordingly *FR 8 Singapore Pty. Ltd. v. Albacore Maritime Inc.*, SD NY, 13 Oct. 2010, 754 F.Supp.2d 628, 636; *Sphere Drake Ins Ltd. v. Clarendon Nat'l Ins. Co.*, 2d Cir, 28 Aug. 2001, 263 F.3d 26, 32, fn. 3; cf. with a detailed overview on international case law, Born, *supra* n. 21, at 580 et seq.
67. *Arsanovia Ltd. v. Cruz City 1 Mauritius Holdings* [2012] EWHC 3702 (Comm), n. 21; *Karl Leibinger, Franz Leibinger v. Stryker Trauma GmbH* [2005] 690 (Comm), 8; *Sonatrach Petroleum Corp. (BVI) v. Ferrell International Ltd.*, 2001 WL 1476318, para. 32; *Sumitomo Heavy Industries v. Oil and Natural Gas Commission* [1994] 1 Lloyd's Rep. 45; *Channel Group v. Balfour Beatty Ltd.* [1993] Adj.L.R. 01/21, n. 67 (House of Lords); regarding the incentive for a clear rule, *see* Born, *supra* n. 21, at 590. Different, however, in a recent case *C v. D* [2007] EWCA Civ 1282, n. 22

only lead to the application of the law of the seat of arbitration in case the arbitration agreement was void under the *lex causae*.[68]

Notwithstanding which of these two views prevails, it has to be distinguished closely between the procedural and the contractual dimension of an arbitration agreement. The *lex causae* approach is in only suitable for the contractual dimension of the arbitration agreement, while the procedural dimension of an arbitration agreement has to be determined according to the law of the seat of arbitration pursuant to Article V(1)(a) NYC. On the other hand, the approach that favours the law of the seat of arbitration, fails to break it down into the (procedural) arbitration statute and the possible application of the contract law at the seat of arbitration regarding the contractual dimension of the arbitration agreement.[69]

This distinction, which is inevitable, becomes apparent especially in Swiss law. While Article 178(1) of the Swiss Law on Private International Law Statute (PILS)[70] contains a substantive provision for the arbitration agreement, Article 178(2) PILS[71] only provides a conflict of laws provision for all further questions of validity of the arbitration agreement. Hence, for all those questions a substantive contract law needs to be determined. Most other national arbitration statutes, such as § 1031 German Civil Procedural Law, only contain form requirements, without specifying the law applicable to other questions of validity. Provisions regarding the law applicable to the interpretation of the arbitration agreement as well as the remedies for a breach of the arbitration agreement are – as far as can be seen – not contained in any arbitration statute.

All the difficulties just described are circumvented by the so called *a-national approach* by French courts, but also partly promoted in literature.[72] According to this approach no particular national law is applicable – except the mandatory (French)

---

et seq.; *Shashoua v. Sharma* [2009] EWHC 957 (Comm), n. 29 et seq., where it was stated that the law applicable to the arbitration clause only rarely differs from the law at the seat of arbitration. See also Collins et al., *supra* n. 64, at paras 16-017, 16-018.

68. See for the leading case *Sulamérica Cia Nacional de Seguros S.A. v. Enesa Engenharia S.A.* [2012] EWCA Civ 638. *Habas Sinai Ve Tibbi Gazlar Istihsal Endustrisi A.S. v. VSC Steel Company Ltd.* [2013] EWHC 4071 (Comm), n. 99 et seq.; *XL Insurance Ltd. v. Owens Corning* [2001] 1 All E.R., 530. On the inconsistent case law in the United Kingdom, see Sabrina Pearson, *Sulamérica v. Enesa, The Hidden Pro-validation Approach Adopted by the English Courts with Respect to the Proper Law of the Arbitration Agreement*, 29 Arb. Int'l 115, 124, 125 (2013), rightly titled as the 'hidden pro-validation approach'. See further Born, *supra* n. 21, at 575.
69. Similarly Kröll, *supra* n. 14, at 59, 82, 83.
70. Article 178(1) Swiss PILS: 'The arbitration agreement must be made in writing, by telegram, telex, telecopier or any other means of communication which permits it to be evidenced by a text.'
71. Article 178(2) Swiss PILS: 'Furthermore, an arbitration agreement is valid if it conforms either to the law chosen by the parties, or to the law governing the subject-matter of the dispute, in particular the main contract, or to Swiss law'.
72. Cass (1re Ch. civ.), *Municipalité de Khoms El Mergeb v. société Dalico*, 20 Dec. 1993, 1993 Rev. Arb. 116, 117; Cass (1re Ch. civ.), *Renault v. société V 2000 (Jaguar France)*, 21 May 1997, 1997 Rev. Arb. 537. Cf. Emmanuel Gaillard & John Savage, *Fouchard Gaillard Goldman on International Commercial Arbitration*, paras 435 et seq., 525 et seq. (The Hague: Kluwer, 1999).

provisions. Rather, the arbitration agreement shall be assessed on the basis of the parties' intent as well as general principles and trade usages in international trade.[73] Although this approach is very appealing due to the fact that it avoids all difficult questions of conflict of laws references,[74] it is nonetheless mostly dismissed as an unnecessary exaggeration of transnational thinking.[75] Furthermore, it does not correspond to the hypothetical parties' intent anymore.[76]

Against this background the question will be discussed in the following, whether and to which aspects of the arbitration agreement the CISG can be applied.

[B] General Applicability of the CISG to Arbitration Agreements

Some authors are of the opinion that the CISG is generally not applicable to arbitration agreements.[77] Beside the *doctrine of separability* it is mainly argued that arbitration agreements fall outside the scope of the CISG due to their procedural nature lacking the sales contract characteristics.[78] As elaborated above, one must distinguish between the procedural and the contractual components of an arbitration agreements. With regard to the contractual dimension the question is whether harmonised or non-harmonised law applies. Article 19(3) (dispute resolution clauses as material alteration of the offer) and Article 81(1) CISG (continuation of the arbitration clause in spite of the avoidance of the main contract) clearly state that dispute resolution clauses are not excluded from the CISG's application.[79] The wording by itself suggests that the CISG puts the arbitration agreement a par with other contractual provisions.[80]

[C] Formal Validity

Most national arbitration statutes still submit arbitration agreements to a form requirement. Only very few states abolished the form requirements for the arbitration

---

73. For an overview, *see* Berger, *supra* n. 58, at 301, 380 et seq.
74. Berger, *supra* n. 58, at 301, 310.
75. Piero Bernardini, *Arbitration Clauses: Achieving Effectiveness in the Law Applicable to the Arbitration Clause*, 197, 202 (van den Berg, Improving the Efficiency of Arbitration Agreements and Awards: 40 Years of Application of the New York Convention, ICCA Congress Series Vol. 9, The Hague: Kluwer, 1999); Berger, *supra* n. 58, at 301, 310. Detailed in Fogt, 26 Am. Rev. Int. Arb. 365, 369 et seq. (2015), with further convincing arguments why this approach has to be dismissed.
76. Bernardini, *supra* n. 75, at 197, 202.
77. *See* for further references Kröll, *supra* n. 14, at 59, 82 et seq.
78. Stefan Kröll, *Selected Problems Concerning the CISG's Scope of Application*, 25 J. L & Comm. 39, 45, 46 (2005) with further references; idem, *supra* n. 14, at 59, 81 f.; BGer, 4C.100/2000, 11 Jul. 2000, CISG-online 627, n. 3.
79. Perales Viscasillas & Ramos Muñoz, *supra* n. 8, at 1366, 1355; Walker, 25 J. L. & Comm. 153, 163 (2005–2006); Robert Koch, *The CISG as the Law Applicable to Arbitration Agreement?*, 267, 280, 281 (B. Andersen & Schroeter, Sharing International Commercial Law across National Boundaries, Festschrift for Albert H. Kritzer on the Occasion of his Eightieth Birthday, London: Wildy, Simmonds & Hill, 2008); Schroeter, *Schlechtriem & Schwenzer Commentary on the CISG* (2016), Intro. to Arts 14–24 paras 16 et seq.
80. Similarly Perales Viscasillas & Ramos Muñoz, *supra* n. 7, at 1355, 1366.

agreement, namely France,[81] Sweden,[82] New Zealand[83] and some Canadian provinces.[84] Also the NYC still contains a form requirement in Article II(1) and (2).

By contrast, according to its Article 11 the CISG is based on the freedom of form principle. Consequently, some authors argue that the freedom of form principle contained in the CISG prevails over any form requirement for arbitration agreements.[85] This view is, however, not compelling.[86]

The form requirements aim particularly at the procedural dimension that is generally governed in all those national arbitration statutes that have not yet implemented the freedom of form principle.[87]

Also by interpretation of the CISG the same result is reached. The application of Article 11 CISG to arbitration agreements was never intended. The freedom of form principle has been disputed since the beginning of the initiatives to harmonise sales law.[88] Objections were mainly raised by former socialist states and countries which have an indirect form requirement tied to the value of the transaction in their national law.[89] The form requirements of an arbitration agreement have never been part of the discussions about the freedom of form.[90]

The possibility to make a reservation according to Article 96 CISG in order to exclude the freedom of form principle further affirms this reasoning. This reservation was mainly made by States that (originally) intended to control their international sales contracts.[91] If the intention had been to submit arbitration agreements to the freedom of form principle of Article 11 CISG most of the contracting states would have been obliged to make such a reservation.[92]

Further, the argument that the CISG prevails as *lex specialis* over national arbitration statutes[93] does not hold up. Rather the contrary is the case. Also from the wording in Article 90 CISG it derives that the CISG does not prevail over the NYC.

---

81. Article 1507 CCP.
82. The Sweden arbitration statute (1999) waives any sort of form requirements for arbitration agreements.
83. New Zealand Arbitration Act 1996, Sch. 1, s. 7(1).
84. Alberta: Alberta Arbitration Act 1991, Art. 5(1); Ontario: Ontario Arbitration Act 1991, Art. 5(3).
85. Walker, 25 J. L. & Comm. 153, 163 (2005–2006); Perales Viscasillas & Ramos Muñoz, *supra* n. 7, at 1355, 1366; Anne-Kathrin Schluchter, *Die Gültigkeit von Kaufverträgen unter dem UN-Kaufrecht*, 91 (Baden-Baden: Nomos, 1996).
86. Of the same opinion Piltz, *supra* n. 18, at § 3 para. 119; Kröll, *supra* n. 14, at 59, 83; Koch, *supra* n. 79, at 267, 276 et seq.
87. Cf. the UNCITRAL Model Law, which offers two options for Art. 7 that consciously reflects both alternatives.
88. Ernst Rabel, *Der Entwurf eines einheitlichen Kaufgesetzes*, RabelsZ 9, 1, 55, 56 (1935).
89. Hans Dölle & Gert Reinhart, *Kommentar zum Einheitlichen Kaufrecht*, Art. 15 paras 14 et seq. (Dölle, Munich: Beck, 1976); such provisions are present for example in the USA: § 2-201(1) UCC; France: Art. 1341 CC. Cf. also Schwenzer, Hachem & Kee, *supra* n. 7, at paras 22.09 et seq.
90. Cf. Schwenzer & Tebel, *The Word Is Not Enough – Arbitration, Choice of Forum and Choice of Law Clauses Under the CISG*, ASA Bull. 4, 740, 748 (2013), *see* fn. 51 with further details on the different positions taken by the delegates throughout the drafting of the CISG.
91. The contracting states, which have originally made an Art. 96 CISG reservation: Argentina, Armenia, Chile, China (withdrawn), Estonia (withdrawn), Latvia (withdrawn), Lithuania (withdrawn), Paraguay, Russian Federation, Ukraine, Hungary and Republic of Belarus.
92. *See* Piltz, *supra* n. 18, at § 2 para. 130.
93. Perales Viscasillas & Ramos Muñoz, *supra* n. 7, at 1355, 1370.

Finally, the same conclusion is reached considering the *most favourable law approach* of Article VII(I) NYC. This provision is dealing with the relation of the NYC to other provisions specifically with regard to recognition and enforcement, however, not with regard to provisions of sales contracts or any other general contractual provisions.[94]

Due to all these reasons it can be assumed that mandatory form requirements of the *lex arbitri* have to be always applied.[95] Whether the CISG is the substantive contract law at the seat of the arbitral tribunal or the *lex causae*, is – like any other applicable contract law – irrelevant.

[D] Substantive Validity

Contrary to the formal validity which depends regularly on the applicable national arbitration statute, the CISG can be applied to questions of substantive validity, when dealing with questions of contract formation (Articles 14 et seq. CISG).[96] As already pointed out, for this discussion only the contractual dimension of the arbitration clause is of importance.

The application of the CISG is unproblematic, if the law governing the main contract is applied. A great number of courts have chosen this approach, without even discussing other viable options.[97] The overwhelming majority of scholars agree on this view.[98] The application of the CISG might not appear as evident if the law of the seat of arbitration is considered to be decisive for the contractual dimension of the arbitration clause. Here the question arises whether to apply the non-harmonised

---

94. Cf. Ulrich Schroeter, *UN-Kaufrecht und Europäisches Gemeinschaftsrecht: Verhältnis und Wechselwirkungen*, § 14 para. 45 (Munich: Sellier, 2005); Thomas Rauscher, *Zuständigkeitsfragen zwischen CISG und Brüssel I*, 933, 950 (Lorenz et al., Festschrift für Andreas Heldrich zum 70. Geburtstag, Munich: Beck, 2005).
95. For a detailed overview, *see* Schwenzer & Tebel, ASA Bull. 4, 740, 749 (2013); also Fogt, 26 Am. Rev. Int. Arb. 365, 396 et seq. (2015).
96. *Filanto S.p.A. v. Chilewich Int'l Corp.*, SD NY, 14 Apr. 1992, CISG-online 45, 789 F.Supp. 1229; LG Hamburg, 19 Jun. 1997, CISG-online 283; Tribunal Supremo (Spain), 17 Feb. 1998, CISG-online 1333; Tribunal Supremo (Spain), 17 Feb. 1998, CISG-online 1335; Koch, *supra* n. 79, at 267, 282.
97. Rechtbank Arnhem, 17 Jan. 2007, CISG-online 1476; *Filanto S.p.A. v. Chilewich International Corp.*, SD NY, 14 Apr. 1992, CISG-online 45; *see* for case law on choice of forum clauses: Cass (1re Ch. civ.), 16 Jul. 1998, CISG-online 344; CA Paris, 13 Dec. 1995, CISG-online 312; *Solea LLC v. Hershey Canada Inc.*, D. Del., 9 May 2008, CISG-online 1769; *Chateau des Charmes Wines Ltd. v. Sabate USA Inc., Sabate S.A.*, 9th Cir., 5 May 2003, CISG-online 767; Gerechtshof 's-Hertogenbosch, 19 Nov. 1996, CISG-online 323, n. 4.4. et seq.; OLG Oldenburg, 20 Dec. 2007, CISG-online 1644; OLG Köln, 24 May 2006, CISG-online 1232; OLG Braunschweig, 28 Oct. 1999, CISG-online 510; LG Landshut, 12 Jun. 2008, CISG-online 1703, n. 31 et seq.; LG Giessen, 17 Dec. 2002, CISG-online 766 (obiter); cf. also *Chateau Des Charmes Wines Ltd. v. Sabate, USA Inc. et al.*, Superior Court of Justice Ontario, 28 Oct. 2005, CISG-online 1139, n. 13; left open by OLG Düsseldorf, 30 Jan. 2004, CISG-online 821.
98. Application of the CISG to dispute resolution clauses: Magnus, J. von Staudingers Kommentar zum Bürgerlichen Gesetzbuch mit Einführungsgesetz und Nebengesetzen – Wiener Kaufrecht (CISG), 2005, Vorbem. zu Arts 14 et seq. para. 8; Schwenzer & Hachem, *Schlechtriem & Schwenzer Commentary on the CISG* (2016), Art. 4 para. 11; Schroeter, *Schlechtriem & Schwenzer Commentary on the CISG* (2016), Intro. to Arts 14–24 paras 18, 19; the same applies to choice of forum clauses: Schroeter, *supra* n. 94, at § 15 para. 24; dissenting Kröll, 25 J. L & Comm. 39, 44, 45 (2005); presumably also Rauscher, *supra* n. 94, at 933, 949 f.

contract law or – if the seat of arbitration is located in a contracting state – the CISG. Supporters of the application of non-harmonised law point out the similarity to arbitration agreements that are concluded independently from a contract.[99] For those always the non-harmonised law and never the CISG would apply. The German Federal Supreme Court has taken a similar stance in a dictum in a recent case in which it decided upon a choice of forum clause pursuant to Article 23 Brussels Regulation.[100]

At least for arbitral tribunals this argument is not convincing. As demonstrated above, arbitral tribunals do not apply the substantive law based on any obligation by international law if all preconditions are met, but rather in absence of a parties' choice of law they apply the law with the closest connection. This rule is not only valid for the selection between different national laws but also applies accordingly for the decision between the non-harmonised and harmonised law of one and the same jurisdiction to be applied to the arbitration agreement. An international dispute, which is governed by the CISG, will regularly be more closely connected to harmonised contract law, which thus is the preferable law.

Even when following the French approach, according to which arbitration agreements are not governed by national but by a-national law, the CISG presents itself as the most viable option of a transnational contract regulation.

[E] Interpretation

Substantive validity and interpretation of an agreement are closely interrelated. The question of what the parties agreed upon cannot be separated from the question whether the parties reached an agreement at all. This is generally the case but especially with regard to the facts that can be taken into account to interpret the parties' conduct. Many Anglo-American legal systems for example apply the *parol evidence rule*[101] according to which oral ancillary agreements cannot serve to interpret the written contract.[102] The CISG, on the contrary, in Article 8(3) CISG explicitly provides for a basis to consider the parties' negotiations, customs, established practices between themselves and subsequent conduct of the parties. The Anglo-American *parol evidence rule* is thus excluded under the CISG.[103] Applying contradicting substantive contract formation provisions and principles of interpretation would lead inevitably to frictions.

---

99. Kröll, 25 J. L & Comm. 39, 45 (2005).
100. BGH, VIII ZR 125/14, 25 Mar. 2015, CISG-online 2588, n. 23.
101. For example., USA: § 2-202 UCC; Singapore: Evidence Act 1997, s. 101; India: Evidence Act 1997, s. 99. Only as rebuttable presumption in England and Wales, cf. Schwenzer, Hachem & Kee, *supra* n. 7, at para. 26.47.
102. CISG Advisory Council, Opinion No. 3, Rapporteur Hyland, *Parol Evidence Rule, Plain Meaning Rule, Contractual Merger Clause and the CISG*, n. 1.2.3; Schwenzer, Hachem & Kee, *supra* n. 7, at paras 26.45 et seq.
103. With a detailed overview on case law and scholarly writings, Schmidt-Kessel, *Schlechtriem & Schwenzer Commentary on the CISG* (2016), Art. 8 para. 33, in fn. 183. On the reasons why the *parol evidence rule* was not incorporated in the CISG, *see* CISG Advisory Council, Opinion No. 3, *supra* n. 102, at n. 2.4. with further references: complexity, unknown to most legal systems and in general strongly criticised.

As a result, the CISG tends to always provide the more suitable provisions tailored to international trade than most of the national laws.[104]

The situation may be different if the applicable national arbitration statute entails specific interpretation rules only and exclusively for arbitration agreements.[105] Such provisions prevail, like form requirements as discussed above, over general contract provisions as *leges speciales*.[106]

[F] Remedies for a Breach of the Arbitration Agreement

Lastly, the question of possible remedies upon a breach of the arbitration agreement is discussed. Can a party claim damages if the other party calls on a national court in violation of the arbitration agreement? Does this possibly result in the right to avoid the whole contract? Again, national arbitration statutes leave these questions open.

Arbitration agreements as well as choice of forum clauses are not merely procedural agreements, but also create contractual obligations.[107] The violation of those contractual obligations in turn may trigger contractual remedies. Accordingly, a solution has to be sought in national contract laws. Once more the choice is to be made between the law of the seat of arbitration and the law applicable to the main contract. An arbitral tribunal has recently upheld a claim for damages due to a breach of the arbitration agreement based on the Swiss Code of Obligations.[108] The Swiss Federal Tribunal affirmed this decision.[109]

Again, the starting point should be the reasonable expectations of the parties. It would be met with confusion if a breach of obligations arising out of the main contract faced different remedies than a breach of the arbitration agreement.[110] As a result one should strive for a congruence in regard to the main contract, be it to apply the *lex causae* or at least when applying the law at the seat of the arbitration when making the choice between the non-harmonised domestic and the harmonised contract law.[111]

§30.04 CONCLUSIONS

Internationally, both the CISG and arbitration are a story of worldwide success. Hardly any other legal framework promotes the international trade as effectively as these two

---

104. Cf. Schmidt-Ahrendts, Belgrade L. Rev. 3, 211, 220 (2011).
105. Such as the *liberal construction principle according to the ordinary understanding of businessmen* as it is known in English law, see on this Collins et al., *supra* n. 64, at para. 16-016.
106. *Premium Nafta Products Ltd. (20th) Defendant et al. v. Fili Shipping Company Ltd. et al.* [2007] EWCA Civ 20, n. 17 f.
107. Cf. also Tan, 47 Va. J. Int'l Law 545, 602 (2006–2007).
108. Simon Gabriel, *Arbitration in Switzerland: The Practitioner's Guide*, 1473, 1475 (Arroyo, Alphen aan der Rijn: Kluwer 2013): awarding of damages on the basis of Art. 97 Swiss CO.
109. BGer, 4A_444/2009, decision of 11 Feb. 2010.
110. Affirmed by Schmidt-Ahrendts, Belgrade L. Rev. 3, 211, 219 (2011), who agrees on the application of Art. 74 CISG in case of a breach of the arbitration agreement.
111. For an application of the CISG: Schmidt-Ahrendts, Belgrade L. Rev. 3, 211, 219 (2011). Dissenting Koch, *supra* n. 79, at 267, 285; Perales Viscasillas & Ramos Muñoz, *supra* n. 7, at 1355, 1346.

international instruments. This increases legal predictability and simultaneously reduces transaction costs.

Arbitrators apply the CISG on a regular basis as substantive law to the international sales contracts. Although the arbitral tribunals are not obliged to apply the CISG on the basis of international law, the CISG is applied due to the parties' choice-of-law or alternatively as suitable law with the closest connection to the dispute.

Further, the CISG plays an important role as the applicable law to the arbitration agreement. Regarding the formal validity arbitration agreements are governed by the applicable law of the seat of arbitration; the freedom of form principle of the CISG is thus not applicable. However, the CISG can be applied to all questions of the substantive validity of an arbitration agreement, its interpretation, as well as the remedies available upon a breach of the agreement.

CHAPTER 31
Multi-party, Multi-contract Rules and the Arbitrators' Role in Finding Consent

Matthew Secomb

Over the last twenty years, the world of international arbitration has fought a pitched battle with multi-party and multi-contract arbitration. It has given rise to complex legal issues – like the competence-competence principle, and separability of the arbitration agreement – while calling out for practical solutions. In other words, Pierre Karrer's cup of tea.[1]

Multi-party, multi-contract arbitration has received a great deal of attention from the international arbitration community. However, it has also suffered from certain misunderstanding. This article attempts to clarify a narrow point in the field of multi-party, multi-contract arbitration: the relationship between consent's nature and multi-party, multi-contract provisions that have been included in arbitral rules over recent years.[2]

Specifically, it aims to clarify that those provisions deal with the question, procedurally, of which parties and what contracts the arbitration covers initially. They do not change fundamentally the arbitrators' powers to deal with multi-party or multi-contract situations. The new provisions do not change questions of which parties consented to arbitration, and under which contracts (or combination of contracts). Those more fundamental questions relate to consent to arbitrate. They determine the back-end issue of who may be bound by the award, and under which contracts claims may be determined.

---

1. Multi-party arbitration is also meaningful to me personally. I first met Pierre Karrer at the Vis moot in 1999. He arbitrated a moot I appeared in and, appropriately, the issue was one of contractual joinder. He delivered some choice, pointed questions, with his usual mischievous glint in his eyes.
2. For example, comprehensive multi-party, multi-contract provisions were included in the 2012 version of the ICC Rules (*see* Arts 7–10) (unless noted otherwise, references to rules are to the version current at the time of publication).

This distinction between the initial determination of the parties and contracts procedurally subject to the arbitration when it starts, and the ultimate determination of who may be bound by the award, and under which contracts, is important. However, the distinction is also sometimes misunderstood. This is because under some rules, arbitrators have been given a dual role. Those rules empower arbitrators to decide procedurally whether a party should be joined or a contract subject to an arbitration, and then decide under the competence-competence principle whether they have jurisdiction over that party or claims arising under that contract. This limited procedural role is very different to the arbitrators' role in determining jurisdiction.

This article first steps back and considers the contrasting aims of business people as compared to the drafters of arbitral rules. It then looks at the procedural question of how the parties and contracts subject to an arbitration are defined at its outset. The next section follows chronologically, considering the arbitrators' jurisdictional role once that definition has been made. It then explains why this all matters. That is, it sets out why it is important that participants in the arbitral process understand the distinction between initial procedural steps, and then jurisdictional decisions. The article finishes with a brief mention of an important contrast with national law provisions that are relevant, and an overall conclusion.

§31.01 MULTI-PARTY/MULTI-CONTRACT ARBITRATION: WHAT BUSINESS PEOPLE CARE ABOUT VERSUS WHAT ARBITRATION RULE DRAFTERS CARE ABOUT

At the outset, it is important to consider what business people think about when it comes to multi-party, multi-contract arbitration. The short answer is very little. But what they do think about is the transaction they are trying to create. And they do care that whatever system of dispute resolution they choose will respect and enforce their agreement.

Business people rarely spell out how they would like disputes resolved in a multi-contract, multi-party situation, even if it is obvious. An example, illustrates this: take an M&A transaction implemented by a share sale agreement and a shareholders' agreement. The two agreements are between the same parties and contain identical arbitration clauses. A disgruntled buyer may wish to start a single arbitration to enforce both the share sale agreement and the shareholders' agreement in the same arbitration. Equally, it may be that the buyer brings an arbitration under the share sale agreement, but that the seller wishes to bring a counterclaim under the shareholders' agreement. While the agreements would unlikely deal expressly with those situations, it would seem obvious that the parties would have wanted any disputes under the two agreements to be resolved together.

If a set of rules did not allow, for example, the seller to bring a counterclaim under the shareholders' agreement, this may frustrate the parties' intentions. It may not give effect to what they intended in terms of dispute resolution when they signed the agreements (even if they did not state it expressly).

However, in other cases, the parties may not intend to allow multi-party, multi-contract arbitration. A good example is a construction project with a classic employer-contractor-subcontractor structure. In that case, the parties almost certainly did not intend the employer and the subcontractor – who are not bound to each other by a contract – to be included in the same arbitration.

Fundamentally, it is the desire to give effect to the parties' intentions that rule drafters have tried to satisfy in multi-party, multi-contract provisions. Rule drafters have tried to create procedural rules that will allow parties to resolve disputes under the transactions as they have envisaged them. This is for a number of reasons, both competitive and otherwise.

On the competitive side, arbitral institutions are increasingly trying to use rule revisions to distinguish themselves. With each amendment to the rules, institutions are trying to innovate, to gain an edge over competing arbitral institutions. Much of the innovation has focused on multi-party and multi-contract arbitration. For example, the SIAC introduced new multi-party, multi-contract provisions in the 2016 revision of their rules.[3] The SIAC describes the new multi-contract provisions as 'a new streamlined process for the commencement of disputes arising out of or in connection with multiple contracts/multiple arbitration agreements'.[4]

In sum, multi-contract and multi-party provisions were introduced to meet a need. That need is allow disputes to be resolved in multi-party, multi-contract situations as the parties intended in their commercial dealings.

§31.02 HOW THE PARTIES AND CONTRACTS SUBJECT TO AN ARBITRATION ARE DEFINED PROCEDURALLY

At any given time, an arbitration has defined parties to it, and covers disputes under identified contracts. National laws and rules dealing with arbitration set out how those parties and contracts are identified. In the 'bad old days' arbitral rules were not very flexible *procedurally* when it came to identifying the parties and contracts that might be the subject of a given arbitration. However, arbitral rules have become more flexible.

[A] The Bad Old Days Before Multi-party, Multi-contract Provisions

The starting point is the time before institutions included multi-party or multi-contract provisions in their rules. At the time, rules allowed for multi-party or multi-contract arbitration in certain circumstances, but they were limited. For example, before the early 2000s, in the ICC system, the claimant identified the parties to the arbitration.[5]

---

3. SIAC Rules, Arts 6–8.
4. SIAC, *Highlights of the SIAC Rules 2016*, http://www.siac.org.sg/images/stories/articles/rules/SIAC%20Rules%202016_Cheat%20Sheet_30June2016.pdf.
5. Anne Marie Whitesell & Eduardo Silva-Romero, *Multiparty and Multicontract Arbitration: Recent ICC Experience*, ICC Court of Arbitration Bulletin: Complex Arbitration – Special Supplement 7, 10 (2003).

The respondent could not add parties to the arbitration once the claimant had defined them in the request for arbitration.

Thus, while objections could be raised to the arbitrators' jurisdiction over the named parties to the arbitration, no procedural mechanism existed that would allow parties to be added (the ICC Court could also effectively remove parties through the prima facie test).

Similar considerations applied to multi-contract arbitration. The claimant could start an arbitration based on several contracts.[6] While the respondent could attempt to introduce a counterclaim under a contract other than that which the claimant relied upon, its ability to do so was limited.[7] Specifically, the respondent's right to bring a counterclaim under another agreement was effectively limited by the ICC Court's prima facie jurisdiction test.[8] Thus, the respondent would need to prove, for example, that the arbitration clause in the new contract was consistent with arbitration clause based on which the arbitration was commenced.

This lack of flexibility would sometimes stifle the parties' intentions when it came to how disputes could be resolved.

[B] The Brave New World of Multi-contract, Multi-party Provisions

Beginning in the late 1990s, drafters started including multi-party and multi-contract provisions in arbitral rules. Drafters were naturally conservative with the first provisions. For example, the 1998 version of the ICC Rules contained very limited grounds for consolidation.[9] The 2012 version, by contrast, contained much more expansive provisions, dealing with joinder, multi-party claims, multi-contract claims and consolidation.[10]

Broadly speaking, three types of mechanisms have been included in rules, namely, those for joinder, intervention and consolidation. While each mechanism is different, they generally[11] have the same effect, namely, that the parties or contracts that are the subject of an arbitration when it is started change. Briefly:

- Joinder is a mechanism under which a further party can be added to an existing arbitration.
- Intervention is a mechanism that allows a party who is not initially a party to the arbitration to become one of its own initiative. (The difference between joinder and intervention is the party who takes the initiative for a party to be

---

6. *Ibid* 14–15.
7. *See* generally, Simon Greenberg, José Ricardo Feris & Christian Albanesi, *Consolidation, Joinder, Cross-Claims Multiparty and Multicontract Arbitrations: Recent ICC Experience*, Multiparty Arbitration, ICC Institute of World Business Law Dossiers (eds Bernard Hanotiau & Eric Schwartz) 161, 166–172 (ICC 2010).
8. *Ibid* 171.
9. ICC Rules (1998), Art. 4(6).
10. ICC Rules, Arts 7–10.
11. As pointed out below, this may not necessarily be the case for consolidation. Consolidation of two arbitrations between the same parties and under the same contracts does not change the arbitration's scope in any meaningful sense.

added. For joinder it is at an existing party's initiative; for intervention it is at the third party's initiative.)
- Consolidation is where two or more arbitrations are combined to make a single arbitration. Consolidation typically leads to the 'consolidated arbitration' having different parties or covering different agreements to the initial arbitrations (although that is not necessarily the case – sometimes two parties each start arbitration against the other, leading to two arbitrations between the same parties under the same agreement).

What is interesting for this article is who decides whether a party can be joined, a party can intervene or two arbitrations can be consolidated. As set out below, different rules designate different decision makers. Some have the institution decide, others the arbitrators, and yet others take a hybrid approach.

[1]   The 'Institution Decides' Approach

Some rule have decisions on joinder, intervention and consolidation decided by the institution. The ICC Rules are a typical, and prominent example of this approach.

In the ICC system, any party to an existing arbitration may file a request to join any third party.[12] If neither the initial parties, nor the party to be joined, object, then the party will be joined. However, if any objection is raised, the ICC Court[13] will decide, in effect, whether the party should be joined.[14] The ICC Court will decide whether it is prima facie satisfied that an arbitration agreement under the ICC Rules which binds all parties the arbitration (old and new) may exist.[15] Thus, for joinder applications, the ICC Court has to be prima facie satisfied that the party to be joined might be bound, by an arbitration agreement, to all of the existing parties to the arbitration. The ICC Rules do not provide for intervention (i.e., joinder can only be initiated by an existing party to the arbitration).

The ICC Rules take a similar approach to the inclusion of claims under new agreements (i.e., other than the contract or contracts on the basis of which the arbitration was initially filed).[16] They provide that claims arising out of two or more contracts can be made in a single arbitration, even if they contain two or more separate arbitration clauses.[17]

Thus, a claimant might bring a claim under one agreement, and then the respondent might make a counterclaim under another agreement. In that case, the

---

12. ICC Rules, Art 7(1).
13. The 2012 ICC Rules contain a 'gate keeper' provision under which the Secretary General can decide whether jurisdictional objections should be submitted to the ICC Court (ICC Rules, Art. 6(2)). For brevity, this paper just refers to the ICC Court.
14. ICC Rules, Art 6(4)(i).
15. ICC Rules, Art 6(4)(i).
16. ICC Rules, Art 9.
17. ICC Rules, Art 9.

respondent's ability to make the counterclaim is subject to a prima facie decision by the ICC Court.[18] The ICC Court will decide whether it is prima facie satisfied that:

(a) ... the arbitration agreements under which those claims are made may be compatible, and
(b) ... all parties to the arbitration may have agreed that those claims can be determined together in a single arbitration.[19]

The net effect is that a respondent who wishes to counterclaim under a new contract will generally only be allowed to do so if it can satisfy the two parts of this test, on a prima facie basis.

Consolidation is dealt with slightly differently. The parties can always agree to consolidate two existing arbitrations.[20] However, if one party seeks consolidation and the other party contests it, the ICC Court has the power to decide whether to consolidate.[21] The ICC Court may consolidate two arbitrations if:

b) all of the claims in the arbitrations are made under the same arbitration agreement;[22] or
c) where the claims in the arbitrations are made under more than one arbitration agreement, the arbitrations are between the same parties, the disputes in the arbitrations arise in connection with the same legal relationship, and the Court finds the arbitration agreements to be compatible.[23]

In practice, these two grounds deal with different circumstances. The first generally deals with the situation that the claims in two arbitrations are all made under the same agreement, but the parties to the two arbitrations are different. Thus, one arbitration might be between A and B, and the other arbitration between A, B *and* C. Thus, consolidation would change the parties to the arbitration. The second deals with the situation where the parties to the two arbitrations are the same, but the claims in them arise under different contracts. So, consolidation would change the contracts subject to the arbitration.

The ICC Rules do not empower the arbitrators to ever join parties or allow intervention.[24]

The CIETAC Rules contain broadly similar provisions, in that it is CIETAC itself that takes a prima facie decision whether to allow joinder, and decides whether arbitrations should be consolidated.[25]

---

18. ICC Rules, Art 6.4(ii). *See* Jason Fry, Simon Greenberg & Francesca Mazza, *The Secretariat's Guide to ICC Arbitration*, para. 3-340 (ICC, 2012).
19. ICC Rules, Art. 6.4(ii) (paragraph break inserted).
20. The rules acknowledge the parties' right to reach this agreement (ICC Rules, Art. 10(a)).
21. ICC Rules, Art. 10.
22. ICC Rules, Art. 10(b).
23. ICC Rules, Art. 10(c).
24. Although joinder could always take place if all parties, existing and new, consent.
25. CIETAC Rules, Arts 18 (joinder) and 19 (consolidation).

[2] The 'Arbitrators Decide' Approach

Other rules allow the arbitrators rather than the institution to decide on these issues. For example, the LCIA Rules allow the tribunal to decide on joinder in certain circumstances.[26] They empower the tribunal:

> to allow one or more third person to be joined in the arbitration as a party provided any such third person and the applicant party have consented to such joinder in writing following the Commencement Date or (if earlier) in the Arbitration Agreement ... .[27]

The LCIA Rules take a similar approach to consolidation. They allow the tribunal:

> (ix) to order, with the approval of the LCIA Court, the consolidation of the arbitration with one or more other arbitrations into a single arbitration subject to the LCIA Rules where all the parties to the arbitrations to be consolidated so agree in writing;
>
> (x) to order, with the approval of the LCIA Court, the consolidation of the arbitration with one or more other arbitrations subject to the LCIA Rules commenced under the same arbitration agreement or any compatible arbitration agreement(s) between the same disputing parties, provided that no arbitral tribunal has yet been formed by the LCIA Court for such other arbitration(s) or, if already formed, that such tribunal(s) is(are) composed of the same arbitrators ... .[28]

Thus, the LCIA Rules also give the tribunal the right to decide on whether arbitrations should be consolidated, albeit subject to the LCIA Court's 'approval' of any decision.

Unsurprisingly, the UNCITRAL Rules also leave joinder decisions to the tribunal, stating:

> The arbitral tribunal may, at the request of any party, allow one or more third persons to be joined in the arbitration as a party provided such person is a party to the arbitration agreement, unless the arbitral tribunal finds, after giving all parties, including the person or persons to be joined, the opportunity to be heard, that joinder should not be permitted because of prejudice to any of those parties. ... .[29]

The JCAA Rules,[30] the Swiss Rules[31] and the NAI Rules,[32] follow a broadly similar approach.

---

26. LCIA Rules, Art. 22(viii).
27. LCIA Rules, Art. 22(viii).
28. LCIA Rules, Art. 22(ix)–(x).
29. UNCITRAL Rules, Art. 17(5).
30. JCAA Rules, Rule 52. Rule 52(4) provides that the tribunal 'may deny joinder'.
31. Swiss Rules, Art. 4(2).
32. NAI Rules, Art. 37.

[3] The Hybrid Approach

Other rules allow both the institution and the tribunal to play a role, depending on the circumstances.

A good example is the HKIAC Rules. Under those rules, who takes any decision on joinder will depend on whether a tribunal is in place.[33] If a joinder issue arises after the tribunal has been constituted, it can decide on the issue.[34] However, if the issue arises before the tribunal has been constituted, the HKIAC itself decides on the joinder issue.[35]

The SIAC Rules,[36] the Spanish Court of Arbitration Rules[37] and the ACICA Rules[38] follow a similar approach (being that the institution decides before the tribunal is constituted).

§31.03 ONCE THE PARTIES AND CONTRACTS SUBJECT TO THE ARBITRATION ARE DEFINED, WHAT HAPPENS TO JURISDICTIONAL OBJECTIONS?

Defining the parties to, and contracts covered by, the arbitration is only the first step. Once that has happened, the next question is whether that will remain the case. It may not, because a party might raise jurisdictional objections. When a party raises jurisdictional objections, under the competence-competence principle, the arbitrators must decide on their own jurisdiction.

Two things need to be considered: first, the way that consent works in multi-party, multi-contract situations and, second, the arbitrators' role when it comes to multi-party, multi-contract arbitration.

[A] Consent's Binary Nature, But with Lots of Combinations and Permutations

Resolving almost all jurisdictional objections requires looking at consent.[39] Consent is, unsurprisingly, binary. A party either consented to arbitrate under certain circumstances, or it did not. And, while consent is binary, it arises in certain circumstances in multi-party arbitration that do not arise in simple, two-party, one-contract arbitrations. Examples of these include:

---

33. HKIAC Rules, Art. 27.
34. HKIAC Rules, Art. 27(1).
35. HKIAC Rules, Art. 27(8).
36. SIAC Rules, Arts 7 (joinder) and 8 (consolidation).
37. Spanish Court of Arbitration Rules, Art. 19.
38. ACICA Rules, Art. 15.
39. Bernard Hanotiau, *Complex Arbitrations: Multiparty, Multicontract, Multi-issue, and Class Action Arbitrations* 7 (Kluwer Law International, 2006).

- Arguments that a party did not consent to being in an arbitration with another party, even if no claims are made between those parties.[40] For example, A might start an arbitration against B, and then B might join C to the arbitration, so it can make claims against it. In those circumstances, A might argue that it does not wish to be involved in an arbitration involving C, even if A and C make no claims against one another. The question would be whether A consented to being in an arbitration with C.
- Arguments that the parties did not agree to have disputes arising under two contracts in the same arbitration. For example A and B might have signed a series of agreements for covering similar subject matter (e.g., a series of individual contracts for the construction of similar ships). The question is whether the parties consented to have disputes under more than one contract resolved in the same arbitration.

Other objections can arise whether or not the arbitration is multi-party or multi-contract. For example, a party can argue that it is not bound by any arbitration agreement (i.e., it never agreed to arbitrate at all). That objection has nothing to do with the arbitration's multi-party, multi-contract nature.

In any given case, it is initially for the arbitrators to determine whether the necessary consent is present.[41] Under the competence-competence principle, arbitrators can decide on their own jurisdiction in any arbitration. However, even if the arbitrators find that they have jurisdiction, national courts can revisit the question of jurisdiction when the award is presented in setting aside or enforcement proceedings.[42]

[B]   Arbitrators' Decisions in Multi-party, Multi-contract Situations

The important thing to understand is that arbitrators are sometimes called upon to make two different decisions on multi-party, multi-contract situations. The first is the hurdle question of whether procedurally, the arbitration's scope should be expanded to include a new party or contract. However, if the rules empower the arbitrators to take that decision, it is a purely procedural one. The arbitrators can decide procedurally, for example, whether a party should be included to the arbitration. However, that decision does not – and certainly should not – prejudge the arbitrators' ultimate decision on whether they have jurisdiction (and, if so, the scope of that jurisdiction).

Rules have different degrees of clarity on the arbitrators' dual role. Article 4(2) of the Swiss Rules, for example, states:

> where a party to pending arbitral proceedings under these Rules requests that one or more third persons participate in the arbitration, the arbitral tribunal shall

---

40. As Gary Born puts it: 'parties agree to arbitrate with particular other parties, according to specific procedures – not to arbitrate with anybody, in any set of proceedings'. Gary Born, *International Commercial Arbitration* 2568 (2nd ed., Kluwer Law International, 2014).
41. Born, *supra* n. 40 2612.
42. Born, *supra* n. 40 2612.

decide on such request, after consulting with all of the parties, including the person or persons to be joined, taking into account all relevant circumstances.[43]

This article, on its face, allows arbitrators to join a party to the arbitration even over an objection. The tribunal needs to take into account 'all relevant circumstances', but does not require the party to be joined to agree to the joinder. In practice, arbitrators require certain criteria to be fulfilled to allow joinder of a party under Article 4(2). If a third party objects to joinder, they will normally require that:

> (a) the third person is a signatory of the arbitration agreement underlying the pending arbitration, or (b) the third person is a signatory of an essentially identical Swiss Rules arbitration agreement with the parties to the arbitration (or at least with the party requesting the joinder) or (c) any
> such arbitration agreement binds the third person as a non-signatory.[44]

However, if arbitrators join a third party under Article 4(2) and that party maintains jurisdictional objections once joined, the arbitrators would assumedly have to decide on those objections in an award. Thus, Article 4(2) seems to provide for the possibility of two decisions: a first on joinder and then a second one on jurisdiction.

The HKIAC Rules are clearer on this point, with Article 27 providing:

> 1. The arbitral tribunal shall have the power to allow an additional party to be joined to the arbitration provided that, prima facie, the additional party is bound by an arbitration agreement under these Rules giving rise to the arbitration, including any arbitration under Article 28 or 29.
> 2. The arbitral tribunal's decision pursuant to Article 27.1 is without prejudice to its power to subsequently decide any question as to its jurisdiction arising from such decision.[45]

These rules clarify the arbitrators' dual role. Their first decision is whether, procedurally, the party should be joined. This does not require a final determination of whether the arbitrators have jurisdiction over that party. Rather, the arbitrators only need to take a prima facie decision on that issue. However, any decision by the arbitrators on joinder should not affect (be 'without prejudice to') the arbitrators' ultimate decision on any jurisdictional objections rose.

§31.04 WHY DOES THIS ALL MATTER? ARBITRATORS' DUAL ROLE FOR MULTI-PARTY, MULTI-CONTRACT ARBITRATION

The above analysis has lessons for arbitrators and arbitration users.

Arbitrators should understand that multi-party, multi-contract provisions in arbitral rules do not change their fundamental nature. They are creatures of contract or, more broadly, consent. Under the competence-competence principle, they must, in any

---

43. Swiss Rules, Art. 4(2).
44. Dorothée Schramm, *Commentary on the Swiss Rules, Article 4* in Manuel Arroyo (ed), *Arbitration in Switzerland: The Practition's Guide* 366–367 (Kluwer Law International 2013).
45. HKIAC Rules, Arts. 27.1 and 27.2.

case determine whether the parties before them consented to arbitration, under the conditions present in that particular arbitration. If the answer is no, they must fully or partially decline jurisdiction.

Multi-party, multi-contract provisions only play a procedural role at the arbitration's outset to determine who are the parties to the arbitration, and what contracts are covered by it. Some rules give arbitrators a role in that determination. However, any decision that the arbitrators take is of a procedural nature, and should not affect the arbitrators' ultimate decision on the more fundamental questions of consent (and thus jurisdiction).

Arbitration users – the parties – must understand that multi-party and multi-contract provisions in rules have really only provided a limited, procedural solution to the problems associated with it international arbitration. They have not changed the nature of consent to arbitration. Thus, using rules with comprehensive multi-party, multi-contract provisions is not necessarily enough to give effect to the parties' intention as to dispute resolution. Rather, parties themselves need to ensure that they set out clearly their intentions for resolving multi-party and multi-contract disputes.

§31.05 THE WILDCARD: NATIONAL LAWS ON CONSOLIDATION

A decision on joinder or consolidation under arbitral rules can be contrasted to applying a national law that allows joinder or consolidation even absent consent.

Few national laws deal expressly with the arbitrators' powers to deal with multi-party or multi-contract arbitration. The most often cited example is Dutch law. Article 1046 of the Dutch Code of Civil Procedure provides:

> If arbitral proceedings have been commenced before an arbitral tribunal in the Netherlands concerning a subject matter which is connected with the subject matter of arbitral proceedings commenced before another arbitral tribunal in the Netherlands, any of the parties may, unless the parties have agree otherwise, request the President of the District Court in Amsterdam to order a consolidation of proceedings.[46]

This provision foresees the possibility of consolidation even absent agreement by the parties.[47] This could be problematic because it allows for a non-consensual form of arbitration. That is, it allows the possibility that the parties be forced to arbitrate with parties with whom they do not have a direct arbitration agreement (although all parties would have to be bound by an arbitration agreement). Born suggests that an award rendered in those circumstances might still be enforceable under the New York Convention.[48] He considers this due to 'the fact that the parties have agreed to arbitrate in an arbitral seat whose legislation provides these procedural mechanism (unless excluded).'[49]

---

46. Dutch Code of Civil Procedure, Art. 1046.
47. Born, *supra* n. 40 2585–2586.
48. Born, *supra* n. 40 2587–2588.
49. Born, *supra* n. 40 2588.

A handful of other national laws contain broadly similar provisions, although most seem to be for domestic arbitration.[50]

The important thing in this context is that provisions of the national law can be very different to arbitral rules. If a national law allows a form of arbitration even absent consent, then the arbitrators would not have to play the same role on jurisdictional issues (i.e., determining whether the parties consented to arbitration).

§31.06 CONCLUSION

In sum, multi-party, multi-contract provisions in rules play an important, but ultimately limited role. They provide procedural mechanisms to determine the parties to, and contracts covered by, the arbitration at its outset. However, they do not change the fundamental need for consent to arbitrate in the conditions present in the arbitration. Those provisions do not change significantly the arbitrators' role. In some circumstances arbitrators are empowered to decide procedurally which parties and contracts will be subject to the arbitration. However, they still need to decide on the more fundamental question of their own jurisdiction.

---

50. *See* e.g., New Zealand Arbitration Act, Sch. 2, Art. 2.

CHAPTER 32
The Emergency Arbitrator

Patricia Shaughnessy

§32.01 INTRODUCTION

This brief chapter considers the challenges of acting as an emergency arbitrator and the powers and duties of this role. An emergency arbitrator is like a doctor who must operate in the emergency room.[1] She must have the ability to quickly organize the procedure under tight time constraints, ensure fairness and efficiency, understand the issues, and wisely make snap decisions that may have significant consequences.

This challenging task requires skills, knowledge and experience to manage the highly expedited procedures and to make difficult and often complex decisions in limited time. Dr. Pierre Karrer epitomizes the type of arbitrator that can manage the challenges of an emergency arbitration. Unfortunately, very few arbitrators share the Dr. Karrer's level of experience, knowledge, skills and temperament. Those who do are often too busy to jump into an emergency arbitrator role in the quick time frame for such an appointment. Fortunately, Dr. Karrer and others that possess this high level of competence (many have contributed to this book), willingly share their knowledge gained from many years of demanding experiences and help to foster new arbitrators. Dr. Karrer has authored many articles sharing his knowledge and experience, but his recent book stands out as a contribution to fostering new arbitrators and arbitrator practitioners.[2]

---

1. This is an expression borrowed from Mark Kantor.
2. Pierre Karrer, *Introduction to International Arbitration Practice: 1001 Questions and Answers* (Kluwer, 2014).

§32.02 BACKGROUND TO EMERGENCY ARBITRATION

Emergency arbitration emerged on the arbitration scene about a decade ago and now has become a standard feature of many, if not most, arbitration institutes. Emergency arbitration allows parties to quickly seek interim measures within the arbitral forum, thus contributing to the autonomy and effectiveness of arbitration. Prior to the arrival of emergency arbitration, the arbitration community sought to enhance arbitration's autonomy, effectiveness and attractiveness by equipping arbitral tribunals with the ability to render interim measures and to facilitate court recognition and enforcement of such measures.[3] Today arbitral interim measures are largely integrated into the procedural and tactical landscape of arbitration. However, during the time needed to constitute the arbitral tribunal, which typically can take between two and four months following the commencement of arbitral proceedings, there exists a risk that the arbitration may be frustrated as the situation for an allegedly aggrieved party may significantly deteriorate.

During this period, in most jurisdictions, parties could seek interim relief from an appropriate court. However, in some cases, national courts may not provide an attractive alternative for a number of factors. A party may not want to use the court that will have jurisdiction as it may present an "unfriendly" or inefficient forum. Even if this is not the case, the courts will use national language and national civil procedures, which may require using local counsel. The national judges may not have the specialized legal or technical knowledge that is relevant to the dispute. The national court forum may have limited opportunities to ensure the privacy of the proceedings.

Emergency arbitration first appeared about a decade ago as an innovation of the ICDR Rules.[4] The SCC launched a more robust approach on January 1, 2010,[5] which was followed by SIAC six months later, the ICC in 2012, and the LCIA in 2014. Emergency Arbitration procedures have now spread around the globe, appearing as part of the regulatory framework of arbitration institutes from Stockholm to Singapore, London to Kigali, Zurich to Beijing.

In the past few years, nearly every arbitral institution that has revised its rules has included provisions for emergency arbitration.[6] While the time periods and details of emergency arbitration procedures vary between institutional rules,[7] the procedures all provide a highly expedited process for obtaining interim measures that precede the

---

3. A noteworthy example is the 2006 amendments to Art. 17 of the UNCITRAL Model Law on International Commercial Arbitration.
4. The ICDR introduced "Emergency Measures of Protection" in 2006. In 1990, the ICC introduced an opt-in Pre-Arbitral Referee Procedure, which has seldom been used. The Netherlands Arbitration Institute (NAI) added Summary Arbitral Proceedings to its rules in 2001.
5. Dr. Pierre Karrer was the Vice-Chair of the Board of the Arbitration Institute of the Stockholm Chamber of Commerce (SCC) from 2006 to 2012 and in this capacity discussed and approved the then very innovative SCC Emergency Arbitration procedure.
6. The UNCITRAL Rules do not provide for the Emergency Arbitration.
7. The SCC Rules provides a short period for the procedure; the Emergency Arbitrator shall make its decision not later than five days following appointment unless the Board grants an extension pursuant to a reasoned request by the Emergency Arbitration. SCC Rules (2017), Appendix II, Art. 8(1). The ICC Rules provide in Appendix V, Art. 6(4), for a period of fifteen days from when the

actual arbitration. In all of the emergency arbitration regimes, the emergency arbitrator is a sole arbitrator specially appointed by the administering Institute through its emergency arbitration rules. The emergency arbitrator has a time-limited mandate and unless the parties agree otherwise, may not be appointed as a member of the tribunal in the subsequent arbitration. Any relief ordered by an emergency arbitrator will be limited in time and will have no binding effect on the decisions of the regular arbitral tribunal constituted in the subsequent arbitration.

There is some variance in the details of the rules. For example, whether the procedure may be obtained prior to filing a request for arbitration, the period for appointing the emergency arbitrator and time for the decision to be made, the form of the decision, and the fees and cost allocations. For example, the ICC emergency arbitrator procedure is more restrictive than the SCC procedure.[8] The ICC procedure is only available when the arbitration agreement was entered into after the effective date for the new rules, for parties that are signatories or successors to the arbitration agreement, and it excludes the procedure in treaty-based arbitration or when the parties have agreed to other pre-arbitral procedures.

Despite the variance of approaches, emergency arbitration provisions have become a common feature of institutional arbitration, although lacking in ad hoc arbitration, notably when conducted pursuant to the UNCITRAL Rules. An interesting question, which will not be pursued here, is whether parties who chose to use the UNCITRAL Rules with the administration of an Arbitration Institute, could also agree in their arbitration agreement to use the Emergency Arbitration procedures of the administering arbitral institute. This chapter will focus on the powers and duties of an Emergency Arbitrator.

§32.03 THE SOURCE OF THE POWERS AND DUTIES OF AN EMERGENCY ARBITRATOR

To assess the powers and duties of an emergency arbitration, a preliminary consideration is the legal nature of emergency arbitration and its relationship to the actual arbitration. In other words, what exactly is an "emergency arbitration"? Is it part of the main arbitration or is it a separate proceeding? Is it arbitration at all? When the parties enter into an arbitration agreement referring to rules on institute that has emergency arbitration procedures, do they make two arbitration agreements – one for emergency arbitration and one for the "regular" arbitration?

The emergency arbitrator derives power from the parties' agreement to arbitrate under arbitral rules that provide for emergency arbitration, just as the "regular" arbitral tribunal derives its power from the agreement to arbitrate. This can be seen as the

---

file was transmitted to the Emergency Arbitrator to make the decision, although the President may extend the time limit pursuant to a reasoned request or on the President's own initiative when necessary.
8. For a discussion of the SCC Emergency Arbitrator Rules, *see*, Patricia Shaughnessy, *Pre-arbitral Urgent Relief: The New SCC Emergency Arbitrator Rule*, Journal of International Arbitration 27(4): 337–360, 2010.

parties delegating their party autonomy to the arbitral institution which they have mutually chosen. If these rules provide for emergency arbitration, then the parties choosing to arbitrate under these rules are deemed to have agreed to these provisions.[9] There have been discussions on whether an emergency arbitrator is an arbitrator at all, but given the broad acceptance of emergency arbitration by the arbitration community, this controversy may become increasingly less relevant. Recent legislation in Singapore, Hong Kong, and South Korea has recognized emergency arbitration and more jurisdictions may follow.[10] A few courts have enforced the decisions of emergency arbitrators, although the nature and enforceability of emergency arbitrator decisions remains controversial.[11]

Perhaps the ultimate test of the nature of emergency arbitration and the enforceability of decisions by emergency arbitrators is whether the international arbitration community, and importantly, state courts, are willing to accept emergency arbitration as a procedure resulting in a final and binding decision that can be enforced as an arbitral interim measure or as an arbitral award. It can be noted that while some institutions such as the SCC provide that the decision may be made in the form of an order or an award, the ICC only allows for a decision in the form of an order, which eliminates the need for scrutiny by the ICC. It is controversial if an interim measure in the form of an award has the necessary finality, let alone an emergency arbitral decision in the form of an award, to be enforced under the New York Convention. However, the UNCITRAL Model Law provides for the recognition and enforcement of arbitral interim orders.[12] Those jurisdictions that have adopted this approach may enforce an emergency arbitrator order if the jurisdiction considers such an emergency arbitrator decision to constitute such an interim measure order.

Recently, a Ukrainian court ordered the enforcement of a SCC emergency arbitration award in an investment case.[13] This was particularly note-worthy because the SCC emergency arbitration rules, similar to some of the other regimes, provide that

---

9. Some rules, such as the ICC do not apply retroactively to arbitration agreements entered into prior to the adoption of emergency arbitration provisions, while others such as the SCC do apply retroactively. See, Patricia Shaughnessy, supra. footnote 8, at page 347.
10. Singapore legislatively recognized emergency arbitration in 2012 through an amendment to its International Arbitration Act (Cap 143A) expanding the definition of 'arbitral tribunal' to include "an emergency arbitrator appointed pursuant to the rules of arbitration agreed to or adopted by the parties ...". In July 2013, Hong Kong amended its Arbitration Ordinance (Cap 609) to add Part 3A, which expressly permits the recognition and enforcement of emergency relief granted by an emergency arbitrator, regardless of whether the seat of arbitration is in Hong Kong or overseas. In July 2016, Korea passed amendments to its Arbitration Act to permit the enforcement of interim measures ordered by an arbitral tribunal seated in Korea, which is understood to apply to orders rendered by emergency arbitrators. See, Eun Young Park and Joel Richardson, Rush to Judgment: Speed v Fairness in International Arbitration, Asian Dispute Review, (© Hong Kong International Arbitration Centre (HKIAC); Hong Kong International Arbitration Centre (HKIAC) 2016(4): 174–180, 2016.
11. Ank Santens and Jaroslav Kudrna, The State of Play of Enforcement of Emergency Arbitrator Decisions, Journal of International Arbitration 34(1): 1–16, 2017.
12. UNCITRAL Model Law on International Commercial Arbitration, with amendments as adopted in 2006, Art. 17 (H) and (I).
13. See, Yaroslav Petrov, JKX vs. Ukraine: An Update on the Enforcement of Emergency Arbitrator's Award, Kluwer Arbitration Blogg, August 12, 2016. The case has been appealed and is pending in a second appeal proceeding.

while the emergency arbitrator's decision is binding upon the parties, it does not have any binding effect on the subsequent tribunal.[14] Upon the reasoned request of a party, the emergency arbitrator may amend or revoke the decision.[15] Notably, a decision of an emergency arbitrator will cease to have any legal effect upon certain events occurring, namely when the emergency arbitrator or the regular arbitral tribunal so decides, when the regular arbitral tribunal makes a final award, when the main arbitration is not commenced within thirty days from the date of the emergency decision, or when the case is not referred to a regular arbitral tribunal within ninety days of the date of the emergency decision.[16]

But even if the enforcement of an emergency arbitrator decision may be uncertain, the procedure may nonetheless have benefits. Reportedly, parties often follow the decisions of the emergency arbitrators without court enforcement in order to avoid additional costs and to show their good faith cooperation with the arbitral process. There may also be increased incentives to settle a case once the parties have received a preliminary assessment of the case by an emergency arbitrator and have had an opportunity to better consider the opposing party's position.

§32.04 THE DEVELOPING PRACTICE OF EMERGENCY ARBITRATION

For the emergency arbitrator, the parties, and their counsel, the emergency proceedings demand full attention and intense effort in a very limited time period. In an attempt to capture some of the practice-oriented aspects of emergency arbitration, I have conducted an unscientific anecdotal study of the impressions and experience of some emergency arbitrators acting under various rules. I have also reviewed some emergency arbitration decisions. It is important to note that most emergency arbitrator decisions are confidential and not available for review. Consequently, my study has been based on limited access to information.

In June 2016, I obtained statistics from some of the prominent arbitral intuitions on their emergency arbitration cases. The arbitral institution representatives all indicated that it is too early to speculate about trends in emergency arbitration based upon the statistics available in these early years of practice.

Based on the June 2016 statistics, the ICDR had accepted to date sixty-seven Emergency Arbitration cases (excluding cases not accepted and cases under the Optional Rules). Of these cases, twenty-nine were wholly or partially won, seventeen were not granted, thirteen were settled, five were withdrawn, and three were pending. In the first half of 2016, six cases were filed, which would seem to indicate that there was an increase in the number of cases than in 2015, where there was a total of seven cases. These statistics indicate that more requests for relief have been granted to some extent than requests have been denied. There is a significant number of cases that have been settled or withdrawn.

---

14. SCC Rules, Appendix II, Art. 9.
15. *Ibid.*
16. SCC Rules, Appendix II, Art. 9(4).

The SIAC reported that as of June 2016, it had received fifty emergency arbitration cases to date. In twenty-one cases, the requested relief was granted, in four cases the relief had been partially granted, in four cases relief was granted by consent, in six cases the request was withdrawn, in fourteen cases the relief was rejected, and as of June 10, 2016 there was one case pending. Interestingly, the SIAC emergency arbitration case load was declining, (although the general case load is increasing), from nineteen cases in 2013, twelve in 2014 and only five in 2015. However, as noted, it is too early to declare a downward trend.

As of June 2016, the SCC had received nine requests for the Emergency Arbitration, bringing the total number of cases since it launched the procedure to twenty-three cases, including five treaty-based cases.[17] Of the total twenty-three cases, eight were wholly or partially granted relief, in fourteen cases the relief was denied, and one case was filed on June 9, 2016 and was pending as of the date of the report. In four cases, the decision was made in the form of an award, one of which was at the joint request of the parties for the decision to be made as an award. Notably, one case had been received in 2015. Reports on emergency arbitration proceedings from earlier years can be found on the SCC website.

The ICC is a relative newcomer to emergency arbitration proceedings having launched the procedure in its 2012 Rules. As of June 2016, it had received thirty-four requests for emergency arbitration, with the following break-down per year: in 2012 the ICC received two requests that were accepted, in 2013 and also in 2014 there were six requests accepted, in 2015 there were ten accepted requests and by June 2016, ten requests were accepted. The ICC performs a preliminary review of emergency arbitration requests to ensure that the requests meet the ICC thresholds for acceptance and thus not all filed requests are reported in the statistics. Five cases were rejected and one case was accepted after the applicant requested a reconsideration and provided proof of succession to the arbitration agreement. It should be recalled that the ICC requires that for an emergency arbitration request to be admissible the following requirements must be met: the arbitration agreement was entered into after the date of entry into force of the 2012 rules, the parties have not opted-out of the emergency arbitrator procedures, there is prima-facie jurisdiction, the parties are signatories to the arbitration agreement or are successors to it, and the emergency arbitration fees of USD 40,000 are paid. It is reported that in just under about half of the accepted cases, the emergency arbitrator granted some relief, either in whole or in part.

The HKIAC is also a relatively newcomer to emergency arbitration and saw its first two cases in 2014, followed by two cases in 2015 and two cases by June 2016. Two of these cases resulted in an emergency decision being issued. In the two other cases, one resulted in an agreement for the emergency arbitrator to execute a Consent Order, by which the emergency proceedings were discontinued. In these cases the emergency arbitrator was quickly appointed, in one case within six hours and the decisions were made within three, seven and eleven days in the cases resulting in a decision. The

---

17. By the end of 2016, the number of Emergency Arbitrator requests totaled thirteen, bringing the number of cases to twenty-seven cases. *See:* http://sccinstitute.com/statistics/ (last visited April 20, 17).

fourth case was pending determination by the emergency arbitrator in June 2016. HKIAC did not proceed with the applications in two other applications, because in one case the applicant failed to pay the application deposit and in the other case, the emergency arbitrator procedures did not apply as the arbitration agreement was entered into before November 1, 2013.

The LCIA included emergency arbitrator provisions in its revised rules that came into effect in October 2014. As of June 2016, there had not been any requests for the appointment of an emergency arbitrator. For some time the LCIA has offered a procedure for the expedited appointment of the arbitral tribunal, which is a different procedure than emergency arbitration. This procedure had seen an increase with thirty applications made in 2015, of which twelve applications were granted, seventeen were denied, and one was withdrawn. This can be compared with ten applications in 2014 and seventeen applications in 2013. It remains to be seen if emergency arbitration gains popularity and hence use in LCIA arbitrations. Perhaps the availability of the expedited appointment of the tribunal affects the attractiveness of emergency arbitration.

§32.05 THE DUTIES AND DECISION-MAKING OF THE EMERGENCY ARBITRATOR

Emergency arbitration requires an experienced arbitrator who can quickly set up the procedures for the case to ensure the due process rights of the parties to be treated equally and to be afforded a reasonable opportunity to be heard in the circumstances. The emergency arbitrator must hit the ground running to arrange and implement the procedure and make a considered and reasoned decision in very tight time-limits. Often the cases are very complex and may involve technical issues and evidence taking. The emergency arbitrators I have interviewed seem to seem to share a sense that the assignment was challenging, stimulating and rewarding, although it demanded their full attention during this intense period and based upon the number of hours spent, the compensation was significantly less than their typical hourly rates.

Claimants often spend some time preparing an application for an emergency arbitrator, while Respondents will have very limited time to respond. Some Claimants, but not all, contact the Secretariat of the arbitral institution in advance to seek information and guidance in preparing the filing. Institutions appreciate receiving a "heads-up" that a filing will soon be made in order to prepare for administering it efficiently. Some of the applications for emergency relief reflect considerable preparation as the submissions may be quite detailed and contain evidentiary information, including witness statements. Once appointed, the emergency arbitrator immediately contacts the parties and requests that a conference call be held to discuss the proceedings and establish the schedule. Emergency arbitrators must expeditiously handle the case while ensuring that the Respondent has a reasonable opportunity to respond. Under most rules, if needed, the emergency arbitrator can make a reasoned request to the arbitral institution to extend the time to make a decision to allow a Respondent more time to prepare a response.

Many of the emergency arbitration procedures provide the emergency arbitrator the same wide discretion that regular arbitrators enjoy when assessing a request for interim measures. For example, both the SCC and the ICC Rules provide that arbitrators, including emergency arbitrators, may grant such relief as deemed appropriate in the circumstances. The conditions or criteria that an emergency arbitrator should consider when assessing a request are typically not set-out in the rules. This often becomes a matter for the parties to plead and argue. Some emergency arbitrators seek guidance in the UNCITRAL Model Law and Rules detailed approach to the criteria for ordering interim relief. The Model Law approach arguably represents an "internationally accepted" approach or "best practices." In some cases it may represent the approach of the *lex arbitri* if the seat of the emergency arbitration is a so-called Model Law jurisdiction. Some emergency arbitrators have stated that they apply the "universally accepted criteria." Others have looked to the procedural codes of the seat or the legal systems with which they are familiar, often assuming that their home jurisdiction represents a "universal" approach. Some referred to previous institutional practice and others referred to commentators when determining the criteria for determining whether the requested relief should be granted.

But it is not clear exactly what the so-called universal approach may actually require in the details of a particular case and the degree of "proof" that should be required in the expedited frame-work of emergency arbitration. Some emergency arbitration rules imply that a threshold issue is the urgency of the requested measure is such that it cannot await the constitution of the arbitral tribunal. A few emergency arbitrators that I spoke with indicated that this was decisive in their decision-making and noted that an arbitral tribunal would not be able to effectively handle an interim measure request as soon as it was constituted. They consequently found that urgency should be assessed with a generous time estimate for the constitution of the tribunal. Some noted the distinction between procedural urgency and the urgency of the substantive measure. Some viewed the urgency assessment as a double-requirement, first as a threshold issue and later as one of the criteria to be assessed.

All of the emergency arbitrators that I interviewed considered that the Claimant must show that there is a serious risk of suffering irreparable harm if the measure were not granted by the emergency arbitrator rather than awaiting the constitution of the regular arbitral tribunal. Similarly to the "Model Law" approach, the proportionality of the potential harm to the respective parties was a key factor to be considered. Finally, emergency arbitrators considered the potential success on the merits, but the standard varied among those I spoke with. This may be due to linguistic forms of expression, but the linguistic expression can lead to a significant difference in the burden of proof. In light of the early stage of the case and the limited time-frames both for deciding the case and for the duration of the measure if granted, most emergency arbitrators seem to apply a relatively low threshold for determining the reasonable likelihood of success on the merits of the case, finding that a prima facie case was sufficient.

§32.06 CONCLUSION

Emergency arbitration has become an established feature of international arbitration although it remains in a state of development. There is a general increasing trend towards increasing arbitral autonomy and empowering arbitrators, including emergency arbitrators, to order interim measures. Emergency arbitration significantly contributes to the autonomy and effectiveness of arbitration. The powers and duties of an emergency arbitrator should correspond to the powers and duties of the regular tribunal. However such powers and duties must be adapted to the specific challenges and restrictions imposed by the short-time frames and limited mandate of an emergency arbitrator. The duty of an arbitrator to ensure a fair process becomes particularly important in the context of emergency arbitration and requires an experienced and skillful arbitrator. The parties need to know and the arbitrator needs to determine the criteria for granting emergency relief and to apply such criteria in a pragmatic manner while ensuring due process. The sharing of experience will help to develop the practice in this developing area of arbitration law.

CHAPTER 33
Deliberations of Arbitrators

Jingzhou Tao[*]

§33.01 INTRODUCTION

The deliberations of arbitrators is of great importance for the successful conduct of the arbitration proceedings. During the process of deliberations, a variety of questions will arise and there have been no commonly accepted rules regulating these issues. As Redfern and Hunter observe, "...in all that is written and said about arbitration – and nowadays a great deal is written and said – there is very little about how a tribunal of arbitrators goes about reaching its decision"[1] Bernhard Beger figuratively described deliberations process as a "black box" which is a box device whose inner workings are unknown, more precisely a device that can be seen only from the outside.[2] This understanding, of course, refers to the perception from the parties' perspective.

This article deals with the deliberations process and tries to provide an overview of the inner side of the "black box" from an arbitrator's perspective. It focuses on questions usually arise from the deliberation process, such as how to define deliberations of arbitrators? Why arbitrators have a duty to deliberate? What is the purpose of the deliberations? How does the arbitral tribunal operate and reach decisions through deliberations? What is the ideal timing for deliberations? How to deal with the potential clash of arbitrators' views? Under what circumstances would an arbitrator violate his/her confidentiality obligations? The last section summarizes some thumb-up rules that are recommended to be applied to the deliberations process in order to achieve "a

---

[*] The author thanks Mariana Zhong and Nannan Gao for their support and assistance throughout the preparation of this article.
1. Redfern and Hunter on International Arbitration, 5th ed., 2009, para. 9.153.
2. Bernhar Berger, The legal Framework: Rights and Obligations of Arbitrators in the Deliberation, Inside the Black Box: How Arbitral Tribunals Operate and Reach Their Decisions, Bernhad Berger & Michael E. Schneider, ASA Special Series No. 42, 2014, page 7.

unanimously acceptable solution that does the greatest possible measure of justice to the parties."[3]

§33.02 ISSUES RELATING TO DELIBERATIONS OF ARBITRATORS

[A] Arbitrators' Duty to Deliberate

According to the Black's Law Dictionary, deliberation means the act of weighing and examining the reasons for and against a contemplated act or course of conduct or a choice of acts or means. In the context of international arbitration, the arbitral tribunals are generally composed by three arbitrators, and all three-member arbitrators have the inherent duty to deliberate at proper stage of the arbitration in order to achieve and deliver the final award in an impartial way.

Not all national arbitration laws directly provide for the need for deliberation, for instance, the Chinese law does not expressly contain the word deliberation, but rather, refers to it indirectly in Article 53 of the PRC Arbitration Law that an award shall be based on the opinion of the majority of arbitrators, failing which, the award shall be given in accordance with the opinion of the presiding arbitrator – this makes it necessary for the arbitrators to exchange their opinions before rendering the final award. Similar provision could also be found in Article 189 of the Swiss Private International Law: unless the parties have agreed to the procedure and form, the award shall be given by the majority of arbitrators, failing which, by the chairmen. This approach is also commonly seen in arbitration rules. For instance, Article 31 of the ICC Arbitration Rules provides that "When the arbitral tribunal is composed of more than one arbitrator, an award is made by a majority decision. If there is no majority, the award shall be made by the president of the arbitral tribunal alone." The same can be said of Article 49 of the CIETAC Arbitration Rules which establishes that award shall be rendered by all three arbitrators or a majority of the arbitrator and where the arbitral tribunal cannot reach a majority opinion, the arbitral award shall be rendered in accordance with the presiding arbitrator's opinion.

It is widely admitted that final awards should be preceded by deliberations of arbitrators. Arbitrators' duty to deliberate is consistent with their mandate to resolve all disputing issues in the arbitration proceedings. "The services of an arbitrator are principally, and habitually, those of settling a dispute between two or more parties."[4] Arbitrators shall review the file, participate the deliberation process, and make a reasoned award on the dispute. This is the reason why the parties appoint arbitrators and present their cases to them for resolution. The primary expectation of parties choosing an arbitrator is that he or she will be diligently involved throughout the arbitral procedure and apply reasoned judgment in an unbiased way.

---

3. Id.
4. *Von Hoffman (Bernd) v. Finanzamt Trier*, Case No. C-145/96, [1997] E.C.R. I-4857, 17 (E.C.J). *See* para. 2.02 [C][1]; Berlinguer, Impartiality and Independence of Arbitrators in International Practice, 6 AM.Rev.Int'l Arb. 339 (1995).

An arbitrator's duty to deliberate could be viewed to include his/her obligations to fix a date for the deliberations, to organize, prepare and participate in the deliberations, and to deliberate on all the litigious questions.[5] No matter how to phrase it, the existence of adequate deliberations of arbitrators appears to be a critical step of all arbitral tribunal's decision-making process, failing to participate in the deliberations can lead to the eviction of an arbitrator at extreme situation. CIETAC Rules for Evaluating the Behavior of Arbitrators provide that when an arbitrator fails to participate in the deliberations or investigations of the arbitral tribunal without justified reasons, he or she should be given a warning by the arbitration institution, and if the circumstances are severe, withdrawal, replacement or dismissal of the arbitrator may apply.[6] More than that, pathologic deliberations may have consequences for the validity and enforceability of the award.

[B] Different Types of Deliberations

The former Secretary General of the Court of Arbitration of ICC Dr. Yves Derains distinguishes two types of deliberations of arbitrators: harmonious deliberations and pathologic deliberations. According to him, a deliberation can be qualified as being "pathologic" when an arbitrator (or even two arbitrators) does not make decisions based on an objective analysis of the issues submitted to the tribunal but rather on a more or less disguised personal interest. This kind of deliberations may involve the risk of breaching the principle of confidentiality of deliberations and sabotage of the arbitration proceedings. Harmonious deliberations refer to the situation where there is an absolute trust among the members of the arbitral tribunal. Harmonious deliberations do not always lead to consensus among arbitrators, although in most cases the award is unanimous. Indeed, this unanimity may be just a facade, because it may be that the decision was taken by majority, but the dissenting arbitrator considered it not meaningful or necessary to inform the parties of his or her disagreement. This situation may also entail some risks when the interest not to reveal to the parties the differences of opinions are transformed, in the name of harmony, into a desire to find at any price a solution that will satisfy all the members of the tribunal.[7]

---

5. Josa Maria Alonso Puig, Deliberation and Drafting Awards in Internaitonal Arbitration in Liber amicorum Bernardo Cremades / ed. M.Á. Fernández-Ballesteros, David Arias, 2010, page 134.
6. Article 10 CIEATC Rules for Evaluating the Behavior of Arbitrators, "[w]hen an arbitrator commits a violation of the Code of Conduct for Arbitrators or the Case Management Standards for Arbitrators other than those listed above, the Arbitration Commission shall assess the situation in its totality. If it determines that reasonable doubt exists as to the conduct of the arbitrator which might affect the parties' confidence in the Arbitration Commission or damage the image of the Commission, but the violation does not warrant withdrawal, replacement or dismissal of the arbitrator, the Commission shall issue a warning to the arbitrator. Circumstances where an arbitrator shall receive a warning include but are not limited to the following: 4. The arbitrator fails to participate in the deliberations or investigations of the arbitral tribunal or be late for an oral hearing without justified reasons."
7. Yves Derains, The arbitrator's Deliberation, Fifth Annual International Commercial Arbitration Lecture 2012.

Some arbitrators make a distinction between deliberations on procedural issues and those on substantive issues. Procedural issues normally take the form of a procedural order and are decided by a unanimous decision of the tribunal. In most cases, the power to issue a procedural order would be delegated by the tribunal to the chairman. Substantive issues have to be decided by an award which is made unanimously or by a majority decision, or by the chairman of the tribunal alone, depending on the requirements of the arbitration rules. With regard to the deliberations on substantive issues, arbitrators shall strictly observe the principle of confidentiality, "save for extreme circumstances where disclosure is compelled in the interest of justice"[8] or otherwise agreed by the parties. Further discussion on arbitrators' confidentiality duty during deliberation process is provide in section §33.04 herein.

[C] The Purpose of Deliberations

Generally speaking, arbitrators use the opportunity of deliberations to identify the issues to be decided by the tribunal and discuss the facts of case, the evidences, the claims, the allegations and defenses of the parties. It would be wrong to think that the only purpose of deliberations is to reach a consensus on the final outcome of the arbitration. In the process of building a consensus on the final resolution of the dispute, arbitrators are trying to make themselves clearer with the merits and law at issue, in order to prepare themselves for the drafting of the final award. If consensus cannot be achieved, to identify the differences in the arbitrators' positions and to narrow down the different views of the members of the tribunal would significantly contribute to reaching a reasoned final award.

In the case of post hearing deliberations, the process also provides arbitrators an opportunity to identify further needs for submission or clarification from the parties and prepare themselves for the drafting of the final award.

[D] The Form of Deliberations

No strict formality is required for the deliberations of arbitrators. Arbitrators can hold in-person meetings to deliberate, or communicate by emails, tele-conference or skype chats, etc. They could also exchange questionnaires, notes and drafts. The essence of deliberations is the exchange of views of arbitrators, all members of the arbitral tribunal should have adequate opportunity to express their positions, irrespective of the form it takes.

Moreover, it is impractical to set up a unified form of deliberations since arbitrators have to take into account the particular circumstances of each case when choosing an appropriate form of deliberations, such as "the size and complexity

---

8. D. Caron & L. Caplan, The UNCITRAL Arbitration Rules: Commentary 699, 2d ed. 2013.

thereof, the parties' claims, the problems inherent in the proceedings and the essential problems, and the separation between responsibility and quantum."[9]

However, nearly all arbitrators and commentators believe that the most effective form of deliberations is in-person meetings. "An in-person procedural conference, even if it means travel, even if it means time away, will often be more effective than doing a relatively short telephone conference that simply sets procedures going forward."[10] "It is extremely important, in my view, to have a face to face preliminary meeting rather than an audio or video conference, particularly if the members of the arbitral tribunal had not previously met."[11] "The tribunal has to seize the time for face to face deliberations before they separate – the failure to do so can be costly."[12]

Institutional rules seem to impliedly suggest that deliberation would be better off to take place face-to-face, e.g., Article 18(3) of the ICC Rules: " the arbitral tribunal may deliberate at any location it considers appropriate"; Article 16(2) of the LCIA Rules: "the arbitral tribunal may hold hearings, meetings and deliberations at any convenient geographical place of its discretion"; Article 35 of the CIETAC Rules: "the arbitral tribunal may hold deliberations at any place or in any manner that it considers appropriate."

[E] The Timing of Deliberations

"Each arbitration is a world of its own,"[13] the deliberations may be held in different ways and at different stages during the arbitration proceedings due to the particular circumstances of each case. As indicated by Piero Bernardini, the exchange of views, which is the essence of the deliberation process "takes place in the most varied ways and at different times depending on the specificity of the case, the complexity of the case and the time availability of the arbitrators."[14]

The deliberations "may start relatively early in quite open way if the three arbitrators happen to know each other by reason maybe of prior arbitration experience...Normally the dialogue among arbitrators may start on the eve of an evidentiary hearing when the arbitrators happen to meet in person for the hearing and maybe a good point in time in which to review the content and what will be said at the

---

9. Josa Maria Alonso Puig, Deliberation and Drafting Awards in Internaitonal Arbitration in Liber amicorum Bernardo Cremades / ed. M.Á. Fernández-Ballesteros, David Arias, 2010, page 134.
10. David W. Rivkin, Form of Deliberations, Inside the Black Box: How Arbitral Tribunals Operate and Reach Their Decisions, Bernhad Berger & Michael E. Schneider, ASA Special Series No. 42, 2014, page 21.
11. Neal G. Bunni, Peronal Vies on How Arbitral Tribunals Operate and Reach Their Decisions, Inside the Black Box: How Arbitral Tribunals Operate and Reach Their Decisions, Bernhad Berger & Michael E. Schneider, ASA Special Series No. 42, 2014, page 123.
12. Nicolas Ulmer, Six Modest Proposals before you get to the Award, Inside the Black Box: How Arbitral Tribunals Operate and Reach Their Decisions, Bernhad Berger & Michael E. Schneider, ASA Special Series No. 42, 2014, page 118.
13. Josa Maria Alonso Puig, Deliberation and Drafting Awards in Internaitonal Arbitration in Liber amicorum Bernardo Cremades / ed. M.Á. Fernández-Ballesteros, David Arias, 2010, page 135.
14. Piero Bernardini, Organization of Deliberations, Inside the Black Box: How Arbitral Tribunals Operate and Reach Their Decisions, Bernhad Berger & Michael E. Schneider, ASA Special Series No. 42, 2014, page 17.

hearing and prepare a few questions for the witness and the expert to be heard."[15] During this stage, the most important task for arbitrators is to identify and narrow down the issues to be heard during the hearing.

In most cases and under most arbitration rules, it is the duty of the arbitral tribunal to convene a case management conference – at the outset of the arbitration or very early stage - in order to establish the arbitration framework and to clarify the conduct of the arbitration. For example, ICC Arbitration Rules require the arbitral tribunal to draw up a Terms of Reference on the basis of documents or in the presence of the parties and in light of their most recent submissions, as soon as it has received the file from the Secretariat, including the basic information of the parties and the dispute as well as a list of issues to be determined. Most arbitrators believe that "it is not too early at this stage to plan and pave the way for how to approach these issues and methodology by which the decisions may be accomplished," and these deliberations are extremely useful to arrive at an efficient hearing.[16] Arbitrators should express their views in a proactive and constructive manner as such exchange would contribute to a useful relationship between the members within the tribunal.

The deliberations may also take place during the pauses of hearing, after the hearing and in the process of drafting the award. Deliberations would be most necessary during and after the hearing, as Neal G. Bunni indicated in his presentation at the ASA Annual Full Day Conference of 2013. "The deliberations during the hearing would take place as the evidence is adduced and discussions should be held between the arbitrators regarding the matters that need to be ventilated. Deliberations would also take place immediately after the hearing in order to establish the procedure for future deliberations and how they should take place and how to proceed with deciding the substantive issues. This would normally lead to establishing how to prepare the next draft(s) of the award after the post-hearing submissions are received, and how to reach necessary decisions."[17]

For the purpose of this article, deliberations of the arbitrators specifically refers to the discussion among the arbitrators on the substantive issues to be decided in the final award, including decision on challenge of jurisdiction. For such type of deliberations, the author believes the ideal timing of deliberations is right after the main hearing while the arbitrators' memory of the case is still fresh and all arbitrators are gathered together. Otherwise, it would be inconvenient and costly to convene all arbitrators again to an in person deliberation. Many arbitrators and commentators share the same understanding, e.g., "once the evidence is heard, and counsel and the parties take their leave, the case is taken under advisement and deliberations begin. Deliberations must begin immediately – ideally, within the first hours of the close of the final hearing."[18] "Deliberation would also take place immediately after the hearing in order to establish

---

15. Id.
16. Neal G. Bunni, Personal Views on How Arbitral Tribunals Operate and Reach Their Decisions, Inside the Black Box: How Arbitral Tribunals Operate and Reach Their Decisions, Bernhad Berger & Michael E. Schneider, ASA Special Series No. 42, 2014, page 123.
17. Id. page 125.
18. L. Yves Fortier, C.C., Q.C. The Tribunal's Deliberations, The Leading Arbitrator's Guide to International Arbitration, (Second edition), page 479.

the procedure for future deliberations and how they should take place and how to proceed with deciding with substantive issues."[19] "Deliberations at the end ought to take place immediately upon the close of the hearing. The arbitrators are in the same place, and the evidence is fresh. I am very unhappy if I am representing a party and I find that the arbitrators are not going to get together until two or three months after the hearing. I feel that the strength of the testimony that I have presented at the hearing may very well get lost that time."[20]

Some arbitrators may find the idea of having deliberations immediately after the hearing not as acceptable: "I worry that it overemphasizes witness evidence as opposed to the document evidence. I worry that arbitrators do not come to the oral cross-examination hearing really having studied the file," "Honestly, I would be reluctant, particularly in a rather fact-driven case, to start deliberating immediately after the hearing. I think you need time to reflect on what you have heard. You may want to go through the transcript of the hearing."[21]

Deliberations upon close of the main hearing is not meant to press the arbitrators to immediately jump to a conclusion on all issues to be decided, and it is important for the chairman not to rush his co-arbitrators into reaching a definitive decision on all outstanding issues. Rather, deliberations after the main hearing could serve a better role in sorting out the arbitrators' views on specific issues, to prepare the tribunal for drafting the final award and to determine what needs to be further clarified by the parties. After all, it is in the interests of the parties that the arbitrators exchange their views in an efficient and accurate manner.

§33.03 THE ROLE OF THE CHAIRMAN IN THE PROCESS OF DELIBERATIONS

The deliberation process is essentially exchange of views among the three members of the tribunal. During such process, the Chairman plays a vital role in managing the process, coordinating and resolving any potential clashes and also very oftenly, drafting the final award or main sections of it afterwards.

[A] To Be Responsible for Organizing the Deliberations

The Chairman should take the lead to organize the deliberations including inquiring about other arbitrators' schedule and availability, and proposing a place and time for the deliberations. The Chairman should try to accommodate the special needs or

---

19. Neal G. Bunni, Peronal Vies on How Arbitral Tribunals Operate and Reach Their Decisions, Inside the Black Box: How Arbitral Tribunals Operate and Reach Their Decisions, Bernhad Berger & Michael E. Schneider, ASA Special Series No. 42, 2014, page 125.
20. David W. Rivkin, Form of Deliberations, Inside the Black Box: How Arbitral Tribunals Operate and Reach Their Decisions, Bernhad Berger & Michael E. Schneider, ASA Special Series No. 42, 2014, page 21.
21. Andreas Reiner, Comments on the presentation "Drafting the award," Inside the Black Box: How Arbitral Tribunals Operate and Reach Their Decisions, Bernhad Berger & Michael E. Schneider, ASA Special Series No. 42, 2014, page 35.

schedules of all arbitrators, and in the meantime, ensure effective and cost-efficient conduct of the deliberations.

During the deliberation process, the Chairman should ensure that his fellow arbitrators have equal and sufficient opportunities to express their views, regardless of their varying background, expertise, personal experience and/or originality. The Chairman should aim to maintain a balanced floor for each arbitrator to express freely and to discuss in an orderly and efficient way.

[B] To Be Responsible for Managing Potential Clashes Among Arbitrators

As Bernardo Cremades once wrote, "The world of arbitration had tired of the long-standing debate which separated common and civil law as antagonistic, irreconcilable positions" and "Arbitration theory has progressed far beyond the exaggerated differences between the common law adversarial system and the inquisitorial system more characteristic of civil law systems."[22] International commercial arbitration has its own independent operating system which "far beyond the differences between the common law and civil law system," and has formed systematic common practices regarding the conduct of arbitration proceedings.

However, it does not mean that the differences and potential clashes among arbitrators could be simply ignored. Each arbitrator comes from different legal and cultural background, and is inevitably influenced by his or her experiences and personalities in deliberating the case and reaching the decisions. "The difference of opinions are the result of personal convictions by each of them and not simply the reflection of the position of the parties."[23]

It could not be denied that the legal and cultural background of arbitrators may lead to potential clash or biased behavior during deliberations. And "it would be wrong to believe that harmonious deliberation always leads to agreements between the members of the tribunal."[24]

The personality of arbitrators also inevitably come into play. Good arbitrators should always be open minded and prepared to listen. If it turns out that his or her position is wrong or inappropriate, he or she should be open to accept other views.

As Ugo Draetta indicated in his book Behind the Scenes in International Arbitrations, the deliberation of arbitrators is the point at which "irreconcilable differences among arbitrators become apparent, which can then lead one of the co-arbitrators to append a dissenting opinion to the award."[25]

---

22. Horacio A. Grigera Naon, Cultural Clashes in International Commercial Arbitration: How Much of a Real Issue?, Liber amicorum Bernardo Cremades / ed. M.Á. Fernández-Ballesteros, David Arias, 2010, page 558.
23. Yves Derains, The arbitrator's Deliberation, Fifth Annual International Commercial Arbitration Lecture 2012, page 920.
24. Id.
25. Ugo Draetta, Behind the Scenes in International Arbitrations, JurisNet, LLC, 2011, page 83.

In case of potential clashes between arbitrators, especially in extreme situations where one or two arbitrators become irritated or irrational, the Chairman has the duty to conciliate and foster a friendly atmosphere to proceed with the deliberations.

[C] To Be Responsible for Drafting the Final Award Afterwards

It is a prevailing practice that the Chairman is entrusted with the main responsibility by his fellow arbitrators to draft the main part(s) of the final award. This may however differ in special situations where another member of the Tribunal has obviously better capacity of the language or more experiences in drafting awards. Therefore, in either situation, it is of great importance for the Chairman to clearly understand during the deliberation process about his fellow arbitrators' views and concerns about the issues to be decided, the reasoning to be discussed and fully explained so that he/she could properly draft the final award on behalf of the tribunal.

§33.04 CONFIDENTIALITY OF ARBITRATORS' DELIBERATIONS

It is also a commonly recognized practice that arbitrators should keep strict confidentiality of their deliberation process. It is intended to, among others, serve the purpose of ensuring that each arbitrator is able to freely express his/her views and observations without worrying that any of his/her comments may subsequently become the subject of challenges by the parties.

Some national arbitration laws expressly require that the deliberations of arbitrators be kept confidential. For example, Article 1479 of the French Code of Civil Procedure provides that "[t]he arbitral tribunal's deliberations shall be confidential." The same can be said of Rule 27 of the Scottish Arbitration Act 2010, which establishes the default rule of private tribunal deliberations that need not be disclosed to parties. It is more common to find the similar provisions in most institutional arbitration rules, e.g., Article 42.2 of the HKIAC Arbitration Rules 2013, Article 30.2 of the LCIA Arbitration Rules 2014 and Article 6 Appendix I of the ICC Rules 2012.[26] In addition, some ethical and professional guidelines also impose the same obligation of confidentiality on arbitrators, e.g., Article 9 of IBA Rules of Ethics, and Canon VI (B) AAA/ABA Code of Ethics.[27]

---

26. Article 42.2 of the HKIAC Arbitration Rules "The deliberations of the arbitral tribunal are confidential"; Art. 30.2 "The deliberations of the Arbitral Tribunal shall remain confidential to its members, save as required by any applicable law and to the extent that disclosure of an arbitrator's refusal to participate in the arbitration is required of the other members of the Arbitral Tribunal under Articles 10, 12, 26 and 27"; Art. 6, Appendix I, 2012 ICC Rules, "The work of the Court is of a confidential nature which must be respected by everyone who participates in that work in whatever capacity."
27. Article 9 IBA Rules of Ethics, "The deliberations of the arbitral tribunal, and the contents of the award itself, remain confidential in perpetuity unless the parties release the arbitrators from this obligation. An arbitrator should not participate in, or give any information for the purpose of assistance in, any proceedings to consider the award unless, exceptionally, he considers it his duty to disclose any material misconduct or fraud on the part of his fellow arbitrators"; Canon

As Gary B. Born observes, "[t]he confidentiality of the arbitral deliberations is central to the adjudicative character and integrity of the arbitral process...Although seldom addressed specifically in applicable rules or legislation, the confidentiality of the arbitrators' deliberations should extend generally to draft awards, internal communications regarding disposition of a case or comments on draft awards, and the content of oral deliberations".[28]

In order to refrain from breaching the confidentiality duties, the arbitrators should be minded to avoid any ex parte communications with a party, including its counsel, relating to any information discussed during the deliberations.

It is worth noting that a recent hot topic arises concerning whether a tribunal secretary should be allowed to attend the tribunal's deliberations. The author will not expand here on this issue.

§33.05 THUMP-UP RULES IN DELIBERATION PROCESS

The following rules are recommended to be applied to arbitrators' deliberations process:

(1) An arbitrator should not become the advocate of his/her appointing party; he/she should be and maintain detached, and form and express his/her views from a neutral perspective for the deliberation.
(2) An arbitrator should fully respect his/her fellow arbitrators, despite their originality/ background/level of education/fields of expertise/experience in arbitration, etc. Deliberations could be effective and meaningful only based on a trustiness and respectful relationship among the arbitrators.
(3) An arbitrator should be minded to conduct the deliberations in a timely and cost-effective manner, so as to control the costs and facilitate the progress of the proceedings.
(4) An arbitrator should be well-prepared for the deliberations, lacking knowledge of the case facts/parties' submissions will seriously lower the efficiency and effectiveness of deliberations and is also disrespectful of other arbitrators.
(5) Arbitrators should aim to conduct the deliberations right after the hearing, or, if not possible, as early as possible.
(6) Arbitrators should always abide by their confidentiality duty and shall not leak any information discussed in or observed from the deliberation process to any party.

VI(B) AAA/ABA Code of Ethics, "The arbitrator should keep confidential all matters relating to the arbitration proceedings and decision."
28. Gary B. Born, International Commercial Arbitration (Second Edition), 2014, page 2809.

CHAPTER 34
The Importance of Languages in International Arbitration and How They Impact Parties' Due Process Rights

Sherlin Tung

§34.01 INTRODUCTION

A wise man once told me that *"the basic concept in law and in international commercial arbitration is that all disputes should be resolved according to, and with, words and comprehension, and not with swords and confrontation."*[1] This wise man, Dr. Pierre Karrer, was my mentor, and he showed me the importance of languages in resolving disputes between parties in an international arbitration proceeding. On occasion of Pierre Karrer's 75th birthday, I am grateful to be able to submit this chapter in honor not only of his career but also the significant impact he has made in the world of arbitration.

A significant rise in international commercial transactions has resulted in a parallel urgent increase in need for an effective and unified dispute resolution system that can settle disputes between international parties.[2] This urgency has led to international commercial arbitration emerging as the leading dispute resolution system for cross-border commercial transactions. International commercial arbitration has the primary advantage over other dispute resolution mechanisms that its awards are enforceable in most countries worldwide due to the Convention on Recognition and

---

1. Karrer, P., *Arbitration and Language Look for the Purpose*, 7, 11 Croatian Arbitration Yearbook 7 (2004).
2. Pathak, H. and Sharma, S., *Rising Importance and Significant of International Commercial Arbitration as an Alternate Dispute Resolution Forum*, 157, Proceedings of the Australia-Middle East Conference and Social Sciences 2016, Dubai (in partnership with the Journal of Developing Areas, Tennessee State University, USA) available at: https://www.aabss.org.au/system/files/published/001264-published-amecbss-2016-dubai.pdf.

Enforcement of Foreign Arbitral Awards of 1958 ("New York Convention").[3] Companies engaged in cross-border commercial transactions are therefore more likely to include arbitration agreements in their contracts as a means to resolve any disputes which may arise.

With the ever-growing amount of cross-border transactions whereby parties from different countries carry out the negotiations and performance of contracts in various countries, the issue of language has become an even more vital component in resolving disputes in international arbitration. The very nature of international arbitration entails parties, arbitrators and any other participant in arbitral proceedings generally being of different nationalities and speaking different languages.[4] There is therefore no doubt that language is central to international arbitration.[5]

This chapter will discuss the importance of languages in international arbitration proceedings and how they have an impact on parties' due process rights. In examining the impact of languages on parties' due process rights in international arbitration, this chapter will be split into three sections. The first section will look at how the use of languages in international business transactions have an impact on international arbitration proceedings. The second section will discuss the concept of due process in international arbitration proceedings. And finally, the third section will focus on how language can impact a party's due process rights in international commercial arbitration proceedings.

§34.02 LANGUAGES IN INTERNATIONAL BUSINESS TRANSACTIONS

Language plays a key role from the start of international business transactions as it reflects the identities and intentions of the parties involved in such transactions. The rise in international business transactions means that parties negotiating such transactions are almost always discussing various details in a language that is not their mother tongue. The diversity in language and cultures of the parties involved can result in misunderstandings and miscommunications. As such, many controversies in international commercial arbitration stem from poor language and are fed by misconceptions about language.[6]

Statements and phrases exchanged between the parties are indicative of their cultures and understandings. The way certain statements and phrases are used by the involved parties also reflect their understandings and intentions in the particular circumstances. In addition to the negotiations process, drafts and ultimately the final versions of international commercial contracts are often exchanged in multiple languages. The use of various languages in every aspect of the negotiation process can

---

3. Convention on the Recognition and Enforcement of Foreign Arbitral Awards, June 10, 1958, 21 U.S.T. 2517, 330 U.N.T.S. 3. (*see also* http://www.newyorkconvention.org/texts).
4. Faienza, V., *The Choice of the Language of the Proceedings: An Underestimated Aspect of the Arbitration?*, Kluwer Arbitration Blog, May 6, 2014, available at: http://kluwerarbitrationblog.com/2014/05/06/the-choice-of-the-language-of-the-proceedings-an-underestimated-aspect-of-the-arbitration/.
5. *Id.*
6. *Id.*

result in discrepancies in the understandings of each party to such transactions. Accordingly, in order to have an accurate understanding of a dispute arising from an international business transaction, it is necessary to take a look at the facts leading up to such dispute.

In order to properly establish such facts, it is important to look at the use of languages during negotiations between the parties, the performance of the contract and after the dispute arises.

[A] Negotiations Between the Parties

The most common perception of the importance of language in arbitration is that of the language to be used during the arbitration proceeding. A simple way for parties to avoid unnecessary costs on an issue unrelated to the dispute should a dispute arise is to agree on a language to be used in an arbitration during their negotiations on their business transaction. Nevertheless, in spite of lengthy negotiations between parties on various aspects of a large international business transaction, the disputes resolution clause of the final contract is almost always the "midnight clause," also known as the "champagne clause," an afterthought and a last minute addition to a complexly negotiated commercial contract.[7]

Only after the most difficult commercial aspects of the contract are negotiated and the champagne is sitting on ice waiting to be opened once the parties have "sealed the deal," do the parties then remember as an afterthought to include a dispute resolution clause.[8] At this point, the thought of a dispute is the furthest thing from the parties' minds and in order to speed up the process, parties hastily throw in a boilerplate dispute resolution clause without considering the specifics of a particular contract.[9] One important specificity often ignored is language and its impact on potential disputes that may arise as the parties are in a celebratory mood and are not in a strategic mindset for the possibility of disputes in the future. Without evidence otherwise, the language used during the parties' negotiations provide strong evidence as to what language should be used during an arbitration proceeding, in the event of no other agreement.

It must be noted, however, that a failure to include a choice of language in a contract and/or arbitration agreement is not the first stage where the issue of language impacts an international arbitral proceeding or parties' due process rights. The arbitral procedure is a search for a true and accurate resolution of controversial positions between disputing parties and language is the necessary medium for reaching this accuracy.[10] However, many obstacles exist which prevent a proper search for the "truth" in international arbitration proceedings. In particular, many disputes in

---

7. Holtz, N. (Retd.), *Beware the Midnight Clause: Hold the Champagne?*, February 19, 2016, available at: http://www.insidecounsel.com/2016/02/19/beware-the-midnight-clause-hold-the-champagne?slreturn = 1492241332.
8. *Id.*
9. *Id.*
10. Ulmer, N., *Language, Truth and Arbitral Accuracy*, 295, Journal of International Arbitration 28(5) (2011) Kluwer Law International.

international commercial arbitrations stem from issues with language and are further fueled by misconceptions about language.

The parties involved in negotiations of an international business transaction are almost never lawyers but instead business people who have little to no background in law. At this point in negotiations, the parties' main focus is to discuss a commercial goal both sides wish to achieve. As such, the negotiations during this stage take place between commercial people who do not give any thought to possible legal implications of what is being discussed.

The language used by the parties at this stage, whether in oral or written form, is important because it reflects what each side understood as being negotiated and the intention of all parties involved. What is exchanged between the parties at this stage plays an even more important role when certain details of such discussions do not make it into the final, signed contract. This is often also result of cultural differences.

From experience, the author understands that it is common for important discussions to occur between European and Chinese counterparts during social events such as dinner or karaoke. Such social events are not always attended by all members of a party's negotiation team, i.e., interpreters and/or lawyers, yet implicit agreements are still made between those present (i.e., CEOs of the respective companies). As the agreements were made during a social event outside of the conference room, it is common that such details fail to make it into the parties' finalized agreement. In spite of this, there is an expectation that such implicit agreements be honored during the course of the contract. When a dispute later arises, however, there is no written evidence of this implicit agreement, and the language exchanged during the negotiation and subsequent understanding between the parties become key in resolving such dispute.

[B]   Performance of an Agreement

The next stage where languages used in international business transactions may have an impact on international arbitration proceedings is during the performance of international commercial contracts. There is a shift in this stage of the transactions with the parties involved in such transactions. Specifically, different parties are involved with the performance of an international commercial contract from those who negotiated and completed such agreement and as such, facts need to also be looked at from a different perspective, the understanding of the parties carrying out performance of the contract.

Generally, negotiations in an international business transaction is conducted by top management and parent companies whereas the performance of such agreements are carried out between lower-level staff members and/or subsidiaries and affiliates that may be located in other countries. In this respect, the parties carrying out the contract often communicate with one another in a different language and may have a different understanding of the other side's intentions. Such a shift in language becomes a factor in the determination of the language of the arbitration proceeding, if needed, and also assists in establishing facts to help the arbitral tribunal in determining a true and accurate resolution for the ongoing dispute.

[C] After the Dispute Arises

Finally, once a dispute arises, the main impact language has with an international arbitration proceeding is what language to be used during such proceeding, unless the parties have already previously agreed to what language governs an arbitration proceeding. It is important for parties to choose the language of an arbitration at the earliest possible stage of the proceeding as it not only makes the arbitration proceeding more efficient, it also ensures proper notice to the parties so that each side can prepare its case accordingly. Choice of language used during an arbitration can also be a strategic move for the parties.

Where there is no party agreement on the language of arbitration, the question arises as to who makes the decision on the language of arbitration. In theory, there are three scenarios: (i) the arbitration institution; (ii) the arbitral tribunal; (iii) or the laws of the place of arbitration. However, the laws of the place of arbitration usually says little on the issue of language in arbitration.[11] In practice, it is almost always the arbitral tribunal which makes the decision, after the parties have provided their views. This is also in line with the leading arbitral rules, which will be discussed in more detail.

The leading arbitral rules mostly provide that if the parties have not agreed on a language for the arbitration, the arbitral tribunal shall make the decision on what language the arbitration will be.[12] There are of course some exceptions with some institutions implementing a default language[13] and others providing for a determination of language in an arbitration proceeding at different stages of such proceeding.[14] Notwithstanding these exceptions, leading arbitral institutions still need to deal with the issue of language when it is not agreed to by the parties and the arbitral tribunal has yet to be constituted.

The ICC, for example, does not have the ICC Court take a decision on the language for the stage of arbitration before the arbitral tribunal is constituted like the LCIA. In the absence of an express language in the arbitration agreement, the ICC provides the parties with the opportunity to agree on a language. Should the parties fail to agree, then the arbitral tribunal is invited to make the decision, once constituted.[15] Before a decision is made, however, the ICC Secretariat will draft its correspondence to the parties in either the language of the contract (if it is one of the languages used by

---

11. Karrer, P., *Arbitration and Language Look for the Purpose*, 9, 11 Croatian Arbitration Yearbook 7 (2004).
12. *See* Art. 15 of the HKIAC Rules, Art. 20 of the ICC Rules, Art. 16 of the ICDR Rules, Art. 17 of the LCIA Rules, Art. 21 of the SCC Rules, Art. 22 of the SIAC Rules and Art. 19 of the UNCITRAL Rules.
13. *See* Art. 81 of the CIETAC Rules, which provide that the language of arbitration will be Chinese, unless the parties have agreed otherwise.
14. *See* Art. 17 of the LCIA Rules which state that the language of the arbitration prior to the constitution of the Arbitral Tribunal will be the prevailing language of the arbitration and, if there are multiple languages, the LCIA Court will take a decision before the matter proceeds.
15. *See* Art. 20 of the ICC Rules.

the Secretariat: English, French, Spanish, Portuguese, German) or in one of the official languages of the ICC Court: English or French.[16]

How the arbitral tribunal makes its decision on what language applies to the arbitration, however, reflects the importance of the languages used by the parties during negotiations and performance of the contract. One factor that is taken into consideration is the language of the arbitration agreement, which is made during the negotiations process.[17] When parties negotiate an agreement, they tend to use a *lingua franca* that is familiar to all parties involved, or at least their legal advisors.[18] While using a language to make an agreement is different from using a language to discuss its meaning and its impact on the rights and obligations of the parties in case of a dispute, it is reasonable to assume that if the parties were comfortable enough to finalize an agreement in a particular language, they also know it well enough for an arbitration.[19] It is safe to say that arbitral tribunals take into consideration the parties' use of language(s) in the events prior to the arbitration dispute, i.e., during the negotiations and performance of the contract, when making their decisions on language of arbitration.

§34.03 DUE PROCESS IN INTERNATIONAL ARBITRATION

When making decisions, arbitral tribunals should try and take all the steps necessary to ensure that their awards, which encompass their decisions during the arbitral procedure, are recognized and enforceable in State courts.[20] One item that needs to be observed throughout the arbitral proceeding is the parties' due process rights.

Due process is a fundamental right that is recognized by courts worldwide. In spite of the varying definitions, at its most fundamental level, the concept refers to the idea that no one should be deprived of his or her rights without the due process of law. Courts worldwide have recognized the following as due process of law: (i) procedural fairness, which includes proper notice to know what an individual is facing, notice of how the trial or hearing will proceed, as well as timeliness and cost efficient proceedings for a decision to be made; (ii) equal treatment; and (iii) the right to be heard, which includes the right to fully present your case, the right to defend yourself and the right to confront the opposing party's witnesses and evidence.[21]

---

16. Fry, J., Greenberg, S. and Mazza, M., *The Secretariat's Guide to ICC Arbitration*, Paris: International Chamber of Commerce (2012) at Sections 3-13 to 3-24.
17. *See* Art. 20 of the 2017 ICC Rules, which provide that the "*Tribunal shall determine the language or languages of the arbitration, due regard being given to all relevant circumstances, including the language of the contract*".
18. Karrer, P., *Arbitration and Language Look for the Purpose*, 12, 11 Croatian Arbitration Yearbook 7 (2004).
19. *Id.*
20. Boog, C. and Moss, B., *The Lazy Myth of the Arbitral Tribunal's Duty to Render an Enforceable Award*, Kluwer Arbitration Blog, January 28, 2013 available at: http://kluwerarbitrati onblog.com/2013/01/28/the-lazy-myth-of-the-arbitral-tribunals-duty-to-render-an-enforceable -award/.
21. Hanotiau, B. and Caprasse, O., *Arbitrability, Due Process, and Public Policy Under Article V of the New York Convention*, 721 – 741 Journal of International Arbitration, 25(6) (2008) and O'Hare,

Due process is seen as a set of criteria that protect a private person in relation to the State and its authorities and are considered to be a constitutional protection of an individual.[22] However, in the context of international arbitration, a different view needs to be taken. International arbitration is an alternative forum for parties to an international contract to definitely resolve disputes without the need for either party to submit to the jurisdiction of a court system to which it is unfamiliar with.[23] The parties have agreed that any dispute which arises will be resolved by an independent and non-governmental decision-maker in the private realm, which produces a final decision, legally binding and enforceable through national courts.[24] The competence of an arbitral tribunal is not based on the powers of the State but rather through the parties' freedom to contract.

Notwithstanding international arbitration taking place in the private realm, due process is not only a requirement for judicial systems but it is also recognized as a fundamental right in international arbitration.[25] A fundamental feature of international arbitration is that arbitral awards are final and binding and determine parties' rights and obligations. Arbitration awards are widely enforceable domestically and internationally. In this respect, States have delegated jurisdictional power to arbitral tribunals indirectly through party agreement.

The necessity of observing parties' due process rights in international commercial arbitration proceedings are memorialized in the New York Convention, the cornerstone of the legal regime for international commercial arbitration.[26] The New York Convention is widely regarded as one of the most successful international treaties ever concluded and the legal foundation for the great success of international arbitration today.[27] The New York Convention provides for mutual recognition and enforcement of arbitral awards by Contracting States, and limits the defenses that may be raised in opposition to the confirmation of an award, in an attempt to eliminate duplicative litigation following an arbitration.[28] As of March 2017, the New York Convention has been ratified by 157 state parties (154 of which are recognized United Nations Member

---

J., *The Denial of Due Process and the Enforceability of CIETAC Awards under the New York Convention – the Hong Kong Experience*, 179–196 Journal of International Arbitration, 13(4) (1996).
22. Kurkela, M. and Turunen, S., *Due Process in International Commercial Arbitration*, 1, 2nd Edition, Oxford University Press, Conflict Management Institute (2010).
23. Born, G., *International Commercial Arbitration (Second Edition)*, 131, 2nd Edition, Kluwer Law International (2014).
24. Id.
25. Fortese, F. and Hemmi, L., *Procedural Fairness and Efficiency in International Arbitration*, 111, Groningen Journal of International Law 3(1) (2015), International Arbitration and Procedure.
26. Born, G., *International Commercial Arbitration (Second Edition)*, 137, 2nd Edition, Kluwer Law International (2014).
27. *Guide to National Rules of Procedure for Recognition and Enforcement of New York Convention Awards* published in the Special Supplement 2008: Guide to National Rules of Procedure for Recognition and Enforcement of New York Convention Awards prepared by the ICC Task Force on National Rules of Procedure for Recognition and Enforcement of Foreign Awards pursuant to the New York Convention (2008).
28. David W. Rivkin, *International Arbitration*, published in Com. Arb. for the 1990S 123, 135 (Richard J. Medalie ed., 1991).

States), which is approximately 80% of the Member States recognized by the United Nations.[29]

Article V of the New York Convention sets out detailed grounds for why recognition or enforcement of an arbitral award may be refused by a Contracting State and a number of these grounds stem from a violation of a party's due process rights during the arbitral proceeding.[30] While the grounds for refusing recognition or enforcement in Article V are exhaustive and construed narrowly, the principle of due process arguably falls under two separate grounds for a National Court to refuse recognition or enforcement of an award – one which is triggered only by a party's request and the second which can be triggered by either a party's request or on the court's initiative.

The first ground is pursuant to Article V(1)(b) of the New York Convention.[31] Upon a party's request, a court may refuse recognition and enforcement of a foreign award when "[t]*he party against whom the award is invoked was not given proper notice of the appointment of the arbitrator or the arbitration proceedings or was otherwise unable to present his case.*"[32] This provision embodies what is known in common law systems as "*due process*" and in civil law systems as "*le principe de la contradiction, du respect des droits de la défense et d'égalité des parties.*"[33]

The second ground falls under Article V(2)(b), which can be triggered either by a party's request or by the Court on its own initiative.[34] An award may be refused recognition and enforcement by a court when "[t]*he recognition or enforcement of the award would be contrary to the public policy of that country.*"[35] While this is the well-known public policy prong of the New York Convention, it is generally admitted that due process also falls under the public policy provision of the New York Convention.[36]

Although there is no dispute that the New York Convention recognizes a lack of due process as grounds for refusing to enforce or recognize a foreign award, the definition of what constitutes due process under the New York Convention is not clear. Though the first ground under Article V(1)(b) of the New York Convention sets out express guidelines for courts to follow, the second ground under Article V(2)(b)

---

29. *See* http://www.newyorkconvention.org/contracting-states/list-of-contracting-states.
30. Section V(1)(b) of the Convention on the Recognition and Enforcement of Foreign Arbitral Awards, June 10, 1958, 21 U.S.T. 2517, 330 U.N.T.S. 3. (*see also* http://www.newyorkconvention.org/texts).
31. Van den Berg, A., "*Refusals of Enforcement Under the New York Convention of 1958: the Unfortunate Few*" published in Special Supplement 1999: Arbitration in the Next Decade: Proceedings of the International Court of Arbitration's 75th Anniversary Conference, page 75 (1999).
32. Article V(1)(b) of the Convention on the Recognition and Enforcement of Foreign Arbitral Awards, June 10, 1958, 21 U.S.T. 2517, 330 U.N.T.S. 3. (*see also* http://www.newyorkconvention.org/texts).
33. Hanotiau, B. and Caprasse, O. (2008).
34. Article V(2)(b) of the Convention on the Recognition and Enforcement of Foreign Arbitral Awards, June 10, 1958, 21 U.S.T. 2517, 330 U.N.T.S. 3. (*see also* http://www.newyorkconvention.org/texts).
35. *Id.*
36. Hanotiau, B. and Caprasse, O., (2008).

provides little, if any guidance, in light of the fact that public policy standards vary and are based on the jurisdiction in which a party tries to enforce an award.

It also bears mention that Article V(1)(e) of the New York Convention provides that a court may also refuse recognition or enforcement of an award upon a party's request when "[t]*he award...has been set aside or suspended by a competent authority of the country in which, or under the law of which, that award was made.*"[37] Depending on the place of arbitration, a violation of due process may also result in an award being set aside and ultimately not enforced or recognized under the New York Convention.

Notwithstanding the lack of an express definition, violations of the public policy prong are frequently invoked, as part of procedural public policy.[38] The Paris Court of Appeals often refers to these invocations as *"compliance with the fundamental notions of due process within the French understanding of international public policy."*[39] From 1973 until 2008, no less than 136 reported court decisions were found worldwide where due process was raised as a ground to oppose enforcement.[40] While Courts have rarely refused to enforce foreign awards on this basis, case law demonstrates that courts will recognize the violation of due process in very serious cases and refuse to recognize or enforce an award.[41]

For example, in 1993 and 1996, two CIETAC awards were refused recognition and enforcement by the High Court of the Supreme Court of Hong Kong based on the grounds that CIETAC had failed to provide the parties to the arbitration the opportunity to present their case.[42] In both cases, the arbitral tribunals set about making their own inquiries or obtaining experts reports, subsequently rendering the awards without permitting the parties to the proceedings the opportunity to address this evidence.[43]

In 2008, the Quebec Superior Court partially annulled an award rendered by an ICC arbitral tribunal because the arbitral tribunal violated the parties' due process rights by awarding a remedy that neither party requested.[44] Also, in 2012 an ICC award was also partially annulled by the Swiss Federal Tribunal because the sole arbitrator inadvertently overlooked one parties' post-hearing submission due to technical difficulties.[45] The Swiss Federal Tribunal found that the parties' due process right to be

---

37. Article V(1)(e) of the Convention on the Recognition and Enforcement of Foreign Arbitral Awards, June 10, 1958, 21 U.S.T. 2517, 330 U.N.T.S. 3. (*see also* http://www.newyorkconvention.org/texts).
38. Hantotiau, B. and Caprasse, O., (2008).
39. Id.
40. Verbist H., *Challenges on Grounds of Due Process Pursuant to Article V(1)(b) of the New York Convention* published in: Gaillard, E. and Di Pietro, D. eds. *Enforcement of Arbitration Agreements and International Arbitral Awards: The New York Convention in Practice*, London: Cameron May (2008).
41. Id.
42. *Pak lito Investments Limite v. Klockner East Asia Ltd.*, 1993 and *Apex Tech Investments Limited v. Chuang's development (China) Limited*, 1996.
43. O'Hare, J., *The Denial of Due Process and the Enforceability of CIETAC Awards under the New York Convention – the Hong Kong Experience*, 179–196 Journal of International Arbitration, 13(4).
44. *Holding Tusculum BV v. Louis Dreyfus* (2008).
45. *X.____ v. Z.____ Inc.*, 2012.

heard on issues raised in its post-hearing brief was violated and therefore annulled parts of the awards which dealt with the issues not addressed by the sole arbitrator.[46]

It is clear that a violation of a parties' due process rights are grounds for an arbitral award to be set aside or not enforced. While there has been an increase in concern for arbitral tribunals to act decisively in certain situations for fear of their arbitration award being challenged on the basis of a party not having had a chance to present its case fully,[47] at the same time, there is also a growing concern with "due process paranoia."[48] In spite of the growing concern on violation of due process rights, only a small percentage of arbitration awards have ultimately not been enforced in countries that are Contracting Parties to the New York Convention.[49]

Notwithstanding the low percentage of awards ultimately not enforced or set aside, the most important players in international arbitrations, the parties, have a unreasonably high fear that an award is ultimately not enforceable or set aside.[50] Companies place extreme importance on the enforceability of an award because awards which are not enforceable or are set aside result in a significant amount of costs for companies.[51] It also results in uncertainty for the company and raises the question of what are the next steps to take in order for a company to enforce its rights. Given the high degree of importance placed by company's on ensuring the enforceability of an award, it is important to look at the impact of languages on a party's due process rights in an international arbitration proceeding.

§34.04 LANGUAGES AND THEIR IMPACT ON PARTIES' DUE PROCESS RIGHTS

As discussed throughout this chapter, language plays a key role in international arbitration starting from the onset of negotiations in international business transactions, through the performance of an international commercial contract and even after a dispute arises. The issue of language during an arbitration proceeding can impact a party's due process rights of procedural fairness, equal treatment and its right to be heard. It is expected that parties to an international arbitration proceeding will not have the same mother tongue and therefore languages in international arbitration can assist in the parties' own strategies for the arbitration proceeding.

---

46. *Id.*
47. Queen Mary University of London *Improvements and Innovations in International Arbitration*, Mistelis, L. and Lagerberg, G. eds., PriceWaterhouseCoopers (2015).
48. Gerbay, R., *Due Process Paranoia*, 6 June 2016, available at: http://kluwerarbitrationblog.com/2016/06/06/due-process-paranoia/.
49. Weigand, F., *Practitioner's Handbook on International Commercial Arbitration* at page 344 (2009).
50. Burford Capital Survey published on June 29, 2016, available at: http://www.4-traders.com/BURFORD-CAPITAL-LIMITED-5668352/news/Burford-Capital-Unenforced-judgments-and-arbitration-awards-cost-14-percent-of-companies-over-50-22755721/.
51. *Id.* finding that unenforced judgments and arbitration awards cost 14% of the companies surveyed costs of over USD 50 million.

[A] Procedural Fairness, Equal Treatment and the Right to Be Heard

Procedural fairness requires that all legal proceedings to be fair and that each party involved in such proceedings be given proper notice.[52] In order to ensure that the parties' are subject to procedural fairness in an international arbitration proceeding, they must understand the arbitration proceeding and be aware of all steps of such proceeding such as the deadline for nominating their arbitrator and for filing submissions. If an arbitration proceeds in a language that is unfamiliar to one (or all) of the parties, they have been deprived of their due process rights of procedural fairness.

Equal treatment of the parties is also another cornerstone of parties' due process rights in international arbitration proceedings. All parties have a right to be treated equally in international arbitration. In an international environment, at least one, if not all of the parties will undoubtedly participate in the arbitration proceeding using a secondary language. It is therefore important that a procedural meeting take place early in the arbitration proceeding between the parties and the arbitral tribunal,[53] particularly if the issue of language of the arbitration still needs to be decided by the tribunal. It is at this procedural meeting, where the parties are afforded an equal opportunity to submit their arguments on what should be the language of arbitration. Without being treated equally in presenting arguments on the issue of language, a party will not be able to express its understanding and intentions during the negotiations and performance of the relevant contract, and a decision on language could be taken without all facts being brought to the arbitral tribunal's attention.

Even in situations where the language of arbitration has already been decided, such meeting between the parties and tribunal remains important as it does not mean that all testimony or evidence should be rendered in that particular language.[54] Witnesses are not deemed parties to the arbitration proceeding. They are third parties and have a right to use their own language to testify.[55] By having a discussion and reaching an agreement early on in the arbitration proceeding on how to deal with witnesses and evidence in a different language, the parties are kept equally aware of what to expect and provided with equal notice of how to deal with such particularities, including time allocation for witnesses who will testify in a different language and need interpreters. It is important to note that equal treatment must be extended to all parties involved in the arbitration but does not need to result in equal responses from the parties. This is an important distinction in international arbitration proceedings where there is a non-responsive party.

Language also plays a significant role in a party's right to be heard in an international arbitration. There are various procedural steps in an arbitration proceeding which impact a party's right to be heard. The first notable procedural step after a

---

52. Fortese, F. and Hemmi, L., *Procedural Fairness and Efficiency in International Arbitration*, 110, Groningen Journal of International Law 3(1) (2015), International Arbitration and Procedure.
53. Karrer, P., *Arbitration and Language Look for the Purpose*, 11, 11 Croatian Arbitration Yearbook 7 (2004).
54. Karrer, P., *Arbitration and Language Look for the Purpose*, 12, 11 Croatian Arbitration Yearbook 7 (2004).
55. Id.

request for arbitration is filed is the constitution of the arbitral tribunal. Parties have a fundamental right to: (i) have a say in who it wishes to appoint as an arbitrator (unless the parties have agreed otherwise);[56] and (ii) an independent and impartial arbitral tribunal vis-à-vis the parties.[57]

A party's right to appoint its arbitrator extends to its right to be heard because its choice in arbitrator is often part of their case strategy. Strategically, parties want to ensure that they are able to nominate an arbitrator who is not only independent and/or impartial to the dispute but also fluent in the language of the arbitration and, ideally, able to understand the other languages relevant to the dispute. For example, a party may wish to choose an arbitrator who is fluent in the language of the other side as well as their own language in order to save on costs of an interpreter and also be on alert when the other side starts speaking in their own native language. In addition to choosing its own arbitrator, the requirement of ensuring that all parties have proper notice of an appointed arbitrator and the right to present their case in a situation where they believe an appointed arbitrator does not meet the independence and/or impartial requirements is also a due process right that must be observed in order to protect the final enforcement of an arbitral award.[58]

Another notable step in the arbitration is the arbitration hearing. As indicated earlier, determination of language of the arbitration proceeding does not mean that witnesses have to testify in the chosen language. The ability for witnesses to testify in their own language with interpreters can also be a part of a party's legal strategy in defending its case. For example, a witness may choose to testify in his/her native language, even if s/he has the ability to testify in the chosen language of an arbitration. The choice of having an interpreter translate every question asked and every response given can result in an uneven advantage for the party who requests interpretation over a party who does not request interpretation. Such advantage includes additional time to process questions asked and additional time to think of how to relay responses.

Another issue arising from language during a hearing is the understanding of the witnesses who are testifying in their native language. The use of interpreters are a way to remedy a situation where witnesses can only testify in a different language however the translation of witness testimony is not always perfect as there will always be phrases and statements which do not have direct translations in other languages. Further, interpreters merely translate the words spoken by the witnesses and not the surrounding emotions or expressions. An interpreter is not able to relay to the tribunal whether a witness is sincere in his/her testimony or gives reason to doubt his/her testimony. There are also situations where the interpreter is unable to comprehend the witness, tribunal or counsel and properly relay the messages conveyed.

---

56. Waincymer, J., *Reconciling Conflicting Rights in International Arbitration: The Right to Choice of Counsel and the Right to an Independent and Impartial Tribunal*, 597 Arbitration International 26(1) (2010).
57. Fouchard, P., Gaillard, E. and Goldman, B. *"Fouchard, Gaillard Goldman on International Commercial Arbitration"*, Kluwer Law International, 1999.
58. Article V(1)(b) of the Convention on the Recognition and Enforcement of Foreign Arbitral Awards, June 10, 1958, 21 U.S.T. 2517, 330 U.N.T.S. 3. (*see also* http://www.newyorkconvention.org/texts).

These issues that arise due to language during an arbitration proceeding impact equal treatment of the parties and also a parties' right to be heard and present its case. A party may not be able to properly present its case and defend itself if its witnesses are not able to properly relay their messages to the arbitral tribunal or if it is not able to properly confront the opposing party's witness and evidence.

[B] CEEG (Shanghai) Solar Science & Technology Co., Ltd. Versus Lumos LLC

One example of how language affects parties' due process rights in international arbitration can be seen in *CEEG (Shanghai) Solar Science & Technology Co., Ltd. v. Lumos, LLC*, a case decided by the 10th Circuit Court of Appeals on 19 July 2016. In this case, the 10th Circuit upheld the U.S. District Court of Colorado's decision declining to recognize a Shanghai International Arbitration Center administered award because the Notice of Commencement of Arbitration sent to the Respondent (who was domiciled in the U.S.) was sent in Chinese rather than English.[59] The 10th Circuit stated that under the circumstances, *"the notice was not reasonably calculated to apprise Lumos of the arbitration proceedings"* in light of the prior practice between the parties of communications in English and the terms of the two agreements, one of which stated the English version of the contract would control and the other which stated that all interactions between the parties and any dispute resolution proceeding would be in English.[60]

The Court issued its decision in spite of the fact that Lumos had actual knowledge that the document received was a notice of arbitration in light of prior email exchanges with CEEG.[61] The Court reasoned that the analysis was not whether a party should know that the documents constituted notice but whether the notice in Chinese was reasonably calculated to apprise a party of the arbitration proceedings. Lumos raised an argument that the process of retaining local counsel took over three weeks after they diligently translated the Chinese notice, which prevented them from properly participating in the arbitration proceeding, including nominating their arbitrator, because they did not have counsel who understood Mandarin Chinese and therefore did not understand the communications from the arbitral institution and were not aware of the deadlines imposed on them.[62]

The CEEG case highlights how language through all stages of an international business transaction impacts parties' due process rights in international arbitration proceedings. The Court based its decision on the language that was not only expressly referred to in the relevant agreements but also the languages used by the parties in their communications during the negotiation process as well as performance of the agreements. Language in this case had an impact on: (i) a party's right to procedural fairness in having proper notice of deadlines and what to expect; (ii) equal treatment of the

---

59. *CEEG (Shanghai) Solar Science & Technology Co. v. Lumos LLC, n/k/a/ Lmos Solar LLC*, 829 F. 3d 1201, 1201 (10th Cir. 2016) at 1207–1208.
60. *Id.*
61. *Id.*
62. *Id.*

parties in that Lumos had to engage Chinese translators and retain Chinese counsel in order to understand the proceeding unlike the other side; and (iii) also a party's right to be heard, as Lumos did not get a chance to present its case in the arbitration proceeding since the arbitration proceeded to the end in spite of its failure to nominate its own arbitrator.

§34.05 CONCLUSION

The rise in international business transactions will undoubtedly result in a rise in international commercial arbitrations. Such arbitration proceedings will continue to see an increase in diversity of parties where no one single language will govern an entire proceeding. Parties must recognize the importance of language from the beginning of negotiations before entering into an international commercial arbitration in order to try and ensure that their due process is maintained during the arbitration proceeding. A hastily put together dispute resolution clause not recognizing the issues presented by language at the end of negotiations will end up costing a party in the long-run.

The realization of the parties' right to a defense and the right to fully present their case to the tribunal depends on whether they can correctly communicate with the arbitral tribunal and follow the proceedings. In order to ensure that they are able to fully present their case, parties need to ensure that take into consideration the issues raised by the existence of multiple languages between the parties, arbitral tribunals and other third parties related to the arbitration dispute.

CHAPTER 35

Proving Legality Instead of Corruption

Marc D. Veit

§35.01 INTRODUCTION

Corruption has become one of the hot topics in international arbitration. The global trend of increased transparency and compliance has now also caught the arbitration community. Over the last years, much has been written on the subject but there is still only a very limited number of cases where arbitral tribunals have found evidence of corruption. This may be linked to the fact that arbitral tribunals have traditionally been reluctant to delve into the issue for a number of reasons.

According to the OECD Foreign Bribery Report,[1] in two-thirds of the cases bribery occurred in only four specific sectors: the extractive, construction, transportation and storage, and information and communication sectors. These are typically the industries in which international arbitration is the dispute resolution method of choice.[2] Anecdotal evidence suggest that a relatively large number of disputes in these industries, in particular, when involving state enterprises and state public officials, indeed have aspects of corruption or bribery. International arbitrators therefore do need appropriate tools to deal with the issue.

Legal writers and arbitral tribunals have been dealing with corruption mainly under two aspects: (i) burden and standard of proof when a party raises allegations of corruption; and (ii) the power and/or duty of arbitrators to conduct *sua sponte* investigations absent any clear allegations of corruption. These two aspects are

---

1. Organisation for Economic Co-operation and Development, OECD Foreign Bribery Report: An Analysis of the Crime of Bribery of Foreign Public Officials, (2014); see also Nicola Bonucci, 'Key Note Presentation: Everything You Always Wanted to Know About Foreign Bribery and Corruption but Were Afraid to Ask', World Arbitration & Mediation Review, Vol. 9 (2015), pp. 239–247, p. 243.
2. 2015 ICC Dispute Resolution Statistics, (2016) *ICC Dispute Resolution Bulletin 2016 No. 1* 9, pp. 9 et seq.

certainly important and they have advanced the discussion into the right direction. However, the published case law shows that arbitral tribunals still have been struggling with applying these concepts, in particular when none of the parties (seriously) pursue clear allegations of corruption. This article suggests a different approach that complements the current thinking to a large extent: instead of having to decide whether or not corruption is present, arbitral tribunals should consider the flipside of the medal, namely, whether there is sufficient evidence that the contract in question is legal.

§35.02 BURDEN AND STANDARD OF PROOF

It is nowadays almost universally accepted that a party bears the burden of proving facts on which it relies in support of its claim or defence. This rule can be found in many national laws[3] and arbitration rules.[4] However, in case of indicia of corruption, some tribunals and commentators have suggested shifting the burden of proof to the party denying corruption to show that it did not commit corruption. The rationale is that corruption is inherently difficult to prove, and innocent parties should be capable of producing countervailing evidence.[5]

The idea of burden-shifting, however, has been widely criticized on the basis that reversing the burden of proof is incompatible with due process.[6] In light of the fact that the burden of proof is a substantive law concept, the answers as to whether a tribunal can shift the burden of proof when it comes to allegations of corruption very often has to be answered under the law applicable on the merits. In that context, the observation of the *Rompetrol v. Romania* tribunal that 'the burden of proof is absolute' may not always be true, but in practice there is certainly great reluctance with arbitral tribunals to shift the burden of proof in cases involving allegations of corruption.

---

3. For example Art. 8 Swiss Civil Code, Art. 9 French Code of Civil Procedure, Art. 2697 Italian Civil Code.
4. For example Art. 27(1) UNCITRAL Rules, Art. 24(1) Swiss Rules, Art. 27 CIArb Arbitration Rules.
5. Andrea Menaker, 'The Evidentiary Challenges', World Arbitration & Mediation Review, Vol. 9 (2015), p. 254; Andrea Menaker, 'Chapter 5: Proving Corruption in International Arbitration' in Domitille Baizeau and Richard H. Kreindler (eds), Addressing Issues of Corruption in Commercial and Investment Arbitration, Dossiers of the ICC Institute of World Business Law, Volume (2015) pp. 77–102, p. 80 with reference to Mills, Karen, 'Corruption and Other Illegality in the Formation and Performance of Contracts and in the Conduct of Arbitration Relating Thereto' in van den Berg, Albert (ed.), ICCA Congress Series 11 (2003) pp. 288, 295; Lamm, Carolyn, Pham, Hansel & Moloo, Rahim, 'Fraud and Corruption in International Arbitration' in Fernandez-Ballesteros, Miguel Angel & Arias, David (eds), Liber Amicorum Bernardo Cremades (2010), pp. 699, 701; Constantine Partasides, 'Proving Corruption in International Arbitration: A Balanced Standard for the Real World,' ICSID Review Foreign Investment Law Journal 25:1 (2010) 47 ¶¶ 60, 63, 66; ICC Case No. 12990, Award of December 2005, ICC Bulletin (Supplement) 24 (2013) 52, 53 ¶ 251; ICC Case No. 6497, Award of 1994, Yearbook of Commercial Arbitration 24a (1999) 71, 73 ¶¶ 3, 4.
6. Alexis Mourre, 'Arbitration and Criminal Law: Reflections on the Duties of the Arbitrator,' Arbitration International, Vol. 22 No. 1 (2006), pp. 95, 103; *Waguih Elie George Siag and Clorinda Vecchi v. Arab Republic of Egypt*, ICSID Case No. ARB/05/15, Award of 1 June 2009, ¶¶ 316–317. Andrea Menaker, 'Chapter 5: Proving Corruption in International Arbitration' in Domitille Baizeau and Richard H. Kreindler (eds), Addressing Issues of Corruption in Commercial and Investment Arbitration, Dossiers of the ICC Institute of World Business Law, Volume (2015) pp. 77–102, p. 80.

Legal authorities show even more ambiguity when it comes to the standard of proof, i.e., the question of how much evidence is needed to prove a certain allegation or claim.[7] Arbitration rules are generally silent on this topic. The standard of proof is primarily a question of the law applicable. Tribunals, however, have varied widely in their views on how to assess evidence of corruption.

In international arbitration, the standard of proof is generally satisfied if the arbitrators are internally convinced that a certain assertion has been established as a fact (civil law approach) or in case the preponderance of evidence/balance of probabilities speaks for instead of against an assertion being made (common law approach). The standard of proof is typically higher in criminal cases where either a standard of *in dubio pro reo* (civil law approach) or beyond a reasonable doubt (common law approach) is required.

There is considerable debate among arbitration practitioners whether in commercial (civil) cases that involve allegations of criminal wrongdoings such as fraud/bribery/corruption, the standard of proof has to be increased or not. A survey of ICC cases that was done in 2003 suggests that in fourteen cases the tribunals heightened the standard of proof when allegations of corruption were at issue, whereas in eleven cases, the tribunals did not.[8]

For example, in ICC Case No. 6401 the tribunal came to the conclusion that only '*clear and convincing evidence*' is sufficient to prove an allegation as serious as fraud.[9] An ad-hoc sole arbitrator stated that '*direct evidence*' is needed to satisfy the standard of proof in such cases.[10] In another award rendered in Switzerland, it was required that fraud and/or bribery be presumed '*with certainty*' in order for the standard of proof to

---

7. Regarding the following assessment concerning the standard of proof cf: Alan Redfern, et al., 'The Standards and Burden of Proof in International Arbitration', Arbitration International, Vol. 10, No. 3 (1994), p. 317; José Rosell and Harvey Prager, 'Illicit Commissions and International Arbitration: The Question of Proof', Arbitration International, Vol. 15 No. 4 (1999), p. 329; Scherer, 'Beweisfragen bei Korruptionsfällen vor internationalen Schiedsgerichten', ASA Bulletin 2001, Vol. 19, p. 648; Abdulhay Sayed, *Corruption in International Trade and Commercial Arbitration*. Kluwer Law International, 2004, Chapter 4: Evidence of Corruption; Haugeneder, Liebscher, Investment Arbitration: Corruption and Investment Arbitration: Substantive Standards and Proof, Austrian Arbitration Yearbook 2009, p. 539; Noradèle Radjai, Where there's smoke, there's fire? Proving illegality in international arbitration, International Bar Association Newsletter, Vol. 15 No. 1, March 2010, p. 139.
8. Antonio Crivellaro, Arbitration Case Law on Bribery, Issues of Arbitrability, Contract Validity, Merits and Evidence, in Dossier of the ICC Institute of World Business Law: Arbitration – Money Laundering, Corruption and Fraud 118 (2003).
9. In ICC Case No. 6401, *Westinghouse v. The Republic of the Philippines*, in Mealey's International Arbitration Report, 7(1), 1992, C-405, p. 34 (cited as *Westinghouse*) the Tribunal stated: '*The party having the burden of persuasion must establish the facts on which it relies by a "preponderance of evidence". In other words, it must have the "superior weight of evidence" and establish that its version of the facts is more likely true than not true. However, in the Philippines and in the United States, fraud in civil cases must be proved to exist by clear and convincing evidence amounting to more than mere preponderance, and cannot be justified by a mere speculation. This is because fraud is never lightly to be presumed.*'
10. Ad-hoc Award 28/7/1995 ASA Bulletin 1995, Vol. 13 No. 4, p. 742 (cited as *Award 28/7/2995*). However, in that case, only a newspaper article was handed to the sole arbitrator to prove the alleged bribery and Claimant had completely fulfilled its obligation to show that it did perform services under the contracts in question.

have been met.[11] This view is seconded by practitioners such as Born who advocates that 'allegations of wrongdoing, particularly serious wrongdoing such as criminal acts, fraud, corruption and the like, require more convincing evidence than other facts.'[12] This heightened standard should also discourage baseless allegations of misconduct.[13] Menaker reports a third concern of arbitral tribunals, namely that many tribunals do fear that a finding of corruption may result in serious consequences for the persons concerned.[14]

However, the danger of imposing a higher standard of proof is that an arbitral tribunal may make it impossible for corruption to be proven. While this may have been of little concern to arbitrators fifteen years ago, tribunals in the current regulatory climate are more concerned. By contrast, there are tribunals which have held that a *'high degree of probability of bribery'*[15] or *'serious indices'*[16] are sufficient to prove corruption.

Over the last years, contract drafters have become increasingly aware of the difficulties associated with proving corrupt practices, in particular when it comes to the standard and burden of proof. Therefore, in jurisdictions that are known to be challenging with regard to corrupt practices increasingly, parties use so-called legality clauses in their agreements with intermediaries that typically require the intermediary to follow anti-corruption norms and to prove in appropriate form that his actions are compliant with the applicable laws.[17] Such clauses can read for example as follows:

> Compliance with Law and Ethics. Distributor shall comply with all legal and regulatory requirements which apply in connection [with] its performance under this Agreement. Distributor expressly agrees that it will cooperate fully with Manufacturer in complying with any applicable laws or regulations, to the extent that Distributor's performance under this Agreement may be subject to such laws or regulations, and to furnish Manufacturer, by affidavit or other reasonable means if requested by Manufacturer, to Manufacturer's reasonable satisfaction, assurances that the appointment of Distributor and Distributor's activities under this Agreement, including payment to Distributor of any commissions, discounts or moneys or consideration contemplated under this Agreement, are proper and lawful under such laws and regulations. Distributor shall conduct its activities under this Agreement in an ethical and professional manner at all times to reflect

---

11. *Société Hilmarton v. Société OTV*, 1994 Rev. Arb., p. 329.
12. Garry Born, International Commercial Arbitration, 2nd edn., 2314 (2009).
13. Abdulhay Sayed, Corruption in International Trade and Commercial Arbitration, 103 (2004).
14. Andrea Menaker, 'The Evidentiary Challenges', World Arbitration & Mediation Review, Vol. 9 (2015), p. 256.
15. ICC Case No. 6497, YCA 1999, p. 71 (cited as *ICC Case No. 6497*): In the end in that case a shift of the burden of proof was assumed by the arbitral tribunal since the consultant did not produce documents requested and then obscured the investigation by an external expert of the same documents.
16. ICC Case No. 8891, Journal du Droit International 4 (2000), p. 1076 (cited as *ICC Case No. 8891*): The serious indices in that case were: no written documentation, no proof of rendering any services of the consultant, very high percentage based commission fee and a short duration of contract.
17. See, e.g., ICC Guidelines on Agents, Intermediaries and Other Third Parties (2010), pp. 6 et seq.

upon the good reputation and name of Manufacturer and its affiliates, recognising that even the appearance of unethical actions is not acceptable.[18]

Legality clauses often shift the burden of proving the legality of the intermediary's actions to the intermediary itself. In addition, the clauses *de-facto* lower the standard of proving corrupt practices as they often provide that already creating the appearance of unethical behaviour may qualify as a breach of contract. While this contractual lowering of the standard of proof may not result in the contract being void (unless a 'normal' standard of proof for corruption is being met), it can at least give a right to the principal to claim damages or to terminate the contract *ex nunc* for breach of contract, in particular if the principal was unaware of the unethical practices.

§35.03 THE ARBITRAL TRIBUNAL'S RIGHT AND DUTY TO RAISE CORRUPTION ISSUES *SUA SPONTE*

The discussion on the burden and standard of proof for corrupt practices primarily becomes relevant if the tribunal is faced with allegations of corruption that have been raised by a party. Indeed, it is uncontroversial that arbitral tribunals have the power and duty to examine such allegations when raised. However, the more interesting question is whether and to what extent the tribunal can and should investigate suspicions of corruption where: (1) neither party has raised the matter but there are indicia that lead the tribunal to suspect corruption; or (2) a party has pleaded or insinuated corruption but made little effort to substantiate its allegations.[19] Analysis of arbitral awards shows that it is quite rare arbitral tribunals have to make findings that a party actually was active in corrupt practices.[20] Either they can avoid the issue (e.g., by declining jurisdiction, settlement, withdrawal of corruption allegations etc.) or then as a general rule, tribunals lack adequate evidence to rule on such allegations, regardless of the standard of proof applied by the tribunal.

This obviously does not come as a surprise. Parties engaged in corrupt practices will try to disguise the true nature of their agreement through seemingly legitimate contracts, such as agency or consultancy agreements, which sometimes are even held in escrow by a lawyer and the parties have access to the agreement only in very well-defined circumstances. It is therefore quite unlikely, but not impossible, to find direct evidence proving corrupt payments. Apart from rare incidents, such as in the *World Duty Free v. Kenya* case,[21] where a witness testifying for the Claimant openly admitted having made 'private payments' to the president, one does normally not find direct evidence of corruption.

---

18. ICC Case No. 16391, Final Award of 6 Dec. 2010 (unpublished).
19. Domitille Baizeau and Tessa Hayes, The Arbitral Tribunal's Duty and Power to Raise and Investigate Corruption *Sua Sponte*, forthcoming, para. 25.
20. Cecily Rose, Questioning the Role of International Arbitration in the Fight against Corruption, JIA, 2014, pp. 183 et seq.
21. *World Duty Free Company Limited v. Kenya*, ICSID Case No. ARB/OO/7, Award 4 Oct. 2006.

Arbitration practitioners have therefore recently argued that arbitral tribunals should be prepared to investigate corruption *sua sponte*.[22] One of the most notable practical examples is the award in the famous *Metal-Tech v. Republic of Uzbekistan* arbitration in which the tribunal describes in detail how it had sought further facts *sua sponte*.[23] One tool that has particularly been advocated to tackle the evidentiary problems of corruption without clear allegations of corrupt practices by one of the parties is to rely on so-called lists of 'red flags' that have been published by the ICC,[24] the US[25] and many others. The lists of red flags include items such as:

- 'A reference check reveals the Third party's flawed background or reputation, or the flawed background or reputation of an individual or enterprise represented by the Third party;
- The operation takes place in a country known for corrupt payments (e.g., the country received a low score on Transparency International's Corruption Perceptions Index);
- The Third party is suggested by a public official, particularly one with discretionary authority over the business at issue;
- Practitioners and institutions have set up checklists of red flags and it is said that arbitrators should start their own investigation in certain circumstances.
- The Third party objects to representations regarding compliance with anti-corruption laws or other applicable laws;
- The Third party has a close personal or family relationship, or business relationship, with a public official or relative of an official;
- The Third party does not reside or have a significant business presence in the country where the customer or project is located;
- Due diligence reveals that the Third party is a shell company or has some other non-transparent corporate structure (e.g. a trust without information about the economic beneficiary);
- The only qualification the Third party brings to the venture is influence over public officials, or the Third party claims that he can help secure a contract because he knows the right people;
- The need for the Third party arises just before or after a contract is to be awarded;
- The Third party requires that his or her identity or, if the Third party is an enterprise, the identity of the enterprise's owners, principals or employees, not be disclosed;
- The Third party's commission or fee seems disproportionate in relation to the services to be rendered;
- The Third party requires payment of a commission, or a significant portion thereof, before or immediately upon the award of a contract;

---

22. Baizeau/Hayes, para. 29; Teresa Giovannini, 'Chapter 8: Ex Officio Powers to Investigate: When Do Arbitrators Cross the Line?', in Domitille Baizeau and Bernd Ehle (eds), Stories from the Hearing Room: Experience from Arbitral Practice (Essays in Honour of Michael E. Schneider) (2015) pp. 59–76, p. 69.
23. *Metal-Tech Ltd v. The Republic of Uzbekistan*, ICSID Case No. ARB/10/3, Award 4 Oct. 2013.
24. ICC Guidelines on Agents, Intermediaries and Other Third Parties, pp. 6 et seq.
25. A Resource Guide to the FCPA U.S. Foreign Corrupt Practices Act (November 2012), http://www.justice.gov/criminal/fraud/fcpa/guide.pdf. For an in-depth analysis, see Vladimir Khvalei, Using Red Flags to Prevent Arbitration from Becoming a Safe Harbour for Contracts that Disguise Corruption, ICC International Court of Arbitration, Special Supplement: Tackling Corruption (2013), pp. 15 et seq.

- The Third party requests an increase in an agreed commission in order for the Third party to 'take care' of some people or cut some red tape; or
- The Third party requests unusual contract terms or payment arrangements that raise local law issues, payments in cash, advance payments, payment in another country's currency, payment to an individual or entity that is not the contracting individual/entity, payment to a numbered bank account or a bank account not held by the contracting individual/entity, or payment into a country that is not the contracting individual/entity's country of registration or the country where the services are performed.[26]

Much has been written about how arbitral tribunals should react when 'red flags' are present. The approach varies from a procedural presumption of corruption, to shifting the burden of proof and making adverse inference.[27]

§35.04 THE LEGALITY TEST: THE FLIPSIDE OF THE MEDAL OR HOW TRIBUNALS CAN DEAL WITH 'RED FLAGS' ABSENT CLEAR ALLEGATIONS OF CORRUPTION

The suggestions found in legal writings as to how to approach 'red flags' are certainly not wrong *per se*. However, they do lack a certain coherence and give little guidance to arbitral tribunals as to which approach is to be preferred in a given case, in particular if none of the parties makes clear allegations of corruption. It has been acknowledged that arbitral tribunals are often inherently ill-suited to the adjudication of corruption allegations.[28] The well-meant proposition that arbitrators should therefore investigate corruption *sua sponte* if 'red flags' are present does not give much guidance either. Equally, it must be acknowledged that the major ethical and also legal risk in not addressing suspicions of corruption is that the tribunal may become complicit in the wrongdoing.[29]

The suggested approach here is that arbitral tribunals, absent clear allegations of corruption, should generally not investigate corruption *sua sponte*. However, if the legality of the transaction is relevant under the applicable law even without the active intervention of one of the parties, e.g., when the contract is null and void under the applicable law (either the law chosen by the parties or other mandatory applicable rules), then the tribunal should indeed put the party implicitly or explicitly relying on the legality of the transaction to proof of the legality. In schematic terms, the legality test should be applied as follows:

---

26. ICC Guidelines on Agents, Intermediaries and Other Third Parties, pp. 6 et seq.
27. Vladimir Khvalei, Using Red Flags to Prevent Arbitration from Becoming a Safe Harbour for Contracts that Disguise Corruption, ICC International Court of Arbitration, Special Supplement: Tackling Corruption (2013), pp. 23 et seq. [Add further references].
28. Cecily Rose, Questioning the Role of International Arbitration in the Fight against Corruption, JIA, 2014, p. 221.
29. Baizeau/Hayes, para. 31.

§35.04   Marc D. Veit

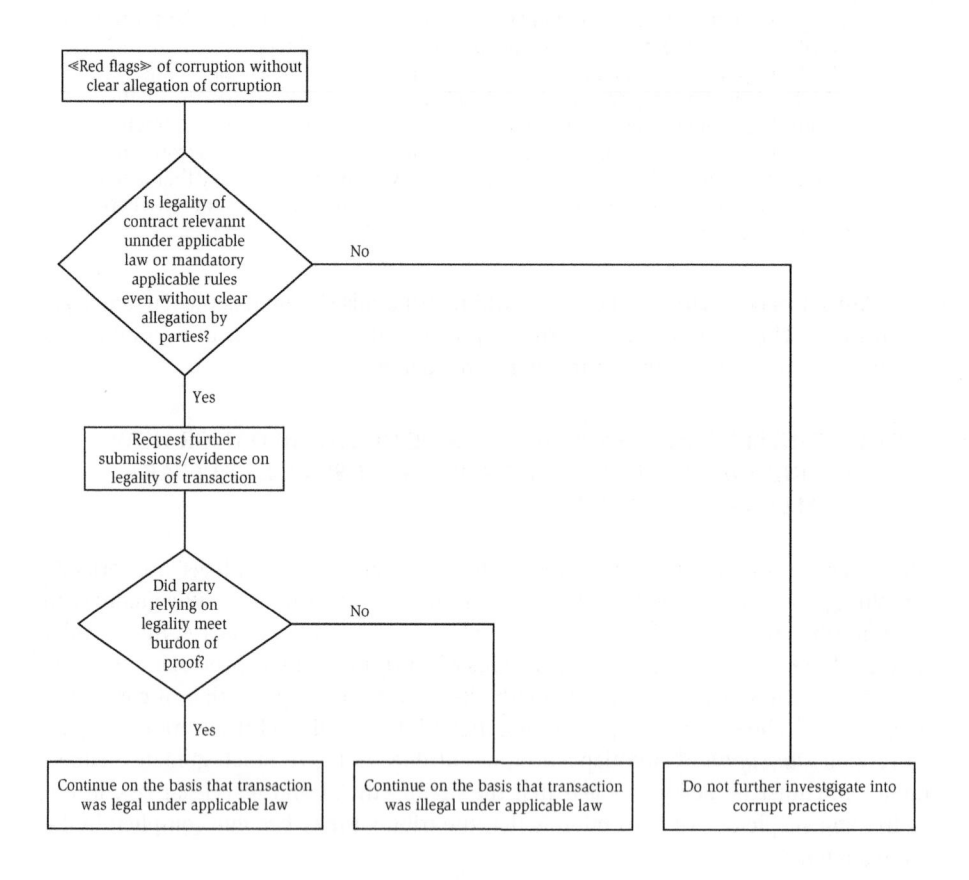

```
┌─────────────────────────────┐
│ «Red flags» of corruption   │
│ without clear allegation    │
│ of corruption               │
└──────────────┬──────────────┘
               │
        ╱──────────────╲
       ╱ Is legality of ╲
      ╱  contract relevannt╲
     ╱   unnder applicable  ╲───── No ──────────────────────┐
     ╲   law or mandatory   ╱                                │
      ╲  applicable rules  ╱                                 │
       ╲ even without clear╱                                 │
        ╲ allegation by   ╱                                  │
         ╲   parties?    ╱                                   │
          ╲──────┬──────╱                                    │
                 │ Yes                                       │
       ┌─────────┴─────────┐                                 │
       │ Request further   │                                 │
       │ submissions/      │                                 │
       │ evidence on       │                                 │
       │ legality of       │                                 │
       │ transaction       │                                 │
       └─────────┬─────────┘                                 │
                 │                                           │
          ╱──────────────╲                                   │
         ╱ Did party      ╲                                  │
        ╱  relying on      ╲── No ──────────┐                │
        ╲  legality meet   ╱                 │                │
         ╲ burdon of      ╱                  │                │
          ╲ proof?       ╱                   │                │
           ╲─────┬─────╱                     │                │
                 │ Yes                       │                │
┌──────────────────────┐  ┌──────────────────────┐  ┌──────────────────────┐
│ Continue on the basis│  │ Continue on the basis│  │ Do not further       │
│ that transaction was │  │ that transaction was │  │ investgigate into    │
│ legal under          │  │ illegal under        │  │ corrupt practices    │
│ applicable law       │  │ applicable law       │  │                      │
└──────────────────────┘  └──────────────────────┘  └──────────────────────┘
```

The first question which the tribunal has to ask itself when being faced with 'red flags' without clear allegation of corruption is whether illegality of the contract or transaction at issue under the applicable law, typically the law chosen by the parties or mandatory applicable rules, is relevant at all.[30] Thus, the issue is whether under the applicable law illegality of the contract makes the contract voidable or automatically void even without further declaration or action by one of the parties. Under many legal systems, including Swiss law,[31] contracts with an illegal purpose such as contracts for

---

30. Thomas K. Sprange, 'Corruption in Arbitration: Sua Sponte Investigations – Duty to Report', in Domitille Baizeau and Richard H. Kreindler (eds), Addressing Issues of Corruption in Commercial and Investment Arbitration, Dossiers of the ICC Institute of World Business Law (2015) p. 134; Baizeau/Hayes, paras 60 et seq.
31. In Switzerland contracts for corruption are void under Art. 20(1) CO: 'A contract is void if its terms are impossible, unlawful or immoral.' However, the Court of Appeals of the Canton of Zurich has held that under Swiss law a contract that was concluded by corruption is not immoral but is only voidable upon request by one of the parties as the contract was entered into under a material error according to Art. 23 CO, Evelyn Wyss and Hans-Caspar von der Crone, Bestechung bei Vertragsschluss, Urteil des Obergerichts des Kantons Zürich vom 17. September 2992, SZW 1/2003, p. 35. Add references from other legal systems.

§35.04

corruption are null and void, whereas contracts that have been obtained by illegal means, e.g., contracts obtained by corruption, are only voidable.

Under the test proposed here, the tribunal should not raise issues of legality of the underlying contract or transaction absent a clear allegation by one of the parties (typically the respondent) if the contract in question is merely voidable if corruption was involved. The danger of an *ultra petita* award in these cases is real. This typically involves contracts that were obtained by corruption, i.e., contracts that are typically concluded between a private party and a government or a state enterprise such as infrastructure supply contracts, concession agreements, PPSAs, etc.

This is in contrast to situations where the suspected corruption leads to the conclusion that the contract is null and void, irrespective of whether one of the parties relies on the illegality. In these situations, tribunals do have a right and indeed the duty to correctly apply the law and invite the parties to submit further evidence as to the legality (or not) of the contract or transaction in question. In arbitral jurisdictions such as Switzerland where the principle of *iura novit arbiter* applies, an arbitral tribunal certainly has the power to raise new issues of law. However, it is recognized today, even in common law jurisdictions, that arbitral tribunals have the power to raise relevant new issues of law, particularly if they concern mandatorily applicable norms, as long as the parties are granted the possibility to respond.[32]

Once the tribunal comes to the conclusion that it has to further deal with the issue of corruption, the next step is to require the party relying on the legality of the contract to submit further evidence as to the legality of the contract or the transaction in question.[33] Focusing on the legality of the transaction instead of embarking on an investigation as to corruption has several advantages.

First, proving corruption is extremely difficult with the methods available to arbitral tribunals. In most cases, there will not be any direct evidence of corruption.

Second, focusing on the legality of the transaction or contract will give the tribunal a further opportunity to look into the details of the transaction and on what was actually done, which amounts were paid, what was done for the amounts received, etc. I vividly remember the case when Pierre and I were sitting on a tribunal and we struggled hard to find out what the reasons were for the substantial payments to the intermediary, what the intermediary had done with the amounts received and what the intermediary's contribution was. We could not find any direct and conclusive evidence of corruption. However, we could not find any reasonable explanation as to the purpose of the contract or the intermediary's duties either. Hence, we proceeded on

---

32. For example Art. 22(1) LCIA Rules, [Add further references].
33. This to some extent was also the approach taken by the *Metal-Tech* tribunal when it ordered the claimant to produce more documents showing background of the transaction. These admissions led the tribunal to exercise its ex-officio powers and order the production of more documents (*Metal-Tech,* paras 239–243, 248–252). Failure by Metal-Tech to comply with the procedural order led the tribunal to conclude that no services had been performed for the money exchanged and that the money had been paid to certain consultants to use their positions and family connections with the Uzbek Government to facilitate Metal-Tech's investment (*Metal-Tech,* paras 311–327).

the basis that the claimant was not able to prove the legality of the contract and dismissed the claim.

Third, focusing on the legality of the transaction instead of requiring proof of corruption has the advantage of not having to apply a different standard of proof than in normal civil cases.

Fourth, a finding that a party did not meet the burden of proving the legitimacy of the transaction as opposed to a finding of corruption may relieve tribunals from fears that their awards will have serious (civil, administrative or criminal) consequences for the persons concerned.

Once the tribunal has assessed the evidence on the legality of the transaction, it will have to determine whether or not it wants to continue its analysis on the basis of whether the transaction was legal or not and draw the appropriate conclusions.

CHAPTER 36
An Arbitrator, a Gorilla and an Elephant Walk into a Room ...

Jeffrey Waincymer

'... If you want to walk straight, do not look at your feet too much. Of course, avoid obstacles, but the best way is to have a goal and to go straight towards it undaunted.'

Pierre Karrer (2014)

§36.01 INTRODUCTION

This book is dedicated to an arbitrator who epitomises the ideals of that profession in practical, scholarly and educational activities. To be exceptional in these endeavours, one must combine a sharp intellect, a clear understanding of arbitration law and theory, a practical and commercial disposition, an ability to adopt an international and comparative perspective in promoting neutrality, or at least in being culturally sensitive, have strong communication skills and an engaging personality, all combined with an ability to identify creative solutions for the inevitable problems that arise from time to time. Or as the above quote suggests, 'walk straight ... have a goal ... and (be) undaunted.'

One of the most significant problems, calling for all of the above skills, together with a nuanced and undaunted response, is what has been described of late as the challenge for an arbitrator when facing 'guerrilla tactics,' or perhaps the tactics of 'gorillas.'

Such behaviour can take many forms. A party might take inappropriate challenges to jurisdiction, make numerous challenges to arbitral independence and impartiality, fail to meet deadlines imposed by the tribunal and call constantly for extensions, fail to properly disclose evidentiary material, change counsel mid-case to create conflict with a tribunal member and make repeated threats as to annulment challenges or blocking of enforcement if tribunal directions are not favourable. In the extreme, there might be physical threats or investigators secretly spying on arbitrators.

It is more likely to be respondents who behave in this way, particularly when there are no counterclaims. Here, it is only the respondent that is at risk of adverse remedies. At times, such persons might fully expect to lose in due course, but wish to delay payment as much as possible. In the extreme, a key strategy may be to bait the arbitrator and lay the groundwork for procedural challenges, either during the hearing, or in an annulment application, or in an application to block enforcement of any adverse award.

Claimants might also undertake aggressive behaviour to try and pressure those with lesser resources to offer unduly favourable settlements. A claimant might have brought a case for an ulterior purpose and may not be arbitrating in good faith. A claimant may have tried to 'get in first' with a weak claim, knowing that a large and valid claim from respondent was imminent.

The problem is seen as being of concern, but one that is difficult to quantify. One survey suggested that 68% of respondents believed that they had experienced guerrilla tactics in arbitration.[1] As the authors note, however, given the problem of defining guerrilla tactics, the survey's affirmative response does not prove that they exist, but merely, that there is a perception of some concern. In any event, from the arbitrator's perspective, it is not a question of how widespread is the phenomenon, but instead, how to respond when faced with such behaviour.

Turning to the title of this chapter, so far we have mentioned the arbitrator and the gorilla, but what is the elephant and how does it come to be in the room? When challenges or threats are made to the tribunal during the currency of proceedings, the elephant in the room is the potential for due process challenges under principles such as those contained in Article 18 of the UNCITRAL Model Law on International Commercial Arbitration. This requires that the parties be treated with equality and that each party have a full or reasonable opportunity to present its case. Similar principles are found in Article 15.1 of the Swiss Arbitration Rules 2012, which stipulate that '(s)ubject to these Rules, the arbitral tribunal may conduct the arbitration in such manner as it considers appropriate, provided that it ensures equal treatment of the parties and their right to be heard.' Article 22.4 of the ICC Rules stipulates that '(i)n all cases, the arbitral tribunal shall act fairly and impartially and ensure that each party has a reasonable opportunity to present its case.' These have been regularly and rightly described as the *magna carta* of international arbitration.[2]

For the practical minded arbitrator, the first question is what authority there is to deal with guerrilla tactics and when and why such authority should be exercised. Many domestic systems provide express rights to judges to take diligence or tardiness into account, in considering procedural applications. Ethical rules and costs discretions

---

1. Edna Sussman and Solomon Ebere, 'All's Fair in Love and War – Or Is It? Perceptions on Ethical Standards for Counsel in International Arbitration', *American Review of International Arbitration* 22 (2011):612.
2. Julian D.M. Lew, Loukas A. Mistelis & Stefan M. Kroll, Comparative International Commercial Arbitration (The Hague: Kluwer Law International, 2003), 95.

allow for orders against counsel or complaints to regulatory bodies. Contempt of court powers can be used in relation to extreme forms of inappropriate behaviour. Where international arbitration is concerned, we are only at the early stages of the employment of such options. Furthermore, many court responses would be inappropriate for arbitration.

As yet, there are no elaborate rules underpinning most arbitrations that expressly deal with these questions, although some small steps have been taken which are discussed below. As with all key questions in arbitration, there will be a need to consider how the *lex arbitri*, party agreement, any arbitral rules, inherent powers, plus relevant guidelines, can be integrated so as to find a valid and coherent theory of arbitral power in such circumstances. Again, as with most questions in arbitration, there can then be different perspectives depending on whether one looks for a more jurisdictional basis of arbitral power, emanating from a *lex arbitri*, or instead see arbitration as essentially consent based. All accept that arbitration is a hybrid and arbitral power and practice must be consistent with both forms of authority, but the different perspectives might call for some variations in the way one responds to provocation.

That should not be a problem with most guerrilla tactics, as the broad powers and obligations to run arbitrations fairly and efficiently emanating from *lex arbitri* and arbitral rules, must be read as being consistent with a good faith presumption of consent to arbitration. Hence, a party who can be presumed to have consented to arbitration in good faith, who then behaves in inappropriate ways, can be said to be in breach of that initial form of consent. New decisions to act in inappropriate ways are not manifestations of consent, but are instead, breaches of it.

Separate consideration might need to be given to powers over the parties, and powers over others. The parties have directly consented to arbitration and have directly or indirectly contracted the arbitrator. Power over party representatives or other third parties who may seek to impact negatively on the case are in a different category. Arbitral powers over such persons must somehow be traced back to basic consent, the bedrock for the tribunal's jurisdiction. If the parties selected a Seat that expressly afforded such powers, that would suffice, although even then, there might be territorial applicability questions as to the right of the laws of a Seat to impact upon counsel from other jurisdictions.

While some still debate the right of a tribunal to control counsel absent some express authority to do so, the better view is to the contrary for the following reasons: There is a broad discretion to control procedure. This is coupled with the sensible presumption that parties who have agreed to arbitration should be presumed to have done so *ab initio* in good faith. The entitlement to counsel or third-party funding or similar third-party involvement, solely arises from the obligation on the tribunal to afford each party a reasonable opportunity to present it's case. Taken together, these should all allow robust arbitrators to conclude that they have such control power over others by reason of their control over the parties.

If that is so, the key is not whether a power exists, but when it may reasonably be exercised. When would purported exercise of such powers offend against the fundamental norms of equal treatment, fairness and a reasonable opportunity to present a case? The 'elephant' tends to relate to challenges under such norms, rather than challenges to the presence of the power in the first place, although the true 'guerrilla/gorilla' would be happy to take any challenge tenably open to it!

Some rules seek to give greater comfort to arbitrators in this context. Such initiatives are not aimed solely or even primarily at guerrilla tactics, although they would purport to embrace such actions. Some have attempted to develop draft standards for counsel. An example is the new LCIA Rules 2014, which expressly mention the right to control legal representatives. A study group of the International Law Association (ILA) on the practice and procedure of international courts and tribunals has also produced the ILA Hague Principles on Ethical Standards for Counsel Appearing Before International Courts and Tribunals. These apply only to arbitrations where a State is a party.[3] A draft code of conduct for Swiss arbitration was postulated some time ago.[4] Another recent development has been the IBA Guidelines on Party Representatives.

While some seek to argue in favour of such detailed written articulation of principles to deal with such guerrilla problems and ethics more generally, most experienced and capable arbitrators understand that such guidelines cannot easily force or allow them to do things that they otherwise were unwilling or unable to do. The first problem with such guidelines is their applicability. Unless the parties expressly agree to be bound by them, they can at most be a guide and then only where their principles otherwise appeal as appropriate objectives of a tribunal's discretionary powers. Even when agreed, such principles must be considered within the context of mandatory due process norms of arbitration, i.e., the elephant can never be banished by express norms alone.

Secondly, such guidelines or rules will tend towards generality, in part because of the difficulty of defining the parameters of ethical behaviour, and secondly, because different legal families take quite different approaches to such matters. Such rules or guidelines will then often tend to raise as many questions as they purport to answer.

Using the IBA Guidelines on Party Representatives as an example, these have sufficient ambiguity to again demand that our ideal arbitrator must exercise good judgment and be undeterred by the challenges that can be based on the wording of the Guidelines themselves. For example, the overriding principle in the Preamble speaks of honesty and the proscription of activities 'designed' to produce unnecessary delay or expense. Reference to intent raises problems of evidence, standard and burden of proof which are all unanswered in the Guidelines. The very applicability of the Guidelines is left open and the Preamble notes the need to integrate these with mandatory laws, professional or disciplinary rules, agreed arbitration rules and other agreements of the parties. Coverage of persons is also unclear. The definition of party representative includes employees of the party, but only those 'who appear in an arbitration on behalf of a Party and make submissions, arguments or representations to the arbitral tribunal on behalf of such Party ...'. There is a grey area covering employee's with various

---

3. http://www.ila-hq.org/en/study-groups/index.cfm/cid/1012.
4. Dessemontet, Draft Code of Conduct for Arbitration Proceedings, paper given at the Study Day of the Swiss Arbitration Association (Berne, 21 Sep. 2007).

degrees of control, consultancy, behind the scenes advice and direct in-house counsel behaviour, not clearly delineated in the above definition.

The Guidelines also purport to invite consideration of possible sanctions, but note carefully that the Guidelines do not purport to indicate what powers tribunals actually have in this regard. A serious drafting generality is the definition of 'misconduct,' which naturally covers matters outlined in the guidelines, but also extends to any other matter considered so by the tribunal. This very open-ended definition leaves scope for fundamentally different views about the nature and circumstances of misconduct. Finally, rules in relation to party representatives do not readily apply to the parties themselves who can often be the key promoters of unreasonable behaviour.

The LCIA Rules 2014 are even further limited to *legal* representatives. The Rules direct each party to ensure that its legal representatives have agreed to comply with the general guidelines as a condition of appearance. This makes appearance rights conditional on promised behaviour. Less clear is whether one could bar counsel from appearing who does not comply with these obligations. Remedial measures in the LCIA Rules are more circumspect and again no indication is given on questions such as standard of proof, what a reasonable opportunity to answer a complaint entails, and whether cross-examination and document production would be allowed.

Furthermore, even in cases where express provisions govern the behaviour of parties and counsel, and where the principles are relatively clear, these will still provide little concrete guidance on specific factual situations. Attention will always need to be given to broad principles of fairness and efficiency, both because these underpin the *magna carta* of arbitration and also, because the many permutations of factual behaviour that might be subject to express supervisory powers, still have to be considered in that context.

In the first instance, it will usually be important to distinguish between inappropriate but well-meaning attempts to bring domestic cultural predilections before unsympathetic international arbitrators and what instead are truly guerrilla tactics aiming to destabilise an arbitration. For example, a respondent might continually seek extensions. That might be done to disrupt and delay or might be for justifiable reasons beyond its control. The respondent might also have selected a lawyer with insufficient experience in arbitration. The respondent might come from a developing country, have little money and be opposed by a multinational corporation with high-class multinational counsel. Hence, our paradigm arbitrator cannot expect simple solutions from arbitral rules or IBA guidelines. Sense and sensibility must always prevail.

The balance of the chapter looks at some particular aspects of this inevitable requirement of an ideal arbitrator.

Examples at the margin of events that are difficult to classify as either zeal or guerrilla tactics, would be common lawyers who seek to engage in excessive and rude cross-examination and who employ continual objections on technical points of evidence. In one's domestic toolkit, that may be highly effective before domestic courts, but before differently disposed international arbitrators, this is simply bad practice. The ideal arbitrator will not take offence, but should simply educate counsel as to what the arbitrator is really concerned to see and hear, in order to afford the relevant party a meaningful opportunity to fully present its case. A misguided counsel is not engaging in guerrilla tactics. A properly warned one that continues to waste time on submissions that will not bear upon the outcome, can more readily be seen as being unduly and perhaps intentionally disruptive.

If the essence is to consider the proper contours of the 'elephant' and the proper responses to guerrilla behaviour, one must also think further about the nature of equality, and fairness and what it means to afford each party a reasonable opportunity to present it's case.

Where equality is concerned, it can first be observed that identical treatment does not mean equality, but that is usually what gorillas demand. Concern for broad casuistic arguments based on the notion of equality, almost certainly prompted the revision of the ICC Rules to replace the concept of 'equality' with a duty to act 'fairly.'[5] True equality or fair treatment in a range of circumstances might thus lead to differing approaches to cross-examination, document production, time-allocation and tribunal questioning.

Where a reasonable opportunity to present one's case is concerned, here again the key word is that of 'opportunity.' As long as the arbitrator manages the process fairly and reasonably, gives parties an opportunity to agree on procedure and in the absence of agreement, allows them to make meaningful and regular suggestions to the tribunal, and as long as timelines are adequate for the purposes of adequate preparation and presentation, the arbitrator can, for example, reject extension applications that are made without just cause, in the knowledge that annulment and enforcement courts should be supportive of such determinations.

A reasonable opportunity should also be limited to an opportunity taken in a timely manner. If counsel has not raised a point at the earliest opportunity, it will often be reasonable to exclude it later on. That should even be so where counsel expressly reserves the right to raise a point at a later stage, unless the tribunal expressly concurred with that option.[6]

It can also be said that the duties on the parties themselves can be considered alongside the rights and duties of the arbitrator, in supporting the above analysis. If one can again presume that parties who have agreed to arbitrate are deemed to have done so in good faith, we can then accept that there are subsidiary duties of diligence, timeliness and co-operation. Some guerrilla tactics may then be said to offend the particular party's own agreement to arbitrate.

Capable arbitrators would also be aware that some approaches that they would wish to adopt as best practice in less adversarial cases, might in fact increase the opportunity for problematic behaviour. A key example is the desirability of inviting parties to seek to agree as much as possible with the arbitral processes to be employed. Commercially minded arbitrators will tend to educate the parties about this prospect and invite agreement on a whole range of matters. This has become ever more important as institutional rules begin to demand efficiency and even proportionality in the way cases are managed by tribunals. The difficulty here is that the more that opportunities are given to parties to agree, the more the 'gorilla' has opportunity to

---

5. ICC Rules 2012, Art. 21.4.
6. *See* for example Walker J in *Jiviaj v. Hashwani* [2015] EWHC 998 (Comm), [2015] All ER 169.

disagree. Once there is no agreement, the tribunal must then make a ruling. If the tribunal then proposes a process contrary to the wishes of the gorilla, the latter can again allude to the 'elephant.'

If the guerrilla tactic is simply non-involvement, all our ideal arbitrator needs to do is to ensure that proper notice has been given and not allow for arguments at later stages as to whether mail or email has been received.

Another form of guerrilla tactics is to try and employ the courts to interfere with the arbitral process. Here we find that most well constructed *lex arbitri* provide sufficient support for our ideal arbitrator. Provisions such as Article 8 of the UNCITRAL Model Law, place limits on a court's ability to interfere with arbitration agreements. The New York Convention is also about recognition of arbitration agreements as well as recognition and enforcement of awards. Recognition of the agreement asks courts to limit their interference. While there is still much uncertainty as to the degree to which courts will interfere, by what applicable law they will determine the validity of an arbitration agreement and what standard of proof they will employ before sending a case away to arbitration, this should not trouble our arbitrator, as nearly all such *lex arbitri* allow the tribunal to continue with the arbitration in the meantime.

Less clear is whether a tribunal should consider anti-suit injunctions generally or whether a tribunal has the power to utilise such measures against court-based guerrilla tactics. Given the lack of limits on the tribunal's own power to continue, it is not thought that such actions are necessary or desirable, even if available. Use of interim measures against the offensive conduct, runs the risk of going beyond the purpose of interim measures powers, or runs the risk of it at least being said to improperly prevent a party's right to present its case.

Often, guerrilla tactics will occur at the hearing itself. This might arise through rudeness, excessive cross-examination, excessive applications and the like. Here again our ideal arbitrator simply needs to 'walk straight', be 'undaunted' and keep the arbitral eye on the guerrilla and not on one's feet, and not on a distracting search for the elephant. Here again there can be no simple rules, but instead polite direction and if necessary firmness, after a reasonable opportunity has been presented. The ideal arbitrator will not only look to see how behaviour would be perceived visually, but also how it might read in a transcript on some later annulment or enforcement application. It will always be a question of judgment and will often call for graded interventionwhen there is rudeness, excessive cross-examination, excessive applications, debates about the meaning of translated evidence, arguments about Chess-clock calculation and the like.

While the above suggests that common sense is the ideal, some would argue that inappropriate behaviour cannot be adequately prevented or responded to, without some meaningful and enforceable sanction powers. Where guerrilla tactics are concerned, that is unlikely to be the case, and in any event, could not be employed absent consideration of the elephant. Here the difficulty is that the mere mention of such potential remedial responses could be asserted to be a threat, which in turn can lead to further baiting by a gorilla. Even tribunals empowered to apply the IBA Guidelines on Party Representatives, may feel loath to seek to exercise sanction powers if in the middle of a case.

A further serious challenge is as to the evidentiary standard that the arbitrator would use when considering express or implied allegations of dishonesty. These might arise through direct allegations of fraudulent misrepresentation, or the suspicion by the arbitrator that counsel or a party are lying when they claim external circumstances beyond their control justifying extensions. In such circumstances, there is not even a global view as to the proper standard of proof in such circumstances. It would be problematic to explore hypotheses from an evidentiary basis mid hearing. Most would at least see the need for an adequate evidentiary basis before such serious adverse conclusions could be drawn. In extreme circumstances, an arbitrator may feel the need to resign.

It is also often improper to draw adverse inferences from such behaviour, unless one can conclude that the only logical corollary of the behaviour, is that information adverse to that party is somehow being withheld or misrepresented. Adverse inferences should never be employed as a punishment for guerrilla tactics if it means treating material evidence as less weighty than it otherwise should be.

Costs sanctions are also unlikely to be effective and will be even less so if not applied at the moment in time when the guerrilla tactic is employed. Yet to do so at that stage, again risks threats of prejudgment, bias and interfering with a party's full opportunity to present its case.

Costs against a party based on the activities of its counsel, can also be problematic if it is not sufficiently clear that counsel was acting on the client's instructions. If such a conclusion is not appropriate on the facts before the tribunal, there is no disincentive to counsel and an innocent party is being punished. Yet to apply the sanction to counsel, requires sufficient evidence that counsel was acting independently. A tribunal can hardly cross-examine the party mid hearing to determine whether that is so.

Another difficulty in using costs discretions to deal with guerrilla tactics is that it undermines or is undermined by loser pays principles where they would otherwise apply. If a guerrilla respondent is simply delaying an inevitable finding against it under a loser pays model, then it will be paying costs in any event. Applying costs against it for numerous extension applications, adds little disincentive. Conversely, if guerrilla tactics were employed by the successful party, adverse costs orders undermine its success, although that can well be justified on policy bases.

Hence, our ideal arbitrator has no safe haven in remedial powers themselves, absent common sense and good judgment. Timely warnings as to how procedures will be conducted and the implications of deadlines is the best way to forestall effective guerrilla tactics and show that a true and robust opportunity has been afforded.

The above analysis has considered the potential for guerrilla tactics by a party or its counsel. A less prevalent but not unheard of phenomenon, is guerrilla tactics by a party-appointed arbitrator. Here, our ideal arbitrator would typically be Chair and can simply handle this by ensuring sufficient opportunities for deliberation and be willing to politely bring these to an end when it is clear that there is no possibility of the minority person shifting the views of the majority and there is no justifiable basis for that person to argue that they have not been sufficiently well heard.

§36.02 CONCLUSION

Even if it can be said with some confidence, that guerrilla tactics are increasing or are at least at a significant level, undue reliance on some rule formulation would be misguided. Broad concepts of fairness, efficiency, equality and opportunity, must be considered on a case-by-case basis. If these questions are being dealt with by an arbitrator facing a party or its counsel who is determined to undermine the process, the arbitrator's actions, both in terms of process, demeanour and determinations, must attempt to the utmost, to dissuade such behaviour, deny applications where they should be denied, and still maximise enforceability of the ultimate award.

In a festschrift for Michael Schneider, Pierre presented a chapter entitled 'Diffusing Unusual Incidents Before They Grow Unmanageable.' In elegant fashion, he identified a number of circumstances where challenges might arise. In only some cases, was an indication given as to what the impeccable arbitrator did in such scenarios. In all cases, the immediate response was not to see the events as 'dramatic and dangerous.' Most could 'be solved on the spot with a touch of humour, rather than drama and outwitting the parties or one of them.' Often the approach was to call for a break, ask the pertinent question, make an elegant side comment and where necessary, be prepared to consciously depart from rules that might otherwise be seen as fundamental, but only where that was necessary to ensure that the problem did not grow to one that would derail the arbitral process.

An ideal arbitrator can only effectively do so to by walking straight, not looking at their own feet and not being intimidated. While they should not look at their own feet in doing so, following the footsteps of Pierre Karrer would be an entirely different and sensible strategy.

CHAPTER 37
Procedural Order No. 1: From Swiss Watch to Arbitrators' Toolkit

Janet Walker & Doug Jones, AO

§37.01 INTRODUCTION

In designing a process to fit the arbitration, timing is everything. Only as details of the dispute emerge do relevant options for the process become clear. However, as the parties' cases take shape, so too do the implications of the procedural options come into sharp relief. This can complicate efforts to obtain agreement on the process. Procedural Order No. 1 usually follows soon after the formation of the tribunal. This has come to be regarded as the best time to consider the options for the procedure and to chart the course for the arbitration. This essay revisits the emphasis on Procedural Order No. 1 and suggests other points during the arbitration when the procedure might be established.

We are pleased to join in paying tribute to Pierre Karrer and his reputation for promoting a managerial and pragmatic role for arbitrators. We hope to contribute to the debate over best practices in designing an efficient arbitral process and to add our voices to those who would dispel the perception that leading Swiss arbitrators are prone to presenting the parties with a fully formed process in 'Procedural Order No. 1'. We hope to foster the continuing spirit of innovation, which our good friend Pierre would agree is among the core roles, powers and duties of Arbitrators.

§37.02 SETTLING THE PROCEDURE BEFORE THE ARBITRATION BEGINS

The range of procedural options available to arbitrators has generated a tension between the *push* to standardise the process in accordance with current trends and the *pull* to customise a bespoke process for the instant case. Those familiar with current trends may overlook opportunities to customise the procedure or misjudge the right moment to make procedural choices.

Sometimes enthusiastic commercial lawyers are unable to resist settling aspects of the procedure in the arbitration agreement. Out of bad experience or lack of experience, they seize the opportunity to specify features of the procedure only to find later that the specifications are unsuitable for the dispute that actually emerges. By carving these features into the stone of the arbitration agreement, they make it difficult to make adjustments without compromising the finality of the award. By transforming what seems likely to be a desirable feature into a mandatory requirement, they create the risk that the award will be set aside or challenged on enforcement as 'not in accordance with the agreement of the parties'.[1] Three common examples illustrate the importance of waiting until the time is right to settle the procedure of the arbitration.

First, parties hope to maintain a conciliatory approach for as long as possible when a difference emerges. They may provide for one or more non-binding forms of dispute resolution before an arbitration may be commenced. Contracting for negotiation or for mediation as preliminary stages may encourage parties to find ways to avoid more costly and adversarial forms of dispute resolution. However, lack of clarity on the triggering event for the arbitration stage can frustrate an aggrieved party's right to seek an arbitrated resolution.[2] Secondly, the freedom to select a tribunal with specialised knowledge and experience suitable for the disputes likely to arise is an attractive feature of arbitration. However, including these attributes in the clause can restrict the pool of arbitrators qualified to serve when the time comes to select them.[3] Thirdly, the benefits of securing a prompt result are obvious. However, including time limits in the arbitration clause for concluding the arbitration can risk depriving a tribunal of jurisdiction before it has achieved that result. Drafting a clause that creates this risk can provoke dilatory tactics that could bring it about.[4]

These examples show the wisdom of leaving much of the procedure until after the arbitration agreement has been deployed, and they offer one reason why Procedural Order No. 1 has achieved its well-deserved status as the focal point for settling much of the arbitral procedure.

§37.03 SETTLING THE PROCEDURE AT THE COMMENCEMENT OF THE ARBITRATION

The importance placed on the first Case Management Conference and on Procedural Order No. 1 for establishing the procedure for the arbitration has significant, if not overwhelming support of the leading arbitral institutions. This can be seen in the Swiss

---

1. Convention on the Recognition and Enforcement of Foreign Arbitral Awards (New York, 1958), Art. V(1)(d).
2. Christopher Boog, 'How to Deal with Multi-tiered Dispute Resolution Clauses: Note on the Swiss Federal Supreme Court's Decision 4A_18/2007 of 6 June 2007', (2008) ASA Bulletin 103.
3. Nigel Blackaby and Constantine Partasides QC, et al., *Redfern and Hunter on International Arbitration.* 6 ed., 234.
4. Richard Kreindler and Timothy Kautz, 'Agreed Deadlines and the Setting Aside of Arbitral Awards' (1997) ASA Bulletin 576.

Rules, the London Court of International Arbitration (LCIA) Rules and the ICC Commission Report on Techniques for Controlling Time and Costs in Arbitration.

Under the 2012 version of the Swiss Rules of International Arbitration, the tribunal is given broad discretion to conduct the arbitration in such manner as it considers appropriate, and it may hold hearings for the presentation of evidence or for oral argument at any stage of the proceedings. However, the Rules provide that '[a]t an early stage of the arbitral proceedings, and in consultation with the parties, the arbitral tribunal shall prepare a provisional timetable for the arbitral proceedings, which shall be provided to the parties and, for information, to the Secretariat.'[5] The mandatory requirement of a provisional timetable at an early stage implies the fixing of key features of the process, and contrasts with what is otherwise contemplated as a very flexible process.

The 2014 version of the LCIA Rules provide that 'the parties and the Arbitral Tribunal are encouraged to make contact (whether by a hearing in person, telephone conference-call, video conference or exchange of correspondence) as soon as practicable but no later than twenty-one days from receipt of the Registrar's written notification of the formation of the Arbitral Tribunal.' The Rules then encourage the parties to agree on joint proposals for the conduct of the arbitration in consultation with the tribunal.[6] Again, the procedure for the arbitration is expected to be established early on.

The 2015 version of the ICC Commission Report on Techniques for Controlling Time and Costs in Arbitration includes a range of recommendations for means to increase the efficiency and reduce the expense of arbitration. Among these, the Commission notes the requirement of the Rules to convene a case management conference when drawing up the Terms of Reference and in describing the scope of the Case Management Conference suggests that '[w]henever possible, the procedure for the entire arbitration should be determined at the first case management conference and reflected in the procedural timetable to be established pursuant to Article 24(2) of the Rules.'[7] This is perhaps the clearest example of emphasis on Procedural Order No. 1.

Thus, the received wisdom is that the first Case Management Conference is *the* occasion on which the procedure of the arbitration should be fixed; and Procedural Order No. 1, as a product of that meeting, should comprise a complete procedural framework for the dispute. Much like a finely crafted Swiss watch, the procedure is expected to be set in motion and left to run through the rest of the arbitration.

Before considering other views on the right time to settle the procedure, it is worth mentioning some of the things that can and should be settled early on – at the

---

5. Swiss Chambers' Arbitration Institution, *The Swiss Chambers of Commerce Association for Arbitration and Mediation Swiss Rules of International Arbitration (Swiss Rules)* (Swiss Chambers' Arbitration Institution; 2012), Art. 15, available at https://www.swissarbitration.org/files/33/Swiss-Rules/SRIA_english_2012.pdf.
6. London Court of International Arbitration, *LCIA Arbitration Rules* (London: LCIA, 2014), Art. 14, available at http://www.lcia.org/Dispute_Resolution_Services/lcia-arbitration-rules-2014.aspx.
7. International Chamber of Commerce, *ICC Commission Report: Controlling Time and Costs in Arbitration* (Paris, 2012, International Chamber of Commerce), 10.

time of the first Case Management Conference. Perhaps the most important of these is the overall length of the process. This is usually done by scheduling the main evidentiary hearing. In ICC procedure, in which the parties and the tribunal formally execute Terms of Reference, the Procedural Timetable, which is to be appended to the Terms of Reference is considered a separate document that can be revised without the need for formal agreement of all the counterparties to the Terms of Reference. This underscores the delicate balance between flexibility and certainty in the timetable. Nevertheless, the logistical challenges of rescheduling main evidentiary hearings, and even interim hearings, is sufficient to ensure the participants' commitment to securing and maintaining this aspect of the procedure and, in doing so, to create a temporal framework for many of the other procedural choices that must be made.

Beyond the question of the length of the arbitration, there are a number of administrative features, large and small, that can and should be established at this time. These can include: identifying the parties' representatives and specifying the basis on which they can be changed; and specifying means of communication and the format for documents in hard copy and electronic form, communications protocols, and the like. And beyond this, there is the need to establish a process for exchanges of case by the parties, and to deal, at least in principle, with the possibility of disclosure and expert evidence.

§37.04 RECENT INNOVATIONS IN THE ARBITRATORS' 'TOOLKIT'

Despite the historic emphasis on the period at the commencement of the arbitration (and the issues that can usefully be decided at that time), there are now respected sources that recommend procedures that may be adopted at various stages of the process and not merely at the time of Procedural Order No. 1. The 2012 UNCITRAL Working Group Revisions on Notes on Organizing Arbitral Proceedings and the ICCA Drafting Sourcebook for Logistical Matters in Procedural Orders are two such sources.

The Notes on Organizing Arbitral Proceedings are flexible in the recommendations they make for the process of organising arbitral proceedings. The Notes suggest that the consultations over procedure 'can be held in one or more meetings' although they note that 'a special meeting may be devoted exclusively to such procedural consultations' and may be called a '"preliminary meeting", "pre-hearing conference", "preparatory conference", "pre-hearing review" … *depend(ing) on the stage of the proceedings at which the meeting is taking place*.'[8] (emphasis added) The ICCA Drafting Sourcebook, contains the 'ICCA Checklist: First Procedural Order' which is described as 'a checklist of issues to consider including in a first procedural order in arbitration' advises that 'it may not be appropriate to include all of the issues… [listed]: *some may be better dealt with later*, or not at all.'[9] (emphasis added)

---

8. United Nations Commission On International Trade Law, *UNCITRAL Notes on Organizing Arbitral Proceedings* (New York, United Nations, 2012), 2–3.
9. The ICCA Reports No. 2; ICCA Drafting Sourcebook For Logistical Matters in Procedural Orders, available at http://www.arbitration-icca.org/publications/ICCA_Sourcebook.html.

Chapter 37: Procedural Order No. 1 §37.05[A]

Initiatives such as these emphasise the value of ensuring that the parties and the arbitrators maintain a well-equipped 'toolbox' to design processes that will most effectively bring to conclusion their dispute. The concept of a toolbox enlivens the discussion of which tools should be used at various stages of the dispute and whether or not the process should be wholly constructed at the commencement of the arbitration.

§37.05 ISSUES BEST LEFT UNTIL LATER IN THE ARBITRATION

The challenge faced as the arbitration progresses has previously been understood as one of fine-tuning Procedural Order No. 1. Increasingly, though, it is recognized that the Tribunal's and the parties' understanding of the dispute and how best to resolve it emerges later. Even the best efforts to design a satisfactory procedure at the first procedural meeting will fail to take account of the developing character of the dispute in a number of important ways. Procedural issues that are relevant to the ongoing design of the arbitral process and that need proactive case management as the case develops may include:

(1) The extent of and disputes concerning disclosure – the '#$%&*!' Redfern schedule;
(2) The factual evidence actually needed to decide the issues in dispute;
(3) Expert evidence- nature, extent and manner of development;
(4) The detail of the evidentiary hearing; and
(5) Value or otherwise of written openings; 'educating' the Tribunal.

These are procedures that can best be designed once a more detailed knowledge of the real issues in dispute emerges from the parties' exchange of their cases. They demonstrate the value that can be added by proactive case management between the parties and the tribunal as the case progresses.

[A] The Extent of Disclosure and Disputes Concerning Disclosure: The '@#$%&' Redfern Schedule

Standard procedural orders normally provide for the deployment of the IBA Rules of Evidence with requests for disclosure (if allowed) being made on the basis of the criteria set out in these rules and with disputes about production being ruled upon by tribunals presented with Redfern schedules.[10] The difficulty with this process is that there is rarely an opportunity for the tribunal to engage with the parties on these issues other than on the basis of the summarised material found in the Redfern Schedule. In the absence of an unusually active correspondence between the parties and the

---

10. International Bar Association, *IBA Rules on the Taking of Evidence in International Arbitration* (London: International Bar Association, 2010), Art. 3, Documents, 7–10.

tribunal over interim issues in the arbitration, the tribunal will know little more about the dispute than that provided in the parties' respective statements of case.

Under these circumstances, it may be difficult for the tribunal to make rulings on contested disclosure requests on the basis of its rudimentary understanding of the relevance and materiality of the material sought. There can and should be ways devised for a more detailed but nevertheless efficient engagement between the parties and the tribunal on what is actually needed and why, together with the application at the point of decision of principles of proportionality and cost. For example, a brief procedural hearing may be an efficient means to settle these issues.

It may not be possible for the parties and the Tribunal to anticipate at the outset of the arbitration the nature of the disclosure issues that might arise and how best to resolve them, and thus it may be wise to make allowance in Procedural Order No. 1 for the possibility of revisiting the process should disclosure issues emerge.

[B] The Factual Evidence Actually Needed to Decide the Issues in Dispute

After an initial exchange of the parties' cases in which they present the documentary and witness evidence relied upon, it may be possible to identify what is really in issue between them and to narrow the witness evidence needed to resolve the issues. It may be the case that certain evidence will have ceased to be necessary once the issues are joined.

This provides the opportunity for a further, more detailed exchange between the parties and the tribunal on each party's case. This may also serve as an opportunity for the tribunal to indicate to the parties, without prejudging the case, some areas and issues that seem to it to require particular attention in the presentation of evidence. This could be described as a second case management conference.

Opportunities at this point could include: limiting by agreement the further evidence required; identifying preliminary issues that can be ventilated on the way to a full hearing, and that might provide the opportunity to limit what needs to be addressed at a full evidentiary hearing; and resolving the detail of what might be the subject of expert evidence.

[C] Expert Evidence: Nature, Extent and Manner of Development

The cost of deploying expert evidence is significant in many arbitrations. Many expert witnesses command higher fees than the legal representatives of the parties. The capacity of tribunals to deal with the competing views of experts of like discipline may be challenged where the experts have been asked different questions, or have been given access to different materials, or have based their opinions on different witness evidence.

The adversarial nature of arbitration may drive counsel to press experts to take positions that ultimately prove untenable. This can occur when an expert is instructed to opine on the case that counsel hopes will emerge at the hearing, even where that is no more than wishful thinking.

Effective management of expert evidence is a 'hands on' process from the start. Tribunals and parties need to determine the matters on which experts of like discipline will opine. They can then devise ways in which these experts can identify, before expressing views that can be exposed to the tribunal, those aspects of their areas of expertise upon which they can agree, and only after doing that, explain the reasons for their areas of disagreement. Ideally, the experts can be encouraged to prepare a joint report of points on which they agree and then prepare their individual reports on the points on which they differ, rather than beginning by crystallising divergent views, based on different facts, only to be asked afterwards whether there might be some common ground. Since this occurs before the evidentiary hearing and before there has been a determination of the facts on which their evidence is based, it may also be helpful to have their respective views on the various factual scenarios that might emerge at the main hearing. Thus, this management process involves the tribunal ensuring that the experts are working from the same material and that the differences in their opinions, when dependent on witness testimony, are clearly linked to the testimony on which they are based and explain how their respective opinions might vary if other, competing, witness testimony is ultimately accepted by the tribunal.

None of this can safely be prescribed in Procedural Order No. 1, except in outline. This needs to be acknowledged, and subsequent, often regular, case management by the tribunal, foreshadowed.

[D]   The Detail of the Evidentiary Hearing

As mentioned earlier, it is not merely possible but essential for the timing of the evidentiary hearings to be set in Procedural Order No. 1. There are however a number of variables that can satisfactorily be settled only as the hearing approaches.

It is common practice for pre-hearing case management conferences to be held some weeks or a month before the evidentiary hearing. Indeed, Procedural Orders No. 1 typically provide for, a pre-hearing case management conference and often set the date for it. One difficulty that can arise, though, is that pre-hearing case management conferences turn out to have been set far too close to the evidentiary hearing to enable the sound management of issues critical to an effective evidentiary hearing. Examples of such issues, which, if left too late, may fail to be dealt with satisfactorily are:

- the electronic and hard copy format of hearing bundles;
- the preparation of agreed chronologies and *dramatis personae;*
- decisions on which witnesses need not to be called for cross examination;
- the manner of interpretation and the identity of the interpreters; and
- the real issues in dispute upon which decisions are required by the tribunal.

It is suggested that earlier pre-hearing conferences than are usually provided for in Procedural Order No. 1 may improve the cost effectiveness and efficiency of evidentiary hearings. Thus, flexibility for much earlier development of these matters needs to be preserved.

[E] Written Openings and the 'Education' of the Tribunal

The extent to which Tribunals commence an evidentiary hearing familiar with the detail of the material exchanged by the parties has been the subject of some debate. Some interesting suggestions have been made for ways that counsel can ensure that the tribunal is well prepared. A little time ago, Lucy Reed suggested that tribunals be paid to meet in advance of the hearing to hold in what came to be described as a 'Reed Retreat'.[11] More recently, Neil Kaplan has suggested that tribunals would benefit from a preliminary explanation by the parties of their cases before the commencement of an evidentiary hearing. This is described as a 'Kaplan Opening'.[12]

It may be troubling to think that counsel and parties should find it necessary to devise ways to educate a tribunal whose job it is to understand and test the cases put before them for determination. Still, there is often a need to assist even the most conscientious tribunals to understand well the parties' cases, prior to the evidentiary hearing, and, perhaps, to encourage less conscientious tribunals to be adequately prepared. Depending upon the way the parties' cases are developed, particularly if they have not followed a memorial process in which the statements of case are combined with the witness statements, there can also be a legitimate need for the pleadings and the subsequent factual and expert evidence to be woven together in a comprehensive way prior to the evidentiary hearing. This has given rise to the provision in many Procedural Orders No. 1 for written openings by parties to be provided to the tribunal before the evidentiary hearing.

It is suggested that the need for written openings, the preparation of which are time consuming and costly, will often depend upon the quality of the parties' exchanges of case, and may be unnecessary where the respective cases have been prepared in a memorial format. However, the need for written openings can only be assessed accurately after the exchanges of case and should sensibly be planned and provided for at this stage of the proceedings rather than in Procedural Order No. 1. For this reason, as well as those discussed above, it may be helpful to have intermediate case management conferences at which sensible further directions can be developed and at which the process of educating the tribunal can be conducted on an iterative basis.

Alternatives to Reed Retreats and Kaplan Openings could usefully include one or more case management conferences at which the key issues emerging from exchanges of parties' cases can be ventilated. In such case management conferences, all of the issues mentioned above, including identification of necessary factual witness evidence, the preparation of focused expert testimony, the identification of key issues that can usefully be the subject of ventilation and sometimes preliminary decision, and the

---

11. Lucy Reed, 'The Kaplan Lecture 2012 Arbitral Decision-making: Art, Science or Sport?'.
12. Neil Kaplan, 'If It Ain't Broke, Don't Change It' (2014) 80 Arbitration 172.

design of the evidentiary hearing, can all be dealt with in time to ensure that the procedural design of the arbitration process delivers an effective and efficient process suited to the particular dispute.

§37.06 CONCLUSION

Our thesis therefore is that Procedural Order No. 1 is but the first building block of an efficient arbitral process and that there should be recognised a need for ongoing case management and the generation thereafter of as many procedural orders as are required. These procedural orders, following as they do upon telephonic or in person hearings, should not be looked upon as responses to extraordinary and unforeseen developments, or merely opportunities to adjust Procedural Order No. 1. On the contrary, they should serve as regular occasions in which the arbitrators and the parties work together to ensure that the process that they develop serves them well. To be sure, continued engagement such as this with the tribunal requires a level of cooperation that rises above seizing the tactical advantages that might occur to counsel along the way. Achieving and sustaining this degree of cooperation may prove difficult in some arbitrations, but it is an objective well worth aiming to meet.

Reaching into the arbitrators' toolbox at regular intervals may seem a less elegant approach to the process than designing the entire arbitration at the outset. However, arbitrations rarely proceed like clockwork from the first procedural meeting onwards. Regular engagement between parties and the tribunal to address procedural issues and opportunities in a timely fashion as they emerge is a workmanlike way to develop a process that best serves the needs of the each dispute.

CHAPTER 38

The Arbitrator's Jurisdiction at Risk: The Case of Hybrid and Asymmetrical Arbitration Agreements

Jane Willems

§38.01 INTRODUCTION

The cornerstone of international commercial arbitration is party autonomy, a principle which embodies the parties' freedom to select the arbitration mechanism that best suit their needs (institutional or *ad-hoc* arbitration) at an elected seat, and empowers them to determine the substantive and procedural rules applicable for the determination of their dispute. This party autonomy principle, in its various formulations, is universally accepted by international instruments, case law and existing statutes and ensures that international commercial arbitration proceeds in accordance with the parties' intentions and desires.

However, it is practically a cliché to point out that dispute resolution clauses are often referred to as the 'midnight clause', the clause that is pushed to the very end of the agreement and considered, briefly, at the end of contract negotiations. This clause, to which no one pays attention to, can be badly drafted and full of defect, a so-called pathological clause. If not cured, this clause may be found unenforceable. At the other end of the spectrum, some dispute resolution clauses are drafted so carefully – perhaps too carefully – that their very enforceability raises some unexpected results. The enforceability of types of complex arbitration clauses, namely hybrid and asymmetrical arbitration agreements, when tested before arbitrators and in state court, shows the limits and the risks of the parties' possibilities in designing their dispute resolution mechanism.

§38.02 THE ARBITRATOR'S JURISDICTION AND HYBRID ARBITRATION AGREEMENTS

International arbitration is classically divided between 'institutional' and 'ad-hoc' arbitration.[1] Parties intending to settle their disputes by institutional arbitration may choose among the various institutions providing international arbitration services located around the world, and select the arbitration rules promulgated by these arbitration institutions.[2] These institutional arbitration rules govern the appointment of the arbitrator, conduct of the arbitral proceedings, and payment of the parties' arbitration costs. These arbitration institutions, and good practice principles,[3] direct and recommend arbitration users and drafters to refer to their model dispute resolution clauses, so as to avoid any mistakes in the drafting of the arbitration agreement which may render the clause 'pathological' and adversely affect its enforceability.

On the other hand, parties wishing to have recourse to *ad-hoc* arbitration need to agree directly on the rules which will conduct their *ad-hoc* arbitration proceedings, or alternatively, adopt existing sets of *ad-hoc* arbitration rules, such as the UNCITRAL arbitration rules.[4]

The practice of hybrid clauses, built on the principle of party autonomy, and coupled with the unlimited creativity of the parties when drafting their arbitration agreement, consists in the parties selecting among the various arbitration institutions and the available arbitration rules institutional or ad-hoc). The two types of alternative hybrid arbitration clauses provide for the parties' choice to have their chosen arbitration institution administer proceedings under: (i) the rules promulgated by another arbitration institution, or (ii) *ad-hoc* arbitration rules. When parties elect this route, they should recognize that once a dispute arises, any disagreements as to the meaning and the enforceability of these hybrid clauses often leads to lengthy proceedings concerning the validity of the arbitration agreement and of the award, before the arbitral tribunal or the courts.

---

1. 2010 IBA Guidelines for Drafting International Arbitration Clauses (IBA Guidelines), Guideline 1: 'The parties should decide between institutional and *ad hoc* arbitration.'
2. Such international arbitration institutions include the International Chamber of Commerce (ICC), the London Court of International Arbitration (LCIA), the Stockholm Chamber of Commerce (SCC), the China International Economic and Trade Arbitration Commission (CIETAC), the Hong Kong International Arbitration Centre (HKIAC), the Singapore International Arbitration Centre (SIAC), the International Centre for the Settlement of Investment Disputes (ICSID), etc. On institutional and *ad-hoc* arbitration, see, N. Blackaby, C. Partasides QC, A. Redfern and M. Hunter, *Redfern & Hunter on International Arbitration* 6th ed., paras 1.141–1.156; G. Born, *International Commercial Arbitration* (Second Edition), Kluwer Law International 2014, p. 205.
3. IBA Guidelines, Guideline 2: 'The parties should select a set of arbitration rules and use the model clause recommended for these arbitration rules as a starting point.'
4. For recommended *ad-hoc* arbitration clauses, see IBA Guidelines, para. 12; *The Freshfields Guide to Arbitration Clauses in International Contracts* (Third Edition), Paulsson, Rawding, et al. (ed) (2010), pp. 151–153.

[A] The Arbitrator's Jurisdiction and the Parties' Choice of an Institution to Administer Proceedings under Arbitration Rules Promulgated by Another Arbitration Institution

Particularly common hybrid clauses are when parties select an arbitral institution, 'X' to conduct the arbitration in accordance with the rules of institution 'Y': *'SIAC administered under ICC rules'*, *'SCC administered under ICC rules'* or *'CIETAC administered under ICC rules'*. Since 2012, the ICC has stated its reservation to other arbitration institutions administering cases under its institutional arbitration rules.[5] Notwithstanding, others international arbitration institutions, such as the SIAC and the Stockholm Chamber of Commerce (SCC), have enforced the parties' choice to administrate the proceedings under other arbitration institutions' rules.

In the seminal *Alstom v. Insigma* case,[6] the licence agreement granted by Alstom to Insigma (China) contained an arbitration clause that required the parties to submit their dispute to SIAC, but instructed SIAC and the arbitrators to apply ICC rules of arbitration. The arbitration clause provided that the dispute would be: *'... finally resolved by arbitration before the Singapore International Arbitration Centre in accordance with the Rules of Arbitration of the International Chamber of Commerce.'* This 'SIAC administered under ICC rules' clause gave rise to a multi-tier dispute at each stage of the arbitration proceedings. Alstom first filed its claim before the ICC Court and then withdrew it. After an agreement was reached between the parties, the case was filed with SIAC, who proceeded with the confirmation of the arbitrators appointed by the parties. Insigma then challenged the validity of the arbitration clause before the arbitral tribunal. SIAC then informed the arbitral tribunal that it was prepared to administer the arbitration in accordance with the ICC Rules and the SIAC Secretariat, Registrar, and Board of Directors of SIAC, respectively, would perform the functions assigned to the Secretary-General, Secretariat, and the ICC Court under the ICC Rules. With that framework in mind, the arbitral tribunal decided that it had jurisdiction to hear the dispute.

Insigma challenged the award before the Singapore courts. The Singapore High Court qualified this 'SIAC administered under ICC rules' arbitration clause as an *ad-hoc* arbitration clause, whereby SIAC merely 'administered the case' and confirmed its validity. The court further held that the fact that SIAC had performed the role set out in the ICC rules in confirming the party-appointed arbitrators was not significant in that no policy reasons would bar SIAC from agreeing to do so.

A recent decision rendered by a Swedish court in *Government of the Russian Federation v. I.M. Badprim, S.r.l.*[7] has confirmed this enforcement positive approach to

---

5. 2012 ICC Arbitration Rules, Art. 1(2): '... *The Court is the only body authorized to administer arbitrations under the Rules, including the scrutiny and approval of awards rendered in accordance with the Rules.*'
6. *Insigma Technology Co Ltd v. Alstom Technology Ltd* [2009] 1 SLR(R) 23.
7. Svea Court of Appeals, 23 Jan. 2015, T 2454-14, available at (http://www.arbitration.sccinstitute.com). In 2014 CIETAC reported a case involving a 'CIETAC administered ICC rules' clause, See 2014 *Annual Report of International Commercial Arbitration*, China Academy of Arbitration Law, p. 33.

hybrid clauses. In that dispute, the parties' agreement provided for a 'SCC administered under ICC Rules' arbitration clause. The SCC accepted the arbitration filing and the arbitrators proceeded to conduct the arbitration according to the ICC rules. The court subsequently rejected the challenge against the award and confirmed the validity of the hybrid arbitration clause.

More recently in *Top Gains Minerals Macao Commercial Offshore Ltd v. TL Resource Pte Ltd* (HCMP 1622/2015),[8] the High Court of Hong Kong was asked to examine, in the context of a request for interim measure, a 'SIAC administered under ICC rules' arbitration clause providing '... *If the dispute or matter cannot be settled by mutual accord between the Parties, such dispute or claim shall be referred to Singapore International Arbitration Center (SIAC) for arbitration in accordance with the Rules of Conciliation and Arbitration of the International Chamber of Commerce ...* ' The claimant had chosen to file its request for arbitration before the auspices of the ICC and not the SIAC. The High Court of Hong Kong decided not to intervene pending the determination by the ICC arbitral tribunal of its jurisdiction, and estimated that, should the tribunal find it has jurisdiction, it was still possible for the award to be recognized and enforced by the Hong Kong Court at the enforcement and recognition stage.[9]

The pro-validity approach to hybrid clauses adopted by courts located in arbitration-friendly jurisdictions is not accepted, however, in other jurisdictions where the enforcement of the same award may be sought under the 1958 New York Convention. In *Insigma*, when Alstom moved to enforce in the Mainland China the award it had obtained, Insigma objected on the ground that the arbitral tribunal had not been constituted in accordance with the parties' agreement. The Hangzhou Court accepted Insigma's objection and denied the enforcement of the award by holding that the confirmation of the arbitrators by the SIAC, and not by the ICC Court of International Arbitration, as required under the ICC Rules chosen by the parties, failed to comply with the parties' agreement.[10]

Since the institutional arbitration rules provide for the intervention of their own organs at various stages of the arbitration proceedings (in particular when the arbitrators are appointed arbitrators) that may not exist in the other institution selected by the parties to administer the dispute, the choice of hybrid arbitration clauses may create a deadlock, which absent an additional agreement of the parties, raise the risk that either the court of the seat, or the enforcing court, will apply a stricter standard and find that the enforcement of the arbitration clause did not comply with the parties' agreement.

---

8. *Top Gains Minerals Macao Commercial Offshore Tfd v. TL Resource Pte Ltd*, [2015] HKCFI 2101; HCMP 1622/2015 (18 Nov. 2015), para. 5, 12.
9. *Idem*, para. 44.
10. *Alstom Technology Ltd v. Insigma Technology Co Ltd*, Hangzhou Intermediate People's Court, Zhejiang, 6 Feb. 2013, [2011] She Hang Zhong Que Zi No. 7, translated in Albert Jan van den Berg and (eds), *Yearbook Commercial Arbitration* 2014, Vol. XXXIX, pp. 380–383, Kluwer Law International 2014.

[B] The Arbitrator's Jurisdiction and the Parties' Choice of an Institution to Administer the Arbitration under Ad-hoc Arbitration Rules

As set out above, *ad-hoc* arbitration clauses in international commercial arbitration, and in investor-State arbitration, often adopt published sets of *ad-hoc* arbitration rules. The parties may choose any arbitral institution to act as the 'appointing authority'. Absent a choice by the parties, published *ad-hoc* arbitration rules, such as the UNCITRAL arbitration rules, require institutions to fulfil the duties of the 'appointing authority' in the designation of the arbitral tribunal.

In addition to administrating proceedings under their own institutional rules, quite a few international arbitration institutions offer to administer *ad-hoc* cases by acting as the appointing authority and providing full or partial administrative assistance.[11] These administered services are regularly used in *ad-hoc* arbitration, in particular in investor-state arbitration. The parties may, therefore, request arbitral institutions to provide administrative services in support of their arbitration proceedings.

The difficulty with the use of an *ad-hoc* arbitration clause has arisen particularly in the international commercial arbitration practice in the Mainland China where *ad-hoc* arbitration agreements are de facto forbidden. In Mainland China, parties must choose an arbitration institution, failing which, the arbitration agreement is invalid.[12]

Chinese arbitration institutions have published and regularly update their institutional international arbitration rules and publish their model arbitration clauses.[13] Some of these Chinese institutional arbitration rules, however, allow the institution to administer cases under 'other arbitration rules'.[14] This is a pragmatic attempt to attract

---

11. The 2010 UNCITRAL arbitration rules have entrusted the Secretary-General of the Permanent Court of Arbitration (PCA) as the default appointing authority. The PCA indicates on its website it also *'provides full administrative support in arbitrations under the UNCITRAL Arbitration Rules'*. The LCIA indicates it acts as appointing authority as administrator in arbitrations conducted under the UNCITRAL arbitration rules. Some arbitration institutions such as the HKIAC and the Japan Commercial Arbitration Association have promulgated special procedures for the administration of UNCITRAL Rules. For a review on these *ad-hoc* arbitration administration services, *See, 69/90 Recommendations to assist arbitral institutions and other interested bodies with regards to arbitration under the UNCITRAL Arbitration Rules (as revised in 2010),* paras 18–26, United Nations UNCITRAL 2013.
12. Article 16 of the 1994 Chinese arbitration law provides that an arbitration agreement shall include the Arbitration Commission selected by the parties. Article 18 of the 1994 Chinese arbitration law provides that, absent such a choice, the arbitration agreement shall be invalid.
13. 2015 CIETAC Arbitration Rules, 2015 Beijing Arbitration Commission Arbitration Rules, 2015 Shanghai International Arbitration (SHIAC) Arbitration Rules.
14. 2015 CIETAC Arbitration Rules, Art. 4(3): *'Where the parties agree to refer their dispute to CIETAC for arbitration but ... have agreed on the application of other arbitration rules, the parties' agreement shall prevail unless such agreement is inoperative or in conflict with a mandatory provision of the law applicable to the arbitral proceedings. Where the parties have agreed on the application of other arbitration rules, CIETAC shall perform the relevant administrative duties.'* See also, 2014 China (Shanghai) Pilot Free Trade Zone arbitration rules promulgated by the Shanghai International Arbitration Centre (SHIAC), Art. 2(4): *'SHIAC shall perform the functions that should be performed by an arbitration institution referred to in other arbitration rules which are applicable upon parties' agreement.'* See also, the 2015 SHIAC arbitration rules, Art. 2(6).

more Sino-foreign cases to be arbitrated in Mainland China by offering the foreign parties a Chinese seated arbitration forum but administered under international arbitration rules, such as the ICC rules.

Furthermore, some Chinese institutional rules expressly state that the institution will provide administered services for arbitration under the UNCITRAL arbitration rules.[15] In the context of the current arbitration legal framework, the offer of administered services for *ad-hoc* arbitration under the UNCITRAL rules, notably in the new Shanghai Free Trade Zone, constitutes a welcome initiative and the first real attempt to open the Great Wall of excluding *ad-hoc* arbitration.[16]

Two instances confirm that while Chinese local courts have rejected the validity of *ad-hoc* clauses, they have affirmed the validity of 'administered' *ad-hoc* clauses. In the first case, Invista Technologies S.à.r.l. (Invista), a European technology licensor and Zhejiang Yisheng (Yisheng), a Chinese petrochemical company, had agreed in two technology licensing agreements to refer disputes to arbitration under a 'CIETAC administered UNCITRAL rules' clause: *'The arbitration shall take place at China International Economic Trade Arbitration Centre (CIETAC), Beijing, P.R. China and shall be settled according to the UNCITRAL Arbitration Rules as at present in force'*.

When a dispute arose, Invista commenced arbitration by submitting its claim to CIETAC in July 2012. Yisheng subsequently applied to Chinese state courts for a declaration that the arbitration clause was invalid. Following the instructions from the Chinese People's Supreme Court, the Ningbo court held the arbitration agreement was valid.[17] In its judgment dated 17 March 2014,[18] the court found that the terms *'shall take place at CIETAC'* meant that the parties had agreed CIETAC would administer the case under UNCITRAL Rules and therefore the arbitration agreement was valid under Chinese law.

Similarly, in a second instance, also involving a 'CIETAC administered *UNCITRAL Rules*' clause, which had been inserted in a construction contract entered into in 2009.[19] The arbitration clause provided:

---

15. The 2015 SHIAC Arbitration Rules, Art. 2(7) and the 2014 China (Shanghai) Pilot Free Trade Zone arbitration rules promulgated by the Shanghai International Arbitration Centre (SHIAC), Art. 2(5) provides that if the parties agree to adopt the UNCITRAL Rules, SHIAC will become the appointing authority *'and perform other administrative functions'* in accordance with the UNCITRAL Rules or the agreement of the parties.
16. *See*, Tao J. & C. von Wunschheim, 'Art. 16 and 18 of the PRC Arbitration Law: The Great Wall of China for Foreign Arbitration Institutions', 23 *Arb. Int.* 309, 311 (2007).
17. Under the pre-reporting system in China, where a lower court considers a foreign-related arbitration agreement is not enforceable, it must first report its findings to the higher court and if the higher court confirms the finding the Supreme People's court ultimately decides. See, Notice of the Supreme People's Court on Several Issues Regarding the Handling by the People's Courts of Certain Issues Pertaining to International Arbitration and Foreign Arbitration, issued by the Supreme People's Court on and effective from 28 Aug. 1995. For an analysis of the pre-reporting system, *See*, Kun Fan, 'Arbitration in China: Practice, Legal Obstacles and Reforms', 19(2) *ICC Int'l Court of Arb. Bull.* 1–16, at 9 (2008).
18. *Zhejiang Yisheng Petrochemical Co Ltd v. Invista Technologies Sarl*, Ningbo Intermediate People's court, 17 Mar. 2014, [2012] Zhe Yong Zhong Que Zi No. 4.
19. Shanghai 2nd Intermediate People's Court, 23 Jan. 2015, [2013] Hu Er Zhong Min Ren (zhongcai) No. 1, not published.

The parties agree to resolve all differences arising out of or relating to this AGREEMENT through binding arbitration before three arbitrators pursuant to the UNCITRAL Arbitration Rules. The place of arbitration shall be Shanghai, People's Republic of China and the language of the arbitration shall be English. The China International Economic and Trade Arbitration Commission, Shanghai Commission shall administer the arbitration, and also act as the appointing authority when the UNCITRAL Arbitration Rules call for an appointing authority to act... .

The terms of this clause are very similar to the draft model clause provided by UNCITRAL for parties who wish for an institution to 'fully administer' the arbitration under the UNCITRAL arbitration rules.[20] In this case, one party filed a request for arbitration before the Shanghai sub-commission of CIETAC, who accepted the case. The respondent to the arbitration proceedings challenged the validity of this clause before the Shanghai Court seeking a declaration that the clause is invalid under then 1994 Chinese arbitration law because it constituted an *ad-hoc* arbitration agreement. The Shanghai court rejected the challenge and held the clause was valid. The state court considered the phrases '*administer the arbitration*' and '*appointing authority*' taken together meant that the parties had empowered the Shanghai sub-commission of CIETAC with more than the function of administering services generally offered by other arbitration institutions in *ad-hoc* arbitrations. It further found that the Shanghai sub-commission of CIETAC was an arbitration institution able to thoroughly administer the present arbitration proceedings, and that neither the Chinese arbitration law nor the arbitration rules of the Shanghai sub-commission of CIETAC prevented parties from choosing the UNCITRAL arbitration rules. The Shanghai Court interpreted the consent of the parties in light of the object and purpose of the clause, concluded that the parties had indeed chosen an 'arbitration institution' as required by Article 16 of the 1994 Chinese arbitration law, and therefore the contemplated arbitration was not an *ad-hoc* arbitration.

These two decisions are a welcome boost to party autonomy in the Mainland China and contribute a way to limit the prohibition of *ad-hoc* arbitration clauses to 'non-administered' *ad-hoc* clauses.[21] Indeed, clearly neither of the two above cited clauses provide for an institutional arbitration. Instead, in these clauses, the parties had only selected an arbitral institution to administer an *ad-hoc* proceeding. Even if the institutional arbitration rules themselves, as it is the case for the SHIAC rules, contains

---

20. The model clause proposed by UNCITRAL, where the parties choose the institution to fully administer the arbitration under the UNCITRAL arbitration rules, reads: 'Any dispute, controversy or claim arising out of or relating to this contract, or the breach, termination or invalidity thereof, shall be settled by arbitration *in accordance with the UNCITRAL Arbitration Rules administered by [name of the institution]. [Name of the institution] shall act as appointing authority.*' (Emphasis added) *See*, 69/90 *Recommendations to assist arbitral institutions and other interested bodies with regards to arbitration under the UNCITRAL Arbitration Rules (as revised in 2010)*, para. 26, United Nations UNCITRAL 2013.
21. Chinese courts have repeatedly held that *ad-hoc* clauses – providing for instance 'arbitration in Beijing' – are invalid. For reported cases, *See*, Peng X., 'Validity of the Beijing Arbitration Clause', 28(1) *J. Int'l Arb.*, 15–20. For an analysis of the Chinese court practice of 'institutionalizing' these type of pure *ad-hoc* arbitration clauses in order to hold the parties had designated an 'arbitration commission', *See* J. Willems, *Les contrats de joint venture sino-étrangères devant l'arbitre international*, Larcier Ed. 2015, para. 111.

provisions for the administration of *ad-hoc* proceedings, the role of the arbitration institution is limited to the administration of the case and to the appointment of the arbitrators under *ad-hoc* arbitration rules chosen by the parties, and therefore the consent of the parties remains that for an *ad-hoc* arbitration.

§38.03 THE ARBITRATOR'S JURISDICTION AND ASYMMETRICAL ARBITRATION AGREEMENTS

Another aspect of the parties' freedom to design their dispute resolution clause is found in asymmetrical arbitration agreements. Indeed, arbitration agreements may be negotiated with the intent to bind the parties to a dispute resolution mechanism where they accept to postpone the identification of the forum before which the dispute will be heard until after the dispute has arisen. The dispute resolution clause contains an option whereby both parties (bilateral option clauses) or sometimes one party only (asymmetrical/unilateral option clauses), holds the option to bring the dispute between two or more jurisdictions. The option is most often between several arbitration alternatives or between litigation and arbitration.

[A] Optional Arbitration Agreements

The option is defined at common law as the right of election to exercise a privilege.[22] In the context of dispute resolution clauses, an option given to a party – the 'optionee' – empowers it to exercise a right to either litigate, or to arbitrate a dispute.[23] The optionee is granted the privilege to accept or reject the offer made by the other party. The optionee is not bound to the contract if it rejects the offer. Hence, until the optionee elects the arbitration or the litigation option, no contract is formed.[24] In *The Messiniaki Berger* where a bilateral option clause was inserted in the contract, Bingham J. held: '*The clause confers an option, which may be not exercised. … [U]ntil an election is made*

---

22. Black's Law Dictionary, Sixth Edition, p. 1094.
23. On asymmetrical arbitration agreements, see, D. Draguiev, 'Unilateral Jurisdiction Clauses: The Case for Invalidity, Severability or Enforceability', 31 *J. of Int. Arb.* 1, 19–25 (2014); S. Nesbitt, H. Quinlan, 'The Status and Operation of Unilateral or Optional Arbitration Clauses', 22(1) *Arb. Int'l.* 133–149; M. Scherer, 'A Cross-Channel Divide over Unilateral Dispute Resolution Clauses', *Jurisdictional Choices in Time of Trouble*, Dossiers ICC Institute of World Business Law, 2014, pp. 10–20; A. Scott Rau, 'Asymmetrical Arbitration Clauses', *Ibid.* pp. 21–55; C. Drahozal, 'Nonmutual Agreements to Arbitrate', 27 *J. Corp L.* 537 (2002); C. Nardinocchi, 'Asymmetrical Arbitration Clauses: A Risk for Pathology?', *Versailles Int' Arb. & Bus. L. Rev.* 109–131 (2014); D. Foster, 'Asymmetrical Arbitration Agreements: Are They Worth the Risk?', *The European, Middle East and African Review* 2014, *Global Arbitration Review* 2014; J. Barbet, P. Rosher, 'La validité des clauses optionnelles', 2010 *Rev. Arb.* 45–83.
24. HG Beale, ed, *Chitty on Contracts: General Principles*, vol. 1, 32nd ed (London, UK: Thomson Reuters, 2015) at 2–134. However, it is worth noting that in the context of landed property transactions, agreements containing an option become contracts at the time they are signed and not when the option is exercised, *See* Chitty, at 2-020.

there is no agreement to arbitrate, but once the election is made (and the option exercised) a binding arbitration agreement comes into existence.'[25]

Bilateral option clauses are routinely enforced by courts and allow either party to trigger the option upon crystallization of the dispute.[26] However, the exercise of asymmetrical dispute resolution clauses and arbitration clauses has given rise to abundant case law. Under English arbitration law, the validity of unilateral arbitration clauses is well settled and courts have held that the fact that one only party holds the option does not affect the validity of the arbitration agreement in itself, as there is no requirement for an arbitration agreement to be 'mutual'.[27]

Contemporary international investment agreements (International investment agreements (IIA), multilateral or bilateral investment treaties (BITs) grant the foreign investor a right of action against the host state. The dispute resolution clauses contained in these treaties offer the investor a unilateral option to choose before which forum to bring its investment dispute against the host state. The option includes the host states' domestic courts or international arbitration under the auspices of different arbitration institutions (ICSID, SCC, etc.)[28] The validity of these asymmetrical arbitration clauses is not disputed. Their practicability resides in the fact that the investor alone may initiate the dispute and act as claimant under the IIA, whereas the host state

---

25. *Westfal-Larsen & Co A/S v. Ikerigi Compania Naviers SA (The Messiniaki Bergen)* [1983] 1 All ER 382. Here, clause 40(b) of the contract in question provided that any dispute arising under the contract was to be decided by the English courts, provided that 'either party may elect to have the dispute referred to [arbitration]' Bingham J. found that clause 40(b) was not merely an agreement to make an agreement to arbitrate and once a valid election to arbitrate was made no further agreement was necessary or contemplated for the arbitration to take place.
26. See *Thermodyn v. M-Real Alizay*, French Supreme Court, Cass Civ. 1ère, 12 Jun. 2013, the cause provided: '*If the dispute is not settled ..., each party may choose to have recourse to arbitration or to a court action before the court of where the buyer has its seat. The dispute shall be submitted and finally by the arbitration rules of the London Court of International Arbitration (LCIA) which is integrated by reference into this Article ... [... Si le différend n'est pas réglé ..., chaque partie pourra choisir de recourir à l'arbitrage ou à une action devant la cour du lieu du siège de l'acheteur. Le différend devra être soumis et réglé de façon définitive par le règlement d'arbitrage de la London Court of International Arbitration (LCIA), qui est intégré dans cet Article par référence...].*' In this case, the Court held that the court had jurisdiction over the dispute since the litigation/arbitration option offered a faculty to both parties and the reference to the LCIA did not allow to reconsider the '*purely optional nature of the recourse to arbitration [... n'était pas de nature à remettre en cause le caractère purement optionnel du recours à l'arbitrage].*'
27. *Pittalis v. Sherefettin* [1986] QB 686, Fox L.J.: '*I can see no reason why, if an agreement between two persons confers to one of them alone the right to refer the matter to arbitration, the reference should not constitute an arbitration. There is a fully bilateral agreement which constitutes a contract to refer. The fact that the option is exercisable by one of the parties only seems to me to be irrelevant.*' See also, *The Stena Pacifica* [1990] 2 Lloyd's Law Reports p. 234; *Lobb Partnership Limited v. Aintree Racecourse Company Limited* [2000] 1 Building Law Reports 65.
28. North American Free Trade Agreement, U.S.-Can.-Mex., 17 Dec. 1992, Art. 1120: '*... a disputing investor may submit the claim to arbitration under: (a) the ICSID Convention, provided that both the disputing Party and the Party of the investor are parties to the Convention; (b) the Additional Facility Rules of ICSID, provided that either the disputing Party or the Party of the investor, but not both, is a party to the ICSID Convention; or (c) the UNCITRAL Arbitration Rules.*' 32 I.L.M. 289 (1993). Agreement among Japan, Korea and the People's Republic of China for the Promotion, Facilitation and Protection of Investment, 11 May 2012, Art. 15(3): '*The investment dispute shall at the request of the disputing investor be submitted to either: (a) a competent court of the disputing Contracting Party; (b) arbitration in accordance with the ICSID Convention, if the ICSID Convention is available; (c) arbitration under the ICSID Additional Facility Rules, if the ICSID*

acts as the respondent. In addition, in order to prevent the introduction by the investor/claimant of the same dispute under several *fora*, IIAs also often contain a so-called fork-in-the-road provision, which aims at making the investor's choice of forum final and exclusive.[29]

The exercise of asymmetrical arbitration clauses in international commercial arbitration is therefore connected with a 'risk' of parallel proceedings, both where the clauses provide for a general option of forum or where they act as an exception to the general forum.

[B] The Enforceability of Asymmetrical Clauses Providing for a General Option of Forum

In international commercial arbitration, the option may be granted to the benefit of the party who will act as claimant if a dispute arises. In this situation, when drafting the contract, the parties cannot foresee which of them will be the claimant in a future dispute and so both parties may act as claimant and exercise the option.[30] The case *China Nat. Metal Product v. Apex Digital*[31] illustrates the risk of parallel arbitration proceedings, and of multiple awards, when enforcing unilateral option clauses. In this case, the purchase orders under a series of written sales agreements, contained a CIETAC arbitration clause with three alternative *fora 'at the claimant's option'*, namely (1) CIETAC in Beijing; (2) CIETAC sub-commission in Shenzhen; or (3) CIETAC sub-commission in Shanghai, the clause read:

> All dispute[s] arising from or in connection with this Contract shall be submitted to [CIETAC] for arbitration which shall be conducted by [CIETAC] in Beijing or by its Shenzhen Sub-Commission in Shenzhen or by its Shanghai Sub-Commission in Shanghai at the Claimant's option in accordance with [CIETAC's] arbitration rules in effect at the time of applying for arbitration... .

The obvious difficulty arises when each party, intending to be the claimant, moved to initiate arbitration proceedings before different *fora*. In *China Nat. Metal v. Apex Digital*, Apex filed a request for arbitration against China Nat Metal before the CIETAC Sub-commission in Shanghai. China Nat Metal subsequently filed a request for arbitration with CIETAC Beijing. The two CIETAC ran parallel and resulted in two different arbitral awards, with the Beijing arbitration panel ruling for China Nat Metal last.

Additional Facility Rules are available; (d) arbitration under the UNCITRAL Arbitration Rules; or (e) if agreed with the disputing Contracting Party, any arbitration in accordance with other arbitration rules...'

29. For an example of a fork-in-the-road provision, See 2009 China-Belgium BIT, art. 8(2): '... *the choice of the proceedings will be final [le choix de la procédure sera définitif].*' See also, ICSID Convention, Art. 26. For an application, See, *Pantechniki S.A. Contractors & Engineers v. Republic of Albania*, ICSID Case No. ARB/07/21.
30. C. Nardinocchi, 'Asymmetrical Arbitration Clauses: A Risk for Pathology?', *Versailles Int'l Arb. & Bus. L. Rev.* 109–131 (2014).
31. *China Nat. Metal v. Apex Digital, Inc.*, 379 F. 3d 796.

Having prevailed in its arbitration proceedings in Beijing against Apex, China Nat. Metal sought to enforce the CIETAC award in the United States under the 1958 New York Convention. In the US court, Apex objected to the enforcement, arguing that it had agreed to arbitrate in one of three *fora*, and not in multiple *fora*. Apex contended that since it was the claimant (in that it had filed first), its option was final. The clause therefore required China Nat. Metal to counterclaim before the forum selected by Apex, as claimant, and not to exercise the option subsequently as a claimant. The Court of Appeals of the 9th Circuit did not agree with Apex, and held that, since CIETAC had permitted the two separate, but related, arbitrations to proceed along parallel paths, the award should be enforced and Apex and China Nat. Metal were both claimants in their respective arbitrations.

This case raises the classic issue of parallel proceedings in international commercial arbitration where absent a clear wording stating that the first claimant's filing will determine the final forum, or the power of the arbitration institution to consolidate the pending arbitration proceedings, the parties run the risk of conflicting arbitral awards.

[C] The Enforceability of Asymmetrical Clauses Providing for an Exception to the General Forum

The option may also be granted to a designated party (Party A), chosen at the time the contract is entered into, to hold the privilege to opt out of the general choice of jurisdiction otherwise agreed upon by both parties. Under the first scenario, an identified party, Party A, holding the option, may refer the dispute to arbitration as an exception to the agreement to resolve the dispute through the courts. Under the second scenario, Party A may refer the dispute to the court as an exception to the arbitration agreement.

Under the first scenario, the choice of court agreement is subject to a unilateral option to arbitrate, therefore Party A may unilaterally opt to refer the dispute to arbitration. In *NB Three Shipping*,[32] the dispute resolution clause inserted in the charter-party (under the amended Barecon 89 Form) granted only the owner, Harebell Shipping Ltd. (as Party A), the privilege over the charterers, *NB Three Shipping* (as Party B), to derogate from the choice of English courts and opt for *ad-hoc* arbitration in London. Clause 47 of the charter-party provided:

> '47.02 The courts of England shall have jurisdiction to settle any disputes which may arise out of or in connection with this Charterparty but [Party A] shall have the option of bringing any dispute hereunder to arbitration...
> '47.10 Any dispute arising from the provisions of this Charterparty or its performance which cannot be resolved by mutual agreement which [Party A] determines to resolve by arbitration shall be referred to arbitration in London or, at [Party A's] option, in another city selected by [Party A] by two arbitrators, one appointed by [Party A] and one by the Charterers [Party B] who shall reach their decision by applying English law. If the arbitrators so

---

32. *NB Three Shipping LTD v. Harebell Shipping Ltd* (*NB Three Shipping*) 2004 All ER (D) 152.

appointed shall not agree they shall appoint an umpire to make such decision.' (Emphasis added)

NB Three Shipping (Party B) brought the dispute against the owners, Harebell Shipping Ltd. (as Party A), before the High Court of England under clause 47.02. Party A, respondents to the court action, then decided to exercise their right to arbitrate the matter, appointed their arbitrator and requested the court to stay the court proceedings on the grounds that the parties were bound to arbitrate the dispute. To the objection of Party B who alleged the option to arbitrate was only available to Party A, when it acted as claimant, the court held that the very purpose of the option granted to one only party was to give that party an advantage and that party may exercise its right to choose between litigation or arbitration and exercise such option even as respondent, after the dispute had arose, by asking the matter be removed from courts and heard in arbitration:

> It seems to me that clause 47.02 gives [Party A] a right to stop or stay a court action brought against them, at their option. This gives the clause some practical effect and was designed to apply in circumstances such as these. If [Party B] seek to bypass the [Party A's] determination to have disputes resolved by arbitration as contemplated by Clause 47.10, then [Party A's] option of bringing the disputes to arbitration remains, continuing [Party A's] control over the issue of arbitration or court. [Party B] can obtain no advantage from 'jumping the starting gun'.

Morison J. found that clause 47.10, which permits only Party A to arbitrate, *'satisfies the requirements of an arbitration agreement since a one sided choice of arbitration is sufficient.'* Morison J. went on to comment that one of the fundamental objectives being exercised in allowing the stay of litigation proceedings (under section 9(1) of the Arbitration Act), is to give the parties autonomy of over their choice of forum and *'... once [Party A] exercise their option the parties have agreed that the disputes should be arbitrated. By refusing a stay the court would not be according to them their autonomy.'*

Under the second scenario, the arbitration agreement is subject to a unilateral option to litigate, and Party A may refer the dispute to the court as an exception to the arbitration agreement. In the case of *Law Debenture Trust Corp Plc v. Elektrim Finance BV*,[33] the dispute resolution clause granted Party A the unilateral right to choose litigation over arbitration:

> '29.2 Any dispute arising out of or in connection with these presents may be submitted by any party to arbitration for final settlement [...].
> 29.4 The place of such arbitration shall be in London [...].
> 29.6 The agreement by all the parties to refer all disputes ... to arbitration ... is exclusive such that neither shall be permitted to bring proceedings in any other court or tribunal ...
> 29.7 Notwithstanding cl 29.2, for the exclusive benefit of the [Party A] and each of the Bondholders, [Party B] hereby agree that [Party A] and each of the Bondholders shall have the exclusive right, at their option, to apply to the

---

33. [2005] APP.L.R. 07/01.

courts of England, who shall have non-exclusive jurisdiction to settle any disputes ...' (Emphasis added)

Elektrim (Party B) commenced an arbitration and Law Debenture (Party A) applied to stay arbitration proceedings commenced by Elektrim (Party B). When Party B applied to stay the litigation proceedings, the Mann J refused and restrained the continuation of the arbitral proceedings. It was held that the contract allowed Party A to exercise the option to force Party B to litigate both as a respondent to an arbitration case *and* in court proceedings after a dispute has arisen. Party B did not have this option. Party A could litigate, but Party B could be forced to arbitrate (unless litigation is started, in which case Party B could counterclaim). Party A, meanwhile, could not be forced to arbitrate if it wished to commence its own proceedings covering the same subject matter.

The enforceability of such clauses is however not shared in all jurisdictions. In the Russian case *CJSC Russian Telephone Company v. Sony Ericsson Mobil Communications Rus LLC*.[34] The disputed resolution clause, inserted in a general distribution contract entered into between two Russian entities, also provided for a unilateral option to litigate the dispute as an exception to an ICC arbitration clause. Under the dispute resolution clause, the buyer, Russian Telephone Company (Party B) was bound to arbitration, while the seller, Sony Ericsson Mobil Communications Rus LLC ('Sony Ericsson', Party A) held the privilege to opt out of the arbitration and apply to court. The arbitration clause provided as follows:

> 'Any dispute arising under this Agreement which cannot be resolved by way of negotiation shall be definitively resolved in accordance with the Rules of Conciliation and Arbitration of the International Chamber of Commerce ... The venue of the arbitration shall be London, and English shall be the language of the proceedings... *This arbitration clause does not limit Sony Ericsson [Party A] the right to apply to a court of competent jurisdiction for recovery of amounts owed for delivered products.*' (Emphasis added)

When a dispute arose, Party B brought the case before a Moscow Court of First Instance, Party A objected to jurisdiction and asked the court to dismiss the case to arbitration based on the option contained in the above stated clause. The Court of First Instance, the review court and the appeal court held, based on party autonomy held the parties were 'free to contract' as they saw fit in, that the arbitration clause was enforceable and refused to consider Party B's claim.

The Supreme Arbitration Court, however, disagreed with the lower courts' decision and sent the case back to the Court of First Instance for review based on the parties' inherent right to be treated equally. The court decided that the unilateral option to litigate was invalid and unenforceable and ruled that the lower courts had not taken

---

34. Judgment of 19 Jun. 2012, No. A40-49223/11-112-401 (Supreme Arbitrazh Court, Russian Federation).

into account the fact that the clause a *forum shopping* right to only one party to the contract, Party A. Hence, the contract created an imbalance between the parties' rights. The Court stressed that equality before the law is one of the basic principles of civil law and the parties should equally be given an opportunity to present to the court all relevant aspects of their case. This would ensure judicial protection and guarantee a fair trial and declared the clause invalid and unenforceable.

CHAPTER 39
Work Ethics of the International Arbitrator, or: The Distinction Between Rendering a Service to the Parties and Being the Parties' Slave

Stephan Wilske

"Dealing with those kind of people taught me how to be not like them, taught me how to be a gentleman."[1]

The pillar of international arbitration who is to be honored by this *liber amicorum*, Pierre A. Karrer, has not only long shown a keen interest in the role and obligations of the international arbitrator;[2] he has also lived such work ethics and served as a role model for future generations (including the author of this humble contribution). At the same time, he is very well aware of the distinction between rendering a service to the parties and being a servant of the parties at their mercy. Accordingly, the author considers it rather fitting to use his contribution to discuss some aspects of work ethics of the international arbitrator and one example of the author's and the jubilee's joint experience where arbitrators were entitled (and maybe even obliged) to reject unreasonable requests by a party.

---

1. Keith Richards as quoted by Jessica Pallington West, *What Would Keith Richards Do? Daily Affirmations From A Rock "N" Roll Survivor*, 163, (Bloomsbury 2009).
2. Pierre A. Karrer, *Don't be Afraid – A Pep Talk*, Arbitration, 24–25, vol. 65, issue 1 (1999); Pierre A. Karrer, *Lawyers' Ethics and Arbitration – Tectonic Plates Clashing*, Croatian Arbitration Yearbook, 47–53, vol. 17 (2010); Pierre A. Karrer, *Responsibility of Arbitrators and Arbitral Institutions*, The Leading Arbitrators' Guide to International Arbitration, ch. 27, 607–620, Lawrence W. Newman, Richard D. Hill (eds.) (2nd ed., Juris Publishing, Inc. 2008); Pierre A. Karrer, *So You Want to Become an Arbitrator? – A Roadmap*, The Journal of World Investment & Trade, 13–15, vol. 4 issue 1 (2003).

§39.01 THE NEW FOCUS ON THE SIGNIFICANCE OF THE "DECISION-MAKERS"

International arbitration faces challenges: Parties complaining of the time and cost incurred (or sometimes right away wasted) in some international arbitrations. In addition, as a consequence of increasing criticism vis-à-vis investment arbitration, the whole idea of international arbitration has become intensely political.[3] In particular – but not really surprisingly, arbitrators become more and more the target of criticism (not only by this author).[4]

The current International Bar Association (IBA) President David W. Rivkin, in a keynote speech opening the Arbitration Week of the Hong Kong International Arbitration Centre on October 27, 2015, even chastised arbitrators for a multitude of sins – including failing to allow sufficient time to hear and decide cases, to familiarize themselves with the facts of disputes in advance, failing to exercise control over counsel, to schedule deliberations soon enough after the hearing and to deliver timely awards that address the matters in issue.[5] His speech – entitled *"A New Contract Between Arbitrators and Parties"* – has been described by one commentator as a *"clarion call for better behaviour"* by arbitrators.[6] ASA President Geisinger has seconded IBA President Rivkin's clarion call,[7] analyzed the *"catalogue of sins"* and concluded that *"[i]t is always possible to do better and the level of service provided by arbitrators is no exception"*.[8] The issue of preoccupied arbitrators and a consequential delay sometimes experienced in receiving arbitral awards has now also been tackled by the International Court of Arbitration of the ICC.[9] Recent scandals about allegedly

---

3. Cf. David W. Rivkin, *A New Contract Between Arbitrators and Parties*, HKIAC Arbitration Week Keynote Address (Oct. 27, 2015).
4. Stephan Wilske, Martin Raible, *The Arbitrator as Guardian of International Public Policy? Should Arbitrators Go Beyond Solving Legal Issues?*, in: The Future of Investment Arbitration, Catherine A. Rogers, Roger P. Alford (eds.) (Oxford University Press 2009), 249, 272 (recommending that international arbitrators should avoid considering themselves as *"guardians of moral values"* but should instead focus on diligently and conscientiously rendering dispute resolution services to state and non-state parties); Stephan Wilske, *Legal Challenges to Delayed Arbitral Awards*, Contemporary Asia Arbitration Journal, 153–186, vol. 6, issue 2 (2013); Stephan Wilske, *The Ailing Arbitrator – Identification, Abuse and Preventing of a Potentially Dangerous Delaying and Obstruction Tool*, Contemporary Asia Arbitration Journal, 279–308, vol. 7, issue 2 (2014).
5. Cf. David W. Rivkin, *A New Contract Between Arbitrators and Parties*, HKIAC Arbitration Week Keynote Address (Oct. 27, 2015); see also Douglas Thomson, *Rivkin Calls for "New Contract" for Arbitrators and Parties*, http://globalarbitrationreview.com/news/article/34855/rivkin-calls-new-contract-arbitrators-parties (accessed May 8, 2016).
6. Douglas Thomson, *Rivkin Calls for "New Contract" for Arbitrators and Parties*, http://globalarbitrationreview.com/news/article/34855/rivkin-calls-new-contract-arbitrators-parties (accessed May 8, 2016) (quoting Christopher Bogart, the CEO of Burford Capital).
7. Elliott Geisinger, *President's Message: A "Clarion Call" Seconded*, ASA Bulletin, 731–739, vol. 4, (2015); see also Elliott Geisinger, *President's Message: Quousque tandem, Arbitrator, abutere patientia nostra?*, ASA Bulletin, 1–7, vol. 1 (2016) (further elaborating on David Rivkin's theme of a "new contract" between parties and arbitrators).
8. Elliott Geisinger, *President's Message: A "Clarion Call" Seconded*, ASA Bulletin, 731, 738, vol. 4 (2015).
9. See the International Court of Arbitration of the ICC's communiqué of Jan. 5, 2016 announcing the release of a note setting out new policies on the financial consequences for arbitral tribunal that

corrupt arbitrators[10] or arbitrators who, in pursuance of their desire to be adequately paid seem to have lost their countenance,[11] are capable of further increasing skepticism vis-à-vis arbitrators. It provides comfort to know that any such criticism could never target our jubilee Pierre A. Karrer, who is the role model of the international arbitrator who takes his mission seriously and would never neglect his mandate because of selfish interests.

§39.02 OFTEN NEGLECTED WORK ETHICS OF ARBITRATORS: THE SO-CALLED SECONDARY VIRTUES

Much has been written about "must have" criteria of international arbitrators such as impartiality and independence, intellectual brilliance, experience,

---

delay without justification the submission of draft awards for scrutiny by the Court (http://www.iccwbo.org/News/Articles/2016/ICC-Court-announces-new-policies-to-foster-transparancy-and-ensure-greater-efficiency/).

10. See Sebastian Perry, *Italian Arbitrator Accused of Corruption*, Global Arbitration Review News (Apr. 18, 2016); *see also* Sebastian Perry, *Italian Arbitrator Disqualified After Bribery Challenge*, http://globalarbitrationreview.com/news/article/35315/italian-arbitrator-disqualified-bribery-challenge/ (accessed on May 13, 2016).

11. Douglas Thomson, *Arbitrators Criticise Court over Treatment of Guinea Award*, Global Arbitration Review News (Jan. 12, 2016), http://globalarbitrationreview.com/news/article/34474/tribunal-criticises-court-treatment-guinea-award/ (accessed on May 17, 2016); Tom Jones, *Attempt to Enforce Guinea Award in the US Continues, After "Repugnant" Set Aside*, Global Arbitration Review News (May 3, 2016), http://globalarbitrationreview.com/news/article/35283/ (accessed on May 17, 2016); Alison Ross, *West African set-aside decision not against U.S. public policy, says court*, Global Arbitration Review News (June 10, 2016), http://globalarbitrationreview.com/article/1036396/west-african-set-aside-decision-not-against-us-public-policy-says-court (discussing the memorandum opinion of the U.S. District Court for the District of Columbia dated June 9, 2016, Civil Action No. 14-1616 (RBW)), but *see also* Anees Naim, Jerome Temme, *Getma: French Supreme Court upholds Paris Court of Appeal decision finding parties' joint liable for arbitrators' fees* (discussing the decision of the French Cour de Cassation of February 1, 2017, Cass. Civ. 1re, 1 Fev. 2017, n° 15-25.687); *see also* Catherine A. Rogers, *When Arbitrators and Institutions Clash, or The Strange Case of Getma v. Guinea*, http://kluwerarbitrationblog.com/2016/05/12/when-arbitrators-and-institutions-clash-or-the-strange-case-of-getma-v-guinea/ (accessed on May 13, 2016) (concluding that "*one challenge that no African arbitral institution should face is arbitrators who deliberately reject that institution's mandatory rules and rulings, and then seek to blame the institution for the post-award consequences of their own actions*"); but *see also* Ibrahim Fadlallah, *La CCJA frappe fort et mal – ou va l'arbitrage OHADA?*, open letter, Dec. 16, 2015 (complaining about incomprehensible hostility towards arbitrators). For a similar case where arbitrators had tried to renegotiate their fees after appointment *see* Supreme Court of New South Wales – Court of Appeal, *Sea Containers Ltd v. ICT Pty Ltd [2002] NSWCA 84* (Apr. 18, 2002), http://www.austlii.edu.au/cgi-bin/sinodisp/au/cases/nsw/NSWCA/2002/84.html?stem=0&synonyms=0&query=carriage%20of%20goods%20or%20sea%20or%20towage (accessed on May 13, 2016) ("*To insist upon a fee without the consent of all parties constitutes misconduct*").

intercultural competence and – in more recent times – availability.[12] Often neglected are the so-called secondary virtues.[13] Some of them will be discussed in the following.

[A] Diligence, Transparency and Predictability

Parties to arbitration are entitled to expect that the arbitral tribunal can be depended upon to take time to read the submissions, consider the arguments made and produce an award that is rational and justified. Parties should reassure themselves that their chosen arbitrator has a proven track record: the hope is that the majority of arbitrators will have conducted themselves reputably in the past, not least of all because they are incentivized to secure reappointments.

Relevant questions in this respect are:

- Does your arbitrator read the submissions? (Completely? How about the exhibits?).
- Does your arbitrator consider the arguments made (not only those he or she personally falls in love with)?
- Does your arbitrator strive to produce an award that is rational and justified?

Luckily, for the jubilee all these questions can be answered in the affirmative. However, by no means should this be taken for granted with respect to all other arbitrator candidates.

[B] Time- and Cost-Consciousness

Many parties will have chosen arbitration as a time- and cost-efficient dispute resolution procedure. Clearly the costs incurred as a result of the proceedings is primarily a matter for the parties and their counsel. However, arbitral tribunals can play a significant, albeit indirect, role in controlling costs through their management of the arbitral process. Conscientious arbitrators will acknowledge the link between time and cost management by establishing a realistic timetable at an early stage. Other ways in which tribunals can intervene to control costs is to delineate the key issues at an early stage and consider making both interim and final costs awards that do not have to follow the traditional "costs follow the event" rule.

Again, relevant questions are as follows:

- Is your arbitrator available when the case so requires?

---

12. Stephan Wilske, Chloë Edworthy, *The Essential Qualities of an Arbitrator – What Appointing Parties Must, Should and May Like to Consider*, Croatian Arbitration Yearbook, 101, 103-108, vol. 23 (2016). *See also* Catherine A. Rogers, *Ethics in International Arbitration*, ch. 8, 311–342 (Oxford University Press 2014) and Catherine A. Rogers, *The Ethics of International Arbitrators, The Leading Arbitrators' Guide to International Arbitration*, ch. 28, 621–649, Lawrence W. Newman, Richard D. Hill (eds.) (2nd ed., Juris Publishing, Inc. 2008).
13. Stephan Wilske, Chloë Edworthy, *The Essential Qualities of an Arbitrator – What Appointing Parties Must, Should and May Like to Consider*, Croatian Arbitration Yearbook, 101, 112-116, vol. 23 (2016).

- Does your arbitrator show awareness of time and cost considerations?
- Is your arbitrator aware that the parties might not be interested in the "perfect" work product or furtherance of his or her academic pet idea?

Nothing is more disappointing for a party than an arbitrator who is not able or not prepared to invest time in the decision of the case for which he or she was appointed. The case might not be important for the arbitrator, but the fate of a company might depend on its correct, or, at least, timely decision. More often than not, it is not only a correct decision which is significant for the parties, but also a decision where time and costs involved have a sound relationship to the amount in dispute. The author is aware of one case where the chairman of the arbitral tribunal invested (or, at least billed) more than 1,200 hours within one year – paid by the hour! – on a case and finally produced a 250 page award. This award looks more like a by-product of the chairman's research project on conflicts of law issues in Chinese arbitration law. A mind-boggling *obiter dicta* in the award promptly triggered another arbitration. Despite all issues being highly contentious between the parties, they did agree not to appoint the same arbitrators again.

Certainly, Pierre A. Karrer is – beyond any doubt – not the type to forget who entrusted him with what mission or to permit inefficiency. This is evidenced by his book *Introduction to International Arbitration Practice* (2014), which manages to answer 1,001 questions in only 247 pages.[14]

[C] Honesty

Honesty is often not considered to be a standalone characteristic. Often it is included in an arbitrator's duty to disclose or his or her failure to advise about a lack of availability. However, to this author it seems of such fundamental significance that it requires separate recognition.

In order to demand honesty of their arbitrators, parties should timely provide arbitrator candidates with as much information about the case and what is expected from the arbitrators. The onus in the first instance is, therefore, on the parties. In so doing, parties will place arbitrator candidates in a position to review whether they have the required qualifications, skills, availability, faculties and experience.

The onus then shifts to the arbitrators who must consider the appointment carefully and in detail and always have in mind Karl-Heinz Böckstiegel's admonishment that there is always the choice to "just say no"[15] to another engagement that might risk one's well-deserved reputation.[16]

Here, the relevant questions are:

---

14. Pierre A. Karrer, *Introduction to International Arbitration Practice – 1001 Questions and Answers*, ch. 2, 45 (Wolters Kluwer 2014).
15. *See* Meg Kinnear, *Current Problems & Developments in Investment Arbitration*, SchiedsVZ 2013, 65, 68.
16. *See also* Jan Paulsson, *The Idea of Arbitration* (2013), 149 ("*It is dishonest to accept appointment without a solid understanding of the relevant domain, or without a considered commitment to give the matter full and timely attention.*").

- Is your arbitrator able to say "no" if a seemingly attractive case is beyond his abilities, physical and mental fitness and availability?
- Will your arbitrator tell the parties when he/she does not understand the facts, a legal argument, the position of a party etc.?
- Does your arbitrator live up to his or her previous commitments?

Again, nothing is more disappointing than the arbitrator who has promised a party in a conversation prior to his appointment not to question the amount in dispute and then is first to insist on an increase of the amount in dispute in the first case management call. Needless to mention, that many arbitrators would have an ego problem with admitting to the parties that he or she simply could not follow a certain technical presentation or legal argument.[17] In such a situation, it is more helpful to be less pretentious[18] and flamboyant and ask the parties, smilingly and modestly, to simply not give up on the arbitrators and try to explain a certain issue once more.[19]

§39.03 ENOUGH IS ENOUGH: NEITHER THE PRIMA DONNA NOR THE PARTIES' SLAVE

While Pierre A. Karrer is rendering his first-class services as arbitrator as required (and often more than that), he is also aware of the fine line between rendering the services required by the arbitrator's mandate and being the parties' slave. In one arbitration under Swiss Rules of International Arbitration seated in Zurich, the jubilee and the author were both serving as party-appointed arbitrators and trying to agree on a mutually acceptable presiding arbitrator. As the dispute was between a German and an American party, it was clear for us that the presiding arbitrator should be of a nationality other than those of the parties. The arbitration clause had provided for English as the language of the arbitration, but had also allowed for submission of documents as evidence in the German language, which made sense because German

---

17. On different species of arbitrator, including *arbiter academicus*, *arbiter mercantilis* and *arbiter technicus see* another Honorary President of ASA, Michael E. Schneider, *President's Message: A Taxonomy of Arbitrators and the New Species of Arbiter Compositus*, Stories from the Hearing Room: Experience from Arbitral Practice – Essays in Honour of Michael E. Schneider, 295–298, Bernd Ehle, Domitille Baizeau (eds.) (Wolters Kluwer 2015). Most probably, our jubilee would qualify as *arbiter arbiter* or *arbiter sapiens* (*id*, 295). *See also* with respect to the limits of a non-arbiter arbiter to follow some experts or wanna-be experts Michael E. Schneider, *President's Message: The Role of Experts in the Adversarial Process and the Arbitrator's Capacity to Absorb Specialized Knowledge*, Stories from the Hearing Room: Experience from Arbitral Practice – Essays in Honour of Michael E. Schneider, 291–293, Bernd Ehle, Domitille Baizeau (eds.) (Wolters Kluwer 2015).
18. *See* the wisdom of England's most influential contemporaneous philosopher and Rock'n'Roll survivor Keith Richards: "*If you just fancy yourself as being a big star, don't bother.*" (Quoted by Jessica Pallington West, *What Would Keith Richards Do? Daily Affirmations From A Rock "N" Roll Survivor*, 96, (Bloomsbury 2009)).
19. While encountering Pierre A. Karrer completely unprepared in a hearing would be an unusual incident, he knows best how to deal with really unusual incidents, *see* Pierre A. Karrer, *Defusing Unusual Incidents Before They Grow Unmanageable*, Stories from the Hearing Room: Experience from Arbitral Practice – Essays in Honour of Michael E. Schneider, ch. 12, 103–109, Bernd Ehle, Domitille Baizeau (eds.) (Wolters Kluwer 2015).

law was the applicable law. We considered it beneficial for the presiding arbitrator to have German language skills – of course, beyond the required English language skills. However, as a presiding arbitrator should be familiar with the applicable German law or, at least, should have easy access to German legal sources, we agreed that the presiding arbitrator should be of Austrian nationality.

The American party – represented by French counsel – objected vigorously, arguing that if the presiding arbitrator were fluent in German, there would be a natural tendency for the three members of the arbitral tribunal to discuss or even to deliberate in German. This allegedly was not the intention of the parties and, therefore, pursuant to the logic of this party, explicitly excluded under the terms of the applicable arbitration clause. This party insisted that the entirety of the arbitration proceedings – including deliberations by the arbitrators – must be conducted in English. Accordingly, this party even argued that the presiding arbitrator should not be an Austrian national, nor be a native or fluent German speaker. Indeed, it was even argued that the presiding arbitrator should have only a limited knowledge, if any, of the German language.

This idea triggered our combined resistance. In a further letter to the party representatives, we stated our belief that in light of the parties' arbitration clause and the Swiss Rules of International Arbitration, broad knowledge of the German language and easy and direct access to applicable German law should not speak against a candidate. To the contrary, in light of the limitations of translations,[20] we strongly recommended that the American party should reconsider its position. Otherwise, Pierre A. Karrer would have been ready to resign in light of such seemingly unreasonable misconceptions by one of the parties. The jubilee's position is even more respectable in light of the fact that the amount in dispute was rather high and – different than in many other arbitration cases – the mandate in this case was even lucrative. Nevertheless, the lesson I learned from Pierre Karrer is that an arbitrator should not give in to party requests that he or she considers misguided.[21]

Similarly, an arbitrator should much more often take a firm position when parties are not playing by the rules or are openly obstructing the proceedings.[22] Or, as Lucy Reed describes it, with respect to the position Pierre A. Karrer is most familiar with: *"[T]he ideal chairperson or sole arbitrator is clearly in command, by actions and by example."*[23] Pierre A. Karrer gives explicit encouragement to make procedural decisions and to make them early on in the proceedings – even if there is a risk of not getting it right:

---

20. Tibor Várady, *Language and Translation in International Commercial Arbitration*, 85–90 (2008); *see also* John P. Bang, David MacArthur, *Lost in Translation*, Korean Arbitration Review, 2nd ed. 11–12, vol. 10 (2013).
21. In this regard, support can, meanwhile, be found in a decision of the Swiss Supreme Court of May 3, 2016, docket no. 4A_42/2016, which held that a party does not have the right to unilaterally dictate the procedure of the arbitral process.
22. Stephan Wilske, Martin Raible, *The Arbitrator as Guardian of International Public Policy? Should Arbitrators Go Beyond Solving Legal Issues?*, in: The Future of Investment Arbitration, Catherine A. Rogers, Roger P. Alford (eds.) (Oxford University Press 2009), 269.
23. Lucy Reed, *Sanctions Available for Arbitrators to Curtail Guerrilla Tactics*, Guerrilla Tactics in International Arbitration, §2.04, 93, 102, Günther J. Horvath, Stephan Wilske (eds.) (Wolters Kluwer 2013). *See also* Leon Kopecký, Victoria Pernt, *A Bid for Strong Arbitrator*, http://www

The more complex the case, the higher the risk that you may not get it absolutely right the first time around. Don't worry. The beauty about procedure is that no harm is done until an award is rendered that is affected by a procedural mistake. If you make a mistake, that is not the end.[24]

By all means, an arbitral tribunal should resist the temptation of simply tolerating, for example, delay tactics by one party, simply because it is much easier for an arbitral tribunal to seek a consensual solution[25] and without ever daring to switch at some point to a more robust "decision-taking" approach.[26]

§39.04 CONCLUSION

The work ethics of the international arbitrator may, in the end all boil down to his or her awareness of arbitration's promise to provide an efficient and final resolution to disputes that would otherwise be plagued with delay, inefficiency and the threat of appellate review.[27] Or, to put it in the words of a philosopher from a culture with which Pierre A. Karrer is quite familiar, i.e., Mencius (Meng Zi):[28]

> The man who cultivates virtue and practices righteousness daily will stand firm in a crooked age.[29]

The author has no doubt that Pierre A. Karrer is one of these firm-standing arbitrators – hopefully for many more years to come.[30]

.lexology.com/library/detail.aspx?g = cd7eb0fa-72a4-4599-bdf2-ff9502068566 (accessed May 13, 2016) (This article was originally published in Kluwer Arbitration Blog on Apr. 15, 2016). ("*Practitioners increasingly face situations where arbitrators seem cautious and reluctant to rule on procedural issues. While such a careful approach may be advisable where arbitrators prudently avoid overstepping their powers, it may, at times, also frustrate parties and practitioners alike.*")

24. Pierre A. Karrer, *Don't Be Afraid – A Pep Talk*, Arbitration, 24, vol. 65, issue 1 (1999).
25. Fabian von Schlabrendorff, *Counsel X's Delay Tactics: What an Arbitral Tribunal Can (and Cannot) Do*, Stories from the Hearing Room: Experience from Arbitral Practice – Essays in Honour of Michael E. Schneider, ch. 20, 153, 163, Bernd Ehle, Domitille Baizeau (eds.) (Wolters Kluwer 2015).
26. On arbitral decision making *see*, e.g., Michael E. Schneider, *President's Message: Arbitral Decision Making – a Look into the Black Box*, Stories from the Hearing Room: Experience from Arbitral Practice – Essays in Honour of Michael E. Schneider, 283–286, Bernd Ehle, Domitille Baizeau (eds.) (Wolters Kluwer 2015).
27. *See* William W. Park, *The Predictability Paradox – Arbitrators and Applicable Law*, in: Fabio Bortolotti, Pierre Mayer (eds.), *The Application of Substantive Law by International Arbitrators*, Dossier XI of the ICC Institute of World Business Law (ICC Publication No. 753E), 2014, 60, 69.
28. Mencius Meng Zi (372 – 289 BC; alt. 385-303/302 BC) was a Chinese philosopher who is the most famous Confucian after Confucius himself.
29. Tsai Chih Chung, *The Sayings of Mencius – Wisdom in a Chaotic Era* (translated by Mary Ng En Tzu), 1991, 108.
30. Hopefully, even though (not only) their musical taste might differ, Pierre A. Karrer might nevertheless be inspired by the non-existing retirement plans of Keith Richards, *Life*, 2010, 545 ("*I can rest on my laurels. ... But then there's that word 'retiring'. I can't retire until I croak.*").